MATHEMATICS

FOR CLASS VII

[*Based on the NCERT syllabus*]

Dr. R.D. SHARMA

B.Sc. (Hons) (Gold Medalist), M.Sc. (Gold Medalist), Ph.D.

Professor and Head of Department of Sciences and Humanities
Delhi Skill and Entrepreneurship University (DSEU)
Aryabhatt DSEU Ashok Vihar Campus, Delhi

DHANPAT RAI PUBLICATIONS (P) LTD.

22, ANSARI ROAD, DARYAGANJ, NEW DELHI-110002

E-Mail : ish.dhanpat@gmail.com

Price : Rs. 375.00

To prevent a pirated book being sold to you, always ask the bookseller to put his stamp on the first page of this book. Buying & Selling pirated books is a criminal offence under Indian Penal Code. This also deprives the author and publisher of their due earnings for providing you the knowledge through this book. Pirated books are also sold as old editions.

ISBN: 978-93-831825-0-3

First Edition: 2001, Reprints: 2002-03; Second Edition: 2004, Reprints: 2005-06; Revised Edition: 2007; Revised Edition: 2008, Reprints: 2009-14; Revised Edition: 2015, Reprints: 2016-21.

This Reprint : 2022

Published by ***Ish Kapur***, for Dhanpat Rai Publications (P) Ltd.

EVERY GENUINE COPY OF THIS BOOK HAS A HSHF

The title of the book has been Laminated by a **High Security Holographic Film (HSHF)** to prevent Piracy. You can see logo of Dhanpat Rai Publications at different angles with special security features.

Important Note: Buying & Selling pirated books which do not carry HSHF is illegal and a criminal offence under the Indian Penal Code. This also deprives the author and the publisher of their due earnings for providing you the knowledge through this book. Pirated books are also sold as old editions.

PREFACE TO THE REVISED EDITION

The Revised edition of the book "MATHEMATICS FOR CLASS VII" has been written strictly according to the latest syllabus prescribed by the NCERT.

In the present edition, at the end of each chapter an exercise containing large number of objective type questions have been added which will help students to test their knowledge and understanding of concepts.

Keeping in mind the mental level of a child, every effort has been made to introduce new concepts in a simple language so that the child understands them easily. Basic concepts have been explained through attractive illustrations relating to our day-to-day life experiences.

The book has been divided into 25 Chapters. The text has been re-written in a lucid manner. The difficulty level of the problems has been reduced and mathematical concepts have been explained in the simplest possible way. Each chapter contains a large number of illustrative examples to understand the applications of concepts. In each section, illustrative examples are followed by an exercise containing an adequate number of unsolved problems. The difficulty level of problms in exercises has also been reduced.

Students are advised to read the theory carefully and solve Illustrative Examples on their own before attempting the Exercises.

I hope that this book will be useful to the students and teachers alike.

I avail this opportunity to convey my sincere thanks to Sh. Ish Kapur of Dhanpat Rai Publications (P) Ltd. for this encouragement and painstaking efforts in bringing out this book in such an excellent form.

In spite of my best efforts to make this edition error free, some printed errors might have gone un-noticed. I shall be grateful to the teachers and students if the same are brought to my notice. You may send your valuable suggestions, feedback or queries by post or through e-mail to **ish.dhanpat@gmail.com** which would be verified by me and the corrections would be incorporated in the subsequent editions.

Any suggestion/criticism to enhance the quality of the book will be gratefully acknowledged.

Dr. R.D. SHARMA

CONTENTS

1

INTEGERS

1.1 INTRODUCTION

In class VI, we have learnt that the numbers

$$\ldots\ldots -3, -2, -1, 0, 1, 2, 3, \ldots\ldots$$

are called integers. The numbers 1, 2, 3, 4, 5, 6, ..., i.e. natural numbers, are called positive integers and the numbers -1, -2, -3, -4, -5, -6, ... are called negative integers. The number 0 is simply an integer. It is neither positive nor negative. We have learnt about addition and subtraction of integers in class VI. In this chapter, we will study about multiplication and division of integers. We will also learn about various properties of these operations on integers.

1.2 MULTIPLICATION OF INTEGERS

In order to multiply integers, we use the following rules:

Rule 1 *The product of two integers of opposite signs is equal to the additive inverse of the product of their absolute values.*

Thus, to find the product of a positive and a negative integer, we find the product of their absolute values and assign minus sign to the product.

For example, (i) $7 \times (-4) = -(7 \times 4) = -28$ (ii) $(-8) \times 5 = -(8 \times 5) = -40$

Rule 2 *The product of two integers with like signs is equal to the product of their absolute values.*

Thus, to find the product of two integers, both positive or both negative, we find the product of their absolute values.

For example, (i) $7 \times 12 = 84$ (ii) $(-8) \times (-13) = 8 \times 13 = 104$

1.2.1 PROPERTIES OF MULTIPLICATION

In class VI, we have learnt properties of multiplication of whole numbers. All properties of multiplication of whole numbers also hold for integers. The multiplication of integers possesses the following properties:

Property 1 *(Closure property): The product of two integers is always an integer.*

That is, for any two integers a and b, $a \times b$ is an integer.

Verification: We have,

(i) $4 \times 3 = 12$, which is an integer. (ii) $3 \times (-5) = -15$, which is an integer.

(iii) $(-7) \times (-6) = 42$, which is an integer.

Property 2 *(Commutativity): For any two integers a and b, we have*

$$a \times b = b \times a$$

That is, multiplication of integers is commutative.

Verification: We have,

(i) $7 \times (-6) = -(7 \times 6) = -42$ and $(-6) \times 7 = -(6 \times 7) = -42$

$\therefore\ 7 \times (-6) = (-6) \times 7$

(ii) $(-5)\times(-9) = 5\times 9 = 45$ and $(-9)\times(-5) = 9\times 5 = 45$

$\therefore\ (-5)\times(-9) = (-9)\times(-5)$.

Property 3 *(Associativity): The multiplication of integers is associative, i.e., for any three integers a, b, c, we have*

$$a\times(b\times c) = (a\times b)\times c$$

Verification: We have,

(i) $(-3)\times\{4\times(-7)\} = (-3)\times(-28) = 3\times 28 = 84$

and, $\{(-3)\times 4\}\times(-7) = (-12)\times(-7) = 12\times 7 = 84$

$\therefore\ (-3)\times\{4\times(-7)\} = \{(-3)\times 4\}\times(-7)$

(ii) $(-2)\times\{(-3)\times(-5)\} = (-2)\times 15 = -(2\times 15) = -30$

and, $\{(-2)\times(-3)\}\times(-5) = 6\times(-5) = -(6\times 5) = -30$

$\therefore\ (-2)\times\{(-3)\times(-5)\} = \{(-2)\times(-3)\}\times(-5)$

Property 4 *(Distributivity of multiplication over addition): The multiplication of integers is distributive over their addition. That is, for any three integers a, b, c, we have*

(i) $a\times(b+c) = a\times b + a\times c$ *(ii)* $(b+c)\times a = b\times a + c\times a$

Verification: We have,

(i) $(-3)\times\{(-5)+2\} = (-3)\times(-3) = 3\times 3 = 9$

and, $(-3)\times(-5) + (-3)\times 2 = (3\times 5) - (3\times 2) = 15 - 6 = 9$

$\therefore\ (-3)\times\{(-5)+2\} = (-3)\times(-5) + (-3)\times 2$.

(ii) $(-4)\times\{(-2)+(-3)\} = (-4)\times(-5) = 4\times 5 = 20$

and, $(-4)\times(-2) + (-4)\times(-3) = (4\times 2) + (4\times 3) = 8 + 12 = 20$

$\therefore\ (-4)\times\{(-2)+(-3)\} = (-4)\times(-2) + (-4)\times(-3)$.

Remark 1 *A direct consequence of the distributivity of multiplication over addition is*

$$a\times(b-c) = a\times b - a\times c$$

Property 5 *(Existence of multiplicative identity): For every integer a, we have*

$$a\times 1 = a = 1\times a$$

The integer 1 is called the multiplicative identity for integers.

Property 6 *(Property of zero): For any integer, we have*

$$a\times 0 = 0 = 0\times a$$

Property 7 *For any integer a, we have*

$$a\times(-1) = -a = (-1)\times a$$

Remark

(i) We know that –a is additive inverse or opposite of a. Thus, to find the opposite or additive inverse or negative of an integer, we multiply the integer by –1.

(ii) Since multiplication of integers is associative. Therefore, for any three integers a, b, c, we have

$$(a\times b)\times c = a\times(b\times c)$$

In what follows, we will write $a\times b\times c$ *for the equal products* $(a\times b)\times c$ *and* $a\times(b\times c)$.

(iii) Since multiplication of integers is both commutative and associative.

Therefore, in a product of three or more integers even if we rearrange the integers, the product will not change.

(iv) When the number of negative integers in a product is odd, the product is negative.

(v) When the number of negative integers in a product is even, the product is positive.

Property 8 *If a, b, c are integers, such that $a > b$, then*

(i) $a \times c > b \times c$, *if c is positive* *(ii)* $a \times c < b \times c$, *if c is negative.*

Property 9 *(i)* $(-a_1) \times (-a_2) \times (-a_3) \times \ldots \times (-a_n) = (a_1 \times a_2 \times a_3 \times \ldots \times a_n)$, *if n is even*

(ii) $(-a_1) \times (-a_2) \times (-a_3) \times \ldots \times (-a_n) = -(a_1 \times a_2 \times a_3 \times \ldots \times a_n)$, *if n is odd*

(iii) $\underbrace{(-1) \times (-1) \times (-1) \times \ldots \times (-1)}_{n\text{-times}} = 1$, *if n is even*

(iv) $\underbrace{(-1) \times (-1) \times (-1) \times \ldots \times (-1)}_{n\text{-times}} = -1$, *if n is odd*

ILLUSTRATIVE EXAMPLES

Example 1 Find each of the following products:

(i) $(-115) \times 8$ (ii) $9 \times (-3) \times (-6)$ (iii) $(-12) \times (-13) \times (-5)$

Solution (i) We have,

$(-115) \times 8 = -(115 \times 8) = -920$

(ii) We have,

$9 \times (-3) \times (-6)$

$= \{9 \times (-3)\} \times (-6)$

$= -(9 \times 3) \times (-6)$

$= -27 \times (-6) = 27 \times 6 = 162$

(iii) We have,

$(-12) \times (-13) \times (-5)$

$= \{(-12) \times (-13)\} \times (-5)$

$= (12 \times 13) \times (-5)$

$= 156 \times (-5) = -(156 \times 5) = -780$

Example 2 Evaluate each of the following products:

(i) $(-1) \times (-2) \times (-3) \times (-4) \times (-5)$ (ii) $(-3) \times (-6) \times (-9) \times (-12)$

(iii) $(-1) \times (-1) \times (-1) \times \ldots$ 50 *times* (iv) $(-1) \times (-1) \times (-1) \times \ldots$ 151 *times*

Solution (i) Since the number of negative integers in the product is odd. Therefore, their product is negative.

Thus, we have

$(-1) \times (-2) \times (-3) \times (-4) \times (-5)$

$= -(1 \times 2 \times 3 \times 4 \times 5)$

$= -(2 \times 3 \times 4 \times 5)$ $[\because 1 \times 2 = 2]$

$= -(6 \times 4 \times 5)$ $[\because 2 \times 3 = 6]$

$= -(24 \times 5) = -120$ $[\because 6 \times 4 = 24]$

(ii) Since the number of negative integers in the given product is even. Therefore, their product is positive. Thus, we have

$(-3) \times (-6) \times (-9) \times (-12)$

$= (3 \times 6 \times 9 \times 12)$

$= (18 \times 9 \times 12)$ $[\because 3 \times 6 = 18]$

$= (162 \times 12) = 1944$ $[\because 18 \times 9 = 162]$

(iii) The number of integers in the given product is even.

$\therefore$ $(-1) \times (-1) \times (-1) \times \ldots 50$ times $= (1 \times 1 \times 1 \times \ldots 50$ times$) = 1$

(iv) The number of integers in the given product is odd.

$\therefore$ $(-1) \times (-1) \times (-1) \times \ldots 151$ times $= -(1 \times 1 \times 1 \times \ldots 151$ times$) = -1$

Example 3 Find the value of

(i) $15625 \times (-2) + (-15625) \times 98$ (ii) $18946 \times 99 - (-18946)$

(iii) $1569 \times 887 - 569 \times 887$

Solution (i) $15625 \times (-2) + (-15625) \times 98$

$= (-15625) \times 2 + (-15625) \times 98$ $[\because 15625 \times (-2) = -(15625 \times 2) = (-15625 \times 2)]$

$= (-15625) \times (2 + 98)$ [Using: $a \times b + a \times c = a \times (b + c)$]

$= (-15625) \times 100$

$= -(15625 \times 100) = -1562500$

(ii) $18946 \times 99 - (-18946)$

$= 18946 \times 99 + 18946$

$= 18946 \times 99 + 18946 \times 1$ $[\because 18946 = 18946 \times 1]$

$= 18946 \times (99 + 1)$ [Using: $a \times b + a \times c = a \times (b + c)$]

$= 18946 \times 100 = 1894600$

(iii) $1569 \times 887 - 569 \times 887$

$= (1569 - 569) \times 887$ $[\because b \times a - c \times a = (b - c) \times a]$

$= 1000 \times 887 = 887000$

EXERCISE 1.1

1. Determine each of the following products:

(i) 12×7 (ii) $(-15) \times 8$ (iii) $(-25) \times (-9)$ (iv) $125 \times (-8)$

2. Find each of the following products:

(i) $3 \times (-8) \times 5$ (ii) $9 \times (-3) \times (-6)$ (iii) $(-2) \times 36 \times (-5)$

(iv) $(-2) \times (-4) \times (-6) \times (-8)$

3. Find the value of:

(i) $1487 \times 327 + (-487) \times 327$ (ii) $28945 \times 99 - (-28945)$

4. Complete the following multiplication table:

Second number

First number

×	–4	–3	–2	–1	0	1	2	3	4
–4									
–3									
–2									
–1									
0									
1									
2									
3									
4									

Is the multiplication table symmetrical about the diagonal joining the upper left corner to the lower right corner?

5. Determine the integer whose product with '–1' is
   (i) 58 (ii) 0 (iii) –225
6. What will be the sign of the product if we multiply together
   (i) 8 negative integers and 1 positive integer?
   (ii) 21 negative integers and 3 positive integers?
   (iii) 199 negative integers and 10 positive integers?
7. State which is greater:
   (i) $(8+9)\times 10$ and $8+9\times 10$ (ii) $(8-9)\times 10$ and $8-9\times 10$
   (iii) $\{(-2)-5\}\times(-6)$ and $(-2)-5\times(-6)$
8. (i) If $a\times(-1)=-30$, is the integer a positive or negative?
   (ii) If $a\times(-1)=30$, is the integer a positive or negative?
9. Verify the following:
   (i) $19\times\{7+(-3)\}=19\times 7+19\times(-3)$
   (ii) $(-23)\ \{(-5)+(+19)\}=(-23)\times(-5)+(-23)\times(+19)$
10. Which of the following statements are true?
   (i) The product of a positive and a negative integer is negative.
   (ii) The product of three negative integers is a negative integer.
   (iii) Of the two integers, if one is negative, then their product must be positive.
   (iv) For all non-zero integers a and b, $a\times b$ is always greater than either a or b.
   (v) The product of a negative and a positive integer may be zero.
   (vi) There does not exist an integer b such that for $a>1$, $a\times b=b\times a=b$.

ANSWERS

1. (i) 84 (ii) –120 (iii) 225 (iv) –1000
2. (i) –120 (ii) 162 (iii) 360 (iv) 384
3. (i) 327000 (ii) 2894500

4. Yes

×	–4	–3	–2	–1	0	1	2	3	4
–4	16	12	8	4	0	–4	–8	–12	–16
–3	12	9	6	3	0	–3	–6	–9	–12
–2	8	6	4	2	0	–2	–4	–6	–8
–1	4	3	2	1	0	–1	–2	–3	–4
0	0	0	0	0	0	0	0	0	0
1	–4	–3	–2	–1	0	1	2	3	4
2	–8	–6	–4	–2	0	2	4	6	8
3	–12	–9	–6	–3	0	3	6	9	12
4	–16	–12	–8	–4	0	4	8	12	16

5. (i) –58 (ii) 0 (iii) 225

6. (i) positive (ii) negative (iii) negative

7. (i) $(8+9)\times 10$ (ii) $(8-9)\times 10$ (iii) $[(-2)-5]\times(-6)$

8. (i) positive (ii) negative 10. (i), (ii), (vi)

1.3 DIVISION OF INTEGERS

We know that division of whole numbers is an inverse process of multiplication. In this section, we shall extend the same idea to integers.

We know that dividing 20 by 5 means finding an integer which when multiplied with 5 gives us 20. Clearly, such an integer is 4. Therefore, we write

$$20 \div 5 = 4 \text{ or, } \frac{20}{5} = 4$$

Similarly, dividing 36 by –9 means, finding an integer which when multiplied with –9 gives 36. Obviously, such an integer is –4. Therefore, we write

$$36 \div (-9) = -4 \text{ or, } \frac{36}{-9} = -4$$

Dividing (–35) by (–7) means, what integer should be multiplied with (–7) to get (–35). Clearly, such an integer is 5. Therefore,

$$(-35) \div (-7) = 5 \text{ or, } \frac{-35}{-7} = 5$$

We have the following definitions:

Dividend The number to be divided is called dividend.

Divisor The number which divides is called the divisor.

Quotient The result of division is called the quotient.

It follows from the above discussion that when dividend is negative and divisor is negative, the quotient is positive. When the dividend is negative and divisor is positive, the quotient is negative.

Thus, we have the following rules for division of integers:

Rule 1 *The quotient of two integers both positive or both negative is a positive integer equal to the quotient of the corresponding absolute values of the integers.*

Thus, for dividing two integers with like signs, we divide their values regardless of their sign and give plus sign to the quotient.

Rule 2 *The quotient of a positive and a negative integer is a negative integer and its absolute value is equal to the quotient of the corresponding absolute values of the integers.*

Thus, for dividing integers with unlike signs, we divide their values regardless of their sign and give minus sign to the quotient.

1.3.1 PROPERTIES OF DIVISION

Division of integers has the following properties:

(i) *If a and b are integers, then* $a \div b$ *is not necessarily an integer.*
For example, $15 \div 4$, $-14 \div 3$ are not integers.

(ii) *If a is an integer different from 0, then* $a \div a = 1$.

(iii) *For every integer a, we have* $a \div 1 = a$.

(iv) *If a is a non-zero integer, then* $0 \div a = 0$.

(v) *If a is an integer, then* $a \div 0$ *is not meaningful.*

(vi) *If a, b, c are non-zero integers, then* $(a \div b) \div c \neq a \div (b \div c)$, *unless* $c = 1$.

(vii) *If a, b, c are integers, then*

(i) $a > b \Rightarrow a \div c > b \div c$, *if c is positive.*

(ii) $a > b \Rightarrow a \div c < b \div c$, *if c is negative.*

ILLUSTRATIVE EXAMPLES

Example 1 Divide:

(i) 84 by 7 (ii) –91 by 13 (iii) –98 by –14 (iv) 324 by –27

Solution (i) We have,

$$84 \div 7 = \frac{|84|}{|7|} = \frac{84}{7} = 12$$

(ii) We have,

$$-91 \div 13 = -\frac{|-91|}{|13|} = -\frac{91}{13} = -7$$

(iii) We have,

$$-98 \div (-14) = +\frac{|-98|}{|-14|} = \frac{98}{14} = 7$$

(iv) We have,

$$324 \div (-27) = -\frac{|324|}{|-27|} = -\frac{324}{27} = -12$$

Example 2 Find the quotient in each of the following:

(i) $(-1728) \div 12$ (ii) $(-15625) \div (-125)$ (iii) $30000 \div (-100)$

Solution (i) We have,

$$(-1728) \div 12 = -\frac{|-1728|}{|12|} = -\frac{1728}{12} = -144$$

(ii) We have,

$$(-15625) \div (-125) = \frac{|-15625|}{|-125|} = \frac{15625}{125} = 125$$

(iii) We have,

$$30000 \div (-100) = -\frac{|30000|}{|-100|} = -\frac{30000}{100} = -300$$

Example 3 Find the value of

(i) $[32+2\times 17+(-6)]\div 15$ (ii) $||-17|+17|\div||-25|-42|$

Solution (i) We have,

$[32+2\times 17+(-6)]\div 15$

$$= [32+34+(-6)] \div 15 = (66-6) \div 15 = 60 \div 15 = \frac{60}{15} = 4$$

(ii) We have,

$||-17|+17|\div||-25|-42|$

$$= |17+17|\div|25-42| = |34|\div|-17| = 34 \div 17 = \frac{34}{17} = 2$$

Example 4 Simplify: $\{36\div(-9)\}\div\{(-24)\div 6\}$

Solution We have,

$\{36\div(-9)\}\div\{(-24)\div 6\}$

$$= \left\{-\frac{|36|}{|-9|}\right\} \div \left\{-\frac{|24|}{|6|}\right\} = \left\{-\frac{36}{9}\right\} \div \left\{-\frac{24}{6}\right\} = (-4) \div (-4) = \frac{|-4|}{|-4|} = \frac{4}{4} = 1$$

EXERCISE 1.2

1. Divide:
   - (i) 102 by 17
   - (ii) –85 by 5
   - (iii) –161 by –23
   - (iv) 76 by –19
   - (v) 17654 by –17654
   - (vi) (–729) by (–27)
   - (vii) 21590 by –10
   - (viii) 0 by –135
2. Fill in the blanks:
   - (i) $296 \div \ldots = -148$
   - (ii) $-88 \div \ldots = 11$
   - (iii) $84 \div \ldots = 12$
   - (iv) $\ldots\ldots\ldots \div -5 = 25$
   - (v) $\ldots\ldots \div 156 = -2$
   - (vi) $\ldots\ldots\ldots \div 567 = -1$
3. Which of the following statements are true?
   - (i) $0 \div 4 = 0$
   - (ii) $0 \div (-7) = 0$
   - (iii) $-15 \div 0 = 0$
   - (iv) $0 \div 0 = 0$
   - (v) $(-8) \div (-1) = -8$
   - (vi) $-8 \div (-2) = 4$

ANSWERS

1. (i) 6 (ii) –17 (iii) 7 (iv) –4 (v) –1 (vi) 27 (vii) –2159 (viii) 0
2. (i) –2 (ii) –8 (iii) 7 (iv) –125 (v) –312 (vi) –567
3. (i), (ii), (vi)

1.4 OPERATOR PRECEDENCE

In simplifying mathematical expressions consisting of the same type of operation, we perform one operation at a time generally starting from the left towards the right. If an expression has more than one fundamental operations, you cannot perform operations in the order they appear. Some operations have to be performed before the others. That is, each operation has its own precedence. Generally, the order in which we perform operations sequentially from left to right is: division, multiplication, addition, subtraction. This order is expressed in short as 'DMAS' where 'D' stands for division, 'M' for multiplication, 'A' for addition and, 'S' for subtraction.

We first do the divisions and multiplications starting from the left towards the right and then perform additions, subtractions left to right.

The following examples will illustrate the precedence of operations of addition, subtraction, multiplication and division.

ILLUSTRATIVE EXAMPLES

Example 1 Simplify: $24 - 4 \div 2 \times 3$

Solution We have,

$24 - 4 \div 2 \times 3$

$= 24 - 2 \times 3$ [Performing division $-4 \div 2 = -2$]

$= 24 - 6$ [Performing multiplication $2 \times 3 = 6$]

$= 18.$ [Performing subtraction]

Example 2 Simplify: $(-2\ 0) + (-8) \div (-2) \times 3$

Solution We have,

$(-20) + (-8) \div (-2) \times 3$

$= (-20) + 4 \times 3$

$= (-20) + 12$ [Performing multiplication]

$= -8.$ [Performing subtraction]

Example 3 Simplify: $(-5) - (-48) \div (-16) + (-2) \times 6$

Solution We have,

$(-5) - (-48) \div (-16) + (-2) \times 6$

$= (-5) - 3 + (-2) \times 6$ [Performing division]

$= (-5) - 3 + (-12)$ [Performing multiplication]

$= -5 - 3 - 12$

$= -20.$ [Performing addition]

EXERCISE 1.3

Find the value of

1. $36 \div 6 + 3$
2. $24 + 15 \div 3$
3. $120 - 20 \div 4$
4. $32 - (3 \times 5) + 4$
5. $3 - (5 - 6 \div 3)$
6. $21 - 12 \div 3 \times 2$
7. $16 + 8 \div 4 - 2 \times 3$
8. $28 - 5 \times 6 + 2$ = 28−30+2 = 28−28=0
9. $(-20) \times (-1) + (-28) \div 7$
10. $(-2) + (-8) \div (-4)$

11. $(-15)+4\div(5-3)$
12. $(-40)\times(-1)+(-28)\div 7$
13. $(-3)+(-8)\div(-4)-2\times(-2)$
14. $(-3)\times(-4)\div(-2)+(-1)$.

ANSWERS

1. 9	2. 29	3. 115	4. 21	5. 0	6. 13
7. 12	8. 0	9. 16	10. 0	11. –13	12. 36
13. 3	14. –7				

1.5 USE OF BRACKETS

In the previous section, we have learnt about the precedence of fundamental operations of addition, subtraction, multiplication and division. According to it, the order in which operations are to be performed is first division, then multiplication after which addition and finally subtraction. But sometimes in complex expressions, we require a set of operations to be performed prior to the others. For example, if we want an addition to be performed before a division or a multiplication, then we need to use brackets. A bracket indicates that the operations within it are to be performed before the operations outside it. For example, the expression $24 \div 3 \times 4$, as per DMAS rule, is simplified by first dividing 24 by 3 and then multiplying by 4 as shown below:

$$24 \div 3 \times 4 = (24 \div 3) \times 4 = 8 \times 4 = 32.$$

However, if we wish to multiply 3 and 4 first and then divide 24 by the resulting number, we write the expression as $24 \div (3 \times 4)$ and simplify it as

$$24 \div (3 \times 4) = 24 \div 12 = 2.$$

In complex expressions, sometimes, it is necessary to have brackets within brackets. Since same type of brackets one within another can be confusing, so different types of brackets are used. Most commonly used brackets are:

Brackets symbol	Name
( )	Parentheses or common brackets
{ }	Braces or Curly brackets
[ ]	Brackets or square brackets or box brackets
—	Vinculum

The left part of each bracket symbol indicates the start of the bracket and the right part indicates the end of the bracket. In writing mathematical expressions consisting of more than one brackets, parenthesis is used in the innermost part followed by braces and these two are covered by square brackets.

REMOVAL OF BRACKETS In order to simplify expressions involving more than one brackets, we use the following steps:

STEP I *See whether the given expression contains a vinculum or not. If a vinculum is present, then perform operations under it. Otherwise go to next step.*

STEP II *See the innermost bracket and perform operations within it.*

STEP III *Remove the innermost bracket by using following rules:*

Rule 1: *If a bracket is preceded by a plus sign, remove it by writing its terms as they are.*

Rule 2: *If a bracket is preceded by a minus sign, change positive signs within it to negative and vice-versa.*

Rule 3: *If there is no sign between a number and a grouping symbol, then it means multiplication.*

Rule 4: *If there is a number before some brackets then we multiply the number inside the brackets with the number outside the brackets.*

STEP IV *See the next innermost bracket and perform operations within it. Remove the second innermost bracket by using the rules given in step III. Continue this process till all the brackets are removed.*

Let us now illustrate these steps by means of some examples.

ILLUSTRATIVE EXAMPLES

Example 1 Simplify: $27 - [5 + \{28 - (29 - 7)\}]$

Solution We have,

$$27 - [5 + \{28 - (29 - 7)\}]$$

$= 27 - [5 + \{28 - 22\}]$ [Removing the innermost brackets]

$= 27 - [5 + 6]$ [Removing braces]

$= 27 - 11 = 16.$

Example 2 Simplify: $48 - [18 - \{16 - (5 - \overline{4 - 1})\}]$

Solution We have,

$$48 - [18 - \{16 - (5 - \overline{4 - 1})\}]$$

$= 48 - [18 - \{16 - (5 - 3)\}]$ [Removing vinculum]

$= 48 - [18 - \{16 - 2\}]$ [Removing parentheses]

$= 48 - [18 - 14]$ [Removing braces]

$= 48 - 4 = 44.$

Example 3 Simplify: $222 - \left[\frac{1}{3}\{42 + (56 - \overline{8 + 9})\} + 108\right]$

Solution We have,

$$222 - \left[\frac{1}{3}\{42 + (56 - \overline{8 + 9})\} + 108\right]$$

$= 222 - \left[\frac{1}{3}\{42 + (56 - 17)\} + 108\right]$ [Removing vinculum]

$= 222 - \left[\frac{1}{3}\{42 + 39\} + 108\right]$ [Removing parentheses]

$= 222 - \left[\frac{81}{3} + 108\right]$ [Removing braces]

$= 222 - [27 + 108] = 222 - 135 = 87$

Example 4 Simplify: $39 - [23 - \{29 - (17 - \overline{9 - 3})\}]$

Solution We have,

$$39 - [23 - \{29 - (17 - \overline{9 - 3})\}]$$

$= 39-\left[23-\{29-(17-6)\}\right]$ [Removing vinculum]

$= 39-\left[23-\{29-11\}\right]$ [Removing parentheses]

$= 39-[23-18]$ [Removing braces]

$= 39-5 \quad = 34$

Example 5 Simplify:

(i) $118-\left[121\div(11\times 11)-(-4)-\left\{3-\overline{9-2}\right\}\right]$

Solution (i) We have,

$118-\left[121\div(11\times 11)-(-4)-\left\{3-\overline{9-2}\right\}\right]$

$= 118-\left[121\div(11\times 11)-(-4)-\{3-7\}\right]$

$= 118\left[121\div 121-(-4)-\{3-7\}\right]$

$= 118-[1-(-4)-(-4)]$ [Performing division]

$= 118-[1+4+4]=118-9=109$

EXERCISE 1.4

Simplify each of the following:

1. $3-(5-6\div 3)$
2. $-25+14\div(5-3)$
3. $25-\frac{1}{2}\left\{5+4-(3+2-\overline{1+3})\right\}$
4. $27-\left[38-\left\{46-(15-\overline{13-2})\right\}\right]$
5. $36-\left[18-\{14-(15-4\div 2\times 2)\}\right]$
6. $45-\left[38-\{60\div 3-(6-9\div 3)\div 3\}\right]$
7. $23-\left[23-\left\{23-(23-\overline{23-23})\right\}\right]$
8. $2550-\left[510-\left\{270-(90-\overline{80+70})\right\}\right]$
9. $4+\frac{1}{5}\left[\left\{-10\times(25-\overline{13-3})\right\}\div(-5)\right]$
10. $22-\frac{1}{4}\{-5-(-48)\div(-16)\}$
11. $63-\left[(-3)\left\{-2-\overline{8-3}\right\}\right]\div\left[3\{5+(-2)(-1)\}\right]$
12. $\left[29-(-2)\{6-(7-3)\}\right]\div\left[3\times\{5+(-3)\times(-2)\}\right]$
13. Using brackets, write a mathematical expression for each of the following:
    (i) Nine multiplied by the sum of two and five.
    (ii) Twelve divided by the sum of one and three.
    (iii) Twenty divided by the difference of seven and two.
    (iv) Eight subtracted from the product of two and three.
    (v) Forty divided by one more than the sum of nine and ten.
    (vi) Two multiplied by one less than the difference of nineteen and six.

ANSWERS

1. 0 2. −18 3. 21 4. 31 5. 21 6. 26
7. 0 8. 2370 9. 10 10. 24 11. 62 12. 1

13. (i) $9(2+5)$ (ii) $12\div(1+3)$ (iii) $20\div(7-2)$
(iv) $2\times 3-8$ (v) $40\div\{1+(9+10)\}$ (vi) $2\times\{(19-6)-1\}$

OBJECTIVE TYPE QUESTIONS

Mark the correct alternative in each of the following:

1. $(-1)\times(-1)\times(-1)\times(-1)\times......500$ times =

 (a) -1 (b) 1 (c) 500 (d) -500

2. $(-1)+(-1)+(-1)+(-1)+......500$ times =

 (a) 500 (b) 1 (c) -1 (d) -500

3. The additive inverse of -7 is

 (a) -7 (b) $-\frac{1}{7}$ (c) 7 (d) $\frac{1}{7}$

4. The modulus of an integer x is 9, then

 (a) $x=9$ only (b) $x=-9$ only (c) $x=\pm 9$ (d) None of these

5. By how much does 5 exceed -4?

 (a) 1 (b) -1 (c) 9 (d) -9

6. By how much less than -3 is -7?

 (a) 4 (b) -4 (c) 10 (d) -10

7. The sum of two integers is 24. If one of them is -19, then the other is

 (a) 43 (b) -43 (c) 5 (d) -5

8. What must be subtracted from -6 to obtain -14?

 (a) 8 (b) 20 (c) -20 (d) -8

9. What should be divided by 6 to get -18?

 (a) -3 (b) 3 (c) -108 (d) 108

10. Which of the following is correct?

 (a) $-12>-9$ (b) $-12<-9$ (c) $(-12)+9>0$ (d) $(-12)\times 9>0$

11. The sum of two integers is -8. If one of the integers is 12, then the other is

 (a) 20 (b) 4 (c) -4 (d) -20

12. On subtracting -14 from -18, we get

 (a) 4 (b) -4 (c) -32 (d) 32

13. $(-35)\times 2+(-35)\times 8=$

 (a) -350 (b) -70 (c) -280 (d) 350

14. If $x\div 29=0$, then $x=$

 (a) 29 (b) -29 (c) 0 (d) None of these

15. If $x = (-10) + (-10) + \ldots 15$ times and $y = (-2) \times (-2) \times (-2) \times (-2) \times (-2)$, then $x - y =$

(a) 118 (b) −118 (c) −182 (d) 182

16. If $a = (-1) \times (-1) \times (-1) \ldots 100$ times and $b = (-1) \times (-1) \times (-1) \ldots 95$ times, then $a + b =$

(a) −1 (b) −2 (c) 0 (d) 1

17. $||3 - 12| - 4| =$

(a) −5 (b) 5 (c) 7 (d) −7

18. If the difference of an integer a and (− 9) is 5, then

(a) 4 (b) 5 (c) −4 (d) −9

19. The sum of two integers is 10. If one of them is negative, then other has to be

(a) negative (b) positive

(c) may be positive or negative (d) None of these

20. If $x = (-1) \times (-1) \times (-1) \times (-1) \times \ldots 25$ times, $y = (-3) \times (-3) \times (-3)$, then $xy =$

(a) −27 (b) 27 (c) 26 (d) −26

ANSWERS

1. (b)	2. (d)	3. (c)	4. (c)	5. (c)	6. (a)	7. (a)
8. (a)	9. (c)	10. (b)	11. (d)	12. (b)	13. (a)	14. (c)
15. (b)	16. (c)	17. (b)	18. (c)	19. (b)	20. (b)	

THINGS TO REMEMBER

1. The numbers. . . . , –4, –3, –1, 0, 1, 2, 3, 4,. . . . etc. are integers.
2. 1, 2, 3, 4, 5. . . . are positive integers and –1,–2, –3,. . . are negative integers.
3. 0 is an integer which is neither positive nor negative.
4. On an integer number line, all numbers to the right of 0 are positive integers and all numbers to the left of 0 are negative integers.
5. 0 is less than every positive integer and greater than every negative integer.
6. Every positive integer is greater than every negative integer.
7. Two integers that are at the same distance from 0, but on opposite sides of it are called opposite numbers.
8. The greater the number, the lesser is its opposite.
9. The sum of an integer and its opposite is zero.
10. The absolute value of an integer is the numerical value of the integer without regard to its sign. The absolute value of an integer a is denoted by $|a|$ and is given by

$$|a| = \begin{cases} a, \text{ if } a \text{ is positive or } 0 \\ -a, \text{ if } a \text{ is negative} \end{cases}$$

11. The sum of two integers of the same sign is an integer of the same sign whose absolute value is equal to the sum of the absolute values of the given integers.
12. The sum of two integers of opposite signs is an integer whose absolute value is the difference of the absolute values of addend and whose sign is the sign of the addend having greater absolute value.
13. To subtract an integer b from another integer a, we change the sign of b and add it to a.
    Thus, $a - b = a + (-b)$
14. All properties of operations on whole numbers are satisfied by these operations on integers.
15. If a and b are two integers, then $(a - b)$ is also an integer.
16. –a and a are negative or additive inverses of each other.
17. To find the product of two integers, we multiply their absolute values and give the result a plus sign if both the numbers have the same sign or a minus sign otherwise.
18. To find the quotient of one integer divided by another non-zero integer, we divide their absolute values and give the result a plus sign if both the numbers have the same sign or a minus sign otherwise.
19. All the properties applicable to whole numbers are applicable to integers in addition, the subtraction operation has the closure property.
20. Any integer when multiplied or divided by 1 gives itself and when multiplied or divided by –1 gives its opposite.
21. When expression has different types of operations, some operations have to be performed before the others. That is, each operation has its own precedence. The order in which operations are performed is division, multiplication, addition and finally subtraction (DMAS).
22. Brackets are used in an expression when we want a set of operations to be performed before the others.
23. While simplifying an expression containing brackets, the operations within the innermost set of brackets are performed first and then those brackets are removed followed by the ones immediately after them till all the brackets are removed.
24. While simplifying arithmetic expressions involving various brackets and operations, we use BODMAS rule.

THINGS TO REMEMBER

1. The numbers ..., –4, –3, –2, –1, 0, 1, 2, 3, 4, ... are integers.
2. 1, 2, 3, 4, ... are positive integers and –1, –2, –3, ... are negative integers.
3. 0 is an integer which is neither positive nor negative.

[illegible]

2

FRACTIONS

2.1 INTRODUCTION

We have learnt about the concept of fraction in the earlier class. We have also studied about types of fractions (proper, improper and mixed), comparison of fractions, equivalent fractions, representation of fractions on the number line, addition and subtraction of fractions.

In this chapter, we will learn the multiplication and division of fractions. Let us first recall, in brief, what we have learnt about fractions in the earlier class.

2.2 RECAPITULATION

FRACTION *A fraction is a number representing a part of a whole. The whole may be a single object or a group of objects.*

The fraction representing three parts out of 7 equal parts in which the whole is divided is denoted by $\frac{3}{7}$ and is read as "*three-sevenths*". In the fraction $\frac{3}{7}$, 3 is called the numerator and 7 is called the denominator. Similarly, $\frac{2}{5}$ is a fraction with numerator 2 and denominator 5 and $\frac{12}{7}$ is a fraction with numerator 12 and denominator 7.

PROPER FRACTION *A fraction whose numerator is less than the denominator, is called a proper fraction.*

For example, $\frac{7}{9}, \frac{3}{11}, \frac{2}{5}$ etc. are proper fractions.

IMPROPER FRACTION *A fraction whose numerator is more than or equal to the denominator, is called an improper fraction.*

For example, $\frac{17}{5}, \frac{47}{31}, \frac{195}{111}$ etc. are improper fractions.

MIXED FRACTION *A combination of a whole number and a proper fraction is called a mixed fraction.*

For example, $2\frac{3}{5}, 7\frac{4}{15}, 21\frac{6}{29}$ etc. are mixed fractions.

In the mixed fraction $3\frac{2}{5}$, 3 is the whole number and $\frac{2}{5}$ is the proper fraction with numerator 2 and denominator 5.

In order to convert a mixed fraction into an improper fraction, we may use the following formula:

$$\text{Improper fraction} = \frac{(\text{Whole number} \times \text{Denominator}) + \text{Numerator}}{\text{Denominator}}$$

For example, (i) $3\frac{2}{5} = \frac{3 \times 5 + 2}{5} = \frac{15 + 2}{5} = \frac{17}{5}$ (ii) $9\frac{5}{4} = \frac{9 \times 4 + 5}{4} = \frac{36 + 5}{4} = \frac{41}{4}$

In order to express an improper fraction as a mixed fraction, we first divide the numerator by denominator and obtain the quotient and remainder and then we write the mixed fraction as

$$\text{Quotient}\frac{\text{Remainder}}{\text{Denominator}}$$

For example, (i) $\frac{19}{4} = 4\frac{3}{4}$ [∵ Quotient = 4, Remainder = 3]

(ii) $\frac{47}{15} = 3\frac{2}{15}$ [∵ Quotient = 3, Remainder = 2]

<u>Remark</u> *If the numerator and denominator of a fraction are both multiplied by the same non-zero number, then its value does not change.*

i.e., $\frac{4}{5} = \frac{4 \times 2}{5 \times 2} = \frac{4 \times 3}{5 \times 3} = \frac{4 \times 4}{5 \times 4} = \frac{4 \times 5}{5 \times 5} = \frac{4 \times 6}{5 \times 6}$ *etc.*

If the numerator and denominator of a fraction are both divided by their common factor, then its value does not change.

i.e., $\frac{6}{10} = \frac{6 \div 2}{10 \div 2} = \frac{3}{5}, \frac{9}{24} = \frac{9 \div 3}{24 \div 3} = \frac{3}{8}$ *etc.*

EQUIVALENT FRACTIONS *A given fraction and various fractions obtained by multiplying (or dividing) its numerator and denominator by the same non-zero number, are called equilvalent fractions.*

For example, $\frac{3 \times 2}{4 \times 2} = \frac{6}{8}, \frac{3 \times 3}{4 \times 3} = \frac{9}{12}, \frac{3 \times 4}{4 \times 4} = \frac{12}{16}$ etc. are equivalent fractions equivalent to the fraction $\frac{3}{4}$.

We have,

$$\frac{8}{28} = \frac{8 \div 4}{28 \div 4} = \frac{2}{7}, \frac{10}{35} = \frac{10 \div 5}{35 \div 5} = \frac{2}{7}$$

∴ $\frac{8}{28}$ and $\frac{10}{35}$ are equivalent fractions equivalent to the fraction $\frac{2}{7}$

If $\frac{a}{b}$ and $\frac{c}{d}$ are two equivalent fractions, then

$$a \times d = b \times c$$

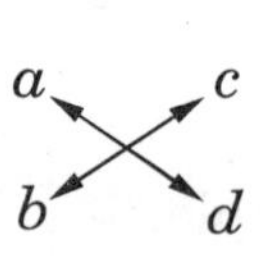

i.e., $\frac{a}{b} = \frac{c}{d} \Leftrightarrow a \times d = b \times c$

LIKE FRACTIONS *Fractions having the same denominators are called like fractions.*

For example, $\frac{2}{15}, \frac{7}{15}, \frac{11}{15}$ etc are like fractions.

UNLIKE FRACTIONS *Fractions with different denominators are called unlike fractions.*

For example, $\frac{2}{13}, \frac{7}{24}, \frac{9}{125}$ etc are unlike fractions.

FRACTION IN LOWEST TERMS *A fraction is in its lowest terms if its numerator and denominator have no common factor other than 1.*

In other words, a fraction is in its lowest terms or in lowest form, if the HCF of its numerator and denominator is 1.

In order to reduce a fraction to its lowest terms, we divide its numerator and denominator by their HCF.

ILLUSTRATION 1 Reduce $\frac{144}{180}$ to its lowest form.

Solution First we find the HCF of 144 and 180 by factorization method.

The factors of 144 are: 1, 2, 3, 4, 6, 8, 9, 12, 16, 18, 24, 36, 48, 72 and 144

The factors of 180 are: 1, 2, 3, 4, 5, 6, 10, 12, 15, 18, 30, 36, 45, 60, 90 and 180

The common factors of 144 and 180 are: 1, 2, 3, 4, 6, 12, 18 and 36

$\therefore$ HCF of 144 and 180 is 36.

Now, $\frac{144}{180} = \frac{144 \div 36}{180 \div 36}$ [Dividing numerator and denominator by the HCF of 144 and 180 i.e., 36]

$\Rightarrow \frac{144}{180} = \frac{4}{5}$

2.2.1 COMPARING FRACTIONS

In order to compare fractions, we may use the following steps:

STEP I *Find the LCM of the denominators of the given fractions.*

STEP II *Convert each fraction to its equivalent fraction with denominator equal to the LCM obtained in step I.*

STEP III *Arrange the fractions in ascending or descending order by arranging numerators in ascending or descending order.*

ILLUSTRATION 1 Which is larger $\frac{3}{4}$ or $\frac{5}{12}$?

Solution Let us first find the LCM of 4 and 12.

We have,

2	4	12
2	2	6
3	1	3
	1	1

$\therefore$ LCM of 4 and 12 is $2 \times 2 \times 3 = 12$.

Now we convert the given fractions to equivalent fractions with denominator 12.

We have,

$$\frac{3}{4}=\frac{3\times 3}{4\times 3}=\frac{9}{12}$$

We know that $9>5$

$$\therefore \quad \frac{9}{12}>\frac{5}{12} \Rightarrow \frac{3}{4}>\frac{5}{12}$$

ILLUSTRATION 2 Arrange the following fractions in ascending order $\frac{5}{8},\frac{5}{6},\frac{7}{4},\frac{3}{5}$

Solution Let us first find the LCM of the denominators:

We have,

2	5 8 6 4
2	5 4 3 2
	5 2 3 1

$\therefore \quad LCM = 2\times 2\times 5\times 2\times 3 = 120$

Now, we convert each fraction to its equivalent fraction with denominator 120.

We have,

$$\frac{3}{5}=\frac{3\times 24}{5\times 24}=\frac{72}{120} \qquad [\because\ 120\div 5=24]$$

$$\frac{5}{8}=\frac{5\times 15}{8\times 15}=\frac{75}{120} \qquad [\because\ 120\div 8=15]$$

$$\frac{5}{6}=\frac{5\times 20}{6\times 20}=\frac{100}{120} \qquad [\because\ 120\div 6=20]$$

$$\frac{7}{4}=\frac{7\times 30}{4\times 30}=\frac{210}{120} \qquad [\because\ 120\div 4=30]$$

We know that

$72<75<100<210.$

$$\Rightarrow \quad \frac{72}{120}<\frac{75}{120}<\frac{100}{120}<\frac{210}{120}$$

$$\Rightarrow \quad \frac{3}{5}<\frac{5}{8}<\frac{5}{6}<\frac{7}{4}$$

Remark *If two fractions have the same numerator but different denominators, the fraction with greater denominator is smaller.*

For example, $\frac{9}{14}<\frac{9}{10}$. Also, $\frac{7}{25}<\frac{7}{18}<\frac{7}{11}<\frac{7}{10}<\frac{7}{8}$.

2.2.2 CONVERSION OF UNLIKE FRACTIONS TO LIKE FRACTIONS

In order to convert unlike fractions to like fractions, we follow the following steps:

STEP I *Find the LCM of the denominators of the given fractions.*

STEP II *Convert each of the given fractions into an equivalent fraction having denominator equal to the LCM obtained in step I.*

ILLUSTRATION 1 Convert the unlike fractions $\frac{7}{6}, \frac{5}{9}$ and $\frac{5}{12}$ into like fractions.

Solution We have,

LCM of $(6, 9, 12) = (3 \times 2 \times 3 \times 2) = 36$

$$\begin{array}{r|rrr} 3 & 6 & 9 & 12 \\ \hline 2 & 2 & 3 & 4 \\ \hline & 1 & 3 & 2 \end{array}$$

Now, $\frac{7}{6} = \frac{7 \times 6}{6 \times 6} = \frac{42}{36}; \frac{5}{9} = \frac{5 \times 4}{9 \times 4} = \frac{20}{36}$ and $\frac{5}{12} = \frac{5 \times 3}{12 \times 3} = \frac{15}{36}$

Clearly, $\frac{42}{36}, \frac{20}{36}$ and $\frac{15}{36}$ are like fractions.

2.2.3 ADDITION AND SUBTRACTION OF FRACTIONS

In order to add or subtract like fractions, we add or subtract their numerators and retain the common denominator.

For example,

(i) $\frac{5}{8} + \frac{2}{8} = \frac{5+2}{8} = \frac{7}{8}$

(ii) $\frac{11}{15} - \frac{7}{15} = \frac{11-7}{15} = \frac{4}{15}$

(iii) $\frac{16}{5} - \frac{3}{5} + \frac{2}{5} - \frac{9}{5} = \frac{16-3+2-9}{5} = \frac{18-12}{5} = \frac{6}{5}$

(iv) $4\frac{2}{3} + \frac{1}{3} - 4\frac{1}{3} = \frac{4 \times 3 + 2}{3} + \frac{1}{3} - \frac{4 \times 3 + 1}{3} = \frac{14}{3} + \frac{1}{3} - \frac{13}{3} = \frac{14+1-13}{3} = \frac{15-13}{3} = \frac{2}{3}$

In order to add and subtract unlike fractions, we follow the following steps:

STEP I *Obtain the fractions and their denominators.*

STEP II *Find the LCM of the denominators.*

STEP III *Convert each fraction into an equivalent fraction having its denominator equal to the LCM obtained in step II.*

STEP IV *Add or subtract like fractions obtained in Step III.*

ILLUSTRATION 1 Add : (i) $\frac{7}{10} + \frac{2}{15}$ (ii) $2\frac{2}{3} + 3\frac{1}{2}$

Solution (i) LCM of 10 and 15 is $(5 \times 2 \times 3) = 30$.

So, we convert the given fractions into equivalent fractions with denominator 30.

We have, $\frac{7}{10} = \frac{7 \times 3}{10 \times 3} = \frac{21}{30}$ and, $\frac{2}{15} = \frac{2 \times 2}{15 \times 2} = \frac{4}{30}$

$$\begin{array}{r|rr} 5 & 10 & 15 \\ \hline & 2 & 3 \end{array}$$

$\therefore \quad \frac{7}{10} + \frac{2}{15} = \frac{21}{30} + \frac{4}{30} = \frac{21+4}{30} = \frac{\cancel{25}^{5}}{\cancel{30}_{6}} = \frac{5}{6}$

(ii) We have,

$$2\frac{2}{3}+3\frac{1}{2}$$

$$=\frac{2\times3+2}{3}+\frac{3\times2+1}{2}$$

$$=\frac{8}{3}+\frac{7}{2}$$

$$=\frac{8\times2}{3\times2}+\frac{7\times3}{2\times3}$$ [∵ LCM of 3 and 2 is 6. So, convert each fraction to an equivalent fraction with denominator 6]

$$=\frac{16}{6}+\frac{21}{6}=\frac{16+21}{6}=\frac{37}{6}$$

ILLUSTRATION 2 Simplify: $\frac{15}{16}-\frac{11}{12}$

Solution We have,

LCM of 16 and 12 $=(4\times4\times3)=48$

4	16	12
	4	3

$$\therefore \frac{15}{16}-\frac{11}{12}$$

$$=\frac{15\times3}{16\times3}-\frac{11\times4}{12\times4}$$ [Converting each fraction to an equivalent fraction with denominator 48]

$$=\frac{45}{48}-\frac{44}{48}=\frac{45-44}{48}=\frac{1}{48}$$

ILLUSTRATION 3 Simplify : $4\frac{5}{6}-2\frac{3}{8}+3\frac{7}{12}$

2	6	8	12
3	3	4	6
2	1	4	2
2	1	2	1
	1	1	1

Solution We have,

$$4\frac{5}{6}-2\frac{3}{8}+3\frac{7}{12}$$

$$=\frac{6\times4+5}{6}-\frac{2\times8+3}{8}+\frac{3\times12+7}{12}$$

$$=\frac{29}{6}-\frac{19}{8}+\frac{43}{12}$$

$$=\frac{29\times4}{6\times4}-\frac{19\times3}{8\times3}+\frac{43\times2}{12\times2}$$ [∵ LCM of 6, 8, 12 is $2\times3\times2\times2=24$]

$$=\frac{116}{24}-\frac{57}{24}+\frac{86}{24}=\frac{116-57+86}{24}=\frac{202-57}{24}=\frac{145}{24}$$

ILLUSTRATIVE EXAMPLES

Example 1 Arrange the following fractions in descending order:

(i) $\frac{2}{9},\frac{2}{3},\frac{8}{21}$ (ii) $\frac{1}{5},\frac{3}{7},\frac{7}{10},\frac{13}{28}$

Solution (i) First we convert the given fractions into like fractions i.e. fractions having common denominator. For this, we first find the LCM of the denominators of the given fractions. Denominators are 9, 3, 21

LCM of $(9, 3, 21) = 3\times3\times7 = 63$

3	9	3	21
3	3	1	7
7	1	1	7
	1	1	1

Now, we convert each fraction into equivalent fractions with 63 as its denominator.

We have,

$$\frac{2}{9} = \frac{2\times7}{9\times7} = \frac{14}{63} \qquad [\because 63 \div 9 = 7]$$

$$\frac{2}{3} = \frac{2\times21}{3\times21} = \frac{42}{63} \qquad [\because 63 \div 3 = 21]$$

$$\frac{8}{21} = \frac{8\times3}{21\times3} = \frac{24}{63} \qquad [\because 63 \div 21 = 3]$$

We know that

$$42 > 24 > 14$$

$$\therefore \quad \frac{42}{63} > \frac{24}{63} > \frac{14}{63} \Rightarrow \frac{2}{3} > \frac{8}{21} > \frac{2}{9}$$

(ii) Denominators of the given fractions are : 5, 7, 10, 28

LCM of denominators $= 5\times7\times2\times2 = 140$

We now convert each fraction into an equivalent fraction with 140 as its denominator.

5	5	7	10	28
7	1	7	2	28
2	1	1	2	4
	1	1	1	2

$$\therefore \quad \frac{1}{5} = \frac{1\times28}{5\times28} = \frac{28}{140} \qquad [\because 140 \div 5 = 28]$$

$$\frac{3}{7} = \frac{3\times20}{7\times20} = \frac{60}{140} \qquad [\because 140 \div 7 = 20]$$

$$\frac{7}{10} = \frac{7\times14}{10\times14} = \frac{98}{140} \qquad [\because 140 \div 10 = 14]$$

$$\frac{13}{28} = \frac{13\times5}{28\times5} = \frac{65}{140} \qquad [\because 140 \div 28 = 5]$$

$$\because \quad 98 > 65 > 60 > 28$$

$$\therefore \quad \frac{98}{140} > \frac{65}{140} > \frac{60}{140} > \frac{28}{140} \Rightarrow \frac{7}{10} > \frac{13}{28} > \frac{3}{7} > \frac{1}{5}$$

Remark *We can also arrange the given fractions in descending order by making their numerators the same and using the result that the fraction having greater denominator is smaller, provided that they have the same numerator.*

Example 2 Ramesh solved $\frac{2}{7}$ part of an exercise while Seema solved $\frac{4}{5}$ of it. Who solved less?

Solution In order to know who solved less part of the exercise, we will compare $\frac{2}{7}$ and $\frac{4}{5}$.

We have,

LCM of denominators (i.e., 7 and 5) $= 7\times5 = 35$

Converting each fraction in to an equivalent fraction having 35 as its denominator, we have

$\frac{2}{7}=\frac{2\times5}{7\times5}=\frac{10}{35}$ and $\frac{4}{5}=\frac{4\times7}{5\times7}=\frac{28}{35}$

$\because \quad 10<28$

$\therefore \quad \frac{10}{35}<\frac{28}{35} \Rightarrow \frac{2}{7}<\frac{4}{5}$

Hence, Ramesh solved lesser part than Seema.

Example 3 Michael finished colouring a picture in $\frac{7}{12}$ hour. Vaibhav finished colouring the same picture in $\frac{3}{4}$ hour. Who worked longer? By what fraction was it longer?

Solution In order to know who worked longer, we will compare fractions $\frac{7}{12}$ and $\frac{3}{4}$.

We have,

(LCM of 12 and 4) = 12

4	12	4
	3	1

Converting each fraction into an equivalent fraction with 12 as denominator, we have

$$\frac{7}{12}=\frac{7\times1}{12\times1}=\frac{7}{12} \text{ and } \frac{3}{4}=\frac{3\times3}{4\times3}=\frac{9}{12}$$

$\because \quad 7<9$

$\therefore \quad \frac{7}{12}<\frac{9}{12} \Rightarrow \frac{7}{12}<\frac{3}{4}$

Thus, Vaibhav finished colouring in longer time.

Now, $\frac{3}{4}-\frac{7}{12}=\frac{9}{12}-\frac{7}{12}=\frac{9-7}{12}=\frac{2}{12}=\frac{1}{6}$

Hence, Vaibhav finished colouring in $\frac{1}{6}$ hour more time than Michael.

Example 4 Simplify :

(i) $2-\frac{3}{5}$ (ii) $4+\frac{7}{8}$ (iii) $\frac{9}{11}-\frac{4}{15}$ (iv) $8\frac{1}{2}-3\frac{5}{8}$

Solution (i) We have,

$\therefore \quad 2-\frac{3}{5}=\frac{2}{1}-\frac{3}{5}$ $\left[\because 2=\frac{2}{1}\right]$

$=\frac{2\times5}{1\times5}-\frac{3\times1}{5\times1}$ [$\because$ LCM of 1 and 5 is 5]

$=\frac{10}{5}-\frac{3}{5}=\frac{10-3}{5}=\frac{7}{5}$

(ii) We have,

$\therefore \quad 4+\frac{7}{8}=\frac{4}{1}+\frac{7}{8}$ $\left[\because 4=\frac{4}{1}\right]$

$=\frac{4\times8}{1\times8}+\frac{7\times1}{8\times1}$ [$\because$ LCM of 1 and 8 is 8]

$$= \frac{32}{8} + \frac{7}{8} = \frac{32+7}{8} = \frac{39}{8} = 4\frac{7}{8}$$

(iii) The LCM of 11 and 15 is $11 \times 15 = 165$.

$$\therefore \quad \frac{9}{11} - \frac{4}{15} = \frac{9 \times 15}{11 \times 15} - \frac{4 \times 11}{15 \times 11} = \frac{135}{165} - \frac{44}{165} = \frac{135-44}{165} = \frac{91}{165}$$

(iv) We have,

$$8\frac{1}{2} - 3\frac{5}{8}$$

$$= \frac{17}{2} - \frac{29}{8}$$

$$= \frac{17 \times 4}{2 \times 4} - \frac{29 \times 1}{8 \times 1} \qquad [\because \text{LCM of 2 and 8 is 8}]$$

$$= \frac{68}{8} - \frac{29}{8} = \frac{68-29}{8} = \frac{39}{8} = 4\frac{7}{8}$$

Aliter We have,

$$8\frac{1}{2} - 3\frac{5}{8}$$

$$= \left(8 + \frac{1}{2}\right) - \left(3 + \frac{5}{8}\right)$$

$$= 8 + \frac{1}{2} - 3 - \frac{5}{8}$$

$$= 8 - 3 + \frac{1}{2} - \frac{5}{8}$$

$$= 5 + \frac{1 \times 4}{2 \times 4} - \frac{5 \times 1}{8 \times 1}$$

$$= 5 + \frac{4}{8} - \frac{5}{8}$$

$$= 5 + \frac{4-5}{8}$$

$$= 5 + \frac{(-1)}{8}$$

$$= \frac{5}{1} - \frac{1}{8} = \frac{5 \times 8}{1 \times 8} - \frac{1 \times 1}{8 \times 1} = \frac{40}{8} - \frac{1}{8} = \frac{40-1}{8} = \frac{39}{8} = 4\frac{7}{8}$$

Example 5 Simplify: $4\frac{2}{3} - 3\frac{1}{4} + 2\frac{1}{6}$.

Solution We have,

$$4\frac{2}{3} - 3\frac{1}{4} + 2\frac{1}{6}$$

$$= \frac{14}{3} - \frac{13}{4} + \frac{13}{6}$$

$$= \frac{14\times4}{3\times4} - \frac{13\times3}{4\times3} + \frac{13\times2}{6\times2}$$ [∵ LCM of 3, 4 and 6 is 12, so we convert each fraction into an equivalent fraction with denominator 12]

$$= \frac{56}{12} - \frac{39}{12} + \frac{26}{12} = \frac{56-39+26}{12} = \frac{82-39}{12} = \frac{43}{12} = 3\frac{7}{12}$$

Example 6 Sameera purchased $3\frac{1}{2}$ kg apples and $4\frac{3}{4}$ kg oranges. What is the total weight of fruits purchased by her?

Solution Total weight of the fruits purchased by Sameera is $\left(3\frac{1}{2}+4\frac{3}{4}\right)$ kg.

Now, $3\frac{1}{2}+4\frac{3}{4}$

$$= \frac{7}{2} + \frac{19}{4}$$

$$= \frac{7\times2}{2\times2} + \frac{19\times1}{4\times1}$$

$$= \frac{14}{4} + \frac{19}{4} = \frac{14+19}{4} = \frac{33}{4} = 8\frac{1}{4}$$

Hence, total weight is $8\frac{1}{4}$ kg.

Example 7 Ritu ate $\frac{3}{5}$ part of an apple and the remaining apple was eaten by her brother Somu. How much part of the apple did Somu eat? Who had the larger share? By how much?

Solution We have, Part of an apple eaten by Ritu $= \frac{3}{5}$

∴ Part of an apple eaten by Somu

$$= 1 - \frac{3}{5} = \frac{5}{5} - \frac{3}{5} = \frac{5-3}{5} = \frac{2}{5}$$

Clearly, $\frac{3}{5} > \frac{2}{5}$. So, Ritu had the larger share.

Now,

$$\frac{3}{5} - \frac{2}{5} = \frac{3-2}{5} = \frac{1}{5}$$

∴ Ritu had $\frac{1}{5}$ part more than Somu.

Example 8 In the adjoining Fig. 1, find the perimeters of (i) $\Delta\, ABE$ (ii) the rectangle *BCDE*. Whose perimeter is greater?

Solution (i) We have,

Perimeter of $\Delta\ ABE$

$= AB + BE + EA$

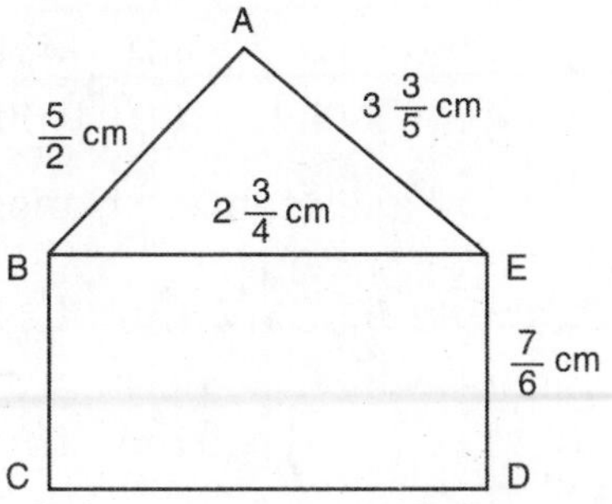

Fig. 1

$$= \left(\frac{5}{2} + 2\frac{3}{4} + 3\frac{3}{5}\right) \text{cm}$$

$$= \left(\frac{5}{2} + \frac{11}{4} + \frac{18}{5}\right) \text{cm}$$

$$= \left(\frac{5\times10}{2\times10} + \frac{11\times5}{4\times5} + \frac{18\times4}{5\times4}\right) \text{cm} \qquad [\because \text{LCM of 2, 4 and 5 is 20}]$$

$$= \left(\frac{50}{20} + \frac{55}{20} + \frac{72}{20}\right) \text{cm} = \frac{50+55+72}{20} \text{cm} = \frac{177}{20} \text{cm} = 8\frac{17}{20} \text{cm}$$

(ii) We have,

Perimeter of rectangle $BCDE$

$= BC + CD + DE + EB$

$$= \left(\frac{7}{6} + 2\frac{3}{4} + \frac{7}{6} + 2\frac{3}{4}\right) \text{cm}$$

$$= \left(\frac{7}{6} + \frac{11}{4} + \frac{7}{6} + \frac{11}{4}\right) \text{cm}$$

$$= \left(\frac{7\times2}{6\times2} + \frac{11\times3}{4\times3} + \frac{7\times2}{6\times2} + \frac{11\times3}{4\times3}\right) \text{cm} \qquad [\because \text{LCM of 6 and 4 is 12}]$$

$$= \left(\frac{14}{12} + \frac{33}{12} + \frac{14}{12} + \frac{33}{12}\right) \text{cm} = \frac{14+33+14+33}{12} \text{cm} = \frac{94}{12} \text{cm} = 7\frac{10}{12} \text{cm} = 7\frac{5}{6} \text{cm}$$

Thus, perimeters of triangle ABE and rectangle $BCDE$ are $\frac{177}{20}$ cm and $\frac{94}{12}$ cm respectively.

In order to determine whose perimeter is greater, we convert $\frac{177}{20}$ and $\frac{94}{12}$ into equivalent fractions with denominators as the LCM of 20 and 12.

We have,

4	20	12
	5	3

LCM of 20 and $12 = (4\times5\times3) = 60$

$$\therefore \quad \frac{177}{20} = \frac{177\times3}{20\times3} = \frac{531}{60} \text{ and } \frac{94}{12} = \frac{94\times5}{12\times5} = \frac{470}{60}$$

$\because \quad 531 > 470$

$\therefore \quad \frac{531}{60} > \frac{470}{60} \Rightarrow \frac{177}{20} > \frac{94}{12}$

Hence, triangle ABE has greater perimeter.

Example 9 Salil wants to put a picture in a frame. The picture is $7\frac{3}{5}$ cm wide. To fit in the frame the picture cannot be more than $7\frac{3}{10}$ cm wide. How much should the picture be trimmed?

Solution We have,

$$\text{Actual width of the picture} = 7\frac{3}{5}\text{ cm} = \frac{38}{5}\text{ cm}$$

$$\text{Required width of the picture} = 7\frac{3}{10}\text{ cm} = \frac{73}{10}\text{ cm}$$

$$\therefore \quad \text{Extra width} = \left(\frac{38}{5} - \frac{73}{10}\right)\text{cm} = \left(\frac{38 \times 2}{5 \times 2} - \frac{73 \times 1}{10 \times 1}\right)\text{cm} = \left(\frac{76}{10} - \frac{73}{10}\right)\text{cm}$$

$$= \frac{76 - 73}{10}\text{ cm} = \frac{3}{10}\text{ cm}$$

Hence, $\frac{3}{10}$ cm width of the picture should be trimmed.

EXERCISE 2.1

1. Compare the following fractions by using the symbol > or < or =:

   (i) $\frac{7}{9}$ and $\frac{8}{13}$ (ii) $\frac{11}{9}$ and $\frac{5}{9}$ (iii) $\frac{37}{41}$ and $\frac{19}{30}$ (iv) $\frac{17}{15}$ and $\frac{119}{105}$

2. Arrange the following fractions in ascending order:

   (i) $\frac{3}{8}, \frac{5}{6}, \frac{6}{8}, \frac{2}{4}, \frac{1}{3}$ (ii) $\frac{4}{6}, \frac{3}{8}, \frac{6}{12}, \frac{5}{16}$

3. Arrange the following fractions in descending order:

   (i) $\frac{4}{5}, \frac{7}{10}, \frac{11}{15}, \frac{17}{20}$ (ii) $\frac{2}{7}, \frac{11}{35}, \frac{9}{14}, \frac{13}{28}$

4. Write five equivalent fractions of $\frac{3}{5}$.

5. Find the sum:

   (i) $\frac{5}{8} + \frac{3}{10}$ (ii) $4\frac{3}{4} + 9\frac{2}{5}$ (iiii) $\frac{5}{6} + 3 + \frac{3}{4}$ (iv) $2\frac{3}{5} + 4\frac{7}{10} + 2\frac{4}{15}$

6. Find the difference of

   (i) $\frac{13}{24}$ and $\frac{7}{16}$ (ii) $\frac{23}{3}$ and 6 (iii) $\frac{18}{20}$ and $\frac{21}{25}$ (iv) $3\frac{3}{10}$ and $2\frac{7}{15}$

7. Find the difference:

(i) $\frac{6}{7}-\frac{9}{11}$ (ii) $8-\frac{5}{9}$ (iii) $9-5\frac{2}{3}$ (iv) $4\frac{3}{10}-1\frac{2}{15}$

8. Simplify:

(i) $\frac{2}{3}+\frac{1}{6}-\frac{2}{9}$ (ii) $12-3\frac{1}{2}$ (iii) $7\frac{5}{6}-4\frac{3}{8}+2\frac{7}{12}$

9. What should be added to $5\frac{3}{7}$ to get 12?

10. What should be added to $5\frac{4}{15}$ to get $12\frac{3}{5}$?

11. Suman studies for $5\frac{2}{3}$ hours daily. She devotes $2\frac{4}{5}$ hours of her time for Science and Mathematics. How much time does she devote for other subjects?

12. A piece of wire is of length $12\frac{3}{4}$m. If it is cut into two pieces in such a way that the length of one piece is $5\frac{1}{4}$m, what is the length of the other piece?

13. A rectangular sheet of paper is $12\frac{1}{2}$ cm long and $10\frac{2}{3}$ cm wide. Find its perimeter.

14. In a "magic square", the sum of the numbers in each row, in each column and along the diagonal is the same. Is this a magic square?

$\frac{4}{11}$	$\frac{9}{11}$	$\frac{2}{11}$
$\frac{3}{11}$	$\frac{5}{11}$	$\frac{7}{11}$
$\frac{8}{11}$	$\frac{1}{11}$	$\frac{6}{11}$

15. The cost of Mathematics book is ₹ $25\frac{3}{4}$ and that of Science book is ₹ $20\frac{1}{2}$. Which costs more and by how much?

16. (i) Provide the number in box □ and also give its simplest form in each of the following:

(i) $\frac{2}{3}\times\square=\frac{10}{30}$ (ii) $\frac{3}{5}\times\square=\frac{24}{75}$.

ANSWER

1. (i) $\frac{7}{9}>\frac{8}{13}$ (ii) $\frac{11}{9}>\frac{5}{9}$ (iii) $\frac{37}{41}>\frac{19}{30}$ (iv) $\frac{17}{15}=\frac{119}{105}$

2. (i) $\frac{1}{3}<\frac{3}{8}<\frac{2}{4}<\frac{6}{8}<\frac{5}{6}$ (ii) $\frac{5}{16}<\frac{3}{8}<\frac{6}{12}<\frac{4}{6}$

3. (i) $\frac{17}{20} > \frac{4}{5} > \frac{11}{15} > \frac{7}{10}$ (ii) $\frac{9}{14} > \frac{13}{28} > \frac{11}{35} > \frac{2}{7}$ 4. $\frac{6}{10}, \frac{9}{15}, \frac{12}{20}, \frac{15}{25}, \frac{18}{30}$

5. (i) $\frac{37}{40}$ (ii) $\frac{283}{20}$ (iii) $\frac{55}{12}$ (iv) $\frac{287}{30}$

6. (i) $\frac{5}{48}$ (ii) $\frac{5}{3}$ (iii) $\frac{3}{50}$ (iv) $\frac{5}{6}$

7. (i) $\frac{3}{77}$ (ii) $\frac{67}{9}$ (iii) $\frac{10}{3}$ (iv) $\frac{19}{6}$

8. (i) $\frac{11}{18}$ (ii) $\frac{17}{2}$ (iii) $\frac{145}{24}$

9. $\frac{46}{7}$ 10. $\frac{22}{3}$ 11. $2\frac{13}{15}$ hours 12. $7\frac{1}{2}$ m

13. $46\frac{1}{3}$ cm 14. Yes 15. Mathematics book by ₹ $5\frac{1}{4}$ 16. (i) $\frac{5}{10}$ (ii) $\frac{8}{15}$

2.3 MULTIPLICATION OF FRACTIONS

Let there be a rectangle of length $7\frac{3}{4}$ cm and breadth $5\frac{1}{2}$ cm. In the previous section, we have learnt how to find the perimeter of the rectangle by using addition of fractions. If we want to calculate the area of the rectangle, we will have to find the product of its length and breadth i.e., $7\frac{3}{4} \times 5\frac{1}{2}$ or, $\frac{31}{4} \times \frac{11}{2}$. This can be calculated if we know how to multiply two fractions. So, we define the multiplication of fractions as follows:

$$\text{Product of two fractions} = \frac{\text{Prodcut of their numerators}}{\text{Product of their denominators}}$$

i.e., $\frac{a}{b} \times \frac{c}{d} = \frac{(a \times c)}{(b \times d)}$

For example,

(i) $\frac{3}{7} \times \frac{4}{5} = \frac{3 \times 4}{7 \times 5} = \frac{12}{35}$ (ii) $\frac{7}{3} \times \frac{5}{2} = \frac{7 \times 5}{3 \times 2} = \frac{35}{6}$

(iii) $5 \times \frac{3}{7} = \frac{5}{1} \times \frac{3}{7} = \frac{5 \times 3}{1 \times 7} = \frac{15}{7}$ (iv) $\frac{5}{12} \times 9 = \frac{5}{12} \times \frac{9}{1} = \frac{5 \times \cancel{9}^{3}}{{}_{4}\cancel{12} \times 1} = \frac{5 \times 3}{4 \times 1} = \frac{15}{4}$

Sometimes for indicating multiplication of two fractions, we use the word 'of' as follows:

$$\frac{1}{2} \text{ of } 8 = \frac{1}{2} \times 8 = \frac{1}{2} \times \frac{8}{1} = \frac{1 \times 8}{2 \times 1} = \frac{8}{2} = 4$$

$$\frac{1}{5} \text{ of } 20 = \frac{1}{5} \times 20 = \frac{1}{5} \times \frac{20}{1} = \frac{1 \times 20}{5 \times 1} = \frac{20}{5} = 4$$

$$\frac{2}{5} \text{ of } 25 = \frac{2}{5} \times 25 = \frac{2}{5} \times \frac{25}{1} = \frac{2 \times 25}{5 \times 1} = \frac{50}{5} = 10$$

$$\frac{2}{3} \text{ of } \frac{5}{7} = \frac{2}{3} \times \frac{5}{7} = \frac{2 \times 5}{3 \times 7} = \frac{10}{21} \text{ etc.}$$

ILLUSTRATIVE EXAMPLES

Example 1 Multiply:

(i) $\frac{2}{9}$ by $\frac{4}{5}$ (ii) $\frac{3}{5}$ by 12 (iii) $2\frac{1}{3}$ by $\frac{2}{5}$ (iv) $5\frac{3}{4}$ by $2\frac{3}{7}$

Solution We have,

(i) $\frac{2}{9}\times\frac{4}{5}=\frac{2\times4}{9\times5}=\frac{8}{45}$

(ii) $\frac{3}{5}\times12=\frac{3}{5}\times\frac{12}{1}=\frac{3\times12}{5\times1}=\frac{36}{5}=7\frac{1}{5}$

(iii) $2\frac{1}{3}\times\frac{2}{5}=\frac{7}{3}\times\frac{2}{5}=\frac{7\times2}{3\times5}=\frac{14}{15}$

(iv) $5\frac{3}{4}\times2\frac{3}{7}=\frac{23}{4}\times\frac{17}{7}=\frac{23\times17}{4\times7}=\frac{391}{28}=13\frac{27}{28}$

Example 2 Multiply and reduce to lowest form (if possible) :

(i) $\frac{2}{3}\times\frac{5}{4}$ (ii) $\frac{1}{3}\times\frac{15}{8}$ (iii) $\frac{4}{5}\times\frac{12}{7}$

Solution We have,

(i) $\frac{2}{3}\times\frac{5}{4}=\frac{{}^{1}\cancel{2}\times5}{3\times\cancel{4}^{2}}=\frac{1\times5}{3\times2}=\frac{5}{6}$

(ii) $\frac{1}{3}\times\frac{15}{8}=\frac{1\times\cancel{15}^{5}}{{}^{1}\cancel{3}\times8}=\frac{1\times5}{1\times8}=\frac{5}{8}$

(iii) $\frac{4}{5}\times\frac{12}{7}=\frac{4\times12}{5\times7}=\frac{48}{35}=1\frac{13}{35}$

Example 3 Simplify :

(i) $5\times\frac{3}{20}\times\frac{2}{15}$ (ii) $\frac{14}{25}\times\frac{35}{51}\times\frac{34}{49}$

Solution We have,

(i) $5\times\frac{3}{20}\times\frac{2}{15}=\frac{5}{1}\times\frac{3}{20}\times\frac{2}{15}=\frac{{}^{1}\cancel{5}\times{}^{1}\cancel{3}\times2}{1\times\cancel{20}_{4}\times\cancel{15}_{5}}=\frac{1\times1\times\cancel{2}^{1}}{1\times\cancel{4}_{2}\times5}=\frac{1}{2\times5}=\frac{1}{10}$

(ii) $\frac{14}{25}\times\frac{35}{51}\times\frac{34}{49}=\frac{{}^{2}\cancel{14}\times{}^{1}\cancel{7}\,\cancel{35}\times\cancel{34}^{2}}{\cancel{25}_{5}\times\cancel{51}_{3}\times\cancel{49}\;\cancel{7}^{1}}=\frac{2\times1\times2}{5\times3\times1}=\frac{4}{15}$

Example 4 Which is greater? $\frac{2}{7}$ of $\frac{3}{4}$ or, $\frac{3}{5}$ of $\frac{5}{8}$.

Solution We have,

$\frac{2}{7}$ of $\frac{3}{4}=\frac{2}{7}\times\frac{3}{4}=\frac{\cancel{2}^{1}\times3}{7\times\cancel{4}_{2}}=\frac{1\times3}{7\times2}=\frac{3}{14}$ and, $\frac{3}{5}$ of $\frac{5}{8}=\frac{3}{5}\times\frac{5}{8}=\frac{3\times\overset{1}{\cancel{5}}}{\underset{1}{\cancel{5}}\times8}=\frac{3\times1}{1\times8}=\frac{3}{8}$

In order to compare these fractions, we convert them into equivalent fractions having same denominator equal to the LCM of 14 and 8.

$$\begin{array}{r|ll} 2 & 14 & 8 \\ \hline & 7 & 4 \end{array}$$

LCM of 14 and 8 $= 2\times 7\times 4 = 56$

$\therefore \quad \frac{3}{14} = \frac{3\times 4}{14\times 4} = \frac{12}{56}$ and $\frac{3}{8} = \frac{3\times 7}{8\times 7} = \frac{21}{56}$

Clearly, $21 > 12$

$\therefore \quad \frac{21}{56} > \frac{12}{56} \Rightarrow \frac{3}{8} > \frac{3}{14}$

Hence, $\frac{3}{5}$ of $\frac{5}{8}$ is greater than $\frac{2}{7}$ of $\frac{3}{4}$.

Aliter We know that if the numerators of two fractions are same, then the fraction having smaller denominator is greater.

$\therefore \quad \frac{3}{8} > \frac{3}{14} \Rightarrow \frac{3}{5}$ of $\frac{5}{8}$ is greater than $\frac{2}{7}$ of $\frac{3}{4}$.

Example 5 Find:

(i) $\frac{3}{5}$ of a rupee (ii) $\frac{3}{4}$ of a year (iii) $\frac{2}{3}$ of a day

(iv) $\frac{5}{8}$ of a kilogram (v) $\frac{2}{3}$ of an hour (vi) $\frac{7}{25}$ of a litre

Solution (i) We have, 1 rupee = 100 paise

$\therefore \quad \frac{3}{5}$ of a rupee $= \frac{3}{5}$ of 100 paise

Now, $\frac{3}{5}$ of $100 = \frac{3}{5}\times 100 = \frac{3}{5}\times\frac{100}{1} = \frac{3\times \cancel{100}^{20}}{\cancel{5}_1\times 1} = \frac{3\times 20}{1\times 1} = 60$

$\therefore \quad \frac{3}{5}$ of a rupee = 60 paise

(ii) We have, 1 year = 12 months

$\therefore \quad \frac{3}{4}$ of a year $= \frac{3}{4}$ of 12 months

Now, $\frac{3}{4}$ of $12 = \frac{3}{4}\times 12 = \frac{3\times \overset{3}{\cancel{12}}}{\underset{1}{\cancel{4}}\times 1} = \frac{3\times 3}{1\times 1} = 9$

$\therefore \quad \frac{3}{4}$ of a year = 9 months

(iii) We have, 1 day = 24 hours

$\therefore \quad \frac{2}{3}$ of a day $= \frac{2}{3}$ of 24 hours

Now, $\frac{2}{3}$ of $24 = \frac{2}{3}\times 24 = \frac{2}{3}\times\frac{24}{1} = \frac{2\times \overset{8}{\cancel{24}}}{\underset{1}{\cancel{3}}\times 1} = \frac{2\times 8}{1\times 1} = 16$

$\therefore \quad \frac{2}{3}$ of a day = 16 hours

(iv) We have, 1 kilogram = 1000 grams

$\therefore \quad \frac{5}{8}$ of a kilogram $= \frac{5}{8}$ of 1000 grams $= \left(\frac{5}{8} \times 1000\right)$ grams

Now, $\frac{5}{8} \times 1000 = \frac{5}{8} \times \frac{1000}{1} = \frac{5 \times \overset{125}{\cancel{1000}}}{\underset{1}{\cancel{8}} \times 1} = \frac{5 \times 125}{1 \times 1} = 625$

$\therefore \quad \frac{5}{8}$ of a kilogram = 625 grams

(v) We have, 1 hour = 60 minutes

$\therefore \quad \frac{2}{3}$ of an hour $= \left(\frac{2}{3} \times 60\right)$ minutes

Now, $\frac{2}{3} \times 60 = \frac{2}{3} \times \frac{60}{1} = \frac{2 \times \overset{20}{\cancel{60}}}{{}_1\cancel{3} \times 1} = \frac{2 \times 20}{1 \times 1} = 40$

$\therefore \quad \frac{2}{3}$ of an hour = 40 minutes

(vi) We have, 1 litre = 1000 ml

$\therefore \quad \frac{7}{25}$ of a litre $= \left(\frac{7}{25} \times 1000\right)$ ml

Now, $\frac{7}{25} \times 1000 = \frac{7}{25} \times \frac{1000}{1} = \frac{7 \times \overset{40}{\cancel{1000}}}{{}_1\cancel{25} \times 1} = 7 \times 40 = 280$

$\therefore \quad \frac{7}{25}$ of a litre = 280 ml.

Example 6 Sugar is sold at ₹ $17\frac{3}{4}$ per kg. Find the cost of $8\frac{1}{2}$ kg of a sugar.

Solution We have,

Cost of 1 kg of sugar = ₹ $17\frac{3}{4}$ = ₹ $\frac{71}{4}$

$\therefore$ Cost of $8\frac{1}{2}$ kg of sugar = ₹ $\left(\frac{71}{4} \times 8\frac{1}{2}\right)$

= ₹ $\left(\frac{71}{4} \times \frac{17}{2}\right)$ = ₹ $\left(\frac{71 \times 17}{4 \times 2}\right)$ = ₹ $\left(\frac{1207}{8}\right)$ = ₹ $150\frac{7}{8}$

Hence, the cost of $8\frac{1}{2}$ kg of sugar is ₹ $150\frac{7}{8}$.

Example 7 A car runs 16 km using 1 litre of petrol. How much distance will it cover using $2\frac{3}{4}$ litres of petrol?

Solution In 1 litre petrol, car runs 16 km

$\therefore$ In $2\frac{3}{4}$ litres of petrol car will travel $= \left(2\frac{3}{4}\times 16\right)$ km $= \left(\frac{11}{\cancel{4}_1}\times\frac{\cancel{16}^4}{1}\right)$ km

$= (11\times 4)$ km $= 44$ km

Hence, car travels 44 km in $2\frac{3}{4}$ litres of petrol.

Example 8 Shikha has read $\frac{3}{4}$ of a book consisting of 288 pages. How many pages are still left?

Solution We have,

Total number of pages in the book = 288

Number of pages read by Shikha $= \frac{3}{4}$ of $288 = \frac{3}{4}\times 288$

$$= \frac{3}{\cancel{4}_1}\times\frac{\cancel{288}^{72}}{1} = 3\times 72 = 216$$

$\therefore$ Number of pages left $= (288 - 216) = 72$

Example 9 A rectangular park is $20\frac{3}{4}$ m long and $15\frac{1}{2}$ m wide. What is the area of the park?

Solution We have,

Length of the park $= 20\frac{3}{4}$ m $= \frac{83}{4}$ m, Width of the park $= 15\frac{1}{2}$ m $= \frac{31}{2}$ m

$\therefore$ Area of the park = Length × Width

$$= \frac{83}{4}\times\frac{31}{2}\text{ m}^2 = \frac{83\times 31}{4\times 2}\text{ m}^2 = \frac{2573}{8}\text{ m}^2 = 321\frac{5}{8}\text{ m}^2$$

Example 10 Find the area of a square field if its each side is $10\frac{3}{4}$ m long.

Solution We have,

Length of the square field $= 10\frac{3}{4}$ m $= \frac{43}{4}$ m.

Breadth of the square field $= 10\frac{3}{4}$ m $= \frac{43}{4}$ m.

$\therefore$ Area of the square field = Length × Breadth

$$= \frac{43}{4} \times \frac{43}{4} \text{ m}^2 = \frac{43 \times 43}{4 \times 4} \text{ m}^2 = \frac{1849}{16} \text{ m}^2 = 115\frac{9}{16} \text{ m}^2$$

Example 11 Priya spends $\frac{3}{5}$ of her income on household expenses and $\frac{1}{7}$ of her income on personal expenses. If her monthly income is ₹ 35000, find her monthly savings.

Solution Priya's total monthly income = ₹ 35000.

$$\text{Monthly expenditure} = \frac{3}{5} \text{ of ₹ } 35000 + \frac{1}{7} \text{ of ₹ } 35000$$

$$= ₹\left(\frac{3}{5} \times 35000\right) + ₹\left(\frac{1}{7} \times 35000\right)$$

$$= ₹\left(\frac{3}{5} \times \frac{35000}{1}\right) + ₹\left(\frac{1}{7} \times \frac{35000}{1}\right)$$

$$= ₹\left(\frac{3 \times \overset{7000}{\cancel{35000}}}{\underset{1}{\cancel{5}} \times 1}\right) + ₹\left(\frac{1 \times \overset{5000}{\cancel{35000}}}{\underset{1}{\cancel{7}} \times 1}\right)$$

$$= ₹ (3 \times 7000) + ₹ (1 \times 5000)$$

$$= ₹ 21000 + ₹ 5000 = ₹ (21000 + 5000) = ₹ 26000$$

$\therefore$ Monthly savings = ₹ (35000 – 26000) = ₹ 9000

Example 12 A carton contains 40 boxes of nails and each box weighs $3\frac{3}{4}$ kg. How much would a carton of nails weigh?

Solution We have,

$$\text{Weight of 1 box} = 3\frac{3}{4} \text{ kg} = \frac{15}{4} \text{ kg}$$

$$\therefore \text{ Weight of 40 boxes} = \left(\frac{15}{4} \times 40\right) \text{kg} = \left(\frac{15}{4} \times \frac{40}{1}\right) \text{kg} = \frac{15 \times \overset{10}{\cancel{40}}}{\underset{1}{\cancel{4}} \times 1} \text{kg} = 150 \text{ kg}$$

Hence, weight of the carton is 150 kg.

EXERCISE 2.2

1. Multiply:

   (i) $\frac{7}{11}$ by $\frac{3}{5}$ (ii) $\frac{3}{5}$ by 25 (iii) $3\frac{4}{15}$ by 24 (iv) $3\frac{1}{8}$ by $\times 4\frac{10}{11}$

2. Find the product:

   (i) $\frac{4}{7} \times \frac{14}{25}$ (ii) $7\frac{1}{2} \times 2\frac{4}{15}$ (iii) $3\frac{6}{7} \times 4\frac{2}{3}$ (iv) $6\frac{11}{14} \times 3\frac{1}{2}$

3. Simplify:

   (i) $\frac{12}{25} \times \frac{15}{28} \times \frac{35}{36}$ (ii) $\frac{10}{27} \times \frac{39}{56} \times \frac{20}{65}$ (iii) $2\frac{2}{17} \times 7\frac{2}{9} \times 1\frac{33}{52}$

4. Find:

   (i) $\frac{1}{2}$ of $4\frac{2}{9}$ (ii) $\frac{5}{8}$ of $9\frac{2}{3}$ (iii) $\frac{2}{3}$ of $\frac{9}{16}$

5. Which is greater? $\frac{1}{2}$ of $\frac{6}{7}$ or $\frac{2}{3}$ of $\frac{3}{7}$

6. Find:

   (i) $\frac{7}{11}$ of ₹ 330 (ii) $\frac{5}{9}$ of 108 metres (iii) $\frac{3}{7}$ of 42 litres

   (iv) $\frac{1}{12}$ of an hour (v) $\frac{5}{6}$ of an year (vi) $\frac{3}{20}$ of a kg

   (vii) $\frac{7}{20}$ of a litre (viii) $\frac{5}{6}$ of a day (ix) $\frac{2}{7}$ of a week

7. Shikha plants 5 saplings in a row in her garden. The distance between two adjacent saplings is $\frac{3}{4}$ m. Find the distance between the first and the last sapling.

8. Ravish reads $\frac{1}{3}$ part of a book in 1 hour. How much part of the book will he read in $2\frac{1}{5}$ hours?

9. Lipika reads a book for $1\frac{3}{4}$ hours everyday. She reads the entire book in 6 days. How many hours in all were required by her to read the book?

10. Find the area of a rectangular park which is $41\frac{2}{3}$ m long and $18\frac{3}{5}$ m broad.

11. If milk is available at ₹ $17\frac{3}{4}$ per litre, find the cost of $7\frac{2}{5}$ litres of milk.

12. Sharda can walk $8\frac{1}{3}$ km in one hour. How much distance will she cover in $2\frac{2}{5}$ hours?

13. A sugar bag contains 30 kg of sugar. After consuming $\frac{2}{3}$ of it, how much sugar is left in the bag?

14. Each side of a square is $6\frac{2}{3}$ m long. Find its area.

15. There are 45 students in a class and $\frac{3}{5}$ of them are boys. How many girls are there in the class?

ANSWERS

1. (i) $\frac{21}{55}$ (ii) 15 (iii) $78\frac{2}{5}$ (iv) $15\frac{15}{44}$

2. (i) $\frac{8}{25}$ (ii) 17 (iii) 18 (iv) $23\frac{3}{4}$ 3. (i) $\frac{1}{4}$ (ii) $\frac{1}{9}$ (iii) 25

4. (i) $2\frac{1}{9}$ (ii) $6\frac{1}{24}$ (iii) $\frac{3}{8}$ 5. $\frac{1}{2}$ of $\frac{6}{7}$

6. (i) Rs 210 (ii) 60 metres (iii) 18 litres (iv) 5 minutes
(v) 10 months (vi) 150 gms (vii) 350 ml
(viii) 20 hours (ix) 2 days

7. 3 m 8. $\frac{11}{15}$ 9. $10\frac{1}{2}$ hours 10. 775 m^2 11. ₹ $131\frac{7}{20}$

12. 20 km 13. 10 kg 14. $44\frac{4}{9}$ m^2 15. 18

2.4 DIVISION OF FRACTIONS

RECIPROCAL OF A FRACTION *Two fractions are said to be the reciprocal or multiplicative inverse of each other, if their product is 1.*

For example,

(i) $\frac{3}{4}$ and $\frac{4}{3}$ are the reciprocals of each other, because $\frac{3}{4}\times\frac{4}{3}=1$.

(ii) The reciprocal of $\frac{1}{7}$ is $\frac{7}{1}$ i.e.; 7, because $\frac{1}{7}\times\frac{7}{1}=1$

(iii) The reciprocal of $\frac{1}{9}$ is 9, because $\frac{1}{9}\times 9=1$

(iv) The reciprocal of $2\frac{3}{5}$ i.e., $\frac{13}{5}$ is $\frac{5}{13}$, because $2\frac{3}{5}\times\frac{5}{13}=1$.

Reciprocal of 0 does not exist because division by zero is not possible.

Clearly, the reciprocal of a non-zero fraction $\frac{a}{b}$ is the fraction $\frac{b}{a}$.

DIVISION OF FRACTIONS *The division of a fraction $\frac{a}{b}$ by a non-zero fraction $\frac{c}{d}$ is defined as the product of $\frac{a}{b}$ with the multiplicative inverse or reciprocal of $\frac{c}{d}$.*

i.e., $$\frac{a}{b}\div\frac{c}{d}=\frac{a}{b}\times\frac{d}{c}$$

For example,

(i) $\frac{3}{5}\div\frac{5}{9}=\frac{3}{5}\times\frac{9}{5}=\frac{3\times 9}{5\times 5}=\frac{27}{25}$ (ii) $\frac{2}{3}\div 8=\frac{2}{3}\times\frac{1}{8}=\frac{\overset{1}{\cancel{2}}\times 1}{3\times \underset{4}{\cancel{8}}}=\frac{1}{12}$

(iii) $4 \div \frac{6}{7} = \frac{4}{1} \div \frac{6}{7} = \frac{4}{1} \times \frac{7}{6} = \frac{\overset{2}{\cancel{4}} \times 7}{1 \times \underset{3}{\cancel{6}}} = \frac{14}{3} = 4\frac{2}{3}$

(iv) $4\frac{2}{3} \div 3\frac{1}{2} = \frac{14}{3} \div \frac{7}{2} = \frac{14}{3} \times \frac{2}{7} = \frac{\overset{2}{\cancel{14}} \times 2}{3 \times \underset{1}{\cancel{7}}} = \frac{4}{3}$.

ILLUSTRATIVE EXAMPLES

Example 1 Divide:

(i) $\frac{5}{9}$ by $\frac{2}{3}$ (ii) 28 by $\frac{7}{4}$ (iii) 36 by $6\frac{2}{3}$

Solution We have,

(i) $\frac{5}{9} \div \frac{2}{3} = \frac{5}{9} \times \frac{3}{2} = \frac{5 \times \overset{1}{\cancel{3}}}{\underset{3}{\cancel{9}} \times 2} = \frac{5 \times 1}{3 \times 2} = \frac{5}{6}$

(ii) $28 \div \frac{7}{4} = \frac{28}{1} \div \frac{7}{4} = \frac{28}{1} \times \frac{4}{7} = \frac{\overset{4}{\cancel{28}} \times 4}{1 \times \underset{1}{\cancel{7}}} = \frac{4 \times 4}{1 \times 1} = \frac{16}{1}$

(iii) $36 \div 6\frac{2}{3} = 36 \div \frac{20}{3} = \frac{36}{1} \div \frac{20}{3} = \frac{\overset{9}{\cancel{36}}}{1} \times \frac{3}{\underset{5}{\cancel{20}}} = \frac{27}{5} = 5\frac{2}{5}$

Example 2 Simplify:

(i) $\frac{4}{9} \div \frac{2}{3}$ (ii) $3\frac{3}{7} \div \frac{8}{21}$ (iii) $15\frac{3}{7} \div 1\frac{23}{49}$

Solution We have,

(i) $\frac{4}{9} \div \frac{2}{3} = \frac{4}{9} \times \frac{3}{2} = \frac{\overset{2}{\cancel{4}} \times \overset{1}{\cancel{3}}}{\underset{3}{\cancel{9}} \times \underset{1}{\cancel{2}}} = \frac{2 \times 1}{3 \times 1} = \frac{2}{3}$

(ii) $3\frac{3}{7} \div \frac{8}{21} = \frac{24}{7} \div \frac{8}{21} = \frac{24}{7} \times \frac{21}{8} = \frac{\overset{3}{\cancel{24}} \times \overset{3}{\cancel{21}}}{\underset{1}{\cancel{7}} \times \underset{1}{\cancel{8}}} = \frac{3 \times 3}{1 \times 1} = 9$

(iii) $15\frac{3}{7} \div 1\frac{23}{49} = \frac{108}{7} \div \frac{72}{49} = \frac{108}{7} \times \frac{49}{72} = \frac{\overset{3}{\cancel{108}} \times \overset{7}{\cancel{49}}}{\underset{1}{\cancel{7}} \times \underset{2}{\cancel{72}}} = \frac{3 \times 7}{1 \times 2} = \frac{21}{2}$

Example 3 Simplify: $\left(\frac{16}{5} \div \frac{8}{20}\right) + \left(\frac{15}{5} \div \frac{3}{35}\right)$

Solution We have,

$$\left(\frac{16}{5} \div \frac{8}{20}\right) + \left(\frac{15}{5} \div \frac{3}{35}\right) = \left(\frac{16}{5} \times \frac{20}{8}\right) + \left(\frac{15}{5} \times \frac{35}{3}\right)$$

$$= \frac{\overset{2}{\cancel{16}} \times \overset{4}{\cancel{20}}}{\underset{1}{\cancel{5}} \times \underset{1}{\cancel{8}}} + \frac{\overset{5}{\cancel{15}} \times \overset{7}{\cancel{35}}}{\underset{1}{\cancel{5}} \times \underset{1}{\cancel{3}}} = \frac{8}{1} + \frac{35}{1} = \frac{43}{1} = 43$$

Example 4 The cost of $5\frac{2}{5}$ kg of sugar is ₹ $101\frac{1}{4}$, find its cost per kg.

Solution We have,

Cost of $5\frac{2}{5}$ kg of sugar = ₹ $101\frac{1}{4}$

$\Rightarrow$ Cost of $\frac{27}{5}$ kg of sugar = ₹ $\frac{405}{4}$

$\Rightarrow$ Cost of 1 kg of sugar

$$= ₹\left(\frac{405}{4} \div \frac{27}{5}\right) = ₹\left(\frac{405}{4} \times \frac{5}{27}\right)$$

$$= ₹\left(\frac{\overset{15}{\cancel{405}} \times 5}{4 \times \underset{1}{\cancel{27}}}\right) = ₹\,\frac{75}{4} = ₹\,18\frac{3}{4}$$

Hence, the cost of 1 kg of sugar is ₹ $18\frac{3}{4}$.

Example 5 The product of two numbers is $20\frac{5}{7}$. If one of the numbers is $6\frac{2}{3}$, find the other.

Solution We have,

Product of two numbers $= 20\frac{5}{7} = \frac{145}{7}$

One of the numbers $= 6\frac{2}{3} = \frac{20}{3}$

$\therefore$ The other number = (Product of the numbers $\div$ One of the numbers)

$$= \frac{145}{7} \div \frac{20}{3}$$

$$= \frac{145}{7} \times \frac{3}{20} = \frac{\overset{29}{\cancel{145}} \times 3}{7 \times \underset{4}{\cancel{20}}} = \frac{29 \times 3}{7 \times 4} = \frac{87}{28} = 3\frac{3}{28}$$

Hence, the other number is $3\frac{3}{28}$.

Example 6 By what number should $5\frac{5}{6}$ be multiplied to get $3\frac{1}{3}$?

Solution We have,

Product of two numbers $= 3\frac{1}{3} = \frac{10}{3}$

One of the numbers $= 5\frac{5}{6} = \frac{35}{6}$

$\therefore$ The other number = Product of the numbers $\div$ One of the numbers

$\Rightarrow$ The other number $= \frac{10}{3} \div \frac{35}{6} = \frac{10}{3} \times \frac{6}{35} = \frac{\cancel{10}^{2} \times \cancel{6}^{2}}{\cancel{3}_{1} \times \cancel{35}_{7}} = \frac{2 \times 2}{1 \times 7} = \frac{4}{7}$

Hence, required number is $\frac{4}{7}$.

Example 7 If the cost of a notebook is ₹ $8\frac{3}{4}$, how many notebooks can be purchased for ₹ $131\frac{1}{4}$?

Solution We have,

Cost of one note book = ₹ $8\frac{3}{4}$ = ₹ $\frac{35}{4}$

Total amount = ₹ $131\frac{1}{4}$ = ₹ $\frac{525}{4}$

$\therefore$ Number of notebooks $= \frac{\text{Total amount}}{\text{Cost of one notebook}}$

$$= \frac{525}{4} \div \frac{35}{4} = \frac{525}{4} \times \frac{4}{35} = \frac{\cancel{525}^{15} \times \cancel{4}^{1}}{\cancel{4}_{1} \times \cancel{35}_{1}} = 15$$

Example 8 A bucket contains $24\frac{3}{4}$ litres of water. How many $\frac{3}{4}$ litre jugs can be filled from the bucket to get it emptied?

Solution We have,

Volume of water in the bucket = $24\frac{3}{4}$ litres = $\frac{99}{4}$ litres

Capacity of jug = $\frac{3}{4}$ litre

$\therefore$ Number of jugs that can be filled to get the bucket emptied

$$= \frac{99}{4} \div \frac{3}{4} = \frac{99}{4} \times \frac{4}{3} = \frac{\cancel{99}^{33} \times \cancel{4}^{1}}{\cancel{4}_{1} \times \cancel{3}_{1}} = 33$$

Hence, 33 jugs of $\frac{3}{4}$ litre can be filled to get the bucket emptied.

EXERCISE 2.3

1. Find the reciprocal of each of the following fractions and classify them as proper, improper and whole numbers:

(i) $\frac{3}{7}$ (ii) $\frac{5}{8}$ (iii) $\frac{9}{7}$ (iv) $\frac{6}{5}$ (v) $\frac{12}{7}$ (vi) $\frac{1}{8}$

2. Divide:

(i) $\frac{3}{8}$ by $\frac{5}{9}$ (ii) $3\frac{1}{4}$ by $\frac{2}{3}$ (iii) $\frac{7}{8}$ by $4\frac{1}{2}$ (iv) $6\frac{1}{4}$ by $2\frac{3}{5}$

3. Divide:

(i) $\frac{3}{8}$ by 4 (ii) $\frac{9}{16}$ by 6 (iii) 9 by $\frac{3}{16}$ (iv) 10 by $\frac{100}{3}$

4. Simplify:

(i) $\frac{3}{10} \div \frac{10}{3}$ (ii) $4\frac{3}{5} \div \frac{4}{5}$ (iii) $5\frac{4}{7} \div 1\frac{3}{10}$ (iv) $4 \div 2\frac{2}{5}$

5. A wire of length $12\frac{1}{2}$ m is cut into 10 pieces of equal length. Find the length of each piece.

6. The length of a rectangular plot of area $65\frac{1}{3}$ m^2 is $12\frac{1}{4}$ m. What is the width of the plot?

7. By what number should $6\frac{2}{9}$ be multiplied to get $4\frac{4}{9}$?

8. The product of two numbers is $25\frac{5}{6}$. If one of the numbers is $6\frac{2}{3}$, find the other.

9. The cost of $6\frac{1}{4}$ kg of apples is ₹ 400. At what rate per kg are the apples being sold?

10. By selling oranges at the rate of ₹ $5\frac{1}{4}$ per orange, a fruit-seller gets ₹ 630. How many dozens of oranges does he sell?

11. In mid-day meal scheme $\frac{3}{10}$ litre of milk is given to each student of a primary school. If 30 litres of milk is distributed every day in the school, how many students are there in the school?

12. In a charity show ₹ 6496 were collected by selling some tickets. If the price of each ticket was ₹ $50\frac{3}{4}$, how many tickets were sold?

ANSWERS

1. (i) $\frac{7}{3}$, improper (ii) $\frac{8}{5}$, improper (iii) $\frac{7}{9}$, proper (iv) $\frac{5}{6}$, proper
(v) $\frac{7}{12}$, proper (vi) 8, whole number

2. (i) $\frac{27}{40}$ (ii) $4\frac{7}{8}$ (iii) $\frac{7}{36}$ (iv) $2\frac{21}{52}$

3. (i) $\frac{3}{32}$ (ii) $\frac{3}{32}$ (iii) 48 (iv) $\frac{3}{10}$

4. (i) $\frac{9}{100}$ (ii) $5\frac{3}{4}$ (iii) $4\frac{2}{7}$ (iv) $1\frac{2}{3}$

5. $1\frac{1}{4}$ m 6. $5\frac{1}{3}$ m 7. $\frac{5}{7}$ 8. $3\frac{7}{8}$ 9. ₹ 64 10. 10 dozens

11. 100 students 12. 128

OBJECTIVE TYPE QUESTIONS

Mark the correct alternative in each of the following:

1. If a fraction $\frac{a}{b}$ is a lowest terms, then HCF of a and b is

   (a) a (b) b (c) 1 (d) ab

2. The fraction $\frac{84}{98}$ in its lowest terms is

   (a) $\frac{42}{49}$ (b) $\frac{12}{14}$ (c) $\frac{6}{7}$ (d) $\frac{3}{7}$

3. Which of the following is a vulgar fraction?

   (a) $\frac{7}{10}$ (b) $\frac{13}{1000}$ (c) $2\frac{9}{10}$ (d) $\frac{7}{9}$

4. Which of the following fraction is an irreducible (or in its lowest terms)?

   (a) $\frac{91}{104}$ (b) $\frac{105}{112}$ (c) $\frac{51}{85}$ (d) $\frac{43}{83}$

5. Which of the following is a proper fraction?

   (a) $\frac{13}{17}$ (b) $\frac{17}{13}$ (c) $\frac{12}{5}$ (d) $1\frac{3}{4}$

6. The reciprocal of the fraction $2\frac{3}{5}$ is

   (a) $2\frac{5}{3}$ (b) $\frac{13}{5}$ (c) $\frac{5}{13}$ (d) $2\frac{2}{5}$

7. $4\frac{1}{3}-2\frac{1}{3}=$

   (a) $2\frac{1}{3}$ (b) 2 (c) $3\frac{1}{3}$ (d) $\frac{1}{2}$

8. $2\frac{3}{5}\div\frac{5}{7}=$

   (a) $\frac{13}{7}$ (b) $\frac{13}{25}$ (c) $\frac{91}{25}$ (d) $\frac{25}{91}$

9. By what number should $1\frac{3}{4}$ be divided to get $2\frac{1}{2}$?

   (a) $\frac{3}{7}$ (b) $1\frac{2}{5}$ (c) $\frac{7}{10}$ (d) $1\frac{3}{7}$

10. By what number $4\frac{3}{5}$ be multiplied to get $2\frac{3}{7}$?

    (a) $\frac{391}{35}$ (b) $\frac{85}{91}$ (c) $\frac{91}{85}$ (d) None of these

11. $\left(5\frac{1}{4}-3\frac{1}{3}\right)=$

(a) $\frac{12}{23}$ (b) 2 (c) $1\frac{11}{12}$ (d) $\frac{11}{12}$

12. The fraction equivalent to $1\frac{2}{3}$ is

(a) $\frac{10}{3}$ (b) $\frac{3}{5}$ (c) $\frac{10}{6}$ (d) $\frac{6}{10}$

13. By what number $9\frac{4}{5}$ be multiplied to get 42?

(a) $\frac{30}{7}$ (b) $\frac{7}{30}$ (c) $4\frac{1}{7}$ (d) $4\frac{3}{7}$

14. Which of the following statements is true?

(a) $\frac{7}{12}<\frac{4}{21}$ (b) $\frac{7}{12}=\frac{4}{21}$ (c) $\frac{7}{12}>\frac{4}{21}$ (d) None of these

15. Which one of the following is the correct statement?

(a) $\frac{3}{4}<\frac{2}{3}<\frac{12}{15}$ (b) $\frac{2}{3}<\frac{3}{4}<\frac{12}{15}$ (c) $\frac{2}{3}<\frac{12}{15}<\frac{3}{4}$ (d) $\frac{12}{15}<\frac{2}{3}<\frac{3}{4}$

16. Which of the following fractions lies between $\frac{2}{3}$ and $\frac{5}{7}$?

(a) $\frac{3}{4}$ (b) $\frac{4}{5}$ (c) $\frac{5}{6}$ (d) None of these

17. Which one of the following is true?

(a) $\frac{1}{2}<\frac{9}{13}<\frac{3}{4}<\frac{12}{17}$ (b) $\frac{3}{4}<\frac{9}{13}<\frac{1}{2}<\frac{12}{17}$

(c) $\frac{1}{2}<\frac{3}{4}<\frac{9}{13}<\frac{12}{17}$ (d) $\frac{1}{2}<\frac{9}{13}<\frac{12}{17}<\frac{3}{4}$

18. The smallest of the fractions $\frac{2}{3},\frac{4}{7},\frac{8}{11}$ and $\frac{5}{9}$ is

(a) $\frac{2}{3}$ (b) $\frac{4}{7}$ (c) $\frac{8}{11}$ (d) $\frac{5}{9}$

19. $9\times\left(-\frac{1}{3}\right)\times(-3)\times\left(-\frac{1}{9}\right)=$

(a) 1 (b) -1 (c) -3 (d) 3

20. Which of the following is correct?

(a) $\frac{2}{3}<\frac{3}{5}<\frac{11}{15}$ (b) $\frac{3}{5}<\frac{2}{3}<\frac{11}{15}$ (c) $\frac{11}{15}<\frac{3}{5}<\frac{2}{3}$ (d) $\frac{3}{5}<\frac{11}{15}<\frac{2}{3}$

21. Which is the smallest of the following fractions?

(a) $\frac{4}{9}$ (b) $\frac{2}{5}$ (c) $\frac{3}{7}$ (d) $\frac{1}{4}$

22. The difference between the greatest and the least fractions out of $\frac{6}{7}, \frac{7}{8}, \frac{8}{9}$ and $\frac{9}{10}$ is

(a) $\frac{3}{70}$ (b) $\frac{1}{56}$ (c) $\frac{1}{40}$ (d) $\frac{1}{72}$

23. Which of the following fractions is greater than $\frac{3}{4}$ and less than $\frac{5}{6}$?

(a) $\frac{2}{3}$ (b) $\frac{1}{2}$ (c) $\frac{4}{5}$ (d) $\frac{9}{10}$

24. Which of the following fractions is more than one-third?

(a) $\frac{23}{70}$ (b) $\frac{205}{819}$ (c) $\frac{26}{75}$ (d) $\frac{118}{335}$

ANSWERS

1. (c)	2. (c)	3. (d)	4. (d)	5. (a)	6. (c)	7. (b)
8. (c)	9. (c)	10. (d)	11. (c)	12. (c)	13. (a)	14. (c)
15. (b)	16. (d)	17. (d)	18. (d)	19. (b)	20. (b)	21. (d)
22. (a)	23. (c)	24. (c)				

THINGS TO REMEMBER

1. *A fraction is a number representing a part of a whole.*
2. *A fraction can be expressed in the form* $\frac{a}{b}$, *where a, b are whole numbers and* $b \neq 0$.
3. *In a fraction* $\frac{a}{b}$, *we call 'a' as numerator and 'b' as denominator.*
4. *A fraction whose numerator is less than the denominator is called a proper fraction.*
5. *A fraction whose numerator is more than or equal to the denominator is called an improper fraction.*
6. *A combination of a whole number and a proper fraction is called a mixed fraction.*
7. *To get a fraction equivalent to a given fraction, we multiply (or divide) its numerator and denominator by the same non-zero number.*
8. *Fractions having the same denominators are called like fractions. Otherwise, they are called unlike fractions.*
9. *A fraction is said to be in its lowest terms if its numerator and denominator have no common factor other than 1.*
10. *To compare fractions, we use the following steps:*
    - *Step I* — *Find the LCM of the denomiantors of the given fractions.*
    - *Step II* — *Convert each fraction to its equivalent fraction with denominator equal to the LCM obtained in step I.*
    - *Step III* — *Arrange the fractions in ascending or descending order by arranging numerators in ascending or descending order.*
11. *To convert unlike fractions into like fractions, we use the following steps:*
    - *Step I* — *Find the LCM of the denomiantors of the given fractions.*
    - *Step II* — *Convert each of the given fractions into an equivalent fraction having denominator equal to the LCM obtained in step I.*
12. *To add (or subtract) fractions, we may use the following steps:*
    - *Step I* — *Obtain the fractions and their denominators.*
    - *Step II* — *Find the LCM of the denominators.*
    - *Step III* — *Convert each fraction into an equivalent fraction having its denominator equal to the LCM obtained in step II.*
    - *Step IV* — *Add (or subtract) like fractions obtained in Step III.*
13. *Product of two fraction* $= \dfrac{\text{Product of their numerators}}{\text{Product of their denominators}}$
14. *Two fractions are said to be reciprocal of each other, if their product is 1. The reciprocal of a non-zero fraction* $\frac{a}{b}$ *is equal to* $\frac{b}{a}$.
15. *The division of a fraction* $\frac{a}{b}$ *by a non-zero fraction* $\frac{c}{d}$ *is the product of* $\frac{a}{b}$ *with the reciprocal of* $\frac{c}{d}$.

3

DECIMALS

3.1 INTRODUCTION

In Class VI, we have learnt about decimal numbers, representation of decimal numbers on the number line, their comparison, addition and subtraction. In this chapter, we will learn about multiplication and division of decimal numbers. Let us first recall various concepts which we have learnt in the earlier class.

3.2 RECAPITULATION

DECIMALS We have learnt in the previous class that the decimals are an extension of our number system. We have also learnt that decimals can be considered as fractions whose denominators are 10, 100, 1000 etc. We may say that the numbers expressed in decimal forms are called decimals. For example, 17.235, 0.149, 125.005, 2534.0 etc are decimal numbers or decimals.

Clearly, each decimal number or decimal has two parts, namely

(i) whole-number part, (ii) decimal part.

Also, these parts are separated by a dot (·), called the decimal point.

In the decimal number 27.54, whole number part is 27 and decimal part is 54.

DECIMAL PLACES *The number of digits contained in the decimal part of a decimal number is known as the number of decimal places.*

For example, 3.75 has two decimal places and 85.325 has three decimal places.

LIKE AND UNLIKE DECIMALS *Decimals having the same number of places are called like decimals i.e. decimals having the same number of digits on the right of the decimal point are known as like decimals. Otherwise, the decimals are unlike decimals.*

For example, 5.25, 15.04, 273.89 are like decimals and 9.5, 18.235, 20.0254 etc are unlike decimals.

It is to note that by annexing zeros on the right side of the extreme right digit of the decimal part of a number does not alter the value of the number. So, unlike decimals can always be converted into like decimals by annexing required number of zeros on the right side of the extreme right digit in the decimal part.

For example, 7.4, 15.35, 49.105 are unlike decimals. These decimals can be re-written as 7.400, 15.350, 49.105. Now, these are like decimals.

3.2.1 COMPARING DECIMALS

In order to compare decimal numbers, we may follow the following steps:

STEP I *Obtain the decimal numbers*

STEP II *Compare the whole parts of the numbers. The number with greater whole part will be greater. If the whole parts are equal, go to next step.*

STEP III *Compare the extreme left digits of the decimal parts of two numbers. The number with greater extreme left digit will be greater. If the extreme left digits of decimal parts are equal, then compare the next digits and so on.*

ILLUSTRATION 1 Which is greater of 48.23 and 39.35?

Solution The given decimals have distinct whole number parts, so we compare whole number parts only.

In 48.23, the whole number part is 48.

In 39.35, the whole number part is 39.

$\because \quad 48 > 39$

$\therefore \quad 48.23 > 39.35.$

ILLUSTRATION 2 Write the following decimals in ascending order:

5.64, 2.54, 3.05, 0.259 and 8.32

Solution Converting the given decimals into like decimals, we get

5.640, 2.540, 3.050, 0.259 and 8.320

Clearly, $0.259 < 2.540 < 3.050 < 5.640 < 8.320$

Hence, the given decimals in the ascending order are:

0.259, 2.54, 3.05, 5.64 and 8.32

A decimal can always be converted into a fraction by using the following steps:

STEP I *Obtain the decimal.*

STEP II *Take the numerator as the number obtained by removing the decimal point from the given decimal.*

STEP III *Take the denominator as the number obtained by inserting as many zeros with 1 (e.g. 10, 100 or 1000 etc.) as there are number of places in the decimal part.*

ILLUSTRATION 3 Express the following decimals as fractions in lowest form:

(i) 0.05 (ii) 3.75 (iii) 0.004 (iv) 5.066

Solution We have,

(i) $0.05 = \frac{05}{100} = \frac{5}{100} = \frac{1}{20}$ (ii) $3.75 = \frac{375}{100} = \frac{15}{4}$

(iii) $0.004 = \frac{4}{1000} = \frac{1}{250}$ (iv) $5.066 = \frac{5066}{1000} = \frac{2533}{500}$

In the beginning of this section, we have mentioned that decimals are fractions with denominators 10, 100, 1000 etc. In order to convert other fractions into decimals, we follow the following steps:

STEP I *Obtain the fraction and convert it into an equivalent fraction with denominator 10 or 100 or 1000 if it is not so.*

STEP II *Write its numerator and mark decimal point after one place or two places or three places from right towards left if the denominator is 10 or 100 or 1000 respectively. If the numerator is short of digits, insert zeros at the left of the numerator.*

ILLUSTRATION 4 Express the following fractions as decimals:

(i) $\frac{2}{10}$ (ii) $\frac{1359}{1000}$ (iii) $7\frac{1}{2}$ (iv) $9\frac{1}{4}$ (v) $12\frac{1}{8}$

Solution Using the above method, we have

(i) $\frac{2}{10} = 0.2$ (ii) $\frac{1359}{1000} = 1.359$

(iii) We have,

$$7\frac{1}{2} = 7 + \frac{1}{2} = 7 + \frac{5 \times 1}{5 \times 2} = 7 + \frac{5}{10} = 7 + 0.5 = 7.5$$

(iv) We have,

$$9\frac{1}{4} = 9 + \frac{1}{4} = 9 + \frac{25 \times 1}{25 \times 4} = 9 + \frac{25}{100} = 9 + 0.25 = 9.25$$

(iv) We have,

$$12\frac{1}{8} = 12 + \frac{1}{8} = 12 + \frac{125 \times 1}{125 \times 8} = 12 + \frac{125}{1000} = 12 + 0.125 = 12.125$$

3.2.2 ADDITION AND SUBTRACTION OF DECIMALS

In order to add or subtract decimals, we may use the following steps:

STEP I *Convert the given decimals to like decimals.*

STEP II *Write the decimals in columns with their decimal points directly below each other so that tenths come under tenths, hundredths come under hundredths and so on.*

STEP III *Add or subtract as we add or subtract whole numbers.*

STEP IV *Place the decimal point, in the answer, directly below the other decimal points.*

ILLUSTRATION 1 Add: 15.44, 7.524 and 25

Solution Converting the given decimals to like decimals, we have 15.440, 7.524 and 25.000.

Now,

$$\begin{array}{r} 15.440 \\ +\ \ 7.524 \\ +\ 25.000 \\ \hline 47.964 \end{array}$$

ILLUSTRATION 2 Aakash bought vegetables weighing 10 kg. Out of this 3 kg 500 g is onion, 2 kg 75 g is tomato and the rest is potato. What is the weight of potato?

Solution We have,

Weight of onion = 3 kg 500 g = 3.500 kg

Weight of tomato = 2 kg 75 g = 2.075 kg

∴ Total weight of onion and tomato is :

$$\begin{array}{r} 3.500 \text{ kg} \\ +\ 2.075 \text{ kg} \\ \hline 5.575 \text{ kg} \end{array}$$

Total weight of vegetables = 10 kg

Weight of potato is = 10 kg – 5.575 kg = 4.425 kg

$$\begin{array}{r} 10.000 \\ -\ 5.575 \\ \hline 4.425 \end{array}$$

ILLUSTRATION 3 Simplify : $36.65 - 15.79 + 85.2 - 57.615$

Solution We have,

$36.65 - 15.79 + 85.2 - 57.615$

$= 36.650 - 15.790 + 85.200 - 57.615$ [Converting the given decimals into like decimals]

$= (36.650 + 85.200) - (15.790 + 57.615)$

$= 121.850 - 73.405$

$= 48.445$

$$\begin{array}{r} 36.650 \\ +\ 85.200 \\ \hline 121.850 \end{array} \qquad \begin{array}{r} 15.790 \\ +\ 57.615 \\ \hline 73.405 \end{array} \qquad \begin{array}{r} 121.850 \\ -\ 73.405 \\ \hline 48.445 \end{array}$$

EXERCISE 3.1

1. Write each of the following as decimals:

   (i) $\frac{8}{100}$ (ii) $20 + \frac{9}{10} + \frac{4}{100}$ (iii) $23 + \frac{2}{10} + \frac{6}{1000}$

2. Convert each of the following into fractions in the lowest form:

   (i) 0.04 (ii) 2.34 (iii) 0.342 (iv) 17.38

3. Express the following fractions as decimals:

   (i) $\frac{23}{10}$ (ii) $25\frac{1}{8}$ (iii) $39\frac{7}{35}$ (iv) $15\frac{1}{25}$

4. Add the following:

   (i) 41.8, 39.24, 5.01 and 62.6 (ii) 18.03, 146.3, 0.829 and 5.324

5. Find the value of:

   (i) $9.756 - 6.28$ (ii) $48.1 - 0.37$ (iii) $108.032 - 86.8$ (iv) $100 - 26.32$

6. Take out 3.547 from 7.2
7. What is to be added to 36.85 to get 59.41?
8. What is to be subtracted from 17.1 to get 2.051?
9. By how much should 34.79 be increased to get 70.15?
10. By how much should 59.71 be decreased to get 34.58?

ANSWERS

1. (i) 0.08 (ii) 20.94 (iii) 23.206
2. (i) $\frac{1}{25}$ (ii) $\frac{117}{50}$ (iii) $\frac{171}{500}$ (iv) $\frac{869}{50}$
3. (i) 2.3 (ii) 25.125 (iii) 39.2 (iv) 15.04
4. (i) 148.65 (ii) 170.483
5. (i) 3.653 (ii) 47.73 (iii) 21.232 (iv) 73.68
6. 3.653 7. 22.56 8. 15.049 9. 35.36 10. 25.13

3.3 MULTIPLICATION OF DECIMALS

In our day-to-day life, we come across many situations where we need to know the multiplication of decimals. For example, if Shikha purchased 2.75 kg potatos at the rate of ₹ 7.50 per kg, then how much money she has to pay? Clearly, money to be paid would be ₹ 7.50 × 2.75. Here, she has to know the multiplication of decimals to know the amount to be paid. In fact, there are many situations where we use the multiplication of decimals.

3.3.1 MULTIPLICATION OF A DECIMAL BY 10, 100, 1000 etc.

We follow the following rules to multiply a decimal by 10, 100, 1000 etc.

Rule I *On multiplying a decimal by 10, the decimal point is shifted to the right by one place.*

Rule II *On multiplying a decimal by 100, the decimal point is shifted to the right by two places.*

Rule III *On multiplying a decimal by 1000, the decimal point is shifted to the right by three places, and so on.*

ILLUSTRATION Find the following products:

(i) 27.05 × 10 (ii) 429.7 × 100 (iii) 31.09 × 1000

Solution We have,

(i) $27.05 \times 10 = 270.5$ [Shifting the decimal point by one place to the right]

(ii) $429.7 \times 100 = 429.70 \times 100$ [$\because 429.7 = 429.70$]

$= 42970$ [Shifting the decimal point by two places to the right]

(iii) $31.09 \times 1000 = 31.090 \times 1000$ [$\because 31.09 = 31.090$]

$= 31090$ [Shifting the decimal point by three places to the right]

3.3.2 MULTIPLICATION OF A DECIMAL BY A WHOLE NUMBER

In order to multiply a decimal by a whole number, we follow the following steps:

STEP I *Multiply the decimal without the decimal point by the given whole number.*

STEP II *Mark the decimal point in the product to have as many places of decimal as are there in the given decimal.*

ILLUSTRATION Find each of the following products:

(i) 3.25 × 12 (ii) 0.524 × 15 (iii) 0.0275 × 17

Solution (i) We have,

$325 \times 12 = 3900$

$\therefore \quad 3.25 \times 12 = 39.00$

$$\begin{array}{r} 325 \\ \times 12 \\ \hline 650 \\ +3250 \\ \hline 3900 \end{array}$$

(ii) We have,

$524 \times 15 = 7860$

$\therefore \quad 0.524 \times 15 = 7.860$

$$\begin{array}{r} 524 \\ \times 15 \\ \hline 2620 \\ +5240 \\ \hline 7860 \end{array}$$

(iii) We have,

$$275 \times 17 = 4675$$

$$\therefore \quad 0.0275 \times 17 = 0.4675$$

$$\begin{array}{r} 275 \\ \times 17 \\ \hline 1925 \\ +2750 \\ \hline 4675 \end{array}$$

3.3.3 MULTIPLICATION OF A DECIMAL BY ANOTHER DECIMAL

In order to multiply a decimal by another decimal, we follow the following steps.

STEP I *Multiply the two decimals without decimal point just like whole numbers.*

STEP II *Insert the decimal point in the product by counting as many places from the right to left as the sum of the number of decimal places of the given decimals.*

ILLUSTRATION 1 Find the product of 9.2 and 6.07.

Solution We have,

$$\begin{array}{r} 92 \\ \times 607 \\ \hline 644 \\ 000 \\ +55200 \\ \hline 55844 \end{array}$$

$\therefore \quad 92 \times 607 = 55844$

Since the sum of the decimal places in the given decimals is 1 + 2 = 3.
So, the product must contain 3 places of decimals.
Hence, $9.2 \times 6.07 = 55.844$

ILLUSTRATION 2 Multiply 0.0345 by 0.0237

Solution We have,

$$\begin{array}{r} 345 \\ \times 237 \\ \hline 2415 \\ 10350 \\ +69000 \\ \hline 81765 \end{array}$$

$\therefore \quad 345 \times 237 = 81765$

We observe that the sum of the decimals in the given decimals is 4 + 4 = 8
So, the product must contain 8 places of decimals.
Hence, $0.0345 \times 0.0237 = 0.00081765$

ILLUSTRATIVE EXAMPLES

Example 1 Find the value of :

(i) 3.45×10 (ii) 0.25×10000 (iii) 1000×5.29

(iv) 10000×0.01

Solution (i) We have,

$3.45 \times 10 = 34.5$ [Shifting the decimal point by one place to the right]

(ii) We have,

0.25×10000

$= 0.2500 \times 10000$ [$\because 0.25 = 0.2500$]

$= 2500$ [By shifting the decimal point by four places to the right]

(iii) We have,

$5.29 = 5.290$

$\therefore \quad 1000 \times 5.29 = 1000 \times 5.290$

$\Rightarrow \quad 1000 \times 5.29 = 5290$ [By Shifting the decimal point by three places to the right]

(iv) We have,

$0.01 = 0.0100$

$\therefore \quad 10000 \times 0.01 = 10000 \times 0.0100$

$= 100$ [By shifting the decimal point by four places to the right]

Example 2 Multiply 7.43 by 14.1

Solution In order to find 7.43 × 14.1, we first multiply 743 by 141.

$$\begin{array}{r} 743 \\ \times 141 \\ \hline 743 \\ 29720 \\ +74300 \\ \hline 104763 \end{array}$$

$\therefore \quad 743 \times 141 = 104763$

Sum of decimal places in the given decimals = 2 + 1 = 3. So, we mark the decimal point by counting 3 places from right to left.

Hence, 7.43 × 14.1 = 104.763

Example 3 Find the product 0.008 × 0.74

Solution In order to find the product, we first multiply 8 by 74.

We have, $8 \times 74 = 592$

Now, 0.008 has 3 decimal places and 0.74 has two decimal places.

The sum of the decimal places = 3 + 2 = 5

So, the product must contain 5 places of decimals.

Hence, 0.008 × 0.74 = 0.00592

Example 4 Find the area of a rectangle whose length is 5.7 cm and breadth is 3.5 cm.

Solution We have,

Length of the rectangle = 5.7 cm, Breadth of the rectangle = 3.5 cm

$\therefore$ Area of the rectangle $=$ Length $\times$ Breadth

$= 5.7 \times 3.5 \,\text{cm}^2$

$= 19.95 \,\text{cm}^2$

$$\begin{array}{r} 57 \\ \times 35 \\ \hline 285 \\ +1710 \\ \hline 1995 \end{array}$$

Hence, area of the rectangle is 19.95 cm^2.

Example 5 A two wheeler covers a distance of 55.4 km in one litre of petrol. How much distance will it cover in 7.5 litres of petrol?

Solution We have,

Distance covered in one litre of petrol = 55.4 km

$\therefore$ Distance covered in 7.5 litres of petrol

= (55.4 × 7.5) km = 415.50 km

$$\begin{array}{r} 554 \\ \times 75 \\ \hline 2770 \\ +38780 \\ \hline 41550 \end{array}$$

Example 6 If 1 kg of pure milk contains 0.245 kg of fat. How much fat is there is 14.4 kg of milk?

Solution We have,

Quantity of fat in 1 kg of milk = 0.245 kg

$\therefore$ Quantity of fat in 14.4 kg of milk

$= (0.245 \times 14.4)$ kg = 3.528 kg

$$\begin{array}{r} 245 \\ \times 144 \\ \hline 980 \\ 9800 \\ +24500 \\ \hline 35280 \end{array}$$

EXERCISE 3.2

1. Find the product:
   (i) 4.74 × 10 (ii) 0.45 × 10 (iii) 0.0215 × 10 (iv) 0.0054 × 10
2. Find the product:
   (i) 35.853 × 100 (ii) 42.5 × 100 (iii) 12.075 × 100 (iv) 100 × 0.005
3. Find the product:
   (i) 2.506 × 1000 (ii) 20.708 × 1000 (iii) 0.0529 × 1000 (iv) 1000 × 0.1
4. Find the product:
   (i) 3.4 × 17 (ii) 0.745 × 12 (iii) 28.73 × 47 (iv) 0.0415 × 59
5. Find :
   (i) 1.07 × 0.02 (ii) 211.9 × 1.13 (iii) 10.05 × 1.05 (iv) 13.01 × 5.01

6. Find the area of a rectangle whose length is 5.5 m and breadth is 3.4 m.
7. If the cost of a book is ₹ 25.75, find the cost of 24 such books.
8. A car covers a distance of 14.75 km in one litre of petrol. How much distance will it cover in 15.5 litres of petrol?
9. One kg of rice costs ₹ 42.65. What will be the cost of 18.25 kg of rice?
10. One metre of cloth costs ₹ 152.50. What is the cost of 10.75 metres of cloth?

ANSWERS

1.	(i) 47.4	(ii) 4.5	(iii) 0.215	(iv) 0.054
2.	(i) 3585.3	(ii) 4250	(iii) 1207.50	(iv) 0.5
3.	(i) 2506	(ii) 20708	(iii) 52.9	(iv) 100
4.	(i) 57.8	(ii) 8.94	(iii) 1350.31	(iv) 2.4485
5.	(i) 0.0214	(ii) 239.447	(iii) 10.5525	(iv) 65.1801
6.	18.7 m^2	7. ₹ 618	8. 228.625 km	
9.	₹ 778.3625	10. ₹ 1639.375		

3.4 DIVISION OF DECIMALS

In our day-to-day, life we come across many situations where we need to know the division of decimals. Suppose we are given the area of a rectangle as 58.75 cm^2 and width as 5.45 cm and we are required to find the length. Clearly, length $= \frac{58.75}{5.45}$. Here, we need division of decimals. Similarly, there are many other situations in our day-to-day life where we need division of decimals.

3.4.1 DIVIDING A DECIMAL BY 10, 100, 1000 etc.

In order to divide a decimal by 10, 100, 1000 etc., we follow the following rules:

Rule I *When a decimal is divided by 10, the decimal point is shifted to the left by one place.*

Rule II *When a decimal is divided by 100, the decimal point is shifted to the left by two places.*

Rule III *When a decimal is divided by 1000, the decimal point is shifted to the left by three places.*

ILLUSTRATION Divide:

(i) 12.75 by 10 (ii) 127.5 by 100 (iii) 1275.7 by 1000
(iv) 0.58 by 10 (v) 3.52 by 100 (vi) 6.25 by 1000

Solution We have,

(i) $12.75 \div 10 = \frac{12.75}{10} = 1.275$ [Shifting decimal point to the left by 1 place]

(ii) $127.5 \div 100 = \frac{127.5}{100} = 1.275$ [Shifting decimal point to the left by 2 places]

(iii) $1275.7 \div 1000 = \dfrac{1275.7}{1000} = 1.2757$ [Shifting decimal point to the left by 3 places]

(iv) $0.58 \div 10 = \dfrac{0.58}{10} = 0.058$ [Shifting decimal point to the left by 1 place]

(v) $3.52 \div 100 = \dfrac{3.52}{100} = 0.0352$ [Shifting decimal point to the left by 2 places]

(vi) $6.25 \div 1000 = \dfrac{6.25}{1000} = 0.00625$ [Shifting decimal point to the left by 3 places]

3.4.2 DIVIDING A DECIMAL BY A WHOLE NUMBER

In order to divide a decimal by a whole number, we follow the following steps:

STEP I *Check the whole number part of the dividend.*

STEP II *If the whole number part of the dividend is less than the divisor, then place a 0 in the ones place in the quotient. Otherwise, go to step III.*

STEP III *Divide the whole number part of the dividend.*

STEP IV *Place the decimal point to the right of ones place in the quotient obtained in step I.*

STEP V *Divide the decimal part of the dividend by the divisor. If the digits of the dividend are exhausted, then place zeros to the right of dividend and remainder each time and continue the process.*

Following examples will illustrate the procedure.

ILLUSTRATIVE EXAMPLES

Example 1 Divide 93.45 by 15

Solution We have,

$$\begin{array}{r} 15\overline{)\,93.45\,}(6.23 \\ -90 \\ \hline 34 \\ -30 \\ \hline 45 \\ -45 \\ \hline 0 \\ \hline \end{array}$$

$\therefore \quad 93.45 \div 15 = 6.23$

Example 2 Divide 8.28 by 12

Solution We have,

$$\begin{array}{r} 12\overline{)\,8.28\,}(0.69 \\ 0 \\ \hline 82 \\ -72 \\ \hline 108 \\ -108 \\ \hline 0 \\ \hline \end{array}$$

$\therefore \quad 8.28 \div 12 = 0.69$

Example 3 Divide 0.6204 by 5

Solution We have,

$$
\begin{array}{r}
5\overline{)\,0.62040\,}(0.12408 \\
0 \\
\hline
6 \\
-5 \\
\hline
12 \\
-10 \\
\hline
20 \\
-20 \\
\hline
40 \\
-40 \\
\hline
0 \\
\hline
\end{array}
$$

Thus, $0.6204 \div 5 = 0.12408$

Example 4 Divide 28.82 by 20

Solution We have,

$$\frac{28.82}{20} = \frac{28.82}{2 \times 10} = \frac{28.82}{2} \times \frac{1}{10} = \frac{14.41}{10} = 1.441$$

Hence, $28.82 \div 20 = 1.441$

Example 5 Divide 48.08 by 400.

Solution We have,

$$\frac{48.08}{400} = \frac{48.08}{4} \times \frac{1}{100} = \frac{12.02}{100} = 0.1202$$

Thus, $48.08 \div 400 = 0.1202$

Example 6 Divide 163.44 by 24

Solution We have,

$$
\begin{array}{r}
24\overline{)\,163.44\,}(6.81 \\
-144 \\
\hline
194 \\
-192 \\
\hline
24 \\
-24 \\
\hline
0 \\
\hline
\end{array}
$$

Hence, $163.44 \div 24 = 6.81$

3.4.3 DIVIDING A DECIMAL BY A DECIMAL

In order to divide a decimal by another decimal, we follow the following steps:

STEP I *Multiple the dividend and divisor by 10 or 100 or 1000 etc to convert the divisor into a whole number.*

STEP II *Divide the new dividend by the whole number obtained in step I.*

Following examples will illustrate the above procedure.

ILLUSTRATIVE EXAMPLES

Example 1 Divide 3.28 by 0.4

Solution We have,

$$\frac{3.28}{0.4} = \frac{3.28 \times 10}{0.4 \times 10} = \frac{32.8}{4}$$

$$\begin{array}{r|l} 4 \overline{)\ 32.8} & (8.2 \\ -32 & \\ \hline 8 & \\ -8 & \\ \hline 0 & \end{array}$$

$\therefore \quad 3.28 \div 0.4 = 8.2$

Example 2 Divide 42.8 by 0.02

Solution We have,

$$\frac{42.8}{0.02} = \frac{42.8 \times 100}{0.02 \times 100} = \frac{4280}{2} = 2140$$

Hence, $42.8 \div 0.02 = 2140$

Example 3 Divide 0.00942 by 0.314

Solution We have,

$$\frac{0.00942}{0.314} = \frac{0.00942 \times 1000}{0.314 \times 1000} = \frac{9.42}{314}$$

$$\begin{array}{r|l} 314 \overline{)\ 9.42} & (0.03 \\ 0 & \\ \hline 942 & \\ -942 & \\ \hline 0 & \end{array}$$

Hence, $0.00942 \div 0.314 = 0.03$

Example 4 Divide 0.0216 by 0.6

Solution We have,

$$\frac{0.0216}{0.6} = \frac{0.0216 \times 10}{0.6 \times 10} = \frac{0.216}{6}$$

$$\begin{array}{r|l} 6 \overline{)\ 0.216} & (0.036 \\ 0 & \\ \hline 21 & \\ -18 & \\ \hline 36 & \\ -36 & \\ \hline 0 & \end{array}$$

Hence, $0.0216 \div 0.6 = 0.036$

Example 5 Divide 0.0024 by 0.04

Solution We have,

$$\frac{0.0024}{0.04} = \frac{0.0024 \times 100}{0.04 \times 100} = \frac{0.24}{4}$$

$$
\begin{array}{r}
4\overline{)\,0.24\,}(0.06 \\
0 \\
\hline
24 \\
-24 \\
\hline
0 \\
\hline
\end{array}
$$

Hence, $0.0024 \div 0.04 = 0.06$

Example 6 Divide 6.9168 by 52.4

Solution We have,

$$\frac{6.9168}{52.4} = \frac{6.9168 \times 10}{52.4 \times 10} = \frac{69.168}{524}$$

$$
\begin{array}{r}
524\overline{)\,69.168\,}(0.132 \\
-0 \\
\hline
691 \\
-524 \\
\hline
1676 \\
-1572 \\
\hline
1048 \\
-1048 \\
\hline
0 \\
\hline
\end{array}
$$

Hence, $6.9168 \div 52.4 = 0.132$

Example 7 Divide 1391 by 1.3

Solution We have,

$$\frac{1391}{1.3} = \frac{1391 \times 10}{1.3 \times 10} = \frac{13910}{13}$$

$$
\begin{array}{r}
13\overline{)\,13910\,}(1070 \\
-13 \\
\hline
91 \\
-91 \\
\hline
0 \\
\hline
\end{array}
$$

$\therefore \quad 1391 \div 1.3 = 1070$

Example 8 Divide 42 by 16

Solution We have,

```
       2.625
16 ) 42.000     ← Annexing three zeros
    -32
     100
    - 96
       40
     - 32
        80
      -80
         0
```

Hence, $42 \div 16 = 2.625$

Example 9 Divide (i) 3 by 8 (ii) 3 by 80

Solution (i) We have,

```
    0.375
8 ) 3.000     ← three zeros annexed
    0
    30
   -24
     60
    -56
      40
     -40
       0
```

Hence, $3 \div 8 = 0.375$

(ii) We have,

```
     0.0375
80 ) 3.0000     ← Four zeros annexed
     0
     30
    -00
     300
    -240
      600
     -560
       400
      -400
         0
```

Hence, $3 \div 80 = 0.0375$

Example 10 The cost of 24 pens is ₹ 2986.80. Find the cost of one pen.

Solution We have,

Cost of 24 pens = ₹2986.80

$\therefore$ Cost of 1 pen $= ₹\left(\frac{2986.80}{24}\right) = ₹\ 124.45$

```
24 ) 2986.80 (124.45
     -24
      58
     - 48
      106
      -96
       108
       -96
        120
        120
          0
```

Hence, the cost of one pen is ₹ 124.45

Example 11 A car covers a distance of 89.1 km in 2.2 hours. What is the average distance covered by the car in 1 hour?

Solution We have,

Distance covered by the car in 2.2 hours = 89.1 km

$\therefore$ Distance covered by the car in 1 hour

$$= \frac{89.1}{2.2} \text{ km}$$

$$= \frac{89.1 \times 10}{2.2 \times 10} = \frac{891}{22} \text{ km} = 40.5 \text{ km}$$

```
22 ) 891.0 (40.5
     88
      11
      00
      110
      110
        0
```

Hence, the car covers 40.5 km in 1 hour.

Example 12 Mrs Jain bought 14.5 litres of refined oil for ₹ 1194.80. Find its cost per litre.

Solution We have,

Cost of 14.5 litres of refined oil = ₹ 1194.80

$\therefore$ Cost of 1 litre of refined oil $= ₹\left(\dfrac{1194.80}{14.5}\right)$

$= ₹\left(\dfrac{1194.80 \times 10}{14.5 \times 10}\right)$

$= ₹\left(\dfrac{11948}{145}\right) = 82.40$

```
145 ) 11948.00 (82.40
     -1160
       348
     - 290
       580
      -580
        00
      - 00
         0
```

Hence, the cost of 1 litre of refined oil is Rs 82.40

Example 13 The product of two decimals is 1.8576. If one of the decimals is 0.54, find the other.

Solution We have,

Product of the given decimals = 1.8576

One decimal = 0.54

$\therefore$ The other decimal $= \dfrac{1.8576}{0.54}$

$= \left(\dfrac{1.8576 \times 100}{0.54 \times 100}\right) = \dfrac{185.76}{54} = 3.44$

Hence, the other decimal = 3.44

EXERCISE 3.3

1. Divide:
   (i) 142.45 by 10 (ii) 54.25 by 10 (iii) 3.45 by 10
   (iv) 0.57 by 10 (v) 0.043 by 10 (vi) 0.004 by 10
2. Divide:
   (i) 459.5 by 100 (ii) 74.3 by 100 (iii) 5.8 by 100
   (iv) 0.7 by 100 (v) 0.48 by 100 (vi) 0.03 by 100
3. Divide:
   (i) 235.41 by 1000 (ii) 29.5 by 1000 (iii) 3.8 by 1000
   (iv) 0.7 by 1000
4. Divide:
   (i) 0.45 by 9 (ii) 217.44 by 18 (iii) 319.2 by 2.28
   (iv) 40.32 by 9.6 (v) 0.765 by 0.9 (vi) 0.768 by 1.6
5. Divide:
   (i) 16.64 by 20 (ii) 0.192 by 12 (iii) 163.44 by 24
   (iv) 403.2 by 96 (v) 16.344 by 12 (vi) 31.92 by 228
6. Divide:
   (i) 15.68 by 20 (ii) 164.6 by 200 (iii) 403.80 by 30

7. Divide:
   (i) 76 by 0.019 (ii) 88 by 0.08 (iii) 148 by 0.074
   (iv) 7 by 0.014
8. Divide:
   (i) 20 by 50 (ii) 8 by 100 (iii) 72 by 576
   (iv) 144 by 15
9. A vehicle covers a distance of 43.2 km in 2.4 litres of petrol. How much distance will it travel in 1 litre of petrol?
10. The total weight of some bags of wheat is 1743 kg. If each bag weights 49.8 kg, how many bags are there?
11. Shikha cuts 50 m of cloth into pieces of 1.25 m each. How many pieces does she get?
12. Each side of a rectangular polygon is 2.5 cm in length. The perimeter of the polygon is 12.5 cm. How many sides does the polygon have?
13. The product of two decimals is 42.987. If one of them is 12.46, find the other.
14. The weight of 34 bags of sugar is 3483.3 kg. If all bags weigh equally, find the weight of each bag.
15. How many buckets of equal capacity can be filled from 586.5 litres of water, if each bucket has capacity of 8.5 litres?

ANSWERS

1.	(i) 14.245	(ii) 5.425	(iii) 0.345	(iv) 0.057
	(v) 0.0043	(vi) 0.0004		
2.	(i) 4.595	(ii) 0.743	(iii) 0.058	(iv) 0.007
	(v) 0.0048	(vi) 0.0003		
3.	(i) 0.23541	(ii) 0.0295	(iii) 0.0038	(iv) 0.0007
4.	(i) 0.05	(ii) 12.08	(iii) 140	(iv) 4.2
	(v) 0.85	(vi) 0.48		
5.	(i) 0.832	(ii) 0.016	(iii) 6.81	(iv) 4.2
	(v) 1.362	(vi) 0.14		
6.	(i) 0.784	(ii) 0.823	(iii) 13.46	
7.	(i) 4000	(ii) 1100	(iii) 2000	(iv) 500
8.	(i) 0.4	(ii) 0.08	(iii) 0.125	(iv) 9.6
9.	18 km	10. 35	11. 40	12. 5
13.	3.45	14. 102.45 kg	15. 69	

OBJECTIVE TYPE QUESTIONS

Mark the correct alternative in each of the following:

1. When 0.48 is written in the simplest form of its terms, the sum of its numerator and denominator is
   (a) 148 (b) 74 (c) 37 (d) 147
2. The improper fraction $2\frac{1}{25}$ in decimal form is
   (a) 2.4 (b) 2.04 (c) 2.004 (d) None of these
3. $4 + 4.4 + 44.4 + 4.04 + 444 =$
   (a) 500.84 (b) 577.2 (c) 495.22 (d) 472.88

4. 1.04 as an mixed fraction is

(a) $1\frac{1}{5}$ (b) $1\frac{2}{5}$ (c) $1\frac{1}{25}$ (d) $1\frac{2}{25}$

5. If $24.125 = 24 + \frac{A}{10} + \frac{B}{100} + \frac{C}{1000}$, then $A + B + C =$

(a) 3 (b) 6 (c) 13 (d) 8

6. $0.002 \times 0.5 =$

(a) 0.0001 (b) 0.001 (c) 0.01 (d) 1

7. $3 \times 0.3 \times 0.03 \times 0.003 \times 30 =$

(a) 0.0000243 (b) 0.000243 (c) 0.00243 (d) 0.0243

8. $0.012 \times 0.15 =$

(a) 0.8 (b) 0.08 (c) 0.008 (d) 0.0018

9. $75.57 \div 0.01 =$

(a) 7557 (b) 0.7557 (c) 755.7 (d) 7.557

10. What should be subtracted from 0.1 to get 0.06?

(a) 0.4 (b) 0.04 (c) 0.004 (d) None of these

11. What should be added to 5.09 to get 5.5?

(a) 0.41 (b) 0.59 (c) 0.49 (d) 0.95

12. $0.3 \times 0.3 \times 0.3 =$

(a) 2.7 (b) 0.27 (c) 0.027 (d) None of these

13. $0.25 \times 0.8 =$

(a) 0.02 (b) 0.2 (c) 0.002 (d) 2

14. 5 kg 5 g written in decimal notation is

(a) 5.5 (b) 5.05 (c) 5.005 (d) 5.0005

15. $0.012 \div 1.5 = ?$

(a) 0.8 (b) 0.08 (c) 0.008 (d) None of these

16. $0.02 \times 0.05 =$

(a) 0.1 (b) 0.01 (c) 0.001 (d) 0.0001

17. 5 km 5 m = ?

(a) 5.5 km (b) 5.05 km (c) 5.005 km (d) 5.0005 km

18. The value of $2.2 \times 0.2 \times 0.001$ is

(a) 4.2 (b) 0.00044 (c) 4.4 (d) None of these

19. If $14 \times 4 = 56$, then $0.014 \times 4 =$

(a) 0.56 (b) 5.6 (c) 0.056 (d) None of these

20. 8 ml is equal to

(a) 0.8 l (b) 0.08 l (c) 0.008 l (d) None of these

ANSWERS

1. (c)	2. (b)	3. (a)	4. (c)	5. (d)	6. (b)	7. (c)
8. (d)	9. (a)	10. (b)	11. (a)	12. (c)	13. (b)	14. (c)
15. (c)	16. (c)	17. (c)	18. (b)	19. (c)	20. (c)	

THINGS TO REMEMBERS

1. *Decimals are an extension of our number system.*
2. *Decimals are fractions whose denominators are 10, 100, 1000 etc.*
3. *A decimal has two parts, namely, the whole number part and decimal part.*
4. *The number of digits contained in the decimal part of a decimal number is known as the number of decimal places.*
5. *Decimals having the same number of places are called like decimals, otherwise they are known as unlike decimals.*
6. *We have, 0.1 = 0.10 = 0.100 etc, 0.5 = 0.50 = 0.500 etc and so on. That is by annexing zeros on the right side of the extreme right digit of the decimal part of a number does not alter the value of the number.*
7. *Unlike decimals may be converted into like decimals by annexing the requisite number of zeros on the right side of the extreme right digit in the decimal part.*
8. *Decimal numbers may be compared by using the following steps.*

   Step I *Obtain the decimal numbers*

   Step II *Compare the whole parts of the numbers. The number with greater whole part will be greater. If the whole parts are equal, go to next step.*

   Step III *Compare the extreme left digits of the decimal parts of two numbers. The number with greater extreme left digit will be greater. If the extreme left digits of decimal parts are equal, then compare the next digits and so on.*
9. *A decimal can be converted into a fraction by using the following steps:*

   Step I *Obtain the decimal.*

   Step II *Take the numerator as the number obtained by removing the decimal point from the given decimal.*

   Step III *Take the denominator as the number obtained by inserting as many zeros with 1 (e.g. 10, 100 or 1000 etc.) as there are number of places in the decimal part.*
10. *Fractions can be converted into decimals by using the following steps:*

    Step I *Obtain the fraction and convert it into an equivalent fraction with denominator 10 or 100 or 1000 if it is not so.*

    Step II *Write its numerator and mark decimal point after one place or two places or three places from right towards left if the denominator is 10 or 100 or 1000 respectively. If the numerator is short of digits, insert zeros at the left of the numerator.*
11. *Decimals can be added or subtracted by using the following steps:*

    Step I *Convert the given decimals to like decimals.*

    Step II *Write the decimals in columns with their decimal points directly below each other so that tenths come under tenths, hundredths come and hundredths and so on.*

    Step III *Add or subtract as we add or subtract whole numbers.*

    Step IV *Place the decimal point, in the answer, directly below the other decimal points.*
12. *In order to multiply a decimal by 10, 100, 1000 etc., we use the following rules:*

    Rule I *On multiplying a decimal by 10, the decimal point is shifted to the right by one place.*

    Rule II *On multiplying a decimal by 100, the decimal point is shifted to the right by two places.*

    Rule III *On multiplying a decimal by 1000, the decimal point is shifted to the right by three places, and so on.*

13. *A decimal can be multiplied by a whole number by using following steps:*

Step I *Multiply the decimal without the decimal point by the given whole number.*

Step II *Mark the decimal point in the product to have as many places of decimal as are there in the given decimal.*

14. *To multiply a decimal by another decimal, we follow following steps:*

Step I *Multiply the two decimals without decimal point just like whole numbers.*

Step II *Insert the decimal point in the product by counting as many places from the right to left as the sum of the number of decimal places of the given decimals.*

15. *A decimal can be divided by 10, 100, 1000 ect by using the following rules:*

Rule I *When a decimal is divided by 10, the decimal point is shifted to the left by one place.*

Rule II *When a decimal is divided by 100, the decimal point is shifted to the left by two places.*

Rule III *When a decimal is divided by 1000, the decimal point is shifted to the left by three places.*

16. *A decimal can be divided by a whole number by using the following steps:*

Step I *Check the whole number part of the dividend.*

Step II *If the whole number part of the dividend is less than the divisor, then place a 0 in the ones place in the quotient. Otherwise, go to step III.*

Step III *Divide the whole number part of the dividend.*

Step IV *Place the decimal point to the right of ones place in the quotient obtained in step I.*

Step V *Divide the decimal part of the dividend by the divisor. If the digits of the dividend are exhausted, then place zeros to the right of dividend and remainder each time and continue the process.*

17. *A decimal can be divided by a decimal by using the following steps:*

Step I *Multiple the dividend and divisor by 10 or 100 or 1000 etc. to convert the divisor into a whole number.*

4

RATIONAL NUMBERS

4.1 INTRODUCTION

We know that for two given integers m and n, their sum $m + n$, product $m \times n$ and the difference $m - n$ are always integers. However, it may not always be possible for a given integer to exactly divide another given integer. In other words, the result of division of an integer by a non-zero integer may or may not be an integer. For example, when 9 is divided by 4, the result is not an integer. In fact $\frac{9}{4}$ is a fraction. Thus, there is need to extend the system of integers so that it may also be possible to divide any given integer by any other given integer different from zero (because division by zero is not possible).

In this chapter, we shall introduce the system of rational numbers. We shall also learn comparison of rational numbers and their representation on the number line.

4.2 RATIONAL NUMBERS

In this section, we shall define rational numbers. We shall also show that every integer is a rational number but a rational number need not be an integer.

RATIONAL NUMBER *A number of the form* $\frac{p}{q}$ *or a number which can be expressed in the form* $\frac{p}{q}$, *where p and q are integers and* $q \neq 0$, *is called a rational number.*

In other words, a rational number is any number that can be expressed as the quotient of two integers with the condition that the divisor is not zero.

Each of the numbers $\frac{2}{3}, \frac{-5}{7}, \frac{-11}{-5}, \frac{7}{-9}$ is a rational number.

SOME USEFUL RESULTS

Result I: *Every natural number is a rational number but a rational number need not be a natural number.*

Explanation: We know that

$$1 = \frac{1}{1}, 2 = \frac{2}{1}, 3 = \frac{3}{1} \text{ and so on.}$$

In other words, every natural number n can be written as $n = \frac{n}{1}$, which is the quotient of two integers. Thus, every natural number is a rational number.

Clearly, $\frac{3}{2}, \frac{2}{5}$, etc. are rational numbers but they are not natural numbers.

Hence, every natural number is a rational number but a rational number need not be a natural number.

Result II: *Zero is a rational number.*

Explanation: We know that the integer 0 can be written in any one of the following forms:

$$\frac{0}{1}, \frac{0}{-1}, \frac{0}{2}, \frac{0}{-2}, \frac{0}{3}, \frac{0}{-3}, \frac{0}{4}, \frac{0}{-4} \text{ and so on.}$$

In other words, $0 = \frac{0}{q}$, where q is any non-zero integer.

Thus, 0 can be written as $\frac{p}{q}$, where $p = 0$ and q is any non-zero integer.

Hence, 0 is a rational number.

Result III: *Every integer is a rational number but a rational number need not be an integer.*

Explanation: We know that

$$1 = \frac{1}{1}, 2 = \frac{2}{1}, 3 = \frac{3}{1}, 4 = \frac{4}{1} \text{ and so on. Also, } -1 = \frac{-1}{1}, -2 = \frac{-2}{1}, -3 = \frac{-3}{1} \text{ and so on.}$$

In other words, any integer p can be written as $p = \frac{p}{1}$, which is a rational number. Thus, every integer is a rational number.

Clearly, $\frac{3}{2}, \frac{-5}{3}$, etc. are rational numbers but they are not integers.

Hence, every integer is a rational number but a rational number need not be an integer.

Result IV: *Every fraction is a rational number but a rational number need not be a fraction.*

Explanation: Let $\frac{p}{q}$ be any fraction. Then, p and q are natural numbers.

Since every natural number is an integer. Therefore, p and q are integers. Thus, the fraction $\frac{p}{q}$ is the quotient of two integers such that $q \neq 0$.

Hence, $\frac{p}{q}$ is a rational number.

We know that $\frac{3}{-5}$ is a rational number but it is not a fraction because its denominator is not a natural number.

Since every mixed fraction consisting of an integer part and a fractional part can be expressed as an improper fraction, which is quotient of two integers. Thus, every mixed fraction is also a rational number.

Hence, every fraction is also a rational number.

NUMERATOR AND DENOMINATOR *If $\frac{p}{q}$ is a rational number, then the integer p is known as its numerator and the integer q is called the denominator.*

POSITIVE RATIONAL NUMBER *A rational number is said to be positive if its numerator and denominator are either both positive integers or both negative integers.*

In other words, a rational number is positive, if its numerator and denominator are of the same sign.

Each of the rational numbers $\frac{2}{3}, \frac{5}{9}, \frac{-7}{-12}, \frac{-3}{-11}$ is a positive rational number, but $\frac{3}{-7}, \frac{-4}{5}$ are not positive rational numbers.

ILLUSTRATION 1 Every natural number is a positive rational number.

Solution We know that

$1 = \frac{1}{1}, 2 = \frac{2}{1}, 3 = \frac{3}{1}$ and so on.

In other words, any natural number n can be written as

$n = \frac{n}{1}$, where n and 1 are positive integers.

Hence, every natural number is a positive rational number.

NEGATIVE RATIONAL NUMBER *A rational number is said to be negative if its numerator and denominator are such that one of them is positive integer and another one is a negative integer.*

In other words, a rational number is negative, if its numerator and denominator are of the opposite signs.

Each of the rational numbers $\frac{-3}{7}, \frac{5}{-9}, \frac{-15}{26}$ is a negative rational number.

ILLUSTRATION 2 Every negative integer is a negative rational number.

Solution We know that

$-1 = \frac{-1}{1}, -2 = \frac{-2}{1}, -3 = \frac{-3}{1}$ and so on.

In other words, any negative integer n can be written as $n = \frac{n}{1}$, here n is negative and 1 is positive.

Hence, every negative integer is a negative rational number.

Remark: *The rational number 0 is neither positive nor negative.*

EXERCISE 4.1

1. Write down the numerator of each of the following rational numbers:

   (i) $\frac{-7}{5}$ (ii) $\frac{15}{-4}$ (iii) $\frac{-17}{-21}$ (iv) $\frac{8}{9}$ (v) 5

2. Write down the denominator of each of the following rational numbers:

   (i) $\frac{-4}{5}$ (ii) $\frac{11}{-34}$ (iii) $\frac{-15}{-82}$ (iv) 15 (v) 0

3. Write down the rational number whose numerator is $(-3) \times 4$, and whose denominator is $(34-23) \times (7-4)$.

4. Write the following rational numbers as integers:

   $$\frac{7}{1}, \frac{-12}{1}, \frac{34}{1}, \frac{-73}{1}, \frac{95}{1}$$

5. Write the following integers as rational numbers with denominator 1:

   $$-15, 17, 85, -100$$

6. Write down the rational number whose numerator is the smallest three digit number and denominator is the largest four digit number.

7. Separate positive and negative rational numbers from the following rational numbers:

   $$\frac{-5}{-7}, \frac{12}{-5}, \frac{7}{4}, \frac{13}{-9}, 0, \frac{-18}{-7}, \frac{-95}{116}, \frac{-1}{-9}$$

8. Which of the following rational numbers are positive:

(i) $\frac{-8}{7}$ (ii) $\frac{9}{8}$ (iii) $\frac{-19}{-13}$ (iv) $\frac{-21}{13}$

9. Which of the following rational numbers are negative?

(i) $\frac{-3}{7}$ (ii) $\frac{-5}{-8}$ (iii) $\frac{9}{-83}$ (iv) $\frac{-115}{-197}$

ANSWERS

1. (i) –7 (ii) 15 (iii) –17 (iv) 8 (v) 5
2. (i) 5 (ii) –34 (iii) –82 (iv) 1 (vi) any non-zero integer
3. $\frac{-12}{33}$ 4. 7, –12, 34, –73, 95 5. $\frac{-15}{1}, \frac{17}{1}, \frac{85}{1}, \frac{-100}{1}$ 6. $\frac{100}{9999}$
7. Positive: $\frac{-5}{-7}, \frac{7}{4}, \frac{-18}{-7}, \frac{-1}{-9}$; Negative: $\frac{12}{-5}, \frac{13}{-9}, \frac{-95}{116}$
8. (ii) $\frac{9}{8}$ (iii) $\frac{-19}{-13}$ 9. (i) $\frac{-3}{7}$ (iii) $\frac{9}{-83}$

4.3 SOME USEFUL PROPERTIES OF RATIONAL NUMBERS

In chapter 2, we have learnt that if we multiply the numerator and denominator of a fraction by the same positive integer, the value of the fraction does not change. For example, the fractions $\frac{2}{3}$ and $\frac{6}{9}$ are equal because the numerator and denominator of $\frac{6}{9}$ can be obtained by muliplying each of the numerator and denominator of $\frac{2}{3}$ by 3.

Also, $\frac{2}{3} = \frac{2 \times 5}{3 \times 5} = \frac{10}{15}, \frac{2}{3} = \frac{2 \times 11}{3 \times 11} = \frac{22}{33}$ and so on.

Similarly,

$$\frac{-3}{4} = \frac{-3 \times (-1)}{4 \times (-1)} = \frac{3}{-4}, \frac{-3}{4} = \frac{-3 \times (2)}{4 \times 2} = \frac{-6}{8}, \frac{-3}{4} = \frac{-3 \times (-2)}{4 \times (-2)} = \frac{6}{-8} \text{ and so on.}$$

$$\therefore \quad \frac{-3}{4} = \frac{-3 \times (-1)}{4 \times (-1)} = \frac{-3 \times 2}{4 \times 2} = \frac{-3 \times (-2)}{4 \times (-2)} \text{ and so on.}$$

These illustrations suggest us the following:

Property 1 *If $\frac{p}{q}$ is a rational number and m is a non-zero integer, then*

$$\frac{p}{q} = \frac{p \times m}{q \times m}$$

In other words, a rational number remains unchanged, if we multiply its numerator and denominator by the same non-zero integer.

EQUIVALENT RATIONAL NUMBERS If $\frac{p}{q}$ is a rational number and m is a non-zero integer, then $\frac{p \times m}{q \times m}$ is a rational number equivalent to $\frac{p}{q}$.

For example, rational numbers $\frac{6}{8}, \frac{9}{12}, \frac{15}{20}, \frac{-21}{-28}, \frac{-36}{-48}$ are equivalent to the rational number $\frac{3}{4}$

<u>NOTE</u>: *If the denominator of a rational number is a negative integer, then by using the above property, we can make it positive by multiplying its numerator and denomiator by –1.*

For example, $\frac{3}{-4} = \frac{3 \times (-1)}{(-4) \times (-1)} = \frac{-3}{4}$

We have learnt in chapter 2, that if we divide the numerator and denominator of a fraction by a common divisor, then the value of the fraction does not change. For example,

$$\frac{12}{32} = \frac{12 \div 4}{32 \div 4} = \frac{3}{8}$$

Also,

$$\frac{210}{462} = \frac{210 \div 2}{462 \div 2} = \frac{105}{231} = \frac{105 \div 3}{231 \div 3} = \frac{35}{77} = \frac{35 \div 7}{77 \div 7} = \frac{5}{11}$$

Similarly, we have

$$\frac{-27}{45} = \frac{(-27) \div 3}{45 \div 3} = \frac{-9}{15} = \frac{(-9) \div 3}{15 \div 3} = \frac{-3}{5}, \text{ and } \frac{70}{-84} = \frac{70 \div 2}{(-84) \div 2} = \frac{35}{-42} = \frac{35 \div (-7)}{(-42) \div (-7)} = \frac{-5}{6}$$

These illustrations suggest us the following:

Property 2 *If* $\frac{p}{q}$ *is a rational number and m is a common divisor of p and q, then*

$$\frac{p}{q} = \frac{p \div m}{q \div m}$$

In other words, if we divide the numerator and denominator of a rational number by a common divisor of both, the rational number remains unchanged.

We shall now use the above properties in expressing a given rational number in different forms. Following examples will illustrate the same.

ILLUSTRATIVE EXAMPLES

Example 1 Write each of the following rational numbers with positive denominator:

$$\frac{5}{-7}, \frac{15}{-28}, \frac{-17}{-13}$$

Solution In order to express a rational number with positive denominator, we multiply its numerator and denominator by –1. Therefore,

$$\frac{5}{-7}=\frac{5\times(-1)}{(-7)\times(-1)}=\frac{-5}{7};\ \frac{15}{-28}=\frac{15\times(-1)}{(-28)\times(-1)}=\frac{-15}{28},\text{ and }\frac{-17}{-13}=\frac{(-17)\times(-1)}{(-13)\times(-1)}=\frac{17}{13}$$

Example 2 Express $\frac{-5}{6}$ as a rational number with numerator:

(i) –15 (ii) 10

Solution (i) In order to express $\frac{-5}{6}$ as a rational number with numerator –15, we first find a number which when multiplied by –5 gives –15.

Clearly, such number is $(-15) \div (-5) = 3$

Multiplying the numerator and denominator of $\frac{-5}{6}$ by 3, we have

$$\frac{-5}{6}=\frac{(-5)\times 3}{6\times 3}=\frac{-15}{18}$$

Thus, the required rational number is $\frac{-15}{18}$.

(ii) In order to express $\frac{-5}{6}$ as a rational number with numerator 10, we first find a number which when multiplied by –5 gives 10.

Clearly, such a number is $10 \div (-5) = -2$.

Multiplying the numerator and denominator of $\frac{-5}{6}$ by (–2), we have

$$\frac{-5}{6}=\frac{(-5)\times(-2)}{6\times(-2)}=\frac{10}{-12}$$

Thus, the required rational number is $\frac{10}{-12}$

Example 3 Express $\frac{-4}{5}$ as a rational number with denominator:

(i) 20 (ii) –30

Solution (i) In order to express $\frac{-4}{5}$ as a rational number with denominator 20, we first find a number which when multiplied with 5 gives 20.

Clearly, such a number $= 20 \div 5 = 4$

Multiplying the numerator and denominator of $\frac{-4}{5}$ by 4, we have

$$\frac{-4}{5}=\frac{-4\times 4}{5\times 4}=\frac{-16}{20}$$

(ii) In order to express $\frac{-4}{5}$ as a rational number with denominator –30, we first find the number which when multiplied by 5 gives –30 .

Clearly, such a number $= (-30) \div 5 = -6$

Multiplying the numerator and denominator of $\frac{-4}{5}$ by –6, we have

$$\frac{-4}{5} = \frac{(-4)\times(-6)}{5\times(-6)} = \frac{24}{-30}$$

Example 4 Express $\frac{-48}{60}$ as a rational number with denominator 5.

Solution In order to express $\frac{-48}{60}$ as a rational number with denominator 5, we first find a number which gives 5 when 60 is divided by it.

Clearly, such a number = (60 ÷ 5) = 12

Dividing the numerator and denominator of $\frac{-48}{60}$ by 12, we have

$$\frac{-48}{60} = \frac{-48 \div 12}{60 \div 12} = \frac{-4}{5}$$

Example 5 Express $\frac{42}{-63}$ as a rational number with denominator 3.

Solution In order to express $\frac{42}{-63}$ as a rational number with denominator 3, we first find a number which gives 3 when –63 is divided by it.

Clearly, such a number = (–63) ÷ 3 = –21

Dividing the numerator and denominator of $\frac{42}{-63}$ by –21, we get

$$\frac{42}{-63} = \frac{42 \div (-21)}{(-63) \div (-21)} = \frac{-2}{3}$$

Example 6 Fill in the blanks:

(i) $\frac{5}{-7} = \frac{....}{35} = \frac{....}{-77}$ (ii) $\frac{7}{13} = \frac{35}{....} = \frac{-63}{....}$

Solution (i) We have, 35 ÷ (–7) = –5

$$\therefore \quad \frac{5}{-7} = \frac{5\times(-5)}{-7\times(-5)} = \frac{-25}{-35}$$

Similarly, we have (–77) ÷ (–7) = 11

$$\therefore \quad \frac{5}{-7} = \frac{5\times 11}{-7\times 11} = \frac{55}{-77}$$

Hence, $\frac{5}{-7} = \frac{-25}{35} = \frac{55}{-77}$

(ii) We have, 35 ÷ 7 = 5

$$\therefore \quad \frac{7}{13} = \frac{7\times 5}{13\times 5} = \frac{35}{65}$$

Similarly, we have $(-63) \div 7 = -9$

$$\therefore \quad \frac{7}{13} = \frac{7 \times (-9)}{13 \times (-9)} = \frac{-63}{-117}$$

Hence, $\frac{7}{13} = \frac{35}{65} = \frac{-63}{-117}$

Example 7 In each of the following, find an equivalent form of the rational numbers having a common denominator

(i) $\frac{5}{6}$ and $\frac{7}{9}$ (ii) $\frac{2}{3}, \frac{5}{6}$ and $\frac{7}{12}$

Solution (i) We have to convert $\frac{5}{6}$ and $\frac{7}{9}$ into equivalent rational numbers having common denominator.

Clearly, such a denominator is the LCM of 6 and 9.

We have, $6 = 2 \times 3$ and $9 = 3 \times 3$

$\therefore$ LCM of 6 and 9 is $2 \times 3 \times 3 = 18$

Now, $18 \div 6 = 3$ and $18 \div 9 = 2$

$$\therefore \quad \frac{5}{6} = \frac{5 \times 3}{6 \times 3} = \frac{15}{18} \text{ and } \frac{7}{9} = \frac{7 \times 2}{9 \times 2} = \frac{14}{18}$$

Hence, given rational numbers with common denominator are $\frac{15}{18}$ and $\frac{14}{18}$.

(ii) LCM of 3, 6 and 12 is 12

Also, $12 \div 3 = 4$, $12 \div 6 = 2$

$$\therefore \quad \frac{2}{3} = \frac{2 \times 4}{3 \times 4} = \frac{8}{12} \text{ and } \frac{5}{6} = \frac{5 \times 2}{6 \times 2} = \frac{10}{12}$$

Hence, the given rational numbers with common denominator are $\frac{8}{12}, \frac{10}{12}$ and $\frac{7}{12}$.

EXERCISE 4.2

1. Express each of the following as a rational number with positive denominator:

   (i) $\frac{-15}{-28}$ (ii) $\frac{6}{-9}$ (iii) $\frac{-28}{-11}$ (iv) $\frac{19}{-7}$

2. Express $\frac{3}{5}$ as a rational number with numerator:

   (i) 6 (ii) –15 (iii) 21 (iv) –27

3. Express $\frac{5}{7}$ as a rational number with denominator:

   (i) –14 (ii) 70 (iii) –28 (iv) –84

4. Express $\frac{3}{4}$ as a rational number with denominator:

   (i) 20 (ii) 36 (iii) 44 (iv) −80

5. Express $\frac{2}{5}$ as a rational number with numerator

   (i) −56 (ii) 154 (iii) −750 (iv) 500

6. Express $\frac{-192}{108}$ as a rational number with numerator:

   (i) 64 (ii) −16 (iii) 32 (iv) −48

7. Express $\frac{168}{-294}$ as a rational number with denominator:

   (i) 14 (ii) −7 (iii) −49 (iv) 1470

8. Write $\frac{-14}{42}$ in a form so that the numerator is equal to:

   (i) −2 (ii) 7 (iii) 42 (iv) −70

9. Select those rational numbers which can be written as a rational number with numerator 6:

$$\frac{1}{22}, \frac{2}{3}, \frac{3}{4}, \frac{4}{-5}, \frac{5}{6}, \frac{-6}{7}, \frac{-7}{8}$$

10. Select those rational numbers which can be written as a rational number with denominator 4:

$$\frac{7}{8}, \frac{64}{16}, \frac{36}{-12}, \frac{-16}{17}, \frac{5}{-4}, \frac{140}{28}$$

11. In each of the following, find an equivalent form of the rational number having a common denominator:

   (i) $\frac{3}{4}$ and $\frac{5}{12}$ (ii) $\frac{2}{3}, \frac{7}{6}$ and $\frac{11}{12}$ (iii) $\frac{5}{7}, \frac{3}{8}, \frac{9}{14}$ and $\frac{20}{21}$

ANSWERS

1. (i) $\frac{15}{28}$ (ii) $\frac{-6}{9}$ (iii) $\frac{28}{11}$ (iv) $\frac{-19}{7}$

2. (i) $\frac{6}{10}$ (ii) $\frac{-15}{-25}$ (iii) $\frac{21}{35}$ (iv) $\frac{-27}{-45}$

3. (i) $\frac{-10}{-14}$ (ii) $\frac{50}{70}$ (iii) $\frac{-20}{-28}$ (iv) $\frac{-60}{-84}$

4. (i) $\frac{15}{20}$ (ii) $\frac{27}{36}$ (iii) $\frac{33}{44}$ (iv) $\frac{-60}{-80}$

5. (i) $\frac{-56}{-140}$ (ii) $\frac{154}{385}$ (iii) $\frac{-750}{-1875}$ (iv) $\frac{500}{1250}$

6. (i) $\frac{64}{-36}$ (ii) $\frac{-16}{9}$ (iii) $\frac{32}{-18}$ (iv) $\frac{-48}{27}$

7. (i) $\frac{-8}{14}$ (ii) $\frac{4}{-7}$ (iii) $\frac{28}{-49}$ (iv) $\frac{-840}{1470}$

8. (i) $\frac{-2}{6}$ (ii) $\frac{7}{-21}$ (iii) $\frac{42}{-126}$ (iv) $\frac{-70}{210}$

9. $\frac{1}{22}, \frac{2}{3}, \frac{3}{4}, \frac{-6}{7}$

10. $\frac{7}{8}, \frac{64}{16}, \frac{36}{-12}, \frac{5}{-4}, \frac{140}{28}$

11. (i) $\frac{9}{12}$ and $\frac{5}{12}$ (ii) $\frac{8}{12}, \frac{14}{12}$ and $\frac{11}{12}$ (iii) $\frac{120}{168}, \frac{63}{168}, \frac{108}{168}$ and $\frac{160}{168}$

4.4 LOWEST FORM OF A RATIONAL NUMBER

DEFINITION *A rational number $\frac{p}{q}$ is said to be in the lowest form or simplest form if p and q have no common factor other than 1.*

In other words, a rational number $\frac{p}{q}$ is said to be in the lowest form, if the HCF of p and q is 1, i.e., p and q are relatively prime.

The rational number $\frac{2}{7}$ is in the lowest form, because 2 and 7 have no common factor other than 1. However, the rational number $\frac{12}{40}$ is not in the lowest form, because 4 is a common factor to both numerator and denominator.

Every rational number can be put in the lowest form using the following steps:

STEP I *Obtain the rational number $\frac{p}{q}$ (say).*

STEP II *Find the HCF of p and q.*

STEP III *If $m = 1$, then $\frac{p}{q}$ is in lowest form.*

STEP IV *If $m \neq 1$, then $\frac{p \div m}{q \div m}$ is the lowest form of $\frac{p}{q}$.*

Following examples will illustrate the above procedure.

ILLUSTRATIVE EXAMPLES

Example 1 Find whether the following rational numbers are in the lowest form or not.

(i) $\frac{17}{79}$ (ii) $\frac{24}{320}$

Solution (i) We observe that 17 and 79 have no common factor, i.e., their HCF is 1.

Therefore, $\frac{17}{79}$ is in the lowest form.

(ii) We have,

$24 = 2 \times 2 \times 2 \times 3$ and $320 = 2 \times 2 \times 2 \times 2 \times 2 \times 2 \times 5$

Thus, HCF of 24 and 320 is $2 \times 2 \times 2 = 8$.

Therefore, $\frac{24}{320}$ is not in the lowest form.

Example 2 Express each of the following rational numbers to the lowest form.

(i) $\frac{12}{16}$ (ii) $\frac{-60}{72}$ (iii) $\frac{-24}{-36}$ (iv) $\frac{91}{-364}$

Solution (i) We have,

$12 = 2 \times 2 \times 3$ and $16 = 2 \times 2 \times 2 \times 2$

$\therefore$ HCF of 12 and 16 is $2 \times 2 = 4$.

So, $\frac{12}{16}$ is not in lowest form.

Dividing numerator and denominator by 4, we have

$$\frac{12}{16} = \frac{12 \div 4}{16 \div 4} = \frac{3}{4}$$

$\therefore$ $\frac{3}{4}$ is the lowest form of $\frac{12}{16}$.

(ii) We have,

$60 = 2 \times 2 \times 3 \times 5$ and $72 = 2 \times 2 \times 2 \times 3 \times 3$

$\therefore$ HCF of 60 and 72 is $2 \times 2 \times 3 = 12$

Dividing numerator and denominator of $\frac{-60}{72}$ by 12, we have

$$\frac{-60}{72} = \frac{-60 \div 12}{72 \div 12} = \frac{-5}{6}$$

Hence, $\frac{-5}{6}$ is the lowest form of $\frac{-60}{72}$.

(iii) We have,

$24 = 2 \times 2 \times 2 \times 3$ and $36 = 2 \times 2 \times 3 \times 3$

$\therefore$ HCF of 24 and 36 is $2 \times 2 \times 3 = 12$

Dividing numerator and denominator of $\frac{-24}{-36}$ by 12, we have

$$\frac{-24}{-36} = \frac{-24 \div 12}{-36 \div 12} = \frac{-2}{-3}$$

$\therefore$ $\frac{-2}{-3}$ is the lowest form of $\frac{-24}{-36}$.

(iv) We have,

$91 = 7 \times 13$ and $364 = 2 \times 2 \times 7 \times 13$

$\therefore$ HCF of 91 and 364 is $13 \times 7 = 91$.

Dividing numerator and denominator by 91, we have

$$\frac{91}{-364} = \frac{91 \div 91}{-364 \div 91} = \frac{1}{-4}$$

Hence, $\frac{1}{-4}$ is the lowest form of $\frac{91}{-364}$

Example 3 Fill in the blanks:

$$\frac{90}{165} = \frac{-6}{\ldots\ldots} = \frac{\ldots\ldots}{-55}$$

Solution Here, $90 = 2 \times 3 \times 3 \times 5$ and $165 = 3 \times 5 \times 11$

$\therefore$ HCF of 90 and 165 is 15.

So, $\frac{90}{165}$ is not in lowest form.

Dividing numerator and denominator by 15, we get

$$\frac{90}{165} = \frac{90 \div 15}{165 \div 15} = \frac{6}{11}$$

Thus, the rational number $\frac{90}{165}$ in the lowest form equals $\frac{6}{11}$

Now, $(-6) \div 6 = -1$

$$\therefore \quad \frac{6}{11} = \frac{6 \times -1}{11 \times -1} = \frac{-6}{-11}$$

Similarly, we have $(-55) \div 11 = -5$

$$\therefore \quad \frac{6}{11} = \frac{6 \times -5}{11 \times -5} = \frac{-30}{-55}$$

Hence, $\frac{90}{165} = \frac{-6}{-11} = \frac{-30}{-55}$

EXERCISE 4.3

1. Determine whether the following rational numbers are in the lowest form or not:

   (i) $\frac{65}{84}$ (ii) $\frac{-15}{32}$ (iii) $\frac{24}{128}$ (iv) $\frac{-56}{-32}$

2. Express each of the following rational numbers to the lowest form:

   (i) $\frac{4}{22}$ (ii) $\frac{-36}{180}$ (iii) $\frac{132}{-428}$ (iv) $\frac{-32}{-56}$

3. Fill in the blanks:

   (i) $\frac{-5}{7} = \frac{\ldots.}{35} = \frac{\ldots.}{49}$ (ii) $\frac{-4}{-9} = \frac{\ldots.}{18} = \frac{12}{\ldots.}$

   (iii) $\frac{6}{-13} = \frac{-12}{\ldots.} = \frac{24}{\ldots.}$ (iv) $\frac{-6}{\ldots.} = \frac{3}{11} = \frac{\ldots.}{-55}$

ANSWERS

1. (i), (ii) 2. (i) $\frac{2}{11}$ (ii) $\frac{-1}{5}$ (iii) $\frac{33}{-107}$ (iv) $\frac{4}{7}$

3. (i) $-25 - 35$ (ii) 8, 27 (iii) 26, -52 (iv) $-22, -15$

4.5 STANDARD FORM OF A RATIONAL NUMBER

DEFINITION *A rational number* $\frac{p}{q}$ *is said to be in the standard form if q is positive, and the integers p and q have no common divisor other than 1.*

In order to express a given rational number in the standard form, we follow the following steps:

STEP I *Obtain the rational number.*

STEP II *See whether the denominator of the rational number is positive or not. If it is negative, multiply or divide numerator and denominator both by –1 so that the denominator becomes positive.*

STEP III *Find the greatest common divisor (GCD) of the absolute values of the numerator and the denominator.*

STEP IV *Divide the numerator and denominator of the given rational number by the GCD (HCF) obtained in step III. The rational number so obtained is the standard form of the given rational number.*

The following examples will illustrate the above procedure.

ILLUSTRATIVE EXAMPLES

Example 1 Express each of the following rational numbers in the standard form:

(i) $\frac{-8}{28}$ (ii) $\frac{-12}{-30}$ (iii) $\frac{14}{-49}$ (iv) $\frac{-16}{-56}$

Solution (i) The denominator of the rational number $\frac{-8}{28}$ is positive. In order to express it in the standard form, we divide its numerator and denominator by the greatest common divisor of 8 and 28.

The greatest common divisor of 8 and 28 is 4.

Dividing the numerator and denominator of $\frac{-8}{28}$ by 4, we have

$$\frac{-8}{28} = \frac{(-8) \div 4}{28 \div 4} = \frac{-2}{7}$$

Thus, the standard form of $\frac{-8}{28}$ is $\frac{-2}{7}$.

(ii) The denominator of the rational number $\frac{-12}{-30}$ is negative. So, we first make it positive.

Multiplying the numerator and denominator of $\frac{-12}{-30}$ by –1, we have

$$\frac{-12}{-30} = \frac{(-12) \times (-1)}{(-30) \times (-1)} = \frac{12}{30}$$

The greatest common divisor of 12 and 30 is 6.

Dividing the numerator and denominator of $\frac{12}{30}$ by 6, we get

$$\frac{12}{30} = \frac{12 \div 6}{30 \div 6} = \frac{2}{5}$$

Hence, the standard form of $\frac{-12}{-30}$ is $\frac{2}{5}$.

(iii) The denominator of $\frac{14}{-49}$ is negative. So, we first make it positive.

Multiplying the numerator and denominator of $\frac{14}{-49}$ by –1, we have

$$\frac{14}{-49} = \frac{14 \times (-1)}{(-49) \times (-1)} = \frac{-14}{49}$$

The greatest common divisor of 14 and 49 is 7.

Dividing the numerator and denominator of $\frac{14}{-49}$ by 7, we have

$$\frac{14}{-49} = \frac{(-14) \div 7}{49 \div 7} = \frac{-2}{7}$$

Hence, the standard form of $\frac{14}{-49}$ is $\frac{-2}{7}$.

(iv) The denominator of $\frac{-16}{-56}$ is negative. So, we first make it positive.

Multiplying the numerator and denominator of $\frac{-16}{-56}$ by –1, we have

$$\frac{-16}{-56} = \frac{(-16) \times (-1)}{(-56) \times (-1)} = \frac{16}{56}$$

The greatest common divisor of 16 and 56 is 8.

Dividing the numerator and denominator of $\frac{16}{56}$ by 8, we get

$$\frac{16}{56} = \frac{16 \div 8}{56 \div 8} = \frac{2}{7}$$

Hence, the standard form of $\frac{-16}{-56}$ is $\frac{2}{7}$.

Example 2 Express each one of the following rational numbers in the standard form:

(i) $\frac{-247}{-228}$ (ii) $\frac{299}{-161}$

Solution (i) The denominator of $\frac{-247}{-228}$ is negative. So, we first make it positive.

Multiplying the numerator and denominator of $\frac{-247}{-228}$ by –1, we get

$$\frac{-247}{-228} = \frac{(-247) \times (-1)}{(-228) \times (-1)} = \frac{247}{228}$$

Now, we find the greatest common divisor of 247 and 228 by division method as follows:

12	228	247	1
	−228	−228	
	0	19	

Clearly, the greatest common divisor of 228 and 247 is the last divisor 19.

Dividing the numerator and denominator of $\frac{247}{228}$ by 19, we get

$$\frac{247}{228}=\frac{247\div 19}{228\div 19}=\frac{13}{12}$$

Hence, the standard form of $\frac{-247}{-228}$ is $\frac{13}{12}$.

(ii) The denominator of $\frac{299}{-161}$ is negative. So, we first make it positive.

Multiplying the numerator and denominator of $\frac{299}{-161}$ by −1, we have

$$\frac{299}{-161}=\frac{299\times(-1)}{(-161)\times(-1)}=\frac{-299}{161}$$

Now, we find the greatest common divisor of 299 and 161 by division method:

1	161	299	1
	−138	−161	
	23	138	6
		−138	
		0	

Clearly, the greatest common divisor of 299 and 161 is the last divisor equal to 23.

Dividing the numerator and denominator of $\frac{-299}{161}$ by 23, we get

$$\frac{-299}{161}=\frac{(-299)\div 23}{161\div 23}=\frac{-13}{7}$$

Hence, the standard form of $\frac{-299}{161}$ is $\frac{-13}{7}$.

EXERCISE 4.4

1. Write each of the following rational numbers in the standard form:

(i) $\frac{2}{10}$ (ii) $\frac{-8}{36}$ (iii) $\frac{4}{-16}$ (iv) $\frac{-15}{-35}$

(v) $\frac{299}{-161}$ (vi) $\frac{-63}{-210}$ (vii) $\frac{68}{-119}$ (viii) $\frac{-195}{275}$

ANSWERS

1. (i) $\frac{1}{5}$ (ii) $\frac{-2}{9}$ (iii) $\frac{-1}{4}$ (iv) $\frac{3}{7}$ (v) $\frac{-13}{7}$ (vi) $\frac{3}{10}$

(vii) $\frac{-4}{7}$ (viii) $\frac{-39}{55}$

4.6 EQUALITY OF RATIONAL NUMBERS

In section 4.3, we have learnt that a rational number remains unchanged if we multiply or divide its numerator and denominator by the same non–zero integer. It follows from this that a rational number can be written in several equivalent forms. Two rational numbers are said to be equivalent if one can be obtained from the other either by multiplying or by dividing its numerator and denominator by the same non–zero integer. Now, a very natural question arises: "Given two rational numbers, how to test whether they are equal?". There are many methods to test the equality of two rational numbers. In this section, we shall discuss various methods to test the equality of two rational numbers.

METHOD I

In order to test the equality of two rational numbers, we express both the rational numbers in the standard form. If they have the same standard form they are equal, otherwise they are not equal.

ILLUSTRATION 1 Are the rational numbers $\frac{8}{-12}$ and $\frac{-50}{75}$ equal?

Solution First we express the given rational numbers in the standard form.

We have,

$$\frac{8}{-12} = \frac{8 \times (-1)}{(-12) \times (-1)} \quad \text{[Multiplying the numerator and denominator by } -1]$$

$$\Rightarrow \frac{8}{-12} = \frac{-8}{12}$$

$$\Rightarrow \frac{8}{-12} = \frac{(-8) \div 4}{12 \div 4} \quad \left[\begin{array}{l}\text{Dividing the numerator and denominator by} \\ \text{the greatest common divisor of 8 and 12 i.e. 4}\end{array}\right]$$

$$\Rightarrow \frac{8}{-12} = \frac{-2}{3}$$

$$\text{and, } \frac{-50}{75} = \frac{(-50) \div 25}{75 \div 25} \quad \left[\begin{array}{l}\text{Dividing the numerator and denominator by} \\ \text{the greatest common divisor of 50 and 75 i.e. 25}\end{array}\right]$$

$$\Rightarrow \frac{-50}{75} = \frac{-2}{3}$$

Clearly, the given rational numbers have the same standard form.

$$\therefore \frac{8}{-12} = \frac{-50}{75}$$

ILLUSTRATION 2 Are the rational numbers $\frac{-8}{28}$ and $\frac{28}{-49}$ equal?

Solution In order to test the equality of the given rational numbers, we first express them in the standard form.

We have,

$$\frac{-8}{28} = \frac{(-8) \div 4}{28 \div 4} \quad \left[\begin{array}{l}\text{Dividing the numerator and denominator by}\\ \text{the greatest common divisor of 8 and 28 i.e. 4}\end{array}\right]$$

$$\Rightarrow \quad \frac{-8}{28} = \frac{-2}{7}$$

$$\text{and,} \quad \frac{28}{-49} = \frac{28 \times (-1)}{-49 \times (-1)} \quad \text{[Multiplying the numerator and denominator by } -1\text{]}$$

$$\Rightarrow \quad \frac{28}{-49} = \frac{-28}{49}$$

$$\Rightarrow \quad \frac{28}{-49} = \frac{(-28) \div 7}{(49) \div 7} \quad \left[\begin{array}{l}\text{Dividing the numerator and denominator by}\\ \text{the greatest common divisor of 28 and 49 i.e. 7}\end{array}\right]$$

$$\Rightarrow \quad \frac{28}{-49} = \frac{-4}{7}$$

Clearly, the standard forms of two rational numbers are not same.

Hence, $\frac{-8}{28}$ is not equal to $\frac{28}{-49}$

METHOD II

In this method, denominators of the given rational numbers are made equal by using the following steps:

STEP I *Obtain the two numbers.*

STEP II *Multiply the numerator and denominator of the first number by the denominator of the second number.*

STEP III *Multiply the numerator and denominator of the second number by the denominator of the first number.*

STEP IV *Check the numerators of the two numbers obtained in steps II and III. If their numerators are equal, then the given rational numbers are equal, otherwise they are not equal.*

ILLUSTRATION 3 Are the rational numbers $\frac{-4}{6}$ and $\frac{16}{-24}$ equal?

Solution Multiplying the numerator and denominator of $\frac{-4}{6}$ by the denominator of $\frac{16}{-24}$ i.e. by -24, we have

$\frac{-4}{6} = \frac{-4 \times (-24)}{6 \times (-24)} = \frac{96}{-144}$

Multiplying the numerator and denominator of $\frac{16}{-24}$ by the denominator of $\frac{-4}{6}$ i.e. by 6, we have

$\frac{16}{-24} = \frac{16 \times 6}{(-24) \times 6} = \frac{96}{-144}$

Clearly, the numerators of the above obtained rational numbers are equal. Hence, the given rational numbers are equal.

ILLUSTRATION 4 Show that the rational numbers $\frac{-15}{35}$ and $\frac{4}{-6}$ are not equal.

Solution Multiplying the numerator and denominator of $\frac{-15}{35}$ by the denominator of $\frac{4}{-6}$ i.e. –6, we get

$\frac{-15}{35} = \frac{(-15) \times (-6)}{35 \times (-6)} = \frac{90}{-210}$

Multiplying the numerator and denominator of $\frac{4}{-6}$ by the denominator of $\frac{-15}{35}$ i.e. 35, we get

$\frac{4}{-6} = \frac{4 \times 35}{-6 \times 35} = \frac{140}{-210}$

We find that the numerators of rational numbers $\frac{90}{-210}$ and $\frac{140}{-210}$ are unequal. Hence, the given rational numbers are unequal.

METHOD III

In this method, to test the equality of two rational numbers $\frac{a}{b}$ and $\frac{c}{d}$, we use the following result:

$\frac{a}{b} = \frac{c}{d} \Leftrightarrow a \times d = b \times c$

$\Leftrightarrow$ Numerator of first × Denominator of second

= Numerator of second × Denominator of first

ILLUSTRATION 5 Which of the following pairs of rational numbers are equal?

(i) $\frac{-7}{21}$ and $\frac{3}{-9}$ (ii) $\frac{-8}{-14}$ and $\frac{13}{21}$

Solution (i) The given rational numbers are $\frac{-7}{21}$ and $\frac{3}{-9}$

We have,

Numerator of first × Denominator of second = (–7) × (–9) = 63

and, Numerator of second × Denominator of first = 3 × 21 = 63.

Clearly,

Numerator of first × Denominator of second

= Numerator of second × Denominator of first

Hence, $\frac{-7}{21} = \frac{3}{-9}$.

(ii) The given rational numbers are $\frac{-8}{-14}$ and $\frac{13}{21}$

We have,

Numerator of first × Denominator of second = $-8 \times 21 = -168$

and, Numerator of second × Denominator of first $= 13 \times (-14) = -182$

Clearly,

Numerator of first × Denominator of second

≠ Numerator of second × Denominator of first.

Hence, $\frac{-8}{-14} \neq \frac{13}{21}$.

ILLUSTRATION 6 If $\frac{-5}{7} = \frac{x}{28}$, find the value of x.

Solution We know that $\frac{a}{b} = \frac{c}{d}$ if $ad = bc$.

$\therefore \quad \frac{-5}{7} = \frac{x}{28}$

$\Rightarrow \quad -5 \times 28 = 7 \times x$

$\Rightarrow \quad 7x = -140$

$\Rightarrow \quad \frac{7x}{7} = \frac{-140}{7}$ [Dividing both sides by 7]

$\Rightarrow \quad x = -20$

Aliter In order to write $\frac{-5}{7}$ as a rational number with denominator 28, we first find a number which when multiplied with 7 gives 28.

Clearly, such a number is $28 \div 7 = 4$.

Multiplying the numerator and denominator of $\frac{-5}{7}$ by 4, we have

$$\frac{-5}{7} = \frac{-5 \times 4}{7 \times 4} = \frac{-20}{28}$$

$$\therefore \quad \frac{-5}{7} = \frac{x}{28} \Rightarrow \frac{-20}{28} = \frac{x}{28} \Rightarrow x = -20$$

ILLUSTRATION 7 Fill in the blank: $\frac{-3}{8} = \frac{....}{48}$

Solution In order to fill the required blank, we have to express –3 as a rational number with denominator 48. For this, we first find an integer which when multiplied with 8 gives us 48.

Clearly, such an integer is $48 \div 8 = 6$

Multiplying the numerator and denominator of $\frac{3}{8}$ by 6, we have

$$\frac{-3}{8} = \frac{-3 \times 6}{8 \times 6} = \frac{-18}{48}$$

Hence, the required number is –18.

EXERCISE 4.5

1. Which of the following rational numbers are equal?

   (i) $\frac{-9}{12}$ and $\frac{8}{-12}$ (ii) $\frac{-16}{20}$ and $\frac{20}{-25}$ (iii) $\frac{-7}{21}$ and $\frac{3}{-9}$ (iv) $\frac{-8}{-14}$ and $\frac{13}{21}$

2. If each of the following pairs represents a pair of equivalent rational numbers, find the values of x:

   (i) $\frac{2}{3}$ and $\frac{5}{x}$ (ii) $\frac{-3}{7}$ and $\frac{x}{4}$ (iii) $\frac{3}{5}$ and $\frac{x}{-25}$ (iv) $\frac{13}{6}$ and $\frac{-65}{x}$

3. In each of the following, fill in the blanks so as to make the statement true:

   (i) A number which can be expressed in the form $\frac{p}{q}$, where p and q are integers and q is not equal to zero, is called a .....

   (ii) If the integers p and q have no common divisor other than 1 and q is positive, then the rational number $\frac{p}{q}$ is said to be in the ....

   (iii) Two rational numbers are said to be equal, if they have the same .... form.

   (iv) If m is a common divisor of a and b, then

   $$\frac{a}{b} = \frac{a \div m}{....}$$

   (v) If p and q are positive integers, then $\frac{p}{q}$ is a ...... rational number and $\frac{p}{-q}$ is a ...... rational number.

   (vi) The standard form of –1 is ...

   (vii) If $\frac{p}{q}$ is a rational number, then q cannot be ....

   (viii) Two rational numbers with different numerators are equal, if their numerators are in the same .... as their denominators.

4. In each of the following state if the statement is true (T) or false (F):

   (i) The quotient of two integers is always an integer.

   (ii) Every integer is a rational number.

   (iii) Every rational number is an integer.

   (iv) Every fraction is a rational number.

   (v) Every rational number is a fraction.

   (vi) If $\frac{a}{b}$ is a rational number and m any integer, then $\frac{a}{b} = \frac{a \times m}{b \times m}$

(vii) Two rational numbers with different numerators cannot be equal.

(viii) 8 can be written as a rational number with any integer as denominator.

(ix) 8 can be written as a rational number with any integer as numerator.

(x) $\frac{2}{3}$ is equal to $\frac{4}{6}$.

ANSWERS

1. (ii), (iii) 2. (i) $\frac{15}{2}$ (ii) $\frac{-12}{7}$ (iii) –15 (iv) –30

3. (i) rational number (ii) standard form or lowest form (iii) standard (iv) b ÷ m
(v) positive, negative (vi) $\frac{-1}{1}$ (vii) zero (viii) ratio

4. (i) F (ii) T (iii) F (iv) T (v) F (vi) F
(vii) F (viii) F (ix) F (x) T

4.7 REPRESENTATION OF RATIONAL NUMBERS ON THE NUMBER LINE

In Class VI, we have learnt how to represent integers on the number line. To represent the integers on the number line, we draw a line and mark a point 'O' on it corresponding to the number 'zero' starting from *O*, we mark on it points at equal distances on right as well as on left of *O*. Let *A*, *B*, *C*, *D*, etc. be the points of division on the right of *O* and A', B', C', D', etc. be the points of division on the left of *O* as shown in Fig. 1. If we take *OA* =1 unit, then points *A*, *B*, *C*, *D*, etc. represent the integers 1, 2, 3, 4, etc respectively and the points A', B', C', D', etc. represent the integers –1 , –2 , –3, –4, etc. respectively.

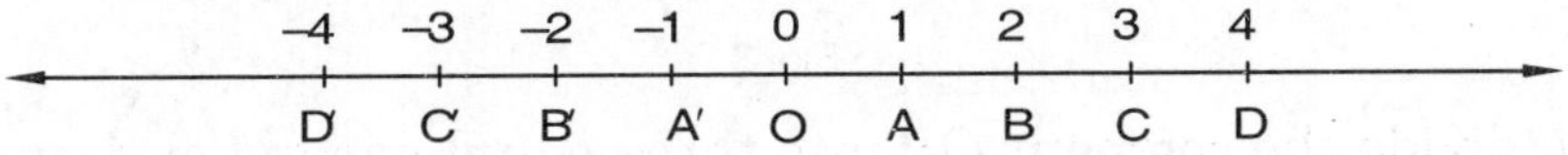

Fig. 1

The point *O* represents integer 0.

Clearly, every positive integer lies to the right of *O* and every negative integer lies to the left of 0.

Rational numbers can also be represented on the number line in the same way.

In order to represent rational numbers on the number line, we draw a line and mark a point *O* on it to represent the rational number zero. The positive rational numbers will be represented by points on the line lying to the right of *O* and negative rational numbers will be represented by points on the line lying to the left of *O*. If we mark a point A on the line to the right of *O* to represent 1, then *OA* =1 unit. Similarly, if we choose a point A' on the line to the left of *O* to represent –1, then OA' =1 unit.

Now, suppose we wish to represent the rational number $\frac{1}{2}$ on the number line. For this, we divide the segment *OA* into two equal parts. Let *P* be the mid-point of segment *OA* . Then $OP = PA = \frac{1}{2}$. Since *O* represents 0 and, *A* represents 1, therefore *P* represents the rational number $\frac{1}{2}$ as shown in Fig 2.

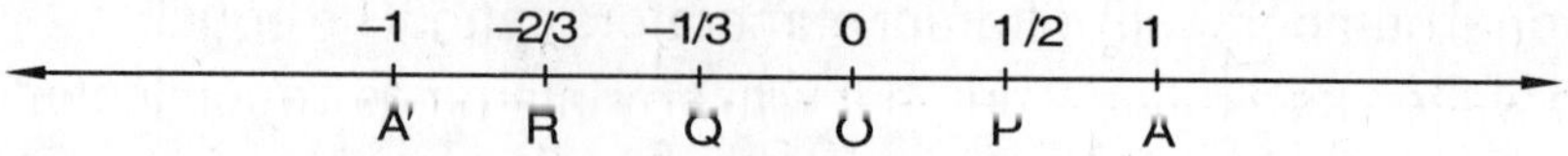

Fig. 2

Similarly, if we want to represent the rational numbers $\frac{-1}{3}$ and $\frac{-2}{3}$ on the number line, we divide the segment OA' into three equal parts. Let Q and R be the points dividing segment OA' into three equal parts. Then, $OQ = QR = RA' = \frac{1}{3}$. Since O represents 0 and A' represents –1. Therefore, Q and R represent $\frac{-1}{3}$ and $\frac{-2}{3}$ respectively.

The following illustrations will illustrate the representation of more rational numbers on the number line.

ILLUSTRATION 1 Represent $\frac{5}{3}$ and $\frac{-5}{3}$ on the number line.

Solution In order to represent $\frac{5}{3}$ and $\frac{-5}{3}$ on the number line, we first draw a number line and mark a point O on it to represent zero. Now, we find the points P and Q on the number line representing the positive integers 5 and –5 respectively as shown in Fig. 3.

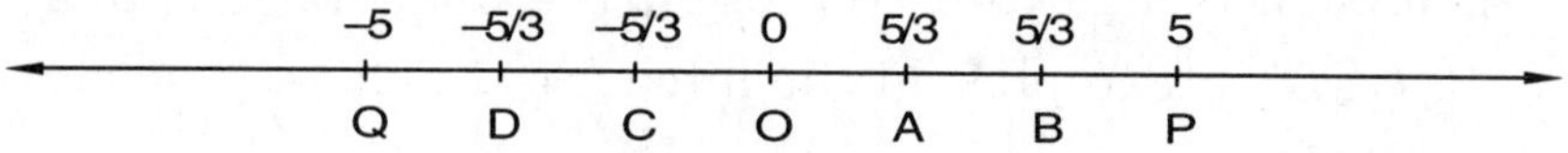

Fig. 3

Now, divide the segment OP into three equal parts. Let A and B be the points of division so that $OA = AB = BP$. By construction, OA is one-third of OP.

Therefore, A represents the rational number $\frac{5}{3}$.

Point Q represents –5 on the number line. Now, divide OQ into three equal parts OC, CD and DQ. The point C is such that OC is one third of OQ. Since Q represents the number –5. Therefore, C represents the rational number $\frac{-5}{3}$.

ILLUSTRATION 2 Represent $\frac{8}{5}$ and $\frac{-8}{5}$ on the number line.

Solution To represent $\frac{8}{5}$ and $\frac{-8}{5}$ on the number line, draw a number line and mark a point O on it to represent zero. Now, mark two points P and Q representing integers 8 and –8 respectively on the number line. Divide the segment OP into five equal parts. Let A, B, C, D be the points of division so that $OA = AB = BC = CD = DP$. By construction, OA is one-fifth of OP. So, A represents the rational number $\frac{8}{5}$.

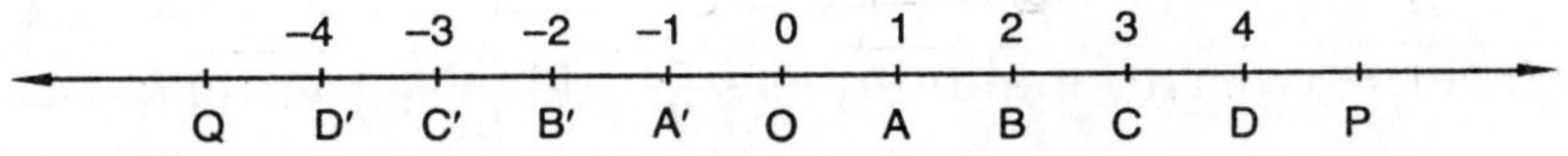

Fig. 4

Now, Q represents –8 on the number line. Divide OQ into five equal parts $OA', A'B', B'C', C'D'$ and $D'Q$. Since Q represents –8. Therefore, A' represents the rational number $\frac{-8}{5}$.

4.8 COMPARISON OF RATIONAL NUMBERS

In the previous classes, we have learnt how to compare two integers and also two fractions. We know that every positive integer is greater than zero and every negative integer is less than zero. Also, every positive integer is greater than every negative integer. Similar to the comparison of integers, we have the following facts about the comparison of rational numbers

(i) Every positive rational number is greater than 0.

(ii) Every negative rational number is less than 0.

(iii) Every positive rational number is greater than every negative rational number.

(iv) Every rational number represented by a point on the number line is greater than every rational number represented by points on its left.

(v) Every rational number represented by a point on the number line is less than every rational number represented by points on its right.

In order to compare any two rational numbers, we can use the following steps:

STEP I *Obtain the given rational numbers.*

STEP II *Write the given rational numbers so that their denominators are positive.*

STEP III *Find the LCM of the positive denominators of the rational numbers obtained in step II.*

STEP IV *Express each rational number (obtained in step II) with the LCM (obtained in step III) as common denominator.*

STEP V *Compare the numerators of rational numbers obtained in step IV. The number having greater numerator is the greater rational number.*

Follwoing examples will illustrate the above procedure.

ILLUSTRATIVE EXAMPLES

Example 1 Which of the two rational numbers $\frac{3}{5}$ and $\frac{-2}{3}$ is greater?

Solution Clearly, $\frac{3}{5}$ is a positive rational number and $\frac{-2}{3}$ is a negative rational number. We know that every positive rational number is greater than every negative rational number.

$$\therefore \quad \frac{3}{5} > \frac{-2}{3}$$

Example 2 Which of the two rational numbers $\frac{5}{7}$ and $\frac{3}{5}$ is greater?

Solution Clearly, denominators of the given rational numbers are positive. The denominators are 7 and 5. The LCM of 7 and 5 is 35. So, we first express each rational number with 35 as common denominator.

$$\therefore \quad \frac{5}{7}=\frac{5\times 5}{7\times 5}=\frac{25}{35} \text{ and } \frac{3}{5}=\frac{3\times 7}{5\times 7}=\frac{21}{35}$$

Now, we compare the numerators of these rational numbers.

$$\therefore \quad 25>21 \Rightarrow \frac{25}{35}>\frac{21}{35} \Rightarrow \frac{5}{7}>\frac{3}{5}$$

Example 3 Which of the two rational numbers $\frac{-4}{9}$ and $\frac{5}{-12}$ is greater?

Solution First we write each one of the given rational numbers with positive denominator.

Clearly, denominator of $\frac{-4}{9}$ is positive. The denominator of $\frac{5}{-12}$ is negative.

So, we express it with positive denominator as follows:

$$\frac{5}{-12}=\frac{5\times(-1)}{(-12)\times(-1)}=\frac{-5}{12}$$

Now, LCM of denominators 9 and 12 is 36.

We write the rational numbers so that they have a common denominator 36 as follows:

$$\frac{-4}{9}=\frac{-4\times 4}{9\times 4}=\frac{-16}{36} \text{ and, } \frac{-5}{12}=\frac{-5\times 3}{12\times 3}=\frac{-15}{36}$$

$$\therefore \quad -15>-16 \Rightarrow \frac{-15}{36}>\frac{-16}{36} \Rightarrow \frac{-5}{12}>\frac{-4}{9} \Rightarrow \frac{5}{-12}>\frac{-4}{9}$$

Example 4 Arrange the rational numbers $\frac{-7}{10}, \frac{5}{-8}, \frac{2}{-3}$ in ascending order:

Solution We first write the given rational numbers so that their denominators are positive.

We have,

2	10	8	3
2	5	4	3
	5	2	3

$$\frac{5}{-8}=\frac{5\times(-1)}{-8\times(-1)}=\frac{-5}{8} \text{ and } \frac{2}{-3}=\frac{2\times(-1)}{(-3)\times(-1)}=\frac{-2}{3}$$

Thus, the given rational numbers with positive denomiantors are

$$\frac{-7}{10}, \frac{-5}{8}, \frac{-2}{3}$$

Now, LCM of the denominators 10, 8 and 3 is $2\times 2\times 5\times 2\times 3=120$

We now write the numbers so that they have a common denominators 120 as follows:

$$\frac{-7}{10}=\frac{-7\times 12}{10\times 12}=\frac{-84}{120}, \frac{-5}{8}=\frac{-5\times 15}{8\times 15}=\frac{-75}{120} \text{ and, } \frac{-2}{3}=\frac{-2\times 40}{3\times 40}=\frac{-80}{120}$$

Comparing the numerators of these numbers, we get

$-84 < -80 < -75$

$$\therefore \quad \frac{-84}{120} < \frac{-80}{120} < \frac{-75}{120} \Rightarrow \frac{-7}{10} < \frac{-2}{3} < \frac{-5}{8} \Rightarrow \frac{-7}{10} < \frac{2}{-3} < \frac{5}{-8}$$

Example 5 Arrange the following rational numbers in descending order:

$$\frac{4}{9}, \frac{-5}{6}, \frac{-7}{-12}, \frac{11}{-24}$$

Solution First we express the given rational numbers in the form so that their denominators are positive.

We have,

$$\frac{-7}{-12} = \frac{(-7)\times(-1)}{(-12)\times(-1)} \quad \text{[Multiplying the numerator and denominator by } -1]$$

$$\Rightarrow \frac{-7}{-12} = \frac{7}{12}$$

$$\text{and, } \frac{11}{-24} = \frac{11\times(-1)}{(-24)\times(-1)} \quad \text{[Multiplying the numerator and denominator by } -1]$$

$$\Rightarrow \frac{-11}{24} = \frac{-11}{24}$$

Thus, given rational numbers are : $\frac{4}{9}, \frac{-5}{6}, \frac{7}{12}, \frac{-11}{24}$

Now, we find the LCM of 9, 6, 12 and 24.

3	9	6	12	24
2	3	2	4	8
2	3	1	2	4
	3	1	1	2

Required LCM = $3 \times 2 \times 2 \times 3 \times 2 = 72$.

We now write the rational numbers so that they have a common denominator 72.

We have,

$$\frac{4}{9} = \frac{4\times 8}{9\times 8} \quad \text{[Multiplying the numerator and denominator by } 72 \div 9 = 8]$$

$$\Rightarrow \frac{4}{9} = \frac{32}{72}$$

$$\frac{-5}{6} = \frac{-5\times 12}{6\times 12} \quad \text{[Multiplying the numerator and denominator by } 72 \div 6 = 12]$$

$$\Rightarrow \frac{-5}{6} = \frac{-60}{72}$$

$\frac{7}{12} = \frac{7 \times 6}{12 \times 6}$ [Multiplying the numerator and denominator by $72 \div 12 = 6$]

$\Rightarrow \frac{7}{12} = \frac{42}{72}$

$\frac{-11}{24} = \frac{-11 \times 3}{24 \times 3}$ [Multiplying the numerator and denominator by $72 \div 24 = 3$]

$\Rightarrow \frac{-11}{24} = \frac{-33}{72}$

Arranging the numerators of these rational numbers in descending order, we have

$42 > 32 > -33 > -60$

$\Rightarrow \frac{42}{72} > \frac{32}{72} > \frac{-33}{72} > \frac{-60}{72} \Rightarrow \frac{-7}{-12} > \frac{4}{9} > \frac{11}{-24} > \frac{-5}{6}$

Hence, the given numbers when arranged in descending order are:

$\frac{-7}{-12}, \frac{4}{9}, \frac{11}{-24}, \frac{-5}{6}$

4.8.1 SOME USEFUL PROPERTIES OF RATIONAL NUMBERS

We have learnt that every rational number different from zero is either positive or negative. So, we have the following properties of rational numbers:

Property 1 *For each rational number x, exactly one of the following is true:*

(i) $x > 0$ *(ii)* $x = 0$ *(iii)* $x < 0$

As we have seen in the previous section that every pair of rational numbers can be compared. So, we have the following properties:

Property 2 *For any two rational numbers x and y, exactly one of the following is true:*

(i) $x > y$ *(ii)* $x = y$ *(iii)* $x < y$

Property 3 *If x, y, z be rational numbers such that* $x > y$ *and* $y > z$*, then* $x > z$.

EXERCISE 4.6

1. Draw the number line and represent the following rational numbers on it:

(i) $\frac{2}{3}$ (ii) $\frac{3}{4}$ (iii) $\frac{3}{8}$ (iv) $\frac{-5}{8}$

(v) $\frac{-3}{16}$ (vi) $\frac{-7}{3}$ (vii) $\frac{22}{-7}$ (viii) $\frac{-31}{3}$

2. Which of the two rational numbers in each of the following pairs of rational numbers is greater?

(i) $\frac{-3}{8}, 0$ (ii) $\frac{5}{2}, 0$ (iii) $\frac{-4}{11}, \frac{3}{11}$ (iv) $\frac{-7}{12}, \frac{5}{-8}$

(v) $\frac{4}{-9}, \frac{-3}{-7}$ (vi) $\frac{-5}{8}, \frac{3}{-4}$ (vii) $\frac{5}{9}, \frac{-3}{-8}$ (viii) $\frac{5}{-8}, \frac{-7}{12}$

3. Which of the two rational numbers in each of the following pairs of rational numbers is smaller?

(i) $\frac{-6}{-13}, \frac{7}{13}$ (ii) $\frac{16}{-5}, 3$ (iii) $\frac{-4}{3}, \frac{8}{-7}$ (iv) $\frac{-12}{5}, -3$

4. Fill in the blanks by the correct symbol out of >, =, or <:

   (i) $\frac{-6}{7}$ ..... $\frac{7}{13}$ (ii) $\frac{-3}{5}$ ..... $\frac{-5}{6}$ (iii) $\frac{-2}{3}$ ..... $\frac{5}{-8}$ (iv) 0..... $\frac{-2}{5}$

5. Arrange the following rational numbers in ascending order:

   (i) $\frac{3}{5}, \frac{-17}{-30}, \frac{8}{-15}, \frac{-7}{10}$ (ii) $\frac{-4}{9}, \frac{5}{-12}, \frac{7}{-18}, \frac{2}{-3}$

6. Arrange the following rational numbers in descending order:

   (i) $\frac{7}{8}, \frac{64}{16}, \frac{36}{-12}, \frac{5}{-4}, \frac{140}{28}$ (ii) $\frac{-3}{10}, \frac{17}{-30}, \frac{7}{-15}, \frac{-11}{20}$

7. Which of the following statements are true:

   (i) The rational number $\frac{29}{23}$ lies to the left of zero on the number line.

   (ii) The rational number $\frac{-12}{-17}$ lies to the left of zero on the number line.

   (iii) The rational number $\frac{3}{4}$ lies to the right of zero on the number line

   (iv) The rational numbers $\frac{-12}{-5}$ and $\frac{-7}{17}$ are on the opposite side of zero on the number line.

   (v) The rational numbers $\frac{-21}{5}$ and $\frac{7}{-31}$ are on the opposite side of zero on the number line.

   (vi) The rational number $\frac{-3}{-5}$ is on the right of $\frac{-4}{7}$ on the number line.

ANSWERS

2. (i) 0 (ii) $\frac{5}{2}$ (iii) $\frac{3}{11}$ (iv) $\frac{-7}{12}$ (v) $\frac{-3}{-7}$ (vi) $\frac{-5}{8}$

   (vii) $\frac{5}{9}$ (viii) $\frac{-7}{12}$

3. (i) $\frac{-6}{-13}$ (ii) $\frac{16}{-5}$ (iii) $\frac{-4}{3}$ (iv) −3

4. (i) < (ii) > (iii) < (iv) >

5. (i) $\frac{-7}{10} < \frac{8}{-15} < \frac{-17}{30} < \frac{3}{5}$ (ii) $\frac{2}{-3} < \frac{-4}{9} < \frac{5}{-12} < \frac{7}{-18}$

6. (i) $\frac{140}{28} > \frac{64}{16} > \frac{7}{8} > \frac{5}{-4} > \frac{36}{-12}$ (ii) $\frac{-3}{10} > \frac{7}{-15} > \frac{-11}{20} > \frac{17}{-30}$

7. (i) F (ii) F (iii) T (iv) T (v) F (vi) T

OBJECTIVE TYPE QUESTIONS

Mark the correct alternative in each of the following:

1. $\frac{44}{-77}$ in standard form is

   (a) $\frac{4}{-7}$ (b) $-\frac{4}{7}$ (c) $-\frac{44}{77}$ (d) None of these

2. $-\frac{102}{119}$ in standard form is

(a) $-\frac{6}{7}$ (b) $\frac{6}{7}$ (c) $-\frac{6}{17}$ (d) None of these

3. A rational number equal to $\frac{-2}{3}$ is

(a) $\frac{-10}{25}$ (b) $\frac{10}{-15}$ (c) $\frac{-9}{6}$ (d) None of these

4. If $\frac{-3}{7} = \frac{x}{35}$, then $x =$

(a) 15 (b) 21 (c) -15 (d) -21

5. Which of the following is correct?

(a) $\frac{5}{9} > \frac{-3}{-8}$ (b) $\frac{5}{9} < \frac{-3}{-8}$ (c) $\frac{2}{-3} < \frac{-8}{7}$ (d) $\frac{4}{-3} > \frac{-8}{7}$

6. If the rational numbers $\frac{-2}{3}$ and $\frac{4}{x}$ represent a pair of equivalent rational numbers, then

(a) 6 (b) -6 (c) 3 (d) -3

7. What is the additive identity element in the set of whole numbers?

(a) 0 (b) 1 (c) -1 (d) None of these

8. What is the multiplicative identity element in the set of whole numbers?

(a) 0 (b) 1 (c) -1 (d) None of these

9. Which of the following is not zero?

(a) 0×0 (b) $\frac{0}{3}$ (c) $\frac{7-7}{3}$ (d) $9 + 0$

10. The whole number nearest to 457 and divisible by 11 is

(a) 450 (b) 451 (c) 460 (d) 462

11. If $-\frac{3}{8}$ and $\frac{x}{-24}$ are equivalent rational numbers, then $x =$

(a) 3 (b) 6 (c) 9 (d) 12

12. If $\frac{27}{-45}$ is expressed as a rational number with denominator 5, then the numerator is

(a) 3 (b) -3 (c) 6 (d) -6

13. Which of the following pairs of rational numbers are on the opposite sides of the zero on the number line?

(a) $\frac{3}{7}$ and $\frac{5}{12}$ (b) $-\frac{3}{7}$ and $\frac{-5}{12}$ (c) $\frac{3}{7}$ and $\frac{-5}{12}$ (d) None of these

14. The rational number equal to $\frac{2}{-3}$ is

(a) $\frac{14}{-18}$ (b) $\frac{-6}{9}$ (c) $\frac{-8}{-12}$ (d) $\frac{3}{-2}$

15. If $-\frac{3}{4} = \frac{6}{x}$, then $x =$

(a) -8 (b) 4 (c) -4 (d) 8

ANSWERS

1. (b)	2. (a)	3. (b)	4. (c)	5. (a)	6. (b)	7. (a)
8. (b)	9. (d)	10. (d)	11. (c)	12. (b)	13. (c)	14. (b)
15. (a)						

THINGS TO REMEMBER

1. *Numbers that can be expressed in the form $\frac{p}{q}$, where q is a non–zero integer and p is any integer are called rational numbers.*
2. *Every integer is a rational number but a rational number need not be an integer.*
3. *Every fraction is a rational number but a fraction need not be a rational number.*
4. *A rational number $\frac{p}{q}$ is said to be in the standard form if q is a positive integer and the integers $\frac{p}{q}$ have no common divisor other than 1.*
5. *A rational number $\frac{p}{q}$ is positive, if p and q are either both positive or both negative.*
6. *A rational number $\frac{p}{q}$ is negative, if p and q are of opposite signs.*
7. *Two rational numbers are equal if they have the same standard form.*
8. *To convert a rational number to an equivalent rational number, either multiply or divide both its numerator and denominator by a non-zero integer.*
9. *If $\frac{x}{y}$ is a rational number and m is any non–zero integer, then $\frac{x}{y} = \frac{x \times m}{y \times m}$*
10. *If $\frac{x}{y}$ is a rational number and m is a common divisor of x and y, then*

$$\frac{x}{y} = \frac{x \div m}{y \div m}$$

11. *If x and y are positive integers, then the rational numbers $\frac{x}{y}$ and $\frac{-x}{-y}$ are both positive and the rational numbers $\frac{-x}{y}$ and $\frac{x}{-y}$ are both negative.*
12. $\frac{a}{b} = \frac{c}{d}$ *only when* $a \times d = b \times c$
13. *If there are two rational numbers with common denominator, then one with the larger numerator is larger than the other.*
14. *Every positive rational number is greater than zero.*
15. *Every negative rational number is less than zero.*
16. *The rational numbers can be represented on the number line.*

5

OPERATIONS ON RATIONAL NUMBERS

5.1 INTRODUCTION

In this chapter, we shall learn about the operations of addition, subtraction, multiplication and division on rational numbers. We shall also learn about the properties of these operations on rational numbers.

5.2 ADDITION OF RATIONAL NUMBERS

In this section, we shall define the operation of addition of rational numbers. The addition of rational numbers is carried out in the same way as that of addition of fractions which you have learnt in earlier classes. If two rational numbers are to be added, we first express each one of them as rational numbers with positive denominator. For addition purpose, we divide the rational numbers into the following two categories:

5.2.1 RATIONAL NUMBERS WITH SAME DENOMINATORS

In order to add two rational numbers having the same denominator, we follow the following steps:

STEP I *Obtain the numerators of two given rational numbers and their common denominator.*

STEP II *Add the numerators obtained in step I*

STEP III *Write a rational number whose numerator is the sum obtained in step II, and whose denominator is the common denominator of the given rational numbers.*

It follows from the above steps that if $\frac{p}{q}$ and $\frac{r}{q}$ are two rational numbers with the same denominator, then

$$\frac{p}{q}+\frac{r}{q}=\frac{p+r}{q}$$

ILLUSTRATIVE EXAMPLES

Example 1 Add $\frac{3}{5}$ and $\frac{13}{5}$.

Solution We have,

$$\frac{3}{5}+\frac{13}{5}=\frac{3+13}{5}=\frac{16}{5} \qquad [\because 3+13=16]$$

Example 2 Add $\frac{7}{9}$ and $\frac{-12}{9}$.

Solution We have,

$$\frac{7}{9}+\frac{-12}{9}=\frac{7+(-12)}{9}=\frac{-5}{9} \qquad [\because 7+(-12)=-5]$$

Example 3 Add $\frac{-5}{9}$ and $\frac{-17}{9}$.

Solution We have,

$$\frac{-5}{9}+\frac{-17}{9}=\frac{(-5)+(-17)}{9}=\frac{-22}{9} \qquad [\because (-5)+(-17)=-22]$$

Example 4 Add $\frac{4}{-11}$ and $\frac{7}{11}$.

Solution We first express $\frac{4}{-11}$ as a rational number with positive denominator.

We have, $\frac{4}{-11}=\frac{4\times(-1)}{(-11)\times(-1)}=\frac{-4}{11}$

Now, $\frac{4}{-11}+\frac{7}{11}=\frac{-4}{11}+\frac{7}{11}=\frac{(-4)+7}{11}=\frac{3}{11}$

5.2.2 NUMBERS WITH DISTINCT DENOMINATORS

To find the sum of two rational numbers which do not have the same denominator, we follow the following steps:

STEP I *Obtain the rational numbers and see whether their denominators are positive or not. If the denominator of one (or both) of the numbers is negative, re–write it so that the denominator becomes positive.*

STEP II *Obtain the denominators of the rational numbers in step I.*

STEP III *Find the LCM of the denominators obtained in step II.*

STEP IV *Express each one of the rational numbers in step I so that the LCM obtained in step III becomes their common denominator.*

STEP V *Write a rational number whose numerator is equal to the sum of the numerators of rational numbers obtained in step IV and denominators as the LCM obtained in step III.*

STEP VI *The rational number obtained in step V is the required sum.*

Following examples will illustrate the above procedure.

ILLUSTRATIVE EXAMPLES

Example 1 Add $\frac{5}{12}$ and $\frac{3}{8}$.

Solution Clearly, denominators of the given numbers are positive.

The L.C.M of denominators 12 and 8 is 24.

Now, we express $\frac{5}{12}$ and $\frac{3}{8}$ into forms in which both of them have the same denominator 24.

We have,

$$\frac{5}{12}=\frac{5\times2}{12\times2}=\frac{10}{24} \text{ and, } \frac{3}{8}=\frac{3\times3}{8\times3}=\frac{9}{24}$$

$$\therefore \quad \frac{5}{12}+\frac{3}{8}=\frac{10}{24}+\frac{9}{24}=\frac{10+9}{24}=\frac{19}{24}$$

Example 2 Add $\frac{7}{9}$ and 4.

Solution We have, $4 = \frac{4}{1}$

Clearly, denominators of the two rational numbers are positive. We now re-write them so that they have a common denominator equal to the LCM of the denominators. LCM of 9 and 1 is 9.

We have, $\frac{4}{1} = \frac{4\times 9}{1\times 9} = \frac{36}{9}$

$\therefore \quad \frac{7}{9} + 4 = \frac{7}{9} + \frac{4}{1} = \frac{7}{9} + \frac{36}{9} = \frac{7+36}{9} = \frac{43}{9}$

Example 3 Add $\frac{3}{8}$ and $\frac{-5}{12}$

Solution The denominators of the given rational numbers are 8 and 12 respectively. The LCM of 8 and 12 is 24.

Now, we rewrite the given rational numbers into forms in which both of them have the same denominator.

$\frac{3}{8} = \frac{3\times 3}{8\times 3} = \frac{9}{24}$ and, $\frac{-5}{12} = \frac{-5\times 2}{12\times 2} = \frac{-10}{24}$

$\therefore \quad \frac{3}{8} + \frac{-5}{12} = \frac{9}{24} + \frac{(-10)}{24} = \frac{9-10}{24} = \frac{-1}{24}$

Example 4 Simplify: $\frac{8}{-15} + \frac{4}{-3}$

Solution We have,

$\frac{8}{-15} + \frac{4}{-3} = \frac{-8}{15} + \frac{-4}{3} \qquad \left[\because \frac{8}{-15} = \frac{8\times(-1)}{(-15)\times(-1)} = \frac{-8}{15} \text{ and, } \frac{4}{-3} = \frac{4\times(-1)}{(-3)\times(-1)} = \frac{-4}{3}\right]$

LCM of 15 and 3 is 15.

Rewriting $\frac{-4}{3}$ in the form in which it has denominator 15, we get

$\frac{-4}{3} = \frac{-4\times 5}{3\times 5} = \frac{-20}{15}$

$\therefore \quad \frac{8}{-15} + \frac{4}{-3} = \frac{-8}{15} + \frac{-4}{3}$

$\Rightarrow \quad \frac{8}{-15} + \frac{4}{-3} = \frac{-8}{15} + \frac{-20}{15} \qquad \left[\because \frac{4}{-3} = \frac{-20}{15}\right]$

$\Rightarrow \quad \frac{8}{-15} + \frac{4}{-3} = \frac{(-8)+(-20)}{15} = \frac{-28}{15}$

Example 5 Simplify: $\frac{7}{-26} + \frac{16}{39}$

Solution We have,

$$\frac{7}{-26}+\frac{16}{39}=\frac{7}{26}+\frac{16}{39} \qquad \left[\because \frac{7}{-26}=\frac{7\times(\ 1)}{(-26)\times(-1)}=\frac{7}{26}\right]$$

LCM of 26 and 39 is 78.

Rewriting $\frac{-7}{26}$ and $\frac{16}{39}$ in forms having the same denominator 78, we get

$$\frac{7}{-26}=\frac{-7\times3}{26\times3}=\frac{-21}{78},\ \frac{16}{39}=\frac{16\times2}{39\times2}=\frac{32}{78}$$

$$\therefore \quad \frac{7}{-26}+\frac{16}{39}=\frac{-7}{26}+\frac{16}{39}=\frac{-21}{78}+\frac{32}{78}=\frac{11}{78}$$

<u>Remark:</u> *If $\frac{p}{q}$ and $\frac{r}{s}$ are two rational numbers such that q and s do not have a common factor other than 1, i.e., HCF of q and s is 1, then*

$$\frac{p}{q}+\frac{r}{s}=\frac{p\times s+r\times q}{q\times s}$$

For example, $\frac{5}{18}+\frac{3}{13}=\frac{5\times13+3\times18}{18\times13}=\frac{65+54}{234}=\frac{119}{234}$

and, $\frac{-2}{11}+\frac{3}{14}=\frac{(-2)\times14+(3\times11)}{11\times14}=\frac{-28+33}{154}=\frac{5}{154}$

EXERCISE 5.1

1. Add the following rational numbers:

(i) $\frac{-5}{7}$ and $\frac{3}{7}$ (ii) $\frac{-15}{4}$ and $\frac{7}{4}$ (iii) $\frac{-8}{11}$ and $\frac{-4}{11}$ (iv) $\frac{6}{13}$ and $\frac{-9}{13}$

2. Add the following rational numbers:

(i) $\frac{3}{4}$ and $\frac{-3}{5}$ (ii) -3 and $\frac{3}{5}$ (iii) $\frac{-7}{27}$ and $\frac{11}{18}$ (iv) $\frac{31}{-4}$ and $\frac{-5}{8}$

3. Simplify:

(i) $\frac{8}{9}+\frac{-11}{6}$ (ii) $\frac{-5}{16}+\frac{7}{24}$ (iii) $\frac{1}{-12}+\frac{2}{-15}$ (iv) $\frac{-8}{19}+\frac{-4}{57}$

4. Add and express the sum as a mixed fraction:

(i) $\frac{-12}{5}+\frac{43}{10}$ (ii) $\frac{24}{7}+\frac{-11}{4}$ (iii) $\frac{-31}{6}+\frac{-27}{8}$

ANSWERS

1. (i) $\frac{-2}{7}$ (ii) -2 (iii) $\frac{-12}{11}$ (iv) $\frac{-3}{13}$

2. (i) $\frac{3}{20}$ (ii) $\frac{-12}{5}$ (iii) $\frac{19}{54}$ (iv) $\frac{-67}{8}$

3. (i) $\frac{-17}{18}$ (ii) $\frac{-1}{48}$ (iii) $\frac{-13}{60}$ (iv) $\frac{-28}{57}$

4. (i) $1\frac{9}{10}$ (ii) $\frac{19}{28}$ (iii) $-8\frac{13}{24}$

5.3 SUBTRACTION OF RATIONAL NUMBERS

If $\frac{a}{b}$ and $\frac{c}{d}$ are two rational numbers, then subtracting $\frac{c}{d}$ from $\frac{a}{b}$ means adding additive inverse (negative) of $\frac{c}{d}$ to $\frac{a}{b}$. The subtraction of $\frac{c}{d}$ from $\frac{a}{b}$ is written as $\frac{a}{b}-\frac{c}{d}$.

Thus, we have

$$\frac{a}{b}-\frac{c}{d}=\frac{a}{b}+\left(\frac{-c}{d}\right) \qquad \left[\because \text{ Additive inverse of } \frac{c}{d} \text{ is } \frac{-c}{d}\right]$$

ILLUSTRATIVE EXAMPLES

Example 1 Subtract $\frac{3}{4}$ from $\frac{5}{6}$.

Solution The additive inverse of $\frac{3}{4}$ is $\frac{-3}{4}$

$$\therefore \quad \frac{5}{6}-\frac{3}{4}=\frac{5}{6}+\frac{(-3)}{4}$$

$$\Rightarrow \quad \frac{5}{6}-\frac{3}{4}=\frac{5\times 2}{6\times 2}+\frac{(-3)\times 3}{4\times 3}=\frac{10}{12}+\frac{-9}{12}=\frac{10+(-9)}{12}=\frac{1}{12}$$

Example 2 Subtract $\frac{-3}{8}$ from $\frac{-5}{7}$.

Solution The additive inverse of $\frac{-3}{8}$ is $\frac{3}{8}$

$$\therefore \quad \frac{-5}{7}-\left(\frac{-3}{8}\right)=\frac{-5}{7}+\frac{3}{8} \qquad \left[\because -\left(\frac{-3}{8}\right)=\frac{3}{8}\right]$$

$$\Rightarrow \quad \frac{-5}{7}-\left(\frac{-3}{8}\right)=\frac{(-5)\times 8+3\times 7}{56}=\frac{-40+21}{56}=\frac{-19}{56}$$

Example 3 Subtract $\frac{-3}{5}$ from $\frac{9}{10}$.

Solution The additive inverse of $\frac{-3}{5}=\frac{3}{5}$

$$\therefore \quad \frac{9}{10}-\left(\frac{-3}{5}\right)=\frac{9}{10}+\frac{3}{5}=\frac{9+3\times 2}{10}=\frac{9+6}{10}=\frac{15}{10}$$

$$\Rightarrow \quad \frac{9}{10}-\left(\frac{-3}{5}\right)=\frac{3}{2} \qquad \text{[Dividing numerator and denominator by 5]}$$

Example 4 The sum of two rational numbers is $\frac{-3}{5}$. If one of the number is $\frac{-9}{20}$, find the other.

Solution Sum of the numbers $= \frac{-3}{5}$, One number $= \frac{-9}{20}$

$\therefore$ The other number = Sum − One number

$$= \frac{-3}{5} - \left(\frac{-9}{20}\right)$$

$$= \frac{-3}{5} + \frac{9}{20} \qquad \left[\because -\left(\frac{-9}{20}\right) = \frac{9}{20}\right]$$

$$= \frac{(-3)\times 4 + 9\times 1}{20} = \frac{-12+9}{20} = \frac{-3}{20}$$

Example 5 What number should be added to $\frac{-5}{8}$ so as to get $\frac{5}{9}$?

Solution Sum of the given number and the required number $= \frac{5}{9}$

Given number $= \frac{-5}{8}$

$\therefore$ Required number = Sum − Given number

$$= \frac{5}{9} + \frac{5}{8} = \frac{5\times 8 + 5\times 9}{72} = \frac{40+45}{72} = \frac{85}{72}$$

Example 6 What should be subtracted from $\frac{-3}{4}$ so as to get $\frac{5}{6}$?

Solution Difference of the given number and the required number $= \frac{-5}{6}$

Given number $= \frac{-3}{4}$

$\therefore$ Required number $= \frac{-3}{4} - \frac{5}{6}$

$$= \frac{-3}{4} + \frac{-5}{6} = \frac{(-3)\times 3 + (-5)\times 2}{12} = \frac{(-9)+(-10)}{12} = \frac{-19}{12}$$

In order to simplify expressions involving the sum or difference of three or more rational numbers, we may use the following steps:

STEP I *Find the LCM of the denominator of all the numbers involved.*

STEP II *Write a rational number whose denominator is the LCM obtained in step I and numerator is computed as follows:*

Divide the LCM obtained in step I by the denominator of first rational number and get a quotient. Multiply the numerator of first rational number by this quoitent. Repeat this procedure for all rational numbers. Retain the given signs of addition and subtraction between the given rational numbers and get an expression involving integers. Simplify this expression to get an integer as the numerator.

STEP III *Reduce the rational number obtained in step II to the lowest form if it is not already so. This rational number so obtained is the required rational number.*

Following examples will illustrate the above procedure.

Example 7 Simplify :

(i) $\frac{-2}{3}+\frac{5}{9}-\frac{-7}{6}$ (ii) $\frac{5}{12}+\frac{-5}{18}-\frac{7}{24}$

Solution (i) We have,

$$\frac{-2}{3}+\frac{5}{9}-\frac{-7}{6}=\frac{-2}{3}+\frac{5}{9}+\frac{7}{6} \qquad \left[\because -\left(\frac{-7}{6}\right)=\frac{7}{6}\right]$$

$$\Rightarrow \frac{-2}{3}+\frac{5}{9}-\frac{-7}{6}=\frac{(-2)\times 6+5\times 2+7\times 3}{18}=\frac{-12+10+21}{18}=\frac{-12+31}{18}=\frac{19}{18}$$

(ii) We have,

$$\frac{5}{12}+\frac{-5}{18}-\frac{7}{24}=\frac{5}{12}+\frac{-5}{18}+\frac{-7}{24}$$

$$\Rightarrow \frac{5}{12}+\frac{-5}{18}-\frac{7}{24}=\frac{5\times 6+(-5)\times 4+(-7)\times 3}{72} \qquad [\because \text{LCM of 12, 18 and 24 is 72}]$$

$$\Rightarrow \frac{5}{12}+\frac{-5}{18}-\frac{7}{24}=\frac{30+(-20)+(-21)}{72}=\frac{30+(-41)}{72}=\frac{-11}{72}$$

EXERCISE 5.2

1. Subtract the first rational number from the second in each of the following:

   (i) $\frac{3}{8}, \frac{5}{8}$ (ii) $\frac{-7}{9}, \frac{4}{9}$ (iii) $\frac{-2}{11}, \frac{-9}{11}$ (iv) $\frac{11}{13}, \frac{-4}{13}$

2. Evaluate each of the following:

   (i) $\frac{2}{3}-\frac{3}{5}$ (ii) $-\frac{4}{7}-\frac{2}{-3}$ (iii) $\frac{4}{7}-\frac{-5}{-7}$ (iv) $-2-\frac{5}{9}$

3. The sum of the two numbers is $\frac{5}{9}$. If one of the numbers is $\frac{1}{3}$, find the other.

4. The sum of two numbers is $\frac{-1}{3}$. If one of the numbers is $\frac{-12}{3}$, find the other.

5. The sum of two numbers is $\frac{-4}{3}$. If one of the numbers is –5, find the other.

6. The sum of two rational numbers is –8. If one of the numbers is $\frac{-15}{7}$, find the other.

7. What should be added to $\frac{-7}{8}$ so as to get $\frac{5}{9}$?

8. What number should be added to $\frac{-5}{11}$ so as to get $\frac{26}{33}$?

9. What number should be added to $\frac{-5}{7}$ to get $\frac{-2}{3}$?

10. What number should be subtracted from $\frac{-5}{3}$ to got $\frac{5}{6}$?

11. What number should be subtracted from $\frac{3}{7}$ to get $\frac{5}{4}$?

12. What should be added to $\left(\frac{2}{3}+\frac{3}{5}\right)$ to get $\frac{-2}{15}$?

13. What should be added to $\left(\frac{1}{2}+\frac{1}{3}+\frac{1}{5}\right)$ to get 3?

14. What should be subtracted from $\left(\frac{3}{4}-\frac{2}{3}\right)$ to get $\frac{-1}{6}$?

15. Simplify:

(i) $\frac{-3}{2}+\frac{5}{4}-\frac{7}{4}$ (ii) $\frac{5}{3}-\frac{7}{6}+\frac{-2}{3}$ (iii) $\frac{5}{4}-\frac{7}{6}-\frac{-2}{3}$ (iv) $\frac{-2}{5}-\frac{-3}{10}-\frac{-4}{7}$

16. Fill in the blanks:

(i) $\frac{-4}{13}-\frac{-3}{26}=$ .... (ii) $\frac{-9}{14}+$.... $=-1$ (iii) $\frac{-7}{9}+$.... $=3$ (iv) ....$+\frac{15}{23}=4$

ANSWERS

1. (i) $\frac{1}{4}$ (ii) $\frac{11}{9}$ (iii) $\frac{-7}{11}$ (iv) $\frac{-15}{13}$

2. (i) $\frac{1}{15}$ (ii) $\frac{2}{21}$ (iii) $\frac{-1}{7}$ (iv) $\frac{-23}{9}$ 3. $\frac{2}{9}$ 4. $\frac{11}{3}$

5. $\frac{11}{3}$ 6. $\frac{-41}{7}$ 7. $\frac{103}{72}$ 8. $\frac{41}{33}$ 9. $\frac{1}{21}$ 10. $\frac{-5}{2}$

11. $\frac{-23}{28}$ 12. $\frac{-7}{5}$ 13. $\frac{59}{30}$ 14. $\frac{1}{4}$

15. (i) -2 (ii) $\frac{-1}{6}$ (iii) $\frac{3}{4}$ (iv) $\frac{33}{70}$

16. (i) $\frac{-5}{26}$ (ii) $\frac{-5}{14}$ (iii) $\frac{34}{9}$ (iv) $\frac{77}{23}$

5.4 MULTIPLICATION OF RATIONAL NUMBERS

In earlier classes, we have learnt how to multiply two fractions. Recall that the product of two given fractions is a fraction whose numerator is the product of the numerators of the given fractions and whose denominator is the product of the denominators of the given fractions. In other words,

$$\text{Product of two given fractions} = \frac{\text{Product of their numerators}}{\text{Product of their denominators}}$$

This rule is also true for the product of rational numbers.

$\therefore$ Product of two rational numbers $= \dfrac{\text{Product of their numerators}}{\text{Product of their denominators}}$

Thus, if $\dfrac{a}{b}$ and $\dfrac{c}{d}$ are any two rational numbers, then

$$\frac{a}{b}\times\frac{c}{d} = \frac{a\times c}{b\times d}$$

ILLUSTRATIVE EXAMPLES

Example 1 Multiply:

(i) $\dfrac{3}{4}$ by $\dfrac{5}{7}$ (ii) $\dfrac{3}{7}$ by $\left(\dfrac{-4}{5}\right)$ (iii) $\left(\dfrac{-5}{9}\right)$ by 4 (iv) $\left(\dfrac{-36}{7}\right)$ by $\left(-\dfrac{28}{9}\right)$

Solution We have,

(i) $\dfrac{3}{4}\times\dfrac{5}{7} = \dfrac{3\times5}{4\times7} = \dfrac{15}{28}$

(ii) $\dfrac{3}{7}\times\left(\dfrac{-4}{5}\right) = \dfrac{3\times-4}{7\times5} = \dfrac{-12}{35}$

(iii) $\left(\dfrac{-5}{9}\right)\times4 = \dfrac{-5}{9}\times\dfrac{4}{1} = \dfrac{(-5)\times4}{9\times1} = \dfrac{-20}{9}$

(iv) $\left(\dfrac{-36}{7}\right)\times\left(-\dfrac{28}{9}\right) = \dfrac{-36}{7}\times\dfrac{-28}{9} = \dfrac{-\overset{-4}{\cancel{36}}\times-\overset{-4}{\cancel{28}}}{\underset{1}{\cancel{7}}\times\underset{1}{\cancel{9}}} = 16$

Example 2 Simplify:

(i) $\dfrac{-8}{7}\times\dfrac{14}{5}$ (ii) $\dfrac{13}{6}\times\dfrac{-18}{91}$ (iii) $\dfrac{-5}{9}\times\dfrac{72}{-125}$ (iv) $\dfrac{-22}{9}\times\dfrac{-51}{-88}$

Solution (i) We have,

$$\frac{-8}{7}\times\frac{14}{5} = \frac{-8\times14}{7\times5} = \frac{-8\times2}{1\times5} = \frac{-16}{5}$$

(ii) We have,

$$\frac{13}{6}\times\frac{-18}{91} = \frac{\overset{1}{\cancel{13}}\times(-\overset{-3}{\cancel{18}})}{\underset{1}{\cancel{6}}\times\underset{7}{\cancel{91}}} = \frac{1\times-3}{1\times7} = \frac{-3}{7}$$

(iii) We have,

$$\frac{-5}{9}\times\frac{72}{-125} = \frac{(-\overset{-1}{\cancel{5}})\times\overset{8}{\cancel{72}}}{\underset{1}{\cancel{9}}\times-\underset{-25}{\cancel{125}}} = \frac{-1\times8}{1\times-25} = \frac{-8}{-25} = \frac{8}{25}$$

(iv) We have,

$$\frac{-22}{9}\times\frac{-51}{-88} = \frac{-22}{9}\times\frac{51}{88} \qquad \left[\because \frac{-51}{-88} = \frac{51}{88}\right]$$

$$\Rightarrow \frac{-22}{9}\times\frac{-51}{-88} = \frac{-\overset{-1}{\cancel{22}}\times\overset{17}{\cancel{51}}}{\underset{3}{\cancel{9}}\times\underset{4}{\cancel{88}}} = \frac{-1\times17}{3\times4} = \frac{-17}{12}$$

Example 3 Simplify:

(i) $\left(\frac{-16}{5}\times\frac{20}{8}\right)-\left(\frac{15}{5}\times\frac{-35}{5}\right)$ (ii) $\left(\frac{-3}{2}\times\frac{4}{5}\right)+\left(\frac{9}{5}\times\frac{-10}{3}\right)-\left(\frac{1\times3}{2\times4}\right)$

Solution (i) We have,

$$\left(\frac{-16}{5}\times\frac{20}{8}\right)-\left(\frac{15}{5}\times\frac{-35}{5}\right)$$

$$=\left(\frac{-\overset{-2}{\cancel{16}}\times\overset{4}{\cancel{20}}}{\underset{1}{\cancel{5}}\times\underset{1}{\cancel{8}}}\right)-\left(\frac{\overset{3}{\cancel{15}}\times-\overset{-7}{\cancel{35}}}{\underset{1}{\cancel{5}}\times\underset{1}{\cancel{5}}}\right)$$

$$=\left(\frac{-2\times4}{1\times1}\right)-\left(\frac{3\times-7}{1\times1}\right)=\frac{-8}{1}-\frac{-21}{1}=-8-(-21)=-8+21=13$$

(ii) We have,

$$\left(\frac{-3}{2}\times\frac{4}{5}\right)+\left(\frac{9}{5}\times\frac{-10}{3}\right)-\left(\frac{1\times3}{2\times4}\right)$$

$$=\frac{-3\times\overset{2}{\cancel{4}}}{\underset{1}{\cancel{2}}\times5}+\frac{\overset{3}{\cancel{9}}\times-\overset{-2}{\cancel{10}}}{\underset{1}{\cancel{5}}\times\underset{1}{\cancel{3}}}-\frac{1\times3}{2\times4}$$

$$=\frac{-3\times2}{1\times5}+\frac{3\times-2}{1\times1}-\frac{3}{8}=\frac{-6}{5}+\frac{-6}{1}-\frac{3}{8}=\frac{-6}{5}+\frac{-6}{1}+\frac{-3}{8}$$

EXERCISE 5.3

1. Multiply:

(i) $\frac{7}{11}$ by $\frac{5}{4}$ (ii) $\frac{5}{7}$ by $\left(\frac{-3}{4}\right)$ (iii) $\frac{(-2)}{9}$ by $\frac{5}{11}$ (iv) $\frac{-3}{17}$ by $\frac{-5}{-4}$

2. Multiply:

(i) $\frac{-5}{17}$ by $\frac{51}{-60}$ (ii) $\frac{-6}{11}$ by $\frac{-55}{36}$ (iii) $\frac{-8}{25}$ by $\frac{-5}{16}$ (iv) $\frac{6}{7}$ by $\frac{-49}{36}$

3. Simplify each of the following and express the result as a rational number in standard form:

(i) $\frac{-16}{21}\times\frac{14}{5}$ (ii) $\frac{7}{6}\times\frac{-3}{28}$ (iii) $\frac{-19}{36}\times16$ (iv) $\frac{-13}{9}\times\frac{27}{-26}$

4. Simplify:

(i) $\left(-5\times\frac{2}{15}\right)-\left(-6\times\frac{2}{9}\right)$ (ii) $\left(\frac{-9}{4}\times\frac{5}{3}\right)+\left(\frac{13}{2}\times\frac{5}{6}\right)$

5. Simplify:

(i) $\left(\frac{13}{9}\times\frac{-15}{2}\right)+\left(\frac{7}{3}\times\frac{8}{5}\right)+\left(\frac{3}{5}\times\frac{1}{2}\right)$ (ii) $\left(\frac{3}{11}\times\frac{5}{6}\right)-\left(\frac{9}{12}\times\frac{4}{3}\right)+\left(\frac{5}{13}\times\frac{6}{15}\right)$

ANSWERS

1. (i) $\frac{35}{44}$ (ii) $\frac{-15}{28}$ (iii) $\frac{-10}{99}$ (iv) $\frac{-15}{68}$ 2. (i) $\frac{1}{4}$ (ii) $\frac{5}{6}$
(iii) $\frac{1}{10}$ (iv) $\frac{-7}{6}$ 3. (i) $\frac{-32}{15}$ (ii) $\frac{-1}{8}$ (iii) $\frac{-76}{9}$ (iv) $\frac{3}{2}$
4. (i) $\frac{2}{3}$ (ii) $\frac{5}{3}$ 5. (i) $\frac{-34}{5}$ (ii) $\frac{-177}{286}$

5.5 RECIPROCAL OF A NON-ZERO RATIONAL NUMBER

For every non-zero rational number $\frac{a}{b}$ there exists a rational number $\frac{b}{a}$ such that

$$\frac{a}{b}\times\frac{b}{a}=1=\frac{b}{a}\times\frac{a}{b}$$

The rational number $\frac{b}{a}$ is called the multiplicative inverse or reciprocal of $\frac{a}{b}$ and is denoted by $\left(\frac{a}{b}\right)^{-1}$.

The reciprocal of $\frac{5}{12}$ is $\frac{12}{5}$ i.e., $\left(\frac{5}{12}\right)^{-1} = \frac{12}{5}$

The reciprocal of $\frac{-3}{7}$ is $\frac{7}{-3}$ i.e., $\left(\frac{-3}{7}\right)^{-1} = \frac{7}{-3}$

The reciprocal of -5 is $\frac{1}{-5}$, since $-5\times\frac{1}{-5} = \frac{-5}{1}\times\frac{1}{-5} = \frac{-5\times1}{-5\times1} = 1$

NOTE: *The reciprocal of 1 is 1 and the reciprocal of –1 is –1. 1 and –1 are the only rational numbers which are their own reciprocals. No other rational number is its own reciprocal.*

Remark: *We know that there is no rational number which when multiplied with 0, gives 1. Therefore, rational number 0 has no reciprocal or multiplicative inverse.*

ILLUSTRATION 1 Write the reciprocal of each of the following rational numbers:

(i) 7 (ii) –11 (iii) $\frac{2}{5}$ (iv) $\frac{-7}{15}$

Solution (i) Reciprocal of 7 is $\frac{1}{7}$ i.e., $7^{-1} = \frac{1}{7}$

(ii) Reciprocal of –11 is $\frac{1}{-11}$ i.e., $(-11)^{-1} = \frac{1}{-11}$

(iii) Reciprocal of $\frac{2}{5}$ is $\frac{5}{2}$ i.e., $\left(\frac{2}{5}\right)^{-1} = \frac{5}{2}$

(iv) Reciprocal of $\frac{-7}{15}$ is $\frac{15}{-7}$ i.e., $\left(\frac{-7}{15}\right)^{-1} = \frac{15}{-7}$

ILLUSTRATION 2 Find the reciprocal of : $\frac{-3}{8}\times\frac{-7}{13}$

Solution We have,

$$\frac{-3}{8}\times\frac{-7}{13}=\frac{(-3)\times(-7)}{8\times 13}=\frac{21}{104}$$

$\therefore$ The reciprocal of $\frac{-3}{8}\times\frac{-7}{13}$ = Reciprocal of $\frac{21}{104}=\frac{104}{21}$

5.6 DIVISION OF RATIONAL NUMBERS

In chapter 2, we have learnt how to divide a fraction by another fraction. Recall that division of fractions is the inverse of multiplication. In case of rational number also, division is the inverse of multiplication as defined below:

DIVISION *If x and y are two rational numbers such that y ≠ 0, then the result of dividing x by y is the rational number obtained on multiplying x by the reciprocal of y.*

When x is divided by y, we write $x \div y$. Thus, $x \div y = x \times \frac{1}{y}$

If $\frac{a}{b}$ and $\frac{c}{d}$ are two rational numbers such that $\frac{c}{d}\neq 0$, then

$$\frac{a}{b}\div\frac{c}{d}=\frac{a}{b}\times\left(\frac{c}{d}\right)^{-1}=\frac{a}{b}\times\frac{d}{c}$$

DIVIDEND *The number to be divided is called the dividend.*

DIVISOR *The number which divides the dividend is called the divisor.*

QUOTIENT *When dividend is divided by the divisor, the result of the division is called the quotient.*

If $\frac{a}{b}$ is divided by $\frac{c}{d}$, then $\frac{a}{b}$ is the dividend, $\frac{c}{d}$ is the divisor and $\frac{a}{b}\div\frac{c}{d}=\frac{a}{b}\times\frac{d}{c}$ is the quotient.

NOTE: *It should be noted that division by 0 is not defined.*

ILLUSTRATIVE EXAMPLES

Example 1 Divide: (i) $\frac{3}{5}$ by $\frac{4}{25}$ (ii) $\frac{-8}{9}$ by $\frac{4}{3}$ (iii) $\frac{-16}{21}$ by $\frac{4}{3}$ (iv) $\frac{-8}{13}$ by $\frac{3}{-26}$

Solution We have,

(i) $$\frac{3}{5}\div\frac{4}{25}=\frac{3}{5}\times\frac{25}{4}=\frac{3\times \overset{5}{\cancel{25}}}{\underset{1}{\cancel{5}}\times 4}=\frac{15}{4}$$

(ii) $$\frac{-8}{9}\div\frac{4}{3}=\frac{-8}{9}\times\frac{3}{4}=\frac{-\overset{2}{\cancel{8}}\times\overset{1}{\cancel{3}}}{\underset{3}{\cancel{9}}\times\underset{1}{\cancel{4}}}=\frac{-2\times 1}{3\times 1}=\frac{-2}{3}$$

(iii) $$\frac{-16}{21}\div\frac{-4}{3}=\frac{-16}{21}\times\frac{3}{-4}=\frac{-\overset{4}{\cancel{16}}\times\overset{1}{\cancel{3}}}{\underset{7}{\cancel{21}}\times(-\underset{1}{\cancel{4}})}=\frac{-4\times 1}{7\times -1}=\frac{-4}{-7}=\frac{4}{7}$$

(iv) $\frac{-8}{13} \div \frac{3}{-26} = \frac{-8}{13} \times \frac{-26}{3} = \frac{-8 \times -26}{13 \times 3} = \frac{8 \times 2}{1 \times 3} = \frac{16}{3}$

Example 2 The product of two rational numbers is $\frac{-28}{81}$. If one of the numbers is $\frac{14}{27}$, find the other.

Solution We have,

Product of two numbers = $\frac{-28}{81}$, One number = $\frac{14}{27}$

So, the other number is obtained by dividing the product by the given number.

∴ Other number

$$= \frac{-28}{81} \div \frac{14}{27} = \frac{-28}{81} \times \frac{27}{14} = \frac{-28 \times 27}{81 \times 14} = \frac{-(\overset{2}{\cancel{28}} \times \overset{1}{\cancel{27}})}{\underset{3}{\cancel{81}} \times \underset{1}{\cancel{14}}} = \frac{-(2 \times 1)}{3 \times 1} = \frac{-2}{3}$$

Example 3 By what number should we multiply $\frac{3}{-14}$, so that the product may be $\frac{5}{12}$.

Solution We have, Product of two numbers = $\frac{5}{12}$, One number = $\frac{3}{-14}$

∴ The other number

$$= \frac{5}{12} \div \frac{3}{-14} = \frac{5}{12} \times \frac{-14}{3} = \frac{5 \times (-14)}{12 \times 3} = \frac{-(5 \times \overset{7}{\cancel{14}})}{\underset{6}{\cancel{12}} \times 3} = \frac{-(5 \times 7)}{6 \times 3} = \frac{-35}{18}$$

EXERCISE 5.4

1. Divide:

(i) 1 by $\frac{1}{2}$ (ii) 5 by $\frac{-5}{7}$ (iii) $\frac{-3}{4}$ by $\frac{9}{-16}$ (iv) $\frac{-7}{8}$ by $\frac{21}{16}$

(v) $\frac{7}{-4}$ by $\frac{63}{64}$ (vi) 0 by $\frac{-7}{5}$ (vii) $\frac{-3}{4}$ by – 6 (viii) $\frac{2}{3}$ by $\frac{-7}{12}$

2. Find the value and express as a rational number in standard form:

(i) $\frac{2}{5} \div \frac{26}{15}$ (ii) $\frac{10}{3} \div \frac{-35}{12}$ (iii) $-6 \div \left(\frac{-8}{17}\right)$ (iv) $\frac{40}{98} \div (-20)$

3. The product of two rational numbers is 15. If one of the numbers is –10, find the other.

4. The product of two rational numbers is $\frac{-8}{9}$. If one of the numbers is $\frac{-4}{15}$, find the other.

5. By what number should we multiply $\frac{-1}{6}$ so that the product may be $\frac{-23}{9}$?

6. By what number should we multiply $\frac{-15}{28}$ so that the product may be $\frac{-5}{7}$?

7. By what number should we multiply $\frac{-8}{13}$ so that the product may be 24?

8. By what number should $\frac{-3}{4}$ be multiplied in order to produce $\frac{2}{3}$?

9. Find $(x+y)\div(x-y)$, if

(i) $x=\frac{2}{3}$, $y=\frac{3}{2}$ (ii) $x=\frac{2}{5}$, $y=\frac{1}{2}$ (iii) $x=\frac{5}{4}$, $y=\frac{-1}{3}$

10. The cost of $7\frac{2}{3}$ metres of rope is ₹ $12\frac{3}{4}$. Find its cost per metre.

11. The cost of $2\frac{1}{3}$ metres of cloth is ₹ $75\frac{1}{4}$. Find the cost of cloth per metre.

12. By what number should $\frac{-33}{16}$ be divided to get $\frac{-11}{4}$?

13. Divide the sum of $\frac{-13}{5}$ and $\frac{12}{7}$ by the product of $\frac{-31}{7}$ and $\frac{-1}{2}$.

14. Divide the sum of $\frac{65}{12}$ and $\frac{8}{3}$ by their difference.

15. If 24 trousers of equal size can be prepared in 54 metres of cloth, what length of cloth is required for each trouser?

ANSWERS

1. (i) 2 (ii) –7 (iii) $\frac{4}{3}$ (iv) $\frac{2}{3}$ (v) $\frac{-16}{9}$ (vi) 0 (vii) $\frac{1}{8}$ (viii) $\frac{-8}{7}$

2. (i) $\frac{3}{13}$ (ii) $\frac{-8}{7}$ (iii) $\frac{51}{4}$ (iv) $-\frac{1}{49}$

3. (i) $\frac{-3}{2}$

4. $\frac{10}{3}$

5. $\frac{46}{3}$

6. $\frac{4}{3}$

7. -39

8. $\frac{-8}{9}$

9. (i) $\frac{-13}{5}$ (ii) -9 (iii) $\frac{11}{19}$

10. ₹ $1\frac{61}{92}$

11. ₹ $32\frac{1}{4}$

12. $\frac{3}{4}$

13. $\frac{-2}{5}$

14. $\frac{97}{33}$

15. $\frac{9}{4}$ metres.

5.7 INSERTION OF RATIONAL NUMBERS BETWEEN TWO GIVEN RATIONAL NUMBERS

In class VI, we have learnt about integers and properties of various operations on them. We have learnt that between two non–consecutive integers m and n there are $(m-n-1)$ integers. However, there is no integer between two consecutive integers. For example, between – 9 and 4 there are 4 – (–9) –1 = 12 integers, namely, – 8 ,–7,– 6 ,– 5 , – 4 , – 3, – 2 ,– 1, 0, 1, 2 and 3 but there is no integer between 4 and 5. Thus, we find that between two given integers there may or may not lie any integer.

In this section, we shall see that between any two rational numbers infinitely many rational numbers can be inserted. This property of rational numbers is known as the dense property.

Let us now try to find some rational numbers lying between two given rational numbers, say between $\frac{-2}{5}$ and $\frac{3}{5}$.

The four rational numbers $\frac{-1}{5}, \frac{0}{5}, \frac{1}{5}$ and $\frac{2}{5}$ lie between $\frac{-2}{5}$ and $\frac{3}{5}$.

If required, we can insert more rational numbers between $\frac{-2}{5}$ and $\frac{3}{5}$ by the technique as discussed below.

The rational numbers $\frac{-2}{5}$ and $\frac{3}{5}$ can also be written as $\frac{-20}{50}$ and $\frac{30}{50}$ respectively.

Clearly, $\frac{-19}{50}, \frac{-18}{50}, \ldots \frac{0}{50}, \frac{1}{50}, \ldots, \frac{29}{50}$ are rational numbers between $\frac{-2}{5}$ and $\frac{3}{5}$.

The total number of these rational numbers is same as the number of integers between -20 and 30, i.e., $30-(-20)-1 = 49$.

Similarly, by re-writing $\frac{-2}{5}$ and $\frac{3}{5}$ as $\frac{-200}{500}$ and $\frac{300}{500}$, we can insert $300-(-200)-1 = 499$ rational numbers between $\frac{-2}{5}$ and $\frac{3}{5}$.

Continuing in this manner, we can insert as many rational numbers between $\frac{-2}{5}$ and $\frac{3}{5}$ as we wish.

ILLUSTRATIVE EXAMPLES

Example 1 Insert 10 rational numbers between $\frac{-3}{11}$ a nd $\frac{8}{11}$.

Solution We know that

$$-3 < -2 < -1 < 0 < 1 < 2 < 3 < 4 < 5 < 6 < 7 < 8$$

$$\therefore \quad \frac{-3}{11} < \frac{-2}{11} < \frac{-1}{11} < \frac{0}{11} < \frac{1}{11} < \frac{2}{11} < \frac{3}{11} < \frac{4}{11} < \frac{5}{11} < \frac{6}{11} < \frac{7}{11} < \frac{8}{11}$$

Hence, 10 rational numbers between $\frac{-3}{11}$ and $\frac{8}{11}$ are :

$$\frac{-2}{11}, \frac{-1}{11}, \frac{0}{11}, \frac{1}{11}, \frac{2}{11}, \frac{3}{11}, \frac{4}{11}, \frac{5}{11}, \frac{6}{11} \text{ and } \frac{7}{11}$$

Example 2 Insert 100 rational numbers between $\frac{-3}{13}$ and $\frac{9}{13}$.

Solution We have,

$$\frac{-3}{13} = \frac{-3\times 10}{13\times 10} = \frac{-30}{130} \text{ and, } \frac{9}{13} = \frac{9\times 10}{13\times 10} = \frac{90}{130}$$

We know that

$$-30 < -29 < -28 < \ldots\ldots -1 < 0 < 1 < 2 < 3 < \ldots\ldots < 70$$

$\Rightarrow \frac{-30}{130} < \frac{-29}{130} < \frac{-28}{130} < \ldots < \frac{-1}{130} < \frac{0}{130} < \frac{1}{130} < \frac{2}{130} < \ldots < \frac{70}{130}$

Hence, 100 rational numbers between $\frac{-3}{13} = \frac{-30}{130}$ and $\frac{9}{13} = \frac{90}{130}$ are:

$\frac{-29}{130}, \frac{-28}{130}, \ldots, \frac{-1}{130}, \frac{0}{130}, \frac{1}{130}, \ldots, \frac{70}{130}$

EXERCISE 5.5

1. Find six rational numbers between $\frac{-4}{8}$ and $\frac{3}{8}$.
2. Find 10 rational numbers between $\frac{7}{13}$ and $\frac{-4}{13}$.
3. State true or false:
   (i) Between any two distinct integers there is always an integer.
   (ii) Between any two distinct rational numbers there is always a rational number.
   (iii) Between any two distinct rational numbers there are infinitely many rational numbers.

ANSWERS

1. $\frac{-3}{8}, \frac{-2}{8}, \frac{-1}{8}, \frac{0}{8}, \frac{1}{8}, \frac{2}{8}$ 2. $\frac{-3}{13}, \frac{-2}{13}, \frac{-1}{13}, \frac{0}{13}, \frac{1}{13}, \frac{2}{13}, \frac{3}{13}, \frac{4}{13}, \frac{5}{13}, \frac{6}{13}$

11. (i) F (ii) T (iii) T

OBJECTIVE TYPE QUESTIONS

Mark the correct alternative in each of the following:

1. What should be added to $\frac{-7}{9}$ to get 2 ?

   (a) $\frac{11}{9}$ (b) $\frac{-11}{9}$ (c) $\frac{-25}{9}$ (d) $\frac{25}{9}$

2. What should be subtracted from $\frac{-2}{3}$ to get $\frac{4}{5}$?

   (a) $\frac{22}{15}$ (b) $\frac{-22}{15}$ (c) $\frac{15}{22}$ (d) $\frac{-15}{22}$

3. Reciprocal of $\frac{-3}{4}$ is

   (a) $\frac{3}{4}$ (b) $\frac{4}{3}$ (c) $\frac{-4}{3}$ (d) None of these

4. The multiplicative inverse of $\frac{4}{-5}$ is

   (a) $-\frac{4}{5}$ (b) $\frac{5}{4}$ (c) $\frac{5}{-4}$ (d) $\frac{-5}{-4}$

5. $1 \div \frac{-5}{7} =$

   (a) $\frac{2}{7}$ (b) $\frac{5}{7}$ (c) $-\frac{2}{7}$ (d) $\frac{-7}{5}$

6. $\frac{-5}{13} + ? = -1$

(a) $\frac{8}{13}$ (b) $\frac{-8}{13}$ (c) $\frac{-18}{13}$ (d) $\frac{18}{13}$

7. $0 \div \frac{3}{5} =$

(a) 0 (b) $\frac{5}{3}$ (c) $\frac{3}{5}$ (d) $-\frac{3}{5}$

8. $-2\frac{3}{7} + 4 = ?$

(a) $\frac{-11}{7}$ (b) $\frac{11}{7}$ (c) $\frac{-45}{7}$ (d) $\frac{45}{7}$

9. If the product of two non-zero rational numbers is 1, then they are

(a) additive inverse of each other (b) multiplicative inverse of each other
(c) reciprocal of each other (d) both (b) and (c)

10. The product $3\frac{1}{7} \times 1\frac{5}{6} \times 1\frac{2}{5} \times 1\frac{1}{11}$ is equal to

(a) $5\frac{8}{5}$ (b) $5\frac{4}{5}$ (c) $8\frac{4}{5}$ (d) $7\frac{4}{5}$

11. $\frac{-7}{13} - \left(\frac{-8}{15}\right) =$

(a) $-\frac{239}{195}$ (b) $\frac{29}{195}$ (c) $\frac{-29}{195}$ (d) None of these

12. $1 \div \frac{1}{3} =$

(a) $\frac{1}{3}$ (b) 3 (c) $1\frac{1}{3}$ (d) $3\frac{1}{3}$

13. $(-2) \div \left(-\frac{5}{3}\right) =$

(a) $\frac{5}{6}$ (b) $-\frac{5}{6}$ (c) $\frac{6}{5}$ (d) $\frac{-6}{5}$

14. If $\frac{x}{2} + \frac{1}{3} = 1$, then $x =$

(a) $\frac{3}{4}$ (b) $\frac{4}{3}$ (c) $-\frac{3}{4}$ (d) $\frac{-4}{3}$

15. $\frac{5}{4} - \frac{7}{6} - \frac{-2}{3} =$

(a) $\frac{3}{4}$ (b) $-\frac{3}{4}$ (c) $\frac{-7}{12}$ (d) $\frac{7}{12}$

ANSWSERS

1. (d) 2. (b) 3. (c) 4. (c) 5. (d) 6. (b) 7. (a)
8. (b) 9. (d) 10. (c) 11. (d) 12. (b) 13. (c) 14. (b)
15. (a)

THINGS TO REMEMBER

1. *For any two rational numbers* $\frac{p}{q}$ *and* $\frac{r}{q}$, *we define :*

$$\frac{p}{q}+\frac{r}{q}=\frac{p+r}{q}$$

2. *For any two rational numbers* $\frac{p}{q}$ *and* $\frac{r}{s}$ *to find* $\frac{p}{q}+\frac{r}{s}$ *first we convert* $\frac{p}{q}$ *and* $\frac{r}{s}$ *to equivalent rational numbers having denominator equal to the LCM of q and s and then they are added.*

3. *For any two rational numbers* $\frac{p}{q}$ *and* $\frac{r}{s}$, *we have* $\frac{p}{q}-\frac{r}{s}=\frac{p}{q}+\left(\text{negative of } \frac{r}{s}\right)$

4. *For any two rational numbers* $\frac{p}{q}$ *and* $\frac{r}{s}$, *we have*

$$\frac{p}{q}\times\frac{r}{s}=\frac{p\times r}{q\times s}$$

5. *The reciprocal of a non-zero rational number* $\frac{p}{q}$ *is* $\frac{q}{p}$ *and we write* $\left(\frac{p}{q}\right)^{-1}=\frac{q}{p}$.

6. *For any two rational numbers* $\frac{p}{q}$ *and* $\frac{r}{s}(\neq 0)$, *we have*

$$\frac{p}{q}\div\frac{r}{s}=\frac{p}{q}\times\frac{s}{r}$$

6

EXPONENTS

6.1 INTRODUCTION

Consider following numbers:

89,000,000,000
1,459,500,000,000
750,000,000,000,000
5,978,043,000,000,000

We find that it is not very convenient to read, understand and compare such large numbers. In order to make such large numbers easy to read, understand and compare, we use exponents. In this chapter, we shall learn about exponents and their uses.

6.2 EXPONENTS

As we know that the continued sum of a number added to itself a number of times can be written as the product of a natural number, equal to the number of times it is added, and the number itself.

For example,

$$5+5+5+5+5+5+5=7\times 5$$

$$(-2)+(-2)+(-2)+(-2)+(-2)+(-2)+(-2)+(-2)+(-2)=9\times(-2)$$

$$\frac{3}{4}+\frac{3}{4}+\frac{3}{4}+\frac{3}{4}+\frac{3}{4}=5\times\frac{3}{4} \text{ etc.}$$

Similarly, the continued product of a number multiplied with itself a number of times can be written as the number raised to the power a natural number, equal to the number of times the number is multiplied with itself.

For example,

$5\times 5\times 5$ can be written as 5^3 and it is read as 5 raised to the power 3 or third power of 5. In 5^3, we call 5 as the base and 3 as the exponent.

Similarly,

$(-2)\times(-2)\times(-2)\times(-2)$ is written as $(-2)^4$

$\frac{2}{3}\times\frac{2}{3}\times\frac{2}{3}\times\frac{2}{3}\times\frac{2}{3}$ is written as $\left(\frac{2}{3}\right)^5$

We have,

$5\times 5\times 5=125$

Also, $5\times 5\times 5$ is written as 5^3.

$\therefore$ $125=5^3$

Similarly,

$$(-2)\times(-2)\times(-2)\times(-2)=16$$

$$\Rightarrow \qquad (-2)^4=16$$

5^3 is known as the exponential form or power notation of 125. Here, 5 is the base and 3 is the exponent.

Similarly, $(-2)^4$ is the exponential form or power notation of 16 with base –2 and exponent 4.

We have,

$$100=10\times10$$
$$1000=10\times10\times10$$
$$10000=10\times10\times10\times10$$
$$100000=10\times10\times10\times10\times10 \text{ etc.}$$

So, the exponential forms of 100, 1000, 10000 and 100000 are as given below:

$$100=10^2 \text{ (read as 10 raised to the power 2)}$$
$$1000=10^3 \text{ (read as 10 raised to the power 3)}$$
$$10000=10^4 \text{ (read as 10 raised to the power 4)}$$
$$100000=10^5 \text{ (read as 10 raised to the power 5)}$$

Some powers have special names. For example,

5^2, which is 5 raised to the power 2, is also read as '5 squared'.

5^3, which is 5 raised to the power 3, is also read as '5 cubed'.

Similarly, 10^2 is read as '10 squared' and 10^3 is read as '10 cubed'.

It follows from the above discussion that for any rational number a, we have

$a\times a=a^2$ (read as 'a squared' or 'a raised to the power 2')

$a\times a\times a=a^3$ (read as 'a cubed' or 'a raised to the power 3')

$a\times a\times a\times a=a^4$ (read as a raised to the power 4 or the 4th power of a)

$a\times a\times a\times a\times a=a^5$ (read as a raised to the power 5 or the 5th power of a)

and so on.

In general, if n is a natural number, then

$$\underbrace{a\times a\times a\times a\times\cdots\times a}_{n\text{-times}}=a^n$$

a^n is called the nth power of a and is also read as 'a raised to the power n'.

<u>NOTE 1</u> *It is evident from the above discussion that*

$a\times a\times a\times b\times b$ *is written as* a^3b^2 *(read as a cubed into b squared)*

$a\times a\times b\times b\times b\times b$ *is written* a^2b^4 *(read as a squared into b raised to the power 4)*

NOTE 2 *For any non-zero rational number a, we define*

(i) $a^1 = a$ (ii) $a^0 = 1$.

ILLUSTRATIVE EXAMPLES

Type I **ON FINDING THE VALUE OF A NUMBER GIVEN IN EXPONENTIAL FORM**

Example 1 Find the value of each of the following:

(i) 11^2 (ii) 9^3 (iii) 5^4

Solution (i) We have,

$$11^2 = 11\times 11 = 121$$

(ii) We have,

$$9^3 = 9\times 9\times 9 = (9\times 9)\times 9 = 81\times 9 = 729$$

(iii) We have,

$$5^4 = 5\times 5\times 5\times 5$$
$$= (5\times 5)\times 5\times 5 = 25\times 5\times 5 = (25\times 5)\times 5 = 125\times 5 = 625$$

Example 2 Find the value of each of the following:

(i) $(-3)^2$ (ii) $(-4)^3$ (iii) $(-5)^4$

Solution (i) We have,

$$(-3)^2 = (-3)\times(-3) = 9$$

(ii) We have,

$$(-4)^3 = (-4)\times(-4)\times(-4) = \big((-4)\times(-4)\big)\times(-4) = 16\times(-4) = -64$$

(iii) We have,

$$(-5)^4 = (-5)\times(-5)\times(-5)\times(-5)$$
$$= \big((-5)\times(-5)\big)\times(-5)\times(-5)$$
$$= 25\times(-5)\times(-5)$$
$$= \big(25\times(-5)\big)\times(-5)$$
$$= (-125)\times(-5) = 125\times 5 = 625$$

Example 3 Simplify:

(i) 2×10^3 (ii) $7^2\times 2^2$ (iii) $2^3\times 5$ (iv) 0×10^2

Solution (i) We have,

$2\times 10^3 = 2\times 1000 = 2000$ $[\because\ 10^3 = 10\times 10\times 10 = 1000]$

(ii) We have,

$7^2\times 2^2 = 49\times 4$ $[\because\ 7^2 = 49,\ 2^2 = 4]$

$= 196$

(iii) We have,

$2^3\times 5 = 8\times 5 = 40$ $[\because\ 2^3 = 2\times 2\times 2 = 8]$

(iv) We have,

$0\times 10^2 = 0\times 100 = 0$ $[\because\ 10^2 = 10\times 10 = 100]$

Example 4 Simplify:

(i) $5^2 \times 3^3$ (ii) $2^4 \times 3^2$ (iii) $3^2 \times 10^4$ (iv) $5^3 \times 2^4$

Solution (i) We have,

$$5^2 \times 3^3 = 25 \times 27 \quad [\because 5^2 = 5 \times 5 = 25 \text{ and } 3^3 = 3 \times 3 \times 3 = 27]$$
$$= 675$$

(ii) We have,

$$2^4 \times 3^2 = 16 \times 9 \quad [\because 2^4 = 2 \times 2 \times 2 \times 2 = 16 \text{ and } 3^2 = 3 \times 3 = 9]$$
$$= 144$$

(iii) We have,

$$3^2 \times 10^4 = 9 \times 10000 \quad [\because 3^2 = 3 \times 3 = 9 \text{ and } 10^4 = 10 \times 10 \times 10 \times 10 = 10000]$$
$$= 90000$$

(iv) We have,

$$5^3 \times 2^4 = 125 \times 16 \quad [\because 5^3 = 5 \times 5 \times 5 = 125 \text{ and } 2^4 = 2 \times 2 \times 2 \times 2 = 16]$$
$$= 2000$$

Example 5 Simplify:

(i) $(-3) \times (-2)^3$ (ii) $(-3)^2 \times (-5)^2$ (iii) $(-2)^3 \times (-10)^3$ (iv) $(-2)^4 \times (-5)^2$

Solution (i) We have,

$$(-3) \times (-2)^3 = (-3) \times (-8) \quad [\because (-2)^3 = (-2) \times (-2) \times (-2) = -8]$$
$$= 24$$

(ii) We have,

$$(-3)^2 \times (-5)^2 = 9 \times 25 \quad [\because (-3)^2 = (-3) \times (-3) = 9 \text{ and } (-5)^2 = (-5) \times (-5) = 25]$$
$$= 225$$

(iii) We have,

$$(-2)^3 \times (-10)^3 = (-8) \times (-1000) \quad \left[\begin{array}{l} \because \quad (-2)^3 = (-2) \times (-2) \times (-2) = -8 \\ \text{and } (-10)^3 = (-10) \times (-10) \times (-10) = -1000 \end{array}\right]$$
$$= 8000$$

(iv) We have,

$$(-2)^4 \times (-5)^2 = 16 \times 25 \quad \left[\begin{array}{l} \because \quad (-2)^4 = (-2) \times (-2) \times (-2) \times (-4) = 16 \\ \text{and } (-5)^2 = (-5) \times (-5) = 25 \end{array}\right]$$
$$= 400$$

Example 6 Simplify:

(i) $(1)^5$ (ii) $(-1)^5$ (iii) $(-1)^6$ (iv) $(-1)^7$

Solution We have,

(i) $(1)^5 = 1 \times 1 \times 1 \times 1 \times 1 = 1$

(ii) $(-1)^5 = (-1) \times (-1) \times (-1) \times (-1) \times (-1)$

$$= \big((-1) \times (-1)\big) \times \big((-1) \times (-1)\big) \times (-1)$$

$$= 1 \times 1 \times (-1) = 1 \times (-1) = -1$$

(iii) $(-1)^6 = (-1)\times(-1)\times(-1)\times(-1)\times(-1)\times(-1)$

$$= ((-1)\times(-1))\times((-1)\times(-1))\times((-1)\times(-1)) = 1\times1\times1 = 1$$

(iv) $(-1)^7 = (-1)\times(-1)\times(-1)\times(-1)\times(-1)\times(-1)\times(-1)$

$$= ((-1)\times(-1))\times((-1)\times(-1))\times((-1)\times(-1))\times(-1)$$

$$= 1\times1\times1\times(-1) = 1\times(-1) = -1$$

Remark 1 *It follows from the above example that*

$$(-1)^{\text{An odd natural number}} = -1 \text{ and, } (-1)^{\text{An even natural number}} = 1$$

i.e., $$(-1)^n = \begin{cases} 1, & \text{if } n \text{ is an even natural number} \\ -1, & \text{if } n \text{ is an odd natural number} \end{cases}$$

Example 7 Express each of the following in the form $\frac{p}{q}$:

(i) $\left(\frac{2}{3}\right)^2$ (ii) $\left(\frac{-3}{4}\right)^3$ (iii) $\left(\frac{-2}{5}\right)^4$

Solution We have,

(i) $\left(\frac{2}{3}\right)^2 = \frac{2}{3}\times\frac{2}{3} = \frac{2\times2}{3\times3} = \frac{4}{9}$

(ii) $\left(\frac{-3}{4}\right)^3 = \left(\frac{-3}{4}\right)\times\left(\frac{-3}{4}\right)\times\left(\frac{-3}{4}\right) = \frac{(-3)\times(-3)\times(-3)}{4\times4\times4} = \frac{-27}{64}$

(iii) $\left(\frac{-2}{5}\right)^4 = \left(\frac{-2}{5}\right)\times\left(\frac{-2}{5}\right)\times\left(\frac{-2}{5}\right)\times\left(\frac{-2}{5}\right) = \frac{(-2)\times(-2)\times(-2)\times(-2)}{5\times5\times5\times5} = \frac{16}{625}$

Remark 2 *If $\frac{a}{b}$ is a rational number and n is a natural number, then*

$$\left(\frac{a}{b}\right)^n = \underbrace{\frac{a}{b}\times\frac{a}{b}\times\frac{a}{b}\times\frac{a}{b}\times\cdots\times\frac{a}{b}}_{(n\text{-times})} = \frac{\overbrace{a\times a\times a\times a\times\cdots\times a}^{(n\text{-times})}}{\underbrace{b\times b\times b\times b\times\cdots\times b}_{(n\text{-times})}} = \frac{a^n}{b^n}$$

$$\therefore \quad \left(\frac{a}{b}\right)^n = \frac{a^n}{b^n}$$

Example 8 Identify the greater number in each of the following:

(i) 5^3 or 3^5 (ii) 2^8 or 8^2 (iii) 2^{10} or 10^2 (iv) 2^{100} or 100^2

Solution (i) We have,

$5^3 = 5\times5\times5 = 125$ and $3^5 = 3\times3\times3\times3\times3 = 243$

$\because$ $243 > 125$

$\therefore$ $3^5 > 5^3$

(ii) We have,

$$2^8 = 2\times2\times2\times2\times2\times2\times2\times2$$
$$= (2\times2)\times(2\times2)\times(2\times2)\times(2\times2)$$
$$= 4\times4\times4\times4 = (4\times4)\times(4\times4) = 16\times16 = 256$$

and, $8^2 = 8\times8 = 64$

$\because$ $256 > 64$

$\therefore$ $2^8 > 8^2$

(iii) We have,

$$2^{10} = 2\times2\times2\times2\times2\times2\times2\times2\times2\times2$$
$$= (2\times2)\times(2\times2)\times(2\times2)\times(2\times2)\times(2\times2)$$
$$= 4\times4\times4\times4\times4 = (4\times4)\times(4\times4)\times4 = 16\times16\times4 = 256\times4 = 1024$$

and, $10^2 = 10\times10 = 100$

$\because$ $1024 > 100$

$\therefore$ $2^{10} > 10^2$

(iv) In (iii) and (iv), we have seen that

$$2^8 > 8^2 \text{ and } 2^{10} > 10^2$$

Similarly, it can be seen that

$$2^{15} > 15^2, 2^{20} > 20^2, 2^{50} > 50^2 \text{ and } 2^{100} > 100^2$$

Example 9 Find the product of the cube of $\frac{-2}{3}$ and the square of $\frac{4}{-5}$.

Solution We have,

$$\left(\text{Cube of } \frac{-2}{3}\right)\times\left(\text{Square of } \frac{4}{-5}\right)$$

$$= \left(\frac{-2}{3}\right)^3 \times \left(\frac{4}{-5}\right)^2$$

$$= \left(\frac{-2}{3}\right)\times\left(\frac{-2}{3}\right)\times\left(\frac{-2}{3}\right)\times\left(\frac{4}{-5}\right)\times\left(\frac{4}{-5}\right)$$

$$= \frac{(-2)\times(-2)\times(-2)}{3\times3\times3}\times\frac{4\times4}{(-5)\times(-5)} = \frac{-8}{27}\times\frac{16}{25} = \frac{-8\times16}{27\times25} = \frac{-128}{675}$$

Example 10 Express the following as a rational number:

$$\left(\frac{1}{2}\right)^3 \times \left(\frac{-3}{5}\right)^3 \times \left(\frac{-4}{9}\right)^2$$

Solution We have,

$$\left(\frac{1}{2}\right)^3 \times \left(\frac{-3}{5}\right)^3 \times \left(\frac{-4}{9}\right)^2$$

$$= \frac{1^3}{2^3} \times \frac{(-3)^3}{5^3} \times \frac{(-4)^2}{9^2} \qquad \left[\because \left(\frac{a}{b}\right)^n = \frac{a^n}{b^n} \text{ See remark 2 on page 6.5}\right]$$

$$= \frac{1}{8} \times \frac{-27}{125} \times \frac{16}{81} = \frac{1 \times -27 \times 16}{8 \times 125 \times 81} = \frac{1 \times -1 \times 2}{1 \times 125 \times 3} = \frac{-2}{375}$$

Example 11 Simplify:

(i) $(-3)^2 \times \left(\frac{-5}{12}\right)^2$ (ii) $\left(\frac{-2}{5}\right)^3 \div \left(\frac{-3}{10}\right)^4$

Solution (i) We have,

$$(-3)^2 \times \left(\frac{-5}{12}\right)^2 = (-3)^2 \times \frac{(-5)^2}{12^2} \qquad \left[\because \left(\frac{a}{b}\right)^n = \frac{a^n}{b^n}\right]$$

$$= 9 \times \frac{25}{144} = 1 \times \frac{25}{16} = \frac{25}{16}$$

(ii) We have

$$\left(\frac{-2}{5}\right)^3 \div \left(\frac{-3}{10}\right)^4 = \frac{\left(\frac{-2}{5}\right)^3}{\left(\frac{-3}{10}\right)^4}$$

$$= \frac{\frac{(-2)^3}{5^3}}{\frac{(-3)^4}{10^4}} \qquad \left[\because \left(\frac{a}{b}\right)^n = \frac{a^n}{b^n}\right]$$

$$= \frac{\frac{-8}{125}}{\frac{81}{10000}} \qquad [\because (-2)^3 = -8, 5^3 = 125, (-3)^4 = 81 \text{ and } 10^4 = 10000]$$

$$= \frac{-8}{125} \times \frac{10000}{81} = \frac{-8 \times 10000}{125 \times 81} = \frac{-8 \times 80}{1 \times 81} = \frac{-640}{81}$$

Example 12 Simplify:

(i) $\left\{\left(\frac{1}{2}\right)^2 - \left(\frac{1}{4}\right)^3\right\} \times 2^3$ (ii) $\left\{(3^2 - 2^2) \div \left(\frac{1}{5}\right)^2\right\}$

Solution (i) We have,

$$\left\{\left(\frac{1}{2}\right)^2-\left(\frac{1}{4}\right)^3\right\}\times 2^3$$

$$=\left\{\frac{1^2}{2^2}-\frac{1^3}{4^3}\right\}\times 2^3 \qquad \left[\because \left(\frac{a}{b}\right)^n=\frac{a^n}{b^n}\right]$$

$$=\left(\frac{1}{4}-\frac{1}{64}\right)\times 8$$

$$=\left(\frac{16-1}{64}\right)\times 8=\frac{15}{64}\times 8=\frac{15\times \overset{1}{\cancel{8}}}{\underset{8}{\cancel{64}}}=\frac{15\times 1}{8}=\frac{15}{8}$$

(ii) We have,

$$\left\{(3^2-2^2)\div\left(\frac{1}{5}\right)^2\right\}=\left\{(9-4)\div\left(\frac{1}{5}\right)^2\right\}$$

$$=5\div\left(\frac{1}{5}\right)^2=\frac{5}{\left(\frac{1}{5}\right)^2}=\frac{5}{\frac{1^2}{5^2}}=\frac{5}{\frac{1}{25}}=5\times\frac{25}{1}=125$$

Example 13 If $a=2$ and $b=3$, then find the values of each of the following:

(i) a^a+b^b (ii) a^b+b^a (iii) $\left(\frac{a}{b}\right)^a$ (iv) $\left(\frac{1}{a}+\frac{1}{b}\right)^a$

Solution We have,

(i) $a^a+b^b=2^2+3^3=2\times 2+3\times 3\times 3=4+27=31$

(ii) $a^b+b^a=2^3+3^2=2\times 2\times 2+3\times 3=8+9=17$

(iii) $\left(\frac{a}{b}\right)^a=\left(\frac{2}{3}\right)^2=\frac{2}{3}\times\frac{2}{3}=\frac{2\times 2}{3\times 3}=\frac{4}{9}$

(iv) $\left(\frac{1}{a}+\frac{1}{b}\right)^a=\left(\frac{1}{2}+\frac{1}{3}\right)^2=\left(\frac{3+2}{6}\right)^2=\left(\frac{5}{6}\right)^2=\frac{5}{6}\times\frac{5}{6}=\frac{5\times 5}{6\times 6}=\frac{25}{36}$

Example 14 Simplify and express each of the following as power of a rational number:

(i) $\left(\frac{2}{3}\right)^3\times\left(-\frac{6}{7}\right)^2\times\left(-\frac{7}{4}\right)\times\frac{3}{2}$ (ii) $-\left(\frac{2}{5}\right)^2\times\left(\frac{5}{7}\right)^2\times\frac{49}{5}+\left(-\frac{4}{5}\right)^3\times\frac{5}{4}\times\frac{3}{4}$

Solution (i) We have,

$$\left(\frac{2}{3}\right)^3\times\left(-\frac{6}{7}\right)^2\times\left(-\frac{7}{4}\right)\times\frac{3}{2}$$

$$=\left(\frac{2}{3}\right)^3\times(-1)^2\times\left(\frac{6}{7}\right)^2\times\left(-\frac{7}{4}\right)\times\frac{3}{2}$$

$= \frac{2^3}{3^3} \times (-1)^2 \times \frac{6^2}{7^2} \times -\frac{7}{4} \times \frac{3}{2}$

$= \frac{8}{27} \times 1 \times \frac{36}{49} \times -\frac{7}{4} \times \frac{3}{2}$

$= \frac{8}{27} \times \frac{36}{49} \times \frac{-7}{4} \times \frac{3}{2} = \frac{8 \times 36 \times -7 \times 3}{27 \times 49 \times 4 \times 2}$

$= \frac{1 \times 36 \times -1 \times 1}{9 \times 7 \times 1 \times 1} = \frac{-36}{9 \times 7} = \frac{-4}{7} = \left(-\frac{4}{7}\right)^1$ $[\because a^1 = a]$

(ii) We have,

$-\left(\frac{2}{5}\right)^2 \times \left(\frac{5}{7}\right)^2 \times \frac{49}{5} + \left(-\frac{4}{5}\right)^3 \times \frac{5}{4} \times \frac{3}{4}$

$= -\frac{2^2}{5^2} \times \frac{5^2}{7^2} \times \frac{49}{5} + (-1)^3 \times \left(\frac{4}{5}\right)^3 \times \frac{5}{4} \times \frac{3}{4}$

$= -\frac{2^2}{5^2} \times \frac{5^2}{7^2} \times \frac{49}{5} + (-1) \times \frac{4^3}{5^3} \times \frac{5}{4} \times \frac{3}{4}$

$= -\frac{4}{25} \times \frac{25}{49} \times \frac{49}{5} + (-1) \times \frac{64}{125} \times \frac{5}{4} \times \frac{3}{4}$

$= -\frac{4}{1} \times \frac{1}{1} \times \frac{1}{5} + (-1) \times \frac{4}{25} \times \frac{1}{1} \times \frac{3}{1}$

$= -\frac{4}{5} - \frac{12}{25} = -\frac{4}{5} - \frac{12}{25} = -\frac{20}{25} - \frac{12}{25} = -\frac{32}{25} = \left(\frac{-32}{25}\right)^1$

Type II ON EXPRESSING NUMBERS IN THE EXPONENTIAL FORM

Example 15 Express each of the following in exponential form:

(i) $(-4) \times (-4) \times (-4) \times (-4) \times (-4) \times (-4)$ (ii) $\frac{3}{5} \times \frac{3}{5} \times \frac{3}{5} \times \frac{3}{5}$

Solution We have,

(i) $(-4) \times (-4) \times (-4) \times (-4) \times (-4) \times (-4) = (-4)^6$

(ii) $\frac{3}{5} \times \frac{3}{5} \times \frac{3}{5} \times \frac{3}{5} = \left(\frac{3}{5}\right)^4$

Example 16 Express each of the following in exponential form:

(i) $2 \times 2 \times 2 \times a \times a$ (ii) $a \times a \times a \times a \times b \times b \times c \times c \times c \times c \times c$

(iii) $a \times a \times a \times \left(\frac{-2}{3}\right) \times \left(\frac{-2}{3}\right)$

Solution We have,

(i) $2 \times 2 \times 2 \times a \times a = 2^3 \times a^2$

(ii) $a \times a \times a \times a \times b \times b \times c \times c \times c \times c \times c = a^4 b^2 c^5$

(iv) $a \times a \times a \times \left(\frac{-2}{3}\right) \times \left(\frac{-2}{3}\right) = a^3 \times \left(\frac{-2}{3}\right)^2$

Example 17 Express each of the following numbers in exponential form:

(i) 128 (ii) 243 (iii) 3125

Solution (i) We have,

2	128
2	64
2	32
2	16
2	8
2	4
	2

$128 = 2\times2\times2\times2\times2\times2\times2$

$\therefore \quad 128 = 2^7$

(ii) We have,

3	243
3	81
3	27
3	9
	3

$243 = 3\times3\times3\times3\times3$

$\therefore \quad 243 = 3^5$

(iii) We have,

5	3125
5	625
5	125
5	25
	5

$3125 = 5\times5\times5\times5\times5$

$\therefore \quad 3125 = 5^5$

Example 18 Express each of the following numbers as a product of powers of their prime factors:

(i) 432 (ii) 648 (iii) 540

Solution (i) Using prime factorisation of 432, we have

2	432
2	216
2	108
2	54
3	27
3	9
	3

$432 = 2\times2\times2\times2\times3\times3\times3$

$\therefore \quad 432 = 2^4\times3^3$

(ii) Using prime factorisation of 648, we have

2	648
2	324
2	162
3	81
3	27
3	9
	3

$648 = 2\times2\times2\times3\times3\times3\times3$

$\therefore \quad 648 = 2^3\times3^4$

(ii) Using prime factorisation of 540, we have

2	540
2	270
3	135
3	45
3	15
	5

$540 = 2\times2\times3\times3\times3\times5$

$\therefore \quad 540 = 2^2\times3^3\times5^1$

Example 19 Express the following numbers as product of powers of their prime factors:

(i) 1000 (ii) 16000 (iii) 3600

Solution (i) Expressing 1000 as the product of prime factors, we have

$$1000 = 2\times2\times2\times5\times5\times5$$

2	1000
2	500
2	250
5	125
5	25
	5

$\therefore$ $1000 = 2^3\times5^3$

<u>Aliter</u> We have,

$$1000 = 10\times10\times10$$

$$= (2\times5)\times(2\times5)\times(2\times5)$$

$$= 2\times2\times2\times5\times5\times5 = 2^3\times5^3$$

(ii) Expressing 16000 as the product of prime factors, we have

$$16000 = 2\times2\times2\times2\times2\times2\times2\times5\times5\times5$$

$$= 2^7\times5^3$$

2	16000
2	8000
2	4000
2	2000
2	1000
2	500
2	250
5	125
5	25
	5

<u>Aliter</u> We have,

$$16000 = 16\times1000$$

$$= 16\times10\times10\times10$$

$$= (2\times2\times2\times2)\times(2\times5)\times(2\times5)\times(2\times5)$$

$$= (2\times2\times2\times2\times2\times2\times2)\times(5\times5\times5)$$

$$= 2^7\times5^3$$

(iii) Expressing 3600 as the product of prime factors, we have

$$3600 = 2\times2\times2\times2\times3\times3\times5\times5$$

$\therefore$ $3600 = 2^4\times3^2\times5^2$

2	3600
2	1800
2	900
2	450
3	225
3	75
5	25
	5

<u>Aliter</u> We have,

$$3600 = 36\times100$$

$$= 4\times9\times10\times10$$

$$= (2\times2)\times(3\times3)\times(2\times5)\times(2\times5)$$

$$= (2\times2\times2\times2)\times(3\times3)\times(5\times5) = 2^4\times3^2\times5^2$$

Example 20 Express each of the following rational numbers in exponential form:

(i) $\frac{27}{64}$ (ii) $\frac{-27}{125}$ (iii) $\frac{-1}{243}$

Solution (i) We have,

$$\frac{27}{64} = \frac{3^3}{4^3} \qquad [\because 27 = 3^3 \text{ and } 64 = 4^3]$$

$$= \left(\frac{3}{4}\right)^3 \qquad \left[\because \frac{a^n}{b^n} = \left(\frac{a}{b}\right)^n\right]$$

(ii) We have,

$$\frac{-27}{125}=\frac{(-3)^3}{5^3} \qquad [\because\ -27=(-3)^3 \text{ and } 125=5^3]$$

$$=\left(\frac{-3}{5}\right)^3$$

(iii) We have,

$$\frac{-1}{243}=\frac{(-1)^5}{3^5} \qquad [\because\ (-1)^5=-1 \text{ and } 3^5=243]$$

$$=\left(\frac{-1}{3}\right)^5$$

EXERCISE 6.1

1. Find the value of each of the following:

   (i) 13^2 (ii) 7^3 (iii) 3^4

2. Find the value of each of the following:

   (i) $(-7)^2$ (ii) $(-3)^4$ (iii) $(-5)^5$

3. Simplify:

   (i) 3×10^2 (ii) $2^2\times5^3$ (iii) $3^3\times5^2$

4. Simplify:

   (i) $3^2\times10^4$ (ii) $2^4\times3^2$ (iii) $5^2\times3^4$

5. Simplify:

   (i) $(-2)\times(-3)^3$ (ii) $(-3)^2\times(-5)^3$ (iii) $(-2)^5\times(-10)^2$

6. Simplify:

   (i) $\left(\frac{3}{4}\right)^2$ (ii) $\left(\frac{-2}{3}\right)^4$ (iii) $\left(\frac{-4}{5}\right)^5$

7. Identify the greater number in each of the following:

   (i) 2^5 or 5^2 (ii) 3^4 or 4^3 (iii) 3^5 or 5^3

8. Express each of the following in exponential form:

   (i) $(-5)\times(-5)\times(-5)$ (ii) $\frac{-5}{7}\times\frac{-5}{7}\times\frac{-5}{7}\times\frac{-5}{7}$ (iiii) $\frac{4}{3}\times\frac{4}{3}\times\frac{4}{3}\times\frac{4}{3}\times\frac{4}{3}$

9. Express each of the following in exponential form:

   (i) $x\times x\times x\times x\times a\times a\times b\times b\times b$ (ii) $(-2)\times(-2)\times(-2)\times(-2)\times a\times a\times a$

   (iiii) $\left(\frac{-2}{3}\right)\times\left(\frac{-2}{3}\right)\times x\times x\times x$

10. Express each of the following numbers in exponential form:

    (i) 512 (ii) 625 (iii) 729

11. Express each of the following numbers as a product of powers of their prime factors:

    (i) 36 (ii) 675 (iii) 392

12. Express each of the following numbers as a product of powers of their prime factors:
    (i) 450 (ii) 2800 (iii) 24000

13. Express each of the following as a rational number of the form $\frac{p}{q}$:
    (i) $\left(\frac{3}{7}\right)^2$ (ii) $\left(\frac{7}{9}\right)^3$ (iii) $\left(\frac{-2}{3}\right)^4$

14. Express each of the following rational numbers in power notation:
    (i) $\frac{49}{64}$ (ii) $-\frac{64}{125}$ (iii) $-\frac{1}{216}$

15. Find the value of each of the following:
    (i) $\left(\frac{-1}{2}\right)^2 \times 2^3 \times \left(\frac{3}{4}\right)^2$ (ii) $\left(\frac{-3}{5}\right)^4 \times \left(\frac{4}{9}\right)^4 \times \left(\frac{-15}{18}\right)^2$

16. If $a = 2$ and $b = 3$, then find the values of each of the following:
    (i) $(a+b)^a$ (ii) $(ab)^b$ (iii) $\left(\frac{b}{a}\right)^b$ (iv) $\left(\frac{a}{b}+\frac{b}{a}\right)^a$

ANSWERS

1. (i) 169 (ii) 343 (iii) 81
2. (i) 49 (ii) 81 (iii) –3125
3. (i) 300 (ii) 500 (iii) 675
4. (i) 90000 (ii) 144 (iii) 2025
5. (i) 54 (ii) –1125 (iii) –3200
6. (i) $\frac{9}{16}$ (ii) $\frac{16}{81}$ (iii) $\frac{-1024}{3125}$
7. (i) 2^5 (ii) 3^4 (iii) 3^5
8. (i) $(-5)^3$ (ii) $\left(\frac{-5}{7}\right)^4$ (iii) $\left(\frac{4}{3}\right)^5$
9. (i) $x^4a^2b^3$ (ii) $(-2)^4 \times a^3$ (iii) $\left(\frac{-2}{3}\right)^2 \times x^3$
10. (i) 2^9 (ii) 5^4 (iii) 3^6
11. (i) $2^2 \times 3^2$ (ii) $3^3 \times 5^2$ (iii) $2^3 \times 7^2$
12. (i) $2 \times 3^2 \times 5^2$ (ii) $2^4 \times 5^2 \times 7$ (iii) $2^6 \times 3^1 \times 5^3$
13. (i) $\frac{9}{49}$ (ii) $\frac{343}{729}$ (iii) $\frac{16}{81}$
14. (i) $\left(\frac{7}{8}\right)^2$ (ii) $\left(-\frac{4}{5}\right)^3$ (iii) $\left(\frac{-1}{6}\right)^3$
15. (i) $\frac{9}{8}$ (ii) $\frac{64}{18225}$
16. (i) 25 (ii) 216 (iii) $\frac{27}{8}$ (iv) $\frac{169}{36}$

6.3 LAWS OF EXPONENTS

In this section, we will learn about various laws of exponents:

6.3.1 MULTIPLYING POWERS WITH THE SAME BASE

Consider the following product of two powers with the same base:

$$3^2 \times 3^4 = (3\times 3)\times(3\times 3\times 3\times 3) = 3\times 3\times 3\times 3\times 3\times 3 = 3^6 = 3^{2+4}$$

In this product LHS is the product of two powers with the same base and exponents 2 and 4 and RHS is the power with the same base and exponent equal to 2 + 4 *i.e.*, the sum of the exponents 2 and 4.

Let us now consider some more products:

$$(-2)^4 \times (-2)^3 = ((-2)\times(-2)\times(-2)\times(-2))\times((-2)\times(-2)\times(-2))$$
$$= (-2)\times(-2)\times(-2)\times(-2)\times(-2)\times(-2)\times(-2) = (-2)^7 = (-2)^{4+3}$$

and,
$$a^3 \times a^5 = (a\times a\times a)\times(a\times a\times a\times a\times a)$$
$$= a\times a\times a\times a\times a\times a\times a\times a = a^8 = a^{3+5}$$

In these products also LHS of each product is the product of two powers with the same base and RHS is the power with the same base and exponent equal to the sum of the exponents of powers on LHS.

The above discussion suggests us the following law of exponents:

FIRST LAW *If a is any non-zero rational number and m, n are natural numbers, then*

$$a^m \times a^n = a^{m+n}$$

Following is the generalised form of the above law:

Generalisation: If a is a non-zero rational number and m, n, p are natural numbers, then

$$a^m \times a^n \times a^p = a^{m+n+p}$$

ILLUSTRATION 1 Simplify and write the answer of each of the following in exponential form:

(i) $5^2 \times 5^3$ (ii) $3^2 \times 3^4 \times 3^8$ (iii) $7^x \times 7^2$ (iv) $\left(\frac{3}{2}\right)^2 \times \left(\frac{3}{2}\right)^5$

Solution We have,

(i) $5^2 \times 5^3 = 5^{2+3} = 5^5$

(ii) $3^2 \times 3^4 \times 3^8 = 3^{2+4+8} = 3^{14}$

(iii) $7^x \times 7^2 = 7^{x+2}$

(iv) $\left(\frac{3}{2}\right)^2 \times \left(\frac{3}{2}\right)^5 = \left(\frac{3}{2}\right)^{2+5} = \left(\frac{3}{2}\right)^7$

6.3.2 DIVIDING POWERS WITH THE SAME BASE

In the above discussion, we have learnt about multiplication of powers with the same base. What happens if powers with the same base are divided. To understand this, let us consider the following division of powers:

$$5^7 \div 5^4 = \frac{5^7}{5^4} = \frac{\cancel{5}\times\cancel{5}\times\cancel{5}\times\cancel{5}\times 5\times 5\times 5}{\cancel{5}\times\cancel{5}\times\cancel{5}\times\cancel{5}} = 5\times 5\times 5 = 5^3 = 5^{7-4}$$

We observe that 5^7 and 5^4 have the same base and $5^7 \div 5^4$ is equal to 5^{7-4}.

Let us now compute some more division of powers having the same base.

We have,

$$(-3)^6 \div (-3)^2 = \frac{(-3)^6}{(-3)^2} = \frac{\cancel{(-3)}\times\cancel{(-3)}\times(-3)\times(-3)\times(-3)\times(-3)}{\cancel{(-3)}\times\cancel{(-3)}}$$

$$= (-3)\times(-3)\times(-3)\times(-3) = (-3)^4 = (-3)^{6-2}$$

and, $$b^9 \div b^3 = \frac{b^9}{b^3} = \frac{\not{b}\times\not{b}\times\not{b}\times b\times b\times b\times b\times b\times b}{\not{b}\times\not{b}\times\not{b}} = b\times b\times b\times b\times b\times b = b^6 = b^{9-3}$$

In all the above divisions of powers with the same base, we find that the divisions of powers with the same base is equal to a power of the same base whose exponent is equal to the difference of exponents of numerator and denominator.

Thus, we have the following law for the division of powers with the same base.

SECOND LAW *If a is any non-zero rational number and m and n are natural numbers such that m>n, then*

$$a^m \div a^n = a^{m-n} \text{ or, } \frac{a^m}{a^n} = a^{m-n}$$

ILLUSTRATION 2 Simplify and write each of the following in exponential form:

(i) $9^{11} \div 9^7$ (ii) $(-7)^{13} \div (-7)^9$ (iii) $\left(\frac{-3}{4}\right)^7 \div \left(\frac{-3}{4}\right)^5$

Solution Using second law of exponents, we have

(i) $9^{11} \div 9^7 = \frac{9^{11}}{9^7} = 9^{11-7} = 9^4$

(ii) $(-7)^{13} \div (-7)^9 = \frac{(-7)^{13}}{(-7)^9} = (-7)^{13-9} = (-7)^4$

(iii) $\left(\frac{-3}{4}\right)^7 \div \left(\frac{-3}{4}\right)^5 = \frac{\left(\frac{-3}{4}\right)^7}{\left(\frac{-3}{4}\right)^5} = \left(\frac{-3}{4}\right)^{7-5} = \left(\frac{-3}{4}\right)^2$

6.3.3 POWER WITH EXPONENT ZERO

Let us now find the value of a power of a non-zero rational number when its exponent is zero.

We know that

$$\frac{3^4}{3^4} = \frac{3\times3\times3\times3}{3\times3\times3\times3} = 1 \qquad \text{...(i)}$$

Also, $\frac{3^4}{3^4} = 3^{4-4}$ [Using second law of exponents]

$$= 3^0 \qquad \text{...(ii)}$$

We find that the left hand sides of (i) and (ii) are same.

So, their right hand sides are equal

$\therefore \quad 3^0 = 1$

Similarly,

$$\frac{7^3}{7^3} = \frac{7\times7\times7}{7\times7\times7} = 1 \text{ and } \frac{7^3}{7^3} = 7^{3-3} = 7^0$$

$$\therefore \quad 7^0 = 1$$

Also for any non-zero rational number a, we have

$$\frac{a^5}{a^5} = \frac{a\times a\times a\times a\times a}{a\times a\times a\times a\times a} = 1 \text{ and } \frac{a^5}{a^5} = a^{5-5} = a^0$$

$$\therefore \quad a^0 = 1$$

It follows from the above discussion that for any non-zero rational number a, we have

$$a^0 = 1$$

6.3.4 POWER OF A POWER

Let us now find what is the power of a power. In order to find it, let us consider the following powers:

$$(3^2)^5 = 3^2\times3^2\times3^2\times3^2\times3^2 \quad \text{[Using definition of power]}$$

$$= 3^{2+2+2+2+2} \quad \text{[Using first law of exponents]}$$

$$= 3^{10} = 3^{2\times5}$$

$$\left\{\left(\frac{3}{2}\right)^3\right\}^2 = \left(\frac{3}{2}\right)^3\times\left(\frac{3}{2}\right)^3 \quad \text{[Using definition of power]}$$

$$= \left(\frac{3}{2}\right)^{3+3} \quad \text{[Using first law of exponents]}$$

$$= \left(\frac{3}{2}\right)^6 = \left(\frac{3}{2}\right)^{3\times2}$$

$$(a^3)^4 = a^3\times a^3\times a^3\times a^3 \quad \text{[Using definition of power]}$$

$$= a^{3+3+3+3} \quad \text{[Using first law of exponents]}$$

$$= a^{12} = a^{3\times4}$$

It follows from the above discussion that the power of a power is equal to the power with the same base and exponent equal to the product of the exponents.

This suggests us the following law.

THIRD LAW *If a is any rational number different from zero and m, n are natural numbers, then*

$$(a^m)^n = a^{m\times n} = (a^n)^m$$

ILLUSTRATION 3 Simplify and write each of the following in exponential form:

(i) $(2^3)^4$ (ii) $\left((-3)^5\right)^3$

(iii) $\left\{\left(\frac{2}{3}\right)^2\right\}^5$ (iv) $(3^2)^5\times(3^4)^2$

Solution Using the third law of exponents, we have

(i) $(2^3)^4 = 2^{3\times 4} = 2^{12}$

(ii) $\left((-3)^5\right)^3 = (-3)^{5\times 3} = (-3)^{15}$

(iii) $\left\{\left(\frac{2}{3}\right)^2\right\}^5 = \left(\frac{2}{3}\right)^{2\times 5} = \left(\frac{2}{3}\right)^{10}$

(iv) $(3^2)^5 \times (3^4)^2 = (3^{2\times 5}) \times (3^{4\times 2})$

$= 3^{10} \times 3^8 = 3^{10+8}$ [Using first law of exponents]

$= 3^{18}$

6.3.5 MULTIPLYING POWERS WITH THE SAME EXPONENTS

In the first law of exponents, we have learnt about the product (or multiplication) of powers with the same base. Now, let us find the product of powers with different bases and same exponents.

Consider the following products:

$$2^3 \times 3^3 = (2\times 2\times 2)\times(3\times 3\times 3)$$
$$= (2\times 3)\times(2\times 3)\times(2\times 3) = 6\times 6\times 6 = 6^3 = (2\times 3)^3$$
$$3^4 \times 5^4 = (3\times 3\times 3\times 3)\times(5\times 5\times 5\times 5)$$
$$= (3\times 5)\times(3\times 5)\times(3\times 5)\times(3\times 5) = 15\times 15\times 15\times 15 = 15^4 = (3\times 5)^4$$
$$2^3 \times b^3 = (2\times 2\times 2)\times(b\times b\times b) = (2\times b)\times(2\times b)\times(2\times b) = (2\times b)^3$$
$$x^5 \times y^5 = (x\times x\times x\times x\times x)\times(y\times y\times y\times y\times y)$$
$$= (x\times y)\times(x\times y)\times(x\times y)\times(x\times y)\times(x\times y)$$
$$= (xy)\times(xy)\times(xy)\times(xy)\times(xy) \qquad [\because\ x\times y = xy]$$
$$= (xy)^5$$

It is evident from the above computations that the product of powers with different bases and same exponents is equal to the power whose base is equal to the product of different bases and exponent equal to the common exponent.

Thus, we have the following law:

FOURTH LAW *If a , b are non-zero rational numbers and n is a natural number, then*

$$a^n \times b^n = (ab)^n$$

Generalisation: If a, b, c are non-zero rational numbers and n is a natural number, then

$$a^n \times b^n \times c^n = (abc)^n$$

ILLUSTRATION 4 Express each of the following products of powers as the exponent of a rational number:

(i) $2^5 \times 3^5$ (ii) $(-4)^3 \times (-2)^3$

(iii) $3^7 \times (-2)^7$ (iv) $\left(\frac{2}{3}\right)^3 \times \left(\frac{3}{5}\right)^3$

(v) $2^3 \times x^3 \times y^3$

Solution Using fourth law of exponents, we have

(i) $2^5 \times 3^5 = (2 \times 3)^5 = 6^5$

(ii) $(-4)^3 \times (-2)^3 = \{(-4) \times (-2)\}^3 = 8^3$

(iii) $3^7 \times (-2)^7 = \{3 \times (-2)\}^7 = (-6)^7$

(iv) $\left(\frac{2}{3}\right)^3 \times \left(\frac{3}{5}\right)^3 = \left(\frac{2}{3} \times \frac{3}{5}\right)^3 = \left(\frac{2}{5}\right)^3$

(v) $2^3 \times x^3 \times y^3 = (2 \times x \times y)^3 = (2xy)^3$

ILLUSTRATION 5 Express each of the following powers as the product of powers:

(i) $(3a)^5$ (ii) $(-4)^7$

Solution We have,

(i) $(3a)^5 = (3 \times a)^5 = 3^5 \times a^5$

(ii) $(-4)^7 = (-1 \times 4)^7 = (-1)^7 \times 4^7$

6.3.6 DIVIDING POWERS WITH THE SAME EXPONENTS

Second law of exponents tells us about the division of powers with the same bases. Let us now find the value of division of powers with different bases and same exponents.

Let us consider the following simplifications:

$$\frac{3^5}{4^5} = \frac{3 \times 3 \times 3 \times 3 \times 3}{4 \times 4 \times 4 \times 4 \times 4} = \frac{3}{4} \times \frac{3}{4} \times \frac{3}{4} \times \frac{3}{4} \times \frac{3}{4} = \left(\frac{3}{4}\right)^5$$

$$\frac{(-2)^3}{3^3} = \frac{(-2) \times (-2) \times (-2)}{3 \times 3 \times 3} = \left(\frac{-2}{3}\right) \times \left(\frac{-2}{3}\right) \times \left(\frac{-2}{3}\right) = \left(\frac{-2}{3}\right)^3$$

It is evident from the above simplifications that the division of powers with same exponents is equal to the power whose base is equal to the division of bases and exponent equal to the same exponent.

Thus, we have the following law of exponents:

FIFTH LAW *If a and b are non-zero rational numbers and n is a natural number, then*

$$\frac{a^n}{b^n} = \left(\frac{a}{b}\right)^n$$

ILLUSTRATION 6 Write each of the following in the form $\frac{p}{q}$:

(i) $\left(\frac{3}{5}\right)^3$ (ii) $\left(\frac{-2}{3}\right)^5$

Solution Using fifth law of exponents, we have

(i) $\left(\frac{3}{5}\right)^3 = \frac{3^3}{5^3} = \frac{3\times3\times3}{5\times5\times5} = \frac{27}{125}$

(ii) $\left(\frac{-2}{3}\right)^5 = \frac{(-2)^5}{3^5} = \frac{(-2)\times(-2)\times(-2)\times(-2)\times(-2)}{3\times3\times3\times3\times3} = \frac{-32}{243}$

Let us now discuss some examples on simplification of expressions by using the laws of exponents.

ILLUSTRATIVE EXAMPLES

Example 1 Using laws of exponents, simplify and write the answer in exponential form:

(i) $2^5\times2^3$ (ii) $3^2\times3^4\times3^8$ (iii) $6^{15}\div6^{10}$ (iv) $(5^3)^2$

(v) $(7^2)^3\div7^3$ (vi) $2^5\times3^5$ (vii) $a^4\times b^4$ (viii) $(2^{20}\div2^{15})\times2^3$

Solution Using the laws of exponents, we have

(i) $2^5\times2^3 = 2^{5+3} = 2^8$ [Using first law]

(ii) $3^2\times3^4\times3^8 = 3^{2+4+8} = 3^{14}$ [Using first law]

(iii) $6^{15}\div6^{10} = \frac{6^{15}}{6^{10}} = 6^{15-10} = 6^5$ [Using second law]

(iv) $(5^3)^2 = 5^{3\times2} = 5^6$ [Using third law]

(v) $(7^2)^3\div7^3 = \frac{(7^2)^3}{7^3} = \frac{7^{2\times3}}{7^3}$ [Using third law]

$= \frac{7^6}{7^3} = 7^{6-3} = 7^3$ [Using second law]

(vi) $2^5\times3^5 = (2\times3)^5 = 6^5$ [Using fourth law]

(vii) $a^4\times b^4 = (a\times b)^4 = (ab)^4$

(viii) $(2^{20}\div2^{15})\times2^3 = \left(\frac{2^{20}}{2^{15}}\right)\times2^3 = 2^{20-15}\times2^3 = 2^5\times2^3 = 2^{5+3} = 2^8$

Example 2 Simplify and express each of the following in exponential form:

(i) $\frac{3^7}{3^4\times3^3}$ (ii) $\left\{(5^2)^3\times5^4\right\}\div5^7$ (iii) $\left(\frac{3^7}{3^2}\right)\times3^5$ (iv) $\frac{4^5\times a^8b^3}{4^5\times a^5b^2}$

Solution (i) We have,

$\frac{3^7}{3^4\times3^3} = \frac{3^7}{3^{4+3}}$ [Using first law]

$= \frac{3^7}{3^7} = 3^{7-7} = 3^0 = 1$

(ii) We have,

$$\{(5^2)^3 \times 5^4\} \div 5^7 = \frac{\{(5^2)^3 \times 5^4\}}{5^7}$$

$$= \frac{5^{2\times 3} \times 5^4}{5^7} \qquad [\because (a^m)^n = a^{mn}]$$

$$= \frac{5^6 \times 5^4}{5^7} = \frac{5^{6+4}}{5^7} = \frac{5^{10}}{5^7} = 5^{10-7} = 5^3$$

(iii) We have,

$$\left(\frac{3^7}{3^2}\right) \times 3^5 = 3^{7-2} \times 3^5 = 3^5 \times 3^5 = 3^{5+5} = 3^{10}$$

(iv) We have,

$$\frac{4^5 \times a^8 b^3}{4^5 \times a^5 b^2} = \left(\frac{4^5}{4^5}\right) \times \left(\frac{a^8}{a^5}\right) \times \left(\frac{b^3}{b^2}\right)$$

$$= 4^{5-5} \times a^{8-5} \times b^{3-2}$$

$$= 4^0 \times a^3 \times b^1$$

$$= 1 \times a^3 \times b \qquad [\because 4^0 = 1 \text{ and } b^1 = b]$$

$$= a^3 b$$

Example 3 Simplify and express each of the following in exponential form:

(i) $2^5 \times 5^5$ (ii) $2^3 \times 2^2 \times 5^5$ (iii) $\{(2^2)^3 \times 3^6\} \times 5^6$ (iv) $\left(\frac{a}{b}\right)^5 \times b^{10}$

Solution We have,

(i) $2^5 \times 5^5 = (2 \times 5)^5 = 10^5$ $[\because a^n \times b^n = (ab)^n]$

(ii) $2^3 \times 2^2 \times 5^5 = (2^3 \times 2^2) \times 5^5 = 2^{3+2} \times 5^5 = 2^5 \times 5^5 = (2 \times 5)^5 = 10^5$

(iii) $\{(2^2)^3 \times 3^6\} \times 5^6 = \{2^{2\times 3} \times 3^6\} \times 5^6$ $[\because (a^m)^n = a^{mn} \therefore (2^2)^3 = 2^{2\times 3}]$

$$= (2^6 \times 3^6) \times 5^6$$

$$= (2 \times 3)^5 \times 5^6 \qquad [\because a^n \times b^n = (ab)^n]$$

$$= 6^6 \times 5^6$$

$$= (6 \times 5)^6 \qquad [\because a^n \times b^n = (ab)^n]$$

$$= 30^6$$

(iv) $\left(\frac{a}{b}\right)^5 \times b^{10} = \frac{a^5}{b^5} \times b^{10}$ $\left[\because \left(\frac{a}{b}\right)^n = \frac{a^n}{b^n}\right]$

$$= a^5 \times \frac{b^{10}}{b^5} = a^5 \times b^{10-5} = a^5 \times b^5 = (ab)^5$$

Example 4 Write exponential form for $8\times8\times8\times8$ taking base as 2.

Solution We have,

$$8\times8\times8\times8=8^4$$

$$=(2^3)^4 \qquad [\because 8=2\times2\times2=2^3]$$

$$=2^{3\times4} \qquad [\because (a^m)^n=a^{mn}]$$

$$=2^{12}$$

Example 5 Simplify and write each of the following in exponential form:

(i) $8^2\div2^3$ (ii) $25^4\div5^3$ (iii) $\dfrac{2^8\times a^5}{4^3\times a^3}$ (iv) $\dfrac{2^3\times3^4\times4}{3\times32}$

Solution We have,

(i) $$8^2\div2^3=\frac{8^2}{2^3}=\frac{(2^3)^2}{2^3} \qquad [\because 8=2\times2\times2=2^3]$$

$$=\frac{2^{3\times2}}{2^3} \qquad [\because (a^m)^n=a^{mn} \therefore (2^3)^2=2^{3\times2}]$$

$$=\frac{2^6}{2^3}=2^{6-3}=2^3$$

(ii) $$25^4\div5^3=\frac{25^4}{5^3}=\frac{(5^2)^4}{5^3} \qquad [\because 25=5\times5=5^2]$$

$$=\frac{5^{2\times4}}{5^3} \qquad [\because (a^m)^n=a^{mn} \therefore (5^2)^4=5^{2\times4}]$$

$$=\frac{5^8}{5^3}=5^{8-3}=5^5$$

(iii) $$\frac{2^8\times a^5}{4^3\times a^3}=\frac{2^8\times a^5}{(2^2)^3\times a^3} \qquad [\because 4=2\times2=2^2]$$

$$=\frac{2^8\times a^5}{2^{2\times3}\times a^3} \qquad [\because (2^2)^3=2^{2\times3}]$$

$$=\left(\frac{2^8}{2^6}\right)\times\left(\frac{a^5}{a^3}\right)=2^{8-6}\times a^{5-3}=2^2\times a^2=(2\times a)^2=(2a)^2$$

(iv) $$\frac{2^3\times3^4\times4}{3\times32}=\frac{2^3\times3^4\times2^2}{3\times2^5} \qquad [\because 4=2\times2=2^2 \text{ and } 32=2\times2\times2\times2\times2=2^5]$$

$$=\frac{2^3\times2^2\times3^4}{2^5\times3}=\frac{2^{3+2}\times3^4}{2^5\times3}$$

$$=\left(\frac{2^5}{2^5}\right)\times\left(\frac{3^4}{3^1}\right)=2^{5-5}\times3^{4-1}=2^0\times3^3=1\times3^3=3^3$$

Example 6 Simplify:

(i) $2^{55} \times 2^{60} - 2^{97} \times 2^{18}$ (ii) $2^3 \times a^3 \times 5a^4$

(iii) $\dfrac{3^n + 3^{n+1}}{3^{n+1} - 3^n}$, where n is a natural number.

Solution (i) We have,

$$2^{55} \times 2^{60} - 2^{97} \times 2^{18} = 2^{55+60} - 2^{97+18} = 2^{115} - 2^{115} = 0$$

(ii) We have,

$$2^3 \times a^3 \times 5a^4 = 2^3 \times 5 \times a^3 \times a^4 = 8 \times 5 \times a^{3+4} = 40 \times a^7 = 40a^7$$

(iii) We have,

$$\frac{3^n + 3^{n+1}}{3^{n+1} - 3^n} = \frac{3^n + 3^n \times 3^1}{3^n \times 3^1 - 3^n} \qquad [\because\ 3^{n+1} = 3^n \times 3^1]$$

$$= \frac{3^n \times 1 + 3^n \times 3}{3^n \times 3 - 3^n \times 1}$$

$$= \frac{3^n(1+3)}{3^n(3-1)} = \frac{3^n \times 4}{3^n \times 2} = \frac{3^n \times 2^2}{3^n \times 2}$$

$$= \frac{3^n}{3^n} \times \frac{2^2}{2} = 3^{n-n} \times 2^{2-1} = 3^0 \times 2^1 = 1 \times 2 = 2.$$

Example 7 Simplify:

(i) $\dfrac{12^4 \times 9^3 \times 4}{6^3 \times 8^2 \times 27}$ (ii) $\dfrac{25 \times 5^2 \times t^8}{10^3 \times t^4}$ (iii) $\dfrac{3^5 \times 10^5 \times 25}{5^7 \times 6^5}$

Solution (i) We have,

$$\frac{12^4 \times 9^3 \times 4}{6^3 \times 8^2 \times 27} = \frac{(2^2 \times 3)^4 \times (3^2)^3 \times 2^2}{(2 \times 3)^3 \times (2^3)^2 \times 3^3} \qquad \left[\begin{matrix}\because\ 12 = 2^2 \times 3, 9 = 3^2, 4 = 2^2, \\ 6 = 2 \times 3, 8 = 2^3 \text{ and } 27 = 3^3\end{matrix}\right]$$

$$= \frac{(2^2)^4 \times 3^4 \times (3^2)^3 \times 2^2}{(2^3 \times 3^3) \times (2^3)^2 \times 3^3} \qquad [\because\ (ab)^n = a^n \times b^n]$$

$$= \frac{2^8 \times 3^4 \times 3^6 \times 2^2}{2^3 \times 3^3 \times 2^6 \times 3^3} \qquad [\because\ (a^m)^n = a^{mn}]$$

$$= \frac{(2^8 \times 2^2) \times (3^4 \times 3^6)}{(2^3 \times 2^6) \times (3^3 \times 3^3)}$$

$$= \frac{2^{8+2} \times 3^{4+6}}{2^{3+6} \times 3^{3+3}} = \frac{2^{10} \times 3^{10}}{2^9 \times 3^6} = \left(\frac{2^{10}}{2^9}\right) \times \left(\frac{3^{10}}{3^6}\right)$$

$$= 2^{10-9} \times 3^{10-6} = 2^1 \times 3^4 = 2 \times 81 = 162$$

(ii) We have,

$$\frac{25\times 5^2\times t^8}{10^3\times t^4}=\frac{5^2\times 5^2\times t^8}{(2\times 5)^3\times t^4}=\frac{5^{2+2}\times t^8}{2^3\times 5^3\times t^4} \qquad [\because (2\times 5)^3 = 2^3\times 5^3]$$

$$=\frac{5^4\times t^8}{5^3\times 2^3\times t^4}=\frac{5^{4-3}\times t^{8-4}}{2^3}=\frac{5^1\times t^4}{2^3}=\frac{5t^4}{8}$$

(iii) We have,

$$\frac{3^5\times 10^5\times 25}{5^7\times 6^5}=\frac{3^5\times (2\times 5)^5\times 5^2}{5^7\times (2\times 3)^5}$$

$$=\frac{3^5\times 2^5\times 5^5\times 5^2}{5^7\times 2^5\times 3^5}$$

$$=\frac{3^5\times 2^5\times 5^7}{3^5\times 2^5\times 5^7}=3^{5-5}\times 2^{5-5}\times 5^{7-7}=3^0\times 2^0\times 5^0=1\times 1\times 1=1$$

Example 8 Express each of the following as a product of prime factors only in exponential form:

(i) 108×192 (ii) 729×64

Solution (i) Using prime factorisations of 108 and 192, we have

$108=2\times 2\times 3\times 3\times 3=2^2\times 3^3$

and, $192=2\times 2\times 2\times 2\times 2\times 2\times 3=2^6\times 3$

2	108
2	54
3	27
3	9
	3

2	192
2	96
2	48
2	24
2	12
2	6
	3

$\therefore \quad 108\times 192=(2^2\times 3^3)\times(2^6\times 3)$

$=(2^2\times 2^6)\times(3^3\times 3^1)$

$=2^{2+6}\times 3^{3+1}$

$=2^8\times 3^4$

(ii) Using prime factorisations of 729 and 64, we have

729×64

$=(3\times 3\times 3\times 3\times 3\times 3)\times(2\times 2\times 2\times 2\times 2\times 2)$

$=3^6\times 2^6$

3	729
3	243
3	81
3	27
3	9
	3

2	64
2	32
2	16
2	8
2	4
	2

Example 9 Compare the following numbers:

(i) 2.7×10^{12} and 1.5×10^8 (ii) 4×10^{14} and 3×10^7

Solution (i) We have,

$2.7\times 10^{12}=2.7\times 10\times 10^{11}=27\times 10^{11}$

and, $1.5\times 10^8=1.5\times 10\times 10^7=15\times 10^7$

$\therefore \quad 2.7\times 10^{12}-1.5\times 10^8=27\times 10^{11}-15\times 10^7$

$=27\times 10^7\times 10^4-15\times 10^7 \qquad [\because 10^{11}=10^{7+4}=10^7\times 10^4]$

$=3\times 10^7(9\times 10^4-5)$

$= 3 \times 10^7 (90000 - 5)$

$= 3 \times 10^7 \times 89995 > 0$

Hence, $2.7 \times 10^{12} > 1.5 \times 10^8$

(ii) We have,

$4 \times 10^{14} - 3 \times 10^7$

$= 4 \times 10^7 \times 10^7 - 3 \times 10^7$ $\quad [\because 10^{14} = 10^{7+7} = 10^7 \times 10^7]$

$= (4 \times 10^7 - 3) \times 10^7 > 0$ $\quad [\because 4 \times 10^7 - 3 > 0]$

$\therefore \quad 4 \times 10^{14} > 3 \times 10^7$

Example 10 Find the values of n in each of the following:

(i) $(2^2)^n = (2^3)^4$ (ii) $2^{5n} \div 2^n = 2^4$ (iii) $2^{n-5} \times 5^{n-4} = 5$

(iv) $2^{n-7} \times 5^{n-4} = 1250$ (v) $5^{n-2} \times 3^{2n-3} = 135$

Solution (i) We have,

$(2^2)^n = (2^3)^4$

$\Rightarrow \quad 2^{2n} = 2^{3\times4}$ $\quad [\because (a^m)^n = a^{mn}]$

$\Rightarrow \quad 2^{2n} = 2^{12}$

$\Rightarrow \quad 2n = 12$ $\quad$ [On equating the exponents]

$\Rightarrow \quad n = \frac{12}{2} = 6$

(ii) We have,

$2^{5n} \div 2^n = 2^4$

$\Rightarrow \quad \frac{2^{5n}}{2^n} = 2^4$

$\Rightarrow \quad 2^{5n-n} = 2^4$ $\quad \left[\because \frac{a^m}{a^n} = a^{m-n}\right]$

$\Rightarrow \quad 2^{4n} = 2^4$

$\Rightarrow \quad 4n = 4$ $\quad$ [On equating the exponents]

$\Rightarrow \quad n = \frac{4}{4} = 1$

(iii) We have,

$2^{n-5} \times 5^{n-4} = 5$

$\Rightarrow \quad \frac{2^n}{2^5} \times \frac{5^n}{5^4} = 5$ $\quad \left[\because 2^{n-5} = \frac{2^n}{2^5} \text{ and } 5^{n-4} = \frac{5^n}{5^4}\right]$

$\Rightarrow \quad \frac{2^n \times 5^n}{2^5 \times 5^4} = 5$

$\Rightarrow \quad (2^n \times 5^n) = 2^5 \times 5^4 \times 5$ $\quad$ [Using cross-multiplication]

$\Rightarrow \quad 2^n \times 5^n = 2^5 \times 5^{4+1}$

$\Rightarrow \quad 2^n \times 5^n = 2^5 \times 5^5$

$\Rightarrow \quad (2\times5)^n = (2\times5)^5$ $[\because\ a^n \times b^n = (ab)^n]$

$\Rightarrow \quad 10^n = 10^5$

$\Rightarrow \quad n = 5$ [On equating the exponents]

Aliter We have,

$2^{n-5} \times 5^{n-4} = 5$

$\Rightarrow \quad 2(2^{n-5} \times 5^{n-4}) = 2\times5$ [Multiplying both sides by 2]

$\Rightarrow \quad 2^{n-5+1} \times 5^{n-4} = 2\times5$

$\Rightarrow \quad 2^{n-4} \times 5^{n-4} = 2\times5$

$\Rightarrow \quad (2\times5)^{n-4} = 2\times5$

$\Rightarrow \quad 10^{n-4} = 10^1$

$\Rightarrow \quad n-4 = 1 \Rightarrow n = 5$

(iv) We have,

$2^{n-7} \times 5^{n-4} = 1250$

$\Rightarrow \quad \frac{2^n}{2^7} \times \frac{5^n}{5^4} = 2\times5^4$ $[\because\ 1250 = 2\times5^4]$

$\Rightarrow \quad \frac{2^n \times 5^n}{2^7 \times 5^4} = 2\times5^4$

$\Rightarrow \quad 2^n \times 5^n = 2^7 \times 5^4 \times 2 \times 5^4$ [Using cross-multiplication]

$\Rightarrow \quad 2^n \times 5^n = 2^{7+1} \times 5^{4+4}$ $[\because\ a^m \times a^n = a^{m+n}]$

$\Rightarrow \quad 2^n \times 5^n = 2^8 \times 5^8$

$\Rightarrow \quad (2\times5)^n = (2\times5)^8$ $[\because\ a^n \times b^n = (a\times b)^n$

$\Rightarrow \quad 10^n = 10^8$

$\Rightarrow \quad n = 8$

(v) We have,

$5^{n-2} \times 3^{2n-3} = 135$

$\Rightarrow \quad \frac{5^n}{5^2} \times \frac{3^{2n}}{3^3} = 3^3 \times 5$ $[\because\ 135 = 3^3 \times 5]$

$\Rightarrow \quad \frac{5^n \times 3^{2n}}{5^2 \times 3^3} = 3^3 \times 5$

$\Rightarrow \quad 5^n \times (3^2)^n = 5^2 \times 3^3 \times 3^3 \times 5$

$\Rightarrow \quad 5^n \times (3^2)^n = 3^{3+3} \times 5^{2+1}$

$\Rightarrow \quad 5^n \times (3^2)^n = 3^6 \times 5^3 = (3^2)^3 \times 5^3 = 5^3 \times (3^2)^3$

$\Rightarrow \quad (5\times3^2)^n = (5\times3^2)^3$

$\Rightarrow \quad (5\times9)^n = (5\times9)^3$

$\Rightarrow \quad 45^n = 45^3$

$\Rightarrow \quad n = 3$

Example 11 If $25^{n-1}+100=5^{2n-1}$, find the value of n.

Solution We have,

$$25^{n-1}+100=5^{2n-1}$$

$$\Rightarrow \quad 5^{2n-1}-25^{n-1}=100$$

$$\Rightarrow \quad \frac{5^{2n}}{5}-\frac{25^n}{25}=10^2$$

$$\Rightarrow \quad \frac{5^{2n}}{5}-\frac{(5^2)^n}{25}=(2\times 5)^2$$

$$\Rightarrow \quad \frac{5^{2n}}{5}-\frac{5^{2n}}{25}=2^2\times 5^2$$

$$\Rightarrow \quad 5^{2n}\times\frac{1}{5}-\frac{5^{2n}}{25}=2^2\times 5^2$$

$$\Rightarrow \quad 5^{2n}\times\left(\frac{1}{5}-\frac{1}{25}\right)=2^2\times 5^2$$

$$\Rightarrow \quad 5^{2n}\times\left(\frac{5-1}{25}\right)=2^2\times 5^2$$

$$\Rightarrow \quad 5^{2n}\times\frac{4}{25}=2^2\times 5^2$$

$$\Rightarrow \quad 5^{2n}\times\frac{2^2}{5^2}=2^2\times 5^2$$

$$\Rightarrow \quad 5^{2n}\times 2^2=2^2\times 5^2\times 5^2$$

$$\Rightarrow \quad 5^{2n}=\frac{2^2\times 5^2\times 5^2}{2^2}$$

$$\Rightarrow \quad 5^{2n}=2^{2-2}\times 5^{2+2}$$

$$\Rightarrow \quad 5^{2n}=2^0\times 5^4 \Rightarrow 5^{2n}=5^4 \Rightarrow 2n=4 \Rightarrow n=\frac{4}{2}=2$$

Example 12 Find n such that

(i) $\left(\frac{2}{3}\right)^3\times\left(\frac{2}{3}\right)^5=\left(\frac{2}{3}\right)^{n-2}$ (ii) $\left(\frac{125}{8}\right)^5\times\left(\frac{125}{8}\right)^n=\left(\frac{5}{2}\right)^{18}$

Solution (i) We have,

$$\left(\frac{2}{3}\right)^3\times\left(\frac{2}{3}\right)^5=\left(\frac{2}{3}\right)^{n-2}$$

$$\Rightarrow \quad \left(\frac{2}{3}\right)^{3+5}=\left(\frac{2}{3}\right)^{n-2}$$

$$\Rightarrow \quad \left(\frac{2}{3}\right)^8 = \left(\frac{2}{3}\right)^{n-2}$$

$\Rightarrow \quad 8 = n - 2$ [On equating the coefficients]

$\Rightarrow \quad n = 8 + 2 = 10$

(ii) We have,

$$\left(\frac{125}{8}\right)^5 \times \left(\frac{125}{8}\right)^n = \left(\frac{5}{2}\right)^{18}$$

$$\Rightarrow \quad \left\{\left(\frac{5}{2}\right)^3\right\}^5 \times \left\{\left(\frac{5}{2}\right)^3\right\}^n = \left(\frac{5}{2}\right)^{18} \qquad \left[\because \frac{125}{8} = \frac{5\times5\times5}{2\times2\times2} = \frac{5^3}{2^3} = \left(\frac{5}{2}\right)^3\right]$$

$$\Rightarrow \quad \left(\frac{5}{2}\right)^{3\times5} \times \left(\frac{5}{2}\right)^{3n} = \left(\frac{5}{2}\right)^{18}$$

$$\Rightarrow \quad \left(\frac{5}{2}\right)^{15} \times \left(\frac{5}{2}\right)^{3n} = \left(\frac{5}{2}\right)^{18}$$

$$\Rightarrow \quad \left(\frac{5}{2}\right)^{15+3n} = \left(\frac{5}{2}\right)^{18}$$

$$\Rightarrow \quad 15 + 3n = 18 \quad \Rightarrow \quad 3n = 18 - 15 \quad \Rightarrow \quad 3n = 3 \quad \Rightarrow \quad n = \frac{3}{3} = 1$$

Example 13 If $\frac{p}{q} = \left(\frac{2}{3}\right)^2 \div \left(\frac{6}{7}\right)^0$, find the value of $\left(\frac{q}{p}\right)^3$.

Solution We have,

$$\left(\frac{p}{q}\right) = \left(\frac{2}{3}\right)^2 \div \left(\frac{6}{7}\right)^0$$

$$\Rightarrow \quad \frac{p}{q} = \left(\frac{2}{3}\right)^2 \div 1 \qquad \left[\because \left(\frac{6}{7}\right)^0 = 1\right]$$

$$\Rightarrow \quad \frac{p}{q} = \left(\frac{2}{3}\right)^2$$

$$\Rightarrow \quad \frac{p}{q} = \frac{2^2}{3^2} = \frac{4}{9}$$

$$\Rightarrow \quad \frac{q}{p} = \frac{9}{4}$$

$$\Rightarrow \quad \frac{q}{p} = \frac{3^2}{2^2}$$

$$\Rightarrow \quad \frac{q}{p} = \left(\frac{3}{2}\right)^2$$

$$\Rightarrow \quad \left(\frac{q}{p}\right)^3 = \left\{\left(\frac{3}{2}\right)^2\right\}^3$$

$$\Rightarrow \quad \left(\frac{q}{p}\right)^3 = \left(\frac{3}{2}\right)^{2\times 3} = \left(\frac{3}{2}\right)^6 = \frac{3^6}{2^6} = \frac{729}{64}$$

Example 14 Find the value of m so that

$$(-3)^{m+1} \times (-3)^5 = (-3)^7$$

Solution We have,

$$(-3)^{m+1} \times (-3)^5 = (-3)^7$$

$$\Rightarrow \quad (-3)^{m+1+5} = (-3)^7$$

$$\Rightarrow \quad (-3)^{m+6} = (-3)^7$$

$$\Rightarrow \quad m+6 = 7 \quad \Rightarrow \quad m = 7-6 = 1$$

EXERCISE 6.2

1. Using laws of exponents, simplify and write the answer in exponential form:

   (i) $2^3 \times 2^4 \times 2^5$ (ii) $5^{12} \div 5^3$ (iii) $(7^2)^3$ (iv) $(3^2)^5 \div 3^4$

   (v) $3^7 \times 2^7$ (vi) $(5^{21} \div 5^{13}) \times 5^7$

2. Simplify and express each of the following in exponential form:

   (i) $\{(2^3)^4 \times 2^8\} \div 2^{12}$ (ii) $(8^2 \times 8^4) \div 8^3$ (iii) $\left(\frac{5^7}{5^2}\right) \times 5^3$ (iv) $\frac{5^4 \times x^{10} y^5}{5^4 \times x^7 y^4}$

3. Simplify and express each of the following in exponential form:

   (i) $\{(3^2)^3 \times 2^6\} \times 5^6$ (ii) $\left(\frac{x}{y}\right)^{12} \times y^{24} \times (2^3)^4$ (iii) $\left(\frac{5}{2}\right)^6 \times \left(\frac{5}{2}\right)^2$ (iv) $\left(\frac{2}{3}\right)^5 \times \left(\frac{3}{5}\right)^5$

4. Write $9 \times 9 \times 9 \times 9 \times 9$ in exponential form with base 3.

5. Simplify and write each of the following in exponential form:

   (i) $(25)^3 \div 5^3$ (ii) $(81)^5 \div (3^2)^5$ (iii) $\frac{9^8 \times (x^2)^5}{(27)^4 \times (x^3)^2}$ (iv) $\frac{3^2 \times 7^8 \times 13^6}{21^2 \times 91^3}$

6. Simplify:

   (i) $(3^5)^{11} \times (3^{15})^4 - (3^5)^{18} \times (3^5)^5$ (ii) $\frac{16 \times 2^{n+1} - 4 \times 2^n}{16 \times 2^{n+2} - 2 \times 2^{n+2}}$

   (iii) $\frac{10 \times 5^{n+1} + 25 \times 5^n}{3 \times 5^{n+2} + 10 \times 5^{n+1}}$ (iv) $\frac{(16)^7 \times (25)^5 \times (81)^3}{(15)^7 \times (24)^5 \times (80)^3}$

7. Find the values of n in each of the following:

   (i) $5^{2n} \times 5^3 = 5^{11}$ (ii) $9 \times 3^n = 3^7$ (iii) $8 \times 2^{n+2} = 32$ (iv) $7^{2n+1} \div 49 = 7^3$

   (v) $\left(\frac{3}{2}\right)^4 \times \left(\frac{3}{2}\right)^5 = \left(\frac{3}{2}\right)^{2n+1}$ (vi) $\left(\frac{2}{3}\right)^{10} \times \left\{\left(\frac{3}{2}\right)^2\right\}^5 = \left(\frac{2}{3}\right)^{2n-2}$

8. If $\frac{9^n \times 3^2 \times 3^n - (27)^n}{(3^3)^5 \times 2^3} = \frac{1}{27}$, find the value of n.

ANSWERS

1.	(i) 2^{12}	(ii) 5^9	(iii) 7^6	(iv) 3^6	(v) 6^7	(vi) 5^{15}
2.	(i) 2^8	(ii) 2^9	(iii) 5^8	(iv) x^3y		
3.	(i) 30^6	(ii) $(2xy)^{12}$	(iii) $\left(\frac{5}{2}\right)^8$	(iv) $\left(\frac{2}{5}\right)^5$		
4.	3^{10}	5. (i) 5^3	(ii) 3^{10}	(iii) $(3x)^4$	(iv) 91^3	
6.	(i) 0	(ii) $\frac{1}{2}$	(iii) $\frac{3}{5}$	(iv) 2		
7.	(i) 4	(ii) 5	(iii) 0	(iv) 2	(v) 4	(vi) 1
8.	4					

6.4 USE OF EXPONENTS IN EXPRESSING LARGE NUMBERS IN STANDARD FORM

In science and engineering and also in many other situations, we often come across numbers which are very large. For example, the mass of the Earth, the distance of Sun from Earth, number of stars in our Galaxy, speed of light etc. are numbers which are very large. Such large numbers are normally approximate, and not exact numbers. For the sake of convenience to read, write and remember such large numbers we write them as a certain number followed by a number of zeros. For example, the speed of light in vacuum is 299792.5 km per second. It is approximated as 300000 km per second or as 300,000,000 metre per second. Similarly, the mass of the earth is 5,976,000,000,000,000,000,000,000 kg. These numbers are not convenient to write and read. To make it convenient, we write these numbers by using exponents with base 10. For example, the speed of light in vacuum may be written as 3×10^8 metre per second or 30×10^7 metre per second or, 300×10^6 metre per second. Thus, every large number can be expressed as $k \times 10^n$, where k is some natural number. However, for the sake of uniformity, we write the numbers in the form $k \times 10^n$, where k is a terminating decimal number greater than or equal to 1 and less than 10 and n is a natural number. Using this notation the speed of light is written as 3×10^8 metre per second, the mass of the Earth is written as 5.976×10^{24} kg, etc.

Such a form of a number is known as its standard form as defined below:

STANDARD FORM *A number is said to be in the standard form, if it is expressed as the product of a number between 1 and 10 (including 1 but excluding 10) and a positive integer power of 10.*

The standard form of a number is also known as Scientific notation.

In order to write large numbers in the standard form, we may use the following steps:

STEP I *Obtain the number and move the decimal point to the left till you get just one digit to the left of the decimal point.*

STEP II *Write the given number as the product of the number so obtained and 10^n, where n is the number of places the decimal point has been moved to the left. If the given number is between 1 and 10, then write it as the product of the number itself and 10^0.*

Following examples will illustrate the above procedure.

ILLUSTRATIVE EXAMPLES

Example 1 Express the following numbers in the standard form:

(i) 3,90,878 (ii) 3,186,500,000 (iii) 65,950,000

Solution (i) We have,

$3,90,878 = 390878.00$

Clearly, the decimal point is moved through five places to obtain a number in which there is just one digit to the left of the decimal point.

$\therefore \quad 390878.00 = 3.90878 \times 10^5$

(ii) We have,

$$3,186,500,000 = 3.186500000 \times 10^9$$
$$= 3.1865 \times 10^9$$

(iii) We have,

$$65,950,000 = 65,950,000.00$$
$$= 6.5950000 \times 10^7$$
$$= 6.595 \times 10^7$$

Example 2 Write the following numbers in the usual form:

(i) 7.54×10^6 (ii) 9.325×10^{12} (iii) 8.4×10^2

Solution We have,

(i) $7.54 \times 10^6 = 7,540,000$

(ii) $9.325 \times 10^{12} = 9,325,000,000,000$

(iii) $8.4 \times 10^2 = 840$

EXERCISE 6.3

1. Express the following numbers in the standard form:
   (i) 3908.78 (ii) 5,00,00,000 (iii) 3,18,65,00,000 (iv) 846×10^7
   (v) 723×10^9
2. Write the following numbers in the usual form:
   (i) 4.83×10^7 (ii) 3.21×10^5 (iii) 3.5×10^3
3. Express the numbers appearing in the following statements in the standard form:
   (i) The distance between the Earth and the Moon is 384,000,000 metres.
   (ii) Diameter of the Earth is 1,27,56,000 metres.
   (iii) Diameter of the Sun is 1,400,000,000 metres.
   (iv) The universe is estimated to be about 12,000,000,000 years old.

ANSWERS

1. (i) 3.90878×10^3 (ii) 5×10^7 (iii) 3.1865×10^9 (iv) 8.46×10^9
   (v) 7.23×10^{11}

2. (i) 4,83,00,000 (ii) 3,21,000 (iii) 3,500

3. (i) 3.84×10^8 m (ii) 1.2756×10^7 m (iii) 1.4×10^9 m (iv) 1.2×10^{10} years old

6.5 DECIMAL NUMBER SYSTEM

In earlier classes, we have learnt about place value and face value of a digit in a number. We have learnt that a natural number can be written as the sum of the place values of all digits of the numbers. For example

$$6847 = 6\times1000 + 8\times100 + 4\times10 + 7\times1$$

Such a form of a natural number is known as its expanded form.

The expanded form of a number can also be expressed in terms of powers of 10 by using

$$10^0 = 1, 10^1 = 10, 10^2 = 100, 10^3 = 1000, 10^4 = 10000 \text{ etc.}$$

For example,

$$6847 = 6\times1000 + 8\times100 + 4\times10 + 7\times1$$

$$\Rightarrow \quad 6847 = 6\times10^3 + 8\times10^2 + 4\times10^1 + 7\times10^0$$

Similarly, we have

$$7504289 = 7\times1000000 + 5\times100000 + 0\times10000 + 4\times1000 + 2\times100 + 8\times10 + 9\times1$$

$$\Rightarrow \quad 7504289 = 7\times10^6 + 5\times10^5 + 0\times10^4 + 4\times10^3 + 2\times10^2 + 8\times10^1 + 9\times10^0.$$

Clearly, each digit of the natural number is multiplied by 10^n, where n is the number of digits to its right and then they are added.

EXERCISE 6.4

1. Write the following numbers in the expanded exponential forms:
   (i) 20068 (ii) 420719 (iii) 7805192 (iv) 5004132
   (v) 927303
2. Find the number from each of the following expanded forms:
   (i) $7\times10^4 + 6\times10^3 + 0\times10^2 + 4\times10^1 + 5\times10^0$
   (ii) $5\times10^5 + 4\times10^4 + 2\times10^3 + 3\times10^0$
   (iii) $9\times10^5 + 5\times10^2 + 3\times10^1$
   (iv) $3\times10^4 + 4\times10^2 + 5\times10^0$

ANSWERS

1. (i) $2\times10^4 + 0\times10^3 + 0\times10^2 + 6\times10^1 + 8\times10^0$
   (ii) $4\times10^5 + 2\times10^4 + 0\times10^3 + 7\times10^2 + 1\times10^1 + 9\times10^0$
   (iii) $7\times10^6 + 8\times10^5 + 0\times10^4 + 5\times10^3 + 1\times10^2 + 9\times10^1 + 2\times10^0$
   (iv) $5\times10^6 + 0\times10^5 + 0\times10^4 + 4\times10^3 + 1\times10^2 + 3\times10^1 + 2\times10^0$
   (v) $9\times10^5 + 2\times10^4 + 7\times10^3 + 3\times10^2 + 0\times10^1 + 3\times10^0$
2. (i) 76045 (ii) 542003 (iii) 900530 (iv) 30405

OBJECTIVE TYPE QUESTIONS

Mark the correct alternative in each of the following:

1. $(6^{-1} - 8^{-1})^{-1} =$

(a) $\frac{1}{24}$ (b) 24 (c) -24 (d) $-\frac{1}{24}$

2. $2^{3^2} =$

(a) 64 (b) 32 (c) 256 (d) 512

3. $(3^{-1} \times 5^{-1})^{-1} =$

(a) $\frac{1}{15}$ (b) $-\frac{1}{15}$ (c) 15 (d) -15

4. $\left(-\frac{3}{5}\right)^{-1} =$

(a) $\frac{3}{5}$ (b) $\frac{5}{3}$ (c) $-\frac{5}{3}$ (d) $-\frac{3}{5}$

5. $(-1)^{301} + (-1)^{302} + (-1)^{303} + \ldots + (-1)^{400}$

(a) 1 (b) 101 (c) 100 (d) 0

6. If $a = 25$, then $a^{25^0} + a^{0^{25}} =$

(a) 25 (b) 26 (c) 24 (d) 0

7. $\left\{\left(\frac{1}{3}\right)^{-3} - \left(\frac{1}{2}\right)^{-3}\right\} \div \left(\frac{1}{4}\right)^{-3} =$

(a) $\frac{19}{64}$ (b) $\frac{64}{19}$ (c) $\frac{27}{16}$ (d) $\frac{-19}{64}$

8. $(25^2 - 15^2)^{3/2} =$

(a) 4000 (b) 8000 (c) 3125 (d) 1024

9. If $\left(\frac{5}{3}\right)^{-5} \times \left(\frac{5}{3}\right)^{11} = \left(\frac{5}{3}\right)^{8x}$, then $x = ?$

(a) $-\frac{1}{2}$ (b) $-\frac{3}{4}$ (c) $\frac{3}{4}$ (d) $\frac{4}{3}$

10. $\left[\left\{\left(-\frac{1}{3}\right)^2\right\}^{-2}\right]^{-1} =$

(a) $\frac{1}{81}$ (b) $\frac{1}{9}$ (c) $-\frac{1}{81}$ (d) $-\frac{1}{9}$

11. $\frac{(144)^{1/2} + (256)^{1/2}}{3^2 - 2} =$

(a) 8 (b) 4 (c) -4 (d) -8

12. $(1+3+5+7+9+11)^{3/2} =$

(a) 36 (b) 216 (c) 256 (d) None of these

13. If $abc = 0$, then $\dfrac{\{(x^a)^b\}^c}{\{(x^b)^c\}^a} =$

(a) 3 (b) 0 (c) -1 (d) 1

14. $(2^3)^4 =$

(a) 2^{4^3} (b) 2^{3^4} (c) $(2^4)^3$ (d) None of these

15. $\{(33)^2 - (31)^2\}^{5/7} =$

(a) 64 (b) 16 (c) 32 (d) 4

16. If $abc = 0$, then find the value of $\{(x^a)^b\}^c$

(a) 1 (b) a (c) b (d) c

17. If $a = 3^{-3} - 3^3$ and $b = 3^3 - 3^{-3}$, then $\dfrac{a}{b} - \dfrac{b}{a}$

(a) 0 (b) 1 (c) -1 (d) 2

18. What should be multiplied to 6^{-2} so that the product may be equal to 216?

(a) 6^4 (b) 6^5 (c) 6^3 (d) 6

19. If $xyz = 0$, then find the value of $(a^x)^{yz} + (a^y)^{zx} + (a^z)^{xy} =$

(a) 3 (b) 2 (c) 1 (d) 0

20. If $2^n = 4096$, then $2^{n-5} =$

(a) 128 (b) 64 (c) 256 (d) 32

21. The number 4,70,394 is standard form is written as

(a) 4.70394×10^5 (b) 4.70394×10^4 (c) 47.0394×10^4 (d) 4703.94×10^2

22. The number 2.35×10^4 in the usual form is written as

(a) 2.35×10^3 (b) 23500 (c) 2350000 (d) 235×10^4

23. If $3^x = 6561$, then $3^{x-3} =$

(a) 81 (b) 243 (c) 729 (d) 27

24. If $2^n = 1024$, then $2^{\frac{n}{2}+2} =$

(a) 64 (b) 128 (c) 256 (d) 512

25. $(8^4 + 8^2)^{1/2} =$

(a) 84 (b) $8\sqrt{77}$ (c) 72 (d) $8\sqrt{65}$

ANSWSERS

1. (b)	2. (d)	3. (c)	4. (c)	5. (d)	6. (b)	7. (a)
8. (b)	9. (c)	10. (a)	11. (b)	12. (b)	13. (d)	14. (c)
15. (c)	16. (a)	17. (a)	18. (b)	19. (a)	20. (a)	21. (a)
22. (b)	23. (b)	24. (b)	25. (d)			

THINGS TO REMEMBER

1. *If a is a non-zero rational number and n is a natural number, then the product*

$$\underbrace{a \times a \times a \times \cdots \times a}_{(n\text{-times})}$$

is denoted by a^n and is read as 'a raised to the power n'. Rational number 'a' is called the base and natural number n is known as the exponent. Also, a^n is known as the exponential form of $\underbrace{a \times a \times a \times \cdots \times a}_{(n\text{-times})}$.

2. *For any non-zero rational number, we have*

$$a^0 = 1 \text{ and } a^1 = a$$

3. *If a and b are non-zero rational numbers and m and n are natural numbers, then following are the laws of exponents:*

(i) $a^m \times a^n = a^{m+n}$ (ii) $\frac{a^m}{a^n} = a^{m-n}$, where $m > n$

(iii) $(a^m)^n = a^{mn} = (a^n)^m$ (iv) $(a \times b)^n = a^n b^n$ (v) $\left(\frac{a}{b}\right)^n = \frac{a^n}{b^n}$

7

ALGEBRAIC EXPRESSIONS

7.1 INTRODUCTION

In class VI, we have learnt about literals and their addition, subtraction, multiplication and division. We have also studied about powers of literals, variables and constants. A symbol having a fixed numeric value is called a constant and a symbol which takes various numerical values is called a variable. A combination of constants and variables connected by the signs of addition, subtraction, multiplication and division is called an algebraic expression. In this chapter, we shall learn about simple algebraic expressions involving one or two variables. We shall also study about their addition and subtraction.

7.2 ALGEBRAIC EXPRESSION

In this section, we shall define an algebraic expression. We shall also define various types of algebraic expressions.

DEFINITION *A combination of constants and variables connected by the signs of fundamental operations of addition, subtraction, multiplication and division is called an algebraic expression.*

TERMS *Various parts of an algebraic expression which are separated by the signs + or – are called the 'terms' of the expression.*

ILLUSTRATION (i) $3x + 2y - 4z$ is an algebraic expression having $3x$, $2y$ and $-4z$ as its terms.

(ii) $5x^3 - 6x^2y + 8xy^3z - 7$ is an algebraic expression consisting of four terms, namely $5x^3$, $-6x^2y$, $8xy^3z$ and -7.

(iii) 4, $3x - 5$, $a^2 + b^2 + c^2 - ab - bc - ca$, $2x^3 + 5x$, $xy + xz$, $xy + yz + zx$, etc. are all algebraic expressions.

7.2.1 TYPES OF ALGEBRAIC EXPRESSIONS

MONOMIAL *An algebraic expression containing only one term is called a monomial.*

For example, $3, 2x, 5x^2y, -6\,abc, \frac{3}{2}ab^2c^3$ are all monomials.

BINOMIAL *An algebraic expression containing two terms is called a binomial.*

For example, $x + 3, 5 - 2x, a^2 - 2abc, x^3 + 7, \frac{2}{3}x^2 + xyz^2$ are all binomials.

Note that $3 + 7$ is not a binomial, because $3 + 7 = 10$, which is a monomial.

TRINOMIAL *An algebraic expression containing three terms is called a trinomial.*

For example, $2x - y + 3, x^2 + y^2 + z^2, 3 + xyz + x^3$ are all trinomials.

Note that $7 + 2x + 9$ is not a trinomial, because $7 + 2x + 9 = 16 + 2x$, which is a binomial.

QUADRINOMIAL *An algebraic expression containing four terms is called a quadrinomial.*

For example, $a^3 + b^3 + c^3 + 3abc, a^2 + b^2 + c^2 + 5, ab + bc + ca + abc$ are all quadrinomials.

POLYNOMIAL *An algebraic expression containing two or more terms is called a polynomial.*

It follows from the above definition that binomial, trinomial and quadrinomial etc. are polynomials.

ILLUSTRATION Identify the monomials, binomials, trinomials and quadrinomials among the following algebraic expressions:

(i) -7 (ii) $x + y$ (iii) $4.5a$ (iv) $a^3 - b^3$

(v) $a^2 + 2ab + b^2$ (vi) $ax + by + c$ (vii) $ax + by + cz + d$

(viii) $3xyz$ (ix) $x + y + z - xyz$

Solution Monomials are: (i), (iii) and (viii) Binomials are: (ii) and (iv)

Trinomials are: (v) and (vi) Quadrinomials are: (vii) and (ix).

7.3 FACTORS AND COEFFICIENTS

FACTORS *Each term in an algebraic expression is a product of one or more number(s) and/or literal number(s). These number(s) and/or literal number(s) are known as the factors of that term.*

ILLUSTRATION 1 (i) The monomial $7x$ is the product of number 7 and literal x. So, 7 and x are factors of the monomial $7x$.

(ii) In the binomial $3xy + 7z$, $3xy$ and $7z$ are two terms. In the term $3xy$, for instance, 3, x and y are its factors. Clearly, number 3 is the numerical factor, and x and y are literal factors.

(iii) In the term $-4xyz$, the numerical factor is -4 whereas x, y and z are literal factors.

(iv) In the binomial expression $-xy + 3$, the term $-xy$ has -1 as the numerical factor while x and y are literal factors. The term 3 has only numerical factor. It has no literal factor.

(v) In the algebraic expression $ab - c^2 - 7$ the term ab has numerical factor as 1 and literal factors are a and b. The term $-c^2$ has numerical factor as -1 and literal factors are c and c^2. The third term -7 has no literal factor.

CONSTANT TERM *A term of the expression having no literal factor is called a constant term.*

ILLUSTRATION 2 (i) In the binomial expression $5x + 7$, the constant term is 7.

(ii) In the trinomial expression $a^2 + b^2 - \frac{3}{4}$, the constant term is $\frac{-3}{4}$.

COEFFICIENT *In a term of an algebraic expression, any of the factors with the sign of the term is called the coefficient of the product of the other factors.*

ILLUSTRATION 3 (i) In the monomial $3xy$, the coefficient of y is $3x$, the coefficient of x is $3y$ and the coefficient of xy is 3.

(ii) Consider the term $-8xy$ in the binomial $-8xy + 7$. The coefficient of x in the term $-8xy$ is $-8y$, the coefficient of y is $-8x$ and the coefficient of xy is -8.

ILLUSTRATION 4 Write down the terms of the expression: $8x^4y - 7x^3yz + \frac{4}{3}x^2yz^2 - 2.5xyz$

What is the coefficient of x^2 in the term $\frac{4}{3}x^2yz^2$?

Solution The given expression has four terms, namely $8x^4y, -7x^3yz, \frac{4}{3}x^2yz^2$ and $-2.5\,xyz$

The coefficient of x^2 in the term $\frac{4}{3}x^2yz^2$ is $\frac{4}{3}yz^2$.

ILLUSTRATION 5 Write down the coefficients of a, ab and abc in the term $4a^4b^2c$ of the algebraic expression $4a^4b^2c - 3a^3b^2c + \frac{3}{2}ab^3c^2$.

Solution The given algebraic expression has three terms, namely, $4a^4b^2c, -3a^3b^2c$ and $\frac{3}{2}ab^3c^2$.

Consider the term $4a^4b^2c$

We have, $4a^4b^2c = 4a \,.\, a^3b^2c$

$\therefore$ Coefficient of a in $4a^4b^2c$ is $4a^3b^2c$

Also, $4a^4b^2c = 4a^3 \,.\, ab \,.\, bc$

$\therefore$ Coefficient of ab in $4a^4b^2c$ is $4a^3bc$

Again, $4a^4b^2c = 4 \,.\, abc \,.\, a^3b$

$\therefore$ Coefficient of abc in $4a^4b^2c$ is $4a^3b$.

7.4 LIKE AND UNLIKE TERMS

LIKE TERMS *The terms having the same literal factors are called like or similar terms.*

UNLIKE TERMS *The terms not having same literal factors are called unlike or dissimilar terms.*

ILLUSTRATION 1 (i) In the algebraic expression $5x^2y + 7xy^2 - 3xy - 4yx^2$, we have $5x^2y$ and $-4yx^2$ as like terms, whereas $7xy^2$ and $-3xy$ are unlike terms.

(ii) In the algebraic expression $a^2 - 3b^2 + 7b^2 - 9a^2 + 6ab + 5$, we have, a^2 and $-9a^2$ as like terms. Also, $-3b^2$ and $7b^2$ are like terms. But a^2, $7b^2$ and $6ab$ are unlike terms.

ILLUSTRATION 2 In the following write down the pairs which contain like terms:

(i) $3x, -7x$ (ii) $16x, 16y$ (iii) $x^2y, -7x^2y$

(iv) $9ab, -6b$ (v) $a^2, 4b^2$ (vi) $a^2b, 3a^2bc$

Solution

(i) In the pair $3x, -7x$ the literal factor x is the same. Hence, the pair $3x, -7x$ contains like terms.

(ii) In the pair $16x, 16y$ the literal factors x and y are not same. So, the pair $16x, 16y$ does not contain like terms.

(iii) Terms x^2y and $-7x^2y$ have the same literal factor x^2y. So, the pair $x^2y, -7x^2y$ is the pair of like terms.

(iv) Since the terms $9ab$ and $-6b$ have literal factors as ab and b. So, the pair $9ab, -6b$ is the pair of unlike terms.

(v) a^2 and $4b^2$ are unlike terms as their literal factors a^2 and b^2 are distinct.

(vi) a^2b and $3a^2bc$ are unlike terms as their literal factors a^2b and a^2bc are distinct.

ILLUSTRATION 3 Identify the like terms and also mention the coefficients of those terms in the following terms: $4xy$, $-5x^2y$, $-3yx$, $2xy^2$

Solution Clearly, terms $4xy$ and $-3yx = -3xy$ have xy as the same literal factor. So, $4xy$ and $-3yx$ are like terms among the given terms. The coefficients of xy in these two terms are 4 and -3 respectively.

Remark *If the coefficient of a term in an algebraic expression is 1, then '1' is usually omitted. For instance, 1a is written as a. Similarly, if the coefficient is –1, then also we omit 1. For instance, –1a is written as –a.*

7.5 FINDING THE VALUE OF AN ALGEBRAIC EXPRESSION

As we have studied in the earlier sections that an algebraic expression involves one or more terms and each term contains one or more literals and some numeric coefficient. Thus, to find the numeric value of an algebraic expression, we need to know the numerical values of all the literals appearing in it.

In order to find the value of an algebraic expression for given values of the literals involved in it, we replace the literals by their numeric values to obtain an arithmetic expression and then evaluate it by usual method of arithmetic.

The process of replacing the literals by their numeric values is called substitution.

The following procedure can be used to find the value of an algebraic expression for the given values of literals involved in it.

PROCEDURE

STEP I *Write the algebraic expression.*

STEP II *Obtain the values of literals involved in the expression.*

STEP III *Replace each literal by its numeric value to obtain an arithmetical expression.*

STEP IV *Simplify the arithmetical expression obtained in step III by the usual method of arithmetic.*

STEP V *The value obtained in step IV is the required value.*

Following illustration will illustrate the above procedure.

ILLUSTRATION 1 If $x = 1$ and $y = 2$, find the values of each of the following algebraic expressions:

(i) $2x + 3$ (ii) $3x - 5y$ (iii) $3x + 2y - 7$ (iv) x^2
(v) x^2y (vi) $x^2 + y^2$ (vii) $-y^2 + 3 - x^2$

Solution Substituting $x = 1$ and $y = 2$ in each of the following expressions, we have

(i) $2x + 3 = 2 \times 1 + 3 = 2 + 3 = 5$

(ii) $3x - 5y = 3 \times 1 - 5 \times 2 = 3 - 10 = -7$

(iii) $3x + 2y - 7 = 3 \times 1 + 2 \times 2 - 7 = 3 + 4 - 7 = 7 - 7 = 0$

(iv) $x^2 = (1)^2 = 1 \times 1 = 1$

(v) $x^2y = (1)^2 \times 2 = 1 \times 2 = 2$

(vi) $x^2 + y^2 = (1)^2 + (2)^2 = 1 + 4 = 5$

(vii) $-y^2 + 3 - x^2 = -(2)^2 + 3 - (1)^2 = -4 + 3 - 1 = -1 - 1 = -2.$

ILLUSTRATION 2 If $x = 1$, $y = -2$ and $z = 3$, find the values of each of the following algebraic expressions:

(i) $x^3 + y^3 + z^3 - 3xyz$ (ii) $3xy^4 - 15x^2y + 4z$

Solution Substituting $x = 1$, $y = -2$ and $z = 3$ in the given expressions, we have

(i) $x^3 + y^3 + z^3 - 3xyz$

$= (1)^3 + (-2)^3 + (3)^3 - 3 \times 1 \times -2 \times 3$

$= 1 + (-8) + 27 - 3 \times -6$

$= 1 - 8 + 27 + 18 = 46 - 8 = 38$

(ii) $3xy^4 - 15x^2y + 4z$

$= 3 \times 1 \times (-2)^4 - 15 \times (1)^2 \times (-2) + 4 \times 3$

$= 3 \times 16 - 15 \times -2 + 4 \times 3 = 48 + 30 + 12 = 90.$

ILLUSTRATION 3 Find the values of each of the following expressions for $a = 1$, $b = 2$ and $c = -1$.

(i) $a^2 + b^2 + 2ab$ (ii) $2a^2 - b^2c + 3abc$

(iii) $a^3 + b^3 + c^3 - 3abc$ (iv) $a^2 + b^2 + c^2 - ab - bc - ca$

Solution Substituting $a = 1$, $b = 2$ and $c = -1$ in the given expressions, we have

(i) $a^2 + b^2 + 2ab = (1)^2 + 2^2 + 2 \times 1 \times 2 = 1 + 4 + 4 = 9$

(ii) $2a^2 - b^2c + 3abc = 2 \times (1)^2 - 2^2 \times (-1) + 3 \times 1 \times 2 \times (-1)$

$= 2 \times 1 - 4 \times (-1) + 6 \times (-1) = 2 + 4 - 6 = 0$

(iii) $a^3 + b^3 + c^3 - 3abc = (1)^3 + (2)^3 + (-1)^3 - 3 \times 1 \times 2 \times (-1)$

$= 1 + 8 - 1 + 6 = 15 - 1 = 14$

(iv) $a^2 + b^2 + c^2 - ab - bc - ca = (1)^2 + (2)^2 + (-1)^2 - 1 \times 2 - 2 \times (-1) - (-1) \times 1$

$= 1 + 4 + 1 - 2 + 2 + 1 = 9 - 2 = 7.$

ILLUSTRATIVE EXAMPLES

Example 1 Identify the monomials, binomials, trinomials and quadrinomials from the following expressions:

(i) $4x^2$ (ii) $x^2 - 1$ (iii) $x^2 - y^2$

(iv) $3x^2 + 4y^2 + 5z$ (v) $ax^2 + bx + c$ (vi) $a^2 + b^2 + c^2 - d^2$

(vii) $3ab^2$ (viii) $a^3 + b^3 - 3ab + 5$ (ix) $-xyz$

(x) $3x - 2$ (xi) $4x - 3x$

Solution

(i) $4x^3$ is a monomial expression as it contains one term only.

(ii) $x^2 - 1$ is a binomial expression because it contains two terms.

(iii) $x^2 - y^2$ is a binomial expression as it consists of two terms.

(iv) $3x^2 - 4y^3 + 5z$ contains three terms. So, it is trinomial.

(v) $ax^2 + bx + c$ contains three terms. So, it is trinomial.

(vi) $a^2 + b^2 + c^2 - d^2$ is quadrinomial, because it contains four terms.

(vii) $3ab^2$ is monomial as it contains just one term.

(viii) $a^3 + b^3 - 3ab + 5$ contains four terms. So, it is quadrinomial.

(ix) $-xyz$ contains just one term. So, it is a monomial.

(x) $3x - 2$ contains two terms. So, it is a binomial expression.

(xi) We have, $4x - 3x = x$. So. it is monomial.

Example 2 Write all the terms of each of the following algebraic expressions:

(i) $3x^5 + 5y^4 - 7x^2y + 7$ (ii) $9y^3 - 2z^3 + 7x^3y - 3xyz$

(iii) $a^5 - 3ab - b^2 + 6$ (iv) $x^2 - x + 1$

Solution (i) $3x^5, 5y^4, -7x^2y$ and 7 are the terms of the algebraic expressions $3x^5 + 5y^4 - 7x^2y + 7$.

(ii) Terms of the algebraic expression $9y^3 - 2z^3 + 7x^3y - 3xyz$ are $9y^3, -2z^3$, $7x^3y$ and $-3xyz$.

(iii) The algebraic expression $a^5 - 3ab - b^2 + 6$ has $a^5, -3ab, -b^2$ and 6 as it terms.

(iv) Various terms of the algebraic expression $x^2 - x + 1$ are $x^2, -x$ and 1.

Example 3 Write down the coefficient of x in each of the following:

(i) $3x$ (ii) $-4ax$ (iii) $5xy^2$

(iv) xyz (v) $-\frac{3}{2}x + 5$ (vi) $-\frac{5}{2}xyz^2$

Solution (i) The coefficient of x in $3x$ is 3.

(ii) The coefficient of x in $-4ax$ is $-4a$

(iii) The coefficient of x in $5xy^2$ is $5y^2$.

(iv) The coefficient of x in xyz is yz

(v) The coefficient of x in $-\frac{3}{2}x + 5$ is $-\frac{3}{2}$

(vi) The coefficient of x in $-\frac{5}{2}xyz^2$ is $-\frac{5}{2}yz^2$

Example 4 Write the numerical coefficient of each term of the following algebraic expressions:

(i) $x^3 - 7x^2y + 5xy^2 - 2$ (ii) $-2a^3 + 7ab^2 - 6ab + 8$

Solution (i) Various terms of the algebraic expression $x^3 - 7x^2y + 5xy^2 - 2$ are x^3, $-7x^2y$, $5xy^2$ and -2. The numerical coefficients of these terms are 1, -7, 5 and -2 respectively.

(ii) Various terms of $-2a^3 + 7ab^2 - 6ab + 8$ are $-2a^3$, $7ab^2$, $-6ab$ and 8. The numerical coefficients of these terms are -2, 7, -6 and 8 respectively.

Example 5 Identify the like terms in each of the following:

(i) $x^2, y^2, 2x^2, z^2$ (ii) $2xy, yz, 3x, \frac{yz}{2}$ (iii) $-2x^2y, x^2z, -yx^2, x^2y^2$

(iv) $cab^2, a^2bc, b^2ac, c^2ab, ab^2c, abc, acb^2$

Solution Recall that the terms having the same literal factors are called like terms.

(i) In $x^2, y^2, 2x^2, z^2$ we have x^2 and $2x^2$ as like terms.

(ii) In $2xy, yz, 3x, \frac{1}{2}yz$ like terms are yz and $\frac{1}{2}yz$.

(iii) $-2x^2y, x^2z, -yx^2, x^2y^2$ like terms are $-2x^2y$ and $-yx^2$

(iv) In cab^2, a^2bc, b^2ac, c^2ab, ab^2c, abc, acb^2 like terms are cab^2, b^2ac, ab^2c and acb^2

Example 6 Identify the like terms in each of the following algebraic expressions:

(i) $x-2y+3z-4x+3xy$ (ii) $3a+2b-c+\frac{3}{2}a-4+3b$

(iii) $xy^2+3x^2y-4x^2y^2-5y^2x-2z^2x+3xz^2$

Solution (i) In the algebraic expression $x-2y+3z-4x+3xy$ like terms are x and $-4x$.

(ii) In the algebraic expression $3a+2b-c+\frac{3}{2}a-4+3b$, the groups of like terms are $3a, \frac{3}{2}a$ and $2b, 3b$.

(iii) In the algebraic expression $xy^2+3x^2y-4-x^2y^2-5y^2x-2z^2x+3xz^2$, the groups of like terms are $xy^2, -5y^2x$ and $-2z^2x, 3xz^2$.

Example 7 Evaluate each of the following algebraic expressions for $x = 2, y = -3, z = -2, a = 2, b = 3$:

(i) $2a^2+ab$ (ii) $2a^2+x^2-y^2$ (iii) $x^3-y^3+z^3$

(iv) $4xy^2-3yz^2+4x^2z$ (v) $x^3+y^3+3xyz+ab$ (vi) $5+4z^3-6y+7a+xy$

Solution Substituting $x=2, y=-3, z=-2, a=2$ and $b=3$ in the given expressions, we have

(i) $2a^2+ab = 2\times(2)^2+2\times3 = 2\times4+2\times3 = 8+6 = 14$

(ii) $2a^2+x^2-y^2 = 2\times(2)^2+2^2-(-3)^2 = 2\times4+4-9 = 8+4-9 = 3$

(iii) $x^3-y^3+z^3 = 2^3-(-3)^3+(-2)^3 = 8-(-27)+(-8) = 8+27-8 = 27$

(iv) $4xy^2-3yz^2+4x^2z = 4\times2\times(-3)^2-3\times(-3)\times(-2)^2+4\times(2)^2\times(-2)$

$= 4\times2\times9-3\times(-3)\times4+4\times4\times-2$

$= 72+36-32 = 76$

(v) $x^3+y^3+3xyz+ab = 2^3+(-3)^3+3\times2\times-3\times-2+2\times3$

$= 8+(-27)+36+6 = 8-27+36+6 = 23$

(vi) $5+4z^3-6y+7a+xy = 5+4\times(-2)^3-6\times(-3)+7\times2+2\times-3$

$= 5+4\times-8+6\times3+7\times2-2\times3$

$= 5-32+18+14-6 = 37-38 = -1$

EXERCISE 7.1

1. Identify the monomials, binomials, trinomials and quadrinomials from the following expressions:

(i) a^2 (ii) a^2-b^2 (iii) $x^3+y^3+z^3$ (iv) $x^3+y^3+z^3+3xyz$

(v) $7+5$ (vi) $abc+1$ (vii) $3x-2+5$ (viii) $2x-3y+4$

(ix) $xy+yz+zx$ (x) ax^3+bx^2+cx+d

2. Write all the terms of each of the following algebraic expressions:

(i) $3x$ (ii) $2x-3$ (iii) $2x^2-7$ (iv) $2x^2+y^2-3xy+4$

3. Identify the like terms and also mention the numerical coefficients of those terms:

(i) $4xy, -5x^2y, -3yx, 2xy^2$ (ii) $7a^2bc, -3ca^2b, -\frac{5}{2}abc^2, \frac{3}{2}abc^2, -\frac{4}{3}cba^2$

4. Identify the like terms in the following algebraic expressions:

(i) $a^2+b^2-2a^2+c^2+4a$ (ii) $3x+4xy-2yz+\frac{5}{2}zy$

(iii) $abc+ab^2c+2acb^2+3c^2ab+b^2ac-2a^2bc+3cab^2$

5. Write the coefficient of x in the following:

(i) $-12x$ (ii) $-7xy$ (iii) xyz (iv) $-7ax$

6. Write the coefficient of x^2 in the following:

(i) $-3x^2$ (ii) $5x^2yz$ (iii) $\frac{5}{7}x^2z$ (iv) $-\frac{3}{2}ax^2+yx$

7. Write the coefficient of:

(i) y in $-3y$ (ii) a in $2ab$ (iii) z in $-7xyz$ (iv) p in $-3pqr$

(v) y^2 in $9xy^2z$ (vi) x^3 in x^3+1 (vii) x^2 in $-x^2$

8. Write the numerical coefficient of each of the following:

(i) xy (ii) $-6yz$ (iii) $7abc$ (iv) $-2x^3y^2z$

9. Write the numerical coefficient of each term in the following algebraic expressions:

(i) $4x^2y-\frac{3}{2}xy+\frac{5}{2}xy^2$ (ii) $-\frac{5}{3}x^2y+\frac{7}{4}xyz+3$

10. Write the constant term of each of the following algebraic expressions:

(i) $x^2y-xy^2+7xy-3$ (ii) a^3-3a^2+7a+5

11. Evaluate each of the following expressions for $x=-2, y=-1, z=3$:

(i) $\frac{x}{y}+\frac{y}{z}+\frac{z}{x}$ (ii) $x^2+y^2+z^2-xy-yz-zx$

12. Evaluate each of the following algebraic expressions for $x=1, y=-1, z=2, a=-2, b=1, c=-2$:

(i) $ax+by+cz$ (ii) $ax^2+by^2-cz^2$ (iii) $axy+byz+cxy$

ANSWERS

1. (i) Monomial (ii) Binomial (iii) Trinomial (iv) Quadrinomial (v) Monomial (vi) Binomial (vii) Binomial (viii) Trinomial (ix) Trinomial (x) Quadrinomial

2. (i) $3x$ (ii) $2x, -3$ (iii) $2x^2, -7$ (iv) $2x^2, y^2, -3xy, 4$

3.
Like terms	Coefficients
(i) $4xy, -3yx$	$4, -3$
(ii) $7a^2bc, -3ca^2b, -\frac{4}{3}cba^2, -\frac{5}{2}abc^2, \frac{3}{2}abc^2$	$7, -3, -\frac{4}{3}, -\frac{5}{2}, \frac{3}{2}$

4. (i) $a^2, -2a^2$ (ii) $-2yz, \frac{5}{2}zy$ (iii) $ab^2c, 2acb^2, b^2ac, 3cab^2$

5. (i) –12 (ii) $-7y$ (iii) yz (iv) $-7a$

6. (i) –3 (ii) $5yz$ (iii) $\frac{5}{7}z$ (iv) $-\frac{3}{2}a$

7. (i) –3 (ii) $2b$ (iii) $-7xy$ (iv) $-3qr$ (v) $9xz$ (vi) 1 (vii) –1

8. (i) 1 (ii) –6 (iii) 7 (iv) –2

9. (i) $4, -\frac{3}{2}, \frac{5}{2}$ (ii) $-\frac{5}{3}, \frac{7}{4}, 3$ 10. (i) –3 (ii) 5 11. (i) $\frac{1}{6}$ (ii) 21

12. (i) –7 (ii) 7 (iii) 2

7.6 OPERATIONS ON ALGEBRAIC EXPRESSIONS

In the previous sections, we have learnt about algebraic expressions and like and unlike terms in an algebraic expression. In this section, we shall study about the fundamental operations of addition and subtraction of algebraic expressions. Since an algebraic expression may consist of like and unlike terms. So, the operations of addition and subtraction of algebraic expressions mean addition or subtraction of like terms. We shall first study addition of like terms.

7.6.1 ADDITION OF POSITIVE LIKE TERMS

To add several positive like terms, we proceed as follows:

STEP I *Obtain all like terms.*

STEP II *Find the sum of the numerical coefficients of all terms.*

STEP III *Write the required sum as a like term whose numerical coefficient is the numerical obtained in step II and literal factor is same as the literal factors of the given like terms.*

ILLUSTRATION 1 Add $4xy$, $12xy$ and $3xy$.

Solution The sum of the numerical coefficients of the given like terms is $4 + 12 + 3 = 19$.

Thus, the sum of the given like terms is another like term whose numerical coefficient is 19.

Hence, $4xy + 12xy + 3xy = 19xy$.

Aliter The sum of the given like terms can also be obtained by using the distributive property of multiplication over addition as discussed below:

$4xy + 12xy + 3xy = (4 + 12 + 3)xy = 19xy$.

ILLUSTRATION 2 Add $3a^2b$, $2a^2b$, $13a^2b$ and a^2b.

Solution The sum of the numerical coefficients of the given like terms is

$3 + 2 + 13 + 1 = 19$

So, the sum of the given like terms is another like term whose numerical coefficient is 19.

Hence, $3a^2b + 2a^2b + 13a^2b + a^2b = 19a^2b$.

Aliter By using the distributive property of multiplication over addition, we have

$3a^2b + 2a^2b + 13a^2b + a^2b = (3 + 2 + 13 + 1)a^2b = 19a^2b$.

7.6.2 ADDITION OF NEGATIVE LIKE TERMS

To add negative like terms, we proceed as follows:

STEP I *Obtain all like terms.*

STEP II *Obtain the sum of the numerical coefficients (without negative sign) of all like terms.*

STEP III *Write an expression as a product of the number obtained is step II, with all the literal coefficients preceded by a minus sign.*

STEP IV *The expression obtained in step III is the required sum.*

ILLUSTRATION 1 Add $-7xy$, $-3xy$ and $-9xy$.

Solution The numerical coefficients (without negative sign) of the given like terms are 7, 3, 9.

$\therefore$ Sum of the numerical coefficients $= 7 + 3 + 9 = 19$.

So, the sum of the given like terms is another like term whose numerical coefficient is 19.

Hence, $-7xy - 3xy - 9xy = -19xy$.

Aliter Using the distributive property of multiplication over addition, we have

$-7xy - 3xy - 9xy = (-7 - 3 - 9)xy = -19xy$.

ILLUSTRATION 2 Add $-4a^2y, -7a^2y, -10a^2y$ and $-3a^2y$.

Solution The sum of the numerical coefficients (without negative sign) is

$4 + 7 + 10 + 3 = 24$

Hence, $-4a^2y - 7a^2y - 10a^2y - 3a^2y = -24a^2y$.

7.6.3 ADDITION OF POSITIVE AND NEGATIVE LIKE TERMS

To add positive and negative like terms, we proceed as follows:

STEP I *Collect all positive like terms and find their sum.*

STEP II *Collect all negative like terms and find their sum.*

STEP III *Obtain the numerical coefficients (without negative sign) of like terms obtained in steps I and II.*

STEP IV *Subtract the numerical coefficient in step II from the numerical coefficient in step I. Write the answer as a product of this number and all the literal coefficients.*

ILLUSTRATION 1 Add $4x^2y$, $8x^2y$ and $-2x^2y$.

Solution We have,

$4x^2y + 8x^2y - 2x^2y$

$= (4x^2y + 8x^2y) - 2x^2y$ [Collecting + ive and – ive like terms together]

$= 12x^2y - 2x^2y$

$= 10x^2y$ [$\because 12 - 2 = 10$]

Aliter $4x^2y + 8x^2y - 2x^2y = (4 + 8 - 2)\,x^2y = 10x^2y$.

ILLUSTRATION 2 Add $4ab, -7ab, -10ab$ and $3ab$.

Solution We have,

$4ab - 7ab - 10ab + 3ab$

$= 4ab + 3ab - 7ab - 10ab$ [Collecting + ive and – ive like terms together]

$= 7ab - 17ab$ [$\because 4ab + 3ab = 7ab$ and $-7ab - 10ab = -17ab$]

$= -10ab$ [$\because 7 - 17 = -10$]

Aliter $4ab - 7ab - 10ab + 3ab = (4 - 7 - 10 + 3)\,ab = -10ab$.

7.7 ADDITION OF ALGEBRAIC EXPRESSIONS WITH LIKE AND UNLIKE TERMS

In adding algebraic expressions containing like and unlike terms, we collect different groups of like terms and find the sum of like terms in each group by the methods discussed above. The collection of like terms can be done by any one of the following two methods:

(i) HORIZONTAL METHOD

In this method, all expressions are written in a horizontal line and then the terms are arranged to collect all the groups of like terms and then added.

(ii) COLUMN METHOD

In this method, each expression is written in a separate row such that their like terms are arranged one below the other in a column. Then the addition of terms is done columnwise. Following illustrations will illustrate these methods.

ILLUSTRATION 1 Add the following:

(i) $3x + 2y$ and $x + y$ (ii) $x + y + 3$ and $3x + 2y + 5$

(iii) $2x + 3y + z$ and $2x - y - z$

Solution (i) *Horizontal Method* *Column Method*

$(3x + 2y) + (x + y)$
$= (3 + 1)x + (2 + 1)y$
$= 4x + 3y$

$$\begin{array}{r} 3x + 2y \\ + \quad x + y \\ \hline 4x + 3y \end{array}$$

(ii) *Horizontal Method* *Column Method*

$(x + y + 3) + (3x + 2y + 5)$
$= (x + 3x) + (y + 2y) + (3 + 5)$
$= (1 + 3)x + (1 + 2)y + (3 + 5)$
$= 4x + 3y + 8$

$$\begin{array}{r} x + y + 3 \\ + \; 3x + 2y + 5 \\ 4x + 3y + 8 \\ \hline \end{array}$$

(iii) *Horizontal Method* *Column Method*

$(2x + 3y + z) + (2x - y - z)$
$= (2x + 2x) + (3y - y) + (z - z)$
$= (2 + 2)x + (3 - 1)y + (1 - 1)z$
$= 4x + 2y + 0z$
$= 4x + 2y.$

$$\begin{array}{r} 2x + 3y + z \\ + \; 2x - y - z \\ 4x + 2y \\ \hline \end{array}$$

ILLUSTRATION 2 Add:

(i) $xy^2 + 4x^2y - 7x^2y - 3xy^2 + 3$ and $x^2y + xy^2$

(ii) $5x^2 + 7y - 6z^2$, $4y + 3x^2$, $9x^2 + 2z^2 - 9y$ and $2y - 2x^2$

Solution (i) We have,

$xy^2 + 4x^2y - 7x^2y - 3xy^2 + 3$
$= xy^2 - 3xy^2 + 4x^2y - 7x^2y + 3$
$= (1 - 3)xy^2 + (4 - 7)x^2y + 3$
$= -2xy^2 - 3x^2y + 3$ ...(i)

Horizontal Method *Column Method*

$= (xy^2 + 4x^2y - 7x^2y - 3xy^2 + 3) + x^2y + xy^2$
$= -2xy^2 - 3x^2y + 3 + x^2y + xy^2$ [Using (i)]
$= -2xy^2 + xy^2 - 3x^2y + x^2y + 3$

$$\begin{array}{r} -2\,xy^2 - 3x^2y + 3 \\ + \quad xy^2 + x^2y \\ \hline - \; xy^2 - 2x^2y + 3 \end{array}$$

$= (-2 + 1)xy^2 + (-3 + 1)x^2y + 3$

$= -xy^2 - 2x^2y + 3$

(ii) *Horizontal Method*

$(5x^2 + 7y - 6z^2) + (4y + 3x^2) + (9x^2 + 2z^2 - 9y) + (2y - 2x^2)$

$= (5x^2 + 3x^2 + 9x^2 - 2x^2) + (7y + 4y - 9y + 2y) + (-6z^2 + 2z^2)$

$= (5 + 3 + 9 - 2)x^2 + (7 + 4 - 9 + 2)y + (-6 + 2)z^2$

$= 15x^2 + 4y - 4z^2$

Column Method

$$\begin{array}{r} 5x^2 + 7y - 6z^2 \\ +\ 3x^2 + 4y \qquad \\ +\ 9x^2 - 9y + 2z^2 \\ -\ 2x^2 + 2y \qquad \\ \hline 15x^2 + 4y - 4z^2 \end{array}$$

7.8 SUBTRACTION OF ALGEBRAIC EXPRESSIONS

To subtract an algebraic expression from another, we should change the signs (from ' + ' to ' – ' or from ' – ' to ' + ') of all the terms of the expression which is to be subtracted and then the two expressions are added.

In the subtraction of two expressions by column method, we indicate the change of sign of every term in the expression to be subtracted below the original sign of each term.

Following examples will illustrate the procedure.

ILLUSTRATIVE EXAMPLES

Example 1 Subtract:

(i) $5x$ from $9x$ (ii) $-7x$ from $5x$ (iii) $-8a$ from $-3a$

Solution (i) $9x - 5x = (9 - 5)x = 4x$

(ii) $5x - (-7x) = 5x + 7x = (5 + 7)x = 12x$

(iii) $-3a - (-8a) = -3a + 8a = (-3 + 8)a = 5a.$

Example 2 Subtract: $a^2 - 3ab$ from $2a^2 - 7ab$

Solution *Horizontal Method*

$(2a^2 - 7ab) - (a^2 - 3ab)$

$= 2a^2 - 7ab - a^2 + 3ab$

$= (2a^2 - a^2) - 7ab + 3ab$

$= a^2 - 4ab.$

Column Method

$$\begin{array}{r} 2a^2 - 7ab \\ a^2 - 3ab \\ -\quad + \quad \\ \hline a^2 - 4ab \end{array}$$

Example 3 Subtract: $x^2 - 3xy + 7y^2 - 2$ from $6xy - 4x^2 - y^2 + 5$

Solution *Horizontal Method*

$(6xy - 4x^2 - y^2 + 5) - (x^2 - 3xy + 7y^2 - 2)$

$= 6xy - 4x^2 - y^2 + 5 - x^2 + 3xy - 7y^2 + 2$

$= (6xy + 3xy) - 4x^2 - x^2 - y^2 - 7y^2 + 5 + 2$

$= 9xy - 5x^2 - 8y^2 + 7$

Column Method

$$\begin{array}{rrrr} 6xy & - 4x^2 & - y^2 & + 5 \\ -3xy & + x^2 & + 7y^2 & - 2 \\ + & - & - & + \\ \hline 9xy & - 5x^2 & - 8y^2 & + 7 \end{array}$$

Example 4 From the sum of $4x^4 - 3x^3 + 6x^2$, $4x^3 + 4x - 3$ and $-3x^4 - 5x^2 + 2x$ subtract $5x^4 - 7x^3 - 3x + 4$.

Solution The sum of $4x^4 - 3x^3 + 6x^2$, $4x^3 + 4x - 3$ and $-3x^4 - 5x^2 + 2x$ is given by

$(4x^4 - 3x^3 + 6x^2) + (4x^3 + 4x - 3) + (-3x^4 - 5x^2 + 2x)$

$= 4x^4 - 3x^4 - 3x^3 + 4x^3 + 6x^2 - 5x^2 + 4x + 2x - 3$

$= x^4 + x^3 + x^2 + 6x - 3$

Now, we have to subtract $5x^4 - 7x^3 - 3x + 4$ from $x^4 + x^3 + x^2 + 6x - 3$.

$\therefore$ Required expression $= (x^4 + x^3 + x^2 + 6x - 3) - (5x^4 - 7x^3 - 3x + 4)$

$= x^4 + x^3 + x^2 + 6x - 3 - 5x^4 + 7x^3 + 3x - 4$

$= (x^4 - 5x^4) + (x^3 + 7x^3) + x^2 + 6x + 3x - 3 - 4$

$= -4x^4 + 8x^3 + x^2 + 9x - 7.$

Example 5 What should be added to $a^2 + 2ab + b^2$ to obtain $4ab + b^2$?

Solution Required expression is equal to the subtraction of $a^2 + 2ab + b^2$ from $4ab + b^2$.

Hence, required expression $= (4ab + b^2) - (a^2 + 2ab + b^2)$

$= 4ab + b^2 - a^2 - 2ab - b^2$

$= 4ab - 2ab + b^2 - b^2 - a^2$

$= 2ab - a^2.$

Example 6 What should be subtracted from $a^3 - 4a^2 + 5a - 6$ to obtain $a^2 - 2a + 1$?

Solution Let P denote the required expression. Then,

$(a^3 - 4a^2 + 5a - 6) - P = a^2 - 2a + 1$

Hence, required expression $P = (a^3 - 4a^2 + 5a - 6) - (a^2 - 2a + 1)$

$= a^3 - 4a^2 + 5a - 6 - a^2 + 2a - 1$

$= a^3 - 4a^2 - a^2 + 5a + 2a - 7$

$= a^3 - 5a^2 + 7a - 7.$

Example 7 How much is $x^3 - 2x^2 + x + 4$ greater than $2x^3 + 7x^2 - 5x + 6$?

Solution Required expression $= (x^3 - 2x^2 + x + 4) - (2x^3 + 7x^2 - 5x + 6)$

$= x^3 - 2x^2 + x + 4 - 2x^3 - 7x^2 + 5x - 6$

$= x^3 - 2x^3 - 2x^2 - 7x^2 + x + 5x + 4 - 6$

$= -x^3 - 9x^2 + 6x - 2.$

Example 8 How much is $2a^2 - 7a + 5$ less than $a^3 - 3a^2 + 2a - 3$?

Solution Required expression $= (a^3 - 3a^2 + 2a - 3) - (2a^2 - 7a + 5)$

$= (a^3 - 3a^2 + 2a - 3) - 2a^2 + 7a - 5$

$= a^3 - 3a^2 - 2a^2 + 2a + 7a - 3 - 5$

$= a^3 - 5a^2 + 9a - 8.$

Example 9 How much does $2a^2 - 5a + 4$ exceed $3a^3 - 5a^2 + 7a - 9$?

Solution Required expression $= (2a^2 - 5a + 4) - (3a^3 - 5a^2 + 7a - 9)$

$= 2a^2 - 5a + 4 - 3a^3 + 5a^2 - 7a + 9$

$= -3a^3 + 2a^2 + 5a^2 - 5a - 7a + 4 + 9$

$= -3a^3 + 7a^2 - 12a + 13.$

EXERCISE 7.2

1. Add the following:
   (i) $3x$ and $7x$ (ii) $-5xy$ and $9xy$
2. Simplify each of the following:
   (i) $7x^3y + 9yx^3$ (ii) $12a^2b + 3ba^2$
3. Add the following:
   (i) $7abc, -5abc, 9abc, -8abc$ (ii) $2x^2y, -4x^2y, 6x^2y, -5x^2y$

4. Add the following expressions:
   (i) $x^3 - 2x^2y + 3xy^2 - y^3,\ 2x^3 - 5xy^2 + 3x^2y - 4y^3$
   (ii) $a^4 - 2a^3b + 3ab^3 + 4a^2b^2 + 3b^4,\ -2a^4 - 5ab^3 + 7a^3b - 6a^2b^2 + b^4$
5. Add the following expressions:
   (i) $8a - 6ab + 5b,\ -6a - ab - 8b$ and $-4a + 2ab + 3b$
   (ii) $5x^3 + 7 + 6x - 5x^2,\ 2x^2 - 8 - 9x,\ 4x - 2x^2 + 3x^3,\ 3x^3 - 9x - x^2$ and $x - x^2 - x^3 - 4$
6. Add the following:

(i)		(ii)	
	$x - 3y - 2z$		$4ab - 5bc + 7ca$
	$5x + 7y - 8z$		$-3ab + 2bc - 3ca$
	$3x - 2y + 5z$		$5ab - 3bc + 4ca$

7. Add $2x^2 - 3x + 1$ to the sum of $3x^2 - 2x$ and $3x + 7$.
8. Add $x^2 + 2xy + y^2$ to the sum of $x^2 - 3y^2$ and $2x^2 - y^2 + 9$.
9. Add $a^3 + b^3 - 3$ to the sum of $2a^3 - 3b^3 - 3ab + 7$ and $-a^3 + b^3 + 3ab - 9$.
10. Subtract:
    (i) $7a^2b$ from $3a^2b$ (ii) $4xy$ from $-3xy$
11. Subtract:
    (i) $-4x$ from $3y$ (ii) $-2x$ from $-5y$
12. Subtract:
    (i) $6x^3 - 7x^2 + 5x - 3$ from $4 - 5x + 6x^2 - 8x^3$
    (ii) $-x^2 - 3z$ from $5x^2 - y + z + 7$ (ii) $x^3 + 2x^2y + 6xy^2 - y^3$ from $y^3 - 3xy^2 - 4x^2y$
13. From
    (i) $p^3 - 4 + 3p^2$, take away $5p^2 - 3p^3 + p - 6$
    (ii) $7 + x - x^2$, take away $9 + x + 3x^2 + 7x^3$
    (iii) $1 - 5y^2$, take away $y^3 + 7y^2 + y + 1$
    (iv) $x^3 - 5x^2 + 3x + 1$, take away $6x^2 - 4x^3 + 5 + 3x$
14. From the sum of $3x^2 - 5x + 2$ and $-5x^2 - 8x + 9$ subtract $4x^2 - 7x + 9$.
15. Subtract the sum of $13x - 4y + 7z$ and $-6z + 6x + 3y$ from the sum of $6x - 4y - 4z$ and $2x + 4y - 7$.
16. From the sum of $x^2 + 3y^2 - 6xy,\ 2x^2 - y^2 + 8xy,\ y^2 + 8$ and $x^2 - 3xy$ subtract $-3x^2 + 4y^2 - xy + x - y + 3$.
17. What should be added to $xy - 3yz + 4zx$ to get $4xy - 3zx + 4yz + 7$?
18. What should be subtracted from $x^2 - xy + y^2 - x + y + 3$ to obtain $-x^2 + 3y^2 - 4xy + 1$?
19. How much is $x - 2y + 3z$ greater than $3x + 5y - 7$?
20. How much is $x^2 - 2xy + 3y^2$ less than $2x^2 - 3y^2 + xy$?
21. How much does $a^2 - 3ab + 2b^2$ exceed $2a^2 - 7ab + 9b^2$?
22. What must be added to $12x^3 - 4x^2 + 3x - 7$ to make the sum $x^3 + 2x^2 - 3x + 2$?
23. If $P = 7x^2 + 5xy - 9y^2$, $Q = 4y^2 - 3x^2 - 6xy$ and $R = -4x^2 + xy + 5y^2$, show that $P + Q + R = 0$.
24. If $P = a^2 - b^2 + 2ab$, $Q = a^2 + 4b^2 - 6ab$, $R = b^2 + b$, $S = a^2 - 4ab$ and $T = -2a^2 + b^2 - ab + a$. Find $P + Q + R + S - T$.

ANSWERS

1. (i) $10x$ (ii) $4xy$ 2. (i) $16x^3y$ (ii) $15a^2b$
3. (i) $3abc$ (ii) $-x^2y$

4. (i) $3x^3 + x^2y - 2xy^2 - 5y^3$ (ii) $-a^4 + 5a^3b - 2a^2b^2 - 2ab^3 + 4b^4$
5. (i) $-2a - 5ab$ (ii) $10x^3 - 7x^2 - 7x - 5$
6. (i) $9x + 2y - 5z$ (ii) $6ab - 6bc + 8ca$
7. $5x^2 - 2x + 8$
8. $4x^2 + 2xy - 3y^2 + 9$
9. $2a^3 - b^3 - 5$
10. (i) $-4a^2b$ (ii) $-7xy$
11. (i) $3y + 4x$ (ii) $-5y + 2x$
12. (i) $-14x^3 + 13x^2 - 10x + 7$ (ii) $6x^2 - y + 4z + 7$ (iii) $2y^3 - 9xy^2 - 6x^2y - x^3$
13. (i) $4p^3 - 2p^2 - p + 2$ (ii) $-7x^3 - 4x^2 - 2$ (iii) $-y^3 - 12y^2 - y$ (iv) $5x^3 - 11x^2 - 4$
14. $-6x^2 - 6x + 2$
15. $-11x + y - 5z - 7$
16. $7x^2 - y^2 - x + y + 5$
17. $3xy + 7yz - 7zx + 7$
18. $2x^2 + 3xy - 2y^2 - x + y + 2$
19. $-2x - 7y + 3z + 7$
20. $x^2 + 3xy - 6y^2$
21. $-a^2 + 4ab - 7b^2$
22. $-11x^3 + 6x^2 - 6x + 9$
23. 0
24. $5a^2 + 3b^2 - 7ab - a + b$

7.9 THE USE OF GROUPING SYMBOLS (OR BRACKETS) IN WRITING ALGEBRAIC EXPRESSIONS

In dealing with algebraic expressions, sometimes it becomes necessary to consider an expression consisting of two or more terms as a single term. For example, if we say that the sum of $2x - y + 3$ and $x + 2y + 1$ is to be subtracted from the sum of $x + y$ and $3x - 4y + 5$. In this case, the sum of $2x - y + 3$ and $x + 2y + 1$ is taken as one term and the sum of $x + y$ and $3x - 4y + 5$ is also taken as one term. By using brackets (grouping symbols), the above statement can be written as

$$\{(2x - y + 3) + (x + 2y + 1)\} - \{(x + y) + (3x - 4y + 5)\}$$

Thus, we need to insert the brackets (or grouping symbols) to perform algebraic operations. We have already learnt in chapter 1 about the use of brackets in expressions consisting of numerals. Exactly in the same way we use brackets in performing operations on algebraic expressions. The different types of brackets which are used in operations on algebraic expressions are:

(i) Parentheses ( )
(ii) Curly bracket or braces { }
(iii) Square bracket [ ]

We shall now illustrate the use of these brackets through following examples.

ILLUSTRATIVE EXAMPLES

Example 1 Put the last two terms of each of the following expressions in the parentheses preceded by a minus sign:

(i) $2x + 3y - 4z + 7$ (ii) $3a - 2b - 7c - 4d$ (iii) $7xy - 4yz + 3zx - 5$

Solution We have,

(i) $2x + 3y - 4z + 7 = 2x + 3y - (4z - 7)$

(ii) $3a - 2b - 7c - 4d = 3a - 2b - (7c + 4d)$

(iii) $7xy - 4yz + 3zx - 5 = 7xy - 4yz - (-3zx + 5)$.

Example 2 Write each of the following statements by using appropriate grouping symbols:

(i) The sum of $x + y$ and $2xy - 3x + 2y$ is subtracted from $xy - x + y$.

(ii) The subtraction of $x + y - 3$ from $3x - 2y + 9$ is subtracted from the sum of $4x + 3y - 9$ and $2x - y + z$.

(iii) The subtraction of $y - 1$ from x is added to $3y$ and its difference from y is subtracted from x.

Solution We have,

(i) The sum of $x + y$ and $2xy - 3x + 2y$ is $(x + y) + (2xy - 3x + 2y)$.

This is subtracted from $xy - x + y$. Therefore, required expression is

$(xy - x + y) - \{(x + y) + (2xy - 3x + 2y)\}$.

(ii) The subtraction of $x + y - 3$ from $3x - 2y + 9$ is

$(3x - 2y + 9) - (x + y - 3)$ ...(i)

The sum of $4x + 3y - 9$ and $2x - y + z$ is

$(4x + 3y - 9) + (2x - y + z)$ ...(ii)

Subtracting (i) from (ii), we obtain

$\{(4x + 3y - 9) + (2x - y + z)\} - \{(3x - 2y + 9) - (x + y - 3)\}$

(iii) The subtraction of $y - 1$ from x is given by $x - (y - 1)$.

When this is added to $3y$, we get

$x - (y - 1) + 3y$

The difference of this from y is

$y - \{x - (y - 1) + 3y\}$

When this is subtracted from x, we obtain

$x - [y - \{x - (y - 1) + 3y\}]$.

Example 3 Place the last two terms in each of the following expressions in parentheses preceded by a '–' sign:

(i) $9a + 5xy - 7x^2 + 8y - 6$ (ii) $-y + z + x^2 - y^2 - a^2$

(iii) $x + y + z - xy - yz - zx$ (iv) $xy^2 + yz^2 + zx^2$

Solution (i) $9a + 5xy - 7x^2 + 8y - 6 = 9a + 5xy - 7x^2 - (-8y + 6)$

(ii) $-y + z + x^2 - y^2 - a^2 = -y + z + x^2 - (y^2 + a^2)$

(iii) $x + y + z - xy - yz - zx = x + y + z - xy - z(y + x)$

(iv) $xy^2 + yz^2 + zx^2 = xy^2 - z(-yz - x^2)$.

EXERCISE 7.3

1. Place the last two terms of the following expressions in parentheses preceded by a minus sign:

(i) $x + y - 3z + y$ (ii) $3x - 2y - 5z - 4$

(iii) $3a - 2b + 4c - 5$ (iv) $7a + 3b + 2c + 4$

(v) $2a^2 - b^2 - 3ab + 6$ (vi) $a^2 + b^2 - c^2 + ab - 3ac$

2. Write each of the following statements by using appropriate grouping symbols:

(i) The sum of $a - b$ and $3a - 2b + 5$ is subtracted from $4a + 2b - 7$.

(ii) Three times the sum of $2x + y - \{5 - (x - 3y)\}$ and $7x - 4y + 3$ is subtracted from $3x - 4y + 7$.

(iii) The subtraction of $x^2 - y^2 + 4xy$ from $2x^2 + y^2 - 3xy$ is added to $9x^2 - 3y^2 - xy$.

ANSWERS

1. (i) $x + y - (3z - y)$ (ii) $3x - 2y - (5z + 4)$ (iii) $3a - 2b - (-4c + 5)$
   (iv) $7a + 3b - (-2c - 4)$ (v) $2a^2 - b^2 - (3ab - 6)$ (vi) $a^2 + b^2 - c^2 - (-ab + 3ac)$
2. (i) $(4a + 2b - 7) - \{(a - b) + (3a - 2b + 5)\}$

   (ii) $(3x - 4y + 7) - 3\left[(2x + y) - \{5 - (x - 3y)\} + (7x - 4y + 3)\right]$

   (iii) $\left\{(2x^2 + y^2 - 3xy) - (x^2 - y^2 + 4xy)\right\} + (9x^2 - 3y^2 - xy)$

7.10 REMOVAL OF BRACKETS

In the previous section, we have seen that when we make operations on two or more algebraic expressions, we use the symbols of groupings, i.e., parentheses, braces and brackets. In simplifying such expressions, we first remove the grouping symbols by using the following rules:

(i) If a ' + ' sign precedes a symbol of grouping, the grouping symbol may be removed without any change in the sign of the terms.

(ii) If a ' – ' sign precedes a symbol of grouping, the grouping symbol may be removed and the sign of each term is changed.

(iii) If more than one grouping symbol is present in an expression, we remove the inner-most grouping symbol first and collect and combine like terms, if any. We continue this process outwards until all the grouping symbols have been removed.

Following examples will illustrate these rules.

ILLUSTRATIVE EXAMPLES

Example 1 Simplify each of the following algebraic expressions:

(i) $(a^2 + b^2 + 2ab) + (a^2 + b^2 - 2ab)$ (ii) $(a^2 + b^2 + 2ab) - (a^2 + b^2 - 2ab)$

Solution (i) Since ' + ' sign precedes the second parentheses, so we remove it as it is.

$\therefore\ (a^2 + b^2 + 2ab) + (a^2 + b^2 - 2ab)$

$= a^2 + b^2 + 2ab + a^2 + b^2 - 2ab$

$= a^2 + a^2 + b^2 + b^2 + 2ab - 2ab$

$= (1 + 1)a^2 + (1 + 1)b^2 + (2 - 2)ab$

$= 2a^2 + 2b^2 + 0ab$

$= 2a^2 + 2b^2$ $[\because 0ab = 0]$

(ii) Since ' – ' sign precedes the second parentheses, so we remove it and change the sign of each term.

$\therefore\ (a^2 + b^2 + 2ab) - (a^2 + b^2 - 2ab)$

$= a^2 + b^2 + 2ab - a^2 - b^2 + 2ab$

$= a^2 - a^2 + b^2 - b^2 + 2ab + 2ab$

$= (1 - 1)a^2 + (1 - 1)b^2 + (2 + 2)ab$

$= 0a^2 + 0b^2 + 4ab$

$= 4ab$ $[0\,a^2 = 0 \text{ and } 0\,b^2 = 0]$

Example 2 Simplify each of the following:

(i) $-5(a+b)+2(2a-b)+4a-7$ (ii) $-3(a+b)+4(2a-3b)-(2a-b)$

Solution We have,

(i) $-5(a+b)+2(2a-b)+4a-7$

$= -5a-5b+2\times 2a-2b+4a-7$

$= -5a-5b+4a-2b+4a-7$

$= -5a+4a+4a-5b-2b-7$

$= (-5+4+4)a+(-5-2)b-7$

$= 3a-7b-7$

(ii) $-3(a+b)+4(2a-3b)-(2a-b)$

$= -3a-3b+8a-12b-2a+b$

$= -3a+8a-2a-3b-12b+b$

$= (-3+8-2)a+(-3-12+1)b$

$= 3a-14b.$

Example 3 Simplify each of the following:

(i) $2x-\{5y-(x-2y)\}$ (ii) $2x-[3y-\{2x-(y-x)\}]$

(iii) $-m-[m+\{m+n-2m-(m-2n)\}-n]$

(iv) $3x^2z-4yz+3xy-\{x^2z-(x^2z-3yz)-4yz-7z\}$

Solution (i) We first remove the innermost grouping symbol ( ) and then braces { }. Thus, we have

$2x-\{5y-(x-2y)\}$

$= 2x-\{5y-x+2y\}$ [Removing ( )]

$= 2x-\{5y+2y-x\}$

$= 2x-\{7y-x\}$

$= 2x-7y+x$ [Removing { }]

$= 2x+x-7y$

$= 3x-7y$

(ii) We first remove the innermost grouping symbol (), then { } and then [ ]. Thus, we have

$2x-[3y-\{2x-(y-x)\}]$

$= 2x-[3y-\{2x-y+x\}]$ [Removing ( )]

$= 2x-[3y-\{3x-y\}]$

$= 2x-[3y-3x+y]$ [Removing { }]

$= 2x-[4y-3x]$

$= 2x-4y+3x$ [Removing [ ]]

$= 2x+3x-4y$

$= 5x-4y$

(iii) We first remove the innermost grouping symbol (), then {} and then []. Thus, we have,

$-m-[m+\{m+n-2m-(m-2n)\}-n]$

$= -m - \left[m + \{m + n - 2m - m + 2n\} - n\right]$ $\left[\text{Removing ( )}\right]$

$= -m - \left[m + \{m - 2m - m + n + 2n)\} - n\right]$

$= -m - \left[m + \{-2m + 3n\} - n\right]$

$= -m - [m - 2m + 3n - n]$ $\left[\text{Removing \{ \}}\right]$

$= -m - [-m + 2n]$

$= -m + m - 2n$ $\left[\text{Removing [ ]}\right]$

$= -2n$

(iv) We first remove the innermost grouping symbol () and then {}.
Thus, we have

$3x^2z - 4yz + 3xy - \left\{x^2z - (x^2z - 3yz) - 4yz - 7z\right\}$

$= 3x^2z - 4yz + 3xy - \left\{x^2z - x^2z + 3yz - 4yz - 7z\right\}$

$= 3x^2z - 4yz + 3xy - \{-yz - 7z\}$

$= 3x^2z - 4yz + 3xy + yz + 7z$ $\left[\text{Removing \{ \}}\right]$

$= 3x^2z - 3yz + 3xy + 7z$

Example 4 Simplify: $15x - \left[8x^3 + 3x^2 - \left\{8x^2 - (4 - 2x - x^3) - 5x^3\right\} - 2x\right]$

Solution We first simplify the innermost grouping symbol ( ), then { } and then [ ]. Thus, we have

$15x - \left[8x^3 + 3x^2 - \left\{8x^2 - (4 - 2x - x^3) - 5x^3\right\} - 2x\right]$

$= 15x - \left[8x^3 + 3x^2 - \left\{8x^2 - 4 + 2x + x^3 - 5x^3\right\} - 2x\right]$

$= 15x - \left[8x^3 + 3x^2 - \left\{8x^2 - 4 + 2x - 4x^3\right\} - 2x\right]$

$= 15x - \left[8x^3 + 3x^2 - 8x^2 + 4 - 2x + 4x^3 - 2x\right]$

$= 15x - \left[8x^3 + 4x^3 + 3x^2 - 8x^2 - 2x - 2x + 4\right]$

$= 15x - \left[12x^3 - 5x^2 - 4x + 4\right]$

$= 15x - 12x^3 + 5x^2 + 4x - 4$

$= -12x^3 + 5x^2 + 15x + 4x - 4 = -12x^3 + 5x^2 + 19x - 4.$

Example 5 Simplify : $5 + \left[x - \left\{2y - (6x + y - 4) + 2x^2\right\} - (x^2 - 2y)\right]$

Solution We first remove the innermost grouping symbol (), then { } and then [ ]. Thus, we have

$5 + \left[x - \left\{2y - (6x + y - 4) + 2x^2\right\} - (x^2 - 2y)\right]$

$= 5 + \left[x - \left\{2y - 6x - y + 4 + 2x^2\right\} - (x^2 - 2y)\right]$

$$= 5 + \left[x - \left\{2y - y - 6x + 4 + 2x^2\right\} - (x^2 - 2y)\right]$$

$$= 5 + \left[x - \left\{y - 6x + 4 + 2x^2\right\} - x^2 + 2y\right]$$

$$= 5 + \left[x - y + 6x - 4 - 2x^2 - x^2 + 2y\right]$$

$$= 5 + \left[x + 6x - y + 2y - 2x^2 - x^2 - 4\right]$$

$$= 5 + \left[(1+6)x + y(-1+2) + x^2(-2-1) - 4\right]$$

$$= 5 + \left[7x + y - 3x^2 - 4\right] = 5 + 7x + y - 3x^2 - 4 \;\; = 1 + 7x + y - 3x^2.$$

Example 6 Simplify and find the value of the following expression when $a = 3$ and $b = 1$:

$$4(a^2 + b^2 + 2ab) - \left[4(a^2 + b^2 - 2ab) - \left\{-b^3 + 4(a - 3)\right\}\right]$$

Solution Proceeding outward from the innermost bracket, we obtain

$$4(a^2 + b^2 + 2ab) - \left[4(a^2 + b^2 - 2ab) - \left\{-b^3 + 4(a - 3)\right\}\right]$$

$$= 4(a^2 + b^2 + 2ab) - \left[4(a^2 + b^2 - 2ab) - \left\{-b^3 + 4a - 12\right\}\right]$$

$$= 4a^2 + 4b^2 + 8ab - \left[4a^2 + 4b^2 - 8ab + b^3 - 4a + 12\right]$$

$$= 4a^2 + 4b^2 + 8ab - 4a^2 - 4b^2 + 8ab - b^3 + 4a - 12$$

$$= 4a^2 - 4a^2 + 4b^2 - 4b^2 + 8ab + 8ab - b^3 + 4a - 12$$

$$= (4 - 4)a^2 + (4 - 4)b^2 + (8 + 8)ab - b^3 + 4a - 12 = 16ab - b^3 + 4a - 12$$

The value of this expression for $a = 3$ and $b = 1$ is

$$16 \times 3 \times 1 - (1)^3 + 4 \times 3 - 12 = 48 - 1 + 12 - 12 = 47$$

EXERCISE 7.4

Simplify each of the following algebraic expressions by removing grouping symbols.

1. $2x + (5x - 3y)$
2. $3x - (y - 2x)$
3. $5a - (3b - 2a + 4c)$
4. $-2\,(x^2 - y^2 + xy) - 3(x^2 + y^2 - xy)$
5. $3x + 2y - \left\{x - (2y - 3)\right\}$
6. $5a - \left\{3a - (2 - a) + 4\right\}$
7. $a - \left[b - \left\{a - (b - 1) + 3a\right\}\right]$
8. $a - \left[2b - \left\{3a - (2b - 3c)\right\}\right]$
9. $-x + \left[5y - \left\{2x - (3y - 5x)\right\}\right]$
10. $2a - \left[4b - \left\{4a - 3(2a - b)\right\}\right]$
11. $-a - \left[a + \left\{a + b - 2a - (a - 2b)\right\} - b\right]$
12. $2x - 3y - \left[3x - 2y - \left\{x - z - (x - 2y)\right\}\right]$
13. $5 + \left[x - \left\{2y - (6x + y - 4) + 2x\right\} - \left\{x - (y - 2)\right\}\right]$
14. $x^2 - \left[3x + \left\{2x - (x^2 - 1)\right\} + 2\right]$
15. $20 - \left[5xy + 3\left\{x^2 - (xy - y) - (x - y)\right\}\right]$
16. $85 - \left[12x - 7(8x - 3) - 2\left\{10x - 5(2 - 4x)\right\}\right]$
17. $xy - \left[yz - zx - \left\{yx - (3y - xz) - (xy - zy)\right\}\right]$

ANSWERS

1. $7x-3y$ 2. $5x-y$ 3. $7a-3b-4c$ 4. $-5x^2-y^2+xy$
5. $2x+4y-3$ 6. $a-2$ 7. $5a-2b+1$ 8. $4a-4b+3c$
9. $-8x+8y$ 10. $-b$ 11. $-2b$ 12. $-x+y-z$
13. $4x-1$ 14. $2x^2-5x-3$ 15. $-3x^2-2xy-6y+3x+20$ 16. $44+104x$
17. $xy+2zx-3y$

OBJECTIVE TYPE QUESTIONS

Mark the correct alternative in each of the following:

1. Which of the following pairs is/are like terms?
   (1) x (2) x^2 (3) $3x^3$ (4) $4x^3$
   (a) 1, 2 (b) 2, 3 (c) 3, 4 (d) None of these
2. Which of the following is not a monomial?
   (a) $2x^2+1$ (b) $3x^4$ (c) ab (d) x^2y
3. The sum of the coefficients in the monomials $3a^2b$ and $-2ab^2$ is
   (a) 5 (b) -1 (c) 1 (d) -6
4. The coefficient of x^2 in $-\frac{5}{3}x^2y$ is equal to
   (a) $-\frac{5}{3}$ (b) $-\frac{5}{3}y$ (c) $\frac{5}{3}$ (d) $\frac{5}{3}y$
5. If *a, b* and *c* are respectively the coefficients of x^2 in $-x^2$, $2x^2+x$ and $2x-x^2$ respectively, then $a+b+c=$
   (a) 0 (b) -2 (c) 2 (d) -1
6. The sum of the coefficients in the terms of $2x^2y-3xy^2+4xy$ is
   (a) -3 (b) 3 (c) 9 (d) 5
7. The product of the coefficients of terms in $-\frac{4}{3}ab^2+\frac{1}{4}bc^2+3ca^2$ is
   (a) 1 (b) $\frac{1}{2}$ (c) -1 (d) 3
8. If *a* and *b* are respectively the sum and product of coefficients of terms in the expression $x^2+y^2+z^2-xy-yz-zx$, then $a+2b=$
   (a) 0 (b) 2 (c) -2 (d) -1
9. If $P=3x^3+3x^2+3x+3$ and $Q=3x^2-3x+3$, then $P-Q=$
   (a) $3x^3$ (b) $3x^3+6x^2+6x+6$ (c) $6x^2+6x+6$ (d) $3x^3+6x$
10. The sum of the values of the expression $2x^2=2x+2$ when $x=-1$ and $x=1$ is
    (a) 6 (b) 8 (c) 4 (d) 2
11. What should be added to $3x^2+4$ to get $9x^2-7$?
    (a) $6x^2-11$ (b) $6x^2+11$ (c) $12x^2-11$ (d) $12x^2+11$
12. How much is a^2-3a greater than $2a^2+4a$?
    (a) a^2-7a (b) a^2+7a (c) $-a^2-7a$ (d) $-a^2+7a$
13. How much is $-2x^2+x+1$ less than x^2+2x-3?
    (a) $-x^2+3x-2$ (b) $3x^2+x-4$ (c) $-3x^2-x+4$ (d) $3x^2+3x-4$

14. What should be added to $xy + yz + zx$ to get $-xy - yz - zx$?

(a) $-2xy - 2yz - 2zx$ (b) $-3xy - yz - zx$

(c) $-3xy - 3yz - 3zx$ (d) $2xy + 2yz + 2zx$

ANSWERS

1. (c)	2. (a)	3. (c)	4. (b)	5. (a)	6. (b)	7. (c)
8. (c)	9. (d)	10. (b)	11. (a)	12. (c)	13. (b)	14. (a)

THINGS TO REMEMBER

1. *The letters which are used to represent numbers are called literal numbers or literals.*
2. *The literal numbers themselves as well as the combinations of literal numbers and numbers obey all the rules (and signs) of addition, subtraction, multiplication and division of numbers along with the properties of these operations.*
3. $x \times y = xy$, $5 \times x = 5x$, $1 \times x = x$, $x \times 4 = 4x$.
4. $a \times a \times a \times .... \times$ *12 times* $= a^{12}$, $y \times y \times y \times ... \times$ *15 times* $= y^{15}$.
5. *In* x^9, *9 is called the index or exponent and* x *is called the base. In* a^5, *the index or exponent is 5 and the base is a.*
6. *A symbol having a fixed numerical value is called a constant.*
7. *A symbol which takes various numerical values is called a variable.*
8. *A combination of constants and variables connected by the signs of fundamental operations of addition, subtraction, multiplication and division is called an algebraic expression.*
9. *Various parts of an algebraic expression which are separated by the signs of '+' or '–' are called the terms of the expression.*
10. *An algebraic expression is called a monomial, a binomial, a trinomial, a quadrinomial according as it contains one term, two terms, three terms and four terms respectively.*
11. *Each term in an algebraic expression is a product of one or more number(s) and/or literal number(s). These number(s) and/or literal number(s) are known as the factors of that term.*
12. *A term of the expression having no literal factor is called a constant term.*
13. *In a term of an algebraic expression any of the factors with the sign of the term is called the coefficient of the product of the factors.*
14. *The terms having the same literal factors are called like or similar terms.*
15. *The terms not having same literal factors are called unlike or dissimilar terms.*
16. *The sum or difference of several like terms is another like term whose coefficient is the sum or difference of those like terms.*
17. *In adding or subtracting algebraic expressions, we collect different groups of like terms and find the sum or difference of like terms in each group.*
18. *To subtract an expression from another, we change the sign (from '+' to '–' and from '–' to '+') of each term of the expression to be subtracted and then add the two expressions.*
19. *When a grouping symbol preceded by '–' sign is removed or inserted, then the sign of each term of the corresponding expression is changed (from '+' to '–' and from '–' to '+').*

8

LINEAR EQUATIONS IN ONE VARIABLE

8.1 INTRODUCTION

In this chapter, we shall study the meaning of an equation and also that of a linear equation. We shall also discuss the meaning of the solution of a linear equation and two methods of obtaining it. One by trial-and-error and another by a systematic method involving addition, subtraction, multiplication or division of some non-zero number on both sides of the equation. In the end of the chapter, we shall study formulation and solution of equations for some real-life problems.

8.2 EQUATIONS

In the earlier chapters, we have come across statements of the following type:

(i) $9+5=14$ (ii) $2\times(3+7)=2\times3+2\times7$ (iii) $(4+7)\times3=4\times3+7\times3$, etc.

All these statements involve the 'equals' symbol '$=$'. Such a statement involving the 'equals' symbol '$=$' is called a statement of equality or simply an equality.

Clearly, none of the above statements involves a literal (variable). Let us now consider the following statements:

(i) 3 added to x is 8.
(ii) 5 subtracted from a number y is 12.
(iii) 7 less than a number x is 4.
(iv) Five times a number p is 32.
(v) A number x divided by 4 gives 3.
(vi) x multiplied by itself is 5 more than it.
(vii) The sum of a number x and twice the number y is 15.
(viii) 4 less from thrice a number m is 14.
(ix) The sum of the number x and its square is 20.

We can re-write the above statements as follows:

(i) $x+3=8$
(ii) $y-5=12$
(iii) $x-7=4$
(iv) $5p=32$
(v) $\frac{x}{4}=3$
(vi) $x^2=5+x$
(vii) $x+2y=15$
(viii) $3m-4=14$
(ix) $x+x^2=20.$

We observe that each one of the above statements is a statement of equality, involving one or more literals (variables). Such statements of equality are called equations as defined below.

EQUATION *A statement of equality which involves one or more literals (variables) is called an equation.*

Clearly, each of the equalities (i) to (ix) is an equation.

Every equation has two sides, namely, the left hand side (written as L.H.S.) and the right hand side (written as R.H.S.)

In the equation $x + 3 = 8$, $x + 3$ is L.H.S. and 8 is R.H.S, whereas in the equation $\frac{x}{4} = 3$, $\frac{x}{4}$ is L.H.S. and 3 is R.H.S. In the equation $x^2 = 5 + x$, x^2 is L.H.S. and $5 + x$ is R.H.S. The literal numbers involved in an equation are called variables or unknowns. Usually the variables are denoted by letters from the later part of the English alphabet, e.g. x, y, z, v, u, w etc.

An equation may contain any number of variables. The equation $x^2 - x = 5$ has only one variable whereas in equation $2x - 3y = 5$ there are two variables x and y.

8.3 LINEAR EQUATIONS

In the previous section, we have studied that an equation may involve any number of variables and the experiments or indices of the variables may be one or more than one. The nomenclature of the equations depends on the highest power of the variable(s) involved.

LINEAR EQUATION *An equation in which the highest power of the variables involved is 1, is called a linear equation.*

For example, equations $3x - 7 = 5$, $\frac{x}{4} + 5 = 3$, $3x - 2y = 7$ and $\frac{x}{2} + \frac{y}{3} = 4$ are linear equations.

The equations $2x^2 + x = 1$, $y + 5 = y^2$ and $x^3 = 8$ are not linear equations, because the highest power of the variable in each equation is greater than one.

In this chapter, we shall study linear equations in one variable only.

ILLUSTRATION Write the L.H.S. and the R.H.S. of each of the following equations:

(i) $x - 3 = 5$ (ii) $3x = 15 - 2x$

(iii) $3x = 21$ (iv) $3x - 4y = 9 + x$

Solution

Equation	L.H.S.	R.H.S.
(i) $x - 3 = 5$	$x - 3$	5
(ii) $3x = 15 - 2x$	$3x$	$15 - 2x$
(iii) $3x = 21$	$3x$	21
(iv) $3x - 4y = 9 + x$	$3x - 4y$	$9 + x$

8.3.1 SOLUTION OF AN EQUATION

Consider the linear equation

$$x - 10 = -7 \quad ...(i)$$

L.H.S. of (i) is $x - 10$ and its R.H.S. is -7.

Let us now evaluate the L.H.S. and R.H.S. for some values of the variables x.

x	L.H.S.	R.H.S.
1	$1-10=-9$	-7
2	$2-10=-8$	-7
3	$3-10=-7$	-7

From the above table, we observe that the L.H.S. equals the R.H.S. only when we substitute 3 for x. For all other values of x, the two sides are not equal. In other words, the equation is satisfied by $x = 3$. Such a value of the variable is called the solution of the equation as defined below.

SOLUTION *A number, which when substituted for the variable in an equation, makes L.H.S. = R.H.S, is said to satisfy the equation and is called a solution or a root of the equation.*

ILLUSTRATION 1 Verify that $x = 3$ is the solution of the equation $2x - 3 = 3$.

Solution Putting $x = 3$ on L.H.S., we have

L.H.S. $= 2 \times 3 - 3 = 6 - 3 = 3$

And, R.H.S. = 3

Thus, for $x = 3$, we have L.H.S. = R.H.S.

Hence, $x = 3$ is the solution of the given equation.

ILLUSTRATION 2 Verify that $y = 9$ is the solution of the equation $\frac{y}{3} + 5 = 8$.

Solution Putting $y = 9$ in L.H.S. of the given equation, we obtain

L.H.S. $= \frac{9}{3} + 5 = 3 + 5 = 8$

And, R.H.S. = 8.

Thus, for $y = 9$, we have L.H.S. = R.H.S.

Hence, $y = 9$ is the solution of the given equation.

8.4 SOLVING LINEAR EQUATIONS

In the previous section, we have studied the meaning of the solution or root of an equation. Note that solving an equation means determining its roots. You will study in higher classes that a linear equation has only one root. Thus, solving a linear equation means finding its root.

In this section, we shall study three methods of solving a linear equation:

(i) By trial-and-error method. (ii) Systematic method (iii) Transposition method.

Let us discuss these methods one by one.

8.4.1 TRIAL-AND-ERROR METHOD

In this method, we often make a guess of the root of the equation. We find the values of L.H.S. and R.H.S. of the given equation for different values of the variable. The value of the variable for which L.H.S. = R.H.S. is the root of the equation.

Following examples illustrate the above method.

ILLUSTRATIVE EXAMPLES

Example 1 Solve the following equations by the trial-and-error method:

(i) $x + 7 = 10$ (ii) $x - 15 = 20$ (iii) $5x = 30$

(iv) $\frac{x}{8} = 9$ (v) $3x + 4 = 5x - 4$ (vi) $\frac{x}{3} + 8 = 11$

Solution Let us evaluate the L.H.S. and R.H.S. of each of the given equations for some values of x and continue to give new values till the L.H.S. becomes equal to the R.H.S.

(i) The given equation is $x + 7 = 10$. We have, L.H.S. $= x + 7$ and R.H.S. $= 10$

x	L.H.S.	R.H.S.	Is L.H.S. = R.H.S.?
1	$1 + 7 = 8$	10	No
2	$2 + 7 = 9$	10	No
3	$3 + 7 = 10$	10	Yes

Clearly, L.H.S. = R.H.S. for $x = 3$.

Hence, $x = 3$ is the solution of given equation.

(ii) The given equation is $x - 15 = 20$, that is, 15 subtracted from x gives 20. So, we substitute values greater than 20. We have L.H.S. $= x - 15$, R.H.S. $= 20$.

x	L.H.S.	R.H.S.	Is L.H.S. = R.H.S.?
25	$25 - 15 = 10$	20	No
30	$30 - 15 = 15$	20	No
34	$34 - 15 = 19$	20	No
35	$35 - 15 = 20$	20	Yes

Clearly, L.H.S. = R.H.S. for $x = 35$.

Hence, $x = 35$ is the solution of the given equation.

(iii) The given equation is $5x = 30$. We have L.H.S. $= 5x$ and R.H.S. $= 30$.

Now,

x	L.H.S.	R.H.S.	Is L.H.S. = R.H.S.?
1	$5 \times 1 = 5$	30	No
2	$5 \times 2 = 10$	30	No
3	$5 \times 3 = 15$	30	No
4	$5 \times 4 = 20$	30	No
5	$5 \times 5 = 25$	30	No
6	$5 \times 6 = 30$	30	Yes

Clearly, L.H.S. = R.H.S for $x = 6$.

Hence, $x = 6$ is the solution of the given equation.

(iv) The given equation is $\frac{x}{8} = 9$ that is, a number divided by 8 gives 9. This means that the number is a multiple of 8.

We have, L.H.S. = $\frac{x}{8}$ and R.H.S. = 9.

x	L.H.S.	R.H.S.	Is L.H.S. = R.H.S.?
32	$\frac{32}{8} = 4$	9	No
40	$\frac{40}{8} = 5$	9	No
48	$\frac{48}{8} = 6$	9	No
64	$\frac{64}{8} = 8$	9	No
72	$\frac{72}{8} = 9$	9	Yes

Clearly, L.H.S. = R.H.S. for $x = 72$.

Hence, $x = 72$ is the solution of the given equation.

(v) The given equation is $3x + 4 = 5x - 4$.

We have, L.H.S. = $3x + 4$ and R.H.S. = $5x - 4$.

x	L.H.S.	R.H.S.	Is L.H.S. = R.H.S.?
1	$3 \times 1 + 4 = 7$	$5 \times 1 - 4 = 1$	No
2	$3 \times 2 + 4 = 10$	$5 \times 2 - 4 = 6$	No
3	$3 \times 3 + 4 = 13$	$5 \times 3 - 4 = 11$	No
4	$3 \times 4 + 4 = 16$	$5 \times 4 - 4 = 16$	Yes

Clearly, L.H.S. = R.H.S. for $x = 4$.

Hence, $x = 4$ is the solution of the given equation.

(vi) The given equation is $\frac{x}{3} + 8 = 11$.

We have, L.H.S. = $\frac{x}{3} + 8$ and R.H.S. = 11.

Since R.H.S. is a natural number. So, $\frac{x}{3}$ must be a natural number. Thus, we give values of x which are multiples of 3.

x	L.H.S.	R.H.S.	Is L.H.S. = R.H.S.?
3	$\frac{3}{3} + 8 = 9$	11	No
6	$\frac{6}{3} + 8 = 10$	11	No
9	$\frac{9}{3} + 8 = 11$	11	Yes

Thus, L.H.S. = R.H.S. for $x = 9$.

Hence, $x = 9$ is the solution of the given equation.

EXERCISE 8.1

1. Verify by substitution that:

   (i) $x = 4$ is the root of $3x - 5 = 7$ (ii) $x = 3$ is the root of $5 + 3x = 14$

   (iii) $x = 2$ is the root of $3x - 2 = 8x - 12$ (iv) $x = 4$ is the root of $\frac{3x}{2} = 6$

   (v) $y = 2$ is the root of $y - 3 = 2y - 5$ (vi) $x = 8$ is the root of $\frac{1}{2}x + 7 = 11$

2. Solve each of the following equations by trial-and-error method:

   (i) $x + 3 = 12$ (ii) $x - 7 = 10$ (iii) $4x = 28$ (iv) $\frac{x}{2} + 7 = 11$

   (v) $2x + 4 = 3x$ (vi) $\frac{x}{4} = 12$ (vii) $\frac{15}{x} = 3$ (viii) $\frac{x}{18} = 20$

ANSWERS

2. (i) 9 (ii) 17 (iii) 7 (iv) 8
   (v) 4 (vi) 48 (vii) 5 (viii) 360

8.5 SYSTEMATIC METHOD

We have learnt about the trial-and-error method of solving linear equations in one variable. As we have seen that this method is time consuming and is not always direct.

In fact, it is a crude method. In the following discussion we shall study a better method of solving linear equations.

An equation can be compared with a weighing balance. The two sides of an equation are two pans and the equality symbol '=' tells us that the two pans are in balance as shown in Fig. 1

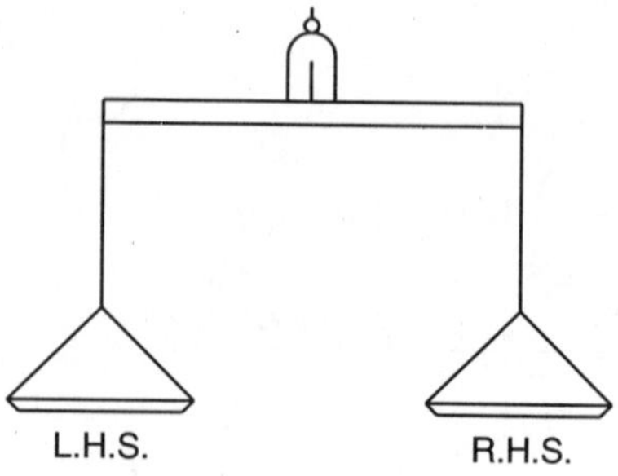

Fig.1

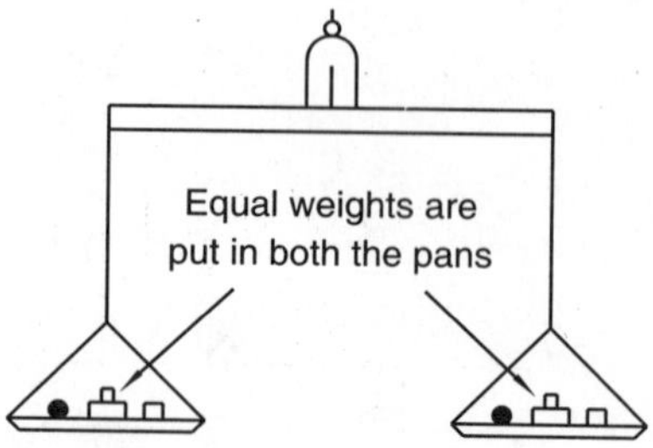

Fig. 2

All of us are familiar with the working of a balance. If equal weights are put in the two pans, we observe that the two pans remain in balance as shown in Fig. 2.

If we remove equal weights from both the pans, we find that the pans still remain in balance as shown in Fig. 3.

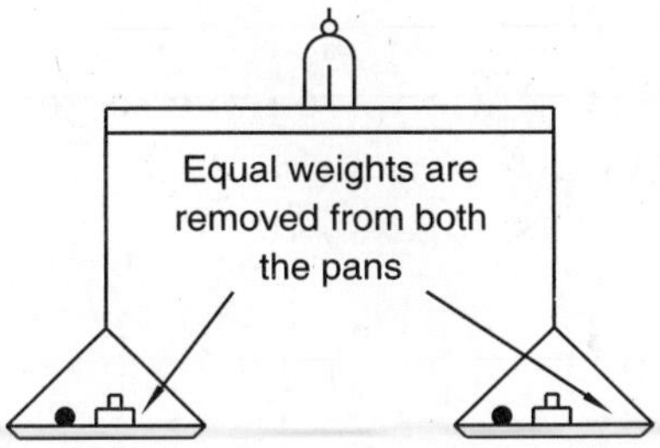

Fig. 3

Since multiplying a number by 4 (say) means adding it four times and dividing a number by 3 means subtracting the same number 3 times from it. Thus, the pans will still remain undisturbed if we multiply or divide the weights in two pans by the same quantity.

Similarly, in the case of an equation, we have the following rules:

Rule 1 *We can add the same number to both sides of the equation, i.e., if* $x + 5 = 7$*, then* $x + 5 + 2 = 7 + 2$.

Rule 2 *We can subtract the same number from both sides of the equation, i.e., if* $x + 5 = 7$*, then* $x + 5 - 2 = 7 - 2$.

Rule 3 *We can multiply both sides of the equation by the same non-zero number, i.e., if* $\frac{x}{3} = 4$*, then* $\frac{x}{3} \times 6 = 4 \times 6$*. Also,* $\frac{x}{3} \times 3 = 4 \times 3$.

Rule 4 *We can divide both sides of the equation by the same non-zero number, i.e., if* $3x = 10$*, then* $\frac{3x}{3} = \frac{10}{3}$*. Also,* $\frac{3x}{5} = \frac{10}{5}$.

Following examples will illustrate the applications of the above rules in solving linear equations.

ILLUSTRATIVE EXAMPLES

Type I EQUATIONS INVOLVING ADDITION

Example 1 Solve the equation $x - 3 = 5$ and check the result.

Solution We have, $x - 3 = 5$.

In order to solve this equation, we have to get x by itself on the L.H.S. To get x by itself on the L.H.S., we need to shift –3. This can be done by adding 3 to both sides of the given equation.

$x - 3 = 5$

$\Rightarrow x - 3 + 3 = 5 + 3$ [Adding 3 to both sides]

$\Rightarrow x + 0 = 8$ $[\because -3 + 3 = 0 \text{ and } 5 + 3 = 8]$

$\Rightarrow x = 8$ $[\because x + 0 = x]$

So, $x = 8$ is the solution of the given equation.

Check Substituting $x = 8$ in the given equation, we get

L.H.S. $= 8 - 3 = 5$ and, R.H.S. $= 5$.

Thus, when $x = 8$, we have L.H.S. = R.H.S.

Example 2 Solve the equation $x - 7 = -2$ and check the result.

Solution We have, $x - 7 = -2$.

In order to solve this equation, we have to get x by itself on the L.H.S. To get x by itself on the L.H.S., we need to shift –7. This can be done by adding 7 to both sides of the given equation. Thus,

$x - 7 = -2$

$\Rightarrow \quad x - 7 + 7 = -2 + 7$ [Adding 7 to both sides]

$\Rightarrow \quad x + 0 = 5$ $[\because \; -7+7=0 \text{ and } -2+7=5]$

$\Rightarrow \quad x = 5$

Thus, $x = 5$ is the solution of the given equation.

Check Substituting $x = 5$ in the given equation, we get

L.H.S. $= 5 - 7 = -2$ and R.H.S. $= -2$

Thus, when $x = 5$, we have L.H.S. = R.H.S.

Type II **EQUATIONS INVOLVING SUBTRACTION**

Example 3 Solve the equation $x + 7 = 5$ and check the result.

Solution In order to solve this equation, we have to obtain x by itself on the L.H.S. To get x by itself on L.H.S., we need to shift 7. This can be done by subtracting 7 from both the sides of the given equation. Thus,

$x + 7 = 5$

$\Rightarrow \quad x + 7 - 7 = 5 - 7$ [Subtracting 7 from both the sides]

$\Rightarrow \quad x + 0 = -2$ $[\because \; 7-7=0 \text{ and } 5-7=-2]$

$\Rightarrow \quad x = -2$ $[\because \; x+0=x]$

Thus, $x = -2$ is the solution of the given equation.

Check Substituting $x = -2$ in the given equation, we get

L.H.S. $= -2 + 7 = 5$ and R.H.S. $= 5$.

Thus, when $x = -2$, we have L.H.S. = R.H.S.

Example 4 Solve the equation $x + 4 = -2$ and check the result.

Solution In order to solve this equation, we have to obtain x by itself on L.H.S. To get x by itself on L.H.S., we need to shift 4. This can be done by subtracting 4 from both sides of the given equation.

Thus, $x + 4 = -2$

$\Rightarrow \quad x + 4 - 4 = -2 - 4$ [Subtracting 4 from both sides]

$\Rightarrow \quad x + 0 = -6$ $[\because \; 4-4=0 \text{ and } -2-4=-6]$

$\Rightarrow \quad x = -6$ $[\because \; x+0=x]$

Thus, $x = -6$ is the solution of the given equation.

Check Substituting $x = -6$ in the given equation, we get

L.H.S. $= -6 + 4 = -2$ and R.H.S. $= -2$

Thus, when $x = -6$, we have L.H.S. = R.H.S.

Type III **EQUATIONS INVOLVING MULTIPLICATION**

Example 5 Solve the equation $\frac{y}{12} = 48$ and check the result.

Solution In order to solve this equation, we have to get y by itself on L.H.S. To get y by itself on L.H.S., we have to remove 12 from L.H.S. This can be done by multiplying both sides of the equation by 12 thus, we have

$$\frac{y}{12} = 48$$

$$\Rightarrow \frac{y}{12} \times 12 = 48 \times 12 \qquad \text{[Multiplying both sides by 12]}$$

$$\Rightarrow y = 576 \qquad \left[\because \frac{y}{12} \times 12 = y \text{ and } 48 \times 12 = 576\right]$$

Thus, $y = 576$ is the solution of the given equation.

Check Putting $y = 576$ in the given equation, we get

L.H.S. $= \frac{576}{12} = 48$ and R.H.S. $= 48$.

Thus, for $y = 576$, we have L.H.S. = R.H.S.

Type IV EQUATIONS INVOLVING DIVISION

Example 6 Solve the equation $15x = 21$ and verify the result.

Solution In order to solve this equation, we have to get x by itself on the L.H.S. For this, 15 has to be removed from the L.H.S. This can be done by dividing both sides of the equation by 15. Thus,

$$15x = 21$$

$$\Rightarrow \frac{15x}{15} = \frac{21}{15} \qquad \text{[Dividing both sides by 15]}$$

$$\Rightarrow x = \frac{7}{5} \qquad \left[\because \frac{15x}{15} = x \text{ and } \frac{21}{15} = \frac{3 \times 7}{3 \times 5} = \frac{7}{5}\right]$$

Thus, $x = \frac{7}{5}$ is the solution of the given equation.

Check Putting $x = \frac{7}{5}$ in the given equation, we get

L.H.S. $= 15 \times \frac{7}{5} = 3 \times 7 = 21$ and R.H.S. $= 21$.

Thus, for $x = \frac{7}{5}$, we have L.H.S. = R.H.S.

Example 7 Solve the equation $\frac{2}{3x} = 18$ and check the result.

Solution We have,

$$\frac{2}{3x} = 18$$

$$\Rightarrow \frac{2}{3x} \times \frac{3}{2} = 18 \times \frac{3}{2} \qquad \left[\text{Multiplying both sides by } \frac{3}{2}\right]$$

$$\Rightarrow \frac{2}{3} \times \frac{3}{2} \times \frac{1}{x} = 27$$

$$\Rightarrow \frac{1}{x} = 27 \Rightarrow x = \frac{1}{27}$$

Thus, $x = 27$ is the solution of the given equation.

Check Putting $x = 27$ in the given equation, we get

L.H.S. $= \frac{2}{3} \times 27 = 18$ and R.H.S. $= 18$.

Thus, for $x = 27$, we have L.H.S. = R.H.S.

Type V **EQUATIONS SOLVABLE BY USING MORE THAN ONE RULE**

In the previous examples, we have discussed those equations which can be solved by using any one of the rules given on page 8.7. Now, we shall discuss some examples of linear equations which can be solved by using two or more of the rules given on page 8.7.

Example 8 Solve the equation $3x + 2 = 11$ and check the result.

Solution We have,

$3x + 2 = 11$

$\Rightarrow 3x + 2 - 2 = 11 - 2$ [Subtracting 2 from both sides]

$\Rightarrow 3x + 0 = 9$

$\Rightarrow 3x = 9$ $[\because 3x + 0 = 3x]$

$\Rightarrow \frac{3x}{3} = \frac{9}{3}$ [Dividing both sides by 3]

$\Rightarrow x = 3$

Thus, $x = 3$ is the solution of the given equation.

Check Putting $x = 3$ in the given equation, we get

L.H.S. $= 3 \times 3 + 2 = 9 + 2 = 11 =$ R.H.S.

Thus, for $x = 3$, we have L.H.S. = R.H.S.

Example 9 Solve the equation $2x - \frac{1}{2} = 3$ and check the result.

Solution We have,

$2x - \frac{1}{2} = 3$

$\Rightarrow 2x - \frac{1}{2} + \frac{1}{2} = 3 + \frac{1}{2}$ $\left[\text{Adding } \frac{1}{2} \text{ to both sides}\right]$

$\Rightarrow 2x + 0 = \frac{7}{2}$

$\Rightarrow 2x = \frac{7}{2}$ $[\because 2x + 0 = 2x]$

$\Rightarrow \frac{2x}{2} = \frac{7}{2} \times \frac{1}{2}$ [Dividing both sides by 2]

$\Rightarrow x = \frac{7}{4}$

Thus, $x = \frac{7}{4}$ is the solution of the given equation.

Check Putting $x = \frac{7}{4}$ in the given equation, we get

$$\text{L.H.S.} = 2\times\frac{7}{4}-\frac{1}{2}=\frac{7}{2}-\frac{1}{2}=\frac{6}{2}=3 \text{ and R.H.S.} = 3$$

Thus, for $x = \frac{7}{4}$, we have L.H.S. = R.H.S.

Example 10 Solve the equation $3(x + 6) = 21$ and check the result.

Solution We have,

$$3(x+6)=21$$

$\Rightarrow$ $3x+18=21$ [On expanding the bracket]

$\Rightarrow$ $3x+18-18=21-18$ [Subtracting 18 from both sides]

$\Rightarrow$ $3x+0=3$

$\Rightarrow$ $3x=3$ [$\because$ $3x+0=3x$]

$\Rightarrow$ $\frac{3x}{3}=\frac{3}{3}$ [Dividing both sides by 3]

$\Rightarrow$ $x=1$

Thus, $x = 1$ is the solution of the given equation.

Check Substituting $x = 1$ in the given equation, we get

L.H.S. = $3(1+6)=3\times 7=21$ and R.H.S. = 21

Thus, for $x = 1$, we have L.H.S. = R.H.S.

Example 11 Solve the equation $16(3x - 5) - 10(4x - 8) = 40$ and verify the result.

Solution We have,

$$16(3x-5)-10(4x-8)=40$$

$\Rightarrow$ $16\times 3x-16\times 5-10\times 4x+10\times 8=40$ [On expanding the brackets]

$\Rightarrow$ $48x-80-40x+80=40$

$\Rightarrow$ $48x-40x-80+80=40$

$\Rightarrow$ $(48-40)x+0=40$

$\Rightarrow$ $8x+0=40$

$\Rightarrow$ $8x=40$

$\Rightarrow$ $\frac{8x}{8}=\frac{40}{8}$ [Dividing both sides by 8]

$\Rightarrow$ $x=5$

Thus, $x = 5$ is the solution of the given equation.

Check Substituting $x = 5$ in the given equation, we get L.H.S.

$= 16(3\times 5-5)-10(4\times 5-8)$

$= 16(15-5)-10(20-8)$

$= 16\times 10-10\times 12$

$= 160-120=40$

and, R.H.S. = 40

Thus, for $x = 5$, we have L.H.S. = R.H.S.

EXERCISE 8.2

Solve each of the following equations and check your answers:

1. $x-3=5$
2. $x+9=13$
3. $x-\frac{3}{5}=\frac{7}{5}$
4. $3x=0$
5. $\frac{x}{2}=0$
6. $x-\frac{1}{3}=\frac{2}{3}$
7. $x+\frac{1}{2}=\frac{7}{2}$
8. $10-y=6$
9. $7+4y=-5$
10. $\frac{4}{5}-x=\frac{3}{5}$
11. $2y-\frac{1}{2}=-\frac{1}{3}$
12. $14=\frac{7x}{10}-8$
13. $3(x+2)=15$
14. $\frac{x}{4}=\frac{7}{8}$
15. $\frac{1}{3}-2x=0$
16. $3(x+6)=24$
17. $3(x+2)-2(x-1)=7$
18. $8(2x-5)-6(3x-7)=1$
19. $6(1-4x)+7(2+5x)=53$
20. $5(2-3x)-17(2x-5)=16$
21. $\frac{x-3}{5}-2=-1$
22. $5(x-2)+3(x+1)=25$

ANSWERS

1. 8	2. 4	3. 2	4. 0	5. 0	6. 1
7. 3	8. 4	9. –3	10. $\frac{1}{5}$	11. $\frac{1}{12}$	12. $\frac{220}{7}$
13. 3	14. $\frac{7}{2}$	15. $\frac{1}{6}$	16. 2	17. –1	18. $\frac{1}{2}$
19. 3	20. $\frac{79}{49}$	21. 8	22. 4		

8.6 TRANSPOSITION METHOD

By transposing a term of an equation, we simply mean changing its sign and carrying it to the other side of the equation. Any term of an equation may be taken to the other side with its sign changed without affecting the equality. This process is called transposition. When we carry a term of an equation from L.H.S. to R.H.S or R.H.S to L.H.S., the plus sign of the term changes into minus sign on the other side and vice-versa.

The transposition method involves the following steps:

STEP I *Obtain the linear equation.*

STEP II *Identify the unknown quantity (variable).*

STEP III *Simplify the L.H.S. and R.H.S by removing grouping symbols (if any).*

STEP IV *Transfer all terms containing the variable on the L.H.S. and constant terms on the R.H.S. of the equation. Note that the signs of the terms will change in carrying them from L.H.S. to R.H.S and vice-versa.*

STEP V *Simplify L.H.S. and R.H.S. in the simplest form so that each side contains just one term.*

STEP VI *Solve the equation obtained in step V by using the rules (given on page 8.7).*

Following examples will illustrate the above procedure.

ILLUSTRATIVE EXAMPLES

Example 1 Solve: $3(x-1) = 2x - 11$ and check the result.

Solution We have,

$3(x-1) = 2x - 11$

$\Rightarrow \quad 3x - 3 = 2x - 11$ [Expanding the bracket on L.H.S.]

$\Rightarrow \quad 3x - 2x = 3 - 11$ [Transposing $2x$ to L.H.S. and -3 to R.H.S.]

$\Rightarrow \quad x = -8$

Thus, $x = -8$ is the solution of the given equation.

Check Substituting $x = -8$ in the given equation, we get

L.H.S. $= 3(-8-1) = 3 \times (-9) = -27$ and, R.H.S. $= 2 \times (-8) - 11 = -16 - 11 = -27$

Thus, for $x = -8$, we have, L.H.S. = R.H.S.

Example 2 Solve: $3(x+3) - 2(x-1) = 5(x-5)$ and check the result.

Solution We have,

$3(x+3) - 2(x-1) = 5(x-5)$

$\Rightarrow \quad 3x + 9 - 2x + 2 = 5x - 25$ [Expanding brackets on both side]

$\Rightarrow \quad 3x - 2x + 9 + 2 = 5x - 25$

$\Rightarrow \quad x + 11 = 5x - 25$ [Simplifying L.H.S. and R.H.S. separately]

$\Rightarrow \quad x - 5x = -25 - 11$ [Transposing $5x$ on L.H.S. and 11 on R.H.S.]

$\Rightarrow \quad -4x = -36$

$\Rightarrow \quad \frac{-4x}{-4} = \frac{-36}{-4}$ [Dividing both sides by -4]

$\Rightarrow \quad x = 9$

Thus, $x = 9$ is the solution of the given equation.

Check Substituting $x = 9$ in the given equation, we get

L.H.S. $= 3(9+3) - 2(9-1) = 3 \times 12 - 2 \times 8 = 36 - 16 = 20$

and, R.H.S. $= 5(9-5) = 5 \times 4 = 20$

Thus, for $x = 9$, we have L.H.S. = R.H.S.

Example 3 Solve: $\frac{x}{2} - 1 = \frac{x}{3} + 4$

Solution We have,

$\frac{x}{2} - 1 = \frac{x}{3} + 4$

$\Rightarrow \quad \frac{x}{2} - \frac{x}{3} = 1 + 4$ [Transposing $\frac{x}{3}$ on L.H.S. and -1 on R.H.S.]

$\Rightarrow \quad \left(\frac{1}{2} - \frac{1}{3}\right)x = 5$

$\Rightarrow \quad \left(\frac{3-2}{6}\right)x = 5$

$\Rightarrow \quad \frac{1}{6}x = 5$

$\Rightarrow \quad 6 \times \frac{1}{6}x = 6 \times 5$ [Multiplying both sides by 6]

$\Rightarrow \quad x = 30$

Thus, $x = 30$ is the solution of the given equation.

Aliter We have,

$$\frac{x}{2} - 1 = \frac{x}{3} + 4$$

Multiplying each term by 6, the L.C.M. of 2 and 3, the given equation becomes

$$6 \times \frac{x}{2} - 6 = 6 \times \frac{x}{3} + 6 \times 4$$

$\Rightarrow \quad 3x - 6 = 2x + 24$

$\Rightarrow \quad 3x - 2x = 6 + 24$ [Transposing $2x$ on L.H.S. and -6 on R.H.S.]

$\Rightarrow \quad x = 30$

Check Substituting $x = 30$ in the given equation, we get

L.H.S. = $\frac{30}{2} - 1 = 15 - 1 = 14$ and, R.H.S. = $\frac{30}{3} + 4 = 10 + 4 = 14$

Thus, L.H.S. = R.H.S when $x = 30$

Example 4 Solve: $\frac{2x-1}{3} + 1 = \frac{x-2}{3} + 2$ and check the result.

Solution We have,

$$\frac{2x-1}{3} + 1 = \frac{x-2}{3} + 2$$

$\Rightarrow \quad \frac{2x}{3} - \frac{1}{3} + 1 = \frac{x}{3} - \frac{2}{3} + 2$

$\Rightarrow \quad \frac{2x}{3} + \frac{3-1}{3} = \frac{x}{3} + \frac{6-2}{3}$

$\Rightarrow \quad \frac{2x}{3} + \frac{2}{3} = \frac{x}{3} + \frac{4}{3}$

$\Rightarrow \quad \frac{2x}{3} - \frac{x}{3} = \frac{4}{3} - \frac{2}{3}$ $\left[\text{Transposing } \frac{x}{3} \text{ on L.H.S. and } \frac{2}{3} \text{ on R.H.S.}\right]$

$\Rightarrow \quad \frac{x}{3} = \frac{2}{3}$

$\Rightarrow \quad \frac{x}{3} \times 3 = \frac{2}{3} \times 3$ [Multiplying both sides by 3]

$\Rightarrow \quad x = 2.$

Thus, $x = 2$ is the solution of the given equation.

Check Substituting $x = 2$ in the given equation, we get

$$\text{L.H.S.} = \frac{2x-1}{3}+1 = \frac{2\times2-1}{3}+1 = \frac{3}{3}+1 = 2$$

$$\text{R.H.S.} = \frac{2-2}{3}+2 = \frac{0}{3}+2 = 0+2 = 2$$

Thus, L.H.S. = R.H.S. when $x = 2$.

Example 5 *Solve:* $\frac{3x}{10}+\frac{2x}{5}=\frac{7x}{25}+\frac{29}{25}$

Solution We have,

$$\frac{3x}{10}+\frac{2x}{5}=\frac{7x}{25}+\frac{29}{25}$$

The denominators on two sides are 10, 5 and 25. Their L.C.M. is 50.
Multiplying both sides of the given equation by 50, we get

$$50\times\left(\frac{3x}{10}+\frac{2x}{5}\right) = 50\times\left(\frac{7x}{25}+\frac{29}{25}\right)$$

$$\Rightarrow \quad 50\times\frac{3x}{10}+50\times\frac{2x}{5} = 50\times\frac{7x}{25}+50\times\frac{29}{25}$$

$$\Rightarrow \quad 15x+20x = 14x+58$$

$$\Rightarrow \quad 35x = 14x+58$$

$$\Rightarrow \quad 35x-14x = 58$$ [On transposing $14x$ to L.H.S.]

$$\Rightarrow \quad 21x = 58$$

$$\Rightarrow \quad \frac{21x}{21} = \frac{58}{21}$$ [Dividing both sides by 21]

$$\Rightarrow \quad x = \frac{58}{21}$$

Thus, $x = \frac{58}{21}$ is the solution of the given equation.

Check Substituting $x = \frac{58}{21}$ in the given equation, we get

$$\text{L.H.S.} = \frac{3x}{10}+\frac{2x}{5}$$

$$= \frac{3}{10}\times\frac{58}{21}+\frac{2}{5}\times\frac{58}{21}$$

$$= \frac{29}{35}+\frac{116}{105} = \frac{29\times3+116}{105} = \frac{87+116}{105} = \frac{203}{105} = \frac{29}{15}$$

and,

$$\text{R.H.S.} = \frac{7x}{25} + \frac{29}{25}$$

$$= \frac{7}{25} \times \frac{58}{21} + \frac{29}{25} = \frac{58}{75} + \frac{29}{25} = \frac{58 + 3 \times 29}{75} = \frac{145}{75} = \frac{29}{15}$$

Thus, for $x = \frac{58}{21}$, we have L.H.S. = R.H.S.

Example 6 Solve: $\frac{12}{7}(x-5) = 24 + 8x$

Solution We have, $\frac{12}{7}(x-5) = 24 + 8x$

Multiplying both sides by 7, we get

$$7 \times \frac{12}{7}(x-5) = 7 \times (24 + 8x)$$

$\Rightarrow$ $12(x-5) = 7(24 + 8x)$

$\Rightarrow$ $12x - 60 = 168 + 56x$

$\Rightarrow$ $12x - 56x = 168 + 60$ [Transposing $56x$ to L.H.S. and – 60 to R.H.S]

$\Rightarrow$ $-44x = 228$

$\Rightarrow$ $\frac{-44x}{-44} = \frac{228}{-44}$ [Dividing both sides by – 44]

$\Rightarrow$ $x = -\frac{57}{11}$

Thus, $x = -\frac{57}{11}$ is the solution of the given equation.

Check Substituting $x = -\frac{57}{11}$ in the given equation, we get

$$\text{L.H.S.} = \frac{12}{7}(x-5)$$

$$= \frac{12}{7} \times \left(\frac{-57}{11} - 5\right)$$

$$= \frac{12}{7} \times \left(\frac{-57-55}{11}\right) = \frac{12}{7} \times -\frac{112}{11} = 12 \times -\frac{16}{11} = -\frac{192}{11}$$

and,

$$\text{R.H.S.} = 24 + 8x$$

$$= 24 + 8 \times -\frac{57}{11} = 24 - \frac{456}{11} = \frac{24 \times 11 - 456}{11} = \frac{264 - 456}{11} = -\frac{192}{11}$$

Thus, L.H.S. = R.H.S. for $x = -\frac{57}{11}$

Example 7 Solve: $\frac{y-8}{3} = \frac{7-4y}{7}$

Solution We have, $\frac{y-8}{3} = \frac{7-4y}{7}$

The denominators on L.H.S. and R.H.S. are 3 and 7 respectively.

Multiplying both sides by the L.C.M. of 3 and 7, that is 21, we get

$$21\left(\frac{y-8}{3}\right) = 21\left(\frac{7-4y}{7}\right)$$

$\Rightarrow \quad 7(y-8) = 3(7-4y)$

$\Rightarrow \quad 7y - 56 = 21 - 12y$

$\Rightarrow \quad 7y + 12y = 21 + 56$ [Transposing $-12y$ to L.H.S. and -56 to R.H.S.]

$\Rightarrow \quad 19y = 77$

$\Rightarrow \quad y = \frac{77}{19}$

Thus, $y = \frac{77}{19}$ is the solution of the given equation.

Check Putting $y = \frac{77}{19}$ in the given equation, we get

$$\text{L.H.S.} = \frac{y-8}{3} = \frac{\frac{77}{19}-8}{3} = \frac{77-152}{19\times 3} = \frac{-75}{57} = \frac{-25}{19}$$

and, R.H.S. $= \frac{7-4y}{7}$

$$= \frac{7-4\times\frac{77}{19}}{7} = \frac{7-\frac{308}{19}}{7} = \frac{133-308}{7\times 19} = \frac{-175}{7\times 19} = \frac{-25}{19}$$

Thus, L.H.S. = R.H.S. for $y = \frac{77}{19}$

Example 8 Solve: $\frac{x-6}{4} - \frac{x-4}{6} = 1 - \frac{x}{10}$

Solution We have, $\frac{x-6}{4} - \frac{x-4}{6} = 1 - \frac{x}{10}$

Multiplying both sides by 60, the L.C.M. of 4, 6 and 10, we get

$$60\left(\frac{x-6}{4}\right) - 60\left(\frac{x-4}{6}\right) = 60\left(1-\frac{x}{10}\right)$$

$\Rightarrow \quad 15(x-6) - 10(x-4) = 60\left(1-\frac{x}{10}\right)$

$\Rightarrow \quad 15x - 90 - 10x + 40 = 60 - 6x$

$\Rightarrow \quad 15x - 10x - 90 + 40 = 60 - 6x$

$\Rightarrow \quad 5x - 50 = 60 - 6x$

$\Rightarrow$ $5x + 6x = 60 + 50$ [Transposing $-6x$ to L.H.S. and -50 to R.H.S.]

$\Rightarrow$ $11x = 110$

$\Rightarrow$ $\frac{11x}{11} = \frac{110}{11}$ [Dividing both sides by 11]

$\Rightarrow$ $x = 10$

Thus, $x = 10$ is the solution of the given equation.

Example 9 Solve: $\frac{3}{4}(7x-1)-\left(2x-\frac{1-x}{2}\right) = x+\frac{3}{2}$

Solution We have,

$$\frac{3}{4}(7x-1)-\left(2x-\frac{1-x}{2}\right) = x+\frac{3}{2}$$

$$\Rightarrow \frac{3}{4}(7x-1)-\left(2x-\frac{1-x}{2}\right) = x+\frac{3}{2}$$

Multiplying both sides by 4, the L.C.M. of 4 and 2, we get

$$3(7x-1)-8x+4\left(\frac{1-x}{2}\right) = 4\left(x+\frac{3}{2}\right)$$

$$\Rightarrow 3(7x-1)-8x+2(1-x) = 4\left(x+\frac{3}{2}\right)$$

$\Rightarrow$ $21x-3-8x+2-2x = 4x+6$ [On expanding brackets]

$\Rightarrow$ $21x-8x-2x-3+2 = 4x+6$

$\Rightarrow$ $11x-1 = 4x+6$

$\Rightarrow$ $11x-4x = 6+1$ [On transposing -1 to R.H.S. and 4x to L.H.S]

$\Rightarrow$ $7x = 7$

$\Rightarrow$ $\frac{7x}{7} = \frac{7}{7}$ [Dividing both sides by 7]

$\Rightarrow$ $x = 1$

Thus, $x = 1$ is the solution of the given equation.

Example 10 Solve: $0.3x + 0.4 = 0.28x + 1.16$

Solution We have,

$0.3x + 0.4 = 0.28x + 1.16$

$\Rightarrow$ $0.3x - 0.28x = 1.16 - 0.4$ [Transposing $0.28\,x$ to LHS and 0.4 to R.H.S]

$\Rightarrow$ $(0.3-0.28)x = 1.16-0.4$

$\Rightarrow$ $0.02x = 0.76$

$\Rightarrow$ $\frac{0.02x}{0.02} = \frac{0.76}{0.02}$ [Dividing both sides by 0.02]

$\Rightarrow$ $x = \frac{76}{2}$

$\Rightarrow$ $x = 38.$

Thus, $x = 38$ is the solution of the given equation.

EXERCISE 8.3

Solve each of the following equations. Also, verify the result in each case.

1. $6x + 5 = 2x + 17$
2. $2(5x - 3) - 3(2x - 1) = 9$
3. $\frac{x}{2} = \frac{x}{3} + 1$
4. $\frac{x}{2} + \frac{3}{2} = \frac{2x}{5} - 1$
5. $\frac{3}{4}(x - 1) = x - 3$
6. $3(x - 3) = 5(2x + 1)$
7. $3x - 2(2x - 5) = 2(x + 3) - 8$
8. $x - \frac{x}{4} - \frac{1}{2} = 3 + \frac{x}{4}$
9. $\frac{6x - 2}{9} + \frac{3x + 5}{18} = \frac{1}{3}$
10. $m - \frac{m - 1}{2} = 1 - \frac{m - 2}{3}$
11. $\frac{(5x - 1)}{3} - \frac{(2x - 2)}{3} = 1$
12. $0.6x + \frac{4}{5} = 0.28x + 1.16$
13. $0.5x + \frac{x}{3} = 0.25x + 7$

ANSWERS

1. 3 2. 3 3. 6 4. –25 5. 9 6. –2
7. 4 8. 7 9. $\frac{1}{3}$ 10. $\frac{7}{5}$ 11. $\frac{2}{3}$ 12. $\frac{9}{8}$
13. 12

8.7 APPLICATIONS OF LINEAR EQUATIONS TO PRACTICAL PROBLEMS

In this section, we shall study formulation and solution of some practical problems. These problems involve relations among unkown quantities (variables) and known quantities (numbers) and are often stated in words. That is why we often refer to these problems as word problems. A word problem is first translated in the form of an equation containing unknown quantities (variables) and known quantities (numbers or constants) and then we solve it by using any one of the methods discussed in the earlier section. The procedure to translate a word problem in the form of an equation is known as the formulation of the problem. Thus, the process of solving a word problem consists of two parts, namely, formulation and solution.

Following steps should be followed to solve a word problem:

STEP I *Read the problem carefully and note what is given and what is required.*
STEP II *Denote the unknown quantity by some letters, say x, y, z, etc.*
STEP III *Translate the statements of the problem into mathematical statements.*
STEP IV *Using the condition (s) given in the problem, form the equation.*
STEP V *Solve the equation for the unknown.*
STEP VI *Check whether the solution satisfies the equation.*

Following examples will illustrate these steps.

ILLUSTRATIVE EXAMPLES

Example 1 5 added to a number gives 9. Find the number.

Formulation: Let the required number be x. Then, 5 added to x is equal to $x + 5$

It is given that when 5 is added to a number, we get 9. Thus, we obtain the following equation:

$$x + 5 = 9$$

Solution We have,

$$x + 5 = 9$$

$\Rightarrow$ $x = 9 - 5$ [On transposing 5 to R.H.S.]

$\Rightarrow$ $x = 4$

Hence, the required number is 4.

Example 2 If 7 is subtracted from five times a number, the result is 63. Find the number.

Formulation: Let the required number be x Then,

Five times $x = 5x$

When 7 is subtracted from five times x, we get $5x - 7$.

It is given that when 7 is subtracted from five times x, the result is 63. So, we obtain the following equation:

$$5x - 7 = 63$$

Solution We have,

$$5x - 7 = 63$$

$\Rightarrow$ $5x = 63 + 7$ [On transposing – 7 to R.H.S]

$\Rightarrow$ $5x = 70$

$\Rightarrow$ $\frac{5x}{5} = \frac{70}{5}$ [Dividing both sides by 5]

$\Rightarrow$ $x = 14$.

Hence, the required number is 14.

Example 3 What is the number which when multipled by 20 gives the product 60?

Formulation: Let the required number be x. Then,

Product of x and $20 = 20\,x$

It is given that when x is multiplied by 20, the product is 60.

Thus, we obtain the following equation:

$$20x = 60$$

Solution We have,

$$20x = 60$$

$\Rightarrow$ $\frac{20x}{20} = \frac{60}{20}$ [Dividing both sides by 20]

$\Rightarrow$ $x = 3$

Hence, the required number is 3.

Example 4 Find the number which when divided by 9 gives 4.

Formulation: Let the required number be x. Then,

$$x \text{ divided by } 9 = \frac{x}{9}$$

It is given that x divided by 9 is 4. So, we obtain the following equation:

$$\frac{x}{9} = 4$$

Solution We have,

$$\frac{x}{9} = 4$$

$$\Rightarrow \quad \frac{x}{9} \times 9 = 4 \times 9 \qquad \text{[Multiplying both sides by 9]}$$

$$\Rightarrow \quad x = 36$$

Hence, the required number is 36.

Example 5 The sum of two consecutive numbers is 53. find the numbers.

Formulation: Let one number be x. Then, the next consecutive number is $x+1$. It is given that the sum of two consecutive numbers is 53. So, we obtain the following equation:

$$x + (x+1) = 53$$

Solution We have,

$$x + (x+1) = 53$$

$$\Rightarrow \quad 2x + 1 = 53$$

$$\Rightarrow \quad 2x = 53 - 1 \qquad \text{[On transposing 1 on R.H.S.]}$$

$$\Rightarrow \quad 2x = 52$$

$$\Rightarrow \quad \frac{2x}{2} = \frac{52}{2} \qquad \text{[Dividing both sides by 2]}$$

$$\Rightarrow \quad x = 26$$

$\therefore$ One number = 26

Another number $= 26 + 1 = 27$.

Example 6 The sum of two consecutive even numbers is 86. Find the numbers.

Formulation: Let one of the even numbers be x. Then, the next consecutive even number $= x + 2$.

Now,

Sum of two consecutive even numbers = 86

$$\Rightarrow \quad x + x + 2 = 86$$

$$\Rightarrow \quad 2x + 2 = 86$$

Solution We have,

$$2x + 2 = 86$$

$$\Rightarrow \quad 2x = 86 - 2 \qquad \text{[On transposing 2 on R.H.S.]}$$

$$\Rightarrow \quad 2x = 84$$

$$\Rightarrow \quad \frac{2x}{2} = \frac{84}{2} \qquad \text{[Dividing both sides by 2]}$$

$$\Rightarrow \quad x = 42.$$

Thus,

One of the even numbers = 42

The other consecutive even number $= x + 2 = 42 + 2 = 44$.

Example 7 The sum of two consecutive odd numbers is 68. Find the numbers.

Formulation. Let one of the odd numbers be x. Then,

The next consecutive odd numbers = $x + 2$.

Now,

Sum of two consecutive odd numbers = 68

$\Rightarrow \quad x + (x + 2) = 68$

$\Rightarrow \quad 2x + 2 = 68$

Solution We have,

$2x + 2 = 68$

$\Rightarrow \quad 2x = 68 - 2$ [On transposing 2 on R.H.S.]

$\Rightarrow \quad 2x = 66$

$\Rightarrow \quad \frac{2x}{2} = \frac{66}{2}$ [Dividing both sides by 2]

$\Rightarrow \quad x = 33.$

Thus, one odd number = 33.

Other odd number $= x + 2 = 33 + 2 = 35.$

Example 8 Find two numbers such that one of them exceeds the other by 9 and their sum is 81.

Formulation: Let the smaller number be x. Then,

Another number = $x + 9$

Now, sum of the numbers = 81

$\Rightarrow \quad x + x + 9 = 81$

$\Rightarrow \quad 2x + 9 = 81$

Solution We have, $2x + 9 = 81$

$\Rightarrow \quad 2x = 81 - 9$ [On transposing 9 on R.H.S.]

$\Rightarrow \quad 2x = 72$

$\Rightarrow \quad \frac{2x}{2} = \frac{72}{2}$

$\Rightarrow \quad x = 36$ [Dividing both sides by 2]

$\therefore$ One number = 36

Another number $= 36 + 9 = 45.$

Example 9 Find a number which when multiplied by 5 is increased by 80.

Formulation: Let the required number be x. Then x multiplied by 5 = $5x$.

It is given that when the number is multiplied by 5, the new number is 80 more than the number x. So, we obtain

$$5x = x + 80$$

Solution We have,

$5x = x + 80$

$\Rightarrow \quad 5x - x = 80$ [On transposing x on L.H.S.]

$\Rightarrow \quad 4x = 80$

$\Rightarrow \quad \frac{4x}{4} = \frac{80}{4}$ [Dividing both sides by 4]

$\Rightarrow \quad x = 20$

Thus, the required number is 20.

Example 10 The sum of ages of father and his son is 75 years. If the age of the son is 25 years, find the age of the father.

Formulation: Let the age of the father be x years.

The age of son = 25 years.

$\therefore$ Sum of the two ages $= (x + 25)$ years.

But the sum of the ages is given as 75 years.

$\therefore \quad x + 25 = 75$

Solution We have,

$x + 25 = 75$

$\Rightarrow \quad x = 75 - 25$ [On transposing 25 on R.H.S.]

$\Rightarrow \quad x = 50$

Thus, the age of the father is 50 years.

Example 11 Rahim's father is three times as old as Rahim. If sum of their ages is 56 years, find their ages.

Formulation: Let Rahim's age be x years. Then,

Rahim's father's age = $3x$ years.

$\therefore$ Sum of their ages $= x + 3x$.

But the sum of their ages is given as 56 years. Therefore, we have the following equation.

$$x + 3x = 56$$

Solution We have, $x + 3x = 56$

$\Rightarrow \quad 4x - 56$

$\Rightarrow \quad \frac{4x}{4} = \frac{56}{4}$ [Dividing both sides by 4]

$\Rightarrow \quad x = 14$

Thus, Rahim's age = 14 years

Rahim's father's age = $3x$ year $= 3 \times 14$ years = 42 years.

Example 12 Mona's father is thrice as old as Mona. After 12 years he will be just twice his daughter. Find their present ages.

Formulation: Let Mona's present age be x years. Then,

Her father's present age = $3x$ years.

Mona's age after 12 years $= (x + 12)$ years.

Mona's father's age after 12 years $= (3x + 12)$ years.

It is given that after 12 years Mona's father will be just twice his daughter. Therefore, we obtain the following equation:

$$3x + 12 = 2\,(x + 12)$$

Solution We have,

$$3x + 12 = 2(x + 12)$$

$\Rightarrow$ $3x + 12 = 2x + 24$ [Expanding bracket on R.H.S.]

$\Rightarrow$ $3x - 2x = 24 - 12$ [Transposing $2x$ on L.H.S. and 12 on R.H.S]

$\Rightarrow$ $x = 12.$

Thus, Mona's present age = 12 years.

Her father's present age $= (3 \times 12)$ years = 36 years.

Example 13 A sum of ₹ 8400 is made up of 50, 20, 10 and 5 rupee notes. The number of 10 rupee notes is five times the number of 5 rupee notes, four times the number of 20 rupee notes and ten times the number of 50 rupee notes. What is the number of notes in each denominator?

Formulation: Let the number of 10 rupee notes be x. Then.

Number of 50 rupee notes $= \frac{x}{10}$.

Number of 20 rupee notes $= \frac{x}{4}$

Number of 5 rupee notes $= \frac{x}{5}$

Now,

Value of x ten rupee notes $=$ ₹ $(10 \times x) =$ ₹ $10x$

Value of $\frac{x}{10}$ fifty rupee notes $=$ ₹ $\left(50 \times \frac{x}{10}\right) =$ ₹ $5x$

Value of $\frac{x}{4}$ twenty rupee notes $=$ ₹ $\left(20 \times \frac{x}{4}\right) =$ ₹ $5x$

Value of $\frac{x}{5}$ five rupee notes $=$ ₹ $\left(5 \times \frac{x}{5}\right) =$ ₹ x

$\therefore$ Total value of all notes $=$ ₹ $(10x + 5x + 5x + x)$

But the total amount is given as ₹ 8400. So, we obtain the following equation:

$$10x + 5x + 5x + x = 8400$$

Solution We have,

$$10x + 5x + 5x + x = 8400$$

$\Rightarrow$ $21x = 8400$

$\Rightarrow$ $\frac{21x}{21} = \frac{8400}{21}$

$\Rightarrow$ $x = 400$

Hence,

Number of ten rupee notes $= 400$

Number of fifty rupee notes $= \frac{x}{10} = \frac{400}{10} = 40$

Number of twenty rupee notes $= \frac{x}{4} = \frac{400}{4} = 100$

Number of five rupee notes $= \frac{x}{5} = \frac{400}{5} = 80.$

Example 14 Ravish owns a plot of rectangular shape. He has fenced it with a wire of length 750 m. The length of the plot exceeds the breadth by 5 m. Find the length and breadth of the plot.

Formulation: Let the breadth of the plot be x metres. Then,

Length = $(x + 5)$ metres.

$\Rightarrow$ Perimeter of the plot $= 2\,(\text{length} + \text{breadth})$

$$= 2(x + 5 + x)$$

$$= 2(2x + 5)$$

$$= (4x + 10)$$

It is given that Ravish has fenced the plot with a wire of length 750 metres. This means that the perimeter of the plot is 750 metres. Thus, we obtain the following equation:

$$4x + 10 = 750.$$

Solution We have, $4x + 10 = 750$

$\Rightarrow \quad 4x = 750 - 10$ [Transposing 10 to R.H.S.]

$\Rightarrow \quad 4x = 740$

$\Rightarrow \quad \frac{4x}{4} = \frac{740}{4}$ [Dividing both sides by 4]

$\Rightarrow \quad x = 185$

Thus, length of the plot = $(x + 5)$ metres = $(185 + 5)$ metres = 190 metres and, breadth of the plot = 185 metres.

Example 15 Sara's mother is three times as old as Sara and four times as old as Sara's sister, Ann. Ann is three years younger than Sara. How old are Sara, Ann and their mother?

Solution Let Sara's age be x years.

It is given that Ann is three years younger than Sara.

$\therefore$ Ann's age $= (x - 3)$ years

It is given that Sara's mother is three times as old as Sara.

$\therefore$ Sara's mother's age $= 3x$ years ... (i)

Also, Sara's mother is four times as old as Ann

$\therefore$ Sara's mother's age $= 4(x - 3)$ years ... (ii)

From (i) and (ii), we have

$$3x = 4(x - 3)$$

$\Rightarrow \quad 3x = 4x - 12$

$\Rightarrow \quad 3x-4x=-12$ [Transposing $4x$ to LHS]

$\Rightarrow \quad -x=-12$ [Dividing both sides by -1]

$\Rightarrow \quad x=12$

$\therefore$ Sara's age = 12years

Ann's age = $(12-3)$ years = 9years

Sara's mother's age = $3x = 3\times 12 = 36$years.

EXERCISE 8.4

1. If 5 is subtracted from three times a number, the result is 16. Find the number.
2. Find the number which when multiplied by 7 is increased by 78.
3. Find three consecutive natural numbers such that the sum of the first and second is 15 more than the third.
4. The difference between two numbers is 7. Six times the smaller plus the larger is 77. Find the numbers.
5. A man says, "I am thinking of a number. When I divide it by 3 and then add 5, my answer is twice the number I thought of". Find the number.
6. If a number is tripled and the result is increased by 5, we get 50. Find the number.
7. Shikha is 3 years younger to her brother Ravish. If the sum of their ages is 37 years, what are their present ages?
8. Mrs. Jain is 27 years older than her daughter Nilu. After 8 years she will be twice as old as Nilu. Find their present ages.
9. A man is 4 times as old as his son. After 16 years, he will be only twice as old as his son. Find the their present ages.
10. The difference in age between a girl and her younger sister is 4 years. The younger sister in turn is 4 years older than her brother. The sum of the ages of the younger sister and her brother is 16. How old are the three children?
11. One day, during their vacation at a beach resort, Shella found twice as many sea shells as Anita and Anita found 5 shells more than sandy. Together sandy and Shella found 16 sea shells. How many did each of them find?
12. Andy has twice as many marbles as Pandy, and Sandy has half as many has Andy and Pandy put together. If Andy has 75 marbles more than Sandy. How many does each of them have?
13. A bag contains 25 paise and 50 paise coins whose total value is Rs 30. If the number of 25 paise coins is four times that of 50 paise coins, find the number of each type of coins.
14. The length of a rectangular field is twice its breadth. If the perimeter of the field is 228 metres, find the dimensions of the field.
15. There are only 25 paise coins in a purse. The value of money in the purse is Rs 17.50. Find the number of coins in the purse.
16. In a hostel mess, 50 kg rice are consumed everyday. If each student gets 400 gm of rice per day, find the number of students who take meals in the hostel mess.

ANSWERS

1. 7 2. 13 3. 16, 17, 18 4. 10, 17 5. 3 6. 15

7. Shikha: 17 years, Ravish 20 years 8. Nilu: 19 years, Mrs. Jain: 46 years

9. Son: 8 years, Man 32 years 10. Brother: 6 years, Younger sister: 10 years, Girl: 14 years.
11. Sandy: 2, Anita: 7, Shella: 14 12. Pandy: 150 Marbles, Andy: 300 Marbles Sandy: 225 Marbles,
13. 50 paise coins : 20, 25 paise coins : 80 14. Length = 76 metres, Breadth = 38 metres
15. 70 16. 125

OBJECTIVE TYPE QUESTIONS

Mark the correct alternative in each of the following:

1. The zero of $3x + 2$ is
   (a) $\frac{2}{3}$ (b) $\frac{3}{2}$ (c) $-\frac{2}{3}$ (d) $\frac{-3}{2}$
2. If $2x - \frac{3}{2} = 5x + \frac{3}{4}$, then $x =$
   (a) $\frac{3}{4}$ (b) $-\frac{3}{4}$ (c) $\frac{4}{3}$ (d) $-\frac{4}{3}$
3. If $\frac{x}{2} - 4 = \frac{x}{3} - 1$, then $x =$
   (a) 3 (b) 6 (c) 18 (d) 2
4. If $\frac{x+2}{x-2} = \frac{2}{3}$
   (a) -10 (b) 10 (c) $\frac{4}{3}$ (d) $-\frac{4}{3}$
5. If $\frac{x}{6} + \frac{x}{4} = \frac{x}{2} + \frac{3}{4}$, then $x =$
   (a) 9 (b) 6 (c) -9 (d) 4
6. If $2x + \frac{5}{3} = \frac{1}{4}x + 4$, then $x =$
   (a) 3 (b) 4 (c) $\frac{3}{4}$ (d) $\frac{4}{3}$
7. If $\frac{x}{2} - \frac{x}{3} = 5$, then $x =$
   (a) 8 (b) 16 (c) 24 (d) 30
8. If $\frac{x-2}{3} = \frac{2x-1}{3} - 1$, then $x =$
   (a) 2 (b) 4 (c) 6 (d) 8
9. The sum of two consecutive whole numbers is 43. The smaller number is
   (a) 21 (b) 22 (c) 23 (d) 24
10. The sum of two consecutive odd numbers is 36. The larger number is
    (a) 17 (b) 15 (c) 19 (d) 21
11. Twice a number when increased by 7 gives 25. The number is
    (a) 7 (b) 9 (c) 10 (d) 8
12. The length of a rectangle is three times its width and its perimeter 56 m. The length is
    (a) 7 m (b) 14 m (c) 21 m (d) 28 m
13. Two-thirds of a number is greater than one-third of the number by 5. The number is
    (a) 10 (b) 5 (c) 15 (d) 12

14. If the sum of a number and its two-fifth is 70. Thenumber is
(a) 70 (b) 50 (c) 60 (d) 90

15. $\frac{2}{3}$ of a number is less than the original number by 20. The number is
(a) 30 (b) 40 (c) 50 (d) 60

16. A number is as much greater than 31 as it is less than 81. The number is
(a) 46 (b) 56 (c) 66 (d) 76

17. Two complementary angles differ by 20°. The smaller angle is
(a) 55° (b) 25° (c) 65° (d) 35°

18. Two supplementary angles differ by 40°. The measure of the larger angle is
(a) 70° (b) 80° (c) 110° (d) 100°

19. The sum of three consecutive odd numbers is 81. The middle number is
(a) 25 (b) 27 (c) 31 (d) 29

20. If $2(2n + 5) = 3(3n - 10)$, then $n =$
(a) 5 (b) 3 (c) 7 (d) 8

ANSWSERS

1. (c)	2. (b)	3. (c)	4. (a)	5. (c)	6. (d)	7. (d)
8. (a)	9. (a)	10. (c)	11. (b)	12. (c)	13. (c)	14. (b)
15. (d)	16. (b)	17. (d)	18. (c)	19. (b)	20. (d)	

THINGS TO REMEMBER

1. *A statement of equality involving one or more variables (literals) is called an equation.*
2. *An equation involving only one literal number (variable) with the highest power one is called a linear equation in one variable.*
3. *While solving an equation we can*
   - *(i) add the same number to both sides of the equation;*
   - *(ii) subtract the same number from both sides of the equation;*
   - *(iii) multiply both sides of the equation by the same non-zero number;*
   - *(iv) divide both sides of the equation by the same non-zero number.*
4. *In an equation, we can drop a term from one side and put it on the other side with the opposite sign. This process is known as transposition.*

9

RATIO AND PROPORTION

9.1 INTRODUCTION

In Class VI, we have gone through the concept of Ratio and Proportion. In this chapter, we will have a brief revision of the same to strengthen our position in the applications of these concepts.

9.2 RATIO

In our daily life, we often come across many situations where we need to compare quantities in terms of their magnitudes/measurements. Generally, we compare two quantities either by finding the difference of their magnitudes or by finding the division of their magnitudes. When we want to see how much more (or less) one quantity is than the other, we find the difference of their magnitudes and such a comparison is known as the comparison by difference. If we want to see how many times more (or less) one quantity is than the other, we find the ratio (or division) of their magnitudes and such a comparison is known as the comparison by division. In fact, when we compare two quantities of the same kind by division, we say that we form a ratio of the two quantities. Suppose Heena's height is 150 cm and her brother Amir's height is 100 cm. If we wish to compare heights of Heena and Amir by difference, then we can say that Heena is 50 cm taller than her brother Amir.

By comparing their heights by division, we can also say that Heena is $\frac{3}{2}$ times taller than her brother Amir. Here we observe that the comparison by division makes better sense than the comparison by taking the difference. When we compare two quantities of the same kind by division, we say that we form a ratio of the two quantities. Thus, we can say that the ratio of the height of Heena to that of Amir is $\frac{150}{100}$. Usually, we use the symbol ':' to express a ratio. Therefore, the ratio of the height of Heena to that of Amir is written as 150 : 100 and it is read as '150 is to 100' or '150 to 100'.

It is evident from the above discussion that a ratio is a fraction that shows how many times a quantity is of another quantity of the same kind.

RATIO *The ratio of two quantities of the same kind and in the same units is a fraction that shows how many times the one quantity is of the other.*

Thus, the ratio of two quantities a and b $(b \neq 0)$ is $a \div b$ or, $\frac{a}{b}$ and is denoted by $a : b$.

In the ratio $a : b$, the quantities (numbers) a and b are called the terms of the ratio. The former 'a' is called the first term or antecedent and the later 'b' is known as the second term or consequent.

We know that a fraction does not change when its numerator and denominator are multiplied or divided by the same non-zero number. So, a ratio does not alter, if its first and second terms are multiplied or divided by the same non-zero number.

$\therefore \quad 150:100 = 15:10$ [Dividing the first and second term by 10]

$150:100 = 300:200$ [Multiplying the first and second term by 2]

RATIO IN THE SIMPLEST FORM *A ratio a : b is said to be in the simplest form if its antecedent a and consequent b have no common factor other than 1.*

A ratio in the simplest form is also called the ratio in the lowest terms.

The ratio 80 : 32 is not in the simplest form, because 16 is a common factor of its antecedent and consequent. The simplest form of this ratio is 5 : 2 (dividing the first and second term by 16).

Usually, a ratio is expressed in the simplest form.

NOTE 1 *In a ratio, we compare two quantities. The comparison becomes meaningless if the quantities being compared are not of the same kind i.e. they are not measured in the same units. It is just meaningless to compare 20 bags with 200 crows. Therefore, to find the ratio of two quantities, they must be expressed in the same units.*

NOTE 2 *Since the ratio of two quantities of the same kind determines how many times one quantity is contained by the other. So, the ratio of any two quantities of the same kind is an abstract quantity. In other words, ratio has no unit or it is independent of the units used in the quantities compared.*

NOTE 3 *The order of the terms in a ratio a : b is very important. The ratio 3 : 2 is different from the ratio 2 : 3.*

Let us now illustrate these ideals through some examples.

ILLUSTRATIVE EXAMPLES

Example 1 Express the ratio 45 : 108 in its simplest form:

Solution In order to express the given ratio in its simplest form we divide its first and second terms by their HCF.

We have,

$$45 = 3 \times 3 \times 5 \text{ and } 108 = 2 \times 2 \times 3 \times 3 \times 3$$

So, HCF of 45 and 108 is $3 \times 3 = 9$.

$$\therefore \quad 45:108 = \frac{45}{108} = \frac{45 \div 9}{108 \div 9} = \frac{5}{12} = 5:12$$

Hence, 45 : 108 in its simplest form is 5 : 12.

Example 2 Shikha and Sumeet take ₹ 600 and ₹ 750 respectively from their parents as monthly pocket expenses. What is the ratio of their expenses in the simplest form?

Solution We have,

Required ratio = ₹ 600 : ₹ 750

$$= \frac{600}{750} = \frac{600 \div 150}{750 \div 150} \quad \left[\begin{array}{l}\text{Dividing the antecedent and consequent} \\ \text{by the HCF of 600 and 750 which is 150}\end{array}\right]$$

$$= \frac{4}{5} = 4:5$$

Example 3 Divide 108 in two parts in the ratio 4 : 5.

Solution We have,

Sum of the terms of the ratio $=(4+5)=9$

$\therefore$ First part $=\frac{4}{9}\times 108=4\times 12=48$

Second part $=\frac{5}{9}\times 108=5\times 12=60$

Aliter Since the given ratio is 4 : 5. So, let the two parts be $4x$ and $5x$. Thus, we have to divide 108 into two parts $4x$ *and* $5x$.

$\therefore$ $4x+5x=108$

$\Rightarrow$ $9x=108$

$\Rightarrow$ $\frac{9x}{9}=\frac{108}{9}$ [Dividing both sides by 9]

$\Rightarrow$ $x=12.$

$\therefore$ First part $=4x=4\times 12=48$

Second part $=5x=5\times 12=60.$

Example 4 Divide ₹ 1250 between Aman and Amit in the ratio 2 : 3.

Solution We have,

Sum of the terms of the ratio $=(2+3)=5$

$\therefore$ Aman's share $=₹\left(\frac{2}{5}\times 1250\right)=₹\,(2\times 250)=₹\,500$

Amit's share $=₹\left(\frac{3}{5}\times 1250\right)=₹\,(3\times 250)=₹\,750.$

Example 5 Two numbers are in the ratio 4 : 5. If the sum of the numbers is 135, find the numbers.

Solution We have,

Sum of the terms of the ratio $=(4+5)=9$

Sum of the numbers $=135.$

$\therefore$ First number $=\frac{4}{9}\times 135=4\times 15=60$

Second number $=\frac{5}{9}\times 135=5\times 15=75.$

Hence, the numbers are 60 and 75.

Example 6 Divide ₹ 1500 among A, B, C in the ratio 3 : 5 : 2.

Solution We have,

Sum of the terms of the ratio $=(3+5+2)=10$

$\therefore$ A's share $=₹\left(\frac{3}{10}\times 1500\right)=₹\,450$

$$B\text{'s share } = ₹\left(\frac{5}{10}\times 1500\right) = ₹\,750$$

$$C\text{'s share } = ₹\left(\frac{2}{10}\times 1500\right) = ₹\,300$$

Example 7 Ratio of the number of male and female workers in a factory is 5 : 3. If there are 115 male workers, determine the number of female workers in the factory.

Solution We have, Male : Female = 5 : 3

So, let there be $5x$ male workers and $3x$ be female workers. It is given that there are 115 male workers.

$\therefore \quad 5x = 115$

$\Rightarrow \quad \frac{5x}{5} = \frac{115}{5}$ [Dividing both sides by 5]

$\Rightarrow \quad x = 23$

$\therefore$ Number of female workers $= 3x = 3\times 23 = 69$

Thus, there are 69 female workers in the factory.

Example 8 The ratio of copper and zinc in an alloy is 5 : 3. If the weight of the copper in the alloy is 30.5 grams, find the weight of zinc in the alloy.

Solution We have,

Weight of copper : Weight of zinc = 5 : 3

So, let the weight of copper in the alloy be $5x$ grams and, Weight of zinc in the alloy be $3x$ grams

But, the weight of the copper in the alloy is given to be 30.5 grams.

$\therefore \quad 5x = 30.5$

$\Rightarrow \quad \frac{5x}{5} = \frac{30.5}{5}$ [Dividing both sides by 5]

$\Rightarrow \quad x = 6.1$

$\therefore$ Weight of zinc in the alloy $= 3x$ grams $= 3\times 6.1$ grams $= 18.3$ grams

<u>Aliter</u> It is given that the alloy contains copper and zinc in the ratio 5 : 3. This means that if the weight of copper in the alloy is 5 grams, then the weight of zinc is 3 grams.

Now,

If the weight of copper in the alloy is 5 gm, then the weight of zinc = 3 gm.

$\therefore$ If the weight of copper is 1 gm, then the weight of the zinc $= \frac{3}{5}$ grams

If the weight of copper is 30.5 gm, then the weight of zinc

$$= \left(\frac{3}{5}\times 30.5\right)\text{ gm} = 18.3\text{ gm}$$

Example 9 If $x : y = 2 : 3$, find the value of $(3x + 2y) : (2x + 5y)$.

Solution We have,

$$x : y = 2 : 3 \Rightarrow \frac{x}{y} = \frac{2}{3}$$

Now,

$$(3x + 2y) : (2x + 5y)$$

$$= \frac{3x + 2y}{2x + 5y}$$

$$= \frac{\dfrac{3x + 2y}{y}}{\dfrac{2x + 5y}{y}}$$ [Dividing numerator and denominator by y]

$$= \frac{3\left(\dfrac{x}{y}\right) + 2}{2\left(\dfrac{x}{y}\right) + 5} = \frac{3 \times \dfrac{2}{3} + 2}{2 \times \dfrac{2}{3} + 5}$$ $\left[\because \dfrac{x}{y} = \dfrac{2}{3}\right]$

$$= \frac{2 + 2}{\dfrac{4}{3} + 5} = \frac{4}{\dfrac{19}{3}} = \frac{12}{19} = 12 : 19$$

Example 10 If $(4x + 5) : (3x + 11) = 13 : 17$, find the value of x.

Solution We have,

$$(4x + 5) : (3x + 11) = 13 : 17$$

$$\Rightarrow \quad \frac{4x + 5}{3x + 11} = \frac{13}{17}$$

$$\Rightarrow \quad 17(4x + 5) = 13(3x + 11)$$

$$\Rightarrow \quad 68x + 85 = 39x + 143$$

$$\Rightarrow \quad 68x - 39x = 143 - 85$$

$$\Rightarrow \quad 29x = 58$$

$$\Rightarrow \quad x = \frac{58}{29} = 2$$

Example 11 What must be added to each term of the ratio 2 : 5 so that it may become equal to 5 : 6?

Solution Let the number to be added be x. Then,

$$(2 + x) : (5 + x) = 5 : 6$$

$$\Rightarrow \quad \frac{2 + x}{5 + x} = \frac{5}{6}$$

$\Rightarrow \quad 6(2+x)=5(5+x)$

$\Rightarrow \quad 12+6x=25+5x$

$\Rightarrow \quad 6x-5x=25-12$

$\Rightarrow \quad x=13$

Hence, the required number is 13.

Example 12 A bag contains ₹ 187 in the form of 1 rupee, 50 paise and 10 paise coins in the ratio 3 : 4 : 5. Find the number of each type of coins.

Solution Let the number of 1 ₹, 50 paise and 10 paise coins be $3x$, $4x$ and $5x$ respectively. Then,

$$3x+4x\times\frac{50}{100}+5x\times\frac{10}{100}=187$$

$$\Rightarrow \quad 3x+2x+\frac{x}{2}=187$$

$$\Rightarrow \quad \frac{11}{2}x=187\Rightarrow x=34$$

$$\therefore \quad 3x=3\times 34=102, 4x=4\times 34=136 \text{ and } 5x=5\times 34=170$$

Hence, the number of 1 ₹, 50 paise and 10 paise coins are 102, 136 and 170 respectively.

EXERCISE 9.1

1. If $x:y=3:5$, find the ratio $3x+4y:8x+5y$.
2. If $x:y=8:9$, find the ratio $(7x-4y):3x+2y$.
3. If two numbers are in the ratio 6 : 13 and their l.c.m. is 312, find the numbers.
4. Two numbers are in the ratio 3 : 5. If 8 is added to each number, the ratio becomes 2 : 3. Find the numbers.
5. What should be added to each term of the ratio 7 : 13 so that the ratio becomes 2 : 3
6. Three numbers are in the ratio 2 : 3 : 5 and the sum of these numbers is 800. Find the numbers.
7. The ages of two persons are in the ratio 5 : 7. Eighteen years ago their ages were in the ratio 8 : 13. Find their present ages.
8. Two numbers are in the ratio 7 : 11. If 7 is added to each of the numbers, the ratio becomes 2 : 3. Find the numbers.
9. Two numbers are in the ratio 2 : 7. If the sum of the numbers is 810, find the numbers.
10. Divide ₹ 1350 between Ravish and Shikha in the ratio 2 : 3.
11. Divide ₹ 2000 among *P, Q, R* in the ratio 2 : 3 : 5.
12. The boys and the girls in a school are in the ratio 7 : 4. If total strength of the school be 550, find the number of boys and girls.
13. The ratio of monthly income to the savings of a family is 7 : 2. If the savings be of ₹ 500, find the income and expenditure.
14. The sides of a triangle are in the ratio 1 : 2 : 3. If the perimeter is 36 cm, find its sides.

15. A sum of ₹ 5500 is to be divided between Raman and Aman in the ratio 2 : 3. How much will each get ?

16. The ratio of zinc and copper in an alloy is 7 : 9. If the weight of the copper in the alloy is 11.7 kg, find the weight of the zinc in the alloy.

17. In the ratio 7 : 8, if the consequent is 40, what is the antecedent?

18. Divide ₹ 351 into two parts such that one may be to the other as 2 : 7.

19. Find the ratio of the price of pencil to that of ball pen, if pencils cost ₹ 16 per score and ball pens cost ₹ 8.40 per dozen.

20. In a class, one out of every six students fails. If there are 42 students in the class, how many pass?

ANSWERS

1. 29 : 49	2. 10 : 21	3. 24, 52	4. 24, 40
5. 5	6. 160, 240, 400	7. 50, 70 yrs	8. 49, 77
9. 180, 630	10. ₹ 540, ₹ 810	11. ₹ 400, ₹ 600, ₹ 1000	
12. Boys 350, Girls 200	13. Income = ₹ 1750, Expenditure = ₹ 1250		
14. 6 cm, 12 cm, 18 cm	15. Raman : ₹ 2200 Aman : ₹ 3300		16. 9.1 kg
17. 35	18. ₹ 78, ₹ 273	19. 8 : 7	20. 35

HINTS TO SELECTED PROBLEMS

6. Let the numbers be $2x$, $3x$, $5x$. Then, $2x + 3x + 5x = 800 \Rightarrow x = 80$

7. Let the present ages be $5x$ and $7x$ years. Then, $\dfrac{5x-18}{7x-18} = \dfrac{8}{13} \Rightarrow x = 10$

8. Let the numbers be $7x$ and $11x$. Then, $\dfrac{7x+7}{11x+7} = \dfrac{2}{3}$

17. Let the antecedent and consequent be $7x$ and $8x$ respectively. Then, consequent $= 40 \Rightarrow 8x = 40 \Rightarrow x = 5$. Therefore, antecedent $= 7x = 7 \times 5 = 35$.

20. Ratio of the number of pass students to the number of fail students = 5 : 1.

9.3 COMPARISON OF RATIOS

In order to compare two given ratios, we follow the following steps:

STEP I *Obtain the given ratios.*

STEP II *Express each one of them in the form of a fraction in the simplest form.*

STEP III *Find the L.C.M. of the denominators of the fractions obtained in step II.*

STEP IV *Obtain first fraction and its denominator. Divide the L.C.M. obtained in step III by the denominator to get a number x (say).*

Now, multiply the numerator and denominator of the fraction by x. Apply the same procedure to the other fraction.

Now, the denominators of all fractions will be same.

STEP V *Compare the numerators of the fractions obtained in step IV. The fraction having larger numerator will be larger than the other.*

Following example will illustrate the above procedure.

ILLUSTRATIVE EXAMPLES

Example 1 Compare the ratios: 5 : 12 and 3 : 8

Solution Writing the given ratios as fractions, we have

$$5:12=\frac{5}{12} \text{ and } 3:8=\frac{3}{8}$$

Now, L.C.M of 12 and 8 is 24.

Making the denominator of each fraction equal to 24, we have

$$\frac{5}{12}=\frac{5\times2}{12\times2}=\frac{10}{24} \text{ and } \frac{3}{8}=\frac{3\times3}{8\times3}=\frac{9}{24}$$

Clearly, 10 > 9

$$\therefore \quad \frac{10}{24}>\frac{9}{24} \Rightarrow \frac{5}{12}>\frac{3}{8}$$

Example 2 Compare the ratios: 7 : 6 and 4 : 9

Solution Writing the given ratios as fractions, we have

$$7:6=\frac{7}{6} \text{ and } 4:9=\frac{4}{9}$$

Now, L.C.M. of 6 and 9 is 18.

Making the denominator of each fraction equal to 18, we have

$$\frac{7}{6}=\frac{7\times3}{6\times3}=\frac{21}{18} \text{ and } \frac{4}{9}=\frac{4\times2}{9\times2}=\frac{8}{18}$$

Clearly, 21 > 8 .

$$\therefore \quad \frac{21}{18}>\frac{8}{18} \Rightarrow \frac{7}{6}>\frac{4}{9}$$

9.4 EQUIVALENT RATIOS

EQUIVALENT RATIO *A ratio obtained by multiplying or dividing the numerator and denominator of a given ratio by the same number is called an equivalent ratio.*

Consider the ratio 6 : 4.

We have,

$$\frac{6}{4}=\frac{6\times2}{4\times2}=\frac{12}{8}, \frac{6}{4}=\frac{6\times3}{4\times3}=\frac{18}{12}, \frac{6}{4}=\frac{6\times4}{4\times4}=\frac{24}{16} \text{ and so on.}$$

Also, $\frac{6}{4}=\frac{6\div2}{4\div2}=\frac{3}{2}$

Thus, $\frac{12}{8}, \frac{18}{12}, \frac{24}{16}, \frac{3}{2}$, etc. are ratios equivalent to the ratio $\frac{6}{4}$.

If $a : b$ and $c : d$ are two equivalent ratios, we write $\frac{a}{b}=\frac{c}{d}$.

ILLUSTRATIVE EXAMPLES

Example 1 Find two equivalent ratios of 6 : 15.

Solution We have,

$$\frac{6}{15} = \frac{6 \div 3}{15 \div 3} = \frac{2}{5}$$

$\therefore$ 2 : 5 is an equivalent ratio of 6 : 15

Also, $\frac{6}{15} = \frac{6 \times 2}{15 \times 2} = \frac{12}{30}$

So, 12 : 30 is an equivalent ratio of 6 : 15.

Hence, 2 : 5 and 12 : 30 are equivalent ratios of 6 : 15.

Example 2 Fill in the following blanks:

$$\frac{14}{21} = \frac{\square}{3} = \frac{6}{\square}$$

Solution In order to find the first missing number, we consider the denominators, 21 and 3.

We have,

$$21 \div 3 = 7$$

So, we divide the numerator and denominator of $\frac{14}{21}$ by 7 to get

$$\frac{14}{21} = \frac{14 \div 7}{21 \div 7} = \frac{2}{3}$$

Hence, first missing number is 2. Consequently, the second ratio is $\frac{2}{3}$.

To find the second missing number, we consider $\frac{2}{3} = \frac{6}{\square}$

We have $6 \div 2 = 3$. So, we multiply the numerator and denominator of $\frac{2}{3}$ by 3 to get $\frac{2}{3} = \frac{2 \times 3}{3 \times 3} = \frac{6}{9}$.

Hence, the second missing number is 9.

Consequently, the third ratio is $\frac{6}{9}$

<u>Aliter</u> Let $\frac{14}{21} = \frac{x}{3} = \frac{6}{y}$. Then,

$$\frac{14}{21} = \frac{x}{3} \Rightarrow 14 \times 3 = 21 \times x \Rightarrow x = \frac{14 \times 3}{21} = 2$$

and, $\frac{14}{21} = \frac{6}{y} \Rightarrow 14 \times y = 21 \times 6 \Rightarrow y = \frac{\overset{3}{\cancel{21}} \times \overset{3}{\cancel{6}}}{\underset{\underset{1}{\cancel{2}}}{\cancel{14}}} = 9$

EXERCISE 9.2

1. Which ratio is larger in the following pairs?
   (i) 3 : 4 or 9 : 16 (ii) 15 : 16 or 24 : 25 (iii) 4 : 7 or 5 : 8
   (iv) 9 : 20 or 8 : 13 (v) 1 : 2 or 13 : 27
2. Give two equivalent ratios of 6 : 8.
3. Fill in the following blanks: $\frac{12}{20} = \frac{\square}{5} = \frac{9}{\square}$

ANSWERS

1. (i) 3 : 4 (ii) 24 : 25 (iii) 5 : 8 (iv) 8 : 13 (v) 1 : 2
2. 3 : 4, 12 : 16 3. 3, 15

9.5 PROPORTION

PROPORTION An equality of two ratios is called a proportion.

Consider the two ratios 6 : 18 and 8 : 24. We find that

6 : 18 = 1 : 3 and 8 : 24 = 1 : 3.

∴ 6 : 18 = 8 : 24

Thus, 6 : 18 = 8 : 24 is a proportion.

Similarly, 40 : 70 = 200 : 350, 180 : 135 = 4 : 3 etc. are proportions.

Four numbers a, b, c, d are said to be in proportion, if the ratio of the first two is equal to the ratio of the last two, i.e., $a : b = c : d$.

If four numbers a, b, c, d are in proportion, then we write

$$a : b :: c : d$$

which is read as 'a is to b as c is to d' or 'a to b as c to d'. Here a, b, c and d are the first, second, third and fourth terms of the proportion. The first and fourth terms of a proportion are called extreme terms or extremes. The second and third terms are called the middle terms or means.

We observe that 2, 6, 18 and 54 are in proportion, because 2 : 6 = 18 : 54. Clearly, 2 and 54 are extremes whereas 6 and 18 are means.

Also, 40, 70, 200 and 350 are in proportion, because 40 : 70 = 200 : 350.

Consider the numbers 40, 70, 200, 350. We find that 40 : 70 = 200 : 350. So, the given numbers are in proportion. Clearly, 40 and 350 are extreme terms and 70 and 200 are middle terms. We find that

Product of extreme terms = $40 \times 350 = 14000$, Product of middle terms = $70 \times 200 = 14000$

∴ Product of extreme terms = Product of middle terms.

Thus, we observe that if four numbers are in proportion, then the product of the extreme terms is equal to the product of the middle terms.

In other words, $a : b = c : d$ *if and only if* $ad = bc$

If $ad \neq bc$, then a, b, c, d are not in proportion.

CONTINUED PROPORTION *Three numbers a, b, c are said to be in continued proportion if a, b, b, c, are in proportion.*

Thus, if a, b, c are in continued proportion, then

a, b, b, c are in proportion, i.e., $a : b :: b : c$

$\Rightarrow$ Product of extreme terms = Product of mean terms

$\Rightarrow$ $a \times c = b \times b$

$\Rightarrow$ $ac = b^2$

$\Rightarrow$ $b^2 = ac.$

MEAN PROPORTIONAL *If a, b, c are in continued proportion, then b is called the mean proportional between a and c.*

Clearly, if b is the mean proportional between a and c, then $b^2 = ac$.

The above concepts are illustrated with the help of the following examples.

ILLUSTRATIVE EXAMPLES

Example 1 Are 30, 40, 45, 60 in proportion?

Solution We have,

$$30:40 = \frac{30}{40} = \frac{3}{4} \quad \text{and,} \quad 45:60 = \frac{45}{60} = \frac{3}{4}$$

$\therefore$ $30:40 = 45:60$

Hence, 30, 40, 45, 60 are in proportion.

Aliter We have,

Product of extremes $= 30 \times 60 = 1800$

Product of means $= 40 \times 45 = 1800$

$\therefore$ Product of extremes = Product of means.

Hence, 30, 40, 45, 60 are in proportion.

Example 2 Are 36, 49, 6, 7 in proportion?

Solution We have,

Product of extremes $= 36 \times 7 = 252$

Product of means $= 49 \times 6 = 294$

Clearly, Product of extremes $\neq$ Product of means

Hence, 36, 49, 6, 7 are not in proportion.

Example 3 Are 4, 12, 36 in continued proportion?

Solution We know that three numbers a, b, c are in continued proportion, if a, b, b, c are in proportion.

Therefore, 4, 12, 36 will be in continued proportion if 4, 12, 12, 36 are in proportion.

We have,

Product of extremes $= 4 \times 36 = 144$

Product of means $= 12 \times 12 = 144$

$\therefore$ Product of extremes = Product of means

$\Rightarrow$ 4, 12, 12, 36 are in proportion

$\Rightarrow$ 4, 12, 36 are in continued proportion.

Example 4 If $3 : x :: 12 : 20$, find the value of x.

Solution We have,

$3 : x :: 12 : 20$

$\Rightarrow$ 3, x, 12, 20 are in proportion

$\Rightarrow$ Product of extremes = Product of means

$\Rightarrow 3 \times 20 = x \times 12$

$\Rightarrow 60 = 12x$

$\Rightarrow \frac{12x}{12} = \frac{60}{12}$ [Dividing both sides by 12]

$\Rightarrow x = 5$

Example 5 The first three terms of a proportion are 3, 5 and 21 respectively. Find its fourth term.

Solution Let the fourth term be x. Then,

3, 5, 21, x are in proportion.

$\Rightarrow$ Product of extremes = Product of means

$\Rightarrow 3 \times x = 5 \times 21$

$\Rightarrow 3x = 5 \times 21$

$\Rightarrow \frac{3x}{3} = \frac{5 \times 21}{3}$ [Dividing both sides by 3]

$\Rightarrow x = 5 \times 7 = 35$

Example 6 What must be added to the numbers 6, 10, 14 and 22 so that they are in proportion?

Solution Let the required number be x. Then,

$6 + x, 10 + x, 14 + x, 22 + x$ are in proportion.

$\Rightarrow$ Product of extremes = Product of means

$\Rightarrow (6 + x)(22 + x) = (10 + x)(14 + x)$

$\Rightarrow 132 + 6x + 22x + x^2 = 140 + 10x + 14x + x^2$

$\Rightarrow 132 + 28x = 140 + 24x$

$\Rightarrow 28x - 24x = 140 - 132$

$\Rightarrow 4x = 8$

$\Rightarrow x = \frac{8}{4} = 2.$

Hence, the required number is 2.

Example 7 For every 12 mangoes that I buy, 3 turn out to be rotten. At this rate, how many rotten mangoes will I have if I buy 100 mangoes?

Solution Suppose I have x rotten mangoes if I buy 100 mangoes. Then, the ratio of rotten mangoes to mangoes bought is $x : 100$.

Since for every 12 mangoes that I buy 3 turn out to be rotten. Therefore, the ratio of rotten mangoes to the mangoes bought is $3 : 12$.

$\therefore \quad x:100 = 3:12$

$\Rightarrow \quad x \times 12 = 100 \times 3$ [$\because$ Product of extremes = Product of means]

$\Rightarrow \quad 12x = 300$

$\Rightarrow \quad x = \frac{300}{12} = 25$

Thus, there will be 25 rotten mangoes, if I buy 100 mangoes.

Example 8 The scale of a map is 1 : 3000000. What is the actual distance between the two towns, if they are 3 cm apart on the map?

Solution The scale of a map is 1 : 3000000 means that if the distance on the map is 1 cm, then the actual distance is 3000000 cm.

We have, $3000000 \text{ cm} = \frac{3000000}{1000 \times 100} \text{ km} = 30 \text{ km}$

Thus, if the distance on the map is 1 cm, the actual distance is 30 km.

Let the actual distance between the two towns be x km. Thus, we have the following information.

Distance on the map	Actual distance
1 cm	30 km
3 cm	x km

$\therefore \quad 1:3 = 30:x$

$\Rightarrow \quad 1 \times x = 3 \times 30$

$\Rightarrow \quad x = 90$

Hence, the actual distance between the two towns is 90 km.

Example 9 If three loaves of bread are consumed by 9 people, how many people will consume 9 loaves of bread?

Solution Suppose x people will consume 9 loaves of bread.

We have,

Number of People	Number of Loaves of bread
9	3
x	9

$\therefore \quad 9:x = 3:9$

$\Rightarrow \quad 9 \times 9 = x \times 3$

$\Rightarrow \quad 81 = 3x$

$\Rightarrow \quad x = \frac{81}{3} = 27$

Hence, 27 people will consume 9 loaves of bread.

EXERCISE 9.3

1. Find which of the following are in proportion?

   (i) 33, 44, 66, 88 (ii) 46, 69, 69, 46 (iii) 72, 84, 186, 217

2. Find x in the following proportions:

   (i) $16:18 = x:96$ (ii) $x:92 = 87:116$

3. The ratio of the income to the expenditure of a family is 7 : 6. Find the savings if the income is ₹ 1400.
4. The scale of a map is 1 : 4000000. What is the actual distance between the two towns if they are 5 cm apart on the map?
5. The ratio of income of a person to his savings is 10 : 1. If his savings of one year are ₹ 6000, what is his income per month?
6. An electric pole casts a shadow of length 20 metres at a time when a tree 6 metres high casts a shadow of length 8 metres. Find the height of the pole.

ANSWERS

1. (i), (iii) 2. (i) $\frac{256}{3}$ (ii) 69 3. ₹ 200
4. 200 km 5. ₹5000 6. 15 metres

HINTS TO SELECTED PROBLEMS

3. Let the expenditure be of ₹ x. Then, $7 : 6 = 1400 : x$.
Now, use, saving = Income – Expenditure
5. Savings per month $= ₹\ \frac{6000}{12} = ₹\ 500$. Let the income per month be ₹ x.
Then, $x : 500 = 10 : 1$.
6. Use : Height of the tree : Length of the shadow of tree = Height of the pole: Length of shadow of pole.

OBJECTIVE TYPE QUESTIONS

Mark the correct alternative in each of the following:

1. If $a : b = 3 : 4$, then $4a : 3b =$
   (a) 4:3 (b) 3:4 (c) 1:1 (d) None of these
2. $\frac{1}{12} : \frac{1}{60} =$
   (a) 4:1 (b) 1:4 (c) 5:1 (d) 1:5
3. The simplest form of 24 : 36 is
   (a) 9:4 (b) 4:9 (c) 3:2 (d) 2:3
4. If $a : b = 4 : 5$ and $b : c = 2 : 3$, then $a : c$
   (a) 4:3 (b) 8:15 (c) 8:9 (d) 5:3
5. If $p : q = 2 : 5$, then $\frac{25p + 14q}{5p + 7q} =$
   (a) 8:5 (b) 5:8 (c) 8:3 (d) 3:8
6. A ratio equivalent to 2 : 5 is
   (a) 6:15 (b) 4:5 (c) 5:2 (d) 5:4
7. If $2a = 3b = 4c$, then $a : b : c =$
   (a) 2:3:4 (b) 3:4:6 (c) 4:3:2 (d) 6:4:3
8. If $2x = 3y$ and $4y = 5z$, then $x : z =$
   (a) 4:3 (b) 8:15 (c) 3:4 (d) 15:8

9. If $\frac{a}{2}=\frac{b}{3}=\frac{c}{4}$, then $a:b:c=$
   (a) 2:3:4 (b) 4:3:2 (c) 3:2:4 (d) None of these
10. If $\frac{1}{a}:\frac{1}{b}:\frac{1}{c}=3:4:5$, then $a:b:c$
   (a) 5:4:3 (b) 20:15:12 (c) 9:12:15 (d) 12:15:20
11. If $a:b=5:7$ and $b:c=6:11$, then $a:b:c=$
   (a) 35:49:66 (b) 30:42:77 (c) 30:42:55 (d) None of these
12. If $x:y=1:1$, then $\frac{3x+4y}{5x+6y}=$
   (a) $\frac{7}{11}$ (b) $\frac{17}{11}$ (c) $\frac{17}{23}$ (d) $\frac{4}{5}$
13. If a : b = 2 : 5, then $\frac{3a+2b}{4a+b}=$
   (a) $\frac{16}{13}$ (b) $\frac{13}{16}$ (c) $\frac{25}{22}$ (d) $\frac{20}{21}$
14. The mean proportional of *a* and *b* is 10 and the value of *a* is four times the value of *b*. The value of $a+b$ $(a>0, b>0)$ is
   (a) 20 (b) 25 (c) 101 (d) 29
15. If $8:x::16:35$
   (a) 35 (b) 70 (c) $\frac{35}{2}$ (d) 24
16. The mean proportional of 6 and 24 is
   (a) 15 (b) 12 (c) 8 (d) 144
17. The boys and girls in a school are in the ratio 9 : 5. If the number of girls is 320, then the total strength of the school is
   (a) 840 (b) 896 (c) 920 (d) 576
18. If the first three terms of a proportion are 3, 5 and 21 respectively, then its fourth term is
   (a) 21 (b) 35 (c) 15 (d) None of these
19. What must be added to each term of the ratio 9 : 16 to make the ratio 2 : 3 ?
   (a) 5 (b) 3 (c) 4 (d) 6
20. What least number is to be subtracted from each term of the ratio 15 : 19 to make the ratio 3:4?
   (a) 3 (b) 5 (c) 6 (d) 9
21. If ₹ 840 is divided between *P* and *Q* in the ratio 3 : 4, then P's share is
   (a) ₹ 340 (b) ₹ 480 (c) ₹ 360 (d) ₹ 400
22. The ages of Ravish and Shikha are in the ratio 3 : 8. Six years hence, their ages will be in the ratio 4 : 9. The present age of Ravish is
   (a) 18 years (b) 15 years (c) 12 years (d) 21 years
23. The present ages of Renu and Ravi are in the ratio 5 : 6. The sum of their present ages is 44 in years. The difference of their ages (in years) is
   (a) 4 (b) 5 (c) 8 (d) 2

24. The third proportional of 3 and 27 is
    (a) 243 (b) 256 (c) 209 (d) 225

ANSWSERS

1. (c)	2. (c)	3. (d)	4. (b)	5. (c)	6. (a)	7. (d)
8. (d)	9. (a)	10. (b)	11. (b)	12. (a)	13. (a)	14. (b)
15. (c)	16. (b)	17. (b)	18. (b)	19. (a)	20. (a)	21. (c)
22. (a)	23. (a)	24. (a)				

THINGS TO REMEMBER

1. *The ratio of a number 'a' to another number 'b' (b ≠ 0) is a fraction* $\frac{a}{b}$ *and is written as a : b.*
2. *In the ratio a : b, the first term is a and the second term is b.*
3. *A ratio is said to be in the simplest form if its two terms have no common factor other than 1.*
4. *The ratio of two numbers is usually expressed in its simplest form.*
5. *The ratio of two quantities is an abstract quantity, i.e., it has no units in itself.*
6. *An equality of two ratios is called a proportion. If a : b = c : d, then we write a : b : : c : d.*
7. *The numbers a, b, c, d are in proportion if the ratio of the first two is equal to the ratio of the last two, i.e., a : b = c : d.*
8. *If four numbers a, b, c, d are in proportion, then a and d are known as extreme terms and b and c are called middle terms.*
9. *Four numbers are in proportion if the product of extreme terms is equal to the product of middle terms, i.e., a : b : : c : d if and only if ad = bc.*
10. *From the terms of a given proportion, we can make three more proportions.*
11. *If a : b = b : c, then a, b, c are said to be in continued proportion.*
12. *If a, b, c are in continued proportion, i.e., a : b : : b : c, then b is called the mean proportional between a and c.*

10

UNITARY METHOD

10.1 UNITARY METHOD

In class VI, we have learnt about unitary method in which we first find the value of one (unit) article from the value of the given number of articles and then we use it to find the value of required number of articles. We have learnt that:

$$\text{Value of one article} = \frac{\text{Value of the given number of articles}}{\text{Number of articles}}$$

and,

Value of required number of articles

= (Value of one article) × (Required number of articles)

Let us recall the unitary method through following examples:

ILLUSTRATIVE EXAMPLES

Example 1 If 6 bowls cost Rs 96. What will be the cost of 15 such bowls?

Solution We have,

Cost of 6 bowls = Rs 96

$\therefore$ Cost of 1 bowl $= \text{Rs } \frac{96}{6}$

Hence, Cost of 15 bowls $= \text{Rs}\left(\frac{96}{6} \times 15\right) = \text{Rs } (16 \times 15) = \text{Rs } 240$

Example 2 The car that Ravish owns can go 150 km in 15 litres of petrol. How for can it go with 50 litres of petrol?

Solution It is given that:

Wtih 15 litres of petrol the car goes 150 km

$\therefore$ With 1 litre of petrol the car goes $\frac{150}{15}$ km

Hence, with 50 litres of petrol it would go

$\left(\frac{150}{15} \times 50\right)$ km $= (10 \times 50)$ km $= 500$ km

Example 3 Shikha earns Rs 3000 for working in 8 days. How much will she earn if she works for 15 days?

Solution We have,

Shikha's earning for 8 days = Rs 3000

$\therefore$ Shikha's earning for 1 day = Rs $\frac{3000}{8}$

Hence, Shikha's earning for 15 days $= \text{Rs}\left(\frac{3000}{8}\times 15\right) = \text{Rs } 5625$

Example 4 25 workers earn Rs 300 per day. What will be the earnings of 20 workers per day at the same rate?

Solution We have,

Per day earning of 25 workers = Rs 300

$\therefore$ Per day earning of 1 worker = Rs $\frac{300}{25}$

Hence, per day earning of 20 workers $= \text{Rs}\left(\frac{300}{25}\times 20\right) = \text{Rs } (12\times 20) = \text{Rs } 240$

Example 5 If 25 metres of cloth cost Rs 1575, how many metres of it can be bought for Rs 2016?

Solution For Rs 1575, cloth bought = 25 m

For Rs 1, cloth bought $= \frac{25}{1575}$ m

For Rs. 2016, cloth bought $= \left(\frac{25}{1575}\times 2016\right) \text{m} = 32 \text{ m}$

Hence, the length of the cloth bought for Rs. 2016 is 32 m.

EXERCISE 10.1

1. 20 chocolates cost Rs 320. Find the cost of 35 such chocolates.
2. The cost of 40 metres of cloth is Rs 200. Find the cost of 50 metres of cloth.
3. A car can cover a distance of 522 km on 36 litres of petrol. How far can it travel on 14 litres of petrol?
4. Travelling 900 km by rail costs Rs 280. What would be the fare for a journey of 360 km when a person travels by the same class?
5. If 6 oil tankers can be filled by a pipe in 4 ½ hours, how long does the pipe take to fill 4 such oil tankers?
6. 3/4 of the salary per month is Rs 600. What is the salary per month?
7. The cost of 32 tables is Rs 23520. Find the number of such tables that can be purchased for Rs 51450.
8. The yield of wheat from 6 hectares is 280 quintals. Find the number of hectares required for a yield of 225 quintals.
9. Fifteen post cards cost Rs 2.25. What will be the cost of 36 post cards? How many postcards can we buy in Rs 45?
10. A rail journey of 75 km costs Rs 215. How much will a journey of 120 km cost?

11. If the sales tax on a purchase worth ₹ 60 is ₹ 4.20. What will be the sales tax on the purchase worth of ₹ 150?

12. 52 packets of 12 pencils each, cost ₹ 499.20. Find the cost of 65 packets of 10 pencils each.

ANSWERS

1. ₹ 560 2. ₹ 250 2. ₹ 203 km. 4. ₹ 112

5. 3 hours 6. ₹ 800 7. 70 8. $4\frac{23}{28}$ hectares 9. ₹ 5.40, 300

10. ₹ 344 11. ₹ 10.50 12. ₹ 520

OBJECTIVE TYPE QUESTIONS

Mark the correct alternative in each of the following:

1. What distance (in m) will a train cover in 1 minute travelling at 72 km/hr?
   (a) 120 (b) 1200 (c) 1400 (d) 720
2. If the cost of 15 mangoes is ₹ 180, then what is the cost of 25 mangoes?
   (a) 220 (b) 360 (c) 200 (d) 300
3. If the cost of 25 pencils is ₹ 75, then the cost of 75 penciles is
   (a) 225 (b) 150 (c) 180 (d) 100
4. The cost of 30 mangoes is less than cost of 40 mangoes by ₹ 50. Find the cost of 50 mangoes in (₹)
   (a) 400 (b) 300 (c) 250 (d) 350
5. 45 cows can graze a field in 12 days. How many cows will graze the same field in 9 days?
   (a) 60 (b) $38\frac{3}{4}$ (c) 54 (d) 45
6. If $\frac{4}{5}$ of a water tank is filled in 1 hour, how much time will be required to fill the rest of it?
   (a) 20 minutes (b) 15 minutes (c) 12 minutes (d) 10 minutes
7. A worker makes a toy every $\frac{2}{3}$ hour. If he works for $7\frac{1}{3}$ hours, then how many toys will he make?
   (a) 11 (b) 16 (c) 18 (d) 22
8. 6 dozen eggs are bought for ₹108. How much will 108 eggs cost?
   (a) ₹171 (b) ₹162 (c) ₹153 (d) ₹180
9. 8 men can finish a piece of work in 40 days. If 2 more men join them, the work will be completed in
   (a) 30 days (b) 32 days (c) 36 days (d) 25 days
10. If 21 cows eat as much as 15 buffaloes, how many cows will eat as much as 35 buffaloes?
    (a) 45 (b) 49 (c) 56 (d) 54
11. If 6 bowls cost ₹ 90, then the cost of 10 such bowls is
    (a) ₹125 (b) ₹175 (c) ₹150 (d) ₹120
12. A car can go 150 km with 25 litres of petrol. How for can it go with 30 litres of petrol?
    (a) 180 km (b) 150 km (c) 210 km (d) 160 km
13. If the cost of 12 books is ₹ 144, then the cost of 18 books is
    (a) ₹ 206 (b) ₹ 216 (c) ₹ 198 (d) ₹ 180
14. If a person travels 150 km in 5 hours, then the time taken by him to travel 180 km is
    (a) 3 (b) 4 (c) 8 (d) 6

15. If a person travels 60 km in 4 hours in a car, then the speed of the car is
(a) 12 km/hr (b) 15 km/hr (c) 20 km/hr (d) 24 km/hr

ANSWERS

1. (b) 2. (d) 3. (a) 4. (c) 5. (a) 6. (b) 7. (a)
8. (b) 9. (b) 10. (b) 11. (c) 12. (a) 13. (b) 14. (d)
15. (b)

THINGS TO REMEMBER

1. *More is the number of articles, more is the value.*

   $\therefore$ *Value of a given number of articles = (Value of one article) $\times$ (Number of articles)*

2. *Less is the number of articles, less is the value.*

   $$\therefore \quad \text{Value of one article} = \frac{\text{Value of a given number of articles}}{\text{Number of articles}}$$

3. *The method of finding first the value of one article from the value of the given number of articles and then the value of the required number of articles is called the unitary method.*

11

PERCENTAGE

11.1 INTRODUCTION

In this chapter, we shall introduce the concept of percentage and shall study percentage as a fraction and also as a ratio. We shall also learn about the conversion of a per cent into a fraction, ratio or decimal and vice-versa.

11.2 PER CENT

The word per cent is an abbreviation of the Latin phrase 'percentum' which means per hundred or hundredths.

Thus, the term per cent means per hundred or for every hundred.

When we say that a man gives 30 per cent of his income as income tax, this means that he gives Rs 30 out of every hundred rupees of his income.

'A trader makes a profit of 15 per cent' means that he gains Rs 15 on every hundred rupees of his investment.

'A boy scored 70 per cent marks in his final examination' means that he obtained 70 marks out of every hundred marks.

The term per cent is sometimes abbreviated as p.c. The symbol% is often used for the term per cent.

Thus, 15 per cent will be written as 15%.

We shall now study per cent as a fraction and also as a ratio.

11.2.1 PER CENT AS A FRACTION

In the previous section, we have discussed that per cent means per hundred or hundredths.

Now,

$$\frac{75}{100} = 75 \times \frac{1}{100} = 75 \text{ hundredths} = 75 \text{ per hundred} = 75\%$$

and, $$\frac{42}{100} = 42 \times \frac{1}{100} = 42 \text{ hundredths} = 42 \text{ per hundred} = 42\%$$

and so on.

It follows from this that:

A fraction with its denominator 100 is equal to that per cent, as the numerator.

11.2.2 PER CENT AS A RATIO

In the previous section, we have learnt that per cent can be treated as a fraction with its denominator as 100. Thus, we have

$$11\% = \frac{11}{100}$$

But, $\frac{11}{100} = 11:100$

$\therefore$ $11\% = 11:100$

Similarly, $8\% = \frac{8}{100} = 8:100$, and $25\% = \frac{25}{100} = 25:100$ etc.

It follows from these that a per cent can also be expressed as a ratio with its second term 100 and first term equal to the given per cent.

11.2.3 CONVERSION OF A PER CENT INTO A FRACTION

In order to convert a per cent into a fraction, we follow the following steps:

STEP I *Obtain the given per cent. Let it be x%.*

STEP II *Drop the per cent sign (i.e %) and divide the number by 100. Thus,* $x\% = \frac{x}{100}$

ILLUSTRATION 1 Express the following per cents as fractions in the simplest forms:

(i) 57% (ii) 36% (iii) 115%

Solution We have,

(i) $57\% = \frac{57}{100}$ (ii) $36\% = \frac{36}{100} = \frac{9}{25}$ (iii) $115\% = \frac{115}{100} = \frac{23}{20}$.

ILLUSTRATION 2 Express each of the following per cents as fractions in the simplest forms:

(i) 0.375% (ii) 0.4% (iii) $16\frac{2}{3}\%$

Solution We have,

(i) $0.375\% = \frac{0.375}{100} = \frac{375}{100000} = \frac{3}{800}$ (ii) $0.4\% = \frac{0.4}{100} = \frac{4}{1000} = \frac{1}{250}$

(iii) $16\frac{2}{3}\% = \frac{50}{3}\% = \frac{(50/3)}{100} = \frac{50}{3} \times \frac{1}{100} = \frac{1}{6}$

11.2.4 CONVERSION OF A FRACTION INTO A PER CENT

In order to convert a fraction into a per cent, we follow the following steps:

STEP I *Obtain the fraction. Let it be* $\frac{a}{b}$.

STEP II *Multiply the fraction by 100 and put the per cent sign% to obtain the required per cent. Thus,* $\frac{a}{b} = \left(\frac{a}{b} \times 100\right)\%$

ILLUSTRATION 1 Express each of the following fractions as per cents:

(i) $\frac{4}{5}$ (ii) $\frac{9}{20}$ (iii) $5\frac{1}{4}$

Solution We have,

(i) $\frac{4}{5}=\left(\frac{4}{5}\times 100\right)=80\%$ (ii) $\frac{9}{20}=\left(\frac{9}{20}\times 100\right)\%=45\%$

(iii) $5\frac{1}{4}=\frac{21}{4}=\left(\frac{21}{4}\times 100\right)\%=525\%$

ILLUSTRATION 2 Express each of the following into per cents:

(i) 0.375 (ii) 0.005 (iii) 2.45

Solution We have,

(i) $0.375=\frac{375}{1000}=\left(\frac{375}{1000}\times 100\right)\%=37.5\%$

(ii) $0.005=\frac{5}{1000}=\left(\frac{5}{1000}\times 100\right)\%=0.5\%$

(iii) $2.45=\frac{245}{100}=\left(\frac{245}{100}\times 100\right)\%=245\%$

NOTE: *From the above illustrations we observe that to convert a decimal into a per cent, we shift the decimal point by two places to the right. This is because the decimal number is multiplied by 100.*

EXERCISE 11.1

1. Express each of the following per cents as fractions in the simplest forms:

(i) 45% (ii) 0.25% (iii) 150% (iv) $6\frac{1}{4}\%$

2. Express each of the following fractions as a per cent:

(i) $\frac{3}{4}$ (ii) $\frac{53}{100}$ (iii) $1\frac{3}{5}$ (iv) $\frac{7}{20}$

ANSWERS

1. (i) $\frac{9}{20}$ (ii) $\frac{1}{400}$ (iii) $\frac{3}{2}$ (iv) $\frac{1}{16}$

2. (i) 75% (ii) 53% (iii) 160% (iv) 35%

11.2.5 CONVERSION OF A RATIO INTO PER CENT AND VICE VERSA

In order to convert a given ratio into a per cent, we proceed as follows:

STEP I *Obtain the ratio, say, a : b.*

STEP II *Convert the given ratio into the fraction* $\frac{a}{b}$.

STEP III *Multiply the fraction obtained in step II by 100 and put per cent sign%.*

ILLUSTRATION 1 Express the following as per cents:

(i) 6 : 5 (ii) 30 : 80 (iii) 3 : 12

Solution We have,

(i) $6:5=\frac{6}{5}=\left(\frac{6}{5}\times 100\right)\%=120\%$ (ii) $30:80=\frac{30}{80}=\left(\frac{30}{80}\times 100\right)\%=37.5\%$

(iii) $3:12=\frac{3}{12}=\left(\frac{3}{12}\times 100\right)\%=25\%$.

In order to convert a given per cent into a ratio, we follow the following steps:

STEP I *Obtain the per cent.*

STEP II *Convert the given per cent into a fraction by dividing it by 100 and removing per cent sign%.*

STEP III *Express the fraction obtained in step II in the simplest form.*

STEP IV *Express the fraction obtained in step III as a ratio.*

ILLUSTRATION 2 Express each of the following per cents as a ratio in the simplest form:

(i) 28% (ii) 52% (iii) 0.4% (iv) $6\frac{2}{3}\%$.

Solution We have,

(i) $28\%=\frac{28}{100}=\frac{7}{25}=7:25$ (ii) $52\%=\frac{52}{100}=\frac{13}{25}=13:25$

(iii) $0.4\%=\frac{0.4}{100}=\frac{4}{1000}=\frac{1}{250}=1:250$ (iv) $6\frac{2}{3}\%=\frac{20}{3}\%=\frac{20}{3}\times\frac{1}{100}=\frac{1}{15}=1:15$.

EXERCISE 11.2

1. Express each of the following ratios as per cents:
   (i) 4 : 5 (ii) 1 : 5 (iii) 11 : 125
2. Express each of the following per cents as ratios in the simplest forms:
   (i) 2.5% (ii) 0.4% (iii) $13\frac{3}{4}\%$

ANSWERS

1. (i) 80% (ii) 20% (iii) $\frac{44}{5}\%$ 2. (i) $\frac{1}{40}$ (ii) $\frac{1}{250}$ (iii) $\frac{11}{80}$

11.2.6 CONVERSION OF PER CENT INTO DECIMAL AND VICE VERSA

In order to convert a given per cent into decimal form, we follow the following steps:

STEP I *Obtain the per cent which is to be converted into decimal.*

STEP II *Express the given per cent as a fraction with denominator as 100.*

STEP III *Write the fraction obtained in step II in decimal form.*

ILLUSTRATION 1 Express each of the following as a decimal:

(i) 65% (ii) 12% (iii) 7.4% (iv) 0.1%

Solution We have,

(i) $65\%=\frac{65}{100}=0.65$ (ii) $12\%=\frac{12}{100}=0.12$

(iii) $7.4\% = \frac{7.4}{100} = 0.074$ (iv) $0.1\% = \frac{0.1}{100} = \frac{1}{1000} = 0.001$.

To convert a given decimal into a per cent, we proceed as follows:

STEP I *Obtain the number in decimal form.*

STEP II *Convert it into a fraction by removing the decimal point. In order to remove decimal, divide by 10 or 100 or 1000 according to the number of digits on the right side of the decimal point 1 or 2 or 3 respectively.*

STEP III *Multiply by 100 and put% sign.*

ILLUSTRATION 2 Express each of the following as per cent :

(i) 0.037 (ii) 0.002 (iii) 1.2

Solution We have,

(i) $0.037 = \frac{37}{1000} = \left(\frac{37}{1000} \times 100\right)\% = 3.7\%$

(ii) $0.002 = \frac{2}{1000} = \left(\frac{2}{1000} \times 100\right)\% = 0.2\%$

(iii) $1.2 = \frac{12}{10} = \left(\frac{12}{10} \times 100\right)\% = 120\%$

EXERCISE 11.3

1. Express each of the following per cents as decimals:

   (i) 12.5% (ii) 75% (iii) 128.8% (iv) 0.05%

2. Express each of the following decimals as a per cent:

   (i) 0.004 (ii) 0.24 (iii) 0.02 (iv) 0.275

3. Write each of the following as whole numbers or mixed numbers:

   (i) 136% (ii) 250% (iii) 300%

ANSWERS

1. (i) 0.125 (ii) 0.75 (iii) 1.288 (iv) 0.0005
2. (i) 0.4% (ii) 24% (iii) 2% (iv) 27.5%
3. (i) $\frac{34}{25}$ (ii) $\frac{5}{2}$ (iii) 3

11.3 FINDING A PERCENTAGE OF A GIVEN NUMBER

As we have discussed earlier that a per cent is a fraction with denominator as 100. So, we can determine what the exact value of a per cent is only when we know the value of the number it is part of. We can use the following stepwise procedure to find the per cent of a given number.

STEP I *Obtain the number, say x.*

STEP II *Obtain the required per cent, say P%.*

STEP III *Multiply x by P and divide by 100 to obtain the required P% of x.*

i.e., $P\% \text{ of } x = \frac{P}{100} \times x$

Following examples will illustrate the above procedure.

ILLUSTRATIVE EXAMPLES

Example 1 Find:

(i) 30% of Rs 180 (ii) 16% of 25 litres

(iii) $4\frac{1}{2}\%$ of Rs 1800 (iv) 10% of 350 km (v) 120% of 20 kg

Solution We know that $P\%$ of x is equal to $\frac{P}{100} \times x$. So, we have

(i) $30\% \text{ of Rs } 180 = \text{Rs}\left(\frac{30}{100} \times 180\right) = \text{Rs } 54$

(ii) $16\% \text{ of } 25 \text{ litres} = \left(\frac{16}{100} \times 25\right) \text{litres} = 4 \text{ litres}$

(iii) $4\frac{1}{2}\% \text{ of Rs } 1800 = \text{Rs}\left(\frac{4\frac{1}{2}}{100} \times 1800\right) = \text{Rs}\left(\frac{\frac{9}{2}}{100} \times 1800\right)$

$= \text{Rs} = \left(\frac{9}{200} \times 1800\right) = \text{Rs } 81.$

(iv) $10\% \text{ of } 350 \text{ km} = \left(\frac{10}{100} \times 350\right) \text{km} = 35 \text{ km}$

(v) $120\% \text{ of } 20 \text{ kg} = \left(\frac{120}{100} \times 20\right) \text{kg} = 24 \text{ kg}$

Example 2 Find a number whose 4% is 72.

Solution Let the required number be x. Then,

$4\% \text{ of } x = 72 \Rightarrow \frac{4}{100} \times x = 72 \Rightarrow x = \frac{100}{4} \times 72 = 1800$

Hence, the required number is 1800.

Example 3 What is the sum of money of which 8% is Rs 480?

Solution Let the required sum of money be Rs x. Then,

8% of Rs x = Rs 480

$\Rightarrow \frac{8}{100} \times x = 480$

$\Rightarrow x = \frac{480 \times 100}{8} = 6000$

Hence, the required sum of money is Rs 6000.

EXERCISE 11.4

1. Find each of the following:

   (i) 7% of Rs 7150 (ii) 40% of 400 kg (iii) 20% of 15.125 litres

   (iv) $3\frac{1}{3}$% of 90 km (v) 2.5% of 600 metres

2. Find the number whose $12\frac{1}{2}$% is 64.

3. What is the number, $6\frac{1}{4}$% of which is 2?

4. If 6 is 50% of a number, what is that number?

ANSWERS

1. (i) Rs 500.50 (ii) 160 kg (iii) 3.025 litres (iv) 3 km (v) 15 metres
2. 512 3. 32 4. 12

11.4 FINDING HOW MUCH PER CENT ONE QUANTITY IS OF ANOTHER QUANTITY

Sometimes we are given two quantities and we want to find what per cent of one quantity is of the other quantity. In other words, we want to find how many hundredths of one quantity should be taken so that it is equal to the second quantity. In such type of problems, we proceed as discussed below:

Let a and b be two numbers and we want to know: what per cent of a is b?

Let x% of a be equal to b. Then,

$$\frac{x}{100}\times a=b \quad \Rightarrow \quad x=b\times\frac{100}{a} \quad \Rightarrow \quad x=\frac{b}{a}\times 100$$

Thus, b is $\left(\frac{b}{a}\times 100\right)\%$ of a.

Following examples will illustrate the above procedure.

ILLUSTRATIVE EXAMPLES

Example 1 What per cent of 25 kg is 3.5 kg?

Solution We have,

$$\text{Required per cent} = \left(\frac{3.5\,\text{kg}}{25\,\text{kg}}\times 100\right) = \frac{3.5\times 100}{25} = \frac{35\times 100}{250} = \frac{35\times 2}{5} = 7\times 2 = 14$$

Hence, 3.5 kg is 14% of 25 kg.

<u>Aliter</u> Let x% of 25 kg be 3.5 kg. Then,

x% of 25 kg = 3.5 kg

$$\Rightarrow \quad \frac{x}{100}\times 25 = 3.5$$

$$\Rightarrow \quad x=\frac{3.5\times 100}{25} \qquad \left[\text{Multiplying both sides by } \frac{100}{25}\right]$$

$\Rightarrow \quad x=\frac{35\times100}{250}=\frac{35\times2}{5}=7\times2=14$

Hence, 3.5 kg is 14% of 25 kg.

Example 2 What per cent of 750 metres is 125 metres?

Solution We have,

$$\text{Required per cent}=\frac{125\text{ metres}}{750\text{ metres}}\times100=\frac{125\times100}{750}=\frac{1\times100}{6}=\frac{50}{3}=16.66$$

Hence, 125 metres is 16.66% of 750 metres.

Aliter Let x% of 750 metres be 125 metres. Then,

x% of 750 = 125

$\Rightarrow \quad \frac{x}{100}\times750=125$

$\Rightarrow \quad x=\frac{125\times100}{750}$ $\left[\text{Multiplying both sides by } \frac{100}{750}\right]$

$\Rightarrow \quad x=\frac{1\times100}{6}=\frac{50}{3}=16.66$

Hence, 125 metres is 16.66% of 750 metres.

Example 3 Express 75 paise as a per cent of Rs 5.

Solution We have, Rs 5 = 500 paise.

Let x% of Rs 5 be 75 paise. Then,

x% of Rs 5 = 75 paise

$\Rightarrow$ x% of 500 paise = 75 paise

$\Rightarrow \quad \frac{x}{100}\times500=75 \Rightarrow x=\frac{75\times100}{500} \Rightarrow x=15$

Hence, 15% of Rs 5 is 75 paise.

Aliter The required per cent $=\left(\frac{75}{500}\times100\right)\%=15\%$

Example 4 Express 18 hours as a per cent of 3 days.

Solution We have, One day = 24 hours

$\therefore \quad 3\text{ days}=(24\times3)\text{ hours}=72\text{ hours}.$

Let x% of 3 days be 18 hours. Then,

x% of 72 hours = 18 hours

$\Rightarrow \quad \frac{x}{100}\times72=18$

$\Rightarrow \quad x=\frac{18\times100}{72}$ $\left[\text{Multiplying both sides by } \frac{100}{72}\right]$

$\Rightarrow \quad x=\frac{1\times100}{4} \Rightarrow x=25$

Hence, 25% of 3 days is equal to 18 hours.

Aliter We have, 3 days = 72 hours.

$\therefore$ Required per cent $=\left(\frac{18}{72}\times 100\right)\% = 25\%$.

Example 5 Find 10% more than Rs 90.

Solution We have,

$$10\% \text{ of Rs } 90 = \text{Rs}\left(\frac{10}{100}\times 90\right) = \text{Rs } 9$$

$\therefore$ 10% more than Rs 90 = Rs 90 + Rs 9 = Rs 99

Example 6 Find 20% less than Rs 70.

Solution We have,

$$20\% \text{ of Rs } 70 = \text{Rs}\left(\frac{20}{100}\times 70\right) = \text{Rs } 14$$

$\therefore$ 20% less than Rs 70 = Rs (70 – 14) = Rs 56

EXERCISE 11.5

1. What per cent of
   (i) 24 is 6? (ii) Rs 125 is Rs 10? (iii) 4 km is 160 metres?
   (iv) Rs 8 is 25 paise? (v) 2 days is 8 hours? (vi) 1 litre is 175 ml?
2. What per cent is equivalent to $\frac{3}{8}$?
3. Find the following:
   (i) 8 is 4% of which number? (ii) 6 is 60% of which number?
   (iii) 6 is 30% of which number? (iv) 12 is 25% of which number?
4. Convert each of the following pairs into percentages and find out which is more?
   (i) 25 marks out of 30, 35 marks out of 40.
   (ii) 100 runs scored off 110 balls, 50 runs scored off 55 balls.
5. Find 20% more than Rs 200.
6. Find 10% less than Rs 150.

ANSWERS

1. (i) 25% (ii) 8% (iii) 4% (iv) 3.125% (v) $16\frac{2}{3}\%$ (vi) 17.50%
2. 37.5% 3. (i) 200 (ii) 10 (iii) 20 (iv) 48
4. (i) 35 marks out of 40 (87.5%) is more than 25 marks out of 30 (83.33%)
   (ii) Both are same (90.91%)
5. Rs 240 6. Rs 135

11.5 SOME WORD PROBLEMS ON PERCENTAGE

In this section, we shall apply the concept of percentage to solve some real-life problems. We shall be using the following formulae for finding increase or decrease per cent:

$$\text{Increase}\% = \left(\frac{\text{Increase}}{\text{Original value}}\times 100\right)\%, \quad \text{Decrease}\% = \left(\frac{\text{Decrease}}{\text{Original value}}\times 100\right)\%$$

Following examples will illustrate the use of the concept of percentage in solving some real-life problems.

ILLUSTRATIVE EXAMPLES

Example 1 Sarita secures 84% marks in Hindi paper. If the maximum marks in the paper are 150, find the marks secured by her in the paper.

Solution Maximum marks in the paper = 150.

Sarita secures 84% marks in the paper.

$\therefore$ Marks secured by Sarita = 84% of 150 $= \frac{84}{100} \times 150 = 126.$

Thus, Sarita secured 126 marks in the paper.

Example 2 55% of the population of a town are males. If the total population of the town is 64100, find the population of females in the town.

Solution We have,

Population of the town = 64100

$\therefore$ 55% of the population $= \frac{55}{100} \times 64100 = 35255$

It is given that 55% of the population are males.

$\therefore$ Number of males = 35255

Hence, number of females in the town = Total population – No. of males

= 64100 – 35255 = 28845

Example 3 In an election, out of 75000 eligible voters 50000 cast their votes. What was the percentage of people casting their votes?

Solution We have,

Total number of eligible voters = 75000

Number of voters who cast their votes = 50000

$\therefore$ Percentage of voters casting their votes $= \frac{50000}{75000} \times 100 = \frac{200}{3} = 66.66$

Hence, 66.66% voters cast their votes.

Example 4 A basket contains 350 eggs. If 12% of the eggs are rotten, find the number of eggs, good enough to be sold.

Solution We have,

Total number of eggs in the basket = 350

Number of rotten eggs = 12% of 350 $= \left(\frac{12}{100} \times 350\right) = 42$

$\therefore$ Number of good eggs = (350 – 42) = 308

Example 5 In a fabric, cotton and synthetic fibres are in the ratio of 2 : 3. What is the percentage of cotton fibre in the fabric?

Solution It is given that the cotton and synthetic fibres are in the ratio 2 : 3. So, let cotton and synthetic fibres be $2x$ and $3x$ respectively.

Total quantity of fibre = $2x + 3x$ = $5x$

Thus, in $5x$ fibres, cotton fibres = $2x$

$\therefore$ Percentage of cotton fibres $= \left(\frac{2x}{5x} \times 100\right)\% = 40\%$

Example 6 A man spends 92% of his monthly income. If he saves Rs 220 per month, what is his monthly income?

Solution Let the total income be Rs x.

We have, Expenditure = 92%

$\therefore$ Saving = (100 – 92)% = 8%

It is given that the man saves Rs 220. This means that 8% of the total income is Rs 220.

i.e., $\frac{8}{100} \times x = 220$

$\Rightarrow \quad x = \frac{220 \times 100}{8} = 2750$

Hence, the man's monthly income = Rs 2750.

Aliter Let his monthly income be Rs 100

Then, his expenditure = Rs 92

$\therefore$ His saving = Rs (100 – 92) = Rs 8

Now, if the saving is Rs 8, then income = Rs 100

If the saving is Rs 220, then income $= \text{Rs}\left(\frac{100}{8} \times 220\right) = \text{Rs } 2750$

Hence, the man's monthly income = Rs 2750.

Example 7 In an examination, 94% of the condidates passed and 114 failed. How many candidates appeared?

Solution Suppose 100 candidates appeared in the examination.

Then, number of passed candidates = 94

Number of failed condidates = (100 – 94) = 6

Thus, if the number of failures is 6, candidates appeared = 100

If the number of failures is 114, candidates appeared $= \left(\frac{100}{6} \times 114\right) = 1900$

Hence, 1900 candidates appeared in the examination.

Aliter We have,

Pass percentage = 94%

$\therefore$ Percentage of failures = 6%

Let the number of candidates appeared be x.

It is given that 114 candidates failed in the examination and the percentage of failures is 6%.

$\therefore$ 6% of x = 114

$\Rightarrow \frac{6}{100} \times x = 114 \Rightarrow x = \frac{114 \times 100}{6} = 1900$

Hence, 1900 candidates appeared in the examination.

Example 8 12% of the employees in a factory are females and the number of male employees is 264. Find the total number of employees. Also, find the number of female employees.

Solution Let the total number of employees be 100

Then, the number of female employees = 12

$\therefore$ Number of male employees = (100 – 12) = 88

Now, if the number of male employees is 88, total number of employees = 100

If the number of male employees is 264,

total number of employees $= \left(\frac{100}{88} \times 264\right) = 300$

Hence, the total number of employees = 300

$\therefore$ Number of female employees = (300 – 264) =36

Aliter Let the total number of employees be x.

It is given that the number of female employees = 12%

Therefore, number of male employees = (100 – 12)% = 88%

It is also given that the total number of male employees is 264

$\therefore$ 88% of x = 264

$\Rightarrow \frac{88}{100} \times x = 264 \quad \Rightarrow x = \frac{264 \times 100}{88} = 300$

Hence, the total number of employees = 300

$\therefore$ Number of female employees = 300 – 264 = 36

Example 9 In a school, 720 are boys and 40% are girls. Find the number of girls.

Solution Let the total number of students be 100. Then,

The number of girls = 40

$\therefore$ Number of boys = 60

Now, if the number of boys is 60, the total number of students = 100

If the number of boys is 720, the total number of students $= \frac{100}{60} \times 720 = 1200$

$\therefore$ Number of girls =1200 – 720 = 480

Aliter Number of girls = 40%

Number of boys = (100 – 40)% = 60%

Girls : Boys = 40 : 60 = 2 : 3

Thus,

If the number of boys is 3, the number of girls = 2

$\therefore$ If the number of boys is 720, the number of girls $= \frac{2}{3} \times 720 = 480$

Example 10 A student scored 3 marks more than what he did in the previous examination in which he had scored 12. Another student scored 12 marks more than he did in the previous examination in which he had scored 84. Who had shown more improvement?

Solution We have,

Percentage improvement in the first examination for the first student

$= \left(\frac{3}{12} \times 100\right)\% = 25\%$

Percentage improvement in the first examination for the second student

$$=\left(\frac{12}{84}\times 100\right)\%=14\frac{2}{7}\%$$

Clearly, $25\% > 14\frac{2}{7}\%$. Thus, the first student had improved more.

Example 11 The size of a bag that could hold 5 kg of sugar has now been increased so that it can hold 6 kg. What is the percentage increase in size?

Solution We have,

Old capacity of the bag = 5 kg.

New capacity of the bag = 6 kg.

$\therefore$ Increase in capacity = New capacity – Old capacity = (6 – 5) kg = 1 kg.

$$\therefore \text{ Percentage increase in size } = \left(\frac{\text{Increase in capacity}}{\text{Old capacity}}\times 100\right)\%$$

$$=\left(\frac{1}{5}\times 100\right)\%=20\%.$$

EXERCISE 11.6

1. Ashu had 24 pages to write. By the evening, he had completed 25% of his work. How many pages were left?
2. A box contains 60 eggs. Out of which $16\frac{2}{3}\%$ are rotten ones. How many eggs are rotten?
3. Rohit obtained 45 marks out of 80. What per cent marks did he get?
4. Mr Virmani saves 12% of his salary. If he receives Rs 15900 per month as salary, find his monthly expenditure.
5. A lawyer willed his 3 sons Rs 250000 to be divided into portions 30%, 45% and 25%. How much did each of them inherit?
6. Rajdhani College has 2400 students, 40% of whom are girls. How many boys are there in the college?
7. Aman obtained 410 marks out of 500 in CBSE XII examination while his brother Anish gets 536 marks out of 600 in IX class examination. Find whose performance is better?
8. Rahim obtained 60 marks out of 75 in Mathematics. Find the percentage of marks obtained by Rahim in Mathematics.
9. In an orchard, $16\frac{2}{3}\%$ of the trees are apple trees. If the number of trees in the orchard is 240, find the number of other type of trees in the orchard.
10. Ram scored 553 marks out of 700 and Gita scored 486 marks out of 600 in science. Whose performance is better?
11. Out of an income of Rs 15000, Nazima spends Rs 10200. What per cent of her income does she save?
12. 45% of the students in a school are boys. If the total number of students in the school is 880, find the number of girls in the school.

13. Mr. Sidhana saves 28% of his income. If he saves Rs 840 per month, find his monthly income.
14. In an examination, 8% of the students fail. What percentage of the students pass? If 1650 students appeared in the examination, how many passed?
15. In an examination, 92% of the candidates passed and 46 failed. How many candidates appeared?

ANSWERS

1. 18 pages	2. 10 eggs	3. $56\frac{1}{4}\%$
4. Rs 13992	5. Rs 75000, Rs 112500, Rs 62500	6. 1440 boys
7. Anish's performance is better	8. 80%	9. 200
10. Gita's performance is better	11. 32%	12. 484 girls
13. Rs 3000	14. 92%, 1518	15. 575

OBJECTIVE TYPE QUESTIONS

Mark the correct alternative in each of the following:

1. $\frac{2}{5}$ as a per cent is
   (a) 30% (b) 35% (c) 40% (d) 45%
2. $\frac{5}{4}$ as a per cent is
   (a) 80% (b) 125% (c) 120% (d) 130%
3. The ratio 3 : 5 as a per cent is
   (a) 60% (b) 50% (c) 40% (d) 80%
4. 12% as a fraction is
   (a) $\frac{3}{25}$ (b) $\frac{4}{25}$ (c) $\frac{3}{20}$ (d) $\frac{6}{25}$
5. $1\frac{1}{4}\%$ as a fraction is
   (a) $\frac{1}{40}$ (b) $\frac{1}{60}$ (c) $\frac{1}{80}$ (d) $\frac{1}{70}$
6. Which of the following fractions is equivalent to 25% ?
   (a) $\frac{1}{4}$ (b) $\frac{1}{5}$ (c) $\frac{1}{3}$ (d) $\frac{1}{2}$
7. If 25% of x is 100, then $x =$
   (a) 100 (b) 200 (c) 300 (d) 400
8. If 8% of a number is 6, then the number is
   (a) 96 (b) 60 (c) 96 (d) 75
9. If x% of 75 is 12, then $x =$
   (a) 8 (b) 10 (c) 12 (d) 16
10. If $\frac{5}{6}$ of 29% of x is 29, then $x =$
    (a) 290 (b) 58 (c) 120 (d) 100
11. What per cent of $\frac{2}{7}$ is $\frac{1}{35}$?

(a) 25 % (b) 20 % (c) 15 % (d) 10 %

12. If $x = 100$, then 120 % of x is
(a) 125 (b) 115 (c) 120 (d) 110

13. 40 % of 150 + 60 % of 150 =
(a) 200 (b) 150 (c) 250 (d) 180

14. 50 % of 150 + 70 % of 300 =
(a) 295 (b) 285 (c) 265 (d) 275

15. 55 % of 1000 ÷ 60% of 2000 =
(a) $\frac{11}{24}$ (b) $\frac{12}{25}$ (c) $\frac{13}{24}$ (d) $\frac{14}{25}$

16. If x% of 2000 = 600, then x=
(a) 60 (b) 30 (c) 40 (d) 50

17. If x% of $\frac{12}{5}$ is $\frac{18}{25}$, then x=
(a) 30 (b) 40 (c) 72 (d) 50

18. The value of 30 % of 60 % of 200 is
(a) 23 (b) 24 (c) 18 (d) 36

19. If $\frac{2}{5}$ of 50 % of x is 10, then x=
(a) 100 (b) 50 (c) 25 (d) 80

20. If $\frac{4}{7}$ of 49 % of x is 21, then x=
(a) 125 (b) 98 (c) 84 (d) 75

21. Which of the following fractions is equivalent to 12.5% ?
(a) $\frac{1}{8}$ (b) $\frac{1}{6}$ (c) $\frac{1}{5}$ (d) $\frac{1}{12}$

22. Ravish saves 55% of his income. If his income is ₹ 11000, then his expenditure is
(a) ₹ 6050 (b) ₹ 7450 (c) ₹ 4950 (d) ₹ 3550

23. If 35 % of a number added to 39 is the number itself, the number is
(a) 60 (b) 65 (c) 75 (d) 105

24. On increasing the salary of a man by 25%, it becomes ₹ 20,000. What was his original salary?
(a) ₹ 15000 (b) ₹ 16000 (c) ₹ 18000 (d) ₹ 25000

25. Rohit scored 180 marks in the first test and 150 marks in the second test. The maximum marks in each test is 200. What is the decrease in his performance in percentage points?
(a) 20 % (b) 15 % (c) 25 % (d) 23 %

ANSWSERS

1. (c)	2. (b)	3. (a)	4. (a)	5. (c)	6. (a)	7. (d)
8. (d)	9. (d)	10. (c)	11. (d)	12. (c)	13. (b)	14. (b)
15. (a)	16. (b)	17. (a)	18. (d)	19. (b)	20. (d)	21. (a)
22. (c)	23. (a)	24. (b)	25. (b)			

THINGS TO REMEMBER

1. *Per cent means per hundred or for every hundred.*
2. *By a certain per cent, we mean that many hundredths.*
3. *A fraction with its denominator as 100 is called a per cent and is equal to that per cent as is the numerator.*
4. *A ratio with its second term 100 is also called a per cent.*
5. *To convert a fraction into a per cent we multiply the fraction by 100.*
6. *To convert a ratio into a per cent, we write it as a fraction and multiply it by 100.*
7. *To convert a decimal into a per cent, we shift the decimal point two places to the right.*
8. *To convert a per cent into a fraction, we drop per cent sign (%) and divide the remainder by 100.*
9. *To convert a per cent into a ratio, we drop per cent sign (%) and form a ratio with the remaining number as the first term and 100 as the second term.*
10. *To convert a per cent into a decimal, we drop per cent sign (%) and shift the decimal point two places to the left.*
11. $$\text{Increase\%} = \left(\frac{\text{Increase}}{\text{Original value}} \times 100\right)\%$$

$$\text{Decrease\%} = \left(\frac{\text{Decrease}}{\text{Original value}} \times 100\right)\%$$

12

PROFIT AND LOSS

12.1 INTRODUCTION

In the previous chapter, we have learnt about percentage and simple problems on computing percentage. In this chapter, we shall learn to apply the concept of percentage to find profit and loss in buying and selling goods in our day-to-day life.

12.2 PROFIT AND LOSS

In our day-to-day life, we buy goods from the shopkeepers in the market which they buy either directly from manufacturers or through wholesalers. In order to earn money, the shopkeepers sell goods at a rate that is higher than the rate at which they bought them. The price at which a shopkeeper buys the goods is called cost price as defined below.

COST PRICE *The money paid by the shopkeeper to buy the goods from a manufacturer or a wholesaler is called the cost price of the shopkeeper and it is abbreviated as C.P.*

As mentioned above that the shopkeepers sell goods at a price that is more than the price at which they bought them. This price is called the selling price as defined below.

SELLING PRICE *The price at which a shopkeeper sells the goods is called the selling price of the shopkeeper and it is abbreviated as S.P.*

If the selling price (S.P.) of an article is greater than the cost price (C.P.), then the shopkeeper makes a gain or profit and the amount of profit is equal to the difference between the selling price and the cost price. Thus, if S.P. > C.P. Then,

$$\text{Profit} = \text{S.P.} - \text{C.P.}$$

$$\Rightarrow \quad \text{S.P.} = \text{Profit} + \text{C.P. and, C.P.} = \text{S.P.} - \text{Profit}$$

If the selling price (S.P.) of an article is less than the cost price (C.P.), then the shopkeeper suffers a loss and the amount of loss is equal to the difference between the cost price (C.P.) and the selling price (S.P.). Thus, if S.P.< C.P., then

$$\text{Loss} = \text{C.P.} - \text{S.P.}$$

$$\Rightarrow \quad \text{S.P.} = \text{C.P.} - \text{Loss and, C.P.} = \text{S.P.} + \text{Loss}$$

Usually, a shopkeeper has to bear some additional expenses such as labour charges, freight charges and maintenance charges for the goods before they are sold. Such charges are called *overhead charges*.

The overhead charges become a part of the cost price. Thus, the effective cost price of the goods is equal to the sum of the actual payment made while purchasing the goods and overhead charges i.e,

Effective cost price = (Payment made while purchasing the goods) + (Overhead charges)

12.2.1 PROFIT PERCENT AND LOSS PERCENT

In order to compare the profit or loss in two or more sales, we usually express profit and loss as a percent of the cost price. The profit percentage is the profit that would be obtained for a C.P. of Rs 100. Similarly, the loss percentage is the loss that would be made for a C.P. of Rs 100.

Thus, we have

$$\text{Profit per cent} = \frac{\text{Profit}}{\text{C.P.}} \times 100, \quad \text{Loss per cent} = \frac{\text{Loss}}{\text{C.P.}} \times 100$$

Following examples will illustrate the computation of profit and loss and also the profit and loss percentages.

ILLUSTRATIVE EXAMPLES

Type I **ON FINDING PROFIT OR LOSS WHEN C.P. AND S.P. ARE GIVEN**

Example 1 Given the following values, find the unknown values:

(i) C.P. = Rs 500, S.P = Rs 600, Profit/Loss = ?

(ii) C.P. = Rs 1270, S.P. = Rs 1250, Profit/Loss = ?

(iii) C.P. = ?, S.P. = Rs 2390, Profit = Rs 120.50

(iv) C.P. = Rs 72, S.P. = ?, Loss = Rs 15.601

Solution (i) We have, C.P. = Rs 500, S.P. = Rs 600

Clearly, S.P. > C.P. So, there will be profit given by

Profit = S.P. – C.P. = Rs (600 – 500) = Rs 100

(ii) We have, C.P = Rs 1270 , S.P. = Rs 1250

Since C.P. > S.P. So, there will be loss given by

Loss = C.P. – S.P. = Rs (1270 – 1250) = Rs 20

(iii) We have, S.P. = Rs 2390 and Profit = Rs 120.50

∴ Profit = S.P. – C .P.

⇒ C.P. = S. P. – Profit

⇒ C.P. = Rs 2390 – Rs 120.50 = Rs (2390 – 120.50) = Rs 2269.50

(iv) We have, C.P. = Rs 72 and Loss = Rs 15.60

∴ Loss = C.P. – S.P.

⇒ S.P. = C.P. – Loss = Rs 72 – Rs 15.60 = Rs (72 – 15.60) = Rs 56.40

Type II **ON COMPUTING C.P. OR S.P. WHEN PROFIT OR LOSS IS GIVEN**

Example 2 Compute the missing enteries in the following table (whereever possible):

	Cost price (C.P.)	*Overhead expenses*	*Selling price (S.P)*	*Profit*	*Loss*
(i)	Rs 450	Rs 70	—	Rs 85	—
(ii)	Rs 8000	Rs 200	—	—	Rs 530
(iii)	Rs 32000	Rs 3000	Rs 38000	—	—
(iv)	Rs 750	Rs 20	—	Rs 50	—
(v)	Rs 1050	Rs 50	—	—	Rs 70

Solution (i) We have, C.P. = Rs 450 and Overhead expenses = Rs 70.

$\therefore$ Effective cost price = Rs (450 + 70) = Rs 520.

Now,

Profit = S.P. – Effective C.P.

$\Rightarrow$ S.P. = Effective C.P. + Profit

$\Rightarrow$ S.P. = Rs (520 + 85) [$\because$ Profit = Rs 85 (given)]

$\Rightarrow$ S.P. = Rs 605

(ii) We have, C.P. = Rs 8000, Overhead expenses = Rs 200 and Loss = Rs 530

Now,

Effective cost price (E.C.P.) = C.P. + Overhead expenses

$\Rightarrow$ Effective cost price (E.C.P.) = Rs (8000 + 200) = Rs 8200

We know that

Loss = E.C.P. – S.P.

$\therefore$ S.P. = E.C.P. – Loss

= Rs (8200 – 530) = Rs 7670

(iii) We have, C.P. = Rs 32000, Overhead expenses = Rs 3000 and S.P. = Rs 38000.

$\therefore$ E.C.P. = C.P. + Overhead expenses

$\Rightarrow$ E.C.P. = Rs (32000 + 3000) = Rs 35000

We have,

S.P. = Rs 38000

Clearly, E.C.P. < S.P. Therefore, there will be profit given by

Profit = S.P. – E.C.P. = Rs (38000 – 35000) = Rs 3000.

(iv) We have, C.P. = Rs 750, Overhead expenses = Rs 20 and Profit = Rs 50.

Now,

E.C.P. = C.P. + Overhead expenses = Rs (750 + 20) = Rs 770.

It is given that there is profit of Rs 50.

$\therefore$ S.P. = E.C.P. + Profit = Rs (770 + 50) = Rs 820.

(v) We have, C.P. = Rs 1050, Overhead expenses = Rs 50 and Loss = Rs 70.

$\therefore$ E.C.P. = C.P. + Overhead expenses = Rs (1050 + 50) = Rs 1100.

It is given that there is loss of Rs 70.

$\therefore$ S.P. = E.C.P. – Loss = Rs(1100 – 70) = Rs 1030

Type III **ON FINDING PROFIT OR LOSS PER CENT**

Example 3 Find the gain or loss percent, if

(i) C.P. = Rs 500 and S.P. = Rs 565 (ii) C.P. = Rs 700 and S.P. = Rs 630

Solution (i) We have, C.P. = Rs 500 and S.P. = Rs 565

Since S.P. > C.P. Therefore, there is gain given by

Gain $= \text{S.P.} - \text{C.P.} = \text{Rs } 565 - \text{Rs } 500 = \text{Rs } 65$

$\therefore$ Gain per cent $= \left(\dfrac{\text{Gain}}{\text{C.P}} \times 100\right)\% = \left(\dfrac{65}{500} \times 100\right)\% = 13\%$

(ii) Since C.P. = Rs 700 and S.P. = Rs 630

Clearly, S.P. < C.P. So, There is loss given by

Loss $= \text{C.P.} - \text{S.P.} = \text{Rs } (700 - 630) = \text{Rs } 70$

$\therefore$ Loss per cent $= \left(\dfrac{\text{Loss}}{\text{C.P}} \times 100\right)\% = \left(\dfrac{70}{700} \times 100\right)\% = 10\%$

Example 4 If the profit made on a packet of tea is Rs 4 and the cost price of the packet is Rs 20, then how much is the profit percentage?

Solution We have, C.P. = Rs 20 and Profit = Rs 4.

$\therefore$ Profit Per cent $= \left(\dfrac{\text{Profit}}{\text{C.P.}} \times 100\right)\% = \left(\dfrac{4}{20} \times 100\right)\% = 20\%$

Example 5 A box of Alphonso mangoes was purchased by a fruit-seller for Rs 300. However, he had to sell them for Rs 255 because they began to get over ripe. What was the loss percentage?

Solution We have, C.P. = Rs 300 and S.P. = Rs 255

Since C.P. > S.P. Therefore, there is loss given by

Loss = C.P. – S.P. = Rs (300 – 255) = Rs 45

Now,

Loss per cent $= \left(\dfrac{\text{Loss}}{\text{C.P.}} \times 100\right)\% = \left(\dfrac{45}{300} \times 100\right)\% = 15\%$

Hence, there was 15% loss.

Example 6 Karim bought 150 dozens pencils at Rs 10 a dozen. His overhead expenses were Rs 100. He sold them at Rs 1.20 each. What was his profit or loss percent?

Solution We have,

Cost price of one dozen pencils = Rs 10

Cost price of 150 dozens pencils = Rs (150 × 10) = Rs 1500

Overhead expenses = Rs 100

$\therefore$ Effective cost price = Rs (1500 + 100) = Rs 1600

Now,

Selling price of one pencil = Rs 1.20

$\therefore$ Selling price of one dozen pencils = Rs (12 × 1.20) = Rs 14.40

$\therefore$ Selling price of 150 dozens pencils = Rs (14.40 × 150) = Rs 2160

Here, S.P. > E.C.P. So, there is profit given by

Profit = S.P. – E.C.P. = Rs 2160 – Rs 16000 = Rs 560

Now, Profit per cent $= \left(\dfrac{\text{Profit}}{\text{E.C.P.}} \times 100\right)\% = \left(\dfrac{560}{1600} \times 100\right)\% = 35\%$

Example 7 Subramaniam bought 100 eggs for Rs 50. Out of these, 4 eggs were found to be broken. He sold the remaining eggs at the rate of Rs 8.50 per dozen. Find his gain or loss percent.

Solution We have,

C.P. of 100 eggs = Rs 50.

It is given that 4 eggs were found to be broken.

$\therefore$ The number of remaining eggs which were sold in the market = 100– 4 = 96.

It is given that the remaining eggs were sold at the rate of Rs 8.50 per dozen.

$\therefore$ S.P. of 12 eggs = Rs 8.50

$\Rightarrow$ S.P. of 1 egg $= \text{Rs } \frac{8.50}{12}$

$\therefore$ S.P. of 96 eggs $= \text{Rs} = \left(\frac{8.50}{12} \times 96\right) = \text{Rs } 68$

Clearly, S.P. > C.P. So, there is gain given by

Gain = S.P. – C.P. = Rs 68 – Rs 50 = Rs 18

$\therefore$ Gain per cent $= \left(\frac{\text{Gain}}{\text{C.P.}} \times 100\right)\% = \left(\frac{18}{50} \times 100\right)\% = 36\%$

Example 8 A grocer buys eggs at 10 for Rs 8 and sells at 8 for Rs 10. Find his gain or loss percent.

Solution We have, L.C.M. of 10 and 8 = 40. So, let the number of eggs bought be 40.

Now,

C.P. of 10 eggs = Rs 8

$\therefore$ C.P. of 40 eggs $= \text{Rs} \left(\frac{8}{10} \times 40\right) = \text{Rs } 32$

Again, S.P. of 8 eggs = Rs 10

$\therefore$ S.P. of 40 eggs $= \text{Rs} \left(\frac{10}{8} \times 40\right) = \text{Rs } 50$

Now, C.P. = Rs 32 and S.P.= Rs 50

Clearly, S.P. > C.P. So, there is gain given by

Gain = S.P. – C.P. = Rs 50 – Rs 32 = Rs 18

$\therefore$ Gain per cent $= \left(\frac{\text{Gain}}{\text{C.P.}} \times 100\right)\% = \left(\frac{18}{32} \times 100\right)\% = \frac{225}{4}\% = 56\frac{1}{4}\%$

Example 9 The selling price of 10 articles is the same as the cost price of 11 articles, find gain percent.

Solution Let the cost price of each article be Rs x

We have,

S.P. of 10 articles = C.P. of 11 articles = Rs $11x$.

C.P. of 10 articles = $10x$

$\therefore$ Gain on the purchase of articles = Rs $11x$ – Rs $10x$ = Rs x

Hence, Gain percent $= \left(\frac{\text{Gain}}{\text{C.P.}} \times 100\right)\% = \left(\frac{x}{10x} \times 100\right)\% = 10\%$

Example 10 Neeru bought 1600 bananas at Rs 3.75 a dozen. She sold 900 of them at 2 for Re 1 and the remaining at 5 for Rs 2. Find her gain or loss percent.

Solution We have,

Cost of one dozen of bananas = Rs 3.75

∴ Cost of 1600 bananas $= \text{Rs}\left(\frac{3.75}{12}\times 1600\right) = \text{Rs}\ \frac{375\times 16}{12} = \text{Rs } 500$

Thus, C.P. of 1600 bananas = Rs 500

Now, Selling price of 900 bananas at the rate of 2 for Re 1 $= \text{Rs}\ \frac{900}{2} = \text{Rs } 450$

Selling price of the remaining i.e., 1600 – 900 = 700 bananas at the rate of 5 for Rs 2

$= \text{Rs}\left(\frac{2}{5}\times 700\right) = \text{Rs } 280$

∴ S.P. of 1600 bananas = Rs (450 + 280) = Rs 730

Since S.P. > C.P. So, there is gain given by

Gain = S.P. – C.P. = Rs (730 – 500) = Rs 230

Hence, Gain percent $= \left(\frac{\text{Gain}}{\text{C.P.}}\times 100\right)\% = \left(\frac{230}{500}\times 100\right)\% = 46\%$

Type IV **ON FINDING THE S.P. WHEN C.P. AND PROFIT OR LOSS PER CENT ARE GIVEN**

Example 11 Bashir bought an article for Rs 1215 and spent Rs 35 on its transportation. At what price should he sell the article to have a gain of 16%?

Solution The effective cost price of the article is equal to the price at which it was bought plus the transportation charge.

∴ C.P. of the given article = Rs (1215 + 35) = Rs 1250

Gain percent = 16%

∴ Gain = 16% of cost price $= \text{Rs}\left(\frac{16}{100}\times 1250\right) = \text{Rs } 200$

∴ S.P. = C.P. + Gain = Rs 1250 + Rs 200 = Rs 1450

Example 12 Krishnamurti bought oranges at Rs 5 a dozen. He had to sell them at a loss of 4%. Find the selling price of one orange.

Solution We have, C.P. of one dozen oranges = Rs 5.

Loss percent = 4%

∴ Loss = 4% of Rs 5 $= \text{Re}\left(\frac{4}{100}\times 5\right) = \text{Re}\left(\frac{1}{5}\right)$

∴ S.P. = C.P. – Loss $= \text{Rs}\left(5-\frac{1}{5}\right) = \text{Rs}\ \frac{24}{5}$

Thus, S.P. of one dozen oranges $= \text{Rs}\ \frac{24}{5}$

∴ S.P. of one orange $= \text{Re}\left(\frac{24}{5}\times\frac{1}{12}\right) = \text{Re}\ \frac{2}{5} = \frac{2}{5}\times 100$ paise = 40 paise

Example 13 A vendor purchased 40 dozen bananas for Rs 250. Out of these, 30 bananas were rotten and could not be sold. At what rate per dozen should he sell the remaining bananas to make a profit of 20%

Solution We have,

C.P. of bananas = Rs 250, Gain required = 20%

$\therefore$ Gain $= 20\%$ of C.P. $= 20\%$ of Rs 250 = Rs $\left(\frac{20}{100} \times 250\right)$ = Rs 50

Now, S.P. = C.P. + Gain

$\Rightarrow$ S.P. = Rs 250 + Rs 50 = Rs 300

Number of good bananas $= (40 \times 12 - 30) = 450$

$\therefore$ S.P. of 450 bananas = Rs 300

$\Rightarrow$ S.P. of 12 bananas = Rs $\left(\frac{300}{450} \times 12\right)$ = Rs 8

Hence, the vendor should sell the remaining bananas at Rs 8 per dozen to make a profit of 20%

Type V ON FINDING THE COST PRICE WHEN S.P. AND PROFIT OR LOSS ARE GIVEN

Example 14 A man sells his scooter for Rs 18000 making a profit of 20%. How much did the scooter cost him?

Solution Let the cost price of the scooter be Rs 100. Then, Profit = Rs 20

$\therefore$ S.P. = C.P. + Profit = Rs 100 + Rs 20 = Rs 120

Thus, if the S.P. is Rs 120, then C.P. = Rs 100

If the S.P. is Rs 18000, then C.P. = Rs $\left(\frac{100}{120} \times 18000\right)$ = Rs 15000

Hence, the cost of the scooter = Rs 15000

Example 15 By selling an A.C. for Rs 18000, I loose 20%. What did I pay for it?

Solution We have, S.P. = Rs 18000, and Loss = 20%

Let the C.P. of A.C. be Rs 100. Then,

Loss = C.P. – S.P.

$\Rightarrow$ S.P. = C.P. – Loss = Rs 100 – Rs 20 = Rs 80

Thus, if the S.P. is Rs 80, then C.P. = Rs 100

If the S.P. is 18000, then C.P. = Rs $\frac{100}{80} \times 18000$ = Rs 22500

Example 16 A farmer sells his product at a loss of 8%. If his S.P. was Rs 27600, what was his actual loss? What was his cost price?

Solution Let the cost price of the product be Rs 100. Then,

Loss = 8% $\Rightarrow$ Loss 8% of Rs 100 = Rs 8

$\therefore$ S.P. = C.P. – Loss = Rs 100 – Rs 8 = Rs 92

Thus, if S.P. is Rs 92, then C.P. = Rs 100

If S.P. is Rs 27600, then C.P. = Rs $\left(\frac{100}{92} \times 27600\right)$ = Rs 30000

Hence, C.P. = Rs 30000.

Actual loss = C.P. – S.P. = Rs 30000 – Rs 27600 = Rs 2400

EXERCISE 12.1

1. Given the following values, find the unknown values:

(i) C.P. = ₹ 1200,	S.P. = ₹ 1350,	Profit/Loss = ?
(ii) C.P. = ₹ 980,	S.P. = ₹ 940,	Profit/Loss = ?
(iii) C.P. = ₹ 720,	S.P. = ?,	Profit = ₹ 55.50
(iv) C.P. = ?	S.P. = ₹ 1254,	Loss = ₹ 32

2. Fill in the blanks in each of the following:

(i) C.P. = ₹ 1265,	S.P. = ₹ 1253,	Loss = ₹ .....
(ii) C.P. = ₹ ....,	S.P. = ₹ 450,	Profit = ₹ 150
(iii) C.P. = ₹ 3355,	S.P. = ₹ 7355,	Profit = ₹ ....
(iv) C.P. = ₹ ....,	S.P. = ₹ 2390,	Loss = ₹ 5.50

3. Calculate the profit or loss and profit or loss per cent in each of the following cases:
   (i) C.P. = ₹ 4560, S.P. = ₹ 5000 (ii) C.P. = ₹ 2600, S.P. = ₹ 2470
   (iii) C.P. = ₹ 332, S.P. = ₹ 350 (iv) C.P. = ₹ 1500, S.P. = ₹ 1500
4. Find the gain or loss per cent, when:
   (i) C.P. = ₹ 4000 and gain = ₹ 40. (ii) S.P. = ₹ 1272 and loss = ₹ 328
   (iii) S.P. = ₹ 1820 and gain = ₹ 420.
5. Find the gain or loss per cent, when:
   (i) C.P. = ₹ 2300, Overhead expenses = ₹ 300 and gain = ₹ 260.
   (ii) C.P. = ₹ 3500, Overhead expenses = ₹ 150 and loss = ₹ 146
6. A grain merchant sold 600 quintals of rice at a profit of 7%. If a quintal of rice cost him ₹ 25 and his total overhead charges for transportation, etc. were ₹ 1000 find his total profit and th selling price of 600 quintals of rice.
7. Naresh bought 4 dozen pencils at ₹ 10.80 a dozen and sold them for 80 paise each. Find hi gain or loss percent.
8. A vendor buys oranges at ₹ 26 per dozen and sells them at 5 for ₹ 13. Find his gain per cent.
9. Mr Virmani purchased a house for ₹ 365000 and spent ₹ 135000 on its repairs. If he sold it fc ₹ 550000, find his gain percent.
10. Shikha purchased a wrist watch for ₹ 840 and sold it to her friend Vidhi for ₹ 910. Find her gai percent.
11. A business man makes a 10% profit by selling a toy costing him ₹ 120. What is the sellin price ?
12. Harish purchased 50 dozen bananas for ₹135. Five dozen bananas could not be sol because they were rotten. At what price per dozen should Harish sell the remaining banana so that he makes a profit of 20% ?
13. A woman bought 50 dozen eggs at ₹ 6.40 a dozen. Out of these 20 eggs were found to b broken. She sold the remaining eggs at 55 paise per egg. Find her gain or loss percent.
14. Jyotsana bought 400 eggs at ₹ 8.40 a dozen. At what price per hundred must she sell them s as to earn a profit of 15% ?

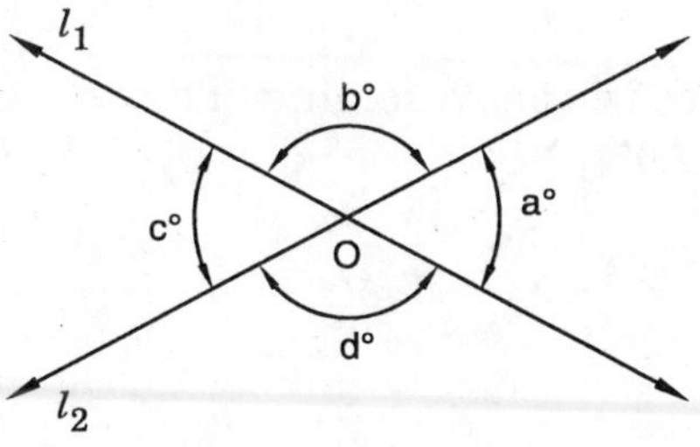

Fig. 10

Solution Since lines l_1 and l_2 intersect at O.

$\therefore \quad \angle a = \angle c$ [Vertically opposite angles]

$\Rightarrow \quad \angle c = 35°$ $[\because \angle a = 35°]$

Clearly, $\angle a + \angle b = 180°$

$\Rightarrow \quad 35° + \angle b = 180°$ $[\because$ $\angle a$ and $\angle b$ are angles of a linear pair$]$

$\Rightarrow \quad \angle b = 180° - 35°$

$\Rightarrow \quad \angle b = 145°$

Since $\angle b$ and $\angle d$ are vertically opposite angles.

$\therefore \quad \angle d = \angle b \Rightarrow \angle d = 145°$ $[\because \angle b = 145°]$

Hence, $b = 145$, $c = 35$ and $d = 145$

Example 9 In Fig. 11, determine the value of y.

Solution Since $\angle COD$ and $\angle EOF$ are vertically opposite angles.

$\therefore \quad \angle COD = \angle EOF$

$\Rightarrow \quad \angle COD = 5y°$ $[\because \angle EOF = 5y°$ (Given)$]$

Now, OA and OB are opposite rays.

$\therefore \quad \angle AOD + \angle DOC + \angle COB = 180°$

$\Rightarrow \quad 2y° + 5y° + 5y° = 180°$

$\Rightarrow \quad 12y° = 180°$

$\Rightarrow \quad y = \dfrac{180}{12} = 15$

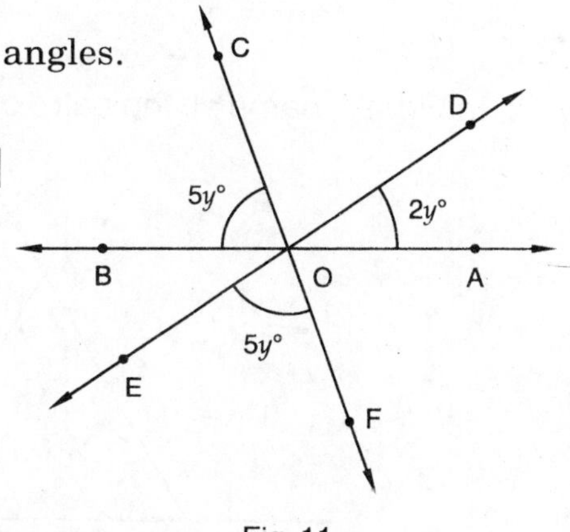

Fig. 11

Hence, $y = 15$.

Example 10 In Fig. 12, two straight lines PQ and RS intersect each other at O. If $\angle POT = 75°$, find the values of a, b and c.

Solution Since OR and OS are in the same line.

$\therefore \quad \angle ROP + \angle POT + \angle TOS = 180°$

$\Rightarrow \quad 4b° + 75° + b° = 180°$

$\Rightarrow \quad 5b° + 75° = 180°$

$\Rightarrow \quad 5b° = 105°$

$\Rightarrow \quad b = 21°$

Since PQ and RS intersect at O. Therefore,

$\angle QOS = \angle POR$ [Vertically opposite angles]

$\Rightarrow \quad a = 4b$

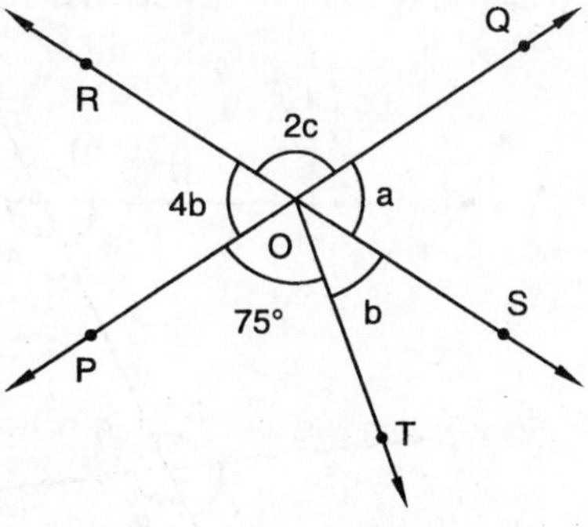

Fig. 12

$\Rightarrow \quad a = 4 \times 21° = 84°$ $[\because b = 21°]$

Now, OR and OS are in the same line. Therefore,

$\angle ROQ + \angle QOS = 180°$ [Linear pair]

$\Rightarrow \quad 2c + a = 180°$

$\Rightarrow \quad 2c + 84° = 180°$ $[\because a = 84°]$

$\Rightarrow \quad 2c = 96°$

$\Rightarrow \quad c = 48°$

Hence, $a = 84°$, $b = 21°$ and $c = 48°$.

EXERCISE 14.1

1. Write down each pair of adjacent angles shown in Fig. 13.

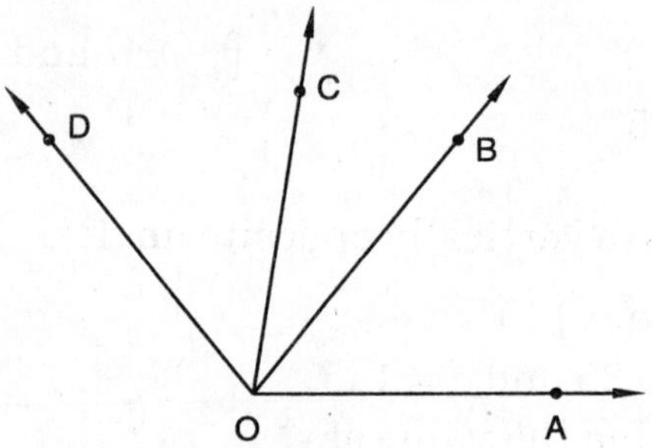

Fig. 13

2. In Fig. 14, name all the pairs of adjacent angles.

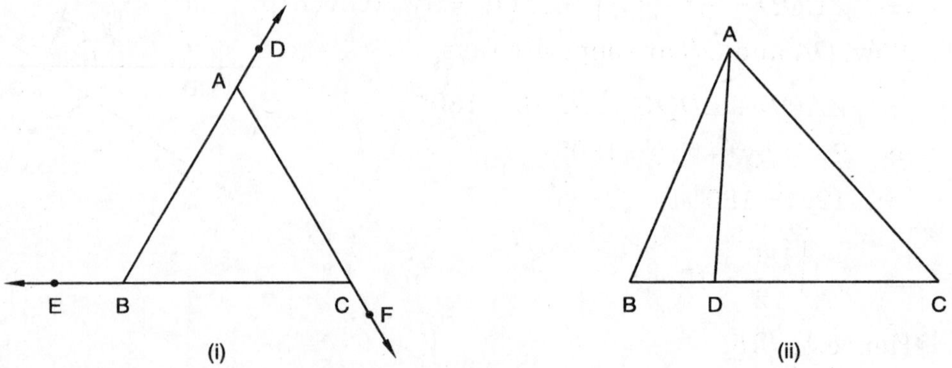

Fig. 14

3. In Fig. 15, write down: (i) each linear pair (ii) each pair of vertically opposite angles.

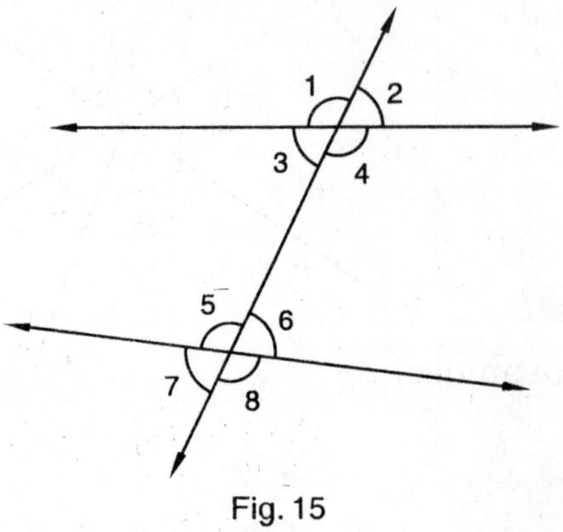

Fig. 15

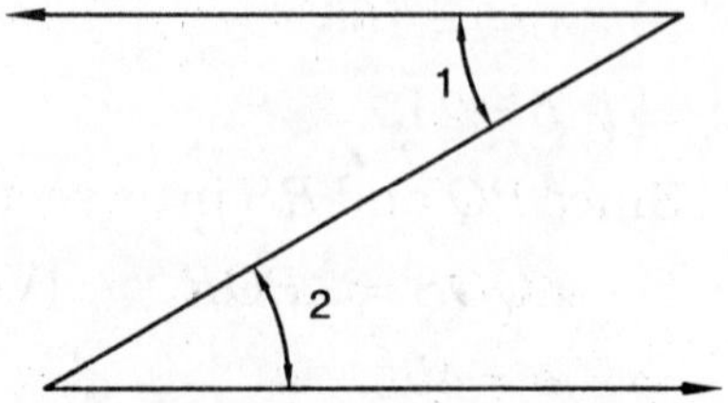

Fig. 16

4. Are the angles 1 and 2 given in Fig. 16 adjacent angles?
5. Find the complement of each of the following angles:
   (i) 35° (ii) 72° (iii) 45° (iv) 85°
6. Find the supplement of each of the following angles:
   (i) 70° (ii) 120° (iii) 135° (iv) 90°
7. Identify the complementary and supplementary pairs of angles from the following pairs:
   (i) 25°, 65° (ii) 120°, 60° (iii) 63°, 27° (iv) 100°, 80°
8. Can two angles be supplementary, if both of them be
   (i) obtuse? (ii) right? (iii) acute?
9. Name the four pairs of supplementary angles shown in Fig. 17.

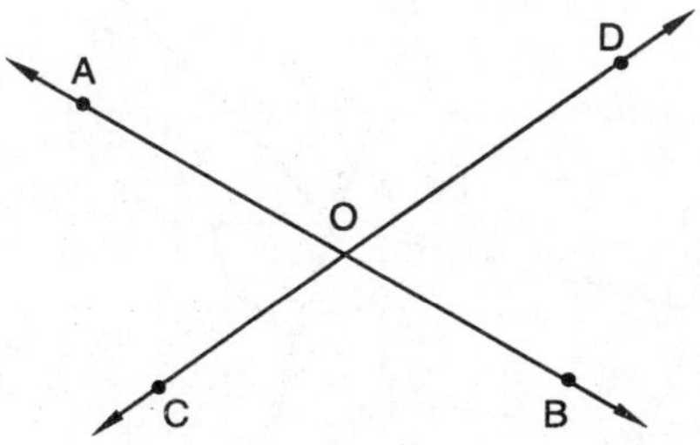

Fig. 17

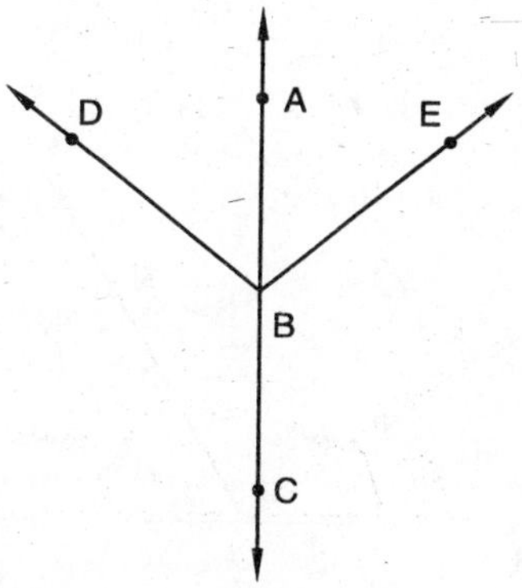

Fig. 18

10. In Fig. 18, A, B, C are collinear points and $\angle DBA = \angle EBA$.
    (i) Name two linear pairs (ii) Name two pairs of supplementary angles.
11. If two supplementary angles have equal measure, what is the measure of each angle?
12. If the complement of an angle is 28°, then find the supplement of the angle.
13. In Fig. 19, name each linear pair and each pair of vertically opposite angles:
14. In Fig. 20, OE is the bisector of $\angle BOD$. If $\angle 1 = 70°$, find the magnitudes of $\angle 2$, $\angle 3$ and $\angle 4$.

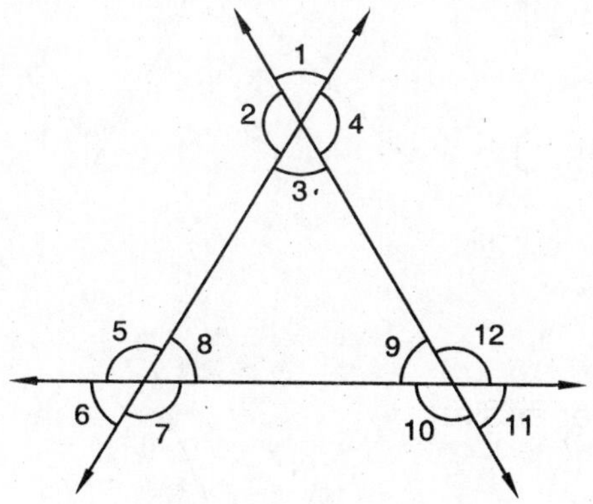

Fig. 19

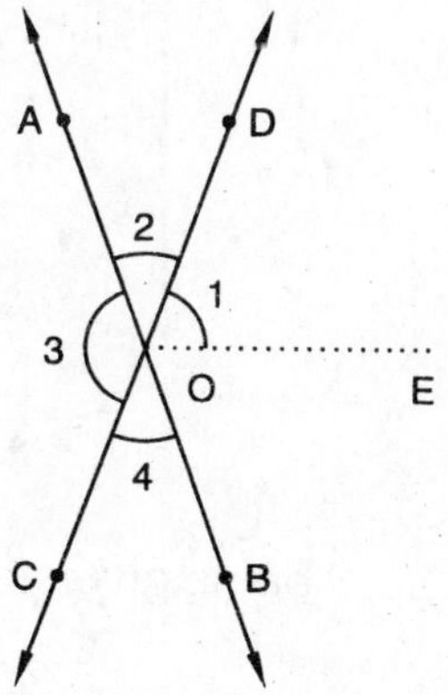

Fig. 20

15. One of the angles forming a linear pair is a right angle. What can you say about its other angle?
16. One of the angles forming a linear pair is an obtuse angle. What kind of angle is the other?
17. One of the angles forming a linear pair is an acute angle. What kind of angle is the other?

18. Can two acute angles form a linear pair?
19. If the supplement of an angle is 65°; then find its complement.
20. Find the value of x in each of the following figures.

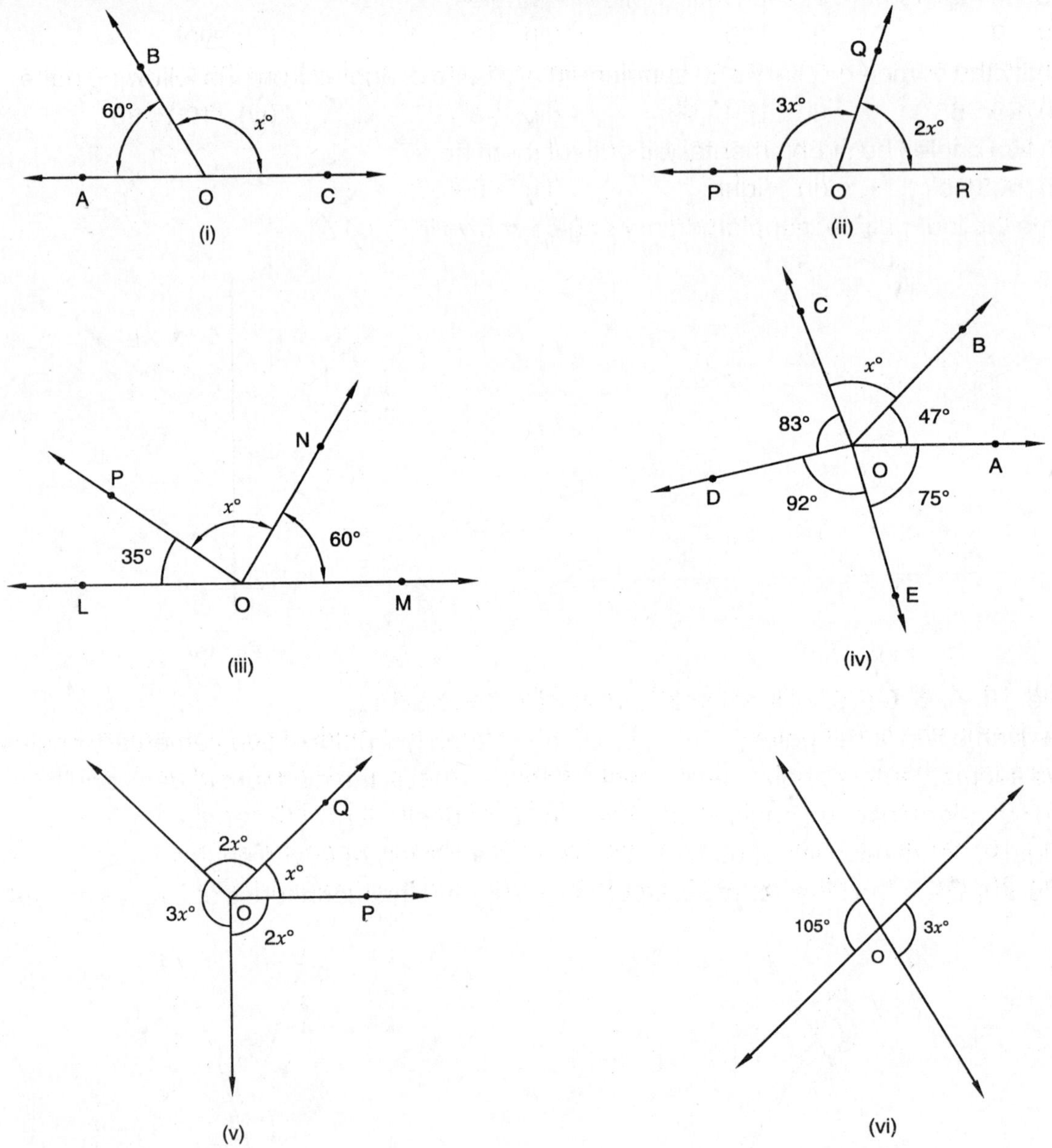

Fig. 21

21. In Fig. 22, it being given that $\angle 1 = 65°$, find all other angles.

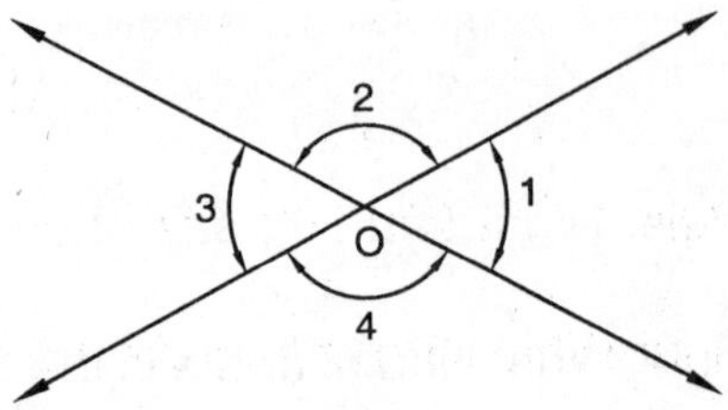

Fig. 22

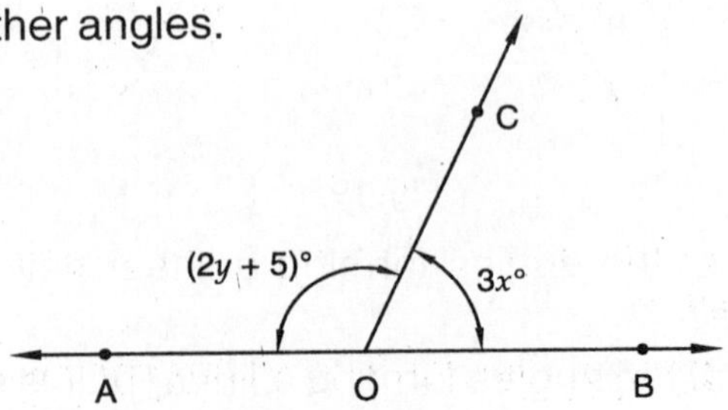

Fig. 23

22. In Fig. 23, *OA* and *OB* are opposite rays:
(i) If $x = 25°$, what is the value of y? (ii) If $y = 35°$, what is the value of x?
23. In Fig. 24, write all pairs of adjacent angles and all the linear pairs.

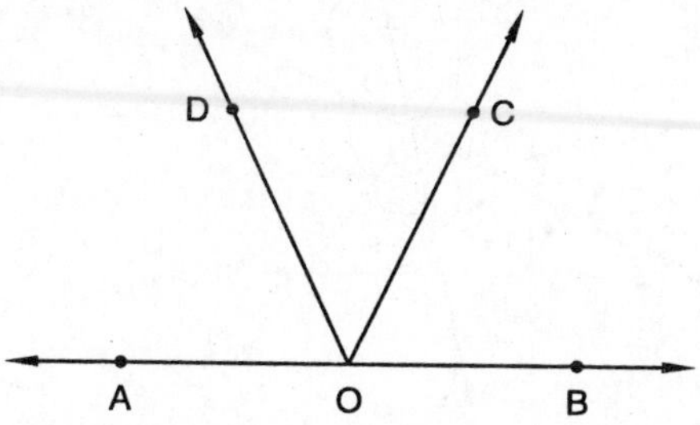

Fig. 24

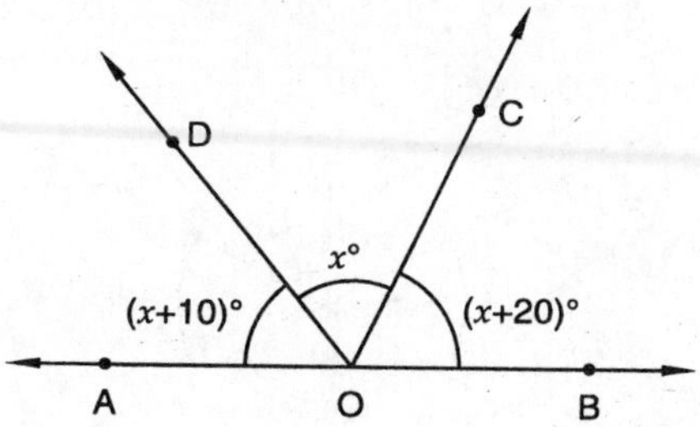

Fig. 25

24. In Fig. 25, find $\angle x$. Further find $\angle BOC$, $\angle COD$ and $\angle AOD$.
25. How many pairs of adjacent angles are formed when two lines intersect in a point?
26. How many pairs of adjacent angles, in all, can you name in Fig. 26?

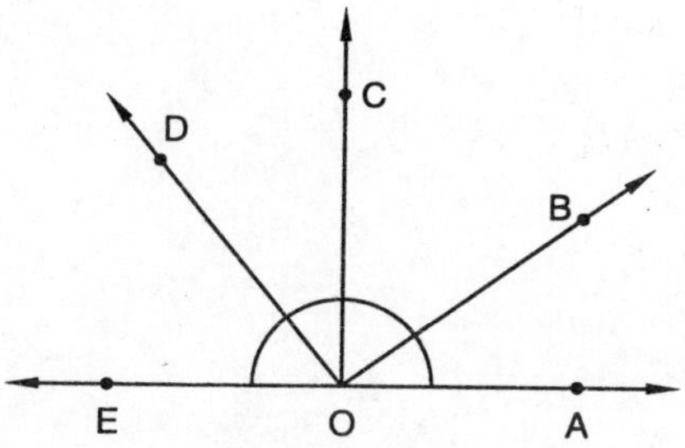

Fig. 26

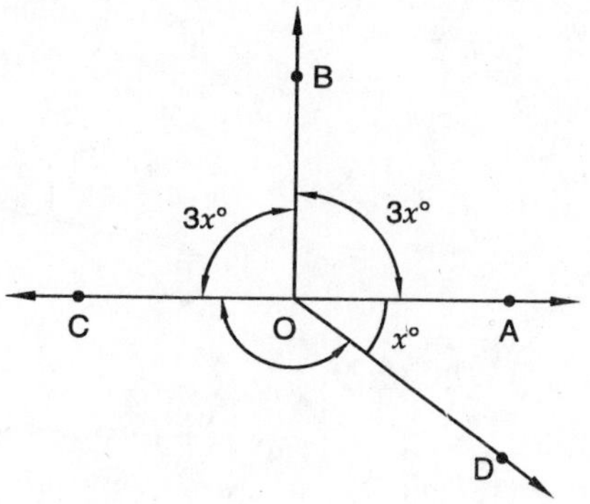

Fig. 27

27. In Fig. 27, determine the value of x.
28. In Fig. 28, *AOC* is a line, find x.

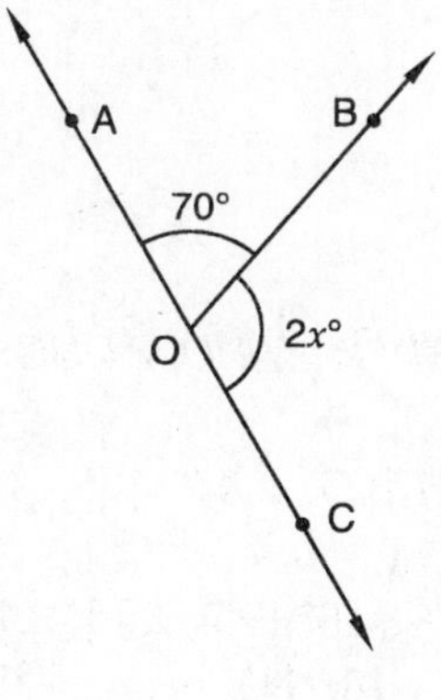

Fig. 28

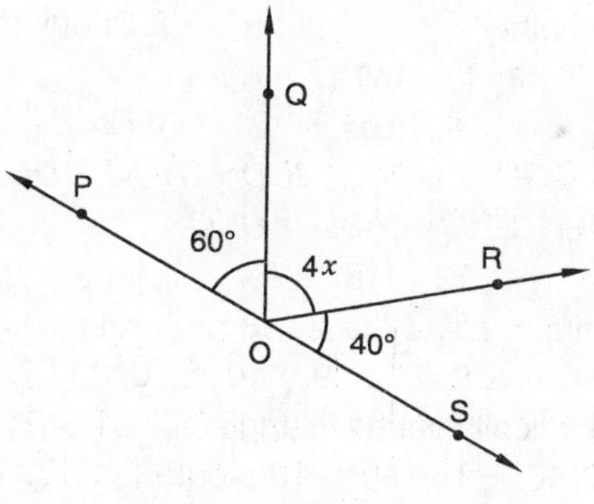

Fig. 29

29. In Fig. 29, *POS* is a line, find x.
30. In Fig. 30, lines l_1 and l_2 intersect at *O*, forming angles as shown in the figure. If $x = 45°$, find the values of y, z and u.

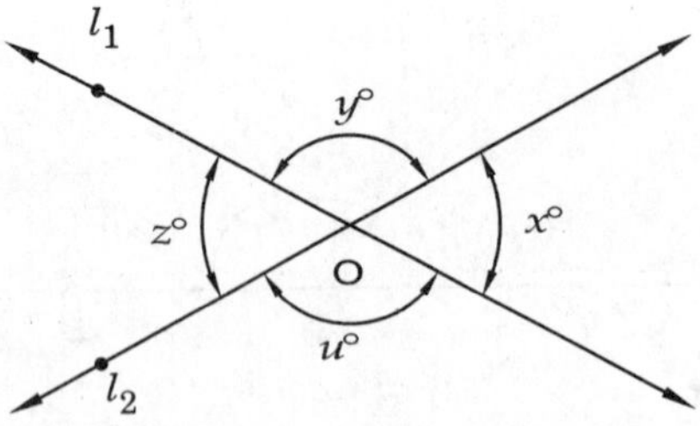

Fig. 30

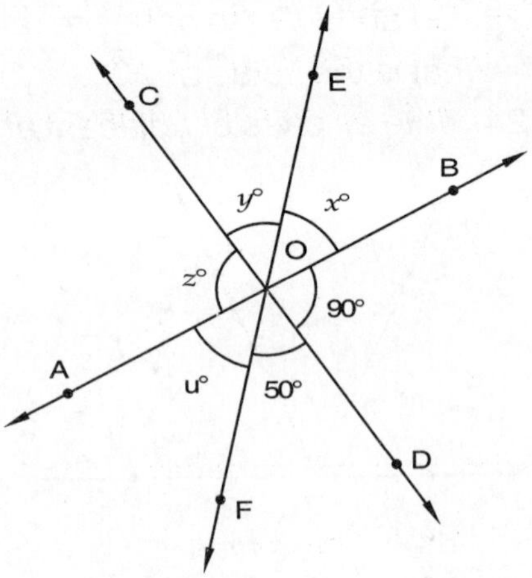

Fig. 31

31. In Fig. 31, three coplanar lines intersect at a point O, forming angles as shown in the figure. Find the values of x, y, z and u.
32. In Fig. 32, find the values of x, y and z.

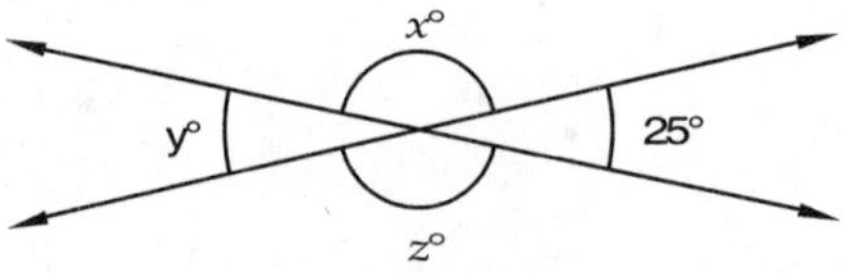

Fig. 32

ANSWERS

1. ∠AOB, ∠BOC; ∠AOC, ∠COD; ∠BOC, ∠COD; ∠AOB, ∠BOD
2. (i) ∠DAC, ∠CAB; ∠ACB, ∠FCB; ∠ABC, ∠ABE
   (ii) ∠ADB, ∠ADC; ∠BAD, ∠DAC
3. (i) ∠1, ∠2; ∠2, ∠4; ∠3, ∠4; ∠1, ∠3; ∠5, ∠6; ∠5, ∠7; ∠7, ∠8; ∠6, ∠8
   (ii) ∠1, ∠4; ∠2, ∠3; ∠5, ∠8; ∠6, ∠7
4. No 5. (i) 55° (ii) 18° (iii) 45° (iv) 5°
6. (i) 110° (ii) 60° (iii) 45° (iv) 90°
7. Complementary Supplementary
   (i), (iii) (ii), (iv)
8. (i) No (ii) Yes (iii) No
9. ∠AOC, ∠COB; ∠COB, ∠BOD; ∠BOD, ∠DOA; ∠DOA, ∠AOC
10. (i) ∠ABE, ∠EBC; ∠ABD, ∠DBC (ii) ∠ABE, ∠EBC; ∠ABD, ∠DBC
11. 90° 12. 118°
13. Linear pairs: ∠1, ∠2; ∠2, ∠3; ∠3, ∠4; ∠4, ∠1; ∠5, ∠6; ∠6, ∠7; ∠7, ∠8; ∠8, ∠5; ∠9, ∠10; ∠10, ∠11; ∠11, ∠12; ∠12, ∠9
    Pairs of vertically opposite angles: ∠1, ∠3; ∠2, ∠4; ∠5, ∠7; ∠6, ∠8°; ∠9, ∠11; ∠10, ∠12
14. 40°, 140°, 40° 15. 90° 16. Acute 17. Obtuse 18. No 19. Does not exist
20. (i) 120° (ii) 36° (iii) 85° (iv) 63° (v) 45° (vi) 35°
21. ∠2 = 115°, ∠3 = 65°, ∠4 = 115°
22. (i) 50° (ii) 35°
23. Adjacent angles: ∠AOD, ∠COD; ∠BOC, ∠COD; ∠AOD, ∠BOD; ∠AOC, ∠BOC
    Linear Pairs: ∠AOD, ∠BOD; ∠AOC, ∠BOC

24. $x = 50°$, $\angle BOC = 70°$, $\angle COD = 50°$, $\angle AOD = 60°$

25. 4 26. 7 27. 30° 28. 55° 29. 20°

30. (i) $y = 135°$, $z = 45°$, $u = 135°$

31. $x = 40°$, $y = 50°$, $z = 90°$, $u = 40°$ 32. $x = 155°$, $y = 25°$, $z = 155°$

14.3 PARALLEL LINES

PARALLEL LINES *Two lines l and m in the same plane are said to be parallel lines if they do not intersect when produced indefinitely in either direction and we write $l \parallel m$ which is read as 'l is parallel to m'.*

Parallel lines

Fig. 33

Clearly, when $l \parallel m$, we have $m \parallel l$.

PARALLEL RAYS *Two rays are parallel if the corresponding lines determined by them are parallel. In other words, two rays in the same plane are parallel if they do not intersect each other even if extended indefinitely beyond their initial points.*

Parallel rays

Fig. 34

In Fig. 34, ray $OA \parallel$ ray PQ.

PARALLEL SEGMENTS *Two segments are parallel if the corresponding lines determined by them are parallel.*

In other words, two segments which are in the same plane and do not intersect each other even if extended indefinitely in both directions are said to be parallel.

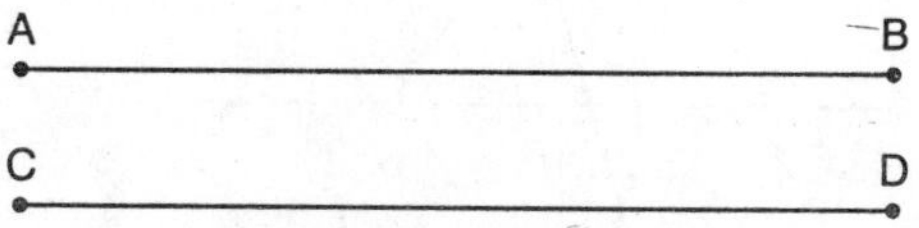

Parallel segments

Fig. 35

In Fig. 35, segment $AB \parallel$ segment CD.

One segment and one ray are parallel if the corresponding lines determined by them are parallel.

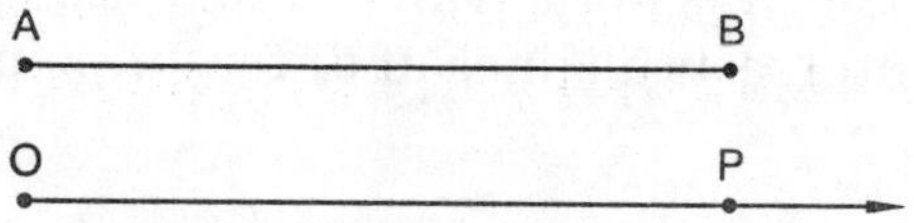

Fig. 36

In Fig. 36 segment $AB \parallel$ ray OP.

The opposite edges of this paper, opposite edges of a black board, the opposite edges of a ruler, railway lines etc. are all examples of parallel line segments.

Remark *It should be noted that if two lines in a plane are not parallel, then they intersect. Thus, two lines in a plane are either parallel or intersecting. However, two rays or two segments or one ray and one segment may neither be parallel nor intersecting. For example, in Fig. 37 (i) rays AB and CD are non-intersecting non-parallel rays, in Fig. 37 (ii), segments PQ and RS are non-parallel non intersecting segments and in Fig. 37 (iii), segment XY and ray UV are non-intersecting non-parallel.*

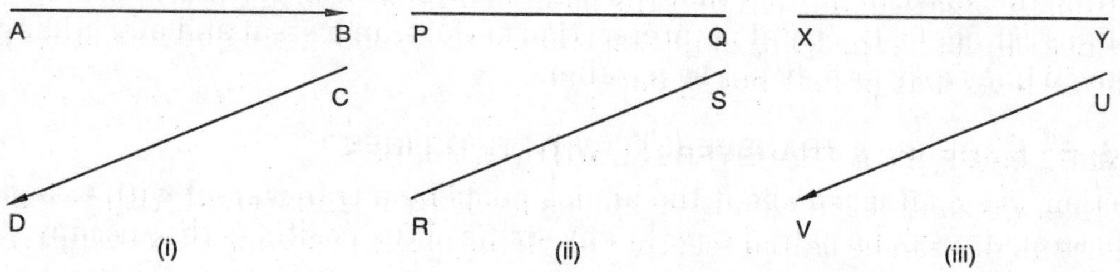

Fig. 37

14.3.1 TRANSVERSALS

TRANSVERSALS *A line intersecting two or more given lines in a plane at different points is called a transversal to the given lines.*

In Fig. 38 (i)-(vi), line l is the transversal to the given lines.

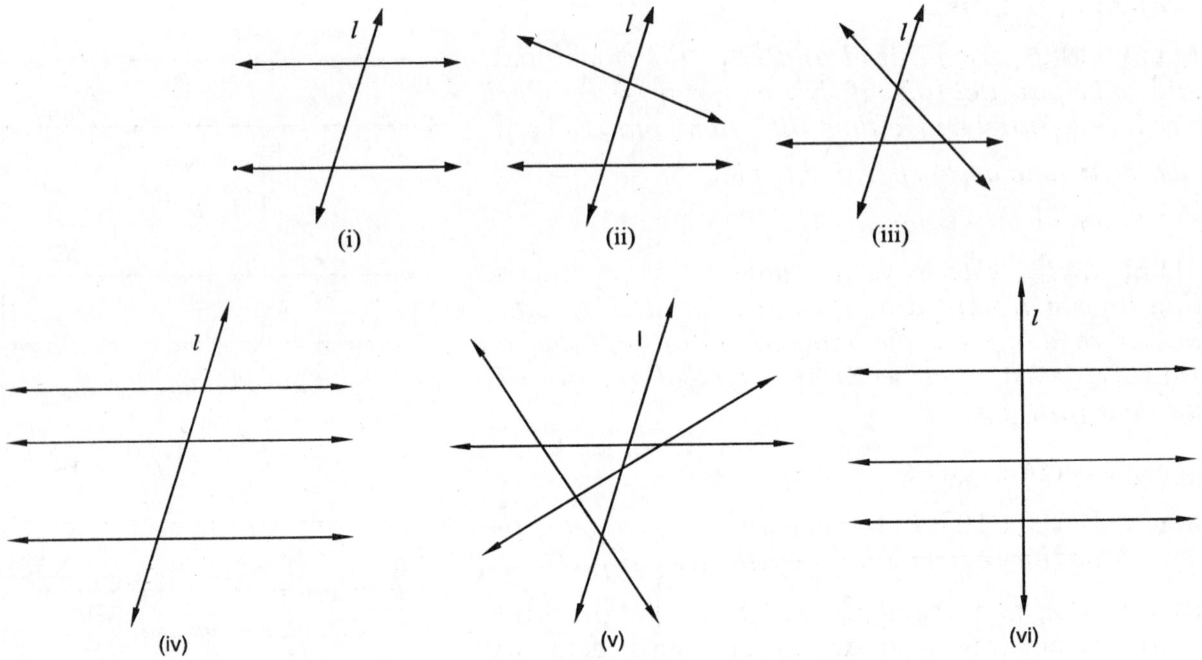

Fig. 38

Line m is not a transversal to the given lines shown in Fig. 39 (i) and (ii), because it does not intersect the lines at different points. In fact, it intersects two lines at the same point.

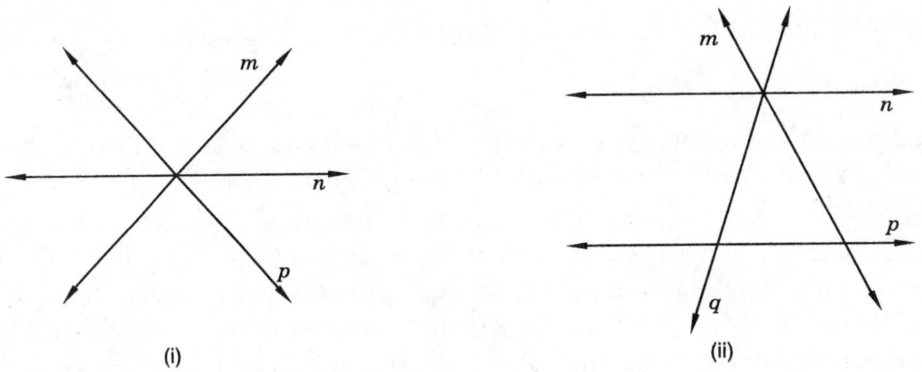

Fig. 39

It follows from the above definition that the point of intersection of the transversal and one of the given lines cannot be the point of intersection of the transversal and any other given line. Also, the given lines may or may not be parallel.

14.3.2 ANGLES MADE BY A TRANSVERSAL WITH TWO LINES

In this section, we shall learn about the angles made by a transversal with two given lines. Some of these angles can be paired together by virtue of the positions they occupy.

Let l and m be two lines and n be a transversal intersecting them at P and Q respectively as shown in Fig. 40.

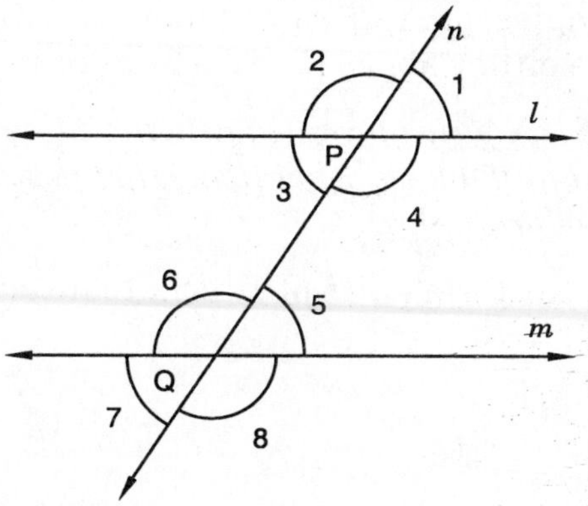

Fig. 40

Clearly, lines l, m and n make eight angles, four at P and the remaining four at Q. We label them 1 to 8 for the sake of convenience and classify them in the following groups:

EXTERIOR ANGLES *The angles whose arms do not include the line segment PQ are called exterior angles.*

In Fig. 41, angles 1, 2, 7 and 8 are exterior angles.

INTERIOR ANGLES *The angles whose arms include line segment PQ are called interior angles.*

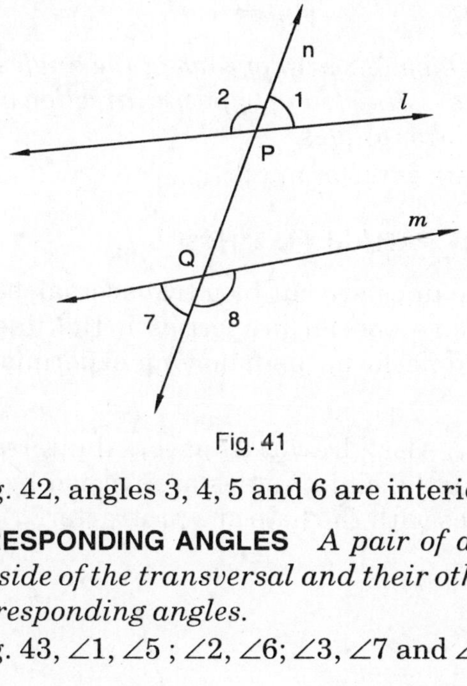

Fig. 41

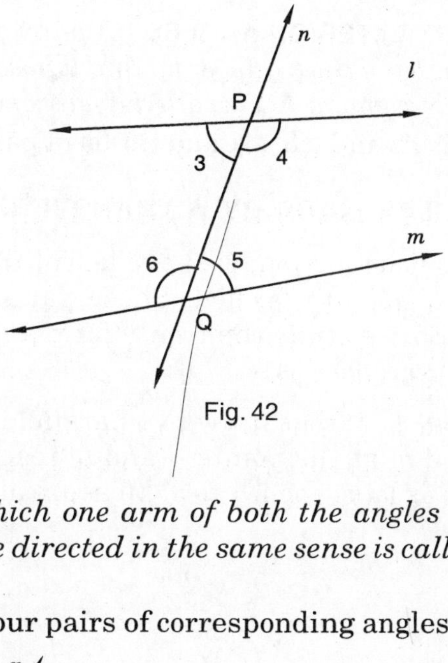

Fig. 42

In Fig. 42, angles 3, 4, 5 and 6 are interior angles.

CORRESPONDING ANGLES *A pair of angles in which one arm of both the angles is on the same side of the transversal and their other arms are directed in the same sense is called a pair of corresponding angles.*

In Fig. 43, $\angle 1$, $\angle 5$; $\angle 2$, $\angle 6$; $\angle 3$, $\angle 7$ and $\angle 4$, $\angle 8$ are four pairs of corresponding angles.

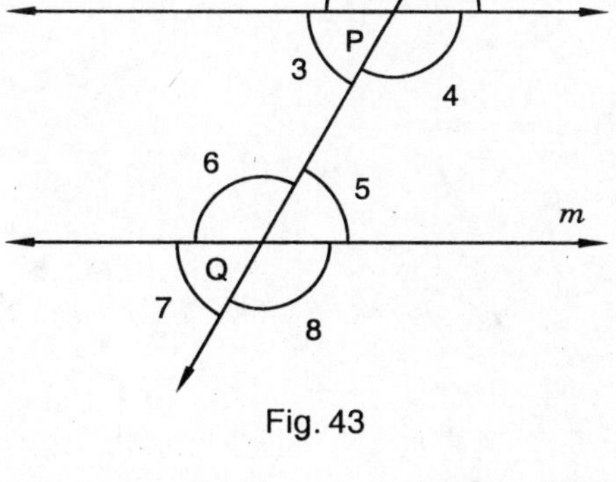

Fig. 43

We can also say that two angles on the same side of a transversal are known as the corresponding angles if both lie either above the two lines or below the two lines.

ALTERNATE INTERIOR ANGLES *A pair of angles in which one arm of each of the angle is on opposite sides of the transversal and whose other arms include segment PQ as shown in Fig. 44 is called a pair of alternate interior angles.*

In Fig. 44, ∠3 and ∠5, ∠4 and ∠6 form pairs of alternate interior angles.

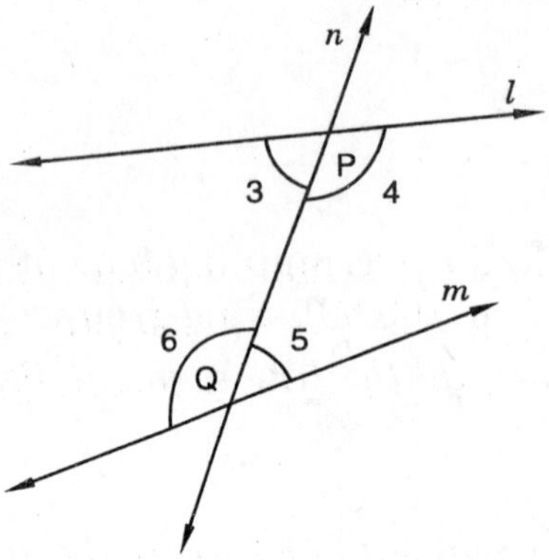

Fig. 44

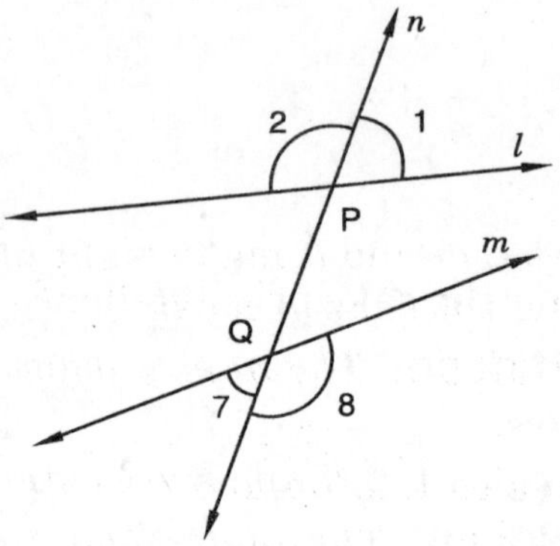

Fig. 45

ALTERNATE EXTERIOR ANGLES *A pair of angles in which one arm of each of the angles is on opposite sides of the transversal and whose other arms are directed in opposite direction and do not include segment PQ is called a pair of alternate exterior angles.*
In Fig. 45, ∠2 and ∠8, ∠1 and ∠7 form pairs of alternate exterior angles.

14.4 ANGLES MADE BY A TRANSVERSAL TO TWO PARALLEL LINES

In the previous section, we have learnt that when two lines are cut by a transversal, several pairs of angles are formed. These pairs of angles have special properties if the lines are parallel. So, we study them only for parallel lines and perform the following experiments to know their properties.

Experiment 1 Let us draw two parallel lines l and m. Also, draw a transversal intersecting lines l and m at the points P and Q respectively. Clearly, eight angles are formed by these lines. Let us label them 1 to 8. Measure all these angles with the help of a protractor.

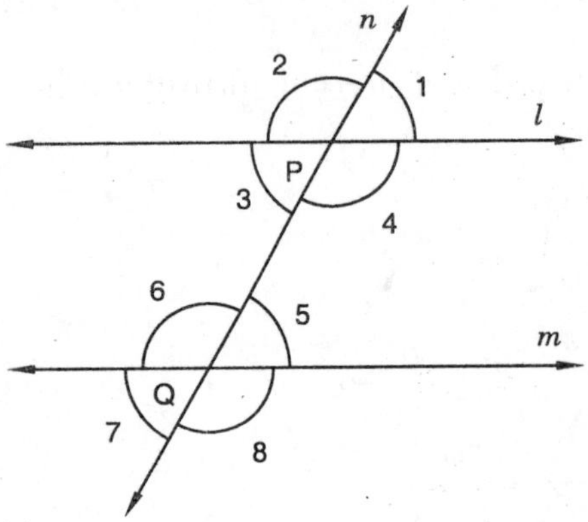

Fig. 46

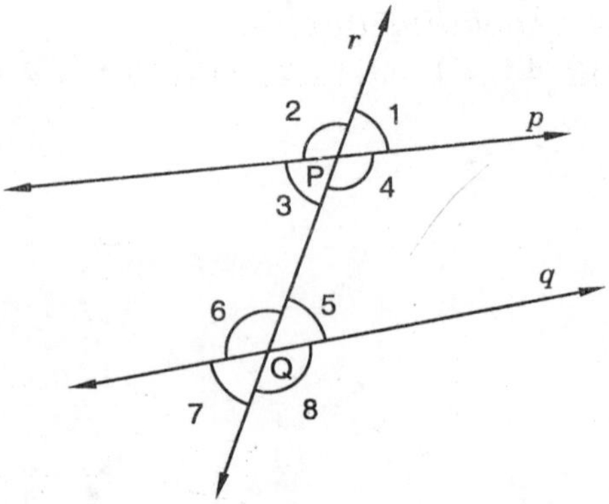

Fig. 47

You will find that:

(i) $\angle 3 = \angle 5$, $\angle 4 = \angle 6$, $\angle 2 = \angle 8$ and $\angle 1 = \angle 7$. That is, pairs of alternate interior and exterior angles are equal.

(ii) $\angle 1 = \angle 5$, $\angle 4 = \angle 8$, $\angle 2 = \angle 6$ and $\angle 3 = \angle 7$. That is, pairs of corresponding angles are equal.

(iii) $\angle 4 + \angle 5 = 180°$ and $\angle 3 + \angle 6 = 180°$. That is, the sum of interior angles on the same side of the transversal is 180°.

We can repeat this experiment by drawing another pair of parallel lines and a transversal to it. We will obtain the same results.

From the above experiment, we observe the following properties of angles formed by a transversal to two parallel lines:

Property 1 *Pairs of alternate (interior or exterior) angles are equal.*

Property 2 *Pairs of corresponding angles are equal.*

Property 3 *The sum of the interior (or exterior) angles on the same side of the transversal is 180°. In other words, the interior (or exterior) angles on the same side of the transversal are supplementary.*

Experiment 2 Let us draw two non-parallel lines p and q. Also, draw a transversal r intersecting lines p and q at P and Q respectively. Clearly, eight angles are formed. Let us label them 1 to 8. Measure all these angles with the help of a protractor.

You will find that:

(i) $\angle 3 \neq \angle 5$, $\angle 4 \neq \angle 6$, $\angle 2 \neq \angle 8$ and $\angle 1 \neq \angle 7$. That is, none of the pairs of alternate angles are equal.

(ii) $\angle 1 \neq \angle 5$, $\angle 4 \neq \angle 8$, $\angle 2 \neq \angle 6$ and $\angle 3 \neq \angle 7$. That is, none of the pairs of the corresponding angles are equal.

(iii) $\angle 3 + \angle 6 \neq 180°$ and $\angle 4 + \angle 5 \neq 180°$. That is, the sum of the interior angles on the same side of the transversal is not equal to 180°.

Thus, we observe that none of the above three properties which are true for parallel lines hold for non-parallel lines. Moreover, we conclude the following:

If *a transversal cuts two lines such that any one of the following conditions holds:*

(i) Pairs of alternate angles are equal.

(ii) Pairs of corresponding angles are equal.

(iii) The sum of the interior angles on the same side of the transversal is 180°.

Then, the two lines are parallel.

The following examples will illustrate the use of the above properties in solving problems.

ILLUSTRATIVE EXAMPLES

Example 1 In Fig. 48, line $l \parallel$ line m, n is transversal and $\angle 1 = 40°$. Find all the other angles marked in the figure.

Solution Since $\angle 1$ and $\angle 5$ are corresponding angles. Therefore,

$$\angle 5 = \angle 1 \Rightarrow \angle 5 = 40° \qquad [\because \angle 1 = 40° \text{ (given)}]$$

$\angle 1$ and $\angle 2$ form a linear pair.

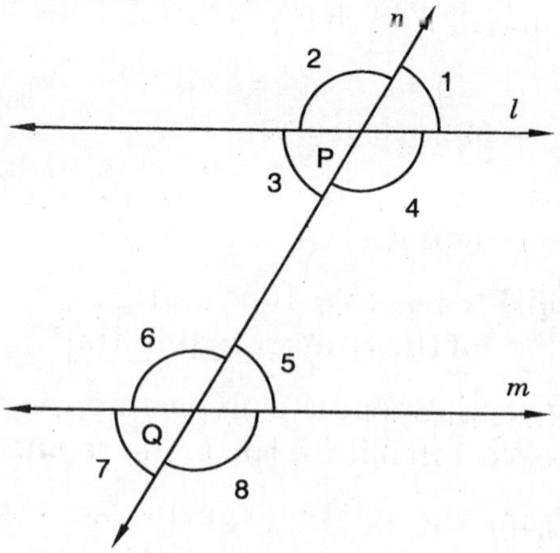

Fig. 48

$\therefore\quad \angle 2 + \angle 1 = 180°$

$\Rightarrow\quad \angle 2 = 180° - \angle 1 = 180° - 40° = 140°$

Again, $\angle 5$ and $\angle 3$ are alternate interior angles. Therefore,

$\angle 3 = \angle 5 \Rightarrow \angle 3 = 40°\qquad [\because \angle 5 = 40°]$

Since $\angle 3$ and $\angle 4$ form a linear pair.

$\therefore\quad \angle 3 + \angle 4 = 180°$

$\Rightarrow\quad \angle 4 = 180° - \angle 3 = 180° - 40° = 140°$

Since $\angle 6$ and $\angle 4$ are alternate interior angles.

$\therefore\quad \angle 6 = \angle 4$

But, $\angle 4 = 140°$

$\therefore\quad \angle 6 = 140°$

Also, $\angle 3$ and $\angle 7$ are corresponding angles. Therefore,

$\angle 7 = \angle 3$

$\Rightarrow\quad \angle 7 = 40°\qquad [\because \angle 3 = 40°]$

Since $\angle 7$ and $\angle 8$ form a linear pair

$\therefore\quad \angle 7 + \angle 8 = 180°$

$\Rightarrow\quad \angle 8 = 180° - \angle 7 = 180° - 40° = 140°\qquad [\because \angle 7 = 40°]$

Hence, we have the following measurements:

$\angle 1 = 40°$, $\angle 2 = 140°$, $\angle 3 = 40°$, $\angle 4 = 140°$, $\angle 5 = 40°$, $\angle 6 = 140°$, $\angle 7 = 40°$ and $\angle 8 = 140°$

Example 2 In Fig. 49, $m \parallel n$ and $\angle 1 = 65°$. Find $\angle 5$ and $\angle 8$.

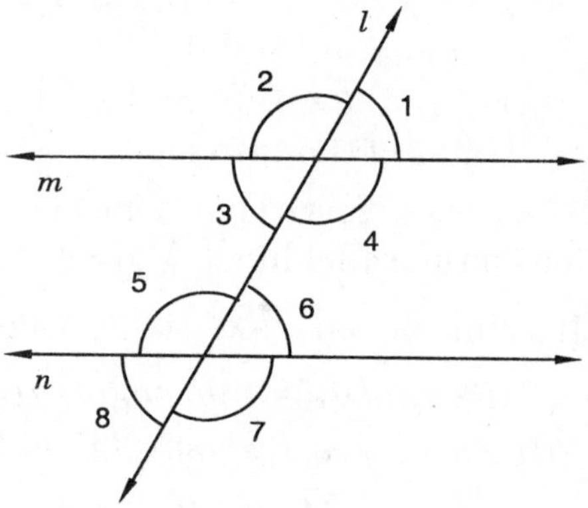

Fig. 49

Solution We have,

$\angle 1 = \angle 3$ [Vertically opposite angles]

and, $\angle 3 = \angle 8$ [Corresponding angles]

$\therefore\quad \angle 1 = \angle 8$

$\Rightarrow\quad \angle 8 = 65°\qquad [\because \angle 1 = 65°\ \text{(given)}]$

Now, $\angle 5 + \angle 8 = 180°$ [Linear pair]

$\Rightarrow\quad \angle 5 + 65° = 180°$

$\Rightarrow\quad \angle 5 = 180° - 65° = 115°$

Thus, $\angle 5 = 115°$ and $\angle 8 = 65°$

Example 3 In Fig. 50, $m \parallel n$ and angles 1 and 2 are in the ratio 3 : 2. Determine all the angles from 1 to 8.

Solution It is given that $\angle 1 : \angle 2 = 3 : 2$.

So, let $\angle 1 = 3x°$ and $\angle 2 = 2x°$

But, $\angle 1$ and $\angle 2$ form a linear pair.

$\therefore\quad \angle 1 + \angle 2 = 180°$

$\Rightarrow\quad 3x° + 2x° = 180°$

$\Rightarrow\quad 5x° = 180°$

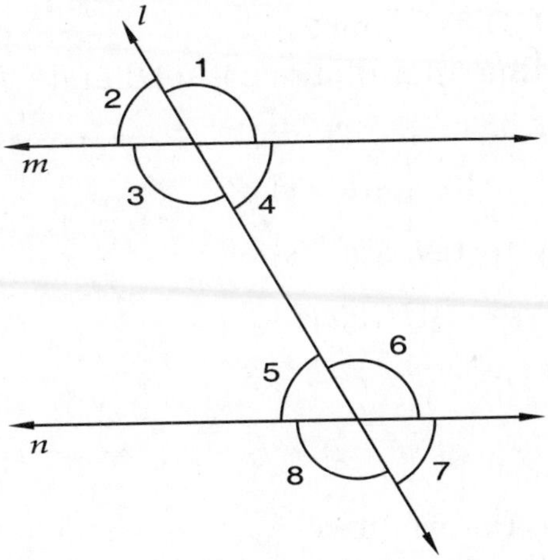

Fig. 50

$\Rightarrow \quad x = \dfrac{180}{5} = 36°$

$\therefore \quad \angle 1 = 3x° = (3 \times 36)° = 108°$

and, $\angle 2 = 2x° = (2 \times 36)° = 72°$

Now, $\angle 1 = \angle 3$ and $\angle 2 = \angle 4$ [Vertically opposite angles]

$\therefore \quad \angle 4 = 72°$ and $\angle 3 = 108°$

Now, $\angle 6 = \angle 1$ and $\angle 4 = \angle 7$ [Corresponding angles]

$\Rightarrow \quad \angle 6 = 72°$ and $\angle 7 = 108°$ [$\because \angle 2 = 72°$]

Again, $\angle 5 = \angle 7$ and $\angle 8 = \angle 6$ [Vertically opposite angles]

$\therefore \quad \angle 5 = 72°$ and $\angle 8 = 108°$

Hence, $\angle 1 = 108°$, $\angle 2 = 72°$, $\angle 3 = 108°$, $\angle 4 = 72°$, $\angle 5 = 72°$, $\angle 6 = 108°$, $\angle 7 = 72°$ and $\angle 8 = 108°$.

Example 4 In Fig. 51, l, m and n are parallel lines intersected by a transversal p at X, Y and Z respectively. Find $\angle 1$, $\angle 2$ and $\angle 3$. Give reasons.

Solution Since parallel lines l and n are intersected by the transversal p at X and Z respectively. Therefore,

$\angle 2 = \angle 4$ [Corresponding angles]

$\Rightarrow \quad \angle 2 = 180° - 50°$ [$\because \angle 4 + 50° = 180°$ (Linear pair)]

$\Rightarrow \quad \angle 2 = 130°$

Since $\angle 2$ and $\angle 3$ are vertically opposite angles.

$\therefore \quad \angle 3 = \angle 2$

$\Rightarrow \quad \angle 3 = 130°$ [$\because \angle 2 = 130°$]

Since parallel lines m and n are intersected by the transversal p at Y and Z respectively. Therefore,

$\angle 1 = \angle 3$ [Alternate interior angles]

$\Rightarrow \quad \angle 1 = 130°$ [$\because \angle 3 = 130°$]

Thus, $\angle 1 = \angle 2 = \angle 3 = 130°$

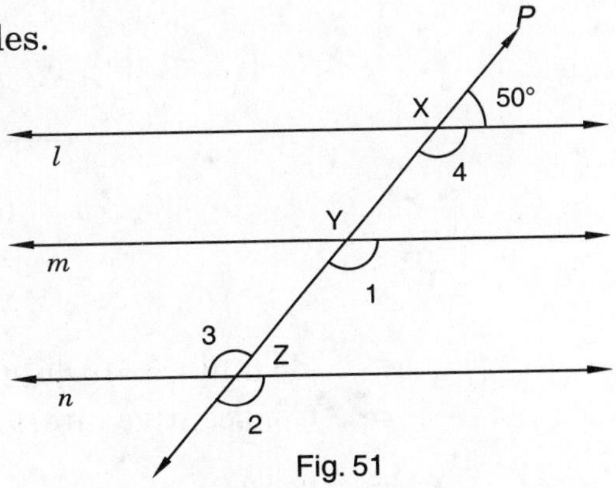

Fig. 51

Example 5 In Fig. 52, $AB \parallel CD$. Determine $\angle a$.

Solution Through O draw a line l parallel to both AB and CD.

Clearly, $\angle a = \angle 1 + \angle 2$ ...(i)

Now, $\angle 1 = 55°$ [Alternate $\angle s$]

and, $\angle 2 = 38°$ [Alternate $\angle s$]

$\therefore \quad \angle a = 55° + 38°$ [Using (i)]

$\Rightarrow \quad \angle a = 93°$

Thus, $\angle a = 93°$.

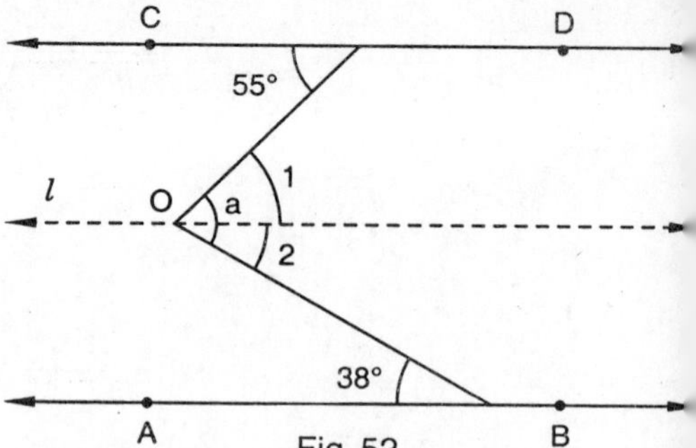

Fig. 52

Example 6 In Fig. 53, $AB \parallel CD$. Determine x.

Solution Through O, draw a line l parallel to both AB and CD. Then,

$\angle 1 = 45°$ and, $\angle 2 = 30°$ [Alternate $\angle s$]

$\therefore \quad \angle BOC = \angle 1 + \angle 2$

$\Rightarrow \quad \angle BOC = 45° + 30° = 75°$

Clearly, x = reflex $\angle BOC$

$\therefore \quad x = 360 - \angle BOC$

$\Rightarrow \quad x = 360° - 75° = 285°$

Hence, $x = 285°$.

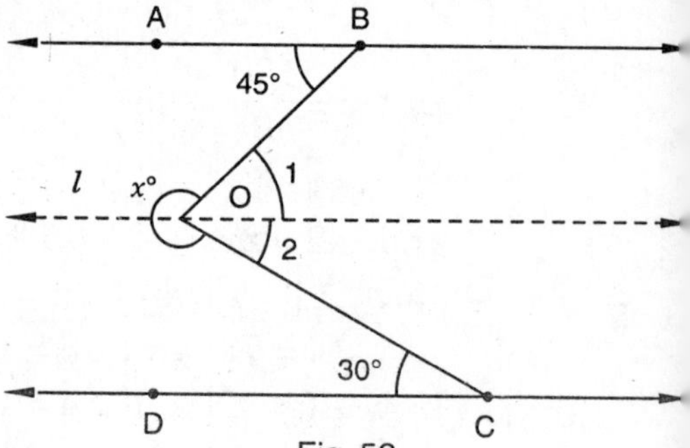

Fig. 53

Example 7 In Fig. 54, if $\angle 2 = 120°$ and $\angle 5 = 60°$, show that $m \parallel n$.

Solution We have,

$\angle 2 = 120°$ and $\angle 5 = 60°$

But, $\angle 2 = \angle 4$ [Vertically opposite angles]

$\therefore \quad \angle 4 = 120°$

$\Rightarrow \quad \angle 4 + \angle 5 = 120° + 60°$ [$\because \angle 5 = 60°$]

$\Rightarrow \quad \angle 4 + \angle 5 = 180°$

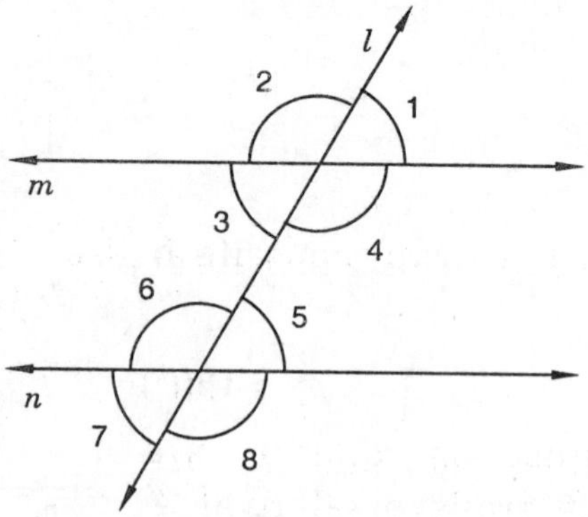

Fig. 54

$\Rightarrow$ $\angle 4$ and $\angle 5$ are supplementary angles.

$\Rightarrow$ Consecutive interior angles are supplementary.

$\Rightarrow$ $m \parallel n$.

Example 8 In Fig. 55, if $\angle 3 = 61°$ and $\angle 7 = 118°$. Is $m \parallel n$?

Solution We have, $\angle 3 = 61°$ and $\angle 7 = 118°$

Since $\angle 3$ and $\angle 4$ form a linear pair.

$\therefore \quad \angle 3 + \angle 4 = 180°$

$\Rightarrow \quad \angle 61° + \angle 4 = 180°$

$\Rightarrow \quad \angle 4 = 180° - 61° \Rightarrow \angle 4 = 119°$

Now, $\angle 4$ and $\angle 7$ are a pair of corresponding angles such that $\angle 4 = 119°$ and $\angle 7 = 118°$

i.e., $\angle 4 \neq \angle 7$.

So, m is not parallel to n.

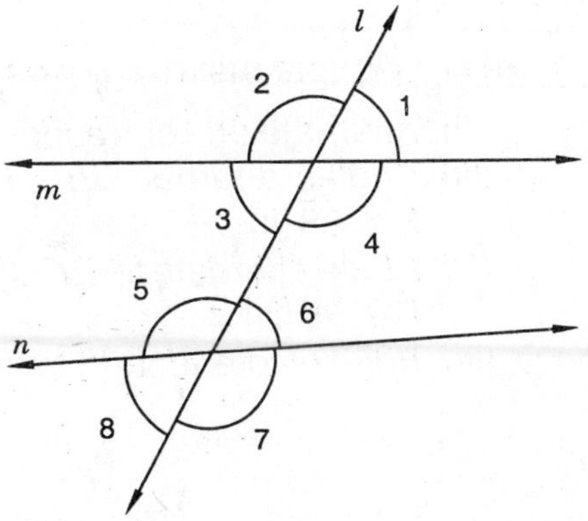

Fig. 55

Example 9 In Fig. 56, give reasons why $l_1 \parallel l_2$. Is $m_1 \parallel m_2$?

Solution Since lines l_1 and l_2 are intersected by a transversal m_2 such that the sum of two consecutive interior angles is 180° i.e. they are supplementary. Therefore, $l_1 \parallel l_2$

From Fig. 56, we observe that the lines m_1 and m_2 are intersected by transversal l_2 such that the alternate interior angles are equal. Therefore, $m_1 \parallel m_2$.

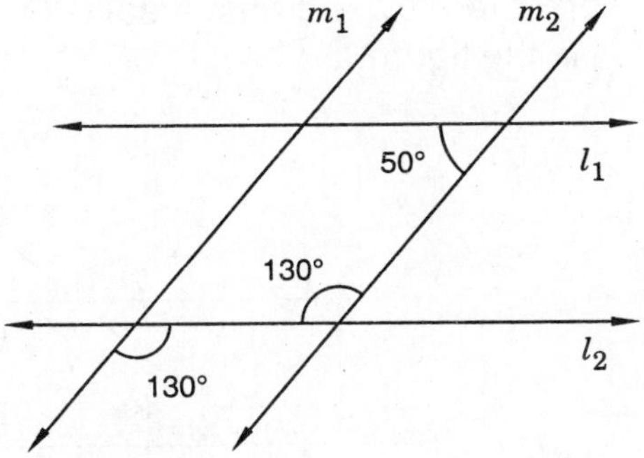

Fig. 56

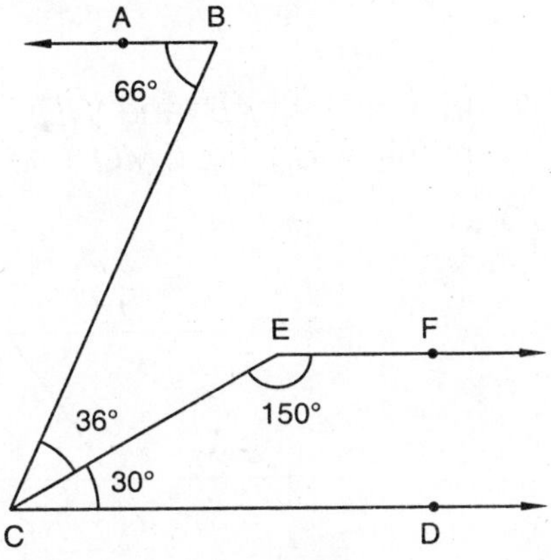

Fig. 57

Example 10 In Fig. 57, show that $AB \parallel EF$.

Solution We have,

$\angle BCD = \angle BCE + \angle ECD$

$\Rightarrow \quad \angle BCD = 36° + 30° = 66°$

$\therefore \quad \angle ABC = \angle BCD$

Thus, lines AB and CD are intersected by the line BC such that $\angle ABC = \angle BCD$ i.e., the alternate angles are equal. Therefore, $AB \parallel CD$ ...(i)

Now, $\angle ECD + \angle CEF = 30° + 150° = 180°$

This shows that the sum of the interior angles on the same side of the transversal CE is 180° i.e. they are supplementary.

$\therefore \quad EF \parallel CD$ ...(ii)

From (i) and (ii), we have $AB \parallel CD$ and $CD \parallel EF$

$\therefore \quad AB \parallel EF$

Hence, $AB \parallel EF$

EXERCISE 14.2

1. In Fig. 58, line n is a transversal to lines l and m. Identify the following:
   - (i) Alternate and corresponding angles in Fig. 58 (i).
   - (ii) Angles alternate to $\angle d$ and $\angle g$ and angles corresponding to angles $\angle f$ and $\angle h$ i Fig. 58 (ii).
   - (iii) Angle alternate to $\angle PQR$, angle corresponding to $\angle RQF$ and angle alternate to $\angle PQE$ i Fig. 58 (iii).
   - (iv) Pairs of interior and exterior angles on the same side of the transversal in Fig. 58 (ii).

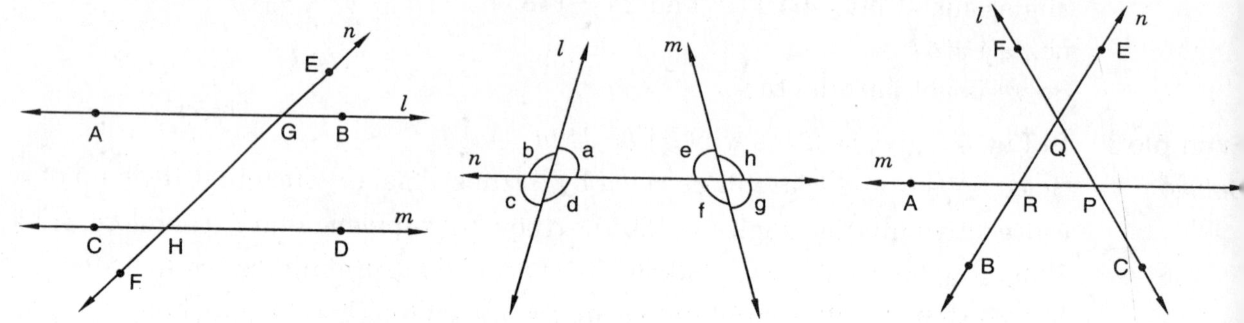

(i) (ii) (iii)

Fig. 58

2. In Fig. 59, AB and CD are parallel lines intersected by a transversal PQ at L and M respectively. If $\angle CMQ = 60°$, find all other angles in the figure.

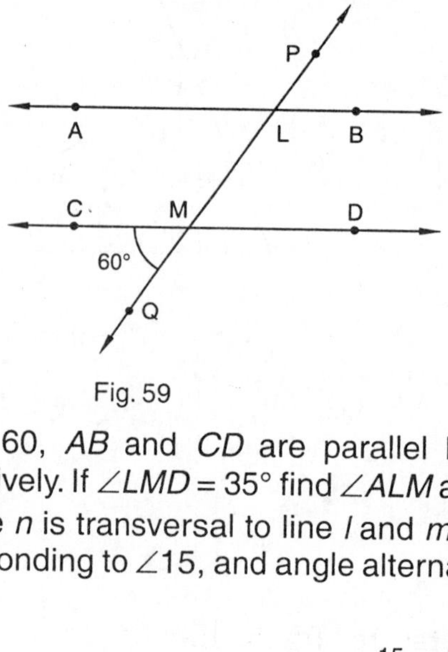

Fig. 59

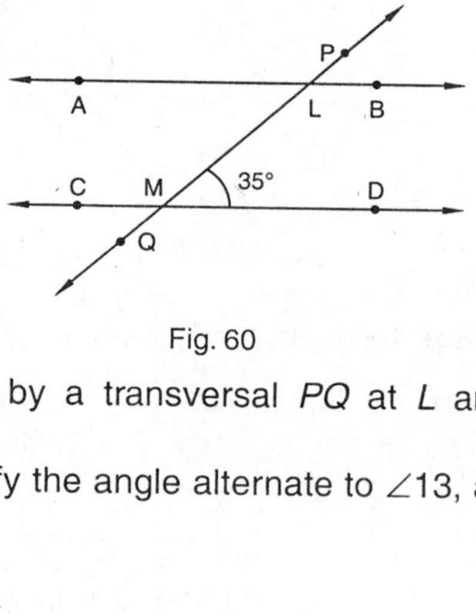

Fig. 60

3. In Fig. 60, AB and CD are parallel lines intersected by a transversal PQ at L and M respectively. If $\angle LMD = 35°$ find $\angle ALM$ and $\angle PLA$.

4. The line n is transversal to line l and m in Fig. 61. Identify the angle alternate to $\angle 13$, angle corresponding to $\angle 15$, and angle alternate to $\angle 15$.

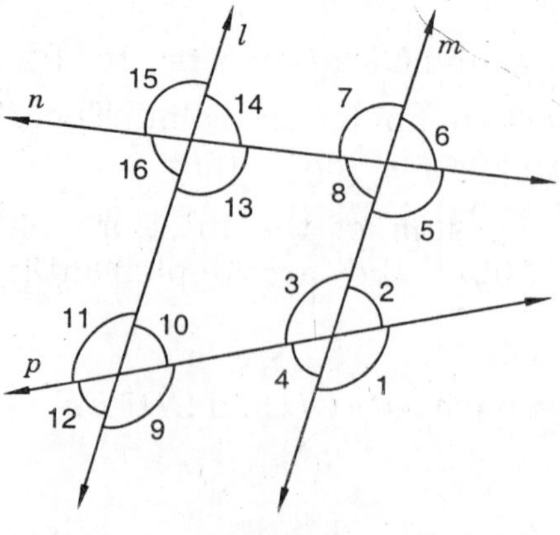

Fig. 61

5. In Fig. 62, line $l \parallel m$ and n is a transversal. If $\angle 1 = 40°$, find all the angles and check that all corresponding angles and alternate angles are equal.

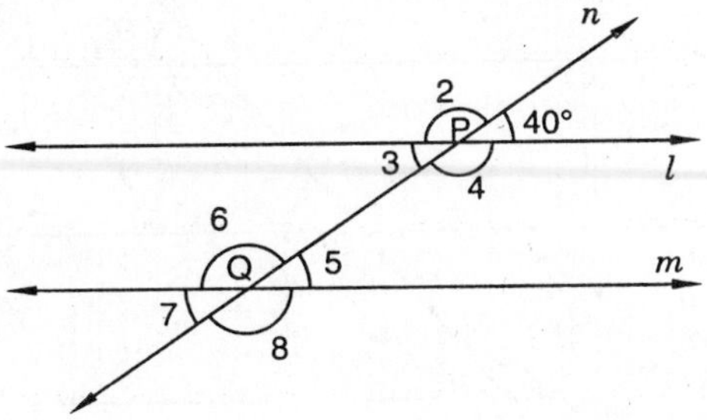

Fig. 62

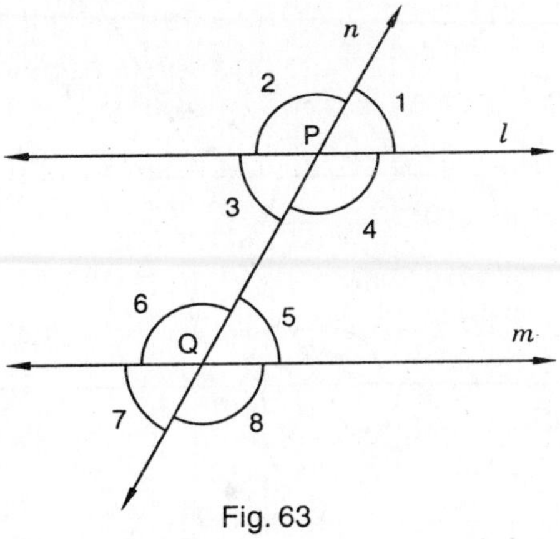

Fig. 63

6. In Fig. 63, line $l \parallel m$ and a transversal n cuts them at P and Q respectively. If $\angle 1 = 75°$, find all other angles.
7. In Fig. 64, $AB \parallel CD$ and a transversal PQ cuts them at L and M respectively. If $\angle QMD = 100°$, find all other angles.

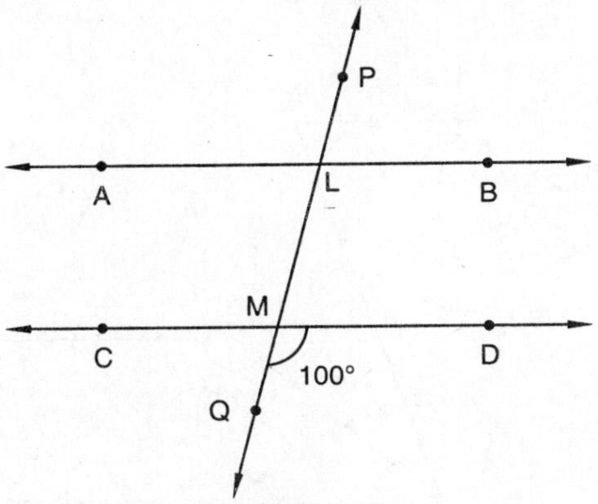

Fig. 64

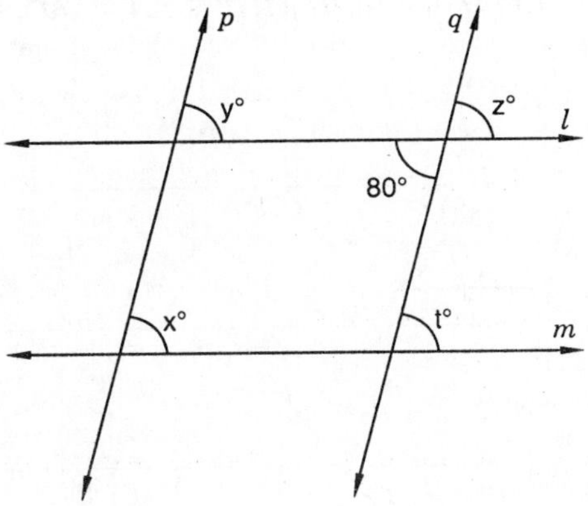

Fig. 65

8. In Fig. 65, $l \parallel m$ and $p \parallel q$. Find the values of x, y, z, t.
9. In Fig. 66, line $l \parallel m$, $\angle 1 = 120°$ and $\angle 2 = 100°$, find out $\angle 3$ and $\angle 4$.

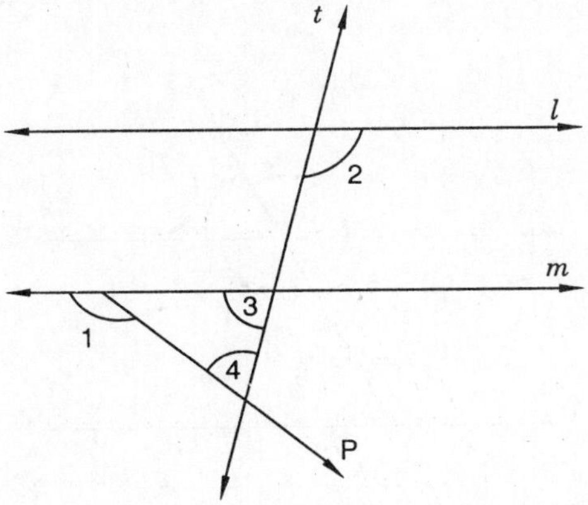

Fig. 66

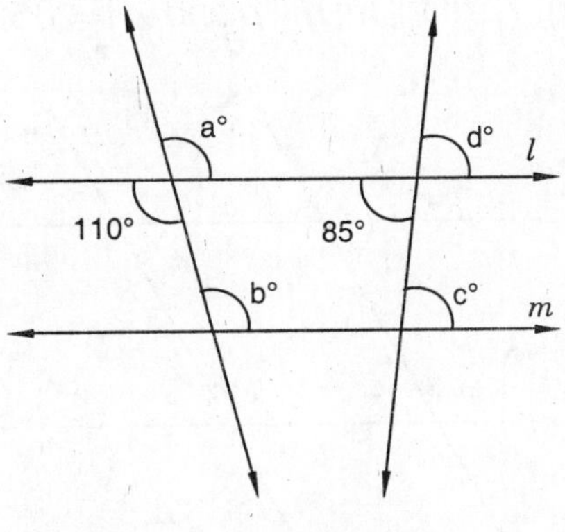

Fig. 67

10. In Fig. 67, line $l \parallel m$. Find the values of a, b, c, d. Give reasons.

11. In Fig. 68, $AB \parallel CD$ and $\angle 1$ and $\angle 2$ are in the ratio 3: 2. Determine all angles from 1 to 8.

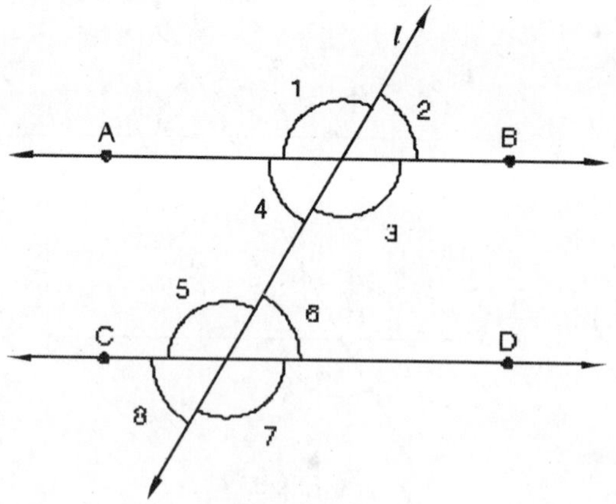

Fig. 68

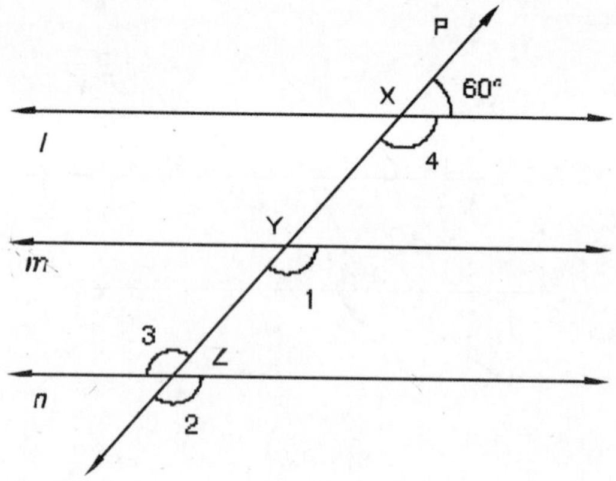

Fig. 69

12. In Fig.69, l, m and n are parallel lines intersected by transversal p at X, Y and Z respectively. Find $\angle 1$, $\angle 2$ and $\angle 3$.

13. In Fig. 70, if $l \parallel m \parallel n$ and $\angle 1 = 60°$, find $\angle 2$.

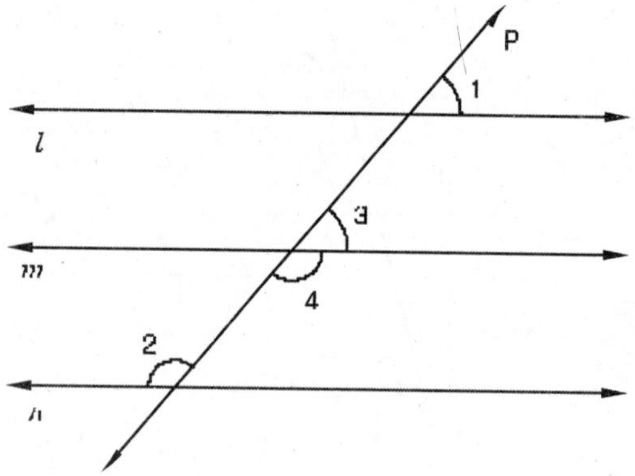

Fig. 70

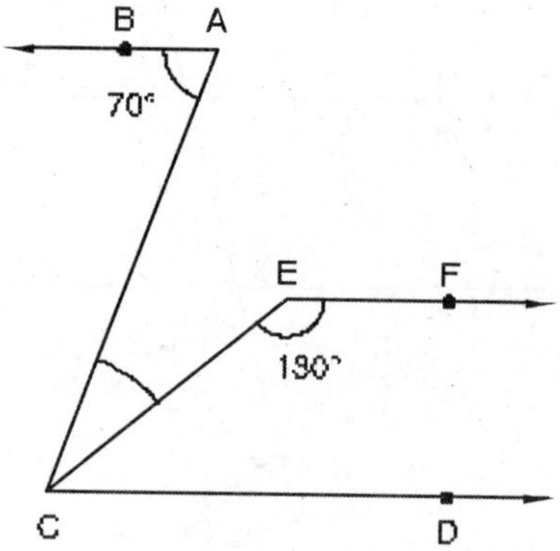

Fig. 71

14. In Fig. 71, if $AB \parallel CD$ and $CD \parallel EF$, find $\angle ACE$.

15. In Fig. 72, if $l \parallel m$, $n \parallel p$ and $\angle 1 = 85°$, find $\angle 2$.

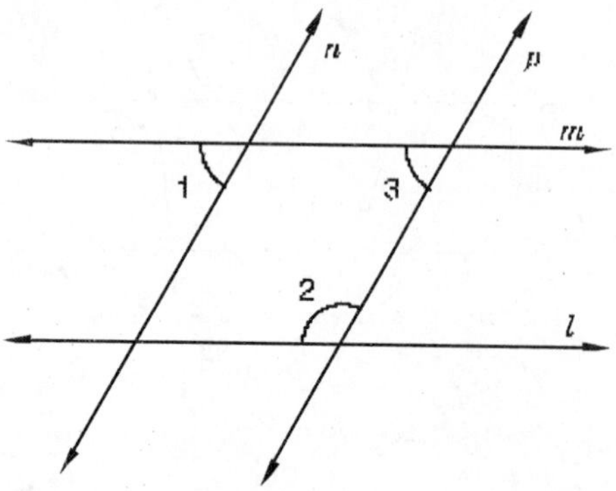

Fig. 72

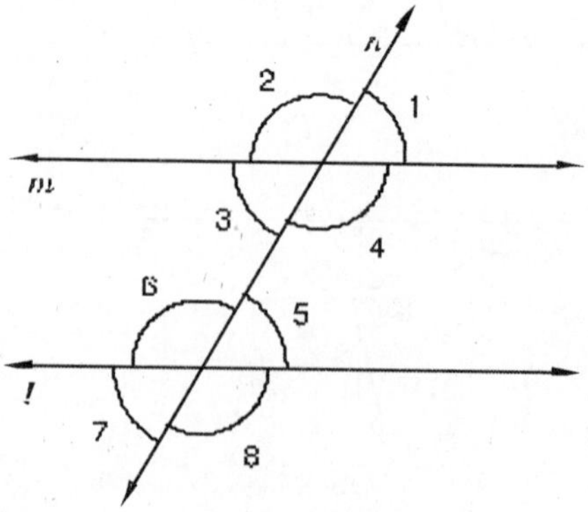

Fig. 73

16. In Fig. 73, a transversal n cuts two lines l and m. If $\angle 1 = 70°$ and $\angle 7 = 80°$, is $l \parallel m$?

17. In Fig. 74, a transversal *n* cuts two lines *l* and *m* such that $\angle 2 = 65°$ and $\angle 8 = 65°$. Are the lines parallel?

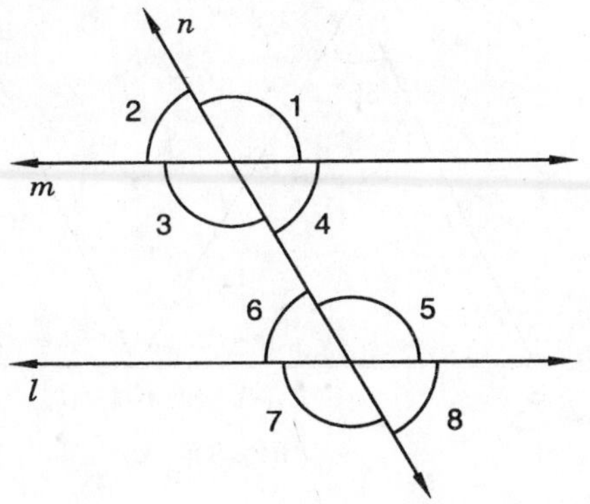

Fig. 74

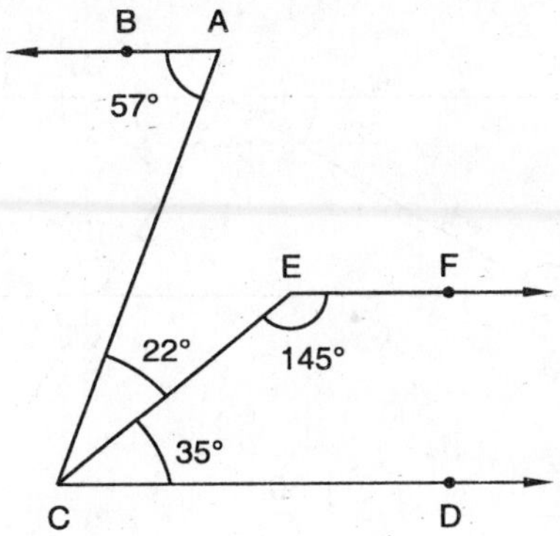

Fig. 75

18. In Fig. 75, show that *AB* || *EF*.

19. In Fig. 76, *AB* || *CD*. Find the values of x, y, z.

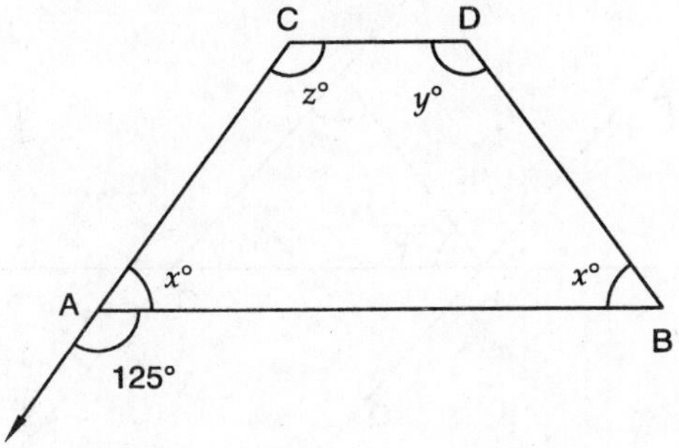

Fig. 76

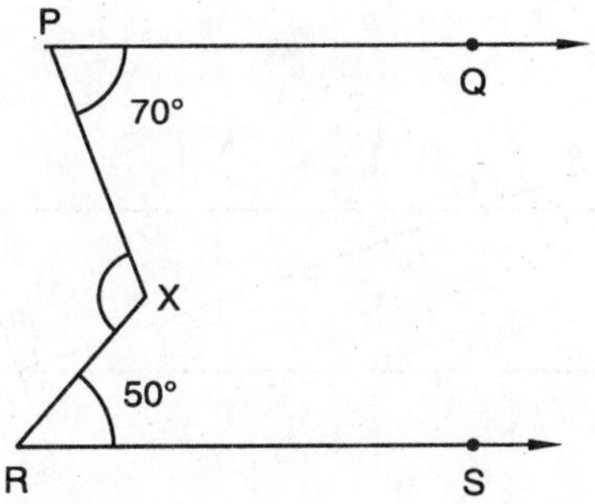

Fig. 77

20. In Fig. 77, find out $\angle PXR$, if *PQ* || *RS*.

21. In Fig. 78, we have

(i) $\angle MLY = 2\angle LMQ$, find $\angle LMQ$. (ii) $\angle XLM = (2x - 10)°$ and $\angle LMQ = x + 30°$, find x.

(iii) $\angle XLM = \angle PML$, find $\angle ALY$ (iv) $\angle ALY = (2x - 15)°$, $\angle LMQ = (x + 40)°$, find x

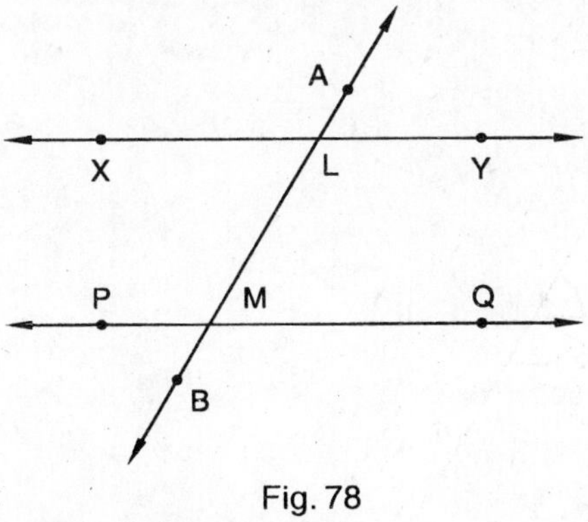

Fig. 78

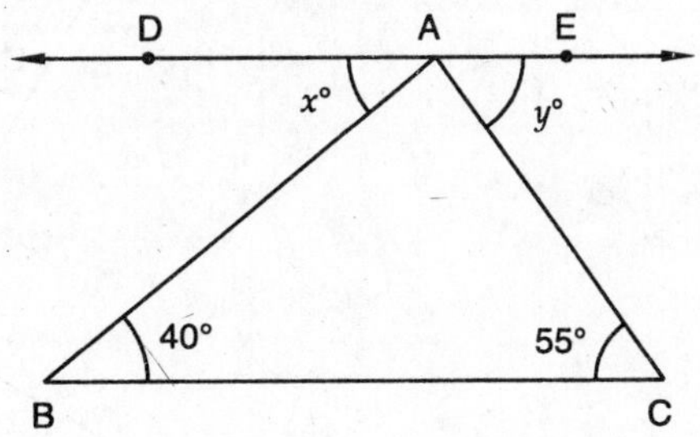

Fig. 79

22. In Fig. 79, *DE* || *BC*. Find the values of x and y.

23. In Fig. 80, line $AC \parallel$ line DE and $\angle ABD = 32°$. Find out the angles x and y if $\angle E = 122°$.

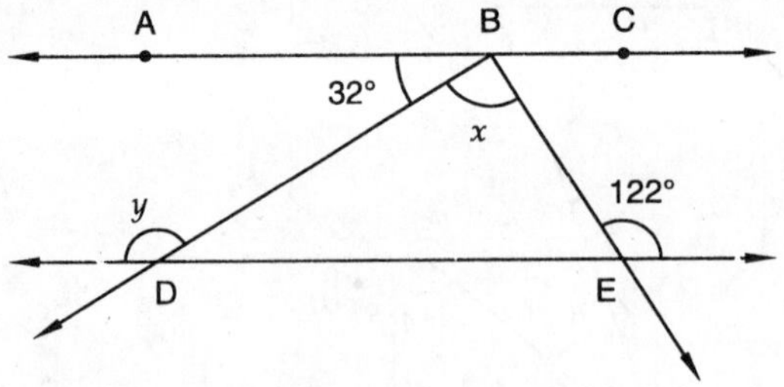

Fig. 80

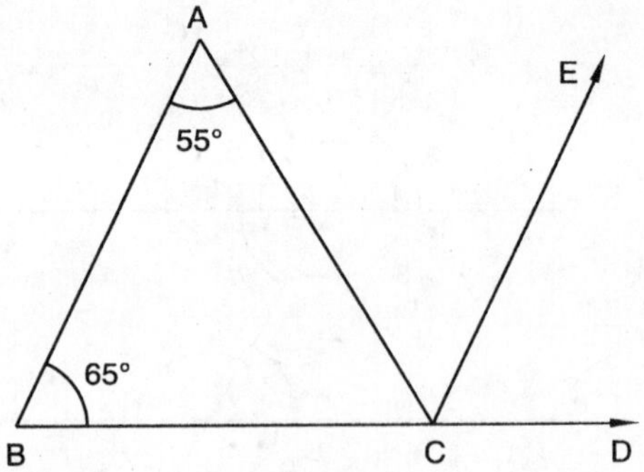

Fig. 81

24. In Fig. 81, side BC of ΔABC has been produced to D and $CE \parallel BA$. If $\angle ABC = 65°$ $\angle BAC = 55°$, find $\angle ACE$, $\angle ECD$ and $\angle ACD$.

25. In Fig. 82, line $CA \perp AB \parallel$ line CR and line $PR \parallel$ line BD. Find $\angle x$, $\angle y$ and $\angle z$.

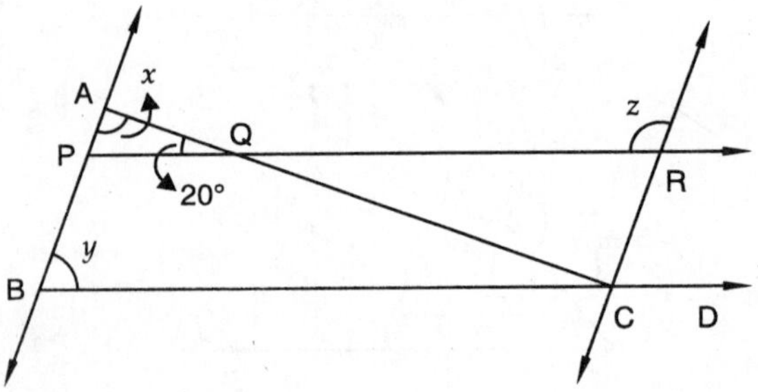

Fig. 82

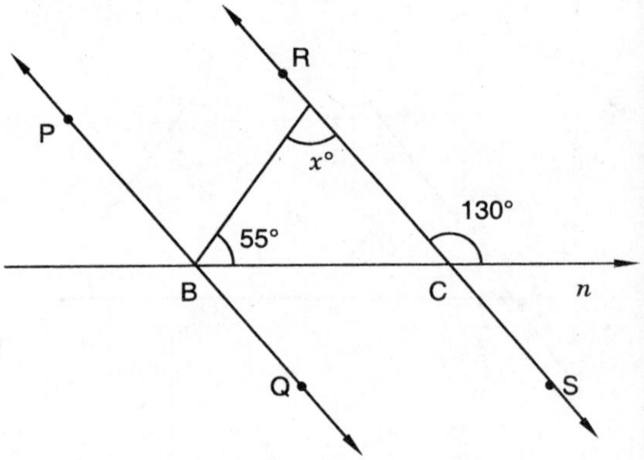

Fig. 83

26. In Fig. 83, $PQ \parallel RS$. Find the value of x.

27. In Fig. 84, $AB \parallel CD$ and $AE \parallel CF$; $\angle FCG = 90°$ and $\angle BAC = 120°$. Find the values of x, y and z.

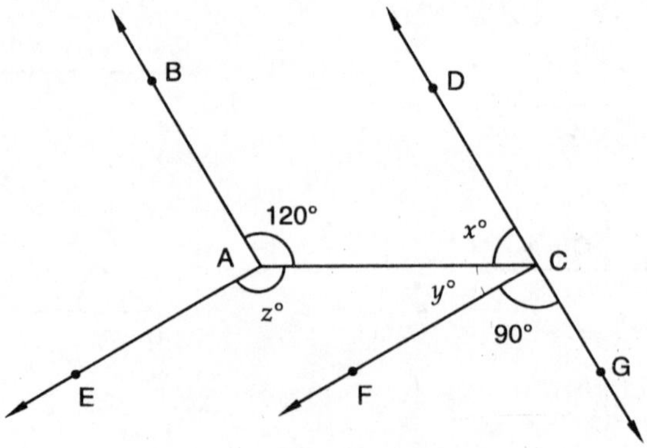

Fig. 84

28. In Fig. 85, *AB* || *CD* and *AC* || *BD*. Find the values of x, y, z.

Fig. 85

29. In Fig. 86, state which lines are parallel and why?

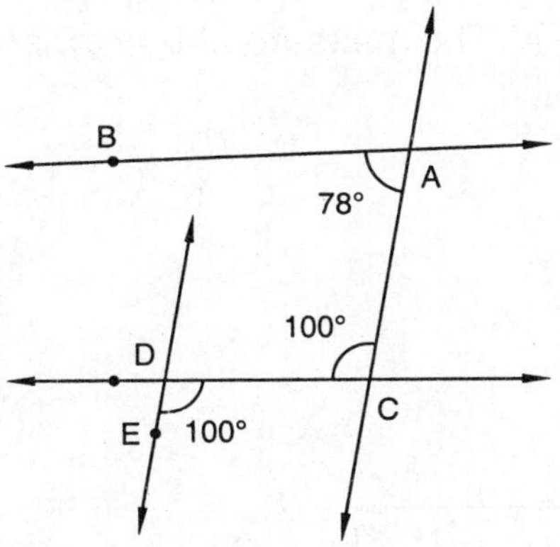

Fig. 86

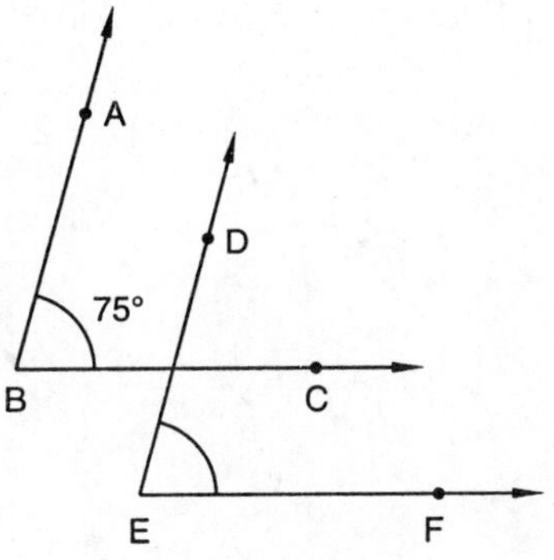

Fig. 87

30. In Fig. 87, the corresponding arms of ∠*ABC* and ∠*DEF* are parallel. If ∠*ABC* = 75°, find ∠*DEF*.

ANSWERS

1. (i) Alternate angles: ∠*BGH* and ∠*CHG*; ∠*AGH* and ∠*DHG*
   Corresponding angles: ∠*EGB* and ∠*GHD*; ∠*EGA* and ∠*GHC*; ∠*BGH* and ∠*DHF*; ∠*AGH* and ∠*CHF*.
   (ii) ∠*e*, ∠*b*, ∠*c*, ∠*a* (iii) ∠*QRA*, ∠*BRA*, ∠*BRA*
   (iv) Interior angles: ∠*d*, ∠*f*; ∠*a*, ∠*e*; Exterior angles: ∠*c*, ∠*g*; ∠*b*, ∠*h*.
2. ∠*QMD* = 120°, ∠*PLB* = 60°, ∠*ALM* = 60°, ∠*MLB* = 120°, ∠*DML* = 60°, ∠*CML* = 120°, ∠*ALP* = 120°
3. ∠*ALM* = 35°, ∠*PLA* = 145° 4. ∠7, ∠7, ∠5
5. ∠2 = 140°, ∠3 = 40°, ∠4 = 140°, ∠5 = 40°, ∠6 = 140°, ∠7 = 40°, ∠8 = 140°
6. ∠2 = 105°; ∠3 = 75°, ∠4 = 105°, ∠5 = 75°, ∠6 = 105°, ∠7 = 75° and ∠8 = 105°
7. ∠*PLB* = 80°, ∠*PLA* = 100°, ∠*ALM* = 80°, ∠*BLM* = 100°, ∠*LMD* = 80°, ∠*LMC* = 100°, ∠*CMQ* = 80°
8. $x = 80°, y = 80°, z = 80°, t = 80°$ 9. ∠3 = 80°, ∠4 = 40°
10. $a = 110°, b = 110°, c = 85°, d = 85°$
11. ∠1 = 108°, ∠2 = 72°, ∠3 = 108°, ∠4 = 72°, ∠5 = 108°, ∠6 = 72°, ∠7 = 108°, ∠8 = 72°
12. ∠1 = 120°, ∠2 = 120°, ∠3 = 120° 13. 120° 14. 20° 15. 95°
16. No 17. Yes 19. $x = 55°, y = 125°, z = 125°$ 20. 120°
21. (i) 60° (ii) 40° (iii) 90° (iv) 55° 22. $x = 40°, y = 55°$
23. $x = 90°, y = 148°$ 24. ∠*ACE* = 55°, ∠*ECD* = 65°, ∠*ACD* = 120°
25. $x = 90°, y = 70°, z = 110°$ 26. 75° 27. $x = 60°, y = 30°, z = 150°$

28. (i) $x = 115°, y = 65°, z = 115°$ (ii) $x = 40°, y = 35°$

29. $AC \parallel DE$, because alternate angles are equal 30. 75°

OBJECTIVE TYPE QUESTIONS

Mark the correct alternative in each of the following:

1. The sum of an angle and one third of its supplementary angle is 90°. The measure of the angle is
   (a) 135° (b) 120° (c) 60° (d) 45°
2. If angles of a linear pair are equal, then the measure of each angle is
   (a) 30° (b) 45° (c) 60° (d) 90°
3. Two complemntary angles are in the ratio 2 : 3. The measure of the larger angle is
   (a) 60° (b) 54° (c) 66° (d) 48°
4. An angle is thrice its supplement. The measure of the angle is
   (a) 120° (b) 105° (c) 135° (d) 150°
5. In Fig. 88 *PR* is a straight line and $\angle PQS : \angle SQR = 7 : 5$. The measure of $\angle SQR$ is
   (a) 60° (b) $62\frac{1}{2}^\circ$ (c) $67\frac{1}{2}^\circ$ (d) 75°

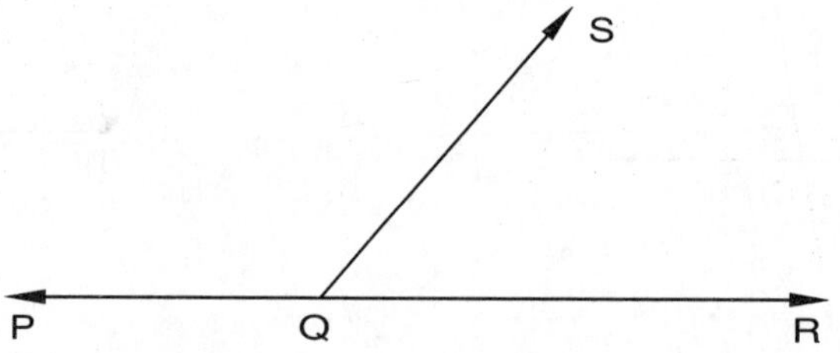

Fig. 88

6. The sum of an angle and half of its complementary angle is 75°. The measure of the angle is
   (a) 40° (b) 50° (c) 60° (d) 80°
7. $\angle A$ is an obtuse angle. The measure of $\angle A$ and twice its supplementary differ by 30°. Then, $\angle A$ can be
   (a) 150° (b) 110° (c) 140° (d) 120°
8. An angle is double of its supplement. The measure of the angle is
   (a) 60° (b) 120° (c) 40° (d) 80°
9. The measure of an angle which is its own complement is
   (a) 30° (b) 60° (c) 90° (d) 45°
10. Two supplementary angles are in the ratio 3 : 2. The smaller angle measures
    (a) 108° (b) 81° (c) 72° (d) 68°
11. In Fig. 89, the value of *x* is
    (a) 75 (b) 65 (c) 45 (d) 55

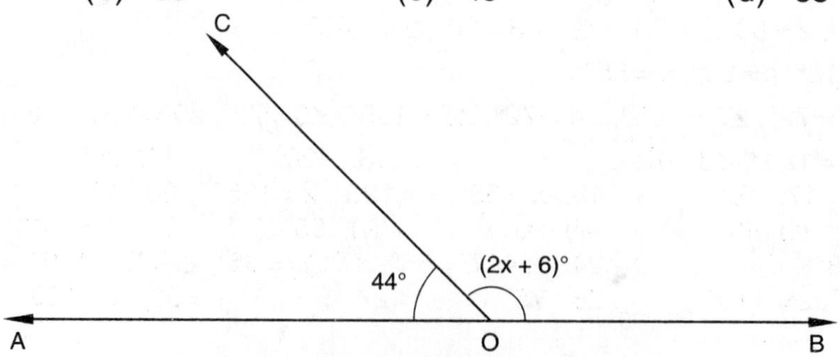

Fig. 89

12. In Fig. 90, *AOB* is a straight line and the ray *OC* stands on it. The value of *x* is
    (a) 16 (b) 26 (c) 36 (d) 46

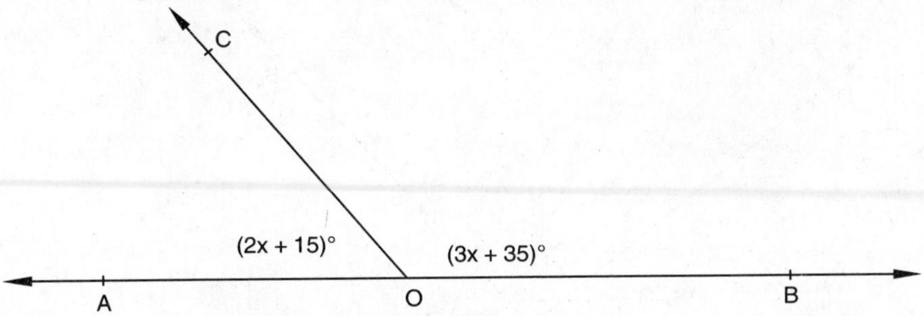

Fig. 90

13. In Fig. 91, *AOB* is a straight line and $4x = 5y$. The value of *x* is
    (a) 100 (b) 105 (c) 110 (d) 115

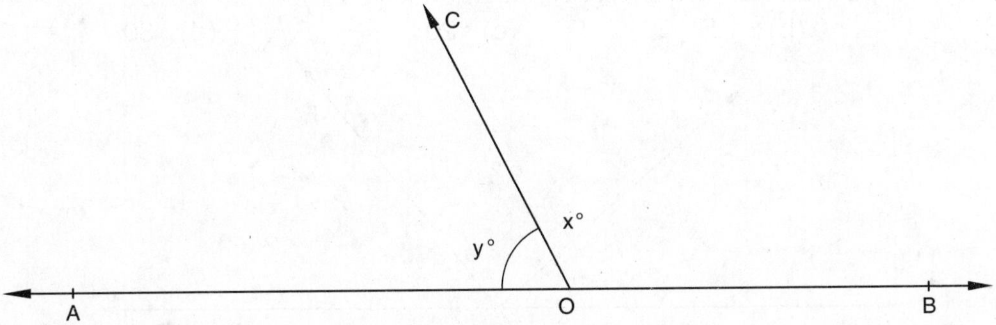

Fig. 91

14. In Fig. 92, *AOB* is a straight line such that $\angle AOC = (3x + 10)°$, $\angle COD = 50°$ and $\angle BOD = (x - 8)°$. The value of *x* is
    (a) 32 (b) 36 (c) 42 (d) 52

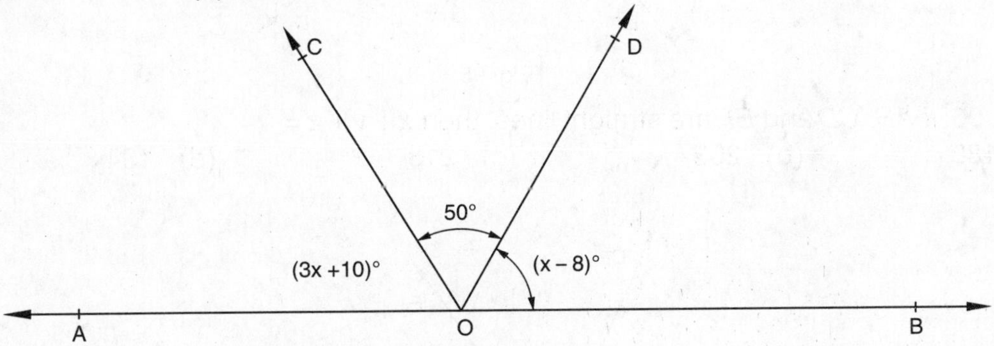

Fig. 92

15. In Fig. 93, if AOC is a straight line, then $x =$
    (a) 42° (b) 52° (c) 142° (d) 38°

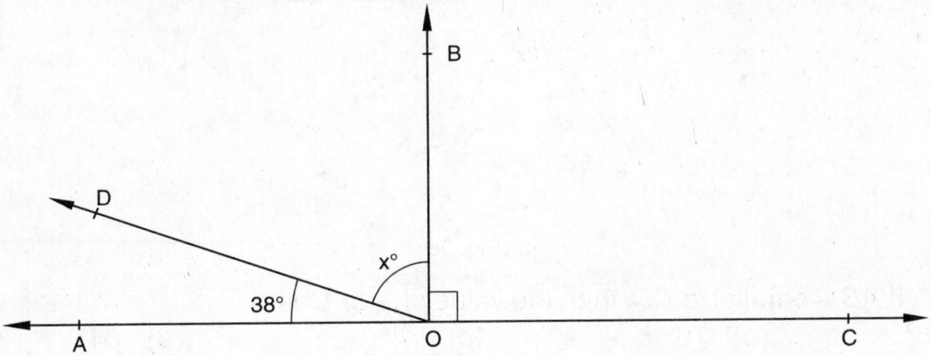

Fig. 93

16. In Fig. 94, if $\angle AOC$ is a straight line, then the value of x is
(a) 15 (b) 18 (c) 20 (d) 16

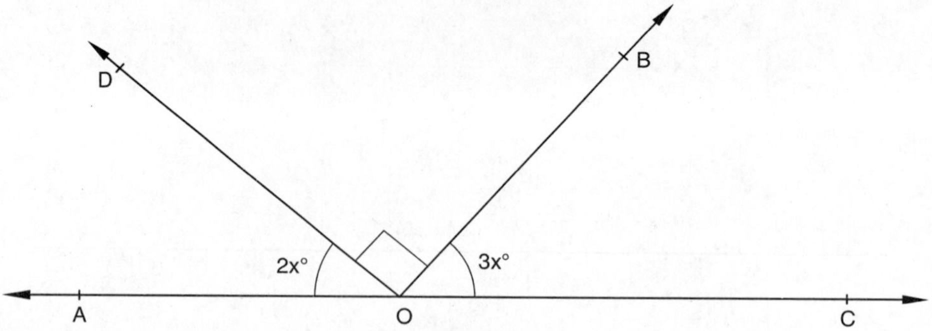

Fig. 94

17. In Fig. 95, if AB, CD and EF are straight lines, then $x =$
(a) 5 (b) 10 (c) 20 (d) 30

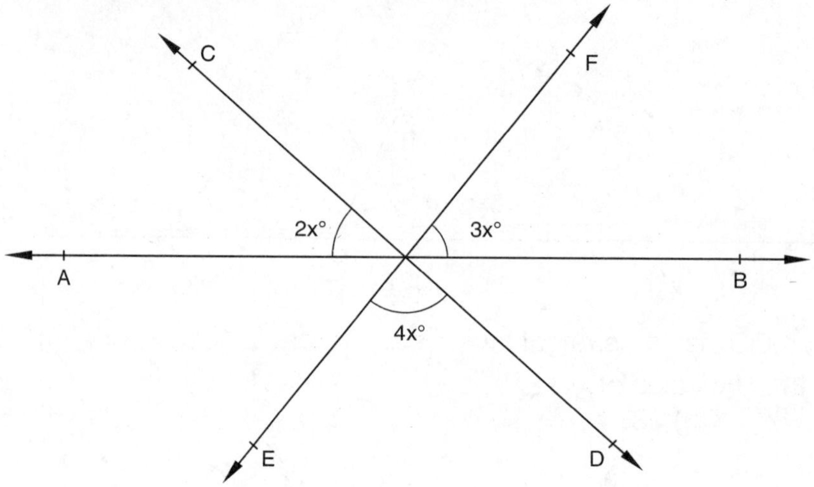

Fig. 95

18. In Fig. 96, if AB, CD and EF are straight lines, then $x + y + z =$
(a) 180 (b) 203 (c) 213 (d) 134

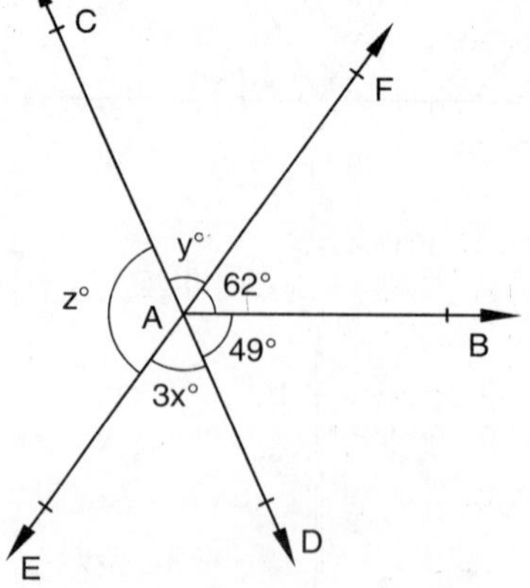

Fig. 96

19. In Fig. 97, if AB is parallel to CD, then the value of $\angle BPE$ is
(a) 106° (b) 76° (c) 74° (d) 84°

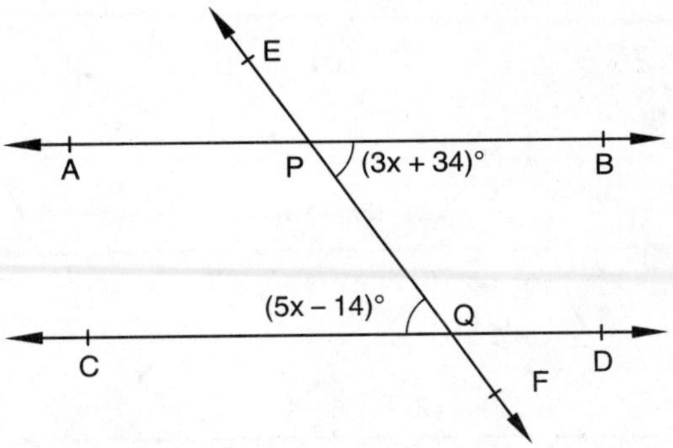

Fig. 97

20. In Fig. 98, if *AB* is parallel to *CD* and *EF* is a transversal, then $x =$
   (a) 19 (b) 29 (c) 39 (d) 49

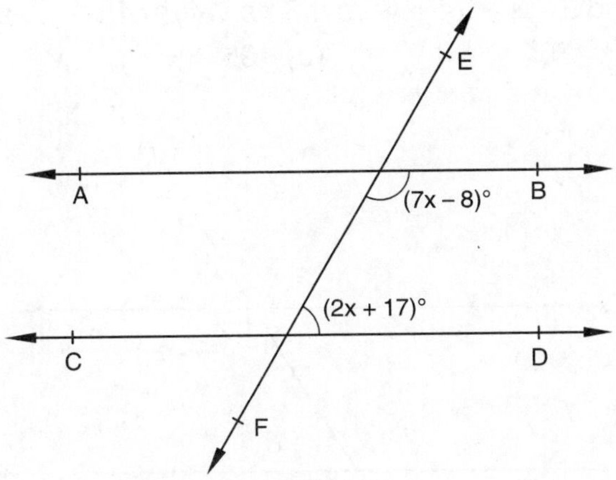

Fig. 98

21. In Fig. 99, $AB \parallel CD$ and *EF* is a transversal intersecting *AB* and *CD* at *P* and *Q* respectively. The measure of $\angle DPQ$ is
   (a) 100° (b) 80° (c) 110° (d) 70°

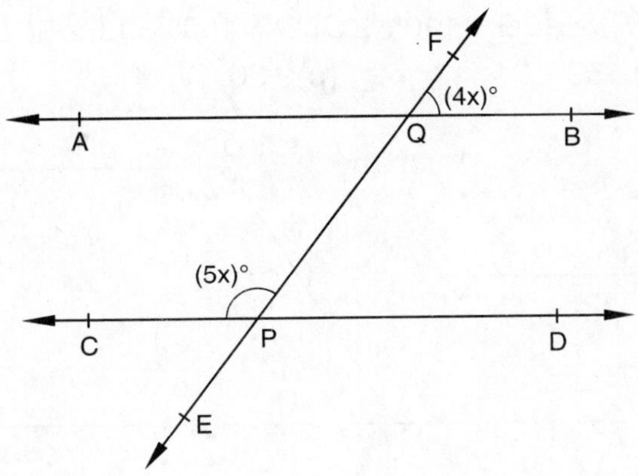

Fig. 99

22. In Fig. 100, $AB \parallel CD$ and EF is a transversal intersecting AB and CD at P and Q respectively. The measure of $\angle DQP$ is

(a) 65 (b) 25 (c) 115 (d) 105

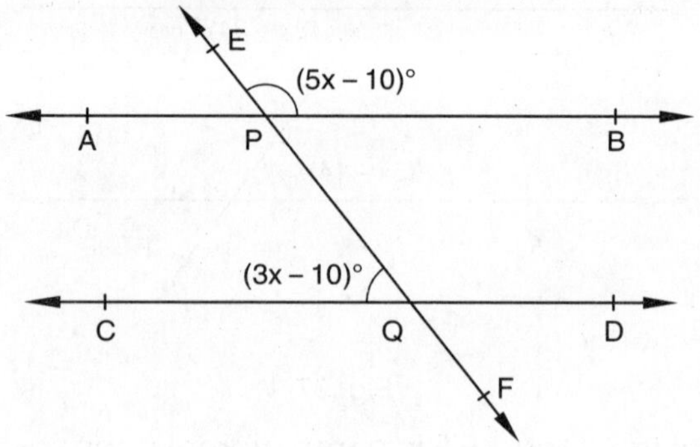

Fig. 100

23. In Fig. 101, $AB \parallel CD$ and EF is a transversal. The value of $y - x$ is

(a) 30 (b) 35 (c) 95 (d) 25

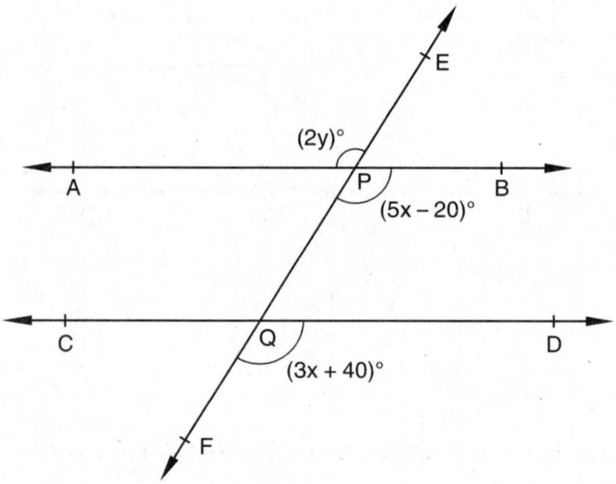

Fig. 101

24. In Fig. 102, $AB \parallel CD \parallel EF$, $\angle ABG = 110°$, $\angle GCD = 100°$ and $\angle BGC = x°$. The value of x is

(a) 35 (b) 50 (c) 30 (d) 40

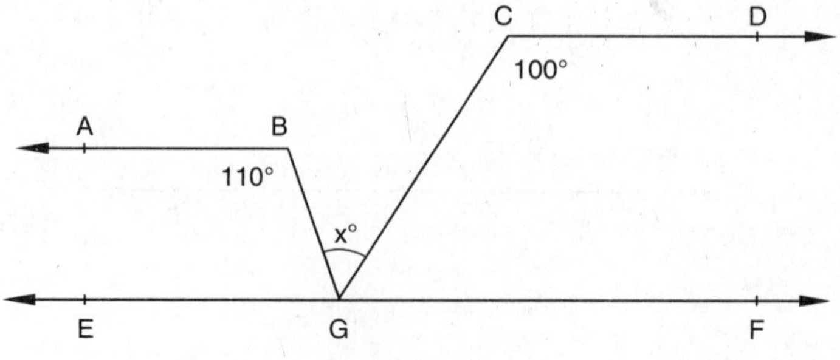

Fig. 102

25. In Fig. 103, $PQ \parallel RS$ and $\angle PAB = 60°$ and $\angle ACS = 100°$. Then, $\angle BAC =$

(a) 40° (b) 60° (c) 80° (d) 50°

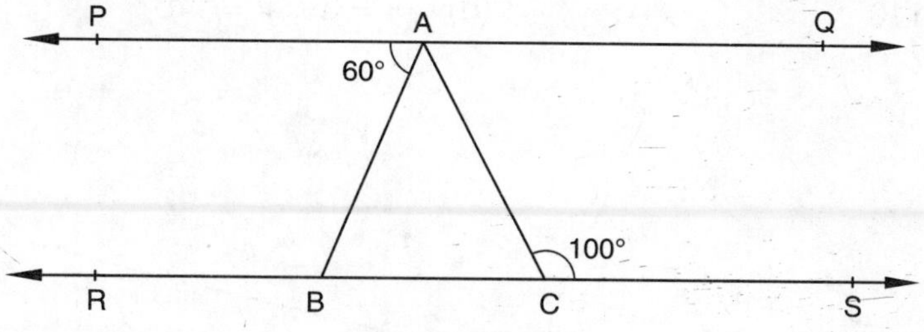

Fig. 103

26. In Fig. 104, $AB \parallel CD$, $\angle OAB = 150°$ and $\angle OCD = 120°$. Then, $\angle AOC =$

(a) 80° (b) 90° (c) 70° (d) 100°

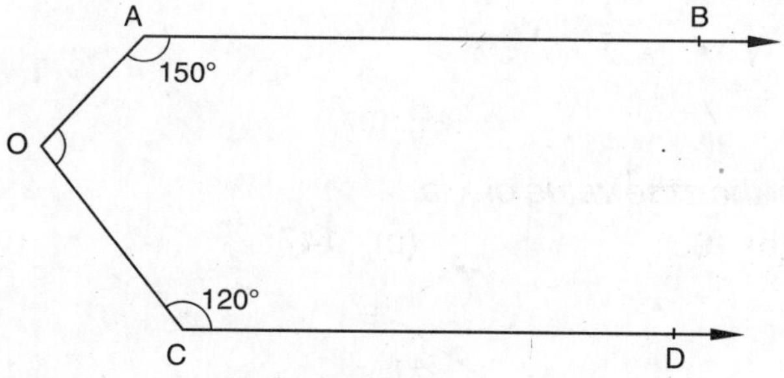

Fig. 104

27. In Fig. 105, if AOB and COD are straight lines. Then, $x + y =$

(a) 120 (b) 140 (c) 100 (d) 160

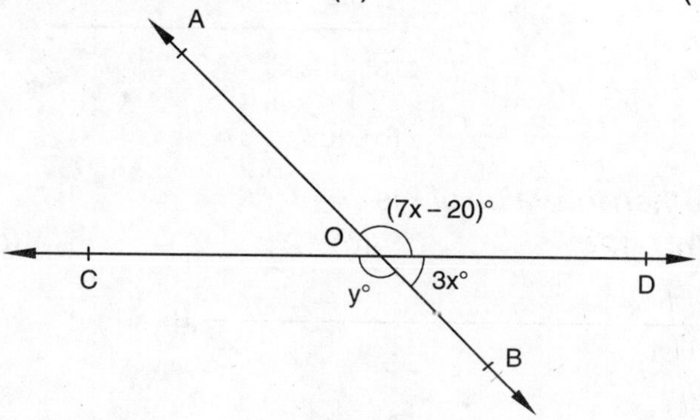

Fig. 105

28. In Fig. 106, the value of x is

(a) 22 (b) 20 (c) 21 (d) 24

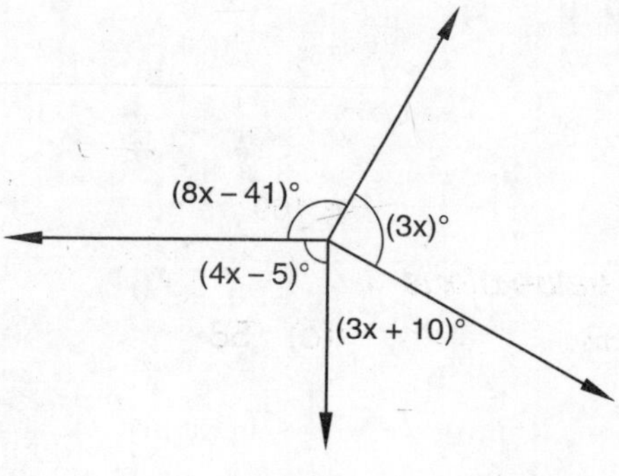

Fig. 106

29. In Fig. 107, if *AOB* and *COD* are straight lines, then

(a) $x = 29, y = 100$ (b) $x = 110, y = 29$

(c) $x = 29, y = 110$ (d) $x = 39, y = 110$

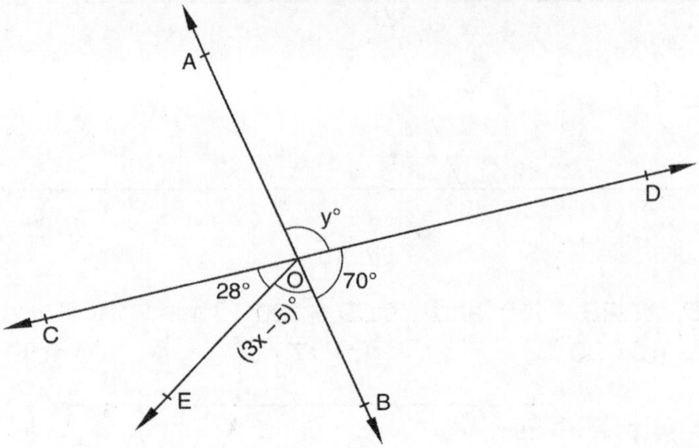

Fig. 107

30. In Fig. 108, if $AB \parallel CD$ *then the value of x is*

(a) 87 (b) 93 (c) 147 (d) 141

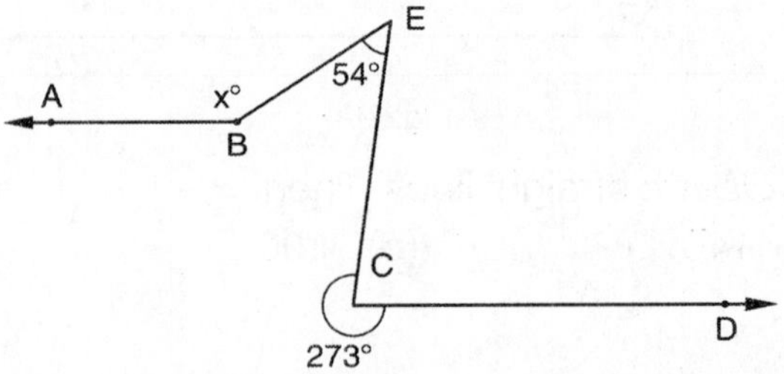

Fig. 108

31. In Fig. 109, if $AB \parallel CD$ *then the value of x is*

(a) 34 (b) 124 (c) 24 (d) 158

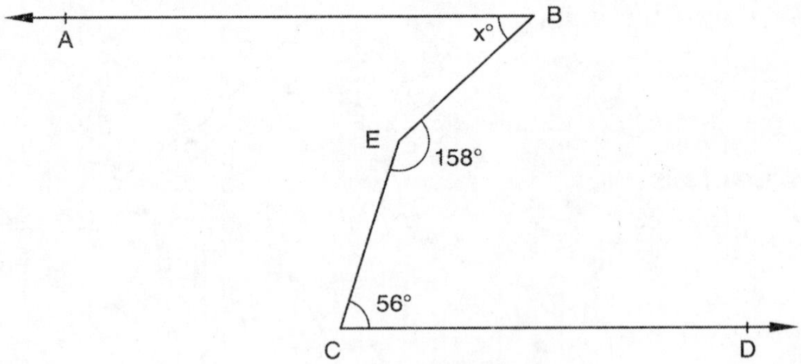

Fig. 109

32. In Fig. 110, if $AB \parallel CD$. *The value of x is*

(a) 122 (b) 238 (c) 58 (d) 119

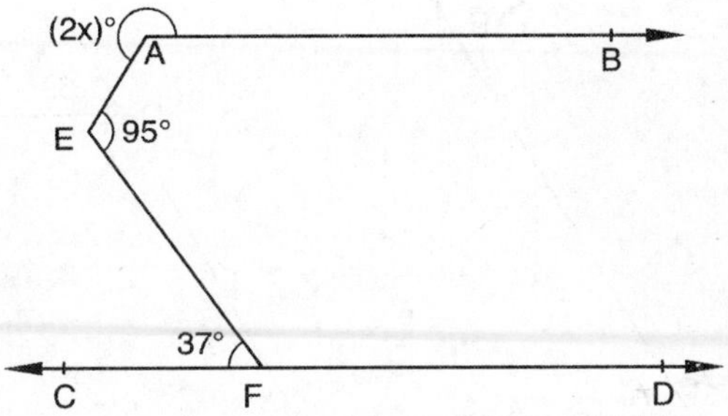

Fig. 110

33. In Fig. 111, if $AB \parallel CD$ then $x =$

(a) 154 (b) 139 (c) 144 (d) 164

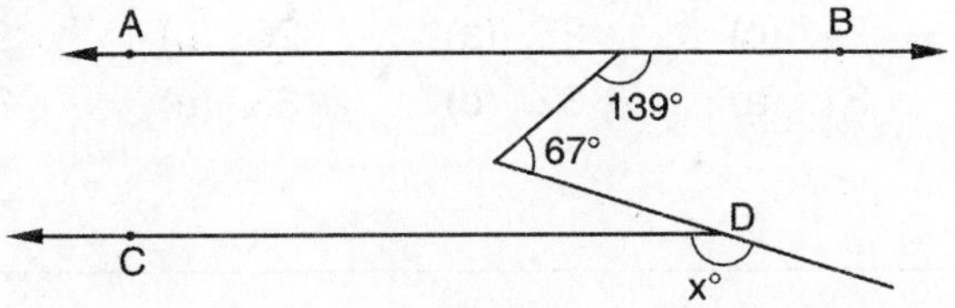

Fig. 111

34. In Fig. 112, if $AB \parallel CD$, then $x =$

(a) 32 (b) 42 (c) 52 (d) 31

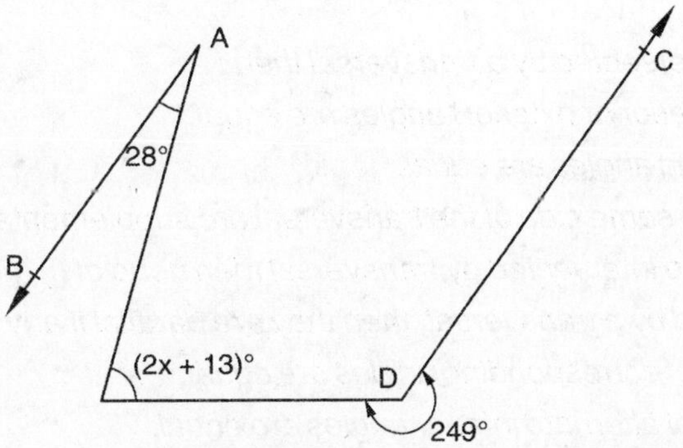

Fig. 112

35. In Fig. 113 if $AC \parallel DF$ and $AB \parallel CE$, then

(a) $x = 145, y = 223$ (b) $x = 223, y = 145$

(c) $x = 135, y = 233$ (d) $x = 233, y = 135$

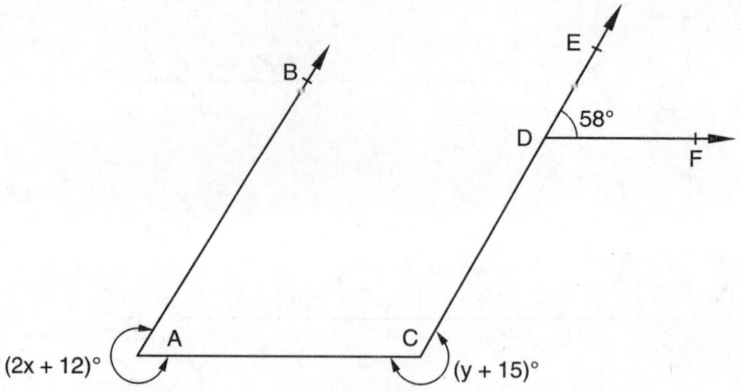

Fig. 113

ANSWSERS

1. (d)	2. (d)	3. (b)	4. (c)	5. (d)	6. (c)	7. (b)
8. (b)	9. (d)	10. (c)	11. (b)	12. (b)	13. (a)	14. (a)
15. (b)	16. (b)	17. (c)	18. (b)	19. (c)	20. (a)	21. (b)
22. (c)	23. (b)	24. (c)	25. (a)	26. (b)	27. (b)	28. (a)
29. (c)	30. (c)	31. (a)	32. (d)	33. (a)	34. (b)	35. (a)

THINGS TO REMEMBER

1. *A line which intersects two or more given lines at distinct points is called a transversal to the given lines.*
2. *Lines in a plane are parallel if they do not intersect when produced indefinitely in either direction.*
3. *The distance between two intersecting lines is zero.*
4. *The distance between two parallel lines is the same everywhere and is equal to the perpendicular distance between them.*
5. *If two parallel lines are intersected by a transversal then*
   - (i) *pairs of alternate (interior or exterior) angles are equal.*
   - (ii) *pairs of corresponding angles are equal.*
   - (iii) *interior angles on the same side of the transversal are supplementary.*
6. *If two non-parallel lines are intersected by transversal then none of (i), (ii) and (iii) hold true in 5.*
7. *If two lines are intersected by a transversal, then they are parallel if any one of the following is true:*
   - (i) *The angles of a pair of corresponding angles are equal.*
   - (ii) *The angles of a pair of alternate interior angles are equal.*
   - (iii) *The angles of a pair of interior angles on the same side of the transversal are supplementary.*

15

PROPERTIES OF TRIANGLES

15.1 INTRODUCTION

In the previous chapter, we have learnt about lines, rays, line segments and angles. In this chapter, we shall study about a plane figure formed by three non-parallel line segments. Such a figure is called a triangle.

15.2 TRIANGLE

TRIANGLE *A plane figure formed by three non-parallel line segments is called a triangle.*

If A, B, C are three non-collinear points in the plane of the paper, then the figure made up by the three line segments AB, BC and CA is called a triangle with vertices A, B and C.

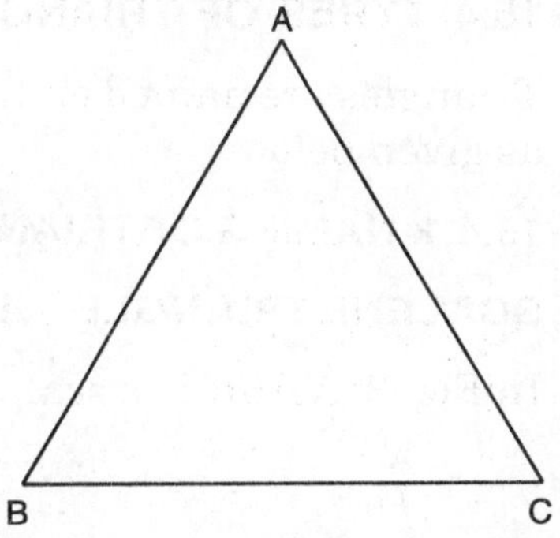

Fig. 1

The triangle with vertices A, B and C is generally denoted by the symbol ΔABC.

Note that the triangle ABC consists of all the points on the line segments AB, BC and CA.

SIDES *The three line segments AB, BC and CA, that form the triangle ABC, are called the sides of the triangle ABC.*

ANGLES *The three angles $\angle BAC$, $\angle ABC$ and $\angle ACB$ are called the angles of ΔABC.*

For the sake of convenience, we shall denote angles $\angle BAC$, $\angle ABC$ and $\angle ACB$ by $\angle A$, $\angle B$, $\angle C$ respectively.

ELEMENTS OR PARTS *The three sides AB, BC, CA and three angles $\angle A$, $\angle B$, $\angle C$ of a ΔABC are together called the six parts or elements of the ΔABC.*

In ΔABC, we observe that the sides AB and AC meet at vertex A and BC is the remaining side. So, we say that 'BC is the side opposite to vertex A and A is the vertex opposite to side BC'.

Similarly, CA is the side opposite to vertex B, and B is the vertex opposite to side CA.

Also, CA is the side opposite to $\angle B$, and $\angle B$ is the angle opposite to side CA.

Clearly, AB is the side opposite to vertex C, and C is the vertex opposite to side AB. We can also say that AB is the side opposite to $\angle C$, and $\angle C$ is the angle opposite to side AB.

15.3 INTERIOR AND EXTERIOR OF TRIANGLE

Consider a triangle ABC. We observe that all points in the plane of ΔABC are divided into following three parts:

(i) The points which lie inside the region enclosed by ΔABC.

(ii) The points which lie on the sides BC, CA and AB of ΔABC.

(iii) The points which lie outside the region enclosed by ΔABC.

So, we define the interior and exterior of a triangle as follows:

INTERIOR *The part made up by all such points P which are enclosed by ΔABC is called the interior of ΔABC.*

EXTERIOR *The part made up by all such points Q which are not enclosed by ΔABC is called the exterior of ΔABC.*

Note that ΔABC is the boundary of its interior.

TRIANGULAR REGION *The interior of ΔABC together with the ΔABC itself, is called the triangular region ABC.*

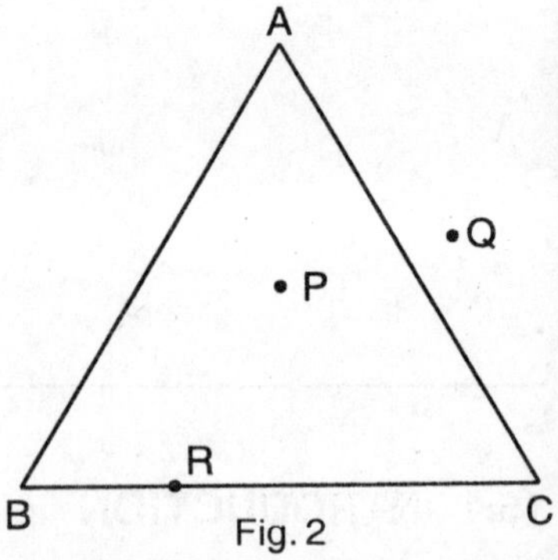

Fig. 2

The part of the plane which consists of all points such as R, i.e., points lying on the sides of the triangle, forms the triangle itself.

It may be noted that if we take any two points X and Y in the interior of ΔABC, then the line segment XY lies entirely in the interior of ΔABC.

15.4 TYPES OF TRIANGLES

Triangles are named on the basis of the lengths of their sides and the measures of their angles as given below:

15.4.1 NAMING OF TRIANGLES BY CONSIDERING THE LENGTHS OF THEIR SIDES

SCALENE TRIANGLE *A triangle whose no two sides are equal, is called a scalene triangle.*

In Fig. 3, ΔABC is a scalene triangle.

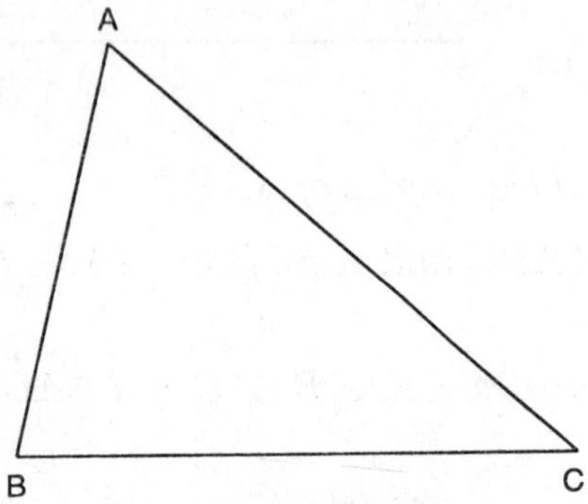

Scalene Triangle

Fig. 3

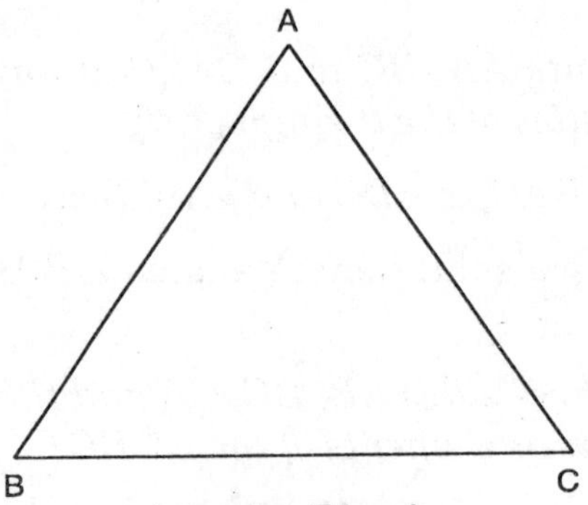

Isosceles Triangle

Fig. 4

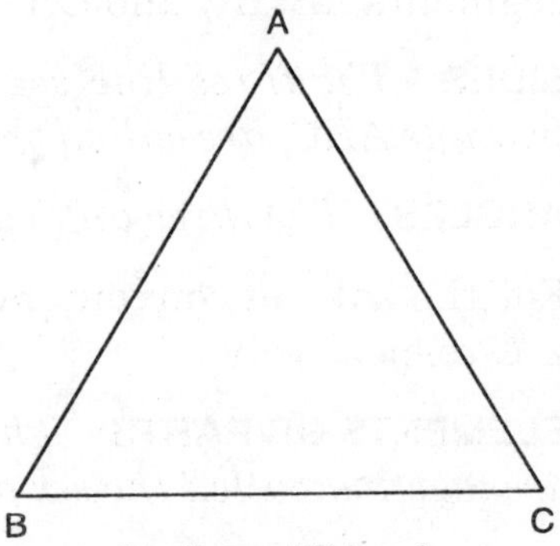

Equilateral Triangle

Fig. 5

ISOSCELES TRIANGLE *A triangle whose two sides are equal is called an isosceles triangle.*

In Fig. 4, ΔABC is an isosceles triangle, where $AB = AC$.

EQUILATERAL TRIANGLE *A triangle whose all sides are equal to one another, is called an equilateral triangle.*

In Fig. 5, ΔABC is an equilateral triangle, where $AB = BC = AC$

NOTE: *It should be noted that an equilateral triangle is isosceles triangle but the converse need not be true.*

15.4.2 NAMING TRIANGLES BY CONSIDERING THE MEASURES OF THEIR ANGLES

ACUTE TRIANGLE *A triangle whose all the angles are acute is called an acute-angled triangle or an acute triangle.*

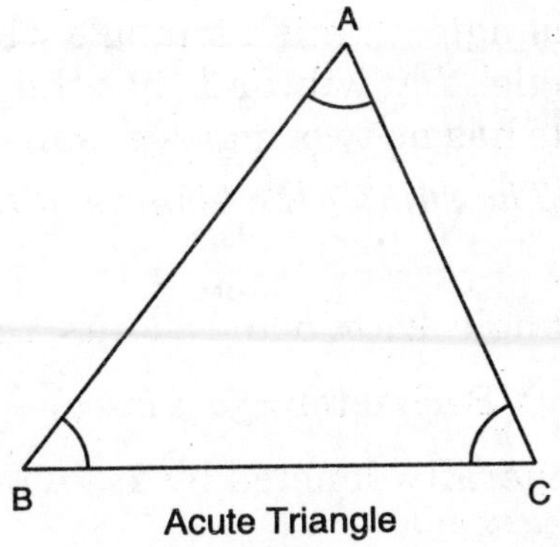

Acute Triangle

Fig. 6

In Fig. 6, ΔABC is an acute-angled triangle where $\angle A$, $\angle B$, $\angle C$ are acute angles.

Note that an equilateral triangle is an acute angled triangle, because the measure of its each angle is 60°

RIGHT TRIANGLE *A triangle whose one angle is a right angle, is called a right-angled triangle or a right triangle.*

The side opposite to the right angle in a right-angled triangle is known as the hypotenuse of the triangle and the other two sides are called the legs of the triangle.

In Fig. 7, ΔPQR is a right-angled triangle, where $\angle P = 90°$.

Note that the remaining two angles of a right-angled triangle are acute.

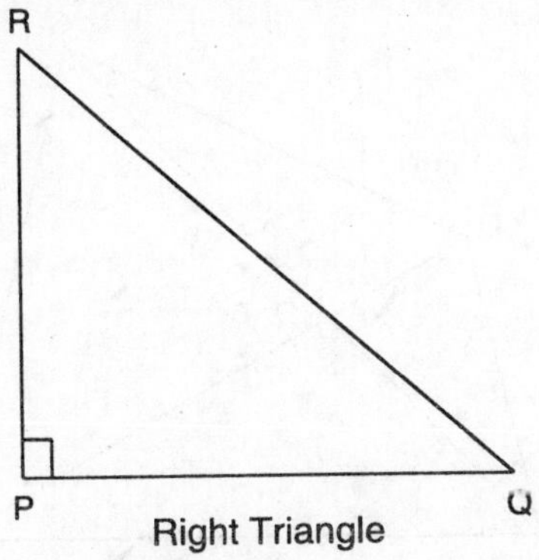

Right Triangle

Fig. 7

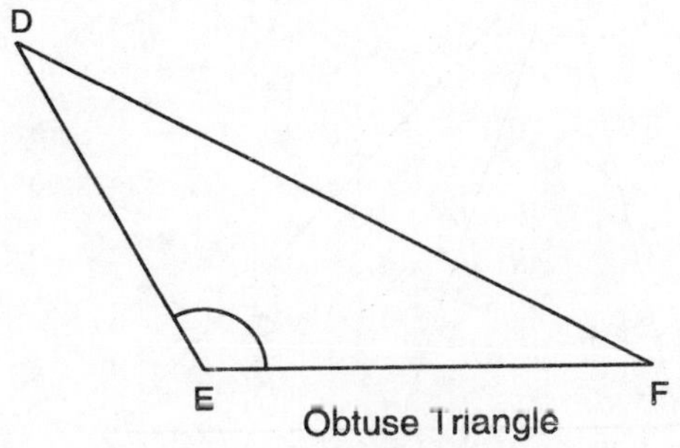

Obtuse Triangle

Fig. 8

OBTUSE TRIANGLE *A triangle whose one angle is obtuse, is called an obtuse-angled triangle or an obtuse triangle.*

In Fig. 8, ΔDEF is an obtuse-angled triangle, where $\angle E$ is an obtuse angle.

Note that in a triangle only one angle can be obtuse and the remaining two angles are acute angles.

Let us perform the following experiments in the support of some facts mentioned in the above discussion.

<u>*Experiment 1*</u> Draw some equilateral triangles and measure each one of the angles of each such triangle. You will find that the measure of each angle is 60°. Thus, the measure of each angle of an equilateral triangle is 60°.

<u>*Experiment 2*</u> Draw an isosceles triangle and measure its angles. You will find that the angles opposite to equal sides are equal. Thus, an isosceles triangle has exactly two equal angles.

Experiment 3 Draw a scalene triangle, that is a triangle whose sides are of different lengths. Measure the angles of this triangle. You will find that the measures of the three angles are different. Thus, a scalene triangle has no two angles equal.

PERIMETER OF A TRIANGLE *The sum of the lengths of the sides of a triangle is called its perimeter.*

If the lengths of the sides of a triangle are a, b and c units, then

$$\text{Perimeter} = (a + b + c)$$

The perimeter of a triangle is generally denoted by $2s$, where s is the semi-perimeter of the triangle. Thus, $2s = a + b + c$

EXERCISE 15.1

1. Take three non-collinear points A, B and C on a page of your notebook. Join AB, BC and CA. What figure do you get? Name the triangle. Also, name
   (i) the side opposite to $\angle B$ (ii) the angle opposite to side AB
   (iii) the vertex opposite to side BC (iv) the side opposite to vertex B.
2. Take three collinear points A, B and C on a page of your note book. Join AB, BC and CA. Is the figure a triangle? If not, why?
3. Distinguish between a triangle and its triangular region.
4. In Fig. 9, D is a point on side BC of a ΔABC. AD is joined. Name all the triangles that you can observe in the figure. How many are they?

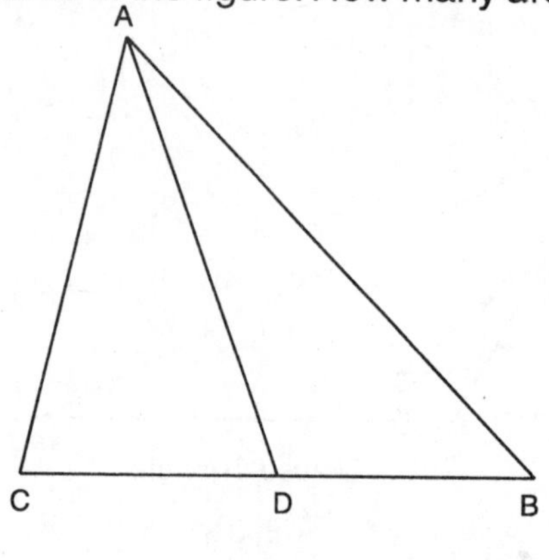

Fig. 9

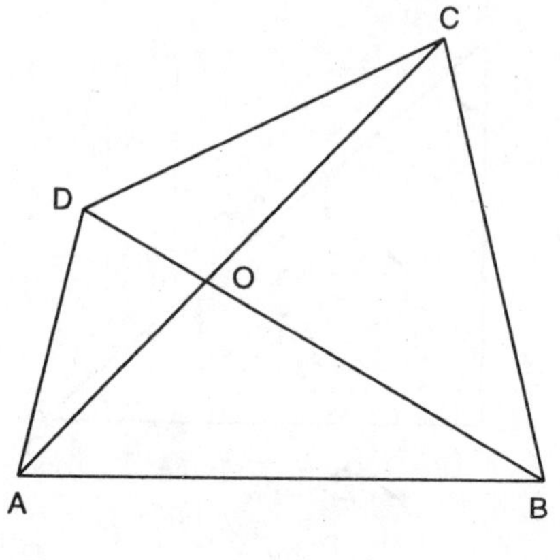

Fig. 10

5. In Fig. 10, A, B, C and D are four points, and no three points are collinear. AC and BD intersect at O. There are eight triangles that you can observe. Name all the triangles.
6. What is the difference between a triangle and triangular region?
7. Explain the following terms:
   (i) Triangle (ii) Parts or elements of a triangle
   (iii) Scalene triangle (iv) Isosceles triangle
   (v) Equilateral triangle (vi) Acute triangle
   (vii) Right triangle (viii) Obtuse triangle
   (ix) Interior of a triangle (x) Exterior of a triangle.
8. In Fig. 11, the length (in cm) of each side has been indicated along the side. State for each triangle whether it is scalene, isosceles or equilateral:

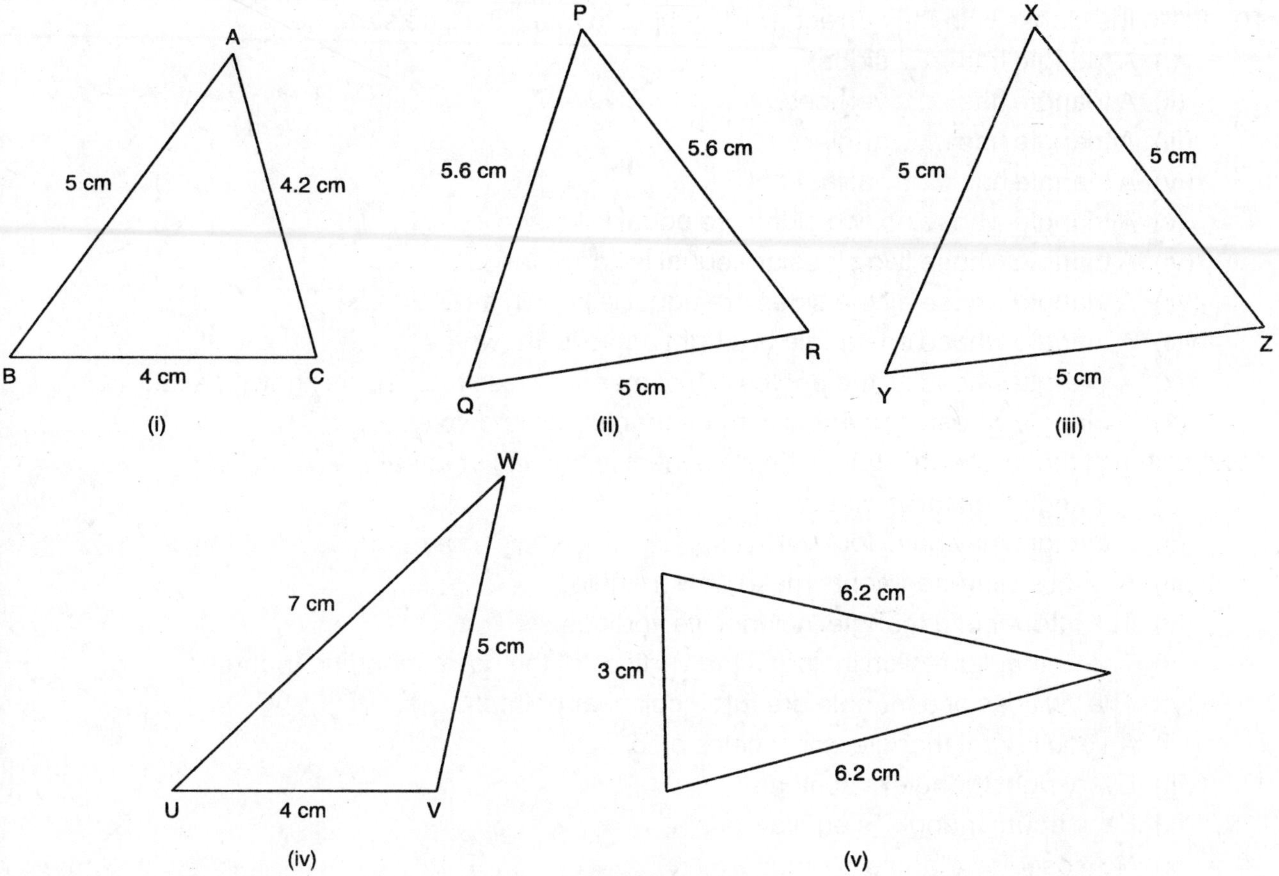

Fig. 11

9. In Fig. 12, there are five triangles. The measures of some of their angles have been indicated. State for each triangle whether it is acute, right or obtuse.

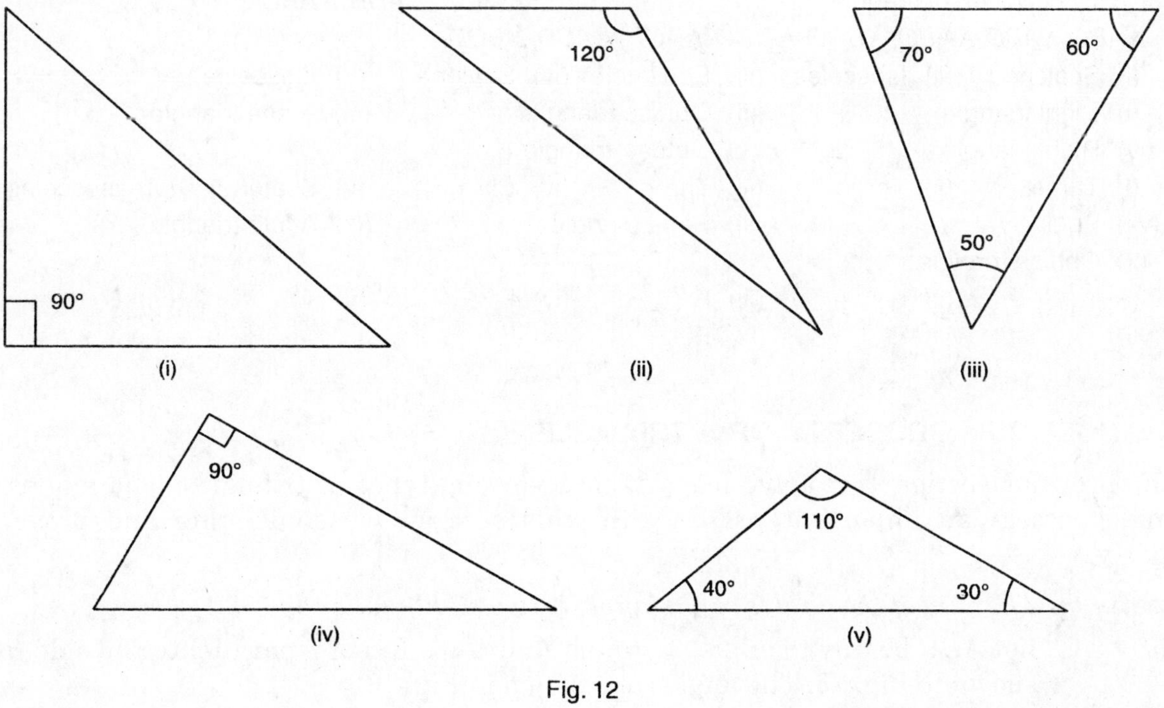

Fig. 12

10. Fill in the blanks with the correct word/symbol to make it a true statement:
   (i) A triangle has .... sides.
   (ii) A triangle has .... vertices.
   (iii) A triangle has .... angles.
   (iv) A triangle has .... parts.
   (v) A triangle whose no two sides are equal is known as ....
   (vi) A triangle whose two sides are equal is known as .....
   (vii) A triangle whose all the sides are equal is known as ....
   (viii) A triangle whose one angle is a right angle is known as ....
   (ix) A triangle whose all the angles are of measure less than 90° is known as .....
   (x) A triangle whose one angle is more than 90° is known as ....

11. In each of the following, state if the statement is true (T) or false (F):
   (i) A triangle has three sides.
   (ii) A triangle may have four vertices.
   (iii) Any three line-segments make up a triangle.
   (iv) The interior of a triangle includes its vertices.
   (v) The triangular region includes the vertices of the corresponding triangle.
   (vi) The vertices of a triangle are three collinear points.
   (vii) An equilateral triangle is isosceles also.
   (viii) Every right triangle is scalene.
   (ix) Each acute triangle is equilateral.
   (x) No isosceles triangle is obtuse.

ANSWERS

1. Triangle, ΔABC (i) AC (ii) $\angle ACB$ (iii) A (iv) AC
2. No, by definition of triangle
4. $\Delta ACD, \Delta ADB, \Delta ABC$; 3
5. $\Delta ABC, \Delta ABD, \Delta ABO, \Delta BCO, \Delta DCO, \Delta AOD, \Delta ACD, \Delta BCD$
8. (i) Scalene (ii) Isosceles (iii) Equilateral (iv) Scalene (v) Isosceles
9. (i) Right triangle (ii) Obtuse triangle (iii) Acute triangle (iv) Right triangle (v) Obtuse-triangle
10. (i) Three (ii) Three (iii) Three (iv) Six (v) Scalene (vi) Isosceles (vii) Equilateral (viii) Right triangle (ix) Acute triangle (x) Obtuse triangle
11. (i) T (ii) F (iii) F (iv) F (v) T (vi) F (vii) T (viii) F (ix) F (x) F

15.5 ANGLE SUM PROPERTY OF A TRIANGLE

In the previous sections, we have learnt about various types of triangles. The angles of a triangle possess an important property. In this section, we shall state and prove this property.

Property *The sum of the angles of a triangle is two right angles or 180°.*

Proof Let ABC be any triangle. Through A, draw a line XY parallel to the side BC as shown in Fig. 13. The angles are shown in Fig. 13.

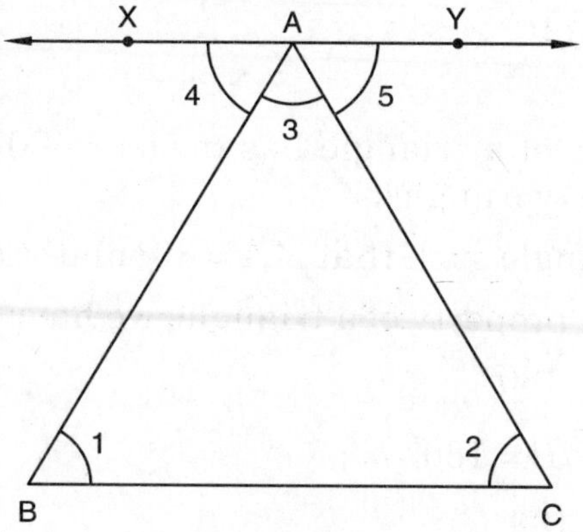

Fig. 13

Since $XY \| BC$ and the transversal AB cuts XY and BC at A and B respectively.

$\therefore \quad \angle 1 = \angle 4$ [$\because$ Alternate interior angles are equal]

Similarly, $XY \| BC$ and the transversal AC cuts XY and BC at A and C respectively.

$\therefore \quad \angle 2 = \angle 5$ [$\because$ Alternate interior angles are equal]

Also, $\angle 3 = \angle 3$

Adding the angles on the respective sides, we get

$\angle 1 + \angle 2 + \angle 3 = \angle 4 + \angle 5 + \angle 3$

But, $\angle 4 + \angle 5 + \angle 3 = 180°$ [By linearity property]

$\therefore \quad \angle 1 + \angle 2 + \angle 3 = 180° = 2$ right angles.

Hence, the sum of the angles of a triangle is two right angles or 180°.

SOME IMPORTANT RESULTS *From the above property, we obtain the following useful results:*

(i) A triangle cannot have more than one right angle.

(ii) A triangle cannot have more than one obtuse angle i.e. if one angle of a triangle is obtuse, then the other two are acute.

(iii) In a right triangle, the other two angles are acute and their sum is 90°.

Following examples will illustrate the applications of the above property.

ILLUSTRATIVE EXAMPLES

Example 1 Two angles of a triangle are of measures 75° and 35°. Find the measure of the third angle.

Solution Let ABC be a triangle such that $\angle B = 75°$ and $\angle C = 35°$. Then, we have to find the measure of the third angle A.

Now, $\angle B = 75°$ and $\angle C = 35°$

$\Rightarrow \quad \angle B + \angle C = 75° + 35° = 110°$

By the angle sum property of a triangle, we have

$\angle A + \angle B + \angle C = 180°$

$\Rightarrow \quad \angle A + 110° = 180°$ [$\because \angle B + \angle C = 110°$]

$\Rightarrow \quad \angle A = 180° - 110°$

$\Rightarrow \quad \angle A = 70°.$

Example 2 One of the angles of a triangle has measure 80° and the other two angles are equal. Find these two angles.

Solution Let ABC be a triangle such that $\angle A = 80°$ and $\angle B = \angle C$.

By the angle sum property of a triangle, we have

$\angle A + \angle B + \angle C = 180°$

$\Rightarrow \quad 80° + \angle B + \angle B = 180°$ $\quad [\because \angle A = 80° \text{ and } \angle C = \angle B]$

$\Rightarrow \quad 80° + 2\angle B = 180°$

$\Rightarrow \quad 2\angle B = 180° - 80°$

$\Rightarrow \quad 2\angle B = 100°$

$$\Rightarrow \quad \angle B = \left(\frac{100}{2}\right)^{o} = 50°$$

Hence, the measure of each of the remaining two angles is 50°.

Example 3 Of the three angles of a triangle, one is twice the smallest and another is three times the smallest. Find the angles.

Solution Let the smallest angle of the given triangle be of $x°$. Then, the other two angles are of measures $2x°$ and $3x°$.

$\therefore \quad x + 2x + 3x = 180°$ $\quad$ [Angle sum property of a triangle]

$\Rightarrow \quad 6x = 180°$

$$\Rightarrow \quad x = \frac{180°}{6} = 30°$$

Hence, the angles of the triangle are 30°, 60° and 90°.

Example 4 Each of the two equal angles of a triangle is twice the third angle. Find the angles of the triangle.

Solution Let the measure of the smallest angle be $x°$. Then each of the other two angles has measure $2x°$.

Since the sum of the angles of a triangle is 180°.

$\therefore \quad x + 2x + 2x = 180$

$\Rightarrow \quad 5x = 180$

$$\Rightarrow \quad \frac{5x}{5} = \frac{180}{5} \quad \Rightarrow \quad x = 36$$

Thus, the angles of the triangle are 36°, 72°, 72°.

Example 5 If the angles of a triangle are in the ratio 2 : 3 : 4, determine three angles.

Solution Let measures of the angles of triangle be $2x°$, $3x°$ and $4x°$. Then,

$2x + 3x + 4x = 180°$ $\quad$ [Sum of the angles of a triangle is 180°]

$\Rightarrow \quad 9x = 180°$

$\Rightarrow \quad x = 20°$

Hence, the angles of the triangle are 40°, 60° and 80°.

Example 6 The sum of two angles of a triangle is equal to its third angle. Determine the measure of the third angle.

Solution Let ABC be a triangle such that

$\angle A + \angle B = \angle C$ ...(i)

We know that

$\angle A + \angle B + \angle C = 180°$ ...(ii)

Putting $\angle A + \angle B = \angle C$ in (ii), we get

$\angle C + \angle C = 180°$

$\Rightarrow \quad 2\angle C = 180°$

$\Rightarrow \quad \angle C = 90°$

Thus, the third angle is of 90°.

Example 7 One of the acute angles of a right triangle is 58°. Find the other acute angle.

Solution Let the measure of the other acute angle be $x°$. Then, the angles of the triangle are 90°, 58° and $x°$.

Since the sum of the angles of a triangle is 180°.

$\therefore \quad 90° + 58° + x = 180°$

$\Rightarrow \quad 148° + x = 180°$

$\Rightarrow \quad x = 180° - 148°$

$\Rightarrow \quad x = 32°$

Hence, the measure of the other acute angle is 32°.

Example 8 In Fig. 14, ΔABC is right-angled at C, and $CD \perp AB$. Also, $\angle A = 65°$. Find
(i) $\angle ACD$ (ii) $\angle BCD$ (iii) $\angle CBD$.

Solution Since ΔABC is right-angled at C. Therefore, $\angle C = 90°$

Also, $\angle A = 65°$ [Given]

Now, sum of the angles of a triangle = 180°

$\therefore \quad \angle A + \angle B + \angle C = 180°$

$\Rightarrow \quad 65° + \angle B + 90° = 180°$

$\Rightarrow \quad \angle B = 180° - (65° + 90°)$

$\Rightarrow \quad \angle B = 180° - 155°$

$\Rightarrow \quad \angle B = 25°$

$\Rightarrow \quad \angle CBD = 25°$

Fig. 14

Since $CD \perp AB$. Therefore, $\angle ADC = \angle CDB = 90°$

In ΔACD, we have

$\angle ACD + \angle CAD + \angle ADC = 180°$

$\Rightarrow \quad \angle ACD + 65° + 90° = 180°$

$\Rightarrow \quad \angle ACD + 155° = 180°$

$\Rightarrow \quad \angle ACD = 180° - 155° = 25°$

In ΔBCD, we have

$\angle BCD + \angle CBD + \angle BDC = 180°$

$\Rightarrow \quad \angle BCD + 25° + 90° = 180°$

$\Rightarrow \quad \angle BCD + 115° = 180°$

$\Rightarrow \quad \angle BCD = 180° - 115°$

$\Rightarrow \quad \angle BCD = 65°$

Hence, $\angle ACD = 25°$, $\angle BCD = 65°$ and $\angle CBD = 25°$.

Example 9 In Fig. 15, D, E are points on sides AB, AC of ΔABC such that $DE \parallel BC$. If $\angle B = 30°$ and $\angle A = 40°$, find $x°, y°, z°$.

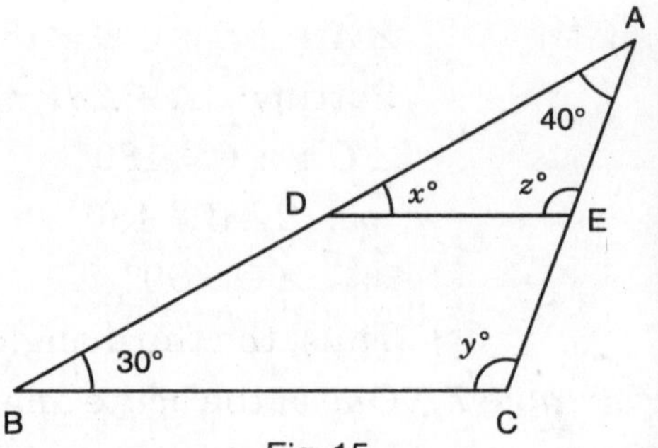

Fig. 15

Solution In ΔABC, we have

$\angle A = 40°$ and $\angle B = 30°$

$\therefore \quad \angle A + \angle B + \angle C = 180°$

$\Rightarrow \quad 40° + 30° + \angle C = 180°$

$\Rightarrow \quad 70° + \angle C = 180°$

$\Rightarrow \quad \angle C = 180° - 70°$

$\Rightarrow \quad \angle C = 110°$

$\Rightarrow \quad y° = 110°$

Now, $DE \parallel BC$ and transversal AB cuts them at D and B respectively.

$\therefore \quad \angle B = \angle ADE$ [Corresponding angles]

$\Rightarrow \quad 30° = x° \quad \Rightarrow x° = 30°$

Again, $DE \parallel BC$ and transversal AC cuts them at E and C respectively.

$\therefore \quad \angle ACB = \angle AED$ [Corresponding angles]

$\Rightarrow \quad y° = z°$

$\Rightarrow \quad z° = 110°$ $[\because y° = 110°]$

Hence, $x° = 30°, y° = 110°$ and $z° = 110°$.

Example 10 The Fig. 16 has been obtained by using two triangles. Find $\angle A + \angle B + \angle C + \angle D + \angle E + \angle F$.

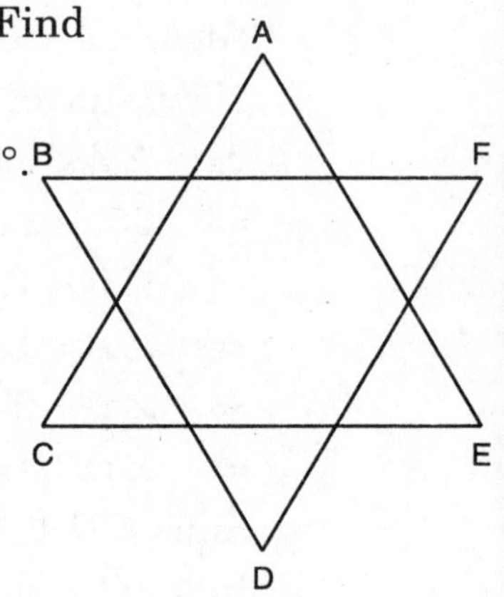

Fig. 16

Solution We know that the sum of the angles of a triangle is 180°.

$\therefore \quad$ In ΔACE, we have $\angle A + \angle C + \angle E = 180°$ ...(i)

In ΔBDF, we have $\angle B + \angle D + \angle F = 180°$ ...(ii)

Adding the corresponding sides of (i) and (ii), we get

$(\angle A + \angle C + \angle E) + (\angle B + \angle D + \angle F)$

$\Rightarrow \quad 180° + 180°$

$\Rightarrow \quad \angle A + \angle B + \angle C + \angle D + \angle E + \angle F = 360°$

Example 11 Fig. 17 is made up of two triangles. Find $\angle DAB + \angle ABC + \angle BCD + \angle CDA$.

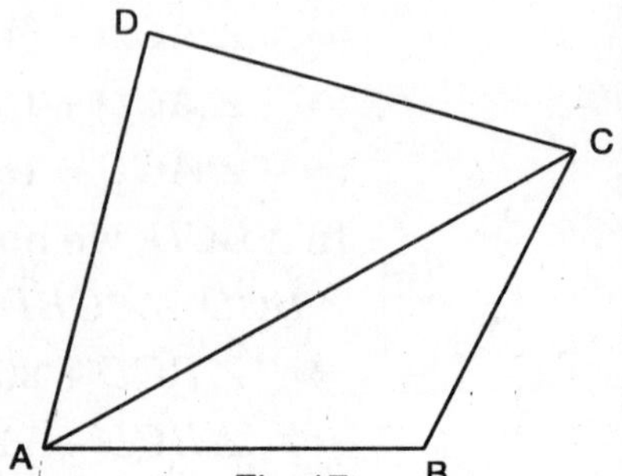

Fig. 17

Solution We know that the sum of the angles of a triangle is 180°.

$\therefore \quad$ In ΔABC, we have

$\angle ABC + \angle BCA + \angle CAB = 180°$ ...(i)

In ΔACD, we have

$\angle DAC + \angle ACD + \angle CDA = 180°$ ...(ii)

Adding the corresponding sides of (i) and (ii), we get

$$(\angle ABC + \angle BCA + \angle CAB) + (\angle DAC + \angle ACD + \angle CDA) = 180° + 180°$$

$$\Rightarrow \angle ABC + (\angle BCA + \angle ACD) + (\angle CAB + \angle DAC) + \angle CDA = 360°$$

$\left[\because \angle BCA + \angle ACD = \angle BCD \text{ and } \angle CAB + \angle DAC = \angle DAB\right]$

$$\Rightarrow \angle ABC + \angle BCD + \angle DAB + \angle CDA = 360°.$$

Example 12 In five cornered Fig. 18, *AD*, *AC* are joined. Find

$\angle EAB + \angle ABC + \angle BCD + \angle CDE + \angle DEA$

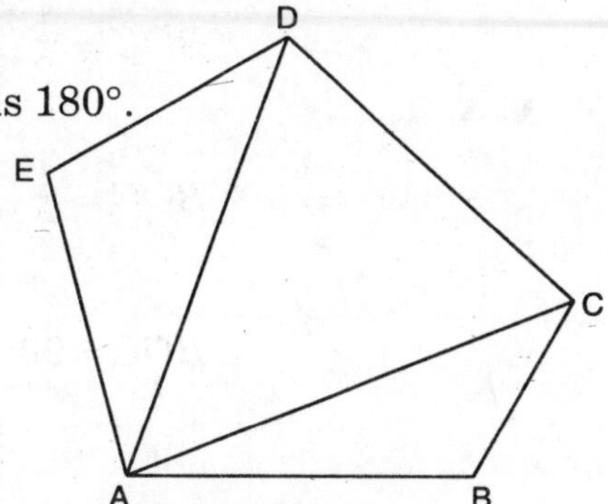

Fig. 18

Solution We know that the sum of the angles of a triangle is 180°.

$\therefore$ In ΔABC, we have

$\angle ABC + \angle BAC + \angle BCA = 180°$ ...(i)

In ΔACD, we have

$\angle ACD + \angle CAD + \angle CDA = 180°$ ...(ii)

In ΔADE, we have

$\angle DAE + \angle ADE + \angle DEA = 180°$ ...(iii)

Adding (i), (ii) and (iii), we get

$$(\angle ABC + \angle BAC + \angle BCA) + (\angle ACD + \angle CAD + \angle CDA) + (\angle DAE + \angle ADE + \angle DEA) = 180° + 180° + 180°.$$

$$\Rightarrow \angle ABC + (\angle BAC + \angle CAD + \angle DAE) + (\angle BCA + \angle ACD) + (\angle CDA + \angle ADE) + \angle DEA = 540°$$

$$\Rightarrow \angle ABC + \angle EAB + \angle BCD + \angle CDE + \angle DEA = 540°.$$

$\left[\because \angle BAC + \angle CAD + \angle DAE = \angle EAB,\ \angle BCA + \angle ACD = \angle BCD \text{ and } \angle CDA + \angle ADE = \angle CDE\right]$

Example 13 The sides *AB* and *AC* of ΔABC are produced to *P* and *Q* respectively. The bisectors of exterior angles at *B* and *C* of ΔABC meet at *O* (Fig. 19). Prove that

$$\angle BOC = 90° - \frac{1}{2}\angle A$$

Solution Since $\angle ABC$ and $\angle CBP$ form a linear pair.

$\therefore \angle ABC + \angle CBP = 180°$ $\left[\because BO \text{ is the bisector of } \angle CBP \therefore \angle CBP = 2\angle 1\right]$

$\Rightarrow \angle B + 2\angle 1 = 180°$

$\Rightarrow 2\angle 1 = 180° - \angle B$

$\Rightarrow \angle 1 = 90° - \frac{1}{2}\angle B$ ...(i)

Again, $\angle ACB$ and $\angle QCB$ form a linear pair.

$\therefore \angle ACB + \angle QCB = 180°$

$\Rightarrow \angle C + 2\angle 2 = 180°$ $\left[\because OC \text{ is the bisector of } \angle QCB \therefore \angle QCB = 2\angle 2\right]$

$\Rightarrow 2\angle 2 = 180° - \angle C$

$\Rightarrow \angle 2 = 90° - \frac{1}{2}\angle C$ ...(ii)

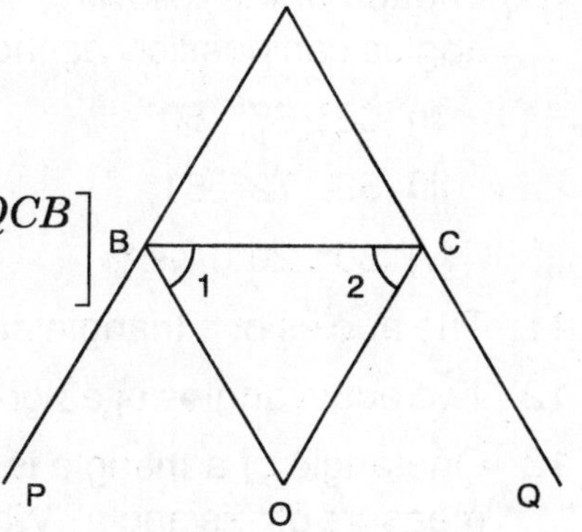

Fig. 19

Now, in ΔBOC, we have

$\angle 1 + \angle 2 + \angle BOC = 180°$

$$\Rightarrow \quad 90^\circ - \frac{1}{2}\angle B + 90^\circ - \frac{1}{2}\angle C + \angle BOC = 180^\circ \qquad \text{[Using (i) and (ii)]}$$

$$\Rightarrow \quad 180^\circ - \frac{1}{2}(\angle B + \angle C) + \angle BOC = 180^\circ$$

$$\Rightarrow \quad \angle BOC = \frac{1}{2}(\angle B + \angle C)$$

$$\Rightarrow \quad \angle BOC = \frac{1}{2}(180^\circ - \angle A) \qquad \begin{bmatrix} \because & \angle A + \angle B + \angle C = 180^\circ \\ \therefore & \angle B + \angle C = 180^\circ - \angle A \end{bmatrix}$$

$$\Rightarrow \quad \angle BOC = 90^\circ - \frac{1}{2}\angle A.$$

EXERCISE 15.2

1. Two angles of a triangle are of measures 105° and 30°. Find the measure of the third angle.
2. One of the angles of a triangle is 130°, and the other two angles are equal. What is the measure of each of these equal angles?
3. The three angles of a triangle are equal to one another. What is the measure of each of the angles?
4. If the angles of a triangle are in the ratio 1 : 2 : 3, determine three angles.
5. The angles of a triangle are $(x-40)^\circ$, $(x-20)^\circ$ and $\left(\frac{1}{2}x - 10\right)^\circ$. Find the value of x.
6. The angles of a triangle are arranged in ascending order of magnitude. If the difference between two consecutive angles is 10°, find the three angles.
7. Two angles of a triangle are equal and the third angle is greater than each of those angles by 30°. Determine all the angles of the triangle.
8. If one angle of a triangle is equal to the sum of the other two, show that the triangle is a right triangle.
9. If each angle of a triangle is less than the sum of the other two, show that the triangle is acute angled.
10. In each of the following, the measures of three angles are given. State in which cases, the angles can possibly be those of a triangle:

    (i) 63°, 37°, 80° (ii) 45°, 61°, 73°

    (iii) 59°, 72°, 61° (iv) 45°, 45°, 90°

    (v) 30°, 20°, 125°
11. The angles of a triangle are in the ratio 3 : 4 : 5. Find the smallest angle.
12. Two acute angles of a right triangle are equal. Find the two angles.
13. One angle of a triangle is greater than the sum of the other two. What can you say about the measure of this angle? What type of a triangle is this?

14. In the six cornered figure, (Fig. 20), AC, AD and AE are joined. Find $\angle FAB + \angle ABC + \angle BCD + \angle CDE + \angle DEF + \angle EFA$.

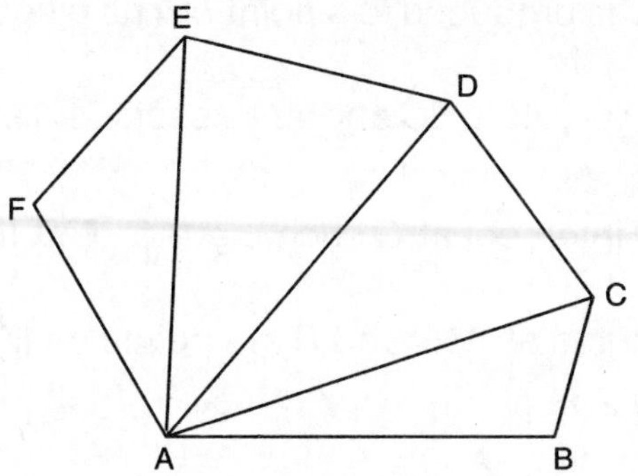

Fig. 20

15. Find x, y, z (whichever is required) in the Figures (Fig. 21) given below, if it is given that $DE \parallel BC$ in Fig. (i) and (iv).

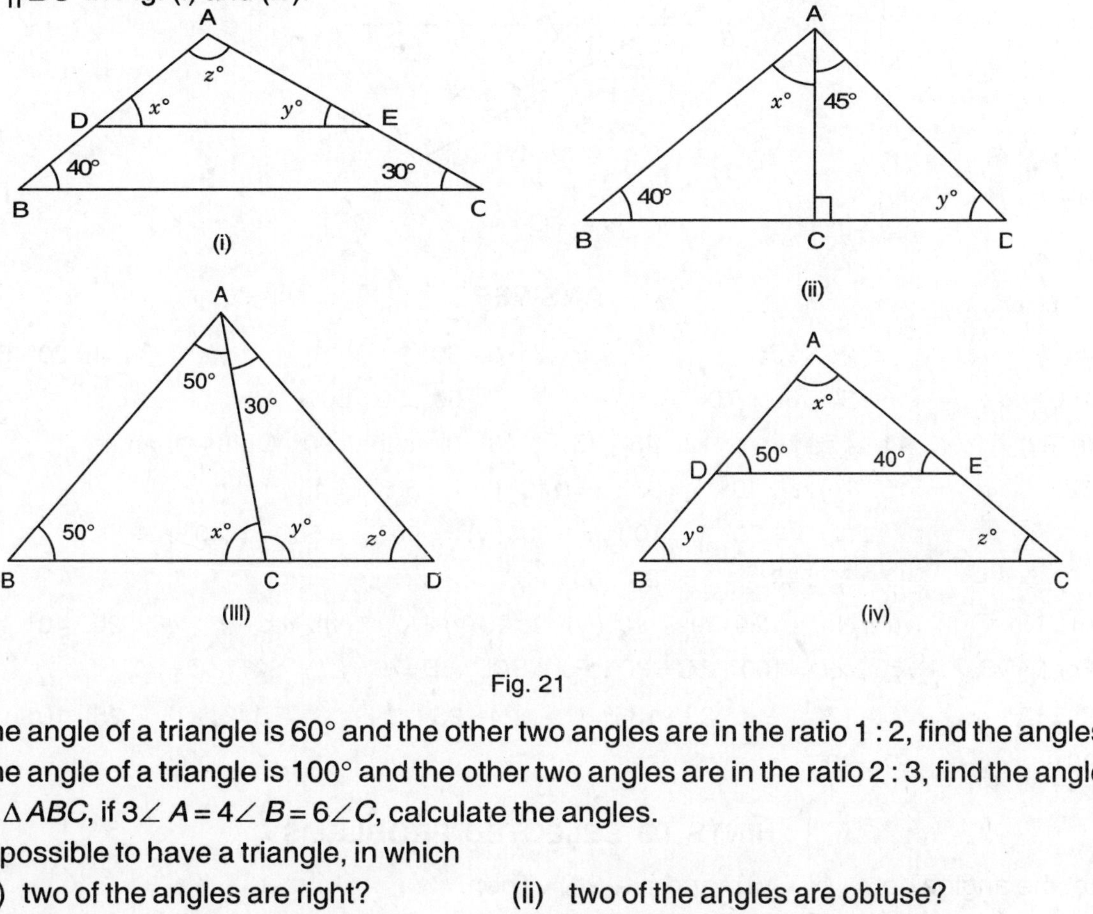

Fig. 21

16. If one angle of a triangle is 60° and the other two angles are in the ratio 1 : 2, find the angles.
17. If one angle of a triangle is 100° and the other two angles are in the ratio 2 : 3, find the angles.
18. In a ΔABC, if $3\angle A = 4\angle B = 6\angle C$, calculate the angles.
19. Is it possible to have a triangle, in which
    (i) two of the angles are right?
    (ii) two of the angles are obtuse?
    (iii) two of the angles are acute?
    (iv) each angle is less than 60°?
    (v) each angle is greater than 60°?
    (vi) each angle is equal to 60°?

    Give reasons in support of your answer in each case.
20. In ΔABC, $\angle A = 100°$, AD bisects $\angle A$ and $AD \perp BC$. Find $\angle B$.
21. In ΔABC, $\angle A = 50°$, $\angle B = 70°$ and bisector of $\angle C$ meets AB in D. Find the angles of the triangles ADC and BDC.
22. In ΔABC, $\angle A = 60°$, $\angle B = 80°$ and the bisectors of $\angle B$ and $\angle C$ meet at O. Find (i) $\angle C$ (ii) $\angle BOC$.

23. The bisectors of the acute angles of a right triangle meet at O. Find the angle at O between the two bisectors
24. In ΔABC, $\angle A = 50°$ and BC is produced to a point D. The bisectors of $\angle ABC$ and $\angle ACD$ meet at E. Find $\angle E$.
25. In ΔABC, $\angle B = 60°$, $\angle C = 40°$, $AL \perp BC$ and AD bisects $\angle A$ such that L and D lie on side BC. Find $\angle LAD$.
26. Line segments AB and CD intersect at O such that $AC \parallel DB$. If $\angle CAB = 35°$ and $\angle CDB = 55°$, find $\angle BOD$.
27. In Fig. 22, ΔABC is right angled at A. Q and R are points on line BC and P is a point such that $QP \parallel AC$ and $RP \parallel AB$. Find $\angle P$.

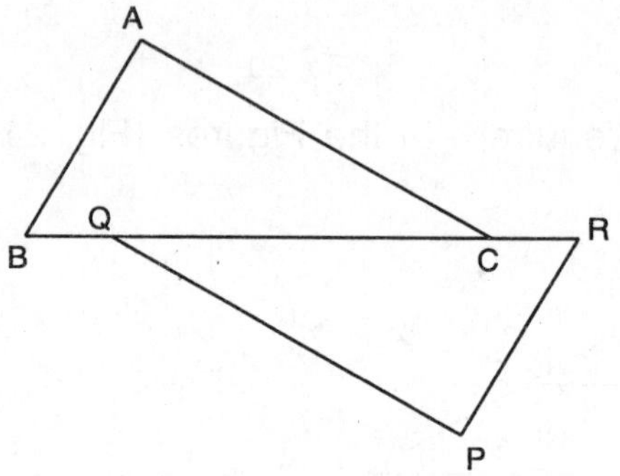

Fig. 22

ANSWERS

1. 45° 2. 25°, 25° 3. 60° 4. 30°, 60°, 90°
5. 100° 6. 50°, 60°, 70° 7. 50°, 50°, 80°
10. (i), (iv) 11. 45° 12. 45°, 45° 13. More than 90°, Obtuse triangle
14. 720° 15. (i) $x = 40°, y = 30°, z = 110°$ (ii) $x = 50°, y = 45°$
(iii) $x = 80°, y = 100°, z = 50°$ (iv) $x = 90°, y = 50°, z = 40°$
16. 40°, 80° 17. 32°, 48° 18. 80°, 60°, 40°
19. (i) No (ii) No (iii) Yes (iv) No (v) No (vi) Yes 20. 40°
21. For ΔADC, $\angle A = 50°$, $\angle D = 100°$, $\angle C = 30°$, For ΔBDC, $\angle B = 70°$, $\angle D = 80°$, $\angle C = 30°$
22. (i) 40° (ii) 120° 23. 135° 24. 25° 25. 10°
26. 90° 27. 90°

HINTS TO SELECTED PROBLEMS

6. Let the angles be $x°$, $(x + 10)°$ and $(x + 20)°$. Then,
$x + (x + 10) + (x + 20) = 180° \Rightarrow 3x + 30 = 180 \Rightarrow 3x = 150 \Rightarrow x = 50.$
So, the angles are 50°, 60° and 70°.
7. Let the angles be $x°$, $x°$ and $x + 30°$. Then,
$x + x + (x + 30) = 180 \Rightarrow 3x + 30 = 180 \Rightarrow x = 50.$
8. Let ABC be a triangle such that $\angle A = \angle B + \angle C$. Then,
$\angle A + \angle B + \angle C = 180° \Rightarrow \angle A + \angle A = 180° \Rightarrow \angle A = 90°$

9. Let $\angle A < \angle B + \angle C$. Then $2\angle A < \angle A + \angle B + \angle C$

$\Rightarrow \quad 2\angle A < 180° \quad \Rightarrow \quad \angle A < 90°$.

Similarly, $\angle B < 90°$ and $\angle C < 90°$.

15.6 EXTERIOR AND INTERIOR OPPOSITE ANGLES OF A TRIANGLE

EXTERIOR ANGLE *If the side BC of a triangle ABC is produced to form ray BX, then $\angle ACX$ is called an exterior angle of ΔABC at C.*

INTERIOR OPPOSITE ANGLES *With respect to exterior angle $\angle ACX$ of ΔABC at C, the angles $\angle BAC$ and $\angle ABC$ are called interior opposite angles or remote interior angles.*

INTERIOR ADJACENT ANGLES *With respect to exterior $\angle ACX$ of ΔABC at C, $\angle ACB$ is called interior adjacent angle.*

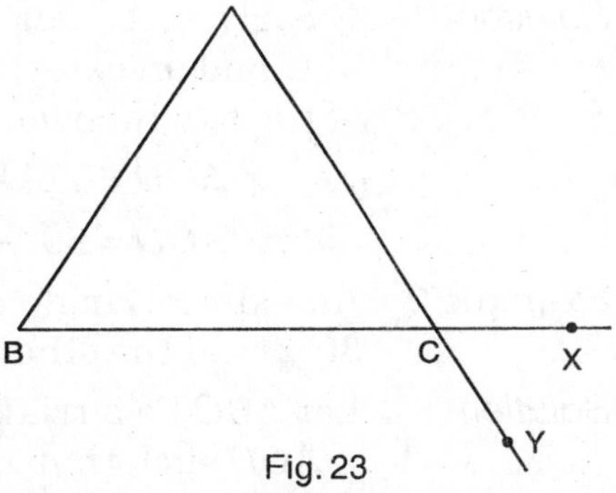

Fig. 23

If we produce side AC to form ray AY, then $\angle BCY$ is also an exterior angle of ΔABC at C. Clearly, $\angle ACX$ and $\angle BCY$ are vertically opposite angles.

$\therefore \quad \angle ACX = \angle BCY$.

Thus, at each vertex of a triangle, we have a pair of exterior angles of the triangle which are equal to each other.

With respect to exterior $\angle BCY$ of ΔABC at C, $\angle ACB$ is the interior adjacent angle and $\angle A$ and $\angle B$ are the two interior opposite angles, same as for exterior $\angle ACX$.

An exterior angle of a triangle is closely related to the interior opposite angles as given below:

THEOREM *(Exterior Angle Property of a Triangle): If a side of a triangle is produced, the exterior angle so formed is equal to the sum of two interior opposite angles.*

Proof Let ABC be a triangle such that its side BC is produced to form ray BX. Then, $\angle ACX = \angle 4$ is the exterior angle of ΔABC at C and $\angle 1$ and $\angle 2$ are two interior opposite angles.

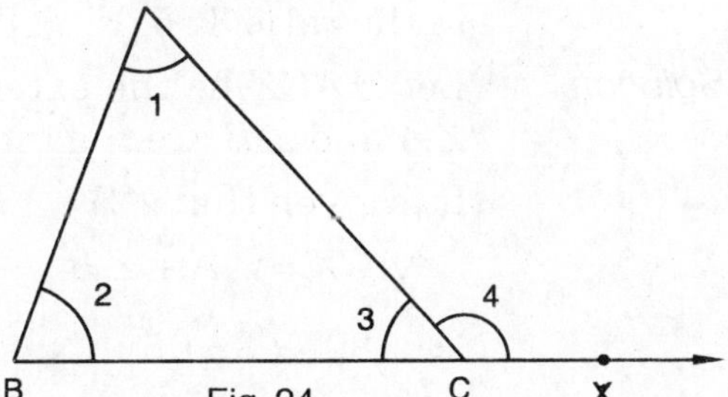

Fig. 24

We have to prove that

$\angle 4 = \angle 1 + \angle 2$

The sum of the angles of a triangle is 180°.

$\therefore \quad \angle 1 + \angle 2 + \angle 3 = 180° \qquad ...(i)$

Also, $\quad \angle 3 + \angle 4 = 180° \qquad ...(ii)$

[$\because$ <3 and <4 form a linear pair]

From (i) and (ii), we get

$\angle 1 + \angle 2 + \angle 3 = \angle 3 + \angle 4$

$\Rightarrow \quad \angle 1 + \angle 2 = \angle 4$ [Subtracting $\angle 3$ from both sides]

Hence, $\angle 4 = \angle 1 + \angle 2$.

<u>An Important Result:</u> *In Fig. 24, we have*

$\angle ACX = \angle A + \angle B \quad \Rightarrow \quad \angle ACX > \angle A$ *and* $\angle ACX > \angle B$.

Thus, in a triangle an exterior angle is greater than either of the interior opposite angles.

Remark *An exterior angle and the interior adjacent angle form a linear pair.*

Let us now discuss some problems to discuss the applications of the above property. Following examples will illustrate the same.

ILLUSTRATIVE EXAMPLES

Example 1 In Fig. 25, two of the angles are indicated. What is the measure of $\angle ACD$?

Solution Clearly, $\angle ACD$ is the exterior angle of ΔABC at C and an exterior angle is equal to the sum of the two interior opposite angles.

$\therefore \quad \angle ACD = \angle A + \angle B$

$\Rightarrow \quad \angle ACD = 60° + 70° = 130°$

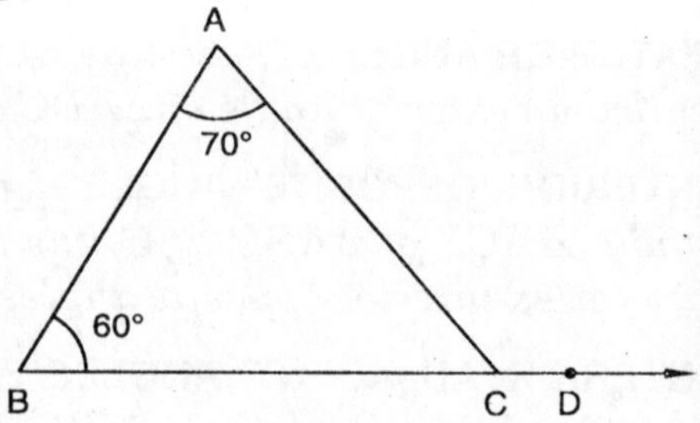

Fig. 25

Example 2 An exterior angle of a triangle is 110°, and one of the interior opposite angles is 30°. Find the other two angles of the triangle.

Solution Let ABC be a triangle whose side BC is produced to D to form an exterior angle $\angle ACD$ such that $\angle ACD = 110°$. (Fig. 26).

Let $\angle B = 30°$. By exterior angle theorem, we have

$\angle ACD = \angle B + \angle A$

$\Rightarrow \quad 110° = 30° + \angle A$

$\Rightarrow \quad \angle A = 110° - 30° = 80°$

Now, $\angle A + \angle B + \angle C = 180°$

$\Rightarrow \quad 80° + 30° + \angle C = 180°$

$\Rightarrow \quad \angle C = 180° - (80° + 30°) = 70°$

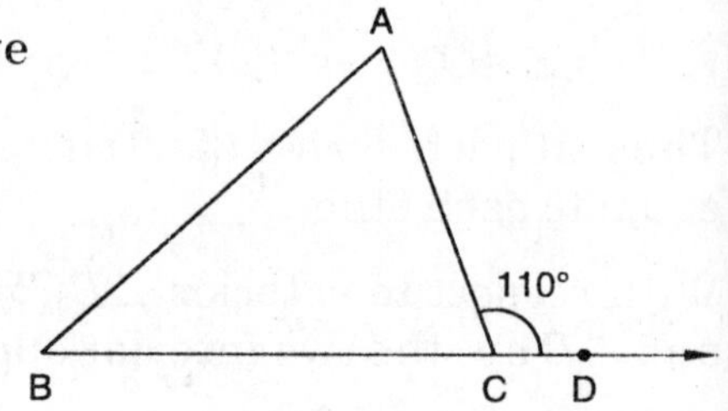

Fig. 26

Hence, the other two angles of the triangle are 80° and 70°.

Example 3 One of the exterior angles of a triangle is 80° and the interior opposite angles are in the ratio 3 : 5. Find the angles of the triangle.

Solution Let $\angle ACX$ be the exterior angle of ΔABC at C such that $\angle ACX = 80°$. Clearly, $\angle A$ and $\angle B$ are the interior opposite angles (Fig. 27).

It is given that $\angle A : \angle B = 3 : 5$. So, let $\angle A = 3x°$ and $\angle B = 5x°$.

$\angle ACX = \angle A + \angle B$

$\Rightarrow \quad 80° = 3x + 5x$ [By exterior angle property]

$\Rightarrow \quad 8x = 80°$

$\Rightarrow \quad \frac{8x}{8} = \frac{80°}{8}$ [Dividing both sides by 8]

$\Rightarrow \quad x = 10°$

$\therefore \quad \angle A = 3x° = 30°$ and $\angle B = 5x° = 50°$

Now, $\angle A + \angle B + \angle C = 180°$

$\Rightarrow \quad 30° + 50° + \angle C = 180°$

$\Rightarrow \quad 80° + \angle C = 180°$

$\Rightarrow \quad \angle C = 180° - 80° = 100°$

Hence, $\angle A = 30°$, $\angle B = 50°$ and $\angle C = 100°$.

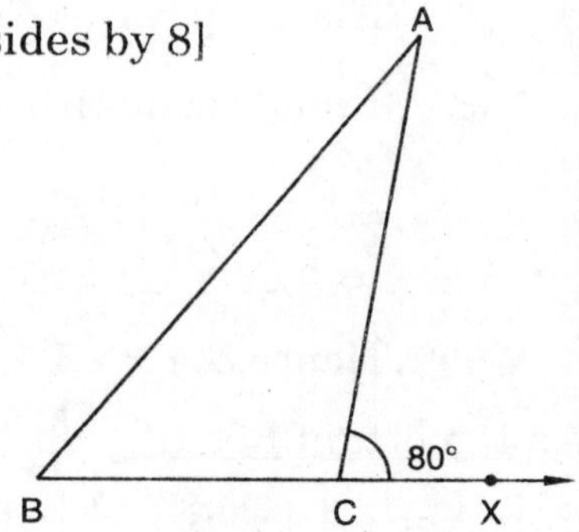

Fig. 27

Example 4 In Fig. 28, the measures of some of the angles are indicated. Find the values of $x°$ and $y°$.

Solution In ΔABC, exterior $\angle CBX$ at B and adjacent interior $\angle CBA$ form a linear pair.

$\therefore \quad \angle CBX + \angle CBA = 180°$

$\Rightarrow \quad 70° + y° = 180°$

$\Rightarrow \quad y° = 180° - 70° = 110°$

$\therefore \quad y° = 110°$

Again, $\angle BCY$ is exterior of ΔABC at C, and $\angle CAB$ and $\angle CBA$ are interior opposite angles.

$\therefore \quad \angle BCY = \angle CAB + \angle CBA$

$\Rightarrow \quad x° = 40° + y°$

$\Rightarrow \quad x° = 40° + 110° \qquad [\because y° = 110°]$

$\Rightarrow \quad x° = 150°$

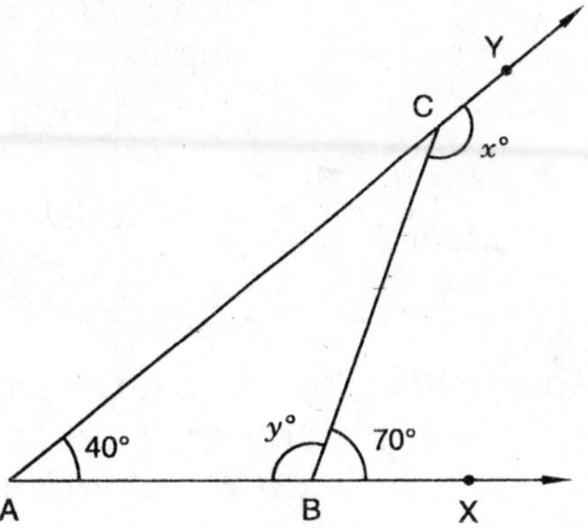

Fig. 28

Hence, we have $x° = 150°$ and $y° = 110°$.

Example 5 In Fig. 29, find $\angle ABD$. Also, if $\angle C = 3\angle ABC$, find $\angle ABC$.

Solution In ΔABD, exterior $\angle BAC$ at A and adjacent interior $\angle BAD$ form a linear pair.

$\therefore \quad \angle BAD + \angle BAC = 180°$

$\Rightarrow \quad \angle BAD + 100° = 180°$

$\Rightarrow \quad \angle BAD = 180° - 100°$

$\Rightarrow \quad \angle BAD = 80°$

In ΔABD, the sum of the angles is 180°.

$\therefore \quad \angle ABD + \angle BAD + \angle ADB = 180°$

$\Rightarrow \quad \angle ABD + 80° + 70° = 180°$

$\Rightarrow \quad \angle ABD + 150° = 180°$

$\Rightarrow \quad \angle ABD = 180° - 150°$

$\Rightarrow \quad \angle ABD = 30°$

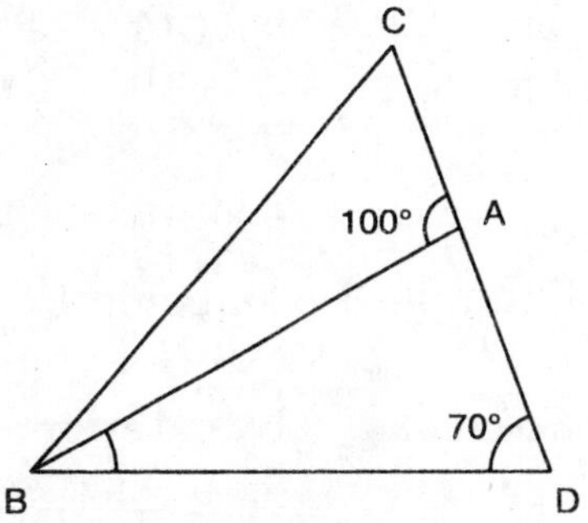

Fig. 29

Again, in ΔABC, we have

$\angle ABC + \angle C + \angle BAC = 180°$

$\Rightarrow \quad \angle ABC + 3\angle ABC + 100° = 180° \qquad [\because C = 3\angle ABC \text{ (Given)}]$

$\Rightarrow \quad 4\angle ABC + 100° = 180°$

$\Rightarrow \quad 4\angle ABC = 180° - 100°$

$\Rightarrow \quad 4\angle ABC = 80°$

$\Rightarrow \quad \angle ABC = \frac{80°}{4} = 20°$

Example 6 In Fig. 30, find: (i) $\angle ACD$ (ii) $\angle AED$

Solution (i) In ΔABC, $\angle ACD$ is the exterior angle at C and $\angle CBA$ and $\angle CAB$ are interior opposite angles.

$\therefore \quad \angle ACD = \angle CBA + \angle CAB$

$\Rightarrow \angle ACD = 40° + 15°$

$\Rightarrow \angle ACD = 55°.$

(ii) In ΔCDE, $\angle AED$ is the exterior angle at E and $\angle ECD$ and $\angle CDE$ are interior opposite angles.

$\therefore \angle AED = \angle ECD + \angle CDE$

$\Rightarrow \angle AED = \angle ACD + \angle CDE$ $[\because \angle ECD = \angle ACD]$

$\Rightarrow \angle AED = 55° + 52° = 107°$

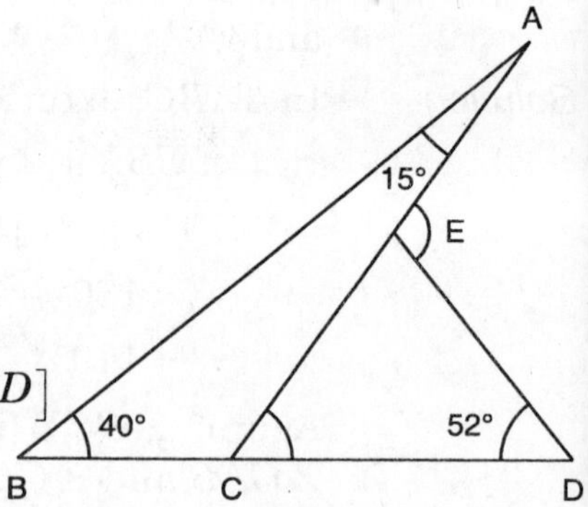

Fig. 30

Example 7 In Fig. 31, the sides BC, CA and AB of a ΔABC, are produced in order, forming exterior angles $\angle ACD$, $\angle BAE$ and $\angle CBF$. Show that $\angle ACD + \angle BAE + \angle CBF = 360°$

Solution By using exterior angle theorem, we have

$\angle ACD = \angle 1 + \angle 2$, $\angle BAE = \angle 2 + \angle 3$,

and, $\angle CBF = \angle 1 + \angle 3$.

Adding these, we get

$\angle ACD + \angle BAE + \angle CBF$

$= (\angle 1 + \angle 2) + (\angle 2 + \angle 3) + (\angle 1 + \angle 3)$

$= 2(\angle 1 + \angle 2 + \angle 3)$

$= 2 \times 180°$ $[\because \angle 1 + \angle 2 + \angle 3 = 180°]$

$= 360°$

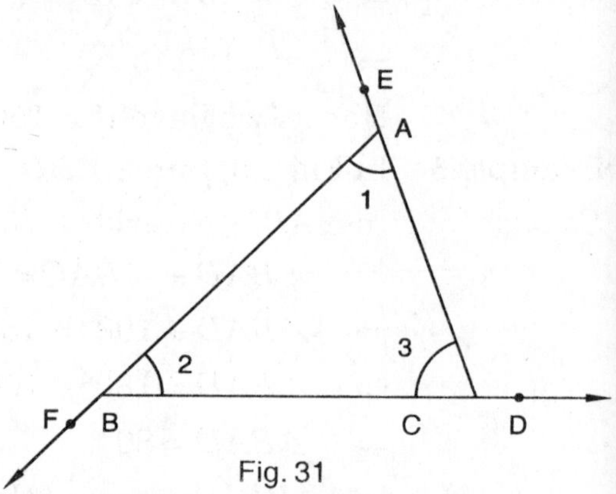

Fig. 31

Example 8 The side BC of a ΔABC is produced on both sides. Show that the sum of the exterior angles so formed is greater than $\angle A$ by two right angles (Fig. 32).

Solution By exterior angle theorem, we have

$\angle 4 = \angle 1 + \angle 3$ and, $\angle 5 = \angle 1 + \angle 2$

Adding these two, we get

$\angle 4 + \angle 5 = (\angle 1 + \angle 3) + (\angle 1 + \angle 2)$

$\Rightarrow \angle 4 + \angle 5 = \angle 1 + (\angle 1 + \angle 2 + \angle 3)$

$\Rightarrow \angle 4 + \angle 5 = \angle 1 + 180°$ $[\because \angle 1 + \angle 2 + \angle 3 = 180°]$

$\Rightarrow \angle 4 + \angle 5 = \angle A + 2 \times 90°$

$\Rightarrow \angle 4 + \angle 5 - \angle A = 2 \times 90°$

$\Rightarrow \angle 4 + \angle 5$ exceeds $\angle A$ by two right angles.

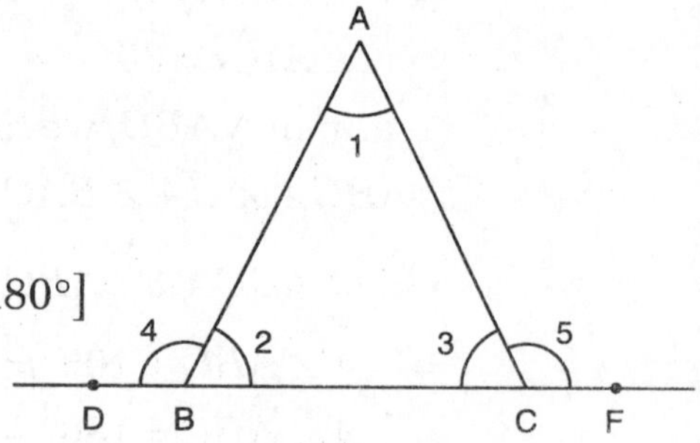

Fig. 32

Example 9 Sides BC, CA and BA of a triangle ABC are produced to D, Q, P respectively as shown in Fig.33. If $\angle ACD = 100°$ and $\angle QAP = 35°$, find all the angles of the triangle.

Solution Since $\angle QAP$ and $\angle BAC$ are vertically opposite angles.

$\therefore \angle BAC = \angle QAP$

$\Rightarrow \angle BAC = 35°$ $[\because \angle QAP = 35°]$

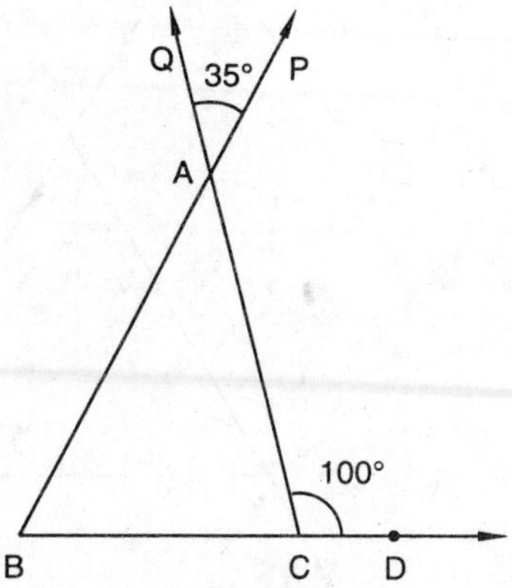

Fig. 33

By exterior angle theorem, we have

$\angle ACD = \angle BAC + \angle CBA$

$\Rightarrow \quad 100° = 35° + \angle CBA$

$\Rightarrow \quad \angle CBA = 100° - 35°$

$\Rightarrow \quad \angle CBA = 65°$

Since $\angle ACB$ and $\angle ACD$ form linear pairs.

$\therefore \quad \angle ACB + \angle ACD = 180°$

$\Rightarrow \quad \angle ACB + 100° = 180°$

$\Rightarrow \quad \angle ACB = 180° - 100° = 80°$

Hence, the angles of the ΔABC are $\angle A = 35°$, $B = 65°$ and $\angle C = 80°$.

Example 10 In Fig. 34, the side BC of ΔABC is produced to form ray BD. Ray CE is drawn parallel to BA. Show directly, without using the angle sum property of a triangle that $\angle ACD = \angle A + \angle B$ and deduce that $\angle A + \angle B + \angle C = 180°$.

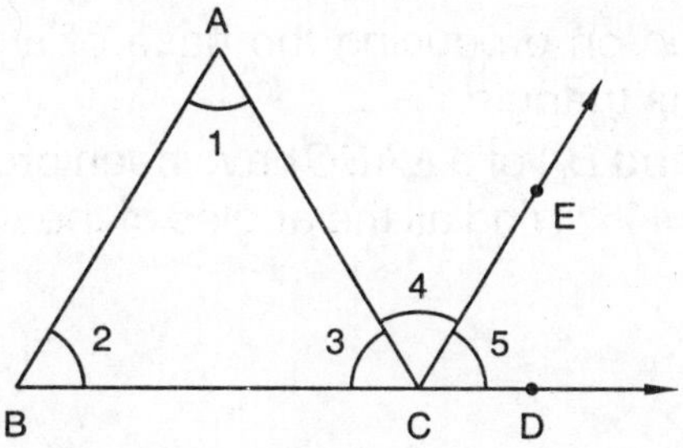

Fig. 34

Solution Since $AB \parallel CE$ and transversal AC cuts them at A and C respectively.

$\therefore \quad \angle 1 = \angle 4$ [Alternate interior angles] ...(i)

Again, $AB \parallel CE$ and transversal BD cuts them at B and C

$\therefore \quad \angle 2 = \angle 5$ [Corresponding angles] ...(ii)

Adding (i) and (ii), we get

$\angle 1 + \angle 2 = \angle 4 + \angle 5$

$\Rightarrow \quad \angle A + \angle B = \angle ACD$ $[\because \angle 4 + \angle 5 = \angle ACD]$

This proves the first part.

$\angle A + \angle B = \angle ACD$

$\Rightarrow \quad \angle A + \angle B + \angle C = \angle ACD + \angle C$ [Adding $\angle C$ on both sides]

$\Rightarrow \quad \angle A + \angle B + \angle C = 180°$ $\left[\begin{array}{l}\because \angle ACD \text{ and } \angle C \text{ form a linear pair} \\ \therefore \angle ACD + \angle C = 180°\end{array}\right]$

EXERCISE 15.3

1. In Fig. 35, $\angle CBX$ is an exterior angle of ΔABC at B. Name
   (i) the interior adjacent angle (ii) the interior opposite angles to exterior $\angle CBX$.
   Also, name the interior opposite angles to an exterior angle at A.

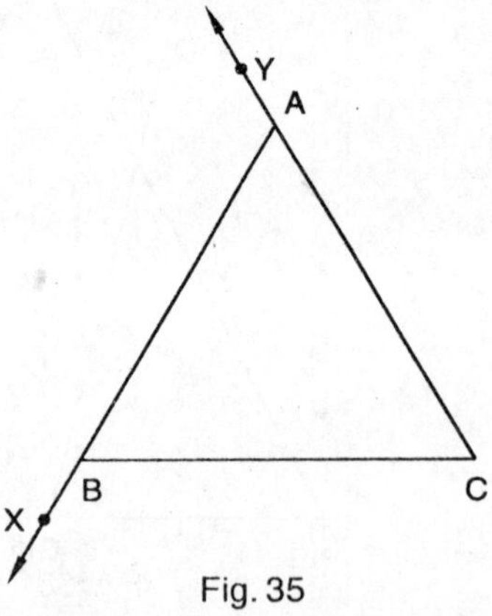

Fig. 35

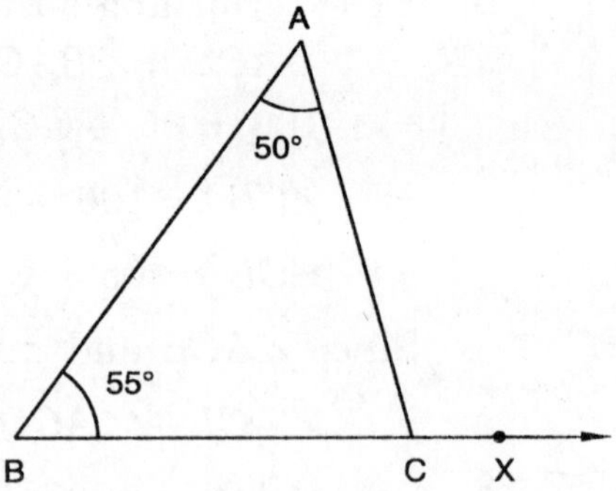

Fig. 36

2. In Fig. 36, two of the angles are indicated. What are the measures of $\angle ACX$ and $\angle ACB$?
3. In a triangle, an exterior angle at a vertex is 95° and its one of the interior opposite angles is 55°. Find all the angles of the triangle.
4. One of the exterior angles of a triangle is 80°, and the interior opposite angles are equal to each other. What is the measure of each of these two angles?
5. The exterior angles, obtained on producing the base of a triangle both ways are 104° and 136°. Find all the angles of the triangle.
6. In Fig. 37, the sides BC, CA and BA of a ΔABC have been produced to D, E and F respectively. If $\angle ACD = 105°$ and $\angle EAF = 45°$; find all the angles of the ΔABC.

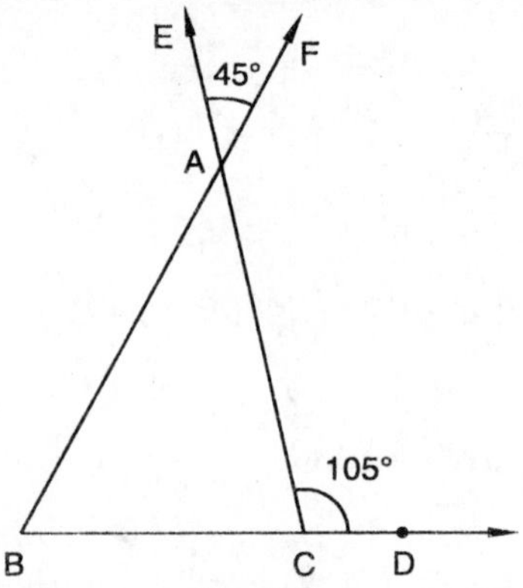

Fig. 37

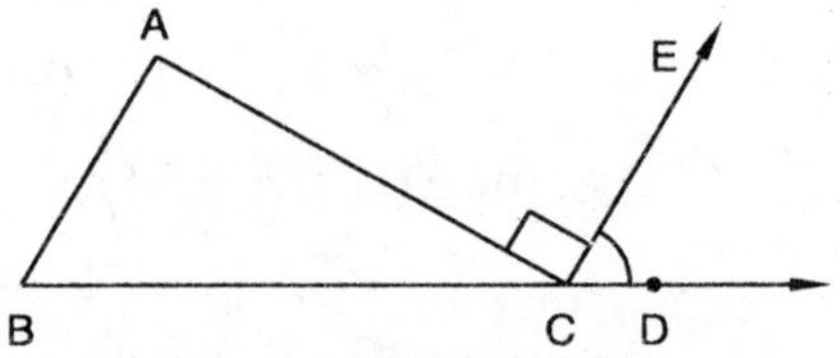

Fig. 38

7. In Fig. 38, $AC \perp CE$ and $\angle A : \angle B : \angle C = 3 : 2 : 1$, find the value of $\angle ECD$.
8. A student when asked to measure two exterior angles of ΔABC observed that the exterior angles at A and B are of 103° and 74° respectively. Is this possible? Why or why not?
9. In Fig. 39, AD and CF are respectively perpendiculars to sides BC and AB of ΔABC. If $\angle FCD = 50°$, find $\angle BAD$.

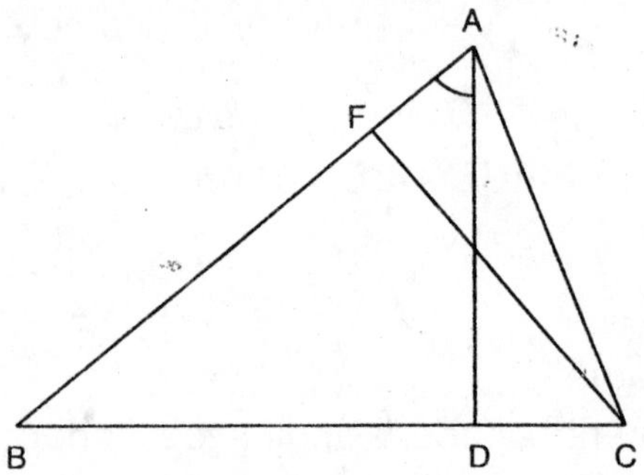

Fig. 39

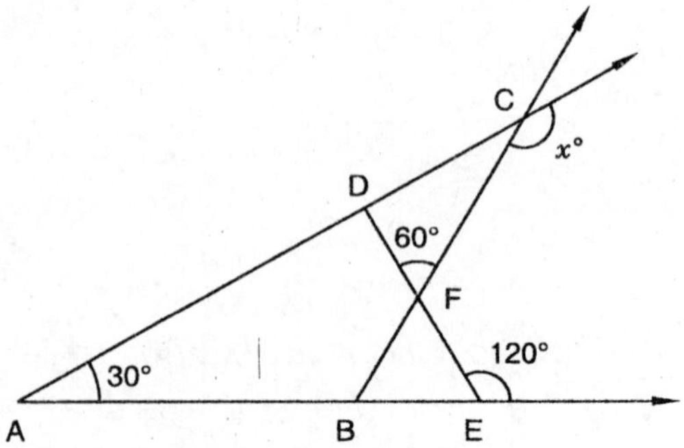

Fig. 40

10. In Fig. 40, measures of some angles are indicated. Find the value of x.

11. In Fig. 41, *ABC* is a right triangle right angled at *A*. *D* lies on *BA* produced and $DE \perp BC$, intersecting *AC* at *F*. If $\angle AFE = 130°$, find
    (i) $\angle BDE$ (ii) $\angle BCA$ (iii) $\angle ABC$

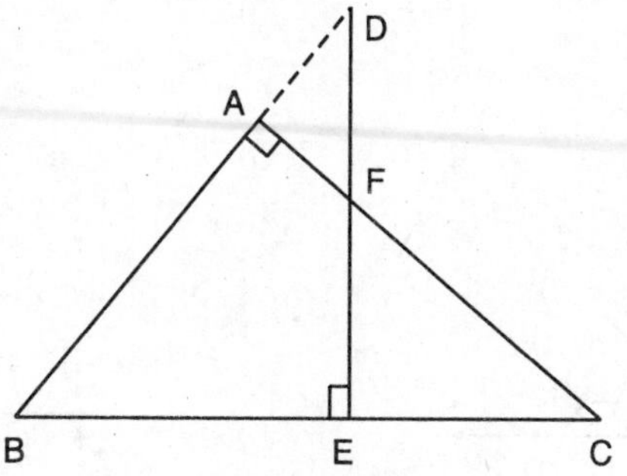

Fig. 41

12. *ABC* is a triangle in which $\angle B = \angle C$ and ray *AX* bisects the exterior angle *DAC*. If $\angle DAX = 70°$, find $\angle ACB$.
13. The side *BC* of ΔABC is produced to a point *D*. The bisector of $\angle A$ meets side *BC* in *L*. If $\angle ABC = 30°$ and $\angle ACD = 115°$, find $\angle ALC$.
14. *D* is a point on the side *BC* of ΔABC. A line *PDQ*, through *D*, meets side *AC* in *P* and *AB* produced at *Q*. If $\angle A = 80°$, $\angle ABC = 60°$ and $\angle PDC = 15°$, find (i) $\angle AQD$ (ii) $\angle APD$.
15. Explain the concept of interior and exterior angles and in each of the figures given below, find x and y (Fig. 42).

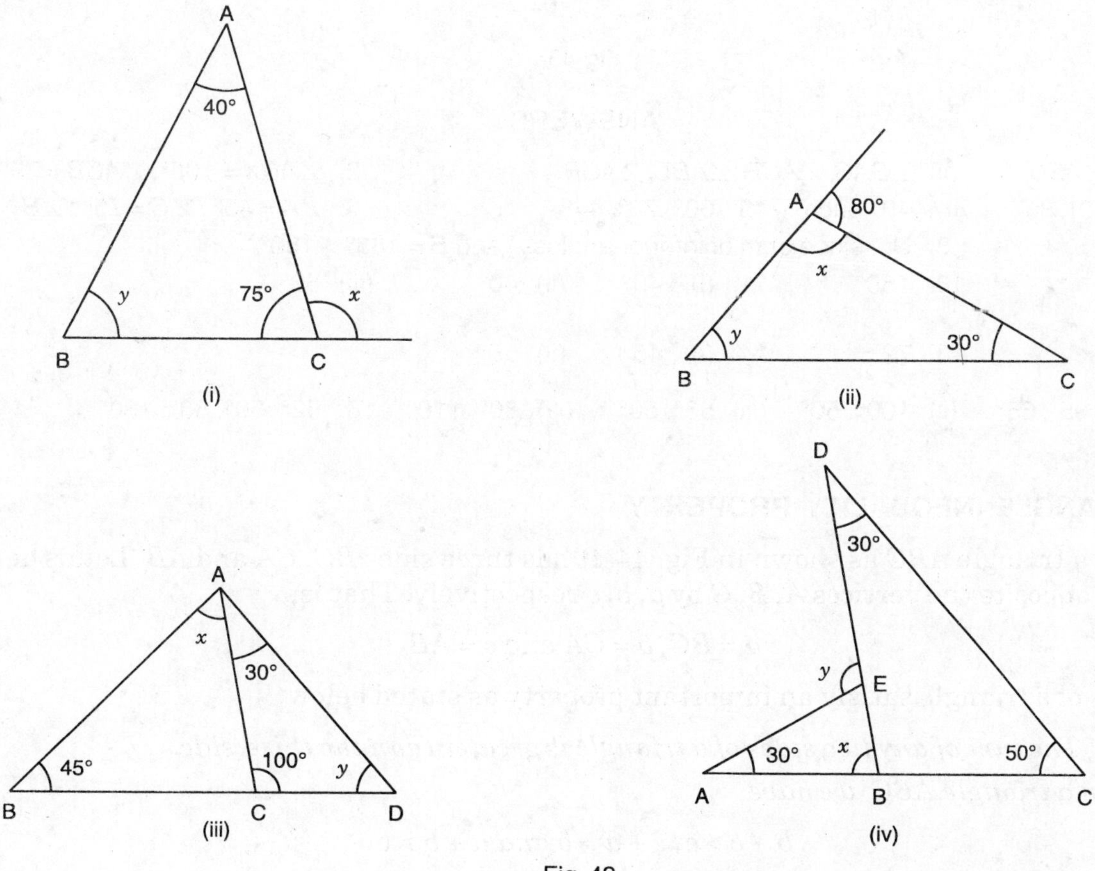

Fig. 42

16. Compute the value of x in each of the following figures:

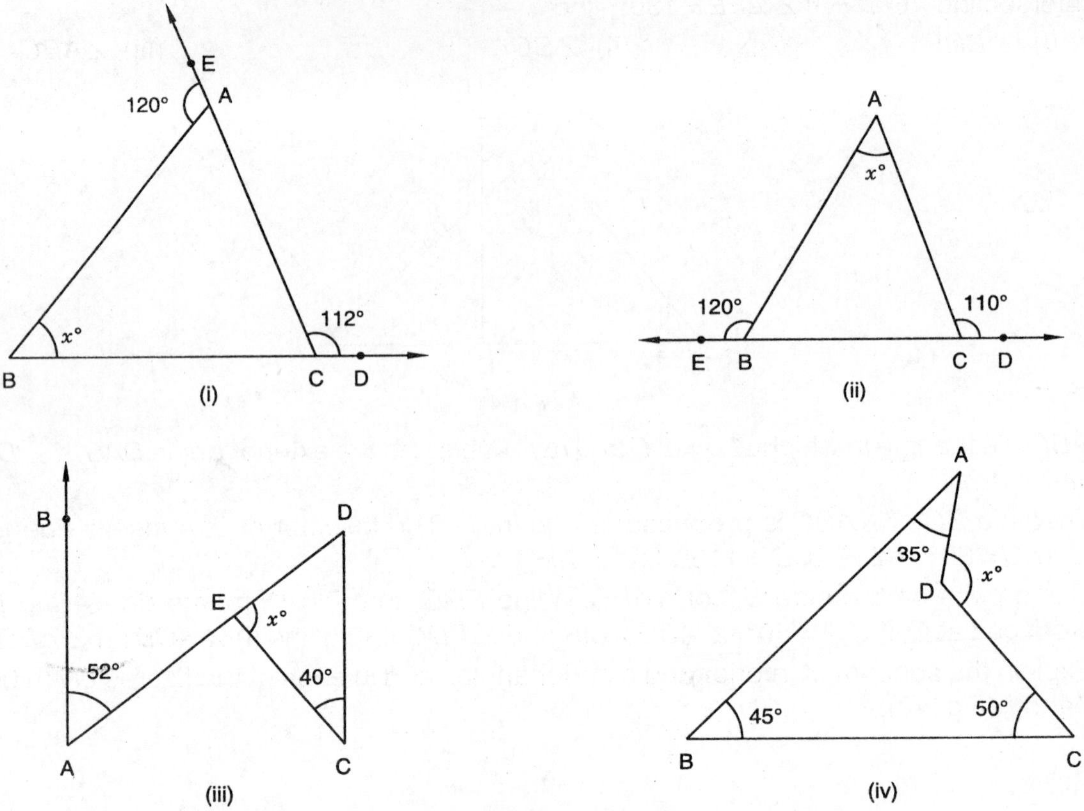

Fig. 43

ANSWERS

1. (i) $\angle ABC$ (ii) $\angle BAC, \angle ACB; \angle ABC, \angle ACB$
2. $\angle ACX = 105°$, $\angle ACB = 75°$
3. 55°, 40°, 85°
4. 40° each
5. 60°, 76°, 44°
6. $\angle A = 45°$; $\angle C = 75°$; $\angle B = 60°$
7. 60°
8. No, since sum of interior angles A and B = 183° > 180°
9. 50°
10. 150°
11. (i) 40° (ii) 40° (iii) 50°
12. 70°
13. $72\frac{1}{2}°$
14. (i) 45° (ii) 55°
15. (i) 105°, 65° (ii) 100°, 50° (iii) 55°, 50° (iv) 80°, 110°
16. 52°, 50°, 88°, 130°

15.7 TRIANGLE INEQUALITY PROPERTY

Consider a triangle ABC as shown in Fig. 44. It has three sides BC, CA and AB. Let us denote the sides opposite the vertices A, B, C by a, b, c respectively. That is,

$$a = BC, b = CA \text{ and } c = AB$$

The sides of a triangle satisfy an important property as stated below:

Property *The sum of any two sides of a triangle is greater than the third side.*

That is, in a triangle ABC, we have

$$b + c > a, c + a > b \text{ and } a + b > c$$

This important property of a triangle is known as Triangle inequality.

In order to verify the above property, let us perform the following experiment.

Experiment Draw any three triangles T_1, T_2 and T_3. Label each one as ΔABC. Measure, in each case, the three sides $a = BC$, $b = CA$ and $c = AB$.

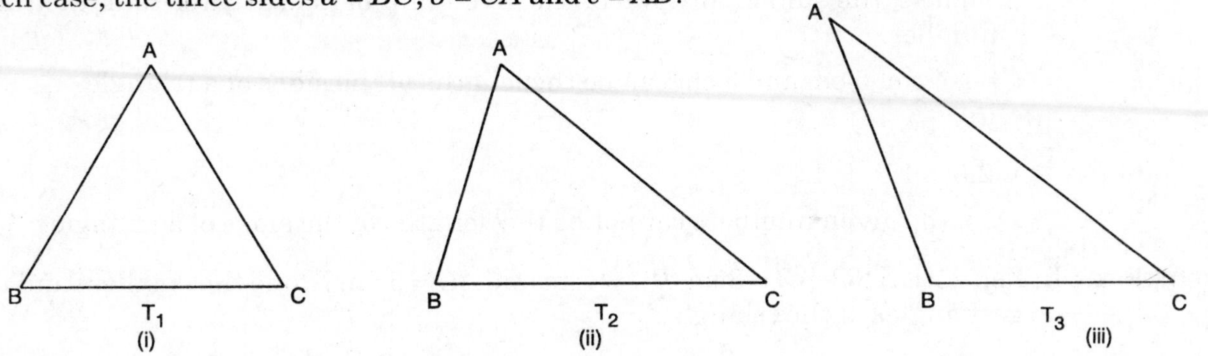

Fig. 44

Tabulate your observations as follows:

Triangle	Side of ΔABC			Computations					
	a	b	c	$b+c$	$b+c-a$	$c+a$	$c+a-b$	$a+b$	$a+b-c$
T_1									
T_2									
T_3									

From the above table you will find that:

(i) each value of $b + c - a$ is positive; (ii) each value of $c + a - b$ is positive ;

(iii) each value of $a + b - c$ is positive.

Now,

$$b + c - a \text{ is positive} \Rightarrow b + c - a > 0 \Rightarrow b + c > a$$

$$c + a - b \text{ is positive} \Rightarrow c + a - b > 0 \Rightarrow c + a > b$$

$$a + b - c \text{ is positive} \Rightarrow a + b - c > 0 \Rightarrow a + b > c$$

Thus, we have verified the following geometrical truth:

The sum of any two sides of a triangle is greater than the third side.

Remark 1 *From the above discussion, we find that three line segments whose lengths are equal to three given numbers, form the sides of a triangle if the sum of the lengths of every pair of two of these is greater than the length of the third.*

Remark 2 *In a triangle, the angle opposite the largest side is the largest.*

ILLUSTRATIVE EXAMPLES

Example 1 In each of the following there are three positive numbers. State if these numbers could possibly be the lengths of the sides of a triangle:

(i) 2, 3, 4 (ii) 4, 5, 3 (iii) 2.5, 1.5, 4

Solution (i) We have,

$2 + 3 > 4$, $2 + 4 > 3$ and $3 + 4 > 2$

That is, the sum of any two of the given numbers is greater than the third number.

So, 2 cm, 3 cm and 4 cm can be the lengths of the sides of a triangle.

(ii) We have,

$4 + 5 > 3, 4 + 3 > 5$ and $5 + 3 > 4$

That is, the sum of any two of the given numbers is greater than the third number.

So, 4 cm, 5 cm and 3 cm can be the lengths of the sides of a triangle.

(iii) We have,

$2.5 + 1.5 \not> 4$.

So, the given numbers cannot be the lengths of the sides of a triangle.

Example 2 In Fig. 45, $\Delta ABC, AB = 3$cm, $BC = 4$cm and $AC = 5$cm. Name the smallest and the largest angles of the triangle.

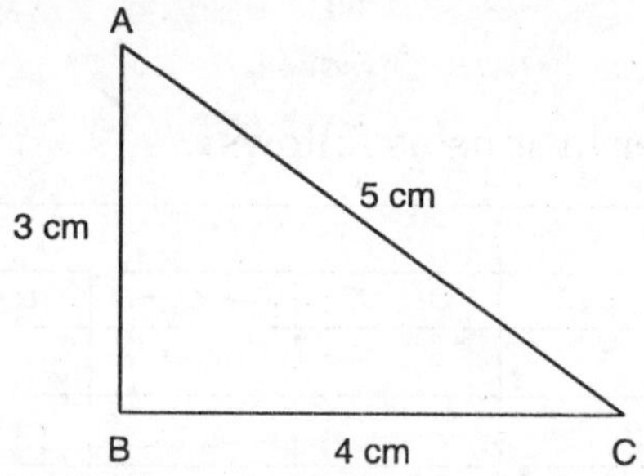

Fig. 45

Solution As the largest angle is always opposite to the largest side. Therefore, $\angle B$ is the largest angle and smallest angle is opposite to smallest side.

$\therefore$ $\angle C$ is the smallest angle.

EXERCISE 15.4

1. In each of the following, there are three positive numbers. State if these numbers could possibly be the lengths of the sides of a triangle:
   (i) 5, 7, 9 (ii) 2, 10, 15 (iii) 3, 4, 5 (iv) 2, 5, 7 (v) 5, 8, 20
2. In Fig. 46, *P* is the point on the side *BC*. Complete each of the following statements using symbol '=', '>' or '<' so as to make it true:

   (i) $AP ... AB + BP$ (ii) $AP .... AC + PC$ (iii) $AP .... \frac{1}{2}(AB + AC + BC)$

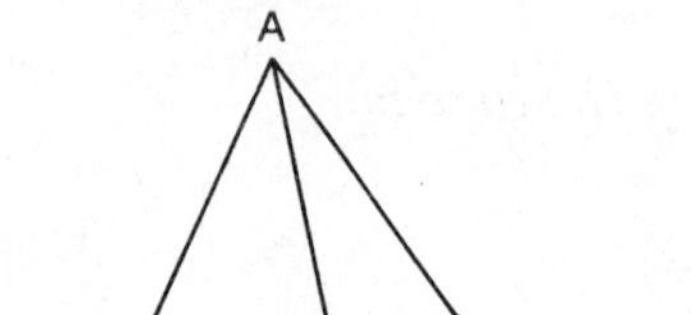

Fig. 46

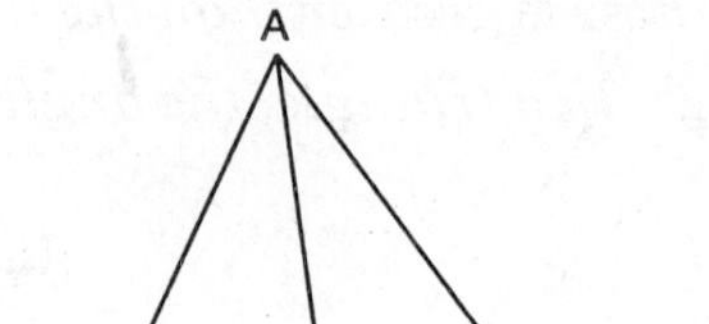

Fig. 47

3. *P* is a point in the interior of ΔABC as shown in Fig. 47. State which of the following statements are true (T) or false (F):
   (i) $AP + PB < AB$ (ii) $AP + PC > AC$ (iii) $BP + PC = BC$

4. O is a point in the exterior of ΔABC. What symbol '>', '<' or '=' will you use to complete the statement $OA + OB$ .. AB? Write two other similar statements and show that

$$OA + OB + OC > \frac{1}{2}(AB + BC + CA)$$

5. In ΔABC, $\angle A = 100°$, $\angle B = 30°$, $\angle C = 50°$. Name the smallest and the largest sides of the triangle.

ANSWERS

1. (i), (iii) 2. (i) < (ii) < (iii) < 3. (i) F (ii) T (iii) F 4. >
5. AC, BC

15.8 PYTHAGORAS THEOREM

Pythagoras, the famous Greek philosopher, was born in about 580 B.C. in Samos, Ionia and lied in about 520 B.C. in Metapontum, Lucania. He gave a wonderful relation between the engths of the sides of a right triangle which is generally known as Pythagoras theorem. Although this theorem was known to the Babylonians 1000 years earlier. But, Pythagoras is believed to have been the first to discover a proof of this theorem. And, for this reason, the theorem bears his name.

STATEMENT *In a right triangle, the square of the hypotenuse equals the sum of the squares of its remaining two sides.*

Thus, if ΔABC is a right triangle right angled at C, so that AB is the hypotenuse and, AC and BC are the sides of the right angle, then

$$(AB)^2 = (BC)^2 + (CA)^2$$

i.e., $(\text{Hypotenuse})^2 = (\text{Base})^2 + (\text{Perpendicular})^2$

or, $c^2 = a^2 + b^2$, where $a = BC$, $b = CA$ and $c = AB$.

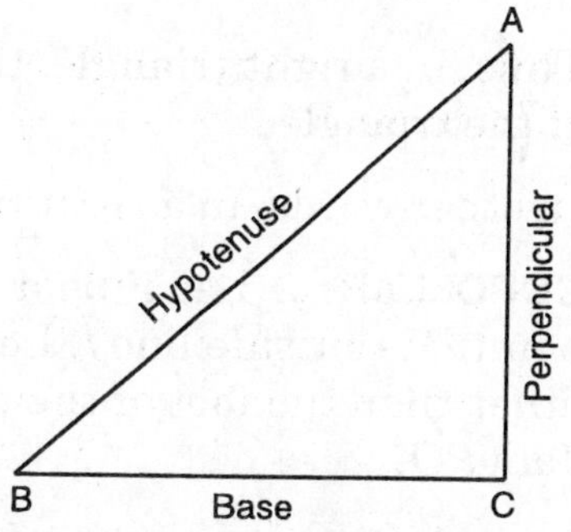

Fig. 48

Verification: In order to verify the above stated theorem, we may perform the following experiment.

Experiment Draw any three right triangles say T_1, T_2 and T_3. Label each as ΔABC with $\angle C$ as the right angle.

In each case, measure the sides a, b and the hypotenuse c of the triangle. Compute a^2, b^2 and c^2 and tabulate the results as follows:

Right Triangle	*Measurements*			*Square of a, b*			*Square of c*	*Difference* $c^2 - (a^2 + b^2)$
	a	b	c	a^2	b^2	$a^2 + b^2$	c^2	
T_1								
T_2								
T_3								

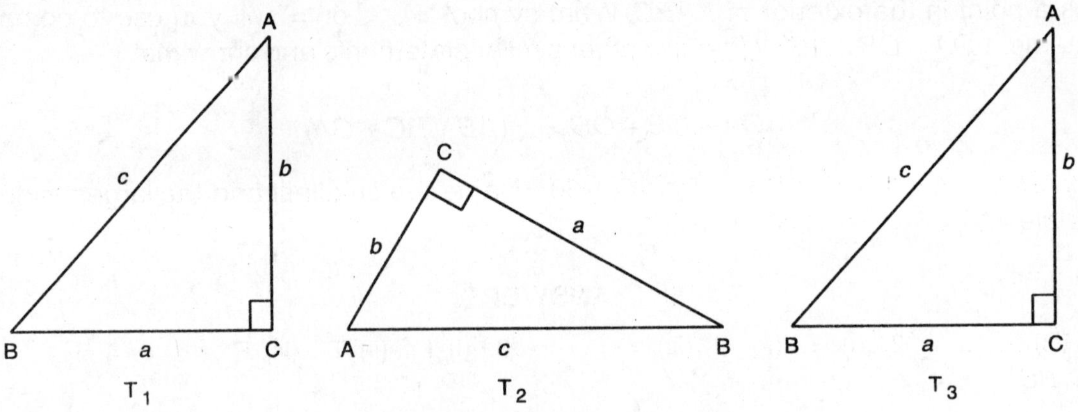

Fig. 49

You will observe that in each case the difference $c^2 - (a^2 + b^2)$ is 0.

$\therefore \quad c^2 = a^2 + b^2$

COROLLARY 1 If ΔABC is a right triangle right angled at C such that $AB = c$, $BC = a$ and $AC = b$, then by Pythagoras theorem, we have

$c^2 = a^2 + b^2$

$\Rightarrow \quad c^2 > a^2$ and $c^2 > b^2$

$\Rightarrow \quad c > a$ and $c > b$

Thus, in a right triangle, the hypotenuse is greater than each one of the remaining two sides of the triangle.

In other words, in a right triangle, the hypotenuse is the longest side.

COROLLARY 2 Let P be a point and l be a line such that the point P is outside line l. Let $PN \perp l$ and let Q be any point on l, other than the foot of the perpendicular drawn from P i.e., N. Join PQ.

Now, ΔPNQ is a right triangle, right-angled at N. So, PQ is the hypotenuse and PN is a side of this right triangle.

$\therefore \quad PN < PQ$ [Using Corrollary 1]

This is true for all points Q, other than N on line l. Hence, we conclude that:

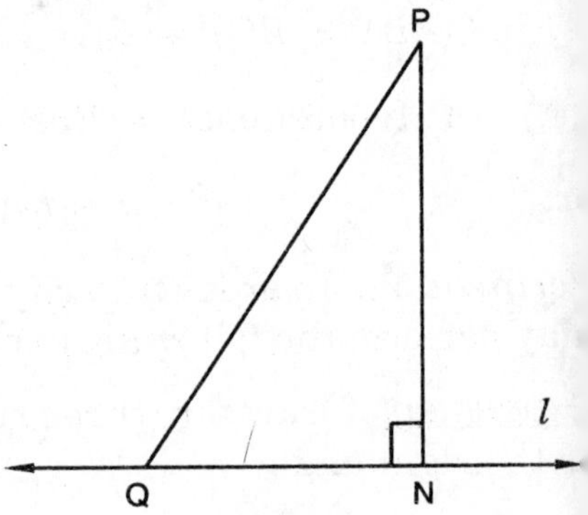

Fig. 50

Of all the line segments that can be drawn to a given line from a point not lying on it, the perpendicular line segment is the shortest.

15.8.1 CONVERSE OF PYTHAGORAS THEOREM

We have learnt that in a right triangle, the square of the hypotenuse is equal to the sum of the squares of the other two sides. Now, a natural question arises: if in a triangle the square of one side is equal to the sum of the squares of the remaining two sides, whether the triangle is a right triangle or not. The answer is in affirmative. In other words, the converse of the Pythagoras theorem is also true.

STATEMENT If the square of one side of a triangle is equal to the sum of the squares of the other two sides, then the triangle is a right triangle with the angle opposite the first side as right angle.

or

If in a ΔABC, we have

$$AB^2 = BC^2 + CA^2$$

then the triangle is a right triangle, right angled at C.

In order to verify the above statement, let us consider the following experiments.

Experiment

(i) Let $a = 3$ cm, $b = 4$ cm and $c = 5$ cm. Then,

$$3^2 + 4^2 = 25 = 5^2$$

$$\Rightarrow \quad a^2 + b^2 = c^2$$

Now, draw ΔABC such that $AB = 5$ cm, $BC = 3$ cm and $CA = 4$ cm and measure $\angle ACB$. You will find that $\angle ACB = 90°$.

$\therefore \quad \Delta ABC$ is a right triangle, right-angled at C.

(ii) Let $a = 12$ cm, $b = 5$ cm and $c = 13$ cm. Then,

$$12^2 + 5^2 = 169 = 13^2$$

$$\Rightarrow \quad a^2 + b^2 = c^2$$

Now, draw a ΔABC such that $BC = 12$ cm, $CA = 5$ cm and $AB = 13$ cm and measure $\angle ACB$.

You will find that $\angle ACB = 90°$. So, the triangle ABC is a right triangle, right-angled at C.

PYTHAGOREAN TRIPLETS *Three positive numbers a, b, c in this order, are said to form a Pythagorean triplet, if* $c^2 = a^2 + b^2$

For example, each one of the triplets (3, 4, 5), (5, 12, 13), (8, 15, 17), (7, 24, 25) and (12, 35, 37) is a pythagorean triplet.

ILLUSTRATIVE EXAMPLES

Example 1 The hypotenuse of a right triangle is 13 cm long. If one of the remaining two sides is of length 5 cm, find the length of another side.

Solution Let ABC be a right triangle, right angled at C

Let $AB = 13$ cm and $BC = 5$ cm.

Then, by Pythagoras theorem, we have

$$AB^2 = BC^2 + AC^2$$

$$\Rightarrow \quad 13^2 = 5^2 + AC^2$$

$$\Rightarrow \quad 169 = 25 + AC^2$$

$$\Rightarrow \quad AC^2 = 169 - 25$$

$$\Rightarrow \quad AC^2 = 144$$

$$\Rightarrow \quad AC = \sqrt{144} \text{ cm} = 12 \text{ cm}.$$

Hence, the length of another side is 12 cm.

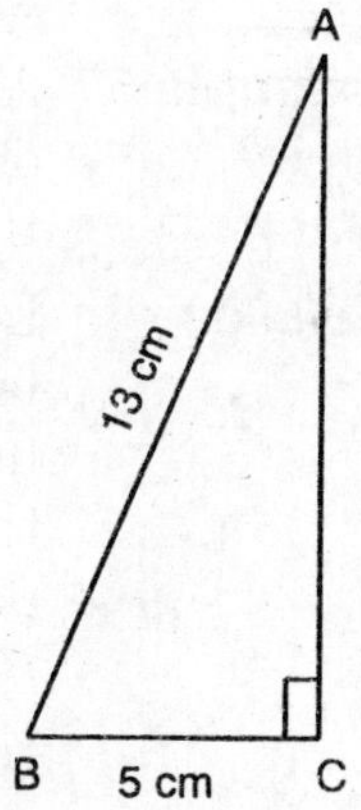

Fig. 51

Example 2 The sides of certain triangles are given below. Determine which of them are right triangles:

(i) $a = 6$ cm, $b = 8$ cm and $c = 10$ cm (ii) $a = 5$ cm, $b = 8$ cm and $c = 11$ cm.

Solution (i) Here the larger side is $c = 10$ cm.

We have: $a^2 + b^2 = 6^2 + 8^2 = 36 + 64 = 100 = c^2$.

So, the triangle with the given sides is a right triangle.

(ii) Here, the larger side is $c = 11$ cm.

Clearly, $a^2 + b^2 = 25 + 64 = 89 \neq c^2$.

So, the triangle with the given sides is not a right triangle.

Example 3 A ladder is placed in such a way that its foot is at a distance of 5 m from a wall and its top reaches a window 12 m above the ground. Determine the length of the ladder.

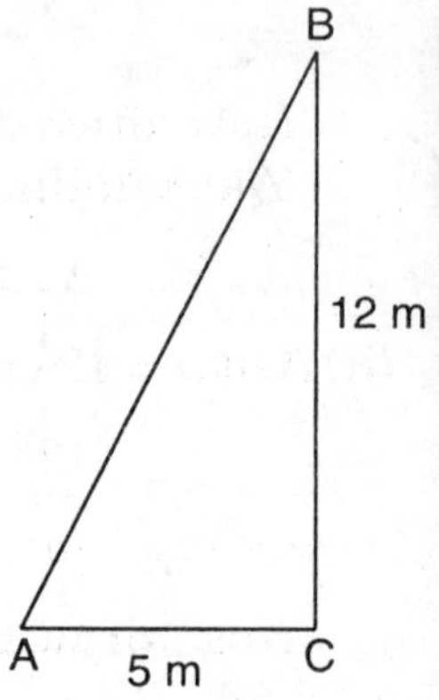

Fig. 52

Solution Let AB be the ladder and B be the window.

Then, $BC = 12$ m and $AC = 5$ m.

Since ΔABC is a right triangle, right-angled at C.

$\therefore \quad AB^2 = AC^2 + BC^2$

$\Rightarrow \quad AB^2 = 5^2 + 12^2 = 169$

$\Rightarrow \quad AB = \sqrt{169}\text{ m} = 13\text{ m}$

Hence, the length of the ladder is 13 m.

Example 4 A ladder 25 m long reaches a window of a building 20 m above the ground. Determine the distance of the foot of the ladder from the building.

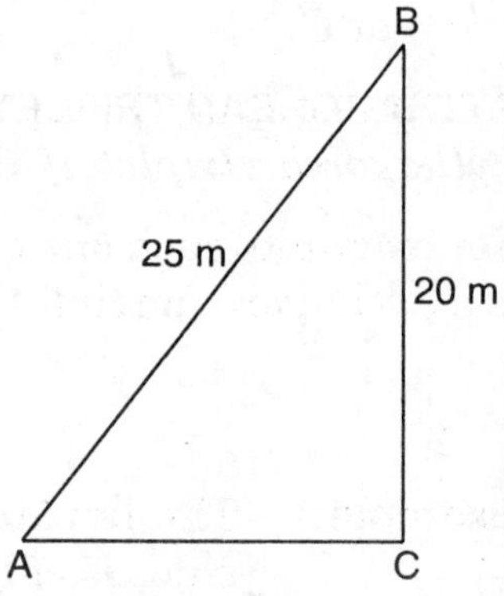

Fig. 53

Solution Suppose that AB is the ladder, B is the window and CB is the building. Then, triangle ABC is a right triangle, with right angle at C

$\therefore \quad AB^2 = AC^2 + BC^2$

$\Rightarrow \quad 25^2 = \text{AC}^2 + 20^2$

$\Rightarrow \quad AC^2 = 625 - 400 = 225$

$\Rightarrow \quad AC = \sqrt{225}\text{ m} = 15\text{ m}.$

Hence, the foot of the ladder is at a distance of 15 m from the building.

Example 5 A ladder 15 m long reaches a window which is 9 m above the ground on one side of a street. Keeping its foot at the same point, the ladder is turned to other side of the street to reach a window 12 m high. Find the width of the street.

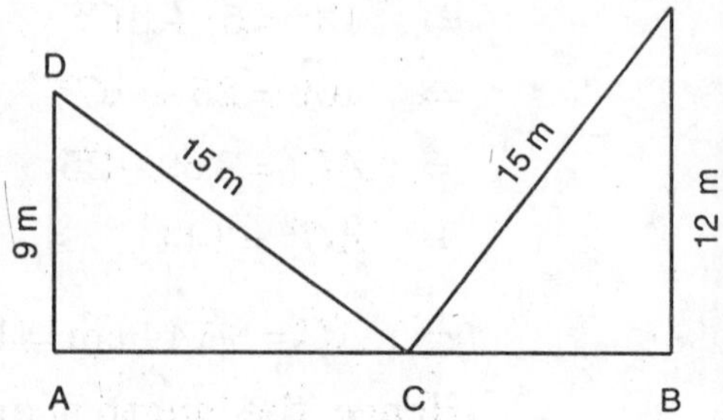

Fig. 54

Solution Let AB be the street and C be the foot of the ladder. Let D and E be the windows at heights of 9 m and 12 m respectively from the ground. Then, CD and CE are the two positions of the ladder. Clearly, $AD = 9$ m, $BE = 12$ m, $CD = CE = 15$ m.

In right ΔACD, right-angled at A we have

$$CD^2 = AC^2 + AD^2$$

$\Rightarrow \quad 15^2 = AC^2 + 9^2$

$\Rightarrow \quad AC^2 = 225 - 81 = 144$

$\Rightarrow \quad AC = \sqrt{144}\text{ m} = 12\text{ m}$

In right $\Delta\, BCE$, right angled at B, we have

$CE^2 = BC^2 + BE^2$

$\Rightarrow \quad 15^2 = BC^2 + 12^2$

$\Rightarrow \quad BC^2 = 225 - 144 = 81$

$\Rightarrow \quad BC = \sqrt{81}\text{ m} = 9\text{ m}$

Hence, width of the street $= AB = AC + CB = (12 + 9)\text{ m} = 21\text{ m}$.

Example 6 A man goes 10 m due east and then 24 m due north. Find the distance from the starting point.

Solution Let the initial position of the man be O and his final position be B. Since the man goes 10 m due east and then 24 m due north. Therefore, $\Delta\, OAB$ is a right triangle, right angled at A such that $OA = 10$ m and $AB = 24$ m.

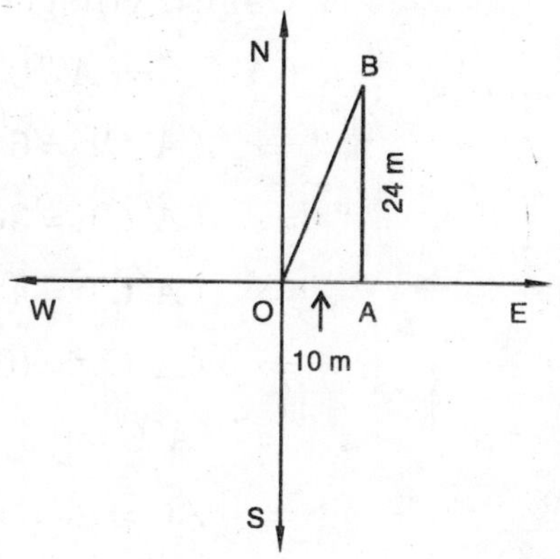

Fig. 55

By Pythagoras theorem, we have

$OB^2 = OA^2 + AB^2$

$\Rightarrow \quad OB^2 = 10^2 + 24^2$

$\Rightarrow \quad OB^2 = 100 + 576 = 676$

$\Rightarrow \quad OB = \sqrt{676}\text{ m} = 26\text{ m}.$

Hence, the man is at a distance of 26 m from the starting point.

Example 7 ABC is an isosceles right triangle, right-angled at C. Prove that: $AB^2 = 2AC^2$.

Solution Since $\Delta\, ABC$ is a right triangle, right-angled at C

$\therefore \quad AB^2 = AC^2 + BC^2$

$\Rightarrow \quad AB^2 = AC^2 + AC^2 \qquad [\because BC = AC]$

$\Rightarrow \quad AB^2 = 2AC^2.$

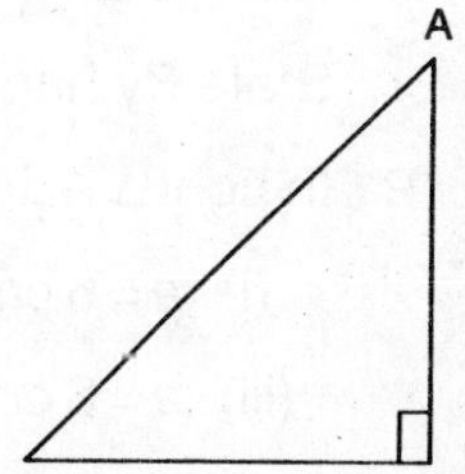

Fig. 56

Example 8 In a $\Delta ABC, AD \perp BC$ and $AD^2 = BD \times CD$. Prove that ΔABC is a right triangle.

Solution In right triangles ADB and ADC, we have

$AB^2 = AD^2 + BD^2 \qquad$ ...(i)

and, $AC^2 = AD^2 + DC^2 \qquad$ ...(ii)

Adding (i) and (ii), we get

$AB^2 + AC^2 = 2AD^2 + BD^2 + DC^2$

$AB^2 + AC^2 = 2BD \times CD + BD^2 + CD^2$

$[\because AD^2 = BD \times CD \text{ (given)}]$

$AB^2 + AC^2 = (BD + CD)^2 = BC^2$

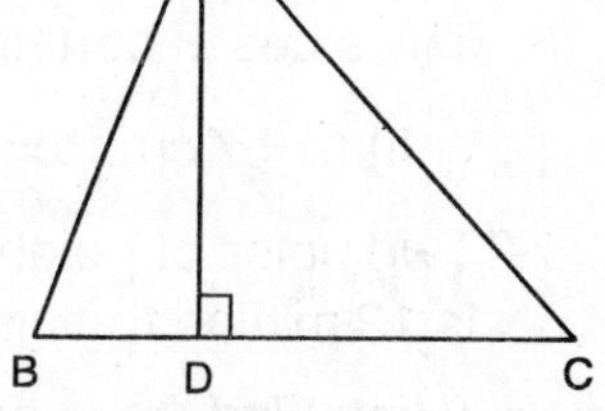

Fig. 57

Thus, in ΔABC, we have

$$AB^2 + AC^2 = BC^2.$$

Hence, ΔABC is a right triangle, right-angled at A.

Example 9 A tree broke at a point but did not separate. Its top touched the ground at a distance of 6 dm from its base. If the point where it broke be at a height 2.5 dm from the ground, what was the total height of the tree before it broke?

Solution Let ACB represent the tree before it broke at the point C, and let the top A touch the ground at A' after it broke. Then, $\Delta\ A'BC$ is a right triangle, right angled at B such that

$A'B = 6$ dm, $BC = 2.5$ dm

Using Pythagoras theorem in $\Delta\ A'BC$, we have

$(A'C)^2 = (A'B)^2 + (BC)^2$

$\Rightarrow\ (A'C)^2 = 6^2 + (2.5)^2$

$\Rightarrow\ (A'C)^2 = 36 + 6.25$

$\Rightarrow\ (A'C)^2 = 42.5$

$\Rightarrow\ (A'C)^2 = (6.5)^2$

$\Rightarrow\ A'C = 6.5$

$\Rightarrow\ AC = A'C = 6.5$ dm $\quad [\because AC = A'C]$

$\therefore\ AB = AC + BC = (6.5 + 2.5)$ dm $= 9$ dm

Hence, the height of the tree before it broke was 9 dm.

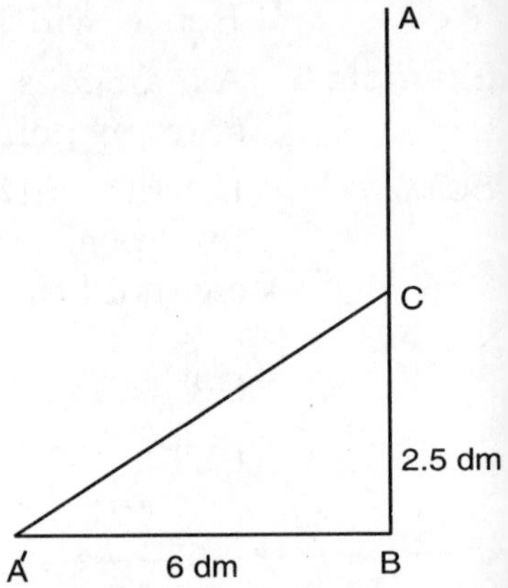

Fig. 58

EXERCISE 15.5

1. State Pythagoras theorem and its converse.
2. In right $\Delta\ ABC$, the lengths of the legs are given. Find the length of the hypotenuse.

   (i) $a = 6$ cm, $b = 8$ cm (ii) $a = 8$ cm, $b = 15$ cm

   (iii) $a = 3$ cm, $b = 4$ cm (iv) $a = 2$ cm, $b = 1.5$ cm
3. The hypotenuse of a triangle is 2.5 cm. If one of the sides is 1.5 cm, find the length of the other side.
4. A ladder 3.7 m long is placed against a wall in such a way that the foot of the ladder is 1.2 m away from the wall. Find the height of the wall to which the ladder reaches.
5. If the sides of a triangle are 3 cm, 4 cm and 6 cm long, determine whether the triangle is right–angled triangle.
6. The sides of certain triangles are given below. Determine which of them are right triangles.

   (i) $a = 7$ cm, $b = 24$ cm and $c = 25$ cm (ii) $a = 9$ cm, $b = 16$ cm and $c = 18$ cm
7. Two poles of heights 6 m and 11 m stand on a plane ground. If the distance between their feet is 12 m, find the distance between their tops.

   [Hint: Find the hypotenuse of a right triangle having the sides (11 – 6) m = 5 m and 12 m]
8. A man goes 15 m due west and then 8 m due north. How far is he from the starting point?

9. The foot of a ladder is 6 m away from a wall and its top reaches a window 8 m above the ground. If the ladder is shifted in such a way that its foot is 8 m away from the wall, to what height does its top reach?
10. A ladder 50 dm long when set against the wall of a house just reaches a window at a height of 48 dm. How far is the lower end of the ladder from the base of the wall?
11. The two legs of a right triangle are equal and the square of the hypotenuse is 50. Find the length of each leg.
12. Verify that the following numbers represent Pythagorean triplet:
    (i) 12 , 35 , 37 (ii) 7, 24, 25 (iii) 27, 36, 45 (iv) 15, 36, 39
13. In a ΔABC, $\angle ABC = 100°$, $\angle BAC = 35°$ and $BD \perp AC$ meets side AC in D. If $BD = 2$ cm, find $\angle C$ and length DC.
14. In a Δ ABC, AD is the altitude from A such that AD = 12 cm, BD = 9 cm and DC = 16 cm. Examine if ΔABC is right angled at A.
15. Draw a triangle ABC, with $AC = 4$ cm, $BC = 3$ cm and $\angle C = 105°$. Measure AB. Is $(AB)^2 = (AC)^2 + (BC)^2$? If not, which one of the following is true:
    $(AB)^2 > (AC)^2 + (BC)^2$ or $(AB)^2 < (AC)^2 + (BC)^2$?
16. Draw a triangle ABC, with $AC = 4$ cm, $BC = 3$ cm and $\angle C = 80°$. Measure AB. Is $(AB)^2 = (AC)^2 + (BC)^2$? If not, which one of the following is true:
    $(AB)^2 > (AC)^2 + (BC)^2$ or $(AB)^2 < (AC)^2 + (BC)^2$?

ANSWERS

2. (i) 10 cm (ii) 17 cm (iii) 5 cm (iv) 2.5 cm
3. 2 cm 4. 3.5 cm 5. No 6. (i) Yes (ii) No
7. 13 m 8. 17 m 9. 6 m 10. 14 dm 11. 5 units
12. (i) Yes (ii) Yes (iii) Yes (iv) Yes
13. 45°, 2 cm 14. Yes 15. No, $AB^2 > (AC^2 + BC^2)$
16. No, $AB^2 < AC^2 + BC^2$

OBJECTIVE TYPE QUESTIONS

Mark the correct alternative in each of the following:

1. If the measures of the angles of a triangle are $(2x)°$, $(3x - 5)°$ and $(4x - 13)°$. Then the value of x is
   (a) 22 (b) 18 (c) 20 (d) 30
2. The angles of a triangle are in the ratio 2 : 3 : 7. The measure of the largest angle is
   (a) 84° (b) 91° (c) 105° (d) 98°
3. In a ΔABC, if $2\angle A = 3\angle B = 6\angle C$, then the measure of the smallest angle is
   (a) 90° (b) 60° (c) 40° (d) 30°
4. In a ΔABC, if $\angle A + \angle B = 150°$ and $\angle B + \angle C = 75°$, then $\angle B =$
   (a) 35° (b) 45° (c) 55° (d) 25°
5. In a ΔABC, if $\angle A - \angle B = 33°$ and $\angle B - \angle C = 18°$, then $\angle B =$
   (a) 35° (b) 45° (c) 56° (d) 55°
6. If the measures of the angles of a triangle are $(2x - 5)°$, $\left(3x - \frac{1}{2}\right)^\circ$ and $\left(30 - \frac{x}{2}\right)^\circ$, then $x =$

(a) $\frac{311}{9}$ (b) $\frac{309}{11}$ (c) $\frac{310}{9}$ (d) $\frac{301}{9}$

7. In Fig. 59, the value of x is
   (a) 84 (b) 74 (c) 94 (d) 57

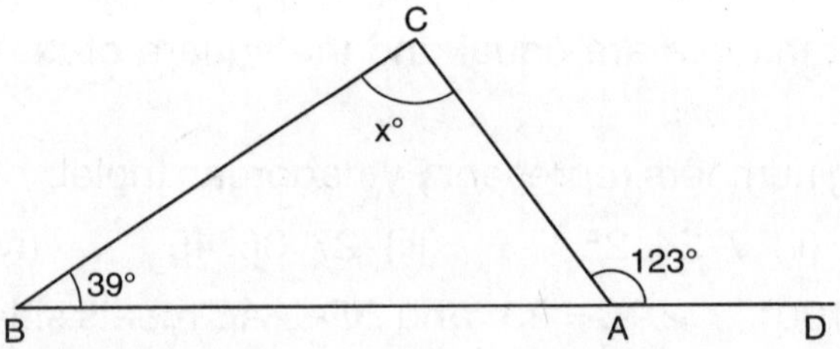

Fig. 59

8. In Fig. 60, the values of x and y are
   (a) $x = 20,\ y = 130$ (b) $x = 40,\ y = 140$
   (c) $x = 20,\ y = 140$ (d) $x = 15,\ y = 140$

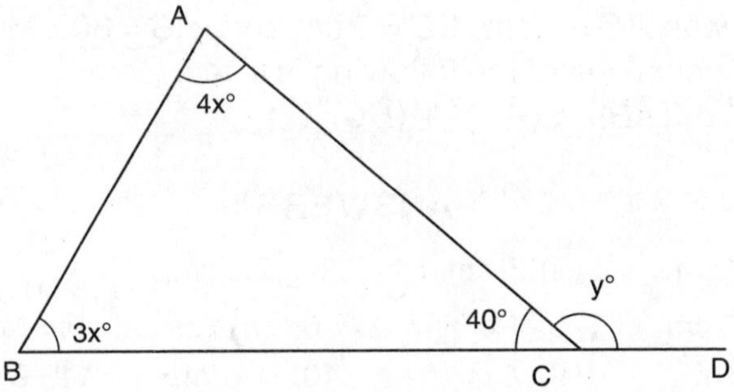

Fig. 60

9. In Fig. 61, the value of x is
   (a) 72° (b) 50 (c) 58 (d) 48

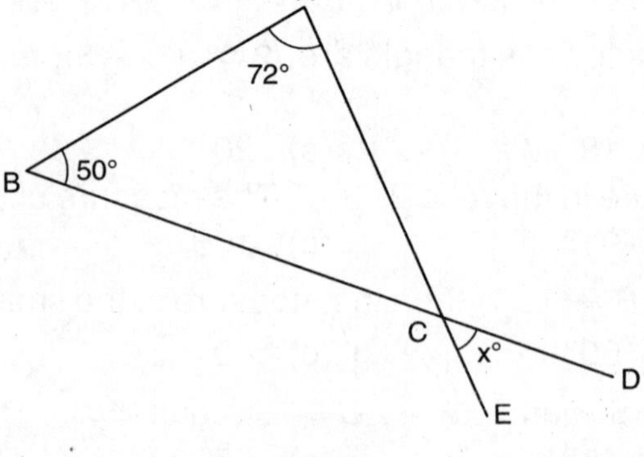

Fig. 61

10. In Fig. 62, if $AB \parallel DE$, then the value of x is
    (a) 25 (b) 35 (c) 40 (d) 45

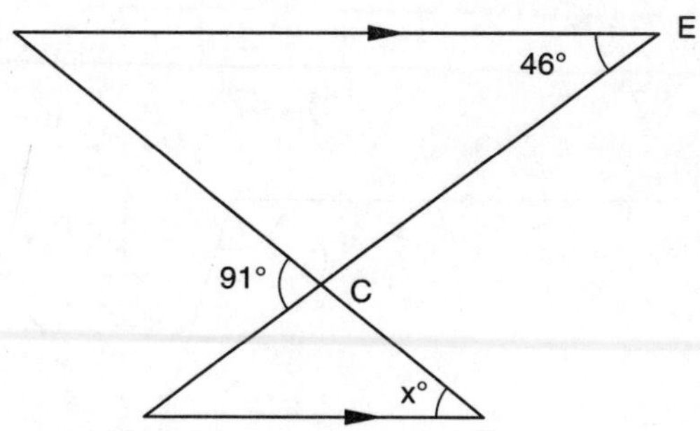

Fig. 62

11. In Fig. 63, if $AB \parallel CD$, the value of x is
    (a) 25 (b) 35 (c) 15 (d) 20

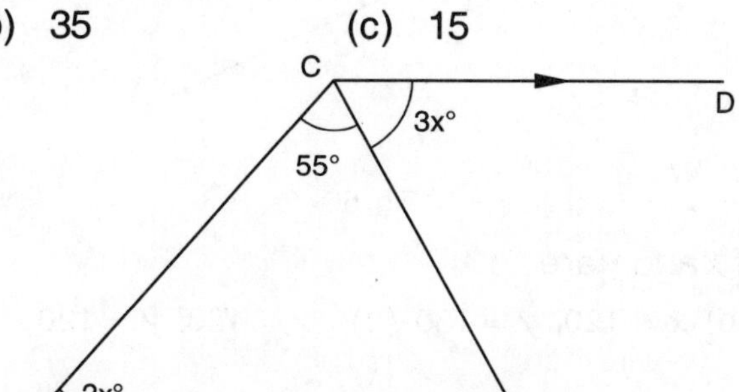

Fig. 63

12. In Fig. 64, if $AB \parallel CD$, the values of x and y are
    (a) $x = 21$, $y = 28$ (b) $x = 21$, $y = 38$ (c) $x = 38$, $y = 21$ (d) $x = 22$, $y = 38$

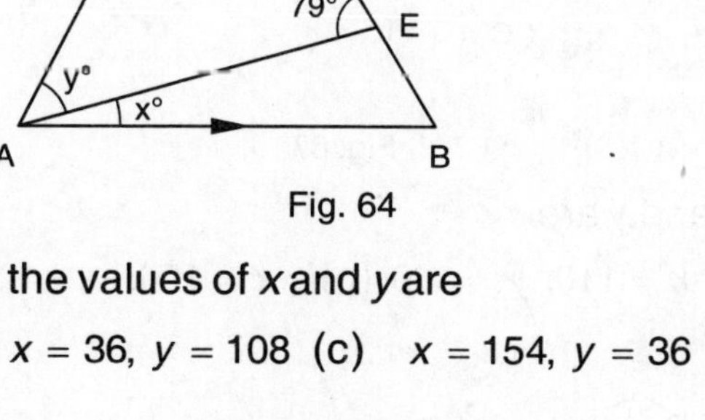

Fig. 64

13. In Fig. 65, if $AB \parallel CE$, then the values of x and y are
    (a) $x = 26$, $y = 144$ (b) $x = 36$, $y = 108$ (c) $x = 154$, $y = 36$ (d) $x = 144$, $y = 26$

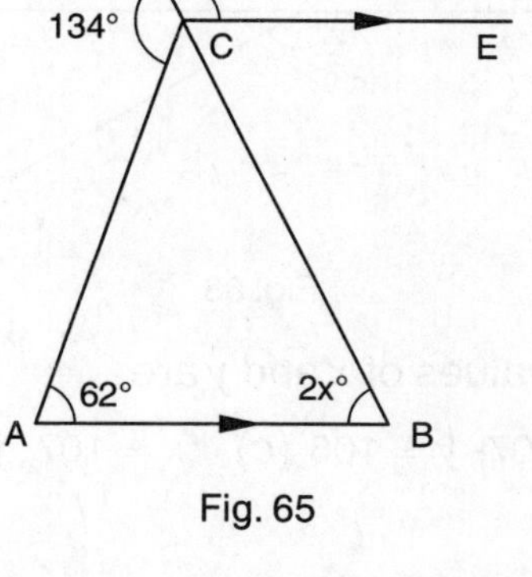

Fig. 65

14. In Fig. 66, if $AF \parallel DE$, then $x =$

 (a) 37 (b) 57 (c) 47 (d) 67

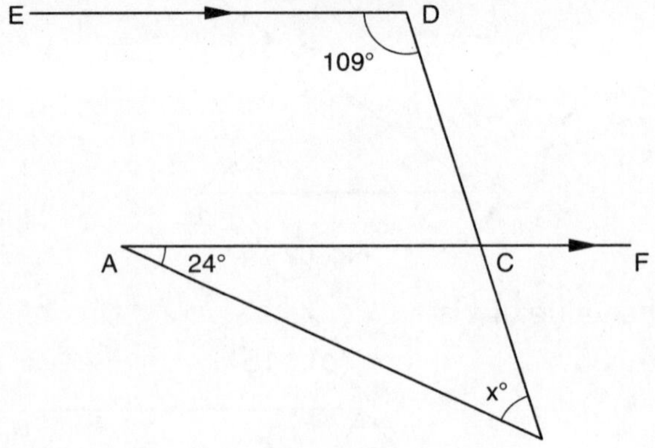

Fig. 66

15. In Fig. 67, the values of x and y are

 (a) $x = 130,\ y = 120$ (b) $x = 120,\ y = 130$ (c) $x = 120,\ y = 120$ (d) $x = 130,\ y = 130$

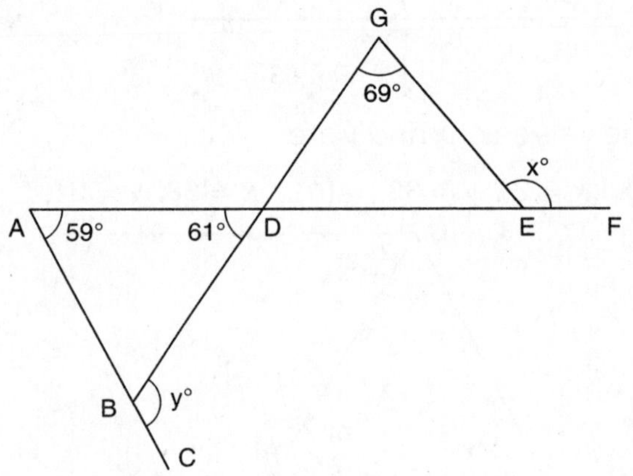

Fig. 67

16. In Fig. 68, the values of x and y are

 (a) $x = 120,\ y = 150$ (b) $x = 110,\ y = 160$ (c) $x = 150,\ y = 120$ (d) $x = 110,\ y = 160$

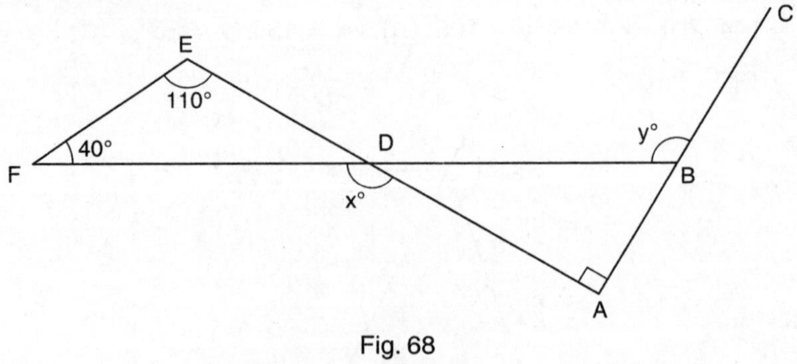

Fig. 68

17. In Fig. 69, if $AB \parallel CD$, then the values of x and y are

 (a) $x = 106,\ y = 307$ (b) $x = 307,\ y = 106$ (c) $x = 107,\ y = 306$ (d) $x = 105, y = 308$

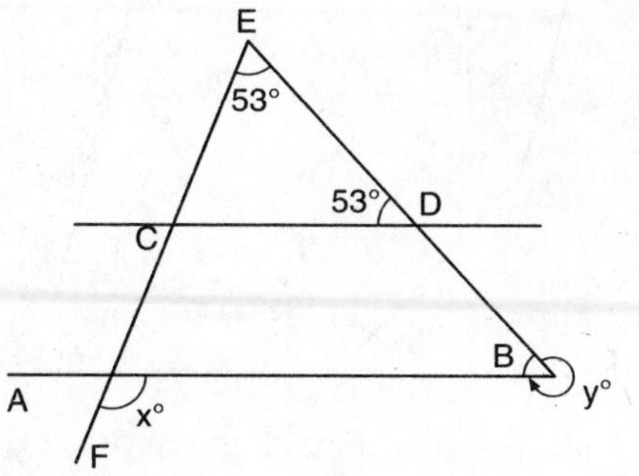

Fig. 69

18. In Fig. 70, if $AB \parallel CD$, then the values of x and y are

(a) $x = 24$, $y = 48$ (b) $x = 34$, $y = 68$ (c) $x = 24$, $y = 68$ (d) $x = 34$, $y = 48$

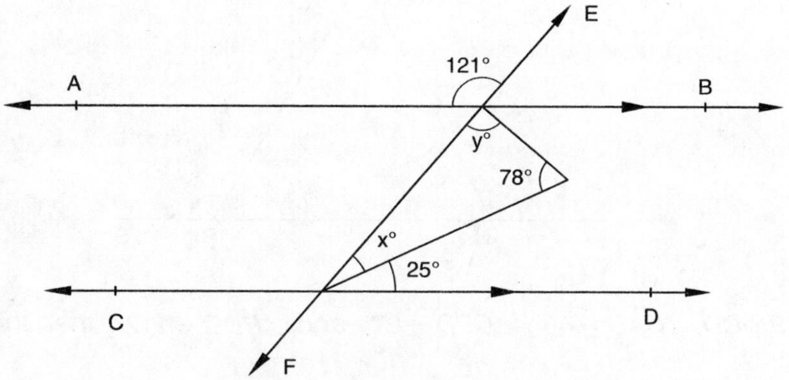

Fig. 70

19. In Fig. 71, if $AB \parallel CD$, then the values of x, y and z are

(a) $x = 56$, $y = 47$, $z = 77$ (b) $x = 47$, $y = 56$, $z = 77$

(c) $x = 77$, $y = 56$, $z = 47$ (d) $x = 56$, $y = 77$, $z = 47$

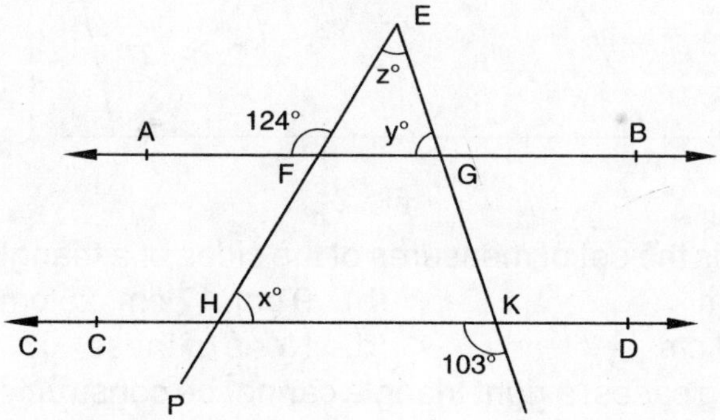

Fig. 71

20. In Fig. 72, if $AB \parallel CD$ and $AE \parallel BD$, then the value of x is

(a) 38 (b) 48 (c) 58 (d) 68

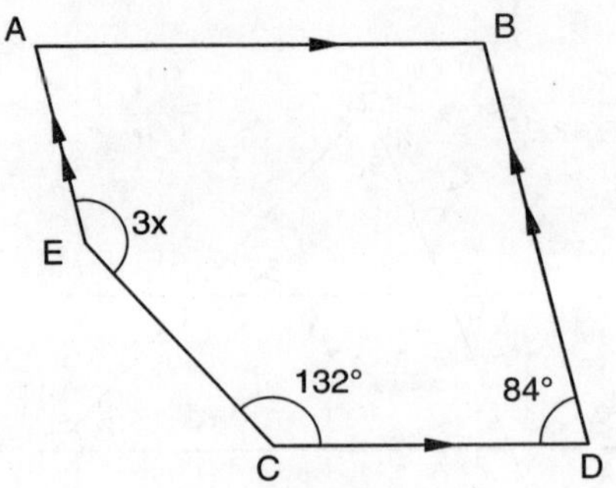

Fig. 72

21. If the exterior angles of a triangle are $(2x + 10)°$, $(3x - 5)°$ and $(2x + 40)°$, then $x =$
    (a) 25 (b) 35 (c) 45 (d) 55
22. In Fig. 73, the value of x is
    (a) 20 (b) 30 (c) 40 (d) 25

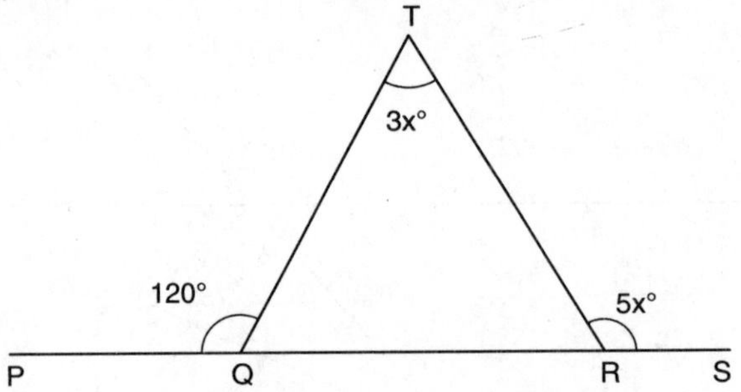

Fig. 73

23. In Fig. 74, if $AB \parallel CD$, $\angle CAB = 49°$, $\angle CBD = 27°$ and $\angle BDC = 112°$, then the values of x and y are
    (a) $x = 41$, $y = 90$ (b) $x = 41$, $y = 63$ (c) $x = 63$, $y = 41$ (d) $x = 90$, $y = 41$

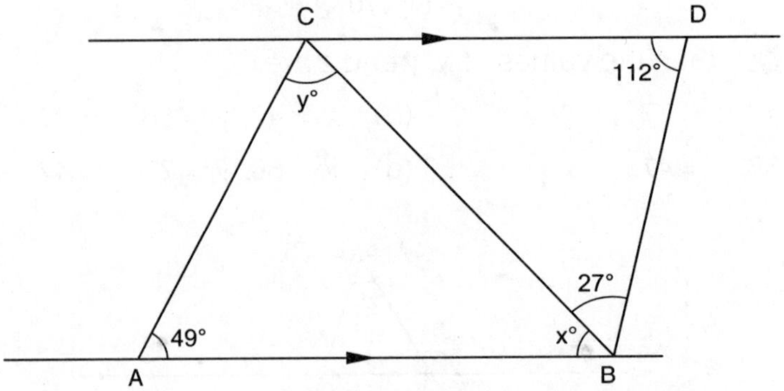

Fig. 74

24. Which of the following is the set of measures of the sides of a triangle?
    (a) 8 cm, 4 cm, 20 cm (b) 9 cm, 17 cm, 25 cm
    (c) 11 cm, 16 cm, 28 cm (d) None of these
25. In which of the following cases, a right triangle cannot be constructed?
    (a) 12 cm, 5 cm, 13 cm (b) 8 cm, 6 cm, 10 cm
    (c) 5 cm, 9 cm, 11 cm (d) None of these
26. Which of the following is/are not Pythagorean triplet (s)?
    (a) 3, 4, 5 (b) 8, 15, 17 (c) 7, 24, 25 (d) 13, 26, 29
27. In a right triangle, one of the acute angles is four times the other. Its measure is
    (a) 68° (b) 84° (c) 80° (d) 72°

28. In which of the following cases can a right triangle *ABC* be constructed?
    (a) $AB = 5$ cm, $BC = 7$ cm, $AC = 10$ cm (b) $AB = 7$ cm, $BC = 8$ cm, $AC = 12$ cm
    (c) $AB = 8$ cm, $BC = 17$ cm, $AC = 15$ cm (d) None of these
29. ΔABC is a right triangle right angled at *A*. If $AB = 24$ cm and $AC = 7$ cm, then $BC =$
    (a) 31 cm (b) 17 cm (c) 25 cm (d) 28 cm
30. If ΔABC is an isosceles right-triangle right angled at *C* such that $AC = 5$ cm. Then, $AB =$
    (a) 2.5 cm (b) $5\sqrt{2}$ cm (c) 10 cm (d) 5 cm
31. Two poles of heights 6 m and 11 m stand vertically on a plane ground. If the distance between their feet is 12 m, the distance between their tops is
    (a) 13 m (b) 14 m (c) 15 m (d) 12.8 m
32. A ladder is placed in such a way that its foot is 15 m away from the wall and its top reaches a window 20 m above the ground. The length of the ladder is
    (a) 35 m (b) 25 m (c) 18 m (d) 17.5 m
33. The hypotenuse of a right triangle is 26 cm long. If one of the remaining two sides is 10 cm long, the length of the other side is
    (a) 25 cm (b) 23 cm (c) 24 cm (d) 22 cm
34. A 15 m long ladder is placed against a wall in such away that the foot of the ladder is 9 m away from the wall. Up to what height does the ladder reach the wall?
    (a) 13 m (b) 10 m (c) 8 m (d) 12 m

ANSWSERS

1. (a)	2. (c)	3. (d)	4. (b)	5. (d)	6. (a)	7. (a)
8. (c)	9. (c)	10. (d)	11. (a)	12. (b)	13. (b)	14. (c)
15. (a)	16. (c)	17. (a)	18. (b)	19. (d)	20. (b)	21. (c)
22. (b)	23. (a)	24. (b)	25. (c)	26. (d)	27. (d)	28. (c)
29. (c)	30. (b)	31. (a)	32. (b)	33. (c)	34. (d)	

THINGS TO REMEMBER

1. A triangle is a figure made up by three line segments joining, in pairs, three non-collinear points. That is, if A, B, C are three non-collinear points, the figure formed by three line segments AB, BC and CA is called a triangle with vertices A, B, C.
2. The three line segments forming a triangle are called the sides of the triangle.
3. The three sides and three angles of a triangle are together called the six parts or elements of the triangle.
4. A triangle whose two sides are equal, is called an isosceles triangle.
5. A triangle whose all sides are equal, is called an equilateral triangle.
6. A triangle whose no two sides are equal, is called a scalene triangle.
7. A triangle whose all the angles are acute is called an acute triangle.
8. A triangle whose one of the angles is a right angle is called a right triangle.
9. A triangle whose one of the angles is an obtuse angle is called an obtuse triangle.
10. The interior of a triangle is made up of all such points P of the plane, as are enclosed by the triangle.
11. The exterior of a triangle is that part of the plane which consists of those points Q, which are neither on the triangle nor in its interior.
12. The interior of a triangle together with the triangle itself is called the triangular region.
13. The sum of the angles of a triangle is two right angles or 180°.
14. If a side of a triangle is produced, the exterior angle so formed is equal to the sum of the interior opposite angles.
15. In any triangle, an exterior angle is greater than either of the interior opposite angles.
16. The sum of any two sides of a triangle is greater than the third side.
17. In a right triangle, if a, b are the lengths of the sides and c that of the hypotenuse, then $c^2 = a^2 + b^2$.
18. If the sides of a triangle are of lengths a, b and c such that $c^2 = a^2 + b^2$, then the triangle is right-angled and the side of length c is the hypotenuse.
19. Three positive numbers a, b, c in this order are said to form a pythagorean triplet, if $c^2 = a^2 + b^2$. Triplets (3, 4, 5) (5, 12, 13), (8, 15, 17), (7, 24, 25) and (12, 35, 37) are some pythagorean triplets.

16

CONGRUENCE

16.1 INTRODUCTION

As you know that in geometry, we learn about geometrical figures, their properties and the relations between them. Every geometrical figure can be described by its shape, size and position. If we are given two geometrical figures, then by simply looking at them we can determine whether they have the same shape or not. When two figures are of same shape, then we try to know whether they are of the same size or not. In order to determine this, we cut the two figures and put one over the other. If they cover each other exactly, then we say that the two figures are of the same shape and same size. When two figures are of the same shape and same size, we say that they are congruent. In this chapter, we shall study the congruence of line segments, angles, squares, rectangles and triangles.

16.2 CONGRUENT FIGURES

The word 'congruent' means 'same shape and size', that is, equal in every respect. Thus, if two figures have exactly the same shape and size, they are said to be congruent. We can also say that two plane figures are congruent if each is a carbon copy of the other. The relation of two figures being congruent, is called congruence. If two figures are congruent, then without bending or changing their positions, we can superpose one figure on the other so that they completely cover each other.

Thus, we can say that:

Two plane figures are congruent, if each when superposed on the other, covers it exactly.

We shall use the symbol '$\cong$' to indicate 'is congruent to'.

Thus, if there are two figures F_1 and F_2, then $F_1 \cong F_2$ means that figure F_1 is congruent to figure F_2.

CONGRUENCE OF LINE SEGMENTS Let there be two line segments *AB* and *CD* as shown in Fig. 1. In order to see whether these two line segments are congruent or not, we take a trace copy of line segment *CD* and then try to superpose it on the line segment *AB*. If they cover exactly, the two line segments are congruent, otherwise not. When *AB* and *CD* cover each other exactly with *C* on *A* and *D* on *B* or *C* on *B* and *D* on *A*, then *AB* and *CD* have the same length.

Thus, in case of line segments, if two line segments have the same length, they are congruent and if they are congruent, they have the same length.

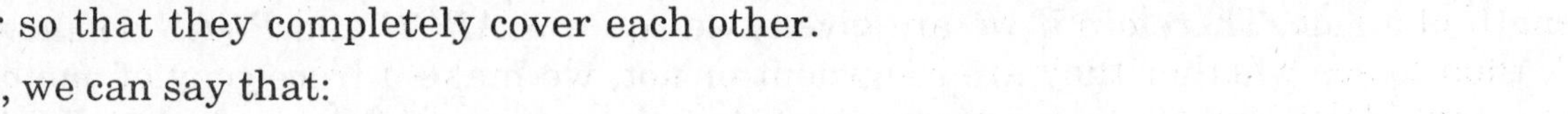

Fig. 1

Hence, we obtain the following result:

Two line segments are congruent, if they have the same length.

That is, line segment $AB \cong$ line segment CD, if $AB = CD$.

CONGRUENCE OF TWO ANGLES Consider two angles $\angle BAC$ and $\angle QPR$ as shown in Fig. 2. In order to see the congruence of these two angles we proceed as follows.

Take a trace copy of $\angle QPR$ and try to superpose it on $\angle BAC$ such that P falls on A and ray PQ falls along ray AB. If now, ray PR falls along ray AC, then $\angle QPR$ covers $\angle BAC$ exactly and we say that $\angle BAC$ and $\angle QPR$ are congruent.

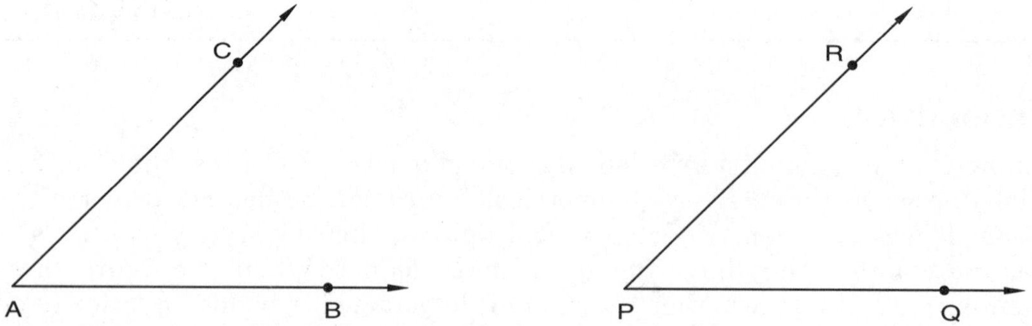

Fig. 2

Clearly, in such a situation $\angle BAC$ and $\angle QPR$ will have the same measure.

Thus, we obtain the following result:

Two angles are congruent, if they have the same measure.

That is,

$\angle BAC \cong \angle QPR$, then $m \angle BAC = m \angle QPR$

CONGRUENCE OF TWO SQUARES We know that two plane figures are congruent, if each when superposed on the other, covers it exactly, that is, they have the same shape and same size. Since all squares have the same shape and the size of a square is determined by the length of a side. Therefore if we are given two squares $ABCD$ and $PQRS$ as shown in Fig. 3, then to see whether they are congruent or not, we make a trace copy of one of the squares, say, $PQRS$ and try to superpose it on the other square $ABCD$ such that P falls on A and side PQ falls on side AB. We find that the square $PQRS$ will cover square $ABCD$ exactly, if $PQ = AB$. Thus, we have the following fact:

Two squares are congruent, if they have the same side length. That is,

square $ABCD \cong$ square $PQRS$, if $AB = PQ$.

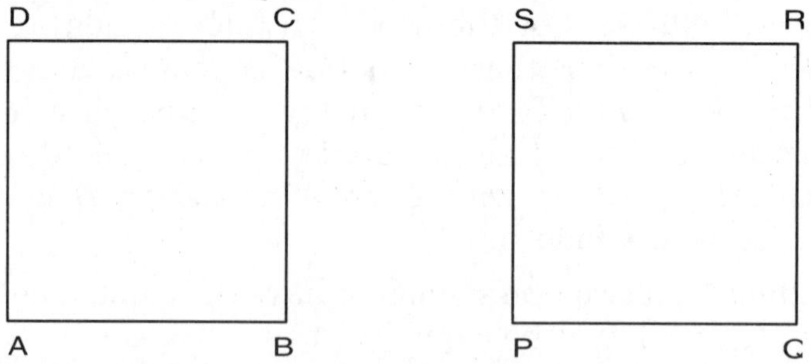

Fig. 3

CONGRUENCE OF TWO RECTANGLES The length and breadth of a rectangle determine its shape and size. In order to see whether two given rectangles $ABCD$ and $PQRS$ are congruent or not, we make a trace copy of rectangle $PQRS$. By superposing it on rectangle $ABCD$, we find that it will cover rectangle $ABCD$ exactly, if $AB = PQ$ and $BC = QR$. That is, rectangles $ABCD$ and $PQRS$ have the same length and breadth. Thus, we have the following fact:

Two rectangles are congruent, if they have the same length and breadth.

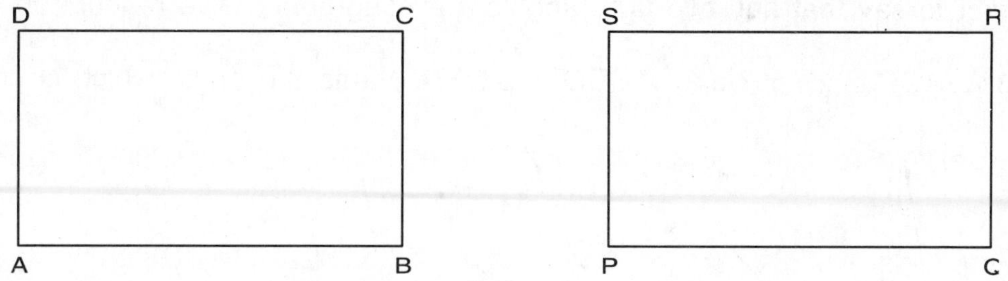

Fig. 4

CONGRUENCE OF TWO CIRCLES We know that all circles have the same shape and the size of a circle is determined by its radius. In order to see whether two given circles C_1 and C_2 (Fig. 5) are congruent or not we make a trace copy of one of the two circles, say C_1, and try to make it cover the second circle. We find that the circle C_2 will cover the circle C_1 exactly, if they are of the same radius. Thus, we have the following fact:

Two circles are congruent if they have the same radius.

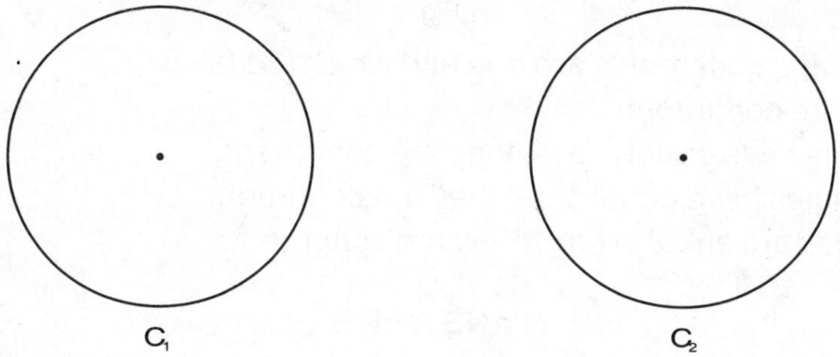

Fig. 5

That is, Circle $C_1 \cong$ Circle C_2, if radius of C_1 = radius of C_2 .

EXERCISE 16.1

1. Explain the concept of congruence of figures with the help of certain examples.
2. Fill in the blanks:
   (i) Two line segments are congruent if ....
   (ii) Two angles are congruent if ......
   (iii) Two squares are congruent if ....
   (iv) Two rectangles are congruent if ......
   (v) Two circles are congruent if ....
3. In Fig. 6, $\angle POQ \cong \angle ROS$, can we say that $\angle POR \cong \angle QOS$

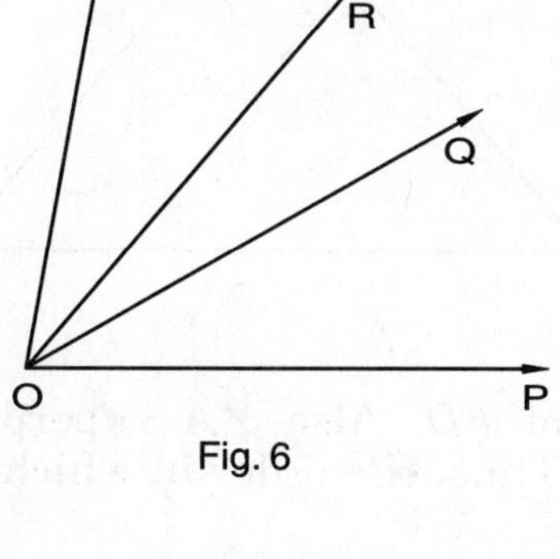

Fig. 6

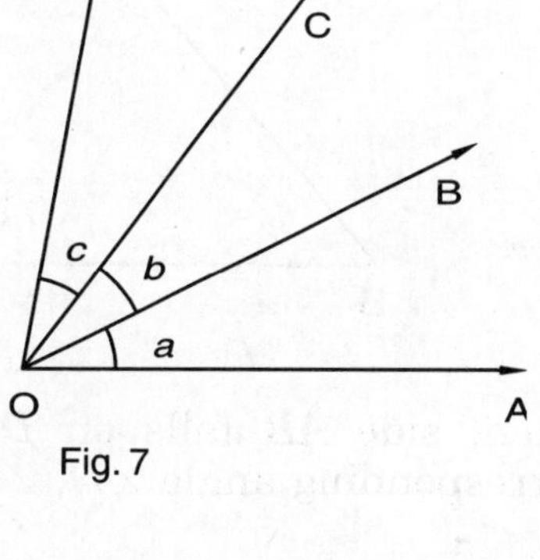

Fig. 7

4. In Fig. 7, $a = b = c$, name the angle which is congruent to $\angle AOC$.
5. Is it correct to say that any two right angles are congruent? Give reasons to justify your answer.
6. In Fig. 8, $\angle AOC \cong \angle PYR$ and $\angle BOC \cong \angle QYR$. Name the angle which is congruent to $\angle AOB$.

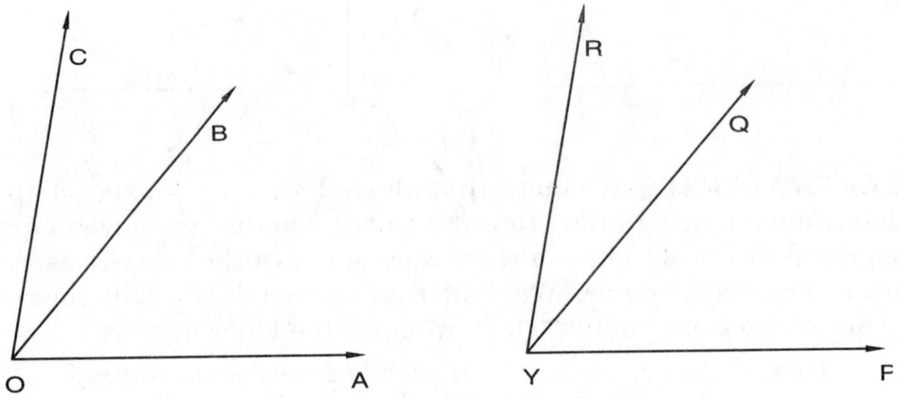

Fig. 8

7. Which of the following statements are true and which are false ;
   (i) All squares are congruent.
   (ii) If two squares have equal areas, they are congruent.
   (iii) If two rectangles have equal area, they are congruent.
   (iv) If two triangles are equal in area, they are congruent.

ANSWERS

2. (i) they are of equal lengths (ii) their measures are equal (iii) they have the same side length (iv) their dimensions are same (v) they have the same radii
3. Yes 4. $\angle BOD$ 5. Yes 6. $\angle PYQ$
7. (i) F (ii) T (iii) F (iv) F

16.3 CONGRUENCE OF TWO TRIANGLES

Two triangles are congruent if and only if one of them can be made to superpose on the other, so as to cover it exactly.

Let ΔABC and ΔDEF be two congruent triangles. Then, we can superpose $\Delta\ ABC$ on $\Delta\ DEF$, so as to cover it exactly. In such a superposition, the vertices of $\Delta\ ABC$ will fall on the vertices of $\Delta\ DEF$, in some order. Let us assume that the vertex A falls on vertex D, vertex B on vertex E and vertex C on vertex F.

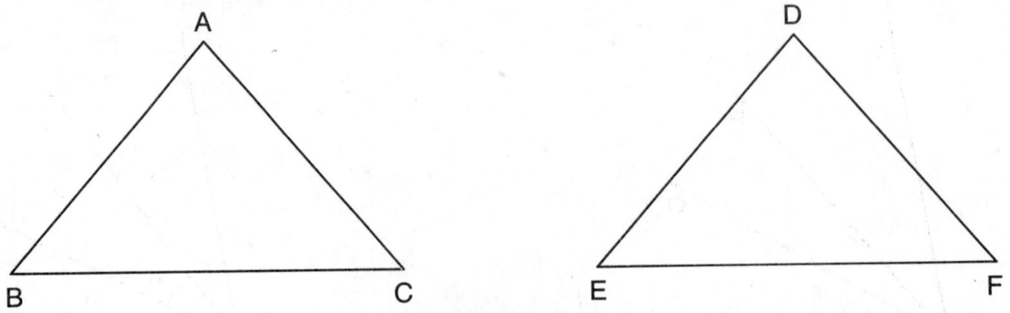

Fig. 9 (a)

Then, side AB falls on DE, BC on EF and CA on FD. Also $\angle A$ superposes on the corresponding angle $\angle D$, $\angle B$ on $\angle E$ and $\angle C$ on $\angle F$. Thus, the order in which the vertices match, automatically determines a correspondence between the sides and angles of the two triangles. And, if the superposition is exact, i.e. the triangles are congruent, the corresponding sides and angles are congruent. Consequently, we get six equalities; three of the corresponding sides and three of the corresponding angles.

It follows from the above discussion that, if ΔABC superposes on ΔDEF exactly such that the vertices of ΔABC fall on the vertices of ΔDEF in the following order

$$A \leftrightarrow D, B \leftrightarrow E, C \leftrightarrow F$$

Then, we have the following six equalities

$AB = DE, BC = EF, CA = FD$ (i.e. Corresponding sides are congruent)

$\angle A = \angle D, \angle B = \angle E, \angle C = \angle F$ (i.e. Corresponding angles are congruent)

In the above discussion we have considered one correspondence between the vertices of triangles ABC and DEF viz. $A \rightarrow D$, $B \rightarrow E$ and $C \rightarrow F$. But there can be many other matchings between the vertices of two triangles as discussed below.

In two triangles ABC and DEF, we have the following six matchings or correspondences between their vertices:

$A \leftrightarrow D, B \leftrightarrow E$ and $C \leftrightarrow F$ written as $ABC \leftrightarrow DEF$
$A \leftrightarrow E, B \leftrightarrow F$ and $C \leftrightarrow D$ written as $ABC \leftrightarrow EFD$
$A \leftrightarrow F, B \leftrightarrow D$ and $C \leftrightarrow E$ written as $ABC \leftrightarrow FDE$
$A \leftrightarrow D, B \leftrightarrow F$ and $C \leftrightarrow E$ written as $ABC \leftrightarrow DFE$
$A \leftrightarrow E, B \leftrightarrow D$ and $C \leftrightarrow F$ written as $ABC \leftrightarrow EDF$
$A \leftrightarrow F, B \leftrightarrow E$ and $C \leftrightarrow D$ written as $ABC \leftrightarrow FED$

If ΔABC is congruent to ΔDEF, then in one of these six matchings ΔABC superposes on ΔDEF exactly and in that particular matching corresponding sides and angles will be congruent. Consequently, we will have three equalities of corresponding sides and three equali-ties of the measures of corresponding angles.

If ΔABC is not congruent to ΔDEF, then ΔABC will not superpose exactly ΔDEF in none of the above six possible matchings. Infact, in each matching at least one part (a side or an angle) of ΔABC will not be equal to the corresponding part of ΔDEF.

From the above discussion we obtain the following general condition for the congruence of two triangles:

Two triangles are congruent if and only if there exists a correspondence between their vertices such that the corresponding sides and the corresponding angles of the two triangles are equal or congruent.

If ΔABC is congruent to ΔDEF and the correspondence $ABC \leftrightarrow DEF$ makes the six pairs of corresponding parts of the two triangles congruent, then we write

$$\Delta ABC \cong \Delta DEF$$

Thus, $\Delta ABC \cong \Delta DEF$ if and only if $AB = DE$, $BC = EF$, $CA = FD$, $\angle A = \angle D$, $\angle B = \angle E$ and $\angle C = \angle F$.

NOTE 1: *In the subsequent discussion, the order of the letters in the names of two triangles will indicate the correspondence between the vertices of two triangles. For example, $\Delta ABC \cong \Delta DEF$ will indicate the correspondence $ABC \leftrightarrow DEF$ and $\Delta ABC \cong \Delta DFE$ will indicate the correspondence $ABC \leftrightarrow DFE$. Thus, we can easily infer the six equalities between the corresponding parts of two triangles from the notation $\Delta ABC \cong \Delta DEF$.*

NOTE 2: *Note that $\Delta PQR \cong \Delta UVW$ will mean that $\angle P = \angle U$, $\angle Q = \angle V$, $\angle R = \angle W$, $PQ = UV$, $QR = VW$ and $PR = UW$.*

16.4 SUFFICIENT CONDITIONS FOR CONGRUENCE OF TWO TRIANGLES

In the previous section, we have learnt that two triangles are congruent if and only if there exists a correspondence between their vertices such that the corresponding sides and corresponding angles of two triangles are congruent or equal, that is, six equalities (three of the corresponding sides and three of the corresponding angles) hold good. Now the question arises: What are the least possible conditions to ensure the congruence of two triangles? Do we need all the six conditions or a less number of conditions will ensure the congruence of two triangles? In this section, we shall see that if three properly chosen conditions out of the six conditions, mentioned in the previous section, are satisfied, then the other three conditions are automatically satisfied. There are four such cases. In each case we have a different combination of three matching parts. Let us now discuss those combinations of three matching parts.

16.4.1 THE SIDE–SIDE–SIDE (SSS) CONGRUENCE CONDITION

Two triangles are congruent, if the three sides of one triangle are respectively equal to the three sides of the other triangle.

In order to verify the above property, let us perform the following experiment.

Experiment: Draw a ΔABC with $AB = 5.5$ cm, $BC = 6.5$ cm and $CA = 4.3$ cm. Draw another ΔPQR with $PQ = 5.5$ cm, $QR = 6.5$ cm and $RP = 4.3$ cm.

Thus, we have

$$AB = PQ, BC = QR \text{ and } CA = RP.$$

Now, make a trace copy of ΔPQR and try to make it cover ΔABC with P on A, Q on B and R on C. You will find that the two triangles cover each other exactly.

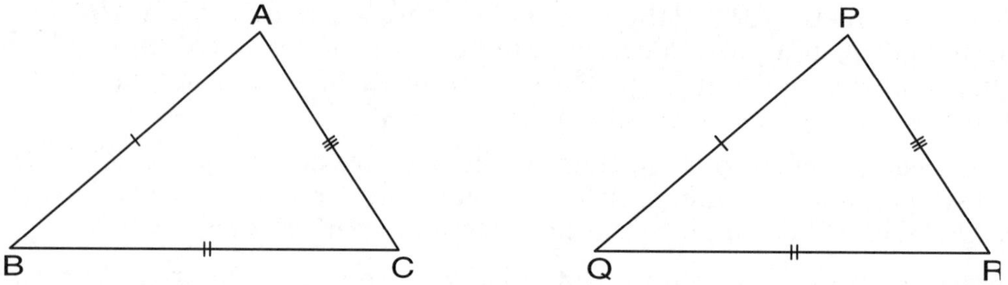

Fig. 9

$\therefore \quad \Delta ABC \cong \Delta PQR$

Remark: *If two triangles are congruent by SSS condition of congruence, then they are identical. So, the corresponding angles (angles opposite to equal sides) will also be equal.*

ILLUSTRATIVE EXAMPLES

Example 1 Without drawing the triangles, state the correspondence between the sides and the angles of the following pairs of congruent triangles:

(i) $\Delta ABC \cong \Delta PQR$ (ii) $\Delta ABC \cong \Delta QRP$

Solution (i) We have,

$\Delta ABC \cong \Delta PQR$

$\Rightarrow \quad A \leftrightarrow P, B \leftrightarrow Q, C \leftrightarrow R$

$\Rightarrow \quad AB = PQ, BC = QR, AC = PR, \angle A = \angle P, \angle B = \angle Q$ and $\angle C = \angle R$

(ii) We have,

$\Delta ABC \cong \Delta QRP$

$\Rightarrow \quad A \leftrightarrow Q, B \leftrightarrow R$ and $C \leftrightarrow P$

$\Rightarrow \quad AB = QR, BC = RP, AC = QP, \ \angle A = \angle Q, \angle B = \angle R$ and $\angle C = \angle P$

Example 2 In the following pairs of triangles (Fig. 10), by applying SSS condition, state which are congruent. State the result in symbolic form:

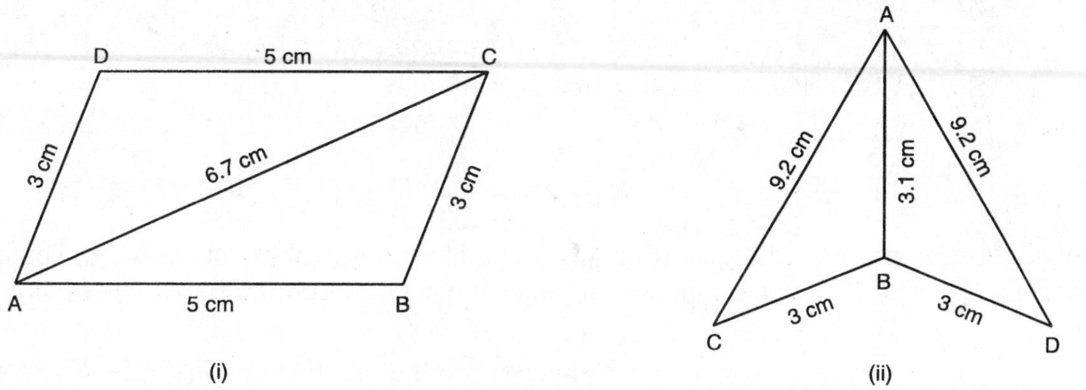

Fig. 10

Solution (i) In triangles ABC and CDA, we have

$AB = CD = 5$ cm, $BC = DA = 3$ cm, and, $AC = AC = 6.7$ cm. (Common)

$\therefore$ By SSS condition of congruence, we have

$$\Delta ABC \cong \Delta CDA$$

(ii) In triangles ABC and ABD, we have

$AC = AD = 9.2$ cm, $BC = BD = 3$ cm and, $AB = AB = 3.1$ cm (Common)

So, by SSS condition of congruence, we have

$$\Delta ABC \cong \Delta ABD$$

Example 3 Which of the following pairs of triangles are congruent? If they are congruent, write out the pairs of equal angles.

(i) $\Delta\ ABC$: $AB = 3$ cm, $BC = 4$ cm, $CA = 2$ cm

$\Delta\ DEF$: $DE = 2$ cm, $EF = 3$ cm and $FD = 4$ cm

(ii) $\Delta\ PQR$: $PQ = 17$ cm, $QR = 15$ cm, $PR = 18$ cm

$\Delta\ DEF$: $DE = 18$ cm, $EF = 17$ cm, $DF = 15$ cm.

Solution (i) In triangles ABC and DEF, we have

$AB = EF = 3$ cm, $BC = FD = 4$ cm and $CA = DE = 2$ cm

So, by SSS condition of congruence, we have

$$\Delta ABC \cong \Delta EFD$$

Since $AB = EF$, therefore angles opposite to these sides are equal.

$\Rightarrow \quad \angle C = \angle D$

Similarly, $BC = FD \quad \Rightarrow \quad \angle A = \angle E$

and, $\quad CA = DE \quad \Rightarrow \quad \angle B = \angle F$

(ii) In triangles PQR and DEF, we have

$PQ = EF = 17$ cm, $QR = FD = 15$ cm and $RP = DE = 18$ cm

So, by SSS condition of congruence, we have

$$\Delta PQR \cong \Delta EFD$$

$\Rightarrow \quad \angle P = \angle E, \angle Q = \angle F$ and $\angle R = \angle D$

Example 4 In Fig. 11, it is given that $AB = CD$ and $AD = BC$.
Provo that $\Delta ADC \cong \Delta CDA$.

Solution In ΔADC and ΔCBA, we have

$AB = CD$ [Given]

$AD = BC$ [Given]

$AC = AC$ [Common side]

So, by SSS criterion of congruence, we have

$\Delta ADC \cong \Delta CBA$

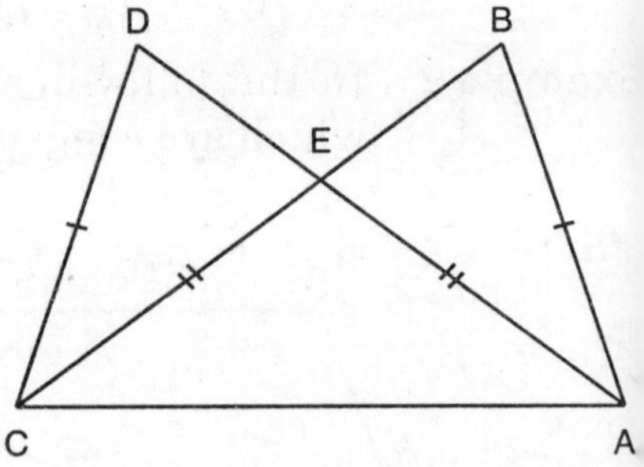

Fig. 11

EXERCISE 16.2

1. In the following pairs of triangles (Fig. 12 to 15), the lengths of the sides are indicated along sides. By applying SSS condition, determine which are congruent. State the result in symbolic form.

(i)

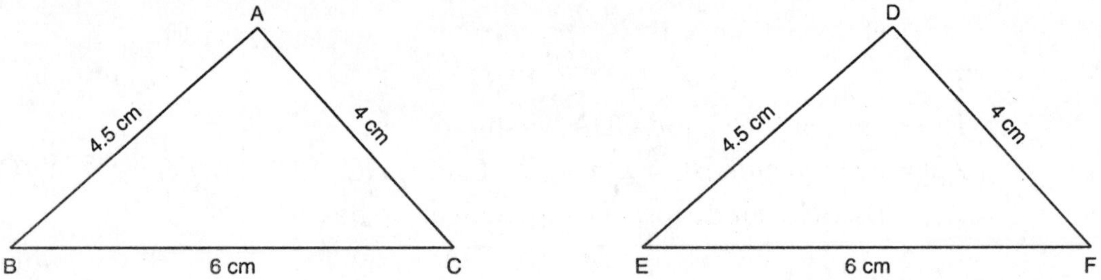

Fig. 12

(ii)

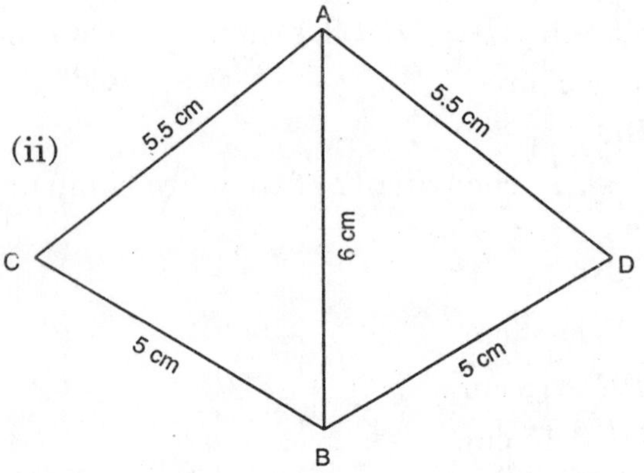

Fig. 13

(iii)

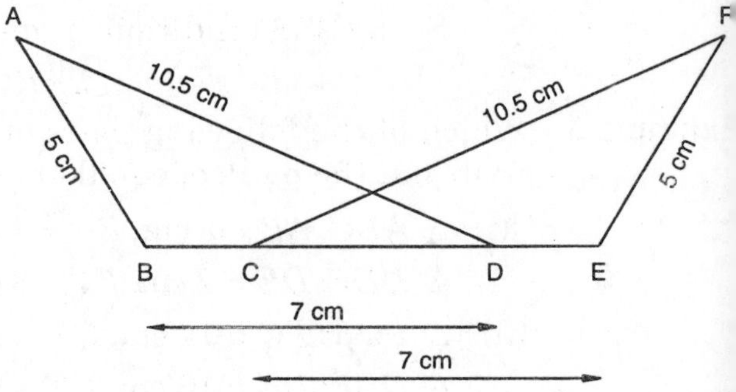

Fig. 14

(iv)

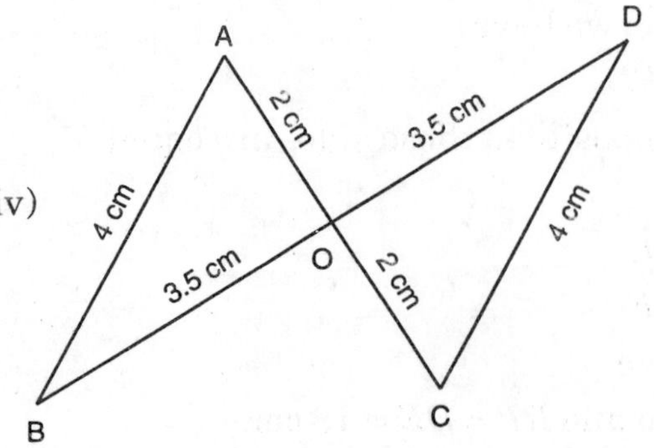

Fig. 15

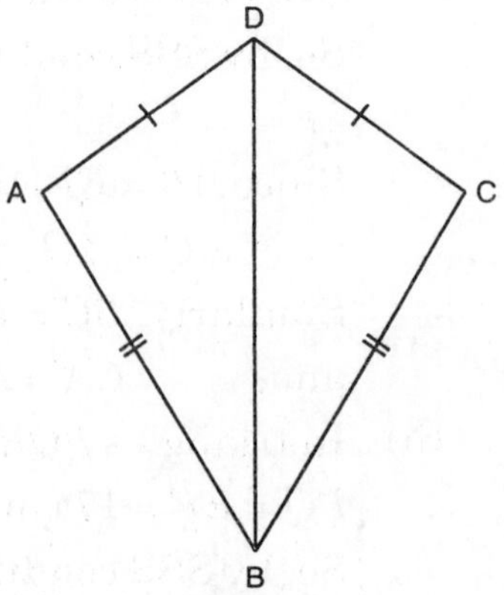

Fig. 16

2. In Fig. 16, $AD = DC$ and $AB = BC$.

(i) Is $\Delta ABD \cong \Delta CBD$?

(ii) State the three parts of matching pairs you have used to answer (i).

3. In Fig. 17, $AB = DC$ and $BC = AD$.

(i) Is $\Delta ABC \cong \Delta CDA$?

(ii) What congruence condition have you used?

(iii) You have used some fact, not given in the question, what is that?

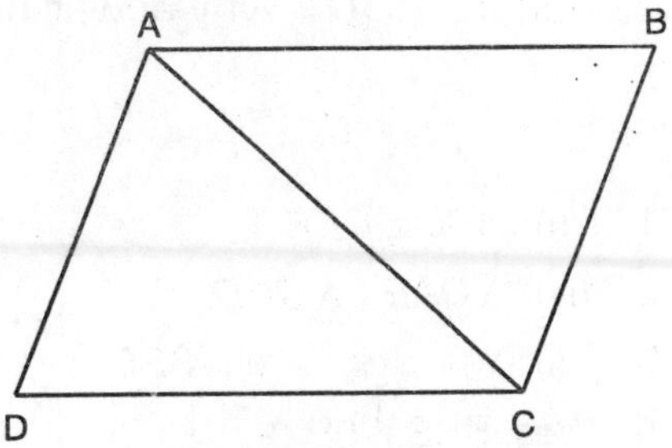

Fig. 17

4. If $\Delta PQR \cong \Delta$ EFD,

(i) Which side of ΔPQR equals ED? (ii) Which angle of ΔPQR equals $\angle E$?

5. Triangles ABC and PQR are both isosceles with $AB = AC$ and $PQ = PR$ respectively. If also, $AB = PQ$ and $BC = QR$, are the two triangles congruent? Which condition do you use? If $\angle B = 50°$, what is the measure of $\angle R$?

6. ABC and DBC are both isosceles triangles on a common base BC such that A and D lie on the same side of BC. Are triangles ADB and ADC congruent? Which condition do you use? If $\angle BAC = 40°$ and $\angle BDC = 100°$; then find $\angle ADB$.

7. ΔABC and ΔABD are on a common base AB, and $AC = BD$ and $BC = AD$ as shown in Fig. 18. Which of the following statements is true?

(i) $\Delta ABC \cong \Delta ABD$

(ii) $\Delta ABC \cong \Delta ADB$

(iii) $\Delta ABC \cong \Delta BAD$

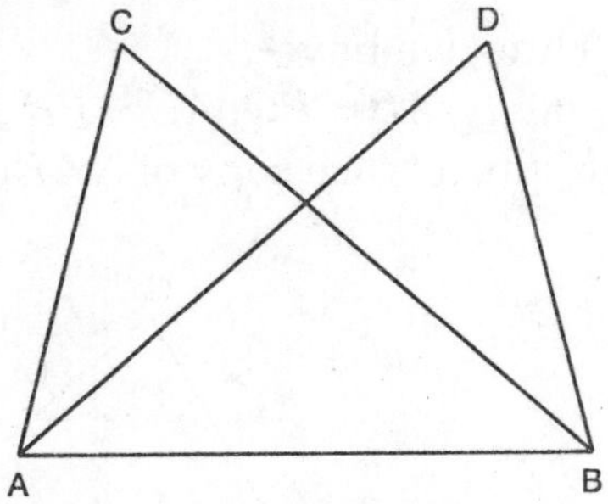

Fig. 18

8. In Fig. 19, ΔABC is isosceles with $AB = AC$, D is the mid-point of base BC.

(i) Is $\Delta ADB \cong \Delta ADC$?

(ii) State the three pairs of matching parts you use to arrive at your answer.

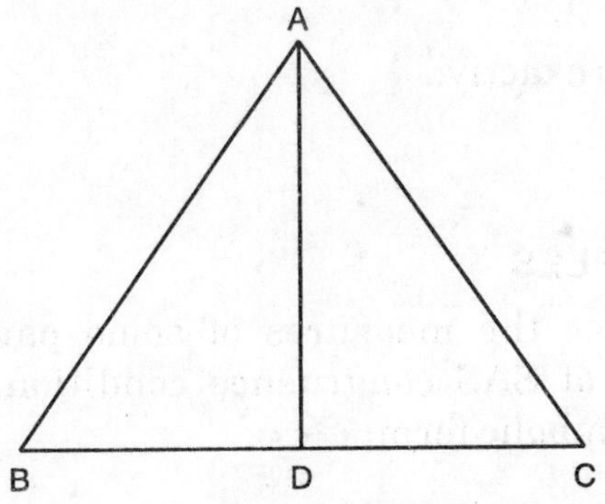

Fig. 19

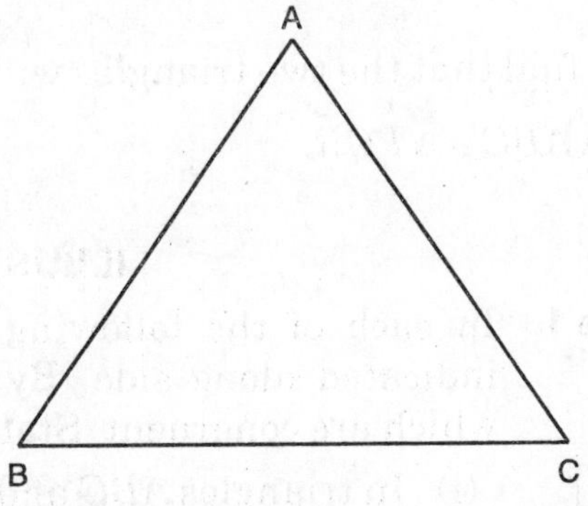

Fig. 20

9. In Fig. 20, ΔABC is isosceles with $AB = AC$. State if $\Delta ABC \cong \Delta ACB$. If yes, state three relations that you use to arrive at your answer.

10. Triangles ABC and DBC have side BC common, $AB = BD$ and $AC = CD$. Are the two triangles congruent? State in symbolic form. Which congruence condition do you use? Does $\angle ABD$ equal $\angle ACD$? Why or why not?

ANSWERS

1. (i) $ABC \cong DEF$ (ii) $ABC \cong ABD$ (iii) $\Delta ABD \cong \Delta FEC$ (iv) $\Delta OAB \cong \Delta OCD$
2. Yes; AB, CB; AD, CD; BD, BD
3. (i) Yes (ii) SSS (iii) AC = CA
4. (i) PR (ii) $\angle P$
5. Yes, SSS, 50°
6. Yes, SSS, 130°
7. (iii)
8. (i) Yes (ii) AB, AC; AD, AD; BD, DC
9. Yes, $AB = AC$, $BC = CB$ and $AC = AB$
10. Yes, $\Delta ABC \cong \Delta$ DBC, SSS, Yes

16.4.2 SAS CONGRUENCE CONDITION

Two triangles are congruent if two sides and the included angle of the one are respectively equal to the two sides and the included angle of the other.

In order to verify the above fact, we perform the following experiment.

Experiment: Draw a ΔABC with $AB = 6$ cm, $AC = 4$ cm and $\angle A = 60°$. Also, draw a ΔPQR with $PQ = 6$ cm, $PR = 4$ cm and $\angle P = 60°$.

Thus, we have

$$AB = PQ, AC = PR \text{ and } \angle A = \angle P$$

Make a trace copy of ΔABC and try to cover ΔPQR with A on P, B on Q and C on R.

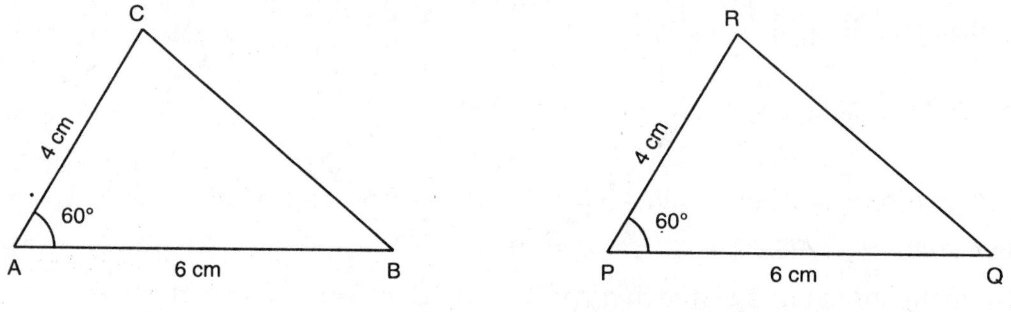

Fig. 21

You will find that the two triangles will cover each other exactly.

Hence, $\Delta ABC \cong \Delta PQR$.

ILLUSTRATIVE EXAMPLES

Example 1 In each of the following pairs of triangles the measures of some parts are indicated along side. By the application of SAS congruence condition, state which are congruent. State the result in symbolic form.

Solution (i) In triangles ABC and PQR, we have

$AB = PQ, AC = PR$ and $\angle A = \angle P = 40°$

So, by SAS-congruence condition, we have

$\Delta ABC \cong \Delta PQR$

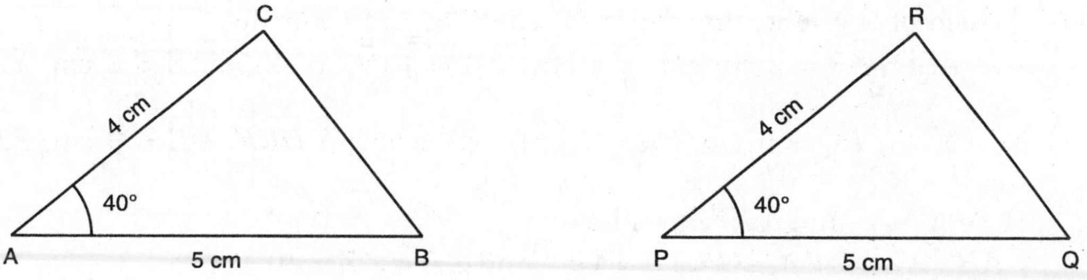

Fig. 22 (i)

(ii) In triangles ABC and PQR, we have

$CB = PQ = 5.5$ cm, $CA = PR = 4$ cm and $\angle C = \angle P = 50°$

So, by SAS congruence condition, we have

$$\Delta CBA \cong \Delta PQR$$

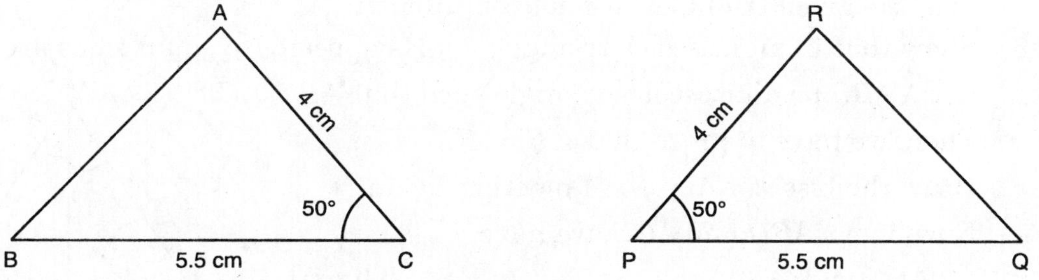

Fig. 22 (ii)

(iii) In triangles ABE and CBD, we have

$AB = CB = 5.2$ cm, $AE = CD = 5$ cm and $\angle A = \angle C = 40°$

So, by SAS congruence condition, we have

$$\Delta EAB \cong \Delta DCB$$

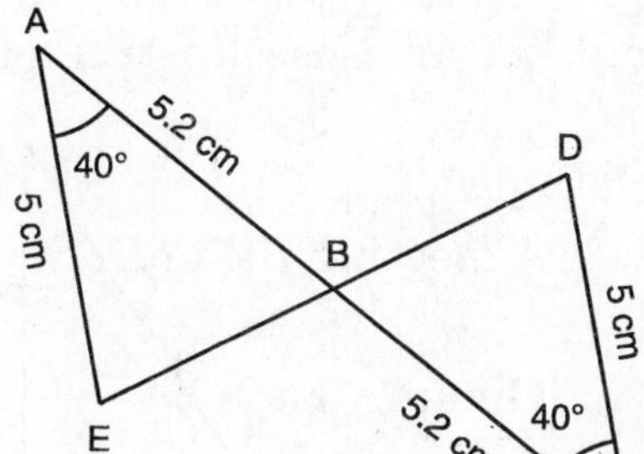

Fig. 22 (iii)

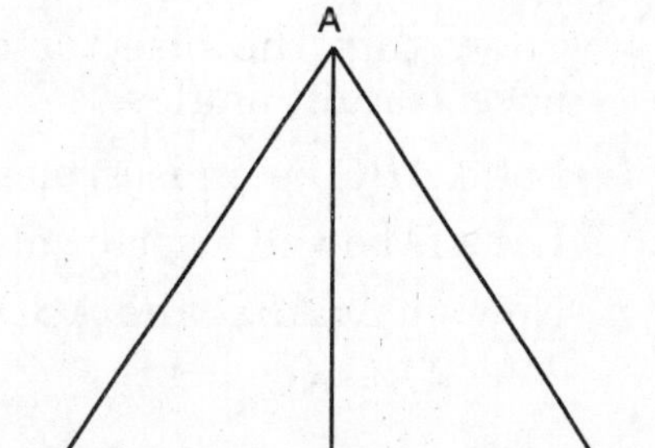

Fig. 22 (iv)

(iv) In triangles ABD and ACD [Fig. 22 (iv)], we have

$BD = CD = 3$ cm, $AD = AD$ and $\angle ADB = \angle ADC = 90°$.

So, by SAS congruence condition, we have

$$\Delta ADB \cong \Delta ADC$$

Example 2 Which of the following pairs of triangles are congruent?

(i) ΔABC: $AB = 2$ cm, $AC = 4$ cm, $\angle A = 40°$; ΔXYZ : $XZ = 2$ cm, $YZ = 4$ cm, $\angle Z = 40°$

(ii) ΔPQR: $PQ = 5$ cm, $PR = 6$ cm, $\angle P = 55°$; ΔDEF: $DE = 6$ cm, $EF = 5$ cm, $\angle D = 55°$

Solution (i) In ΔABC and ΔXYZ, we have

$AB = XZ = 2$ cm, $AC = YZ = 4$ cm and $\angle A = \angle Z = 40°$

Thus, in ΔABC and XYZ, the two sides and included angle of one triangle are equal to two sides and the corresponding included angle of the other.

So, by SAS congruence condition, we have

$\Delta ABC \cong \Delta ZXY$

(ii) In ΔPQR, the included angle between PQ and PR is $\angle P$

In ΔDEF, the included angle between DE and EF is $\angle E$

We have,

$$PQ = EF = 5 \text{ cm and } PR = DE = 6 \text{ cm but } \angle P \neq \angle E$$

So, the given triangles are not congruent.

Example 3 Show that in an isosceles triangle, angles opposite to equal sides are equal.

Solution Let ΔABC be an isosceles triangle such that $AB = AC$.

Then, we have to prove that $\angle B = \angle C$.

Draw the bisector AD of $\angle A$ meeting BC in D.

Now, in Δ s ABD and ACD, we have

$AB = AC$ [Given]

$\angle BAD = \angle CAD$ [$\because$ AD is the bisector of $\angle A$]

and, $AD = AD$ [Common side]

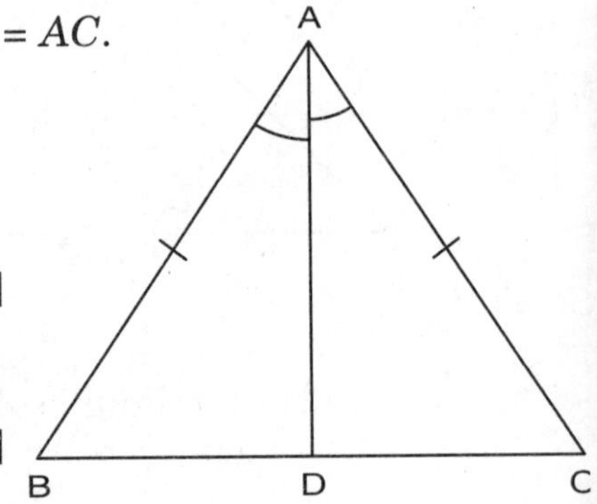

Fig. 23

Therefore, by SAS congruence condition, we have

$\Delta ABD \cong \Delta ACD$

$\Rightarrow$ $\angle B = \angle C$ [Corresponding parts of congruent triangles are equal]

Example 4 Show that the bisector of vertical angle of an isosceles triangle bisects the base at right angles.

Solution Let ΔABC be an isosceles triangle such that $AB = AC$.

Let AD be the bisector of vertical angle $\angle A$ meeting BC in D.

Now, in Δs ABD and ACD, we have

$AB = AC$ [Given]

$\angle BAD = \angle CAD$ [$\because$ AD is the bisector of $\angle A$]

and, $AD = AD$ [Common side]

$\Rightarrow$ $BD = CD$ and $\angle ADB = \angle ADC$

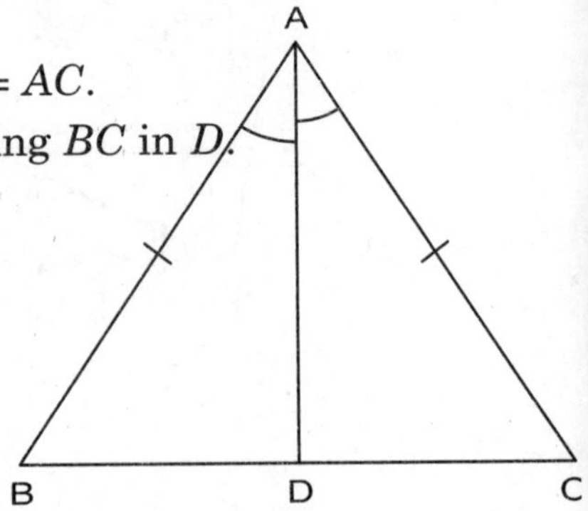

Fig. 24

Therefore, by SAS congruence condition, we have

$\Delta ABD \cong \Delta ACD$

But, $\angle ADB + \angle ADC = 180°$ [Linear pair property]

$\therefore$ $\angle ADB = \angle ADC = 90°$

Hence, AD bisects BC at right angles.

Example 5 In ΔABC, $\angle A = 100°$ and $AB = AC$. Find $\angle B$ and $\angle C$.

Solution We have,

$AB = AC$ [Given]

$\Rightarrow \angle B = \angle C$ [$\because$ Angles opp. to equal sides are equal]

Now,

$\angle A + \angle B + \angle C = 180°$ [$\because$ Sum of angles of a triangle = 180°]

$\Rightarrow \angle A + \angle B + \angle B = 180°$ [$\because \angle B = \angle C$]

$\Rightarrow 100° + 2\angle B = 180°$

$\Rightarrow 2\angle B = 80°$

$\Rightarrow \angle B = 40°$

Hence, $\angle B = \angle C = 40°$

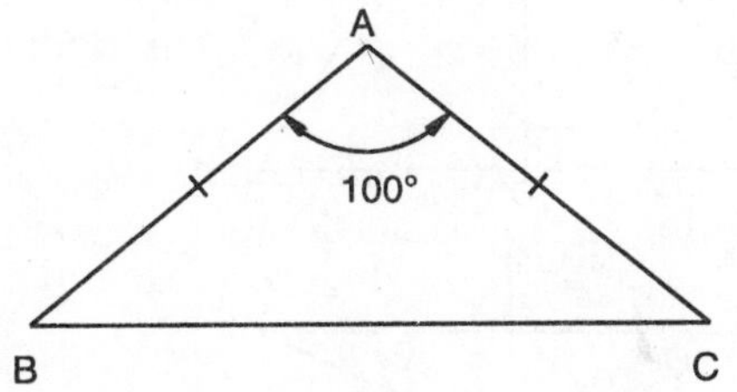

Fig. 25

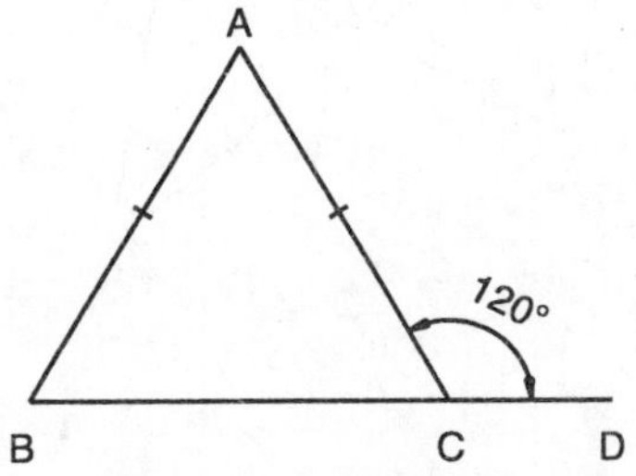

Fig. 26

Example 6 In Fig. 26, $AB = AC$ and $\angle ACD = 120°$. Find $\angle A$.

Solution We have,

$AB = AC$ [Given]

$\Rightarrow \angle B = \angle C$ [$\because$ Angles opposite to equal sides are equal]

Now,

$\angle ACB + \angle ACD = 180°$ [Angles of a linear pair]

$\Rightarrow \angle C + 120° = 180°$ [$\because$ Sum of angles of a triangle is 180°]

$\Rightarrow \angle C = 60°$

$\therefore \angle B = 60°$ [$\because \angle B = \angle C$]

Now,

$\angle A + \angle B + \angle C = 180°$ [$\because$ Sum of angles of a triangle is 180°]

$\Rightarrow \angle A + 60° + 60° = 180°$

$\Rightarrow \angle A = 60°$

Example 7 Prove that measure of each angle of an equilateral triangle is 60°

Solution Let ΔABC be an equilateral triangle. Then, $AB = BC = CA$

Since angles opposite to equal sides of a triangle are equal.

$\therefore AB = BC$

$\Rightarrow \angle C = \angle A$ ...(i)

and, $BC = CA$

$\Rightarrow \angle A = \angle B$ ...(ii)

From (i) and (ii), we get

$\angle A = \angle B = \angle C$

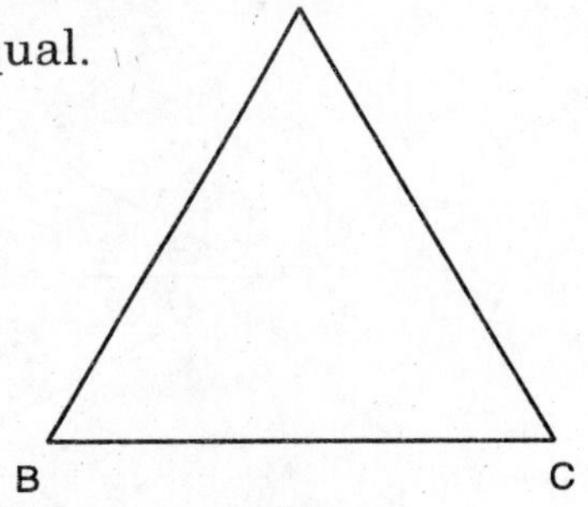

Fig. 27

But, $\angle A + \angle B + \angle C = 180°$ [$\because$ Sum angle property of a triangle]

$\therefore \quad \angle A + \angle A + \angle A = 180°$

$\Rightarrow \quad 3\angle A = 180°$

$\Rightarrow \quad \angle A = 60°$

Hence, $\angle A = \angle B = \angle C = 60°$.

EXERCISE 16.3

1. By applying SAS congruence condition, state which of the following pairs (Fig. 28) of triangles are congruent. State the result in symbolic form

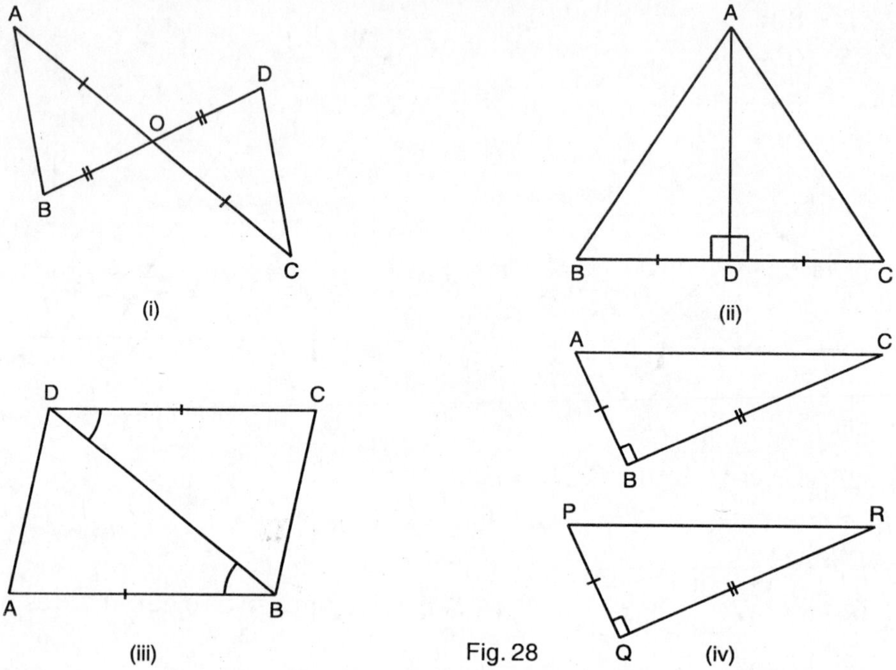

Fig. 28

2. State the condition by which the following pairs of triangles are congruent.

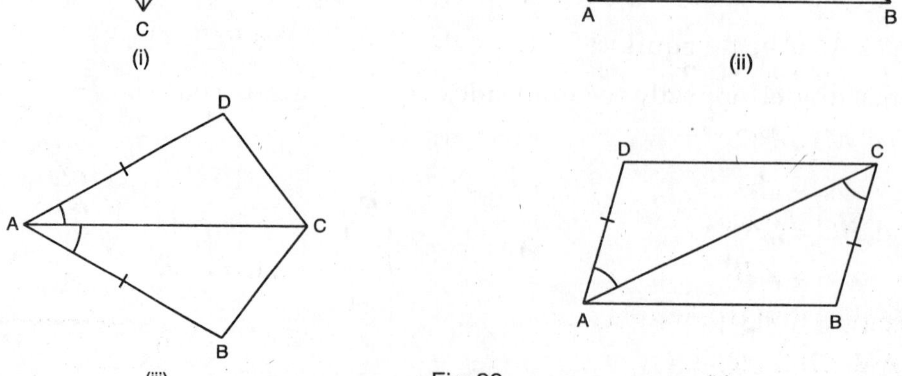

Fig. 29

3. In Fig. 30, line segments AB and CD bisect each other at O. Which of the following statements is true?
   (i) $\Delta AOC \cong \Delta DOB$ (ii) $\Delta AOC \cong \Delta BOD$
   (iii) $\Delta AOC \cong \Delta ODB$.
   State the three pairs of matching parts, you have used to arive at the answer.

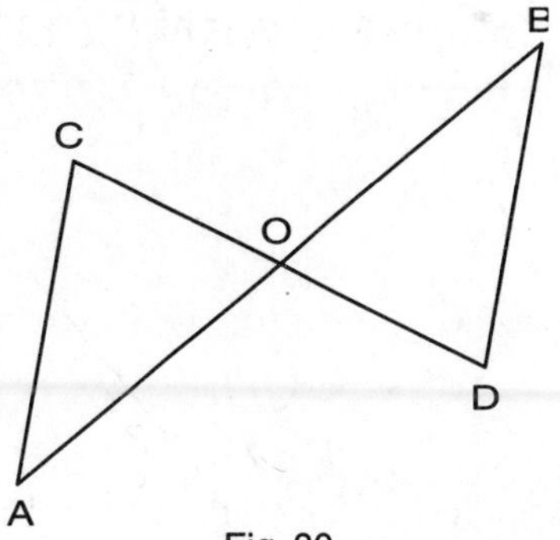

Fig. 30

4. Line-segments AB and CD bisect each other at O. AC and BD are joined forming triangles AOC and BOD. State the three equality relations between the parts of the two triangles, that are given or otherwise known. Are the two triangles congruent? State in symbolic form. Which congruence condition do you use?
5. ΔABC is isosceles with $AB = AC$. Line segment AD bisects $\angle A$ and meets the base BC in D.
   (i) Is $\Delta ADB \cong \Delta ADC$?
   (ii) State the three pairs of matching parts used to answer (i).
   (iii) Is it true to say that $BD = DC$?
6. In Fig. 31, $AB = AD$ and $\angle BAC = \angle DAC$.
   (i) State in symbolic form the congruence of two triangles ABC and ADC that is true.
   (ii) Complete each of the following, so as to make it true:
   (a) $\angle ABC =$ ....
   (b) $\angle ACD =$ ....
   (c) Line segment AC bisects ..... and .....

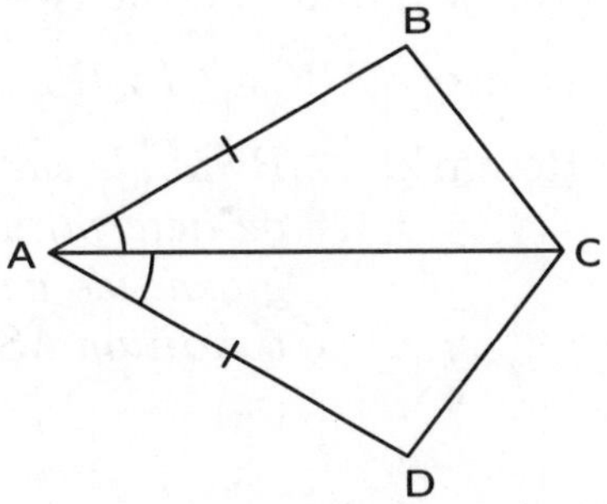

Fig. 31

7. In Fig. 32, $AB \parallel DC$ and $AB = DC$.
   (i) Is $\Delta ACD \cong \Delta CAB$?
   (ii) State the three pairs of matching parts used to answer (i).
   (iii) Which angle is equal to $\angle CAD$?
   (iv) Does it follow from (iii) that $AD \parallel BC$?

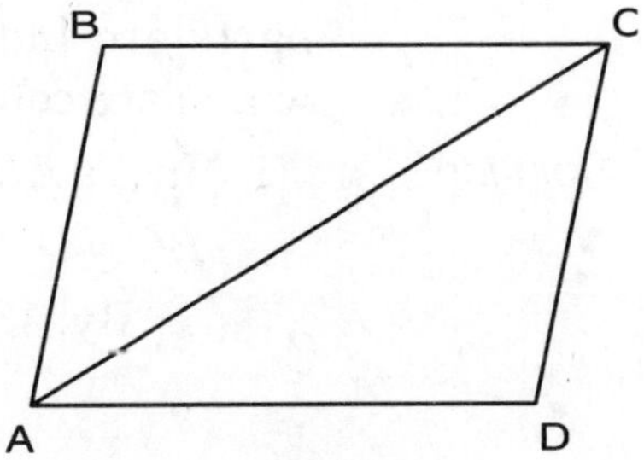

Fig. 32

ANSWERS

1. (i) $\Delta AOB \cong \Delta COD$ (ii) $\Delta ADC \cong \Delta ADB$ (iii) $\Delta ABD \cong \Delta CDB$
   (iv) $\Delta ABC \cong \Delta PQR$
2. (i) SSS (ii) SSS (iii) SAS (iv) SAS
3. (ii) AO, BO; CO, DO; $\angle AOC, \angle BOD$
4. $OA = OB$, $OC = OD$, $\angle AOC = \angle BOD$; Yes ; $\Delta AOC \cong \Delta BOD$; SAS
5. (i) Yes (ii) AB, AC; AD, AD; $\angle BAD = \angle CAD$ (iii) Yes
6. (i) $\Delta ABC \cong \Delta ADC$ (a) $\angle ADC$ (b) $\angle ACB$ (c) $\angle A, \angle C$
7. (i) Yes (ii) AC, CA; DC, BA; $\angle DCA, \angle BAC$ (iii) $\angle ACB$ (iv) Yes

16.4.3 ASA CONGRUENCE CONDITION

Two triangles are congruent if two angles and the included side of the one are respectively equal to the two angles and the included side of the other.

In order to verify the above statement, let us perform the following experiment.

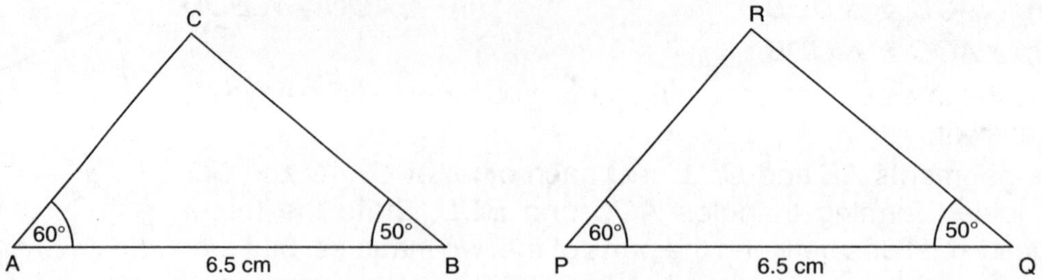

Fig. 32a

Experiment: Draw a ΔABC with $AB = 6.5$ cm, $\angle A = 60°$ and $\angle B = 50°$. Also, draw a ΔPQR with $PQ = 6.5$ cm, $\angle P = 60°$ and $\angle Q = 50°$. Thus, we have two triangles ABC and PQR such that $AB = PQ$, $\angle A = \angle P$ and $\angle B = \angle Q$. Make a trace copy of ΔABC and try to cover ΔPQR with A on P, B on Q and C on R.

You will find that the two triangles will cover each other exactly.

Hence, $\Delta ABC \cong \Delta PQR$.

Remark: *By angle sum property of a triangle, given two angles of a triangle, the third can be determined. Thus, whenever one side and any two angles of a triangle are given, we can change this to the type, two angles and included side, and the condition ASA is applied.*

ILLUSTRATIVE EXAMPLES

Example 1 In each of the following pairs of triangles given in Fig. 33, the measures of some parts are indicated along side. By applying ASA congruence condition, state which are congruent. State the answer in symbolic form.

Solution (i) In Δ's ABC and PQR, we have

$BC = QR = 6$ cm, $\angle ABC = \angle PQR = 50°$ and $\angle ACB = \angle PRQ = 40°$

$\therefore$ By ASA congruence condition, we have

$$\Delta ABC \cong \Delta PQR$$

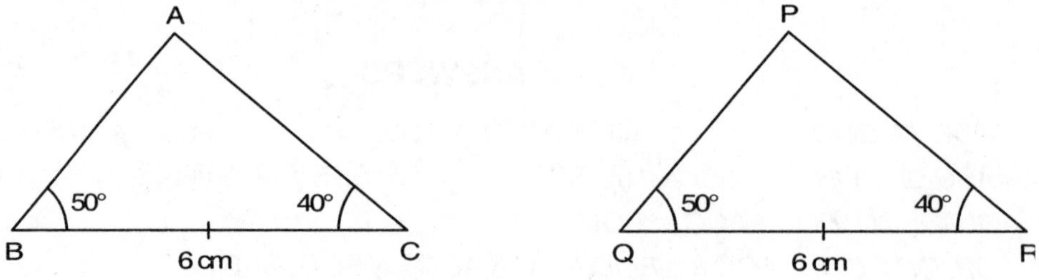

Fig. 33 (i)

(ii) In Δ's PQR and XYZ, we have

$QR = YZ = 5.5$ cm

$\angle PQR = \angle XYZ = 90°$

and, $\angle PRQ = \angle XZY = 40°$

So, by ASA congruence condition, we have

$$\Delta PQR \cong \Delta XYZ$$

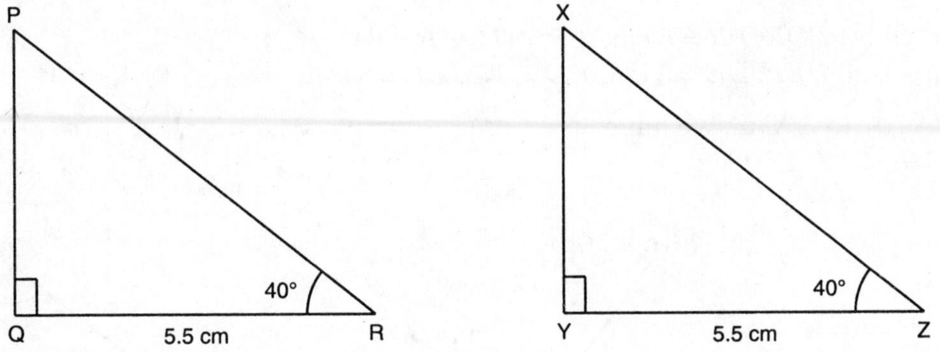

Fig. 33 (ii)

(iii) In Δ's AOD and BOC, we have

$\angle ADO = \angle CBO = 100°$

$\angle AOD = \angle COB$ [Vertically opposite angles]

and, $OB = OD = 2$ cm

So, by ASA congruence condition, we have

$\therefore \ \Delta AOD \cong \Delta COB$

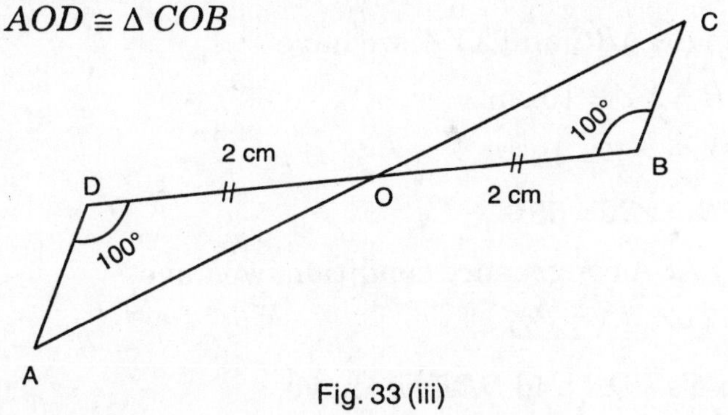

Fig. 33 (iii)

(iv) In Δ's ABC and BAD, we have

$\angle CAB = \angle DBA = 30°$

$\angle ABC = \angle BAD = 55°$

and, $AB = BA$

$\therefore$ By ASA congruence condition, we have

$$\Delta ABC \cong \Delta BAD$$

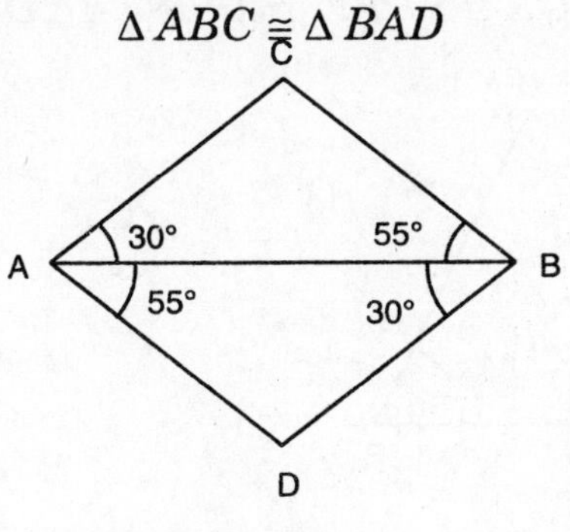

Fig. 33 (iv)

Example 2 Which of the following pairs of triangles are congruent?

(i) ΔABC: $AB = 10$ cm, $\angle A = 40°$, $\angle B = 55°$
ΔXYZ: $XY = 10$ cm, $\angle Y = 40°$, $\angle Z = 85°$

(ii) ΔPQR: $PR = 5$ cm, $\angle P = 37°$, $\angle R = 64°$
ΔDEF: $DE = 5$ cm, $\angle D = 37°$, $\angle F = 64°$

Solution (i) In ΔXYZ, we have

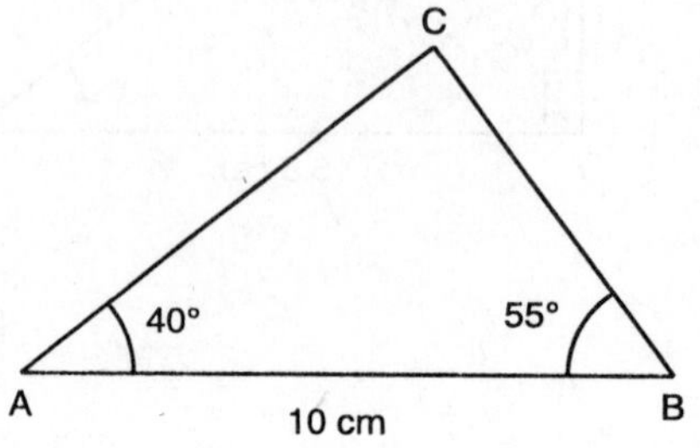

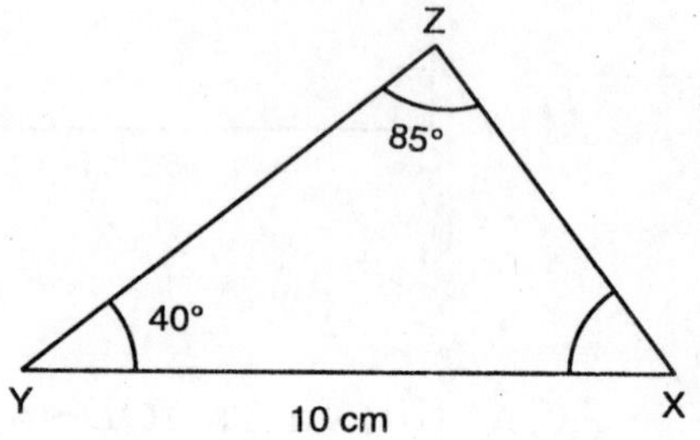

Fig. 34

$\angle Y = 40°$ and $\angle Z = 85°$

$\therefore$ $\angle X = 180° - (\angle Y + \angle Z) = 180° - (40° + 85°) = 55°$

Thus, in Δ s ABC and XYZ, we have

$AB = XY = 10$ cm

$\angle A = \angle Y = 40°$

and, $\angle B = \angle X = 55°$

$\therefore$ By ASA congruence condition, we have

$\Delta ABC \cong \Delta YXZ$

(ii) In Δ's PQR and DEF, we have

$PR = DE = 5$ cm

$\angle P = \angle D = 37°$

and, $\angle R = \angle E = 64°$

$\therefore$ By ASA congruence condition, we have

$\Delta PQR \cong \Delta DFE$ or $\Delta PRQ \cong \Delta DEF$

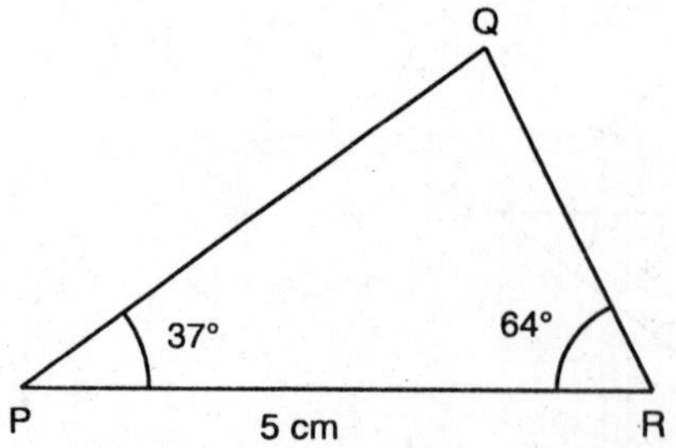

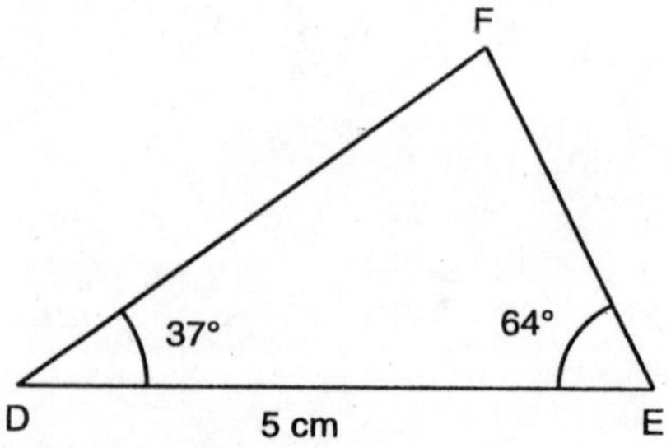

Fig. 34

EXERCISE 16.4

1. Which of the following pairs of triangles are congruent by ASA condition?

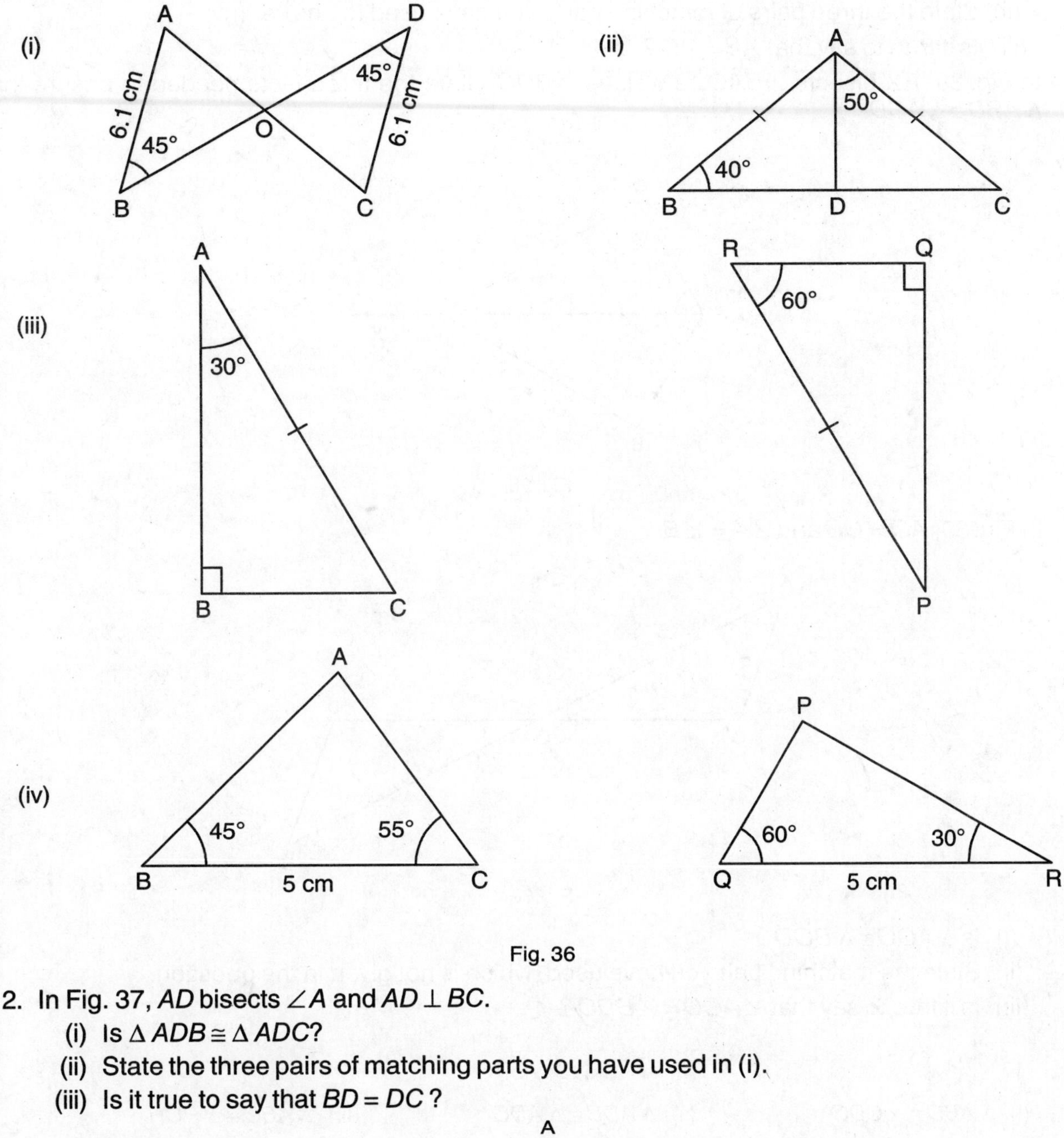

Fig. 36

2. In Fig. 37, AD bisects $\angle A$ and $AD \perp BC$.
   (i) Is $\Delta ADB \cong \Delta ADC$?
   (ii) State the three pairs of matching parts you have used in (i).
   (iii) Is it true to say that $BD = DC$?

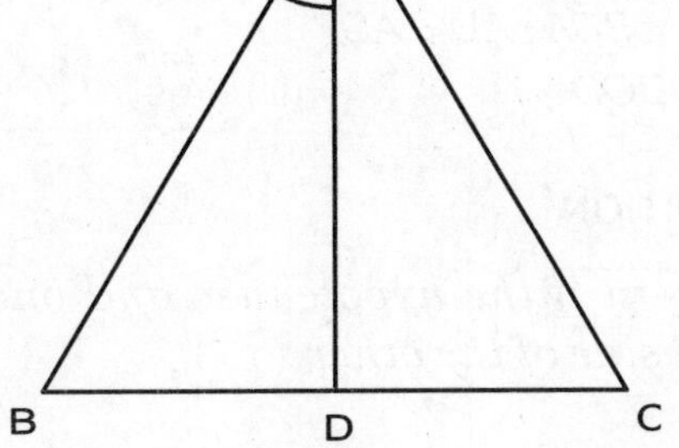

Fig. 37

3. Draw any triangle ABC. Use ASA condition to construct another triangle congruent to it.
4. In ΔABC, it is known that $\angle B = \angle C$. Imagine you have another copy of ΔABC
   (i) Is $\Delta ABC \cong \Delta ACB$?
   (ii) State the three pairs of matching parts you have used to answer (i).
   (iii) Is it true to say that $AB = AC$?
5. In Fig. 38, AX bisects $\angle BAC$ as well as $\angle BDC$. State the three facts needed to ensure that $\Delta ABD \cong \Delta ACD$.

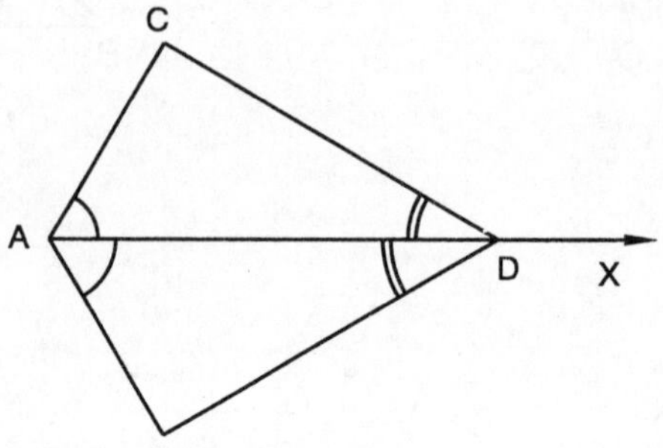

Fig. 38

6. In Fig. 39, $AO = OB$ and $\angle A = \angle B$.

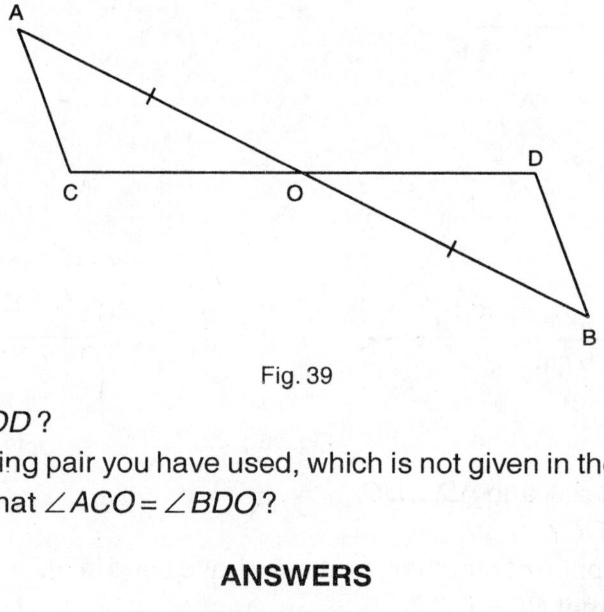

Fig. 39

   (i) Is $\Delta AOC \cong \Delta BOD$?
   (ii) State the matching pair you have used, which is not given in the question.
   (iii) Is it true to say that $\angle ACO = \angle BDO$?

ANSWERS

1. (i) $\Delta ABO \cong \Delta CDO$ (ii) $\Delta ADB \cong \Delta ADC$ (iii) $\Delta ABC \cong \Delta PQR$
   (iv) No
2. (i) Yes (ii) $\angle BAD, \angle CAD; AD, AD; \angle ADB, \angle ADC$ (iii) Yes
4. (i) Yes (ii) $\angle ABC, \angle ACB; \angle ACB, \angle ABC; BC, CD$ (iii) Yes
5. (i) $\angle CAD = \angle BAD, \angle CDA = \angle BDA; AD = AD$
6. (i) Yes (ii) $\angle AOC, \angle BOD$ (iii) Yes

16.4.4 RHS CONGRUENCE CONDITION

Two right triangles are congruent if the hypotenuse and one side of the one are respectively equal to the hypotenuse and one side of the other.

In order to verify the above fact, let us perform the following experiment.

Experiment: Draw a ΔABC such that $\angle C$ is a right angle, hypotenuse AB =10 cm, and side AC = 8 cm. Also, draw a Δ PQR with $\angle R$ = 90° ; hypotenuse PQ =10 cm and side PR =8 cm.

Thus, we have two triangles ABC and PQR such that

$\angle C = \angle R = 90°$, hypotenuse AB = hypotenuse PQ and side AC = side PR as shown in Fig. 40.

Now, make a trace copy of Δ PQR and try to cover ΔABC with P on A, Q on B and R on C. You will find that the two triangles will cover each other exactly. Hence, $\Delta ABC \cong \Delta PQR$.

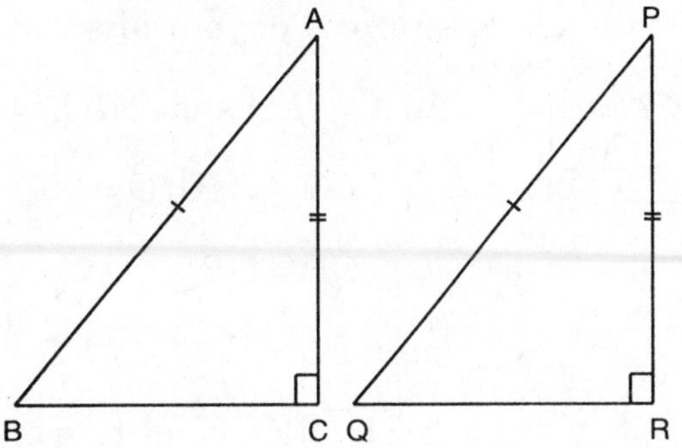

Fig. 40

ILLUSTRATIVE EXAMPLES

Example 1 In each of the following pairs of right triangles, the measures of some parts are indicated along side. State by the application of RHS congruence condition which are congruent. State each result in symbolic form.

Solution (i) In Δ's ADB and BCA, we have

$\angle ADB = \angle BCA = 90°$

$AB = AB$ [Hypotenuse]

and, $AD = BC = 8$ cm

So, by RHS congruence condition, we have

$$\Delta ADB \cong \Delta BCA$$

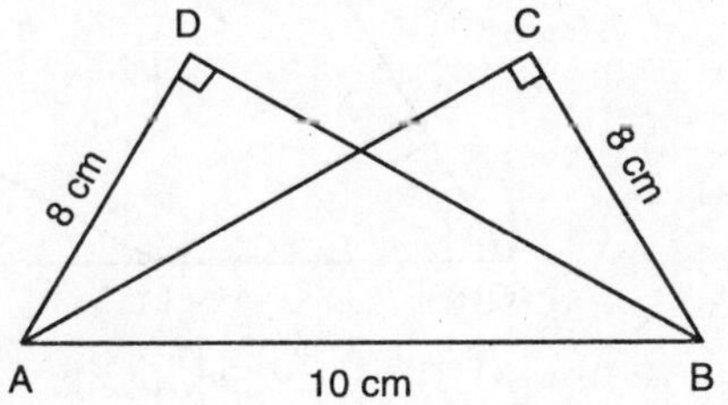

(i)

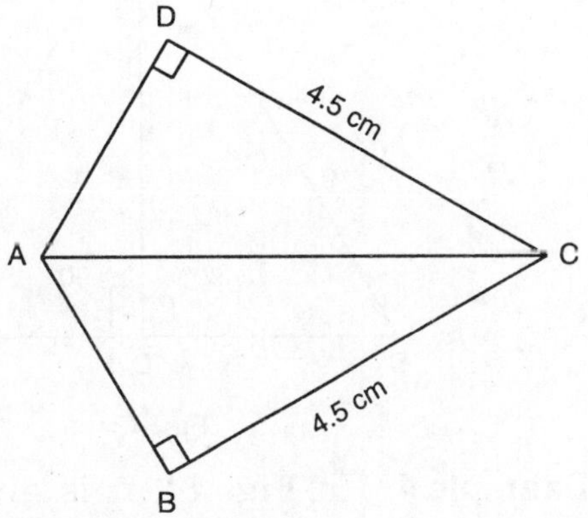

(ii)

Fig. 41

(ii) In Δ s ABC and ADC, we have

$\angle ABC = \angle ADC = 90°$

$AC = AC$ [Hypotenuse]

and, $BC = DC = 4.5$ cm

So, by RHS congruence condition, we have

$$\Delta ABC \cong \Delta ADC$$

Example 2 In Fig. 42, $PL \perp OB$ and $PM \perp OA$ such that $PL = PM$. Is $\Delta PLO \cong \Delta PMO$? Give reasons in support of your answer.

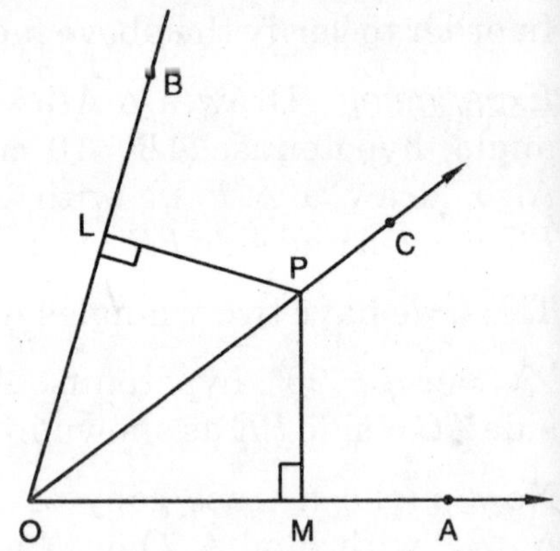

Fig. 42

Solution In Δs PLO and PMO, we have

$\angle PLO = \angle PMO = 90°$

$OP = OP$ [Hypotenuse]

and, $PL = PM$ [Given]

So, by RHS condition of congruence, we have

$$\Delta PLO \cong \Delta PMO.$$

Example 3 If ΔABC is an isosceles triangle such that $AB = AC$, then altitude AD from A on BC bisects BC (Fig. 43).

Solution In right triangles ADB and ADC, we have

Hyp. AB = Hyp. AC [Given]

$AD = AD$ [Common side]

So, by RHS criterion of congruence,

$\Delta ABD \cong \Delta ACD$

$\Rightarrow$ $BD = DC$ [∵ Corresponding parts of above congruent triangles are equal]

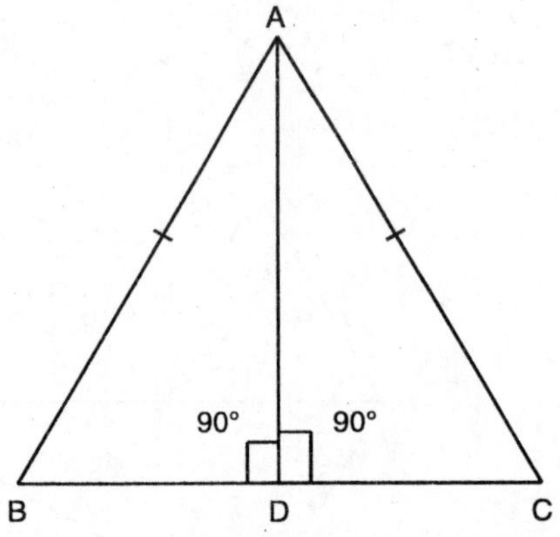

Fig. 43

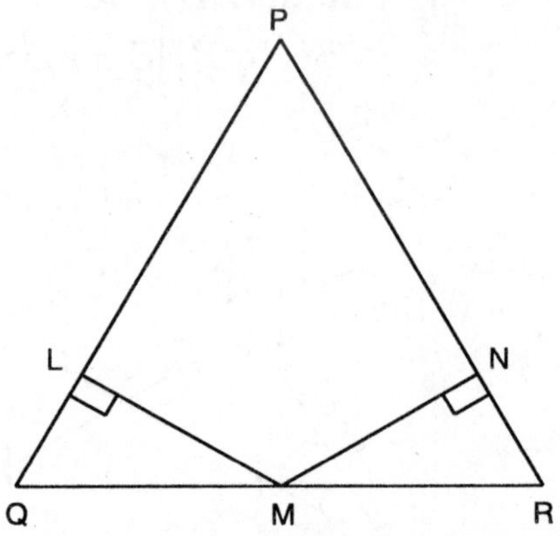

Fig. 44

Example 4 In Fig. 44, it is given that $LM = MN$, $QM = MR$, $ML \perp PQ$ and $MN \perp PR$. Prove that $PQ = PR$.

Solution In right triangles QLM and MNR, we have

Hyp. QM = Hyp. MR [Given]

$LM = MN$ [Given]

So, by RHS criterion of congruence, we have

$\Delta QLM \cong \Delta MNR$

$\Rightarrow$ $\angle Q = \angle R$ [∵ Corresponding parts of congruent triangles are equal]

$\Rightarrow$ $PR = PQ$ [∵ Sides opposite to equal angles are equal]

Example 5 *AD*, *BE* and *CF*, the altitudes of ΔABC are equal. Prove that ΔABC is an equilateral triangle.

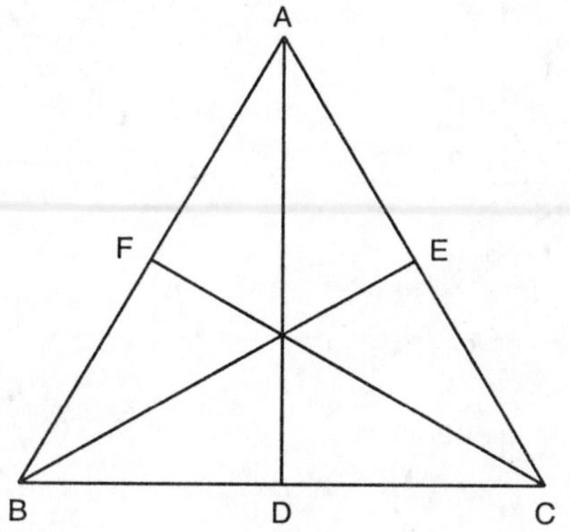

Fig. 45

Solution In right triangles *BCE* and *BFC*, we have

Hyp. BC = Hyp. BC

$BE = CF$ [Given]

So, by RHS criterion of congruence, we have

$\Delta BCE \cong \Delta BFC$

$\Rightarrow \quad \angle B = \angle C$ [$\because$ Corresponding parts of congruent triangles are equal]

$\Rightarrow \quad AC = AB$ ...(i) [$\because$ Sides opposite to equal angles are equal]

Similarly, $\Delta ABD \cong \Delta ABE$

$\Rightarrow \quad \angle B = \angle A$ [Corresponding parts of congruent triangles are equal]

$\Rightarrow \quad AC = BC$ ...(ii) [Sides opposite to equal angles are equal]

From (i) and (ii), we get

$AB = BC = AC$

Hence, ΔABC is an equilateral triangle.

EXERCISE 16.5

1. In each of the following pairs of right triangles, the measures of some parts are indicated along side. State by the application of RHS congruence condition which are congruent. State each result in symbolic form. (Fig. 46)

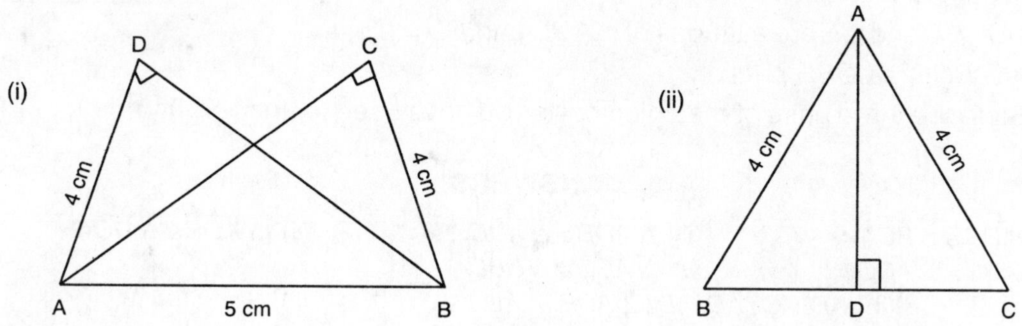

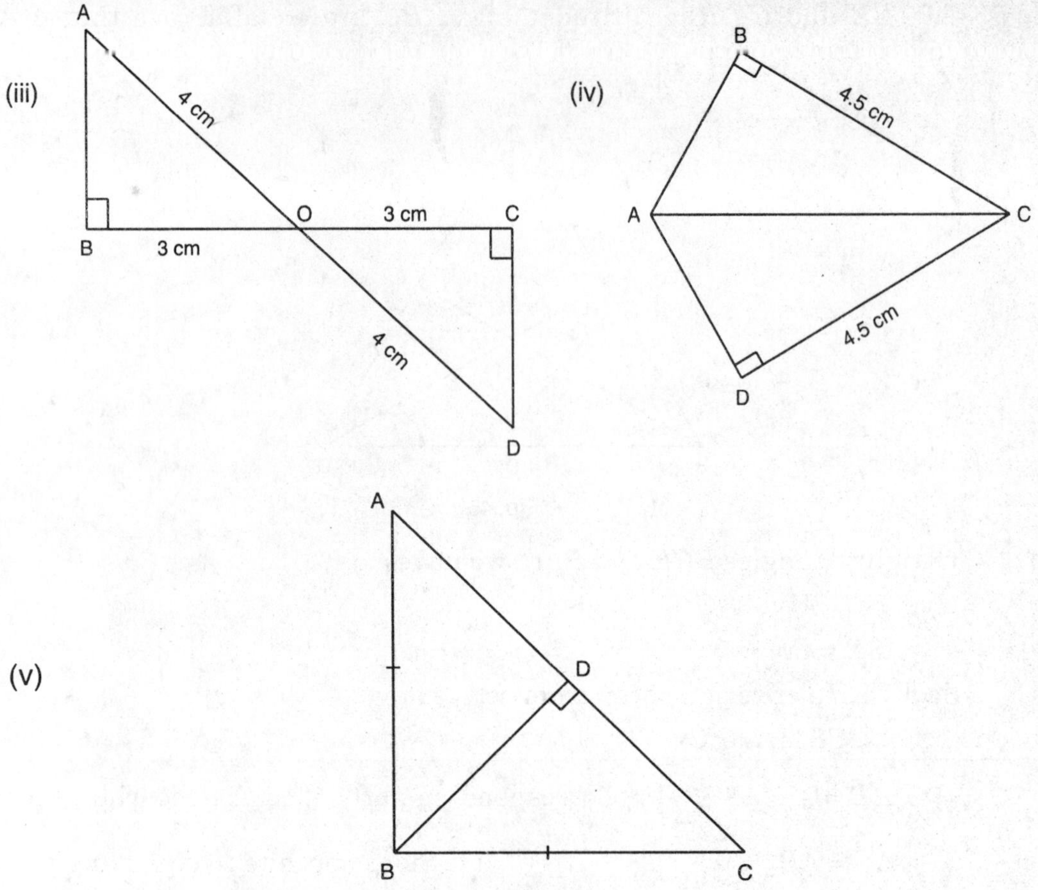

Fig. 46

2. Δ *ABC* is isosceles with $AB = AC$. *AD* is the altitude from *A* on *BC*.
   (i) Is $\Delta ABD \cong \Delta ACD$?
   (ii) State the pairs of matching parts you have used to answer (i).
   (iii) Is it true to say that $BD = DC$?
3. Δ *ABC* is isosceles with $AB = AC$. Also, $AD \perp BC$ meeting *BC* in *D*. Are the two triangles *ABD* and *ACD* congruent? State in symbolic form. Which congruence condition do you use? Which side of ΔADC equals *BD*? Which angle of ΔADC equals $\angle B$?
4. Draw a right triangle *ABC*. Use RHS condition to construct another triangle congruent to it.
5. In Fig. 47, *BD* and *CE* are altitudes of ΔABC and $BD = CE$.
   (i) Is $\Delta BCD \cong \Delta CBE$?
   (ii) State the three pairs of matching parts you have used to answer (i).

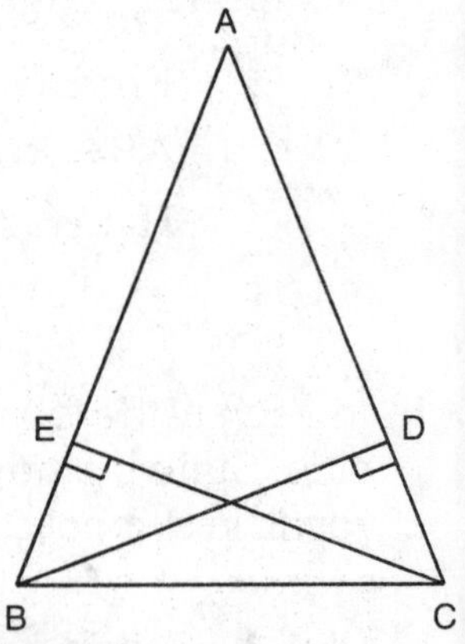

Fig. 47

ANSWERS

1. (i) $\Delta ADB \cong \Delta BCA$ (ii) $\Delta ADB \cong \Delta ADC$ (iii) $\Delta AOB \cong \Delta DOC$
   (iv) $\Delta ABC \cong \Delta ADC$ (v) $\Delta ABD \cong \Delta CBD$
2. (i) Yes (ii) *AB*, *AC*; *AD*, *AD*; $\angle ADB$, $\angle ADC$ (iii) Yes
3. Yes, $\Delta ABD \cong \Delta ACD$, RHS, *CD*, *LC*
5. (i) Yes (ii) *BD*, *CE*; *CB*; *BC*, $\angle BDC$, $\angle CEB$

THINGS TO REMEMBER

1. *Two figures are congruent, if they have exactly the same shape and size.*
2. (i) *Two line segments are congruent, if they have the same length.*
   (ii) *Two angles are congruent, if they have the same measure.*
   (iii) *Two squares are congruent, if they have the same side length.*
   (iv) *Two rectangles are congruent, if they have the same length and breadth.*
   (v) *Two circles are congruent, if they have the same radius.*
3. *Two triangles are congruent, if in matching of their vertices, the three sides and the three angles of one triangle are respectively equal to the corresponding parts of the other.*
4. SSS Congruence Condition: *Two triangles are congruent, if three sides of one triangle are respectively equal to the three sides of the other.*
5. SAS Congruence Condtion: *Two triangles are congruent, if two sides and the included angle of one are respectively equal to the two sides and the included angle of the other.*
6. ASA Congruence Condition: *Two triangles are congruent, if two angles and the included side of the one are respectively equal to the two angles and the included side of the other.*
7. RHS Congruence Condition: *Two right triangles are congruent, if the hypotenuse and one side of the one triangle are respectively equal to the hypotenuse and one side of the other.*
8. *In an isosceles triangle, the angles opposite to equal sides are equal.*
9. *The bisector of the vertical angle of an isosceles triangle bisects the base at right angles.*
10. *Two congruent figures are equal in area but two figures having the same area need not be congruent.*

17

CONSTRUCTIONS

17.1 INTRODUCTION

In the previous class, we have learnt how to draw a line segment, an angle, perpendicular at a point given on a line, perpendicular from a point to a line when the point is outside the line, perpendicular bisector of a line segment, bisector of an angle, a line parallel to a given line etc. In this chapter, we shall learn the construction of triangles when sufficient data is given. In the previous class, we have studied that a triangle has six elements or parts, namely, three sides and three angles. A triangle can always be drawn if we have three elements one of which must be a side.

In the following sections, we shall learn about the simple cases of construction of triangles.

17.2 DRAWING A LINE PARALLEL TO A GIVEN LINE THROUGH A GIVEN POINT OUTSIDE IT

In the previous chapters, we have learnt that if a transversal cuts two parallel lines, then the alternate angles are equal. Therefore, to draw a line parallel to a given line XY through a point P outside it, we proceed as follows:

Steps of Construction

STEP I *Take any point Q on XY.*

STEP II *Join PQ.*

STEP III *With Q as centre, draw an arc cutting XY and PQ at A and B respectively.*

STEP IV *With centre P and the same radius as in step III, draw an arc on the opposite side of QP to cut QP at C.*

STEP V *With centre C and radius equal to AB draw an arc cutting the arc drawn in step IV at D.*

STEP VI *Join PD and produce it in both directions to obtain the required line.*

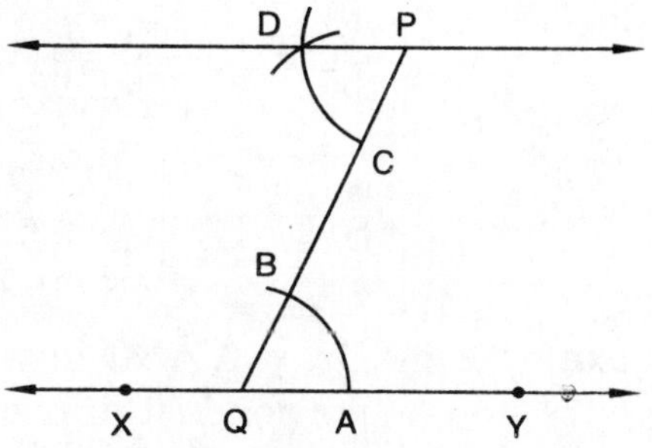

Fig. 1

Validity: Since $\angle DPQ = \angle AQP$ and these are alternate angles. Therefore, $PD \parallel XY$ and PD contains P.

EXERCISE 17.1

1. Draw an $\angle BAC$ of measure 50° such that $AB = 5$ cm and $AC = 7$ cm. Through C draw a line parallel to AB and through B draw a line parallel to AC, intersecting each other at D. Measure BD and CD.
2. Draw a line PQ. Draw another line parallel to PQ at a distance of 3 cm from it.
3. Take any three non-collinear points A, B, C and draw ΔABC. Through each vertex of the triangle, draw a line parallel to the opposite side.

4. Draw two parallel lines at a distance 5 cm apart.

17.3 SSS TRIANGLE CONSTRUCTION

In order to construct a triangle when the lengths of its sides are given, we follow the following steps:

Steps of Construction

STEP I *Draw a line segment of length equal to one of the sides, say BC of the triangle.*

STEP II *With centre B and radius equal to the length of side AB, draw an arc.*

STEP III *With centre C and radius equal to the length of side AC, draw an arc cutting the arc drawn in Step II at A.*

STEP IV *Join AB and AC to obtain the desired triangle ABC.*

The following examples will illustrate the above procedure:

ILLUSTRATIVE EXAMPLES

Example 1 Construct a triangle ABC if the lengths of its sides are given by $AB = 6$ cm, $BC = 7$ cm and $AC = 5$ cm.

Solution To construct the ΔABC, we follow the following steps:

Steps of Construction

STEP I *Draw a line segment BC = 7 cm.*

STEP II *With centre B and radius AB = 6 cm, draw an arc of the circle.*

STEP III *With centre C and radius AC = 5 cm, draw another arc intersecting the arc drawn in step III at A.*

STEP IV *Join AB and AC to obtain the desired triangle.*

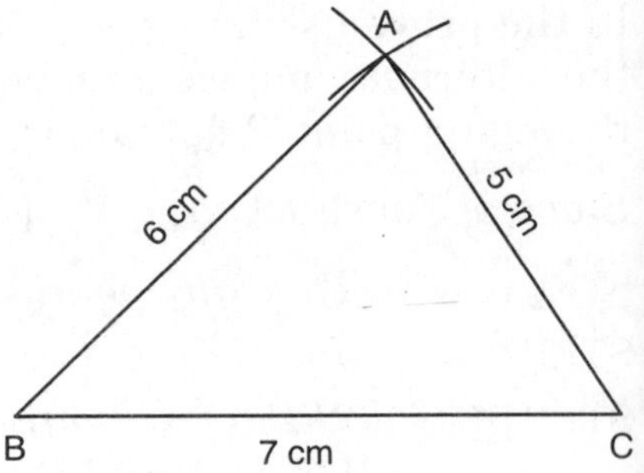

Fig. 2

Example 2 Draw ΔABC in which $AB = 4.5$ cm, $BC = 5$ cm and $CA = 6$ cm. Also, draw the perpendicular bisector of BC.

Solution In order to draw the ΔABC and the perpendicular bisector of BC, we follow the following steps:

Steps of Construction:

STEP I *Draw a line segment BC = 5 cm.*

STEP II *With centre B and radius AB = 4.5 cm, draw an arc of the circle.*

STEP III *With centre C and radius AC = 6 cm, draw an arc intersecting the previously drawn arc at A.*

STEP IV *Join AB and AC to obtain the desired triangle.*

STEP V *With centre B and radius more than* $\frac{1}{2}$*(BC), draw two arcs on both sides of BC.*

STEP VI *With centre C and the same radius as in step V, draw two arcs intersecting the arcs drawn in step V at D and E.*

STEP VII *Join DE to obtain the required perpendicular bisector of BC.*

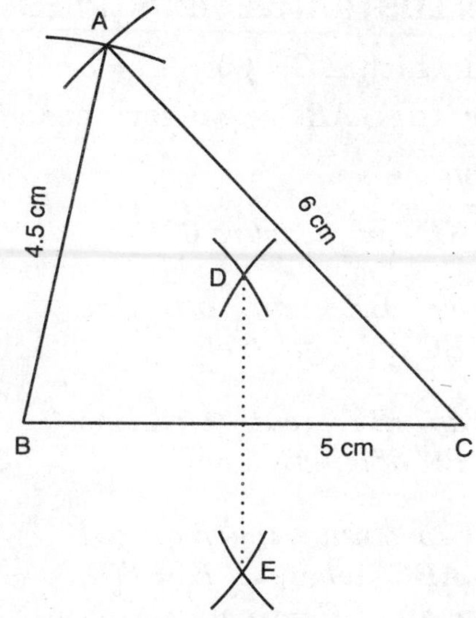

Fig. 3

EXERCISE 17.2

1. Draw Δ *ABC* in which *AB* = 5.5 cm, *BC* = 6 cm and *CA* = 7 cm. Also, draw perpendicular bisector of side *BC*.
2. Draw Δ *PQR* in which *PQ* = 3 cm, *QR* = 4 cm and *RP* = 5 cm. Also, draw the bisector of $\angle Q$.
3. Draw an equilateral triangle one of whose sides is of length 7 cm.
4. Draw a triangle whose sides are of lengths 4 cm, 5 cm and 7 cm. Draw the perpendicular bisector of the largest side.
5. Draw a triangle *ABC* with *AB* = 6 cm, *BC* = 7 cm and *CA* = 8 cm. Using ruler and compass alone, draw (i) the bisector *AD* of $\angle A$ and (ii) perpendicular *AL* from *A* on *BC*.

   Measure *LAD*.
6. Draw Δ *DEF* such that *DE* = *DF* = 4 cm and EF = 6 cm. Measure $\angle E$ and $\angle F$.
7. Draw any trianlge *ABC*. Bisect side *AB* at *D*. Through *D*, draw a line parallel to *BC*, meeting *AC* in *E*. Measure *AE* and *EC*.

17.4 SAS TRIANGLE CONSTRUCTION

In order to construct a triangle when two of its sides, say *AB* and *BC* and the included angle $\angle B$ are given, we follow the following steps:

Steps of Construction

STEP I *Draw $\angle XBY$ of measure equal to that of $\angle B$.*

STEP II *From ray BX, cut off line segment equal to BC.*

STEP III *From ray BY, cut off line segment equal to BA.*

STEP IV *Join AC to obtain the triangle ABC.*

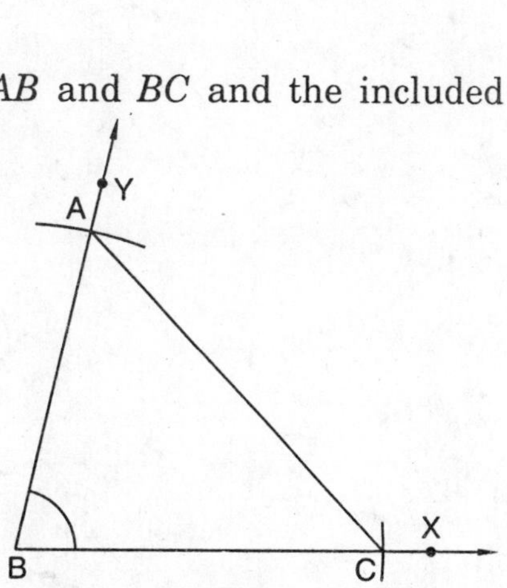

Fig. 4

Following examples will illustrate the above procedure.

ILLUSTRATIVE EXAMPLES

Example 1 Construct ΔABC in which $\angle B = 60°$; $AB = 5$ cm and $BC = 6$ cm.

Solution In order to construct the ΔABC, we follow the following steps:

Steps of Construction:

STEP I *Draw $\angle XBY$ of measure 60°.*

STEP II *From ray BX, cut off line segment BC of length 6 cm.*

STEP IV *From ray BY, cut off line segment BA of length 5 cm.*

STEP IV *Join AC to obtain the required triangle ABC, where $\angle B = 60°$, $AB = 5$ cm and $BC = 6$ cm.*

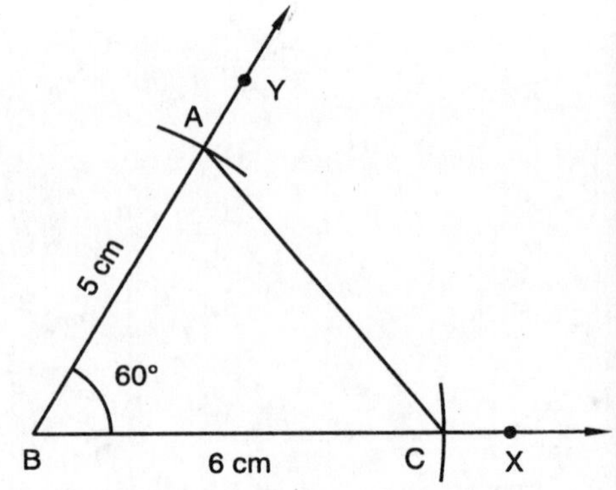

Fig. 5

Example 2 Draw a triangle ABC with $BC = 3.2$ cm, $AB = 3.6$ cm and $\angle B = 120°$. Also draw a perpendiculr from A on BC.

Solution We follow the following steps to construct the required triangle:

Steps of Construction:

STEP I *Draw $\angle XBY$ of measure 120°.*

STEP II *From ray BX, cut off line segment BC of length 3.2 cm.*

STEP III *From ray BY, cut off line segment BA of length 3.6 cm.*

STEP IV *Join CA to obtain the required triangle.*

STEP V *Draw ray BZ.*

STEP VI *With centre A, draw an arc intersecting rays BX and BZ at P and Q respectively.*

STEP VII *With centre P and radius more than $\frac{1}{2}$ (PQ), cut an arc on the opposite of A.*

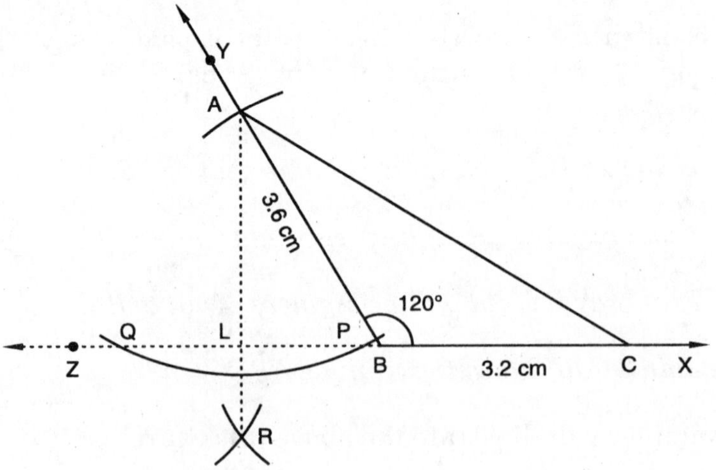

Fig. 6

STEP VIII *With centre Q and the same radius as in step VII, cut an arc which intersects the arc drawn in step VII at R.*

STEP IX *Join AR. If it meets BZ at L, then AL is the required perpendicular from A on BC.*

EXERCISE 17.3

1. Draw $\Delta\, ABC$ in which $AB = 3$ cm, $BC = 5$ cm and $\angle B = 70°$.
2. Draw $\Delta\, ABC$ in which $\angle A = 70°$, $AB = 4$ cm and $AC = 6$ cm. Measure BC.
3. Draw an isosceles triangle in which each of the equal sides is of length 3 cm and the angle between them is 45°.
4. Draw $\Delta\, ABC$ in which $\angle A = 120°$, $AB = AC = 3$ cm. Measure $\angle B$ and $\angle C$.
5. Draw $\Delta\, ABC$ in which $\angle C = 90°$ and $AC = BC = 4$ cm.
6. Draw a triangle ABC in which $BC = 4$ cm, $AB = 3$ cm and $\angle B = 45°$. Also, draw a perpendicular from A on BC.
7. Draw a triangle ABC with $AB = 3$ cm, $BC = 4$ cm and $\angle B = 60°$. Also, draw the bisector of angles C and A of the triangle, meeting in a point O. Measure $\angle COA$.

17.5 ASA TRIANGLE CONSTRUCTION

To construct a triangle when two of its angles, say B and C, and the included side BC are given, we proceed as follows (Fig. 6):

Steps of Construction

STEP I *Draw line segment BC.*

STEP II *Draw $\angle CBX$ of measure equal to that of $\angle B$.*

STEP III *Draw $\angle BCY$ with Y on the same side of BC as X, such that its measure is equal to that of $\angle C$. Let BX and CY intersect at A. Then, $\Delta\, ABC$ is the required triangle.*

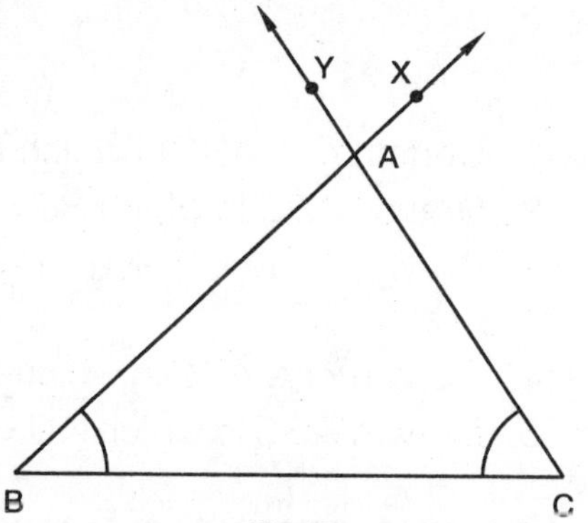

Fig. 7

Following examples will illustrate the above procedure.

ILLUSTRATIVE EXAMPLES

Example 1 Draw ΔABC in which $BC = 6$ cm, $\angle B = 35°$ and $\angle C = 100°$. Measure $\angle A$.

Solution To draw the ΔABC, we follow the following steps:

Steps of Construction:

STEP I *Draw a line segment $BC = 6$ cm.*

STEP II *Draw $\angle CBX$, such that $\angle CBX = 35°$.*

STEP III *Draw $\angle BCY$ with Y on the same side of BC as X, such that $\angle BCY = 100°$.*

STEP IV *Let BX and CY intersect at A. Then Δ ABC is the required triangle.*

By measurement we find that $\angle A = 45°$.

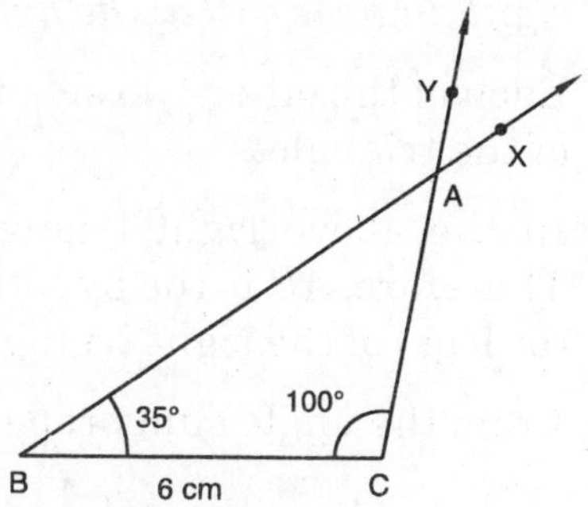

Fig. 8

Example 2 Draw a triangle ABC in which $BC = 5.2$ cm, $\angle B = 60°$ and $\angle A = 100°$.

Solution Here, we are given the side BC, $\angle B$ and $\angle A$. But to draw the triangle, we require $\angle C$.

We know that

$\angle A + \angle B + \angle C = 180°$

$\Rightarrow \quad 100° + 60° + \angle C = 180°$

$\Rightarrow \quad 160° + \angle C = 180°$

$\Rightarrow \quad \angle C = 180° - 160° = 20°$

Thus, we have, $BC = 5.2$ cm, $\angle B = 60°$ and $\angle C = 20°$.

Now, to draw the ΔABC, we follow the following steps:

Steps of Construction:

STEP I *Draw a line segment $BC = 5.2$ cm.*

STEP II *Draw $\angle CBX$, such that $\angle CBX = 60°$.*

STEP III *Draw $\angle BCY$, with Y on the same side of BC as X such that $\angle BCY = 20°$*

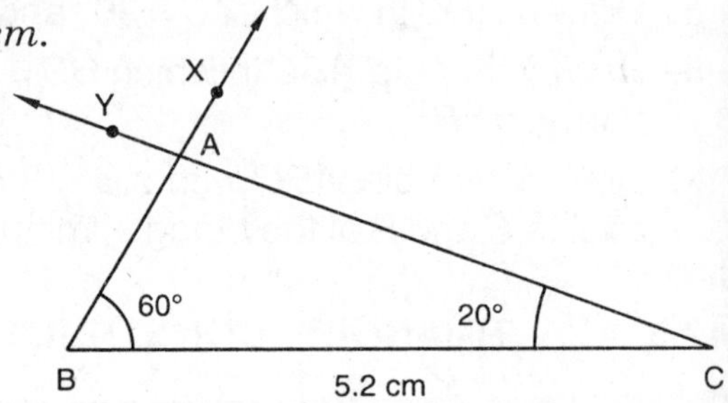

Fig. 9

Let BX and CY intersect at A.

Then ΔABC is the required triangle.

EXERCISE 17.4

1. Construct ΔABC in which $BC = 4$ cm, $\angle B = 50°$ and $\angle C = 70°$.
2. Draw ΔABC in which $BC = 8$ cm, $\angle B = 50°$ and $\angle A = 50°$.
3. Draw ΔPQR in which $\angle Q = 80°$, $\angle R = 55°$ and $QR = 4.5$ cm. Draw the perpendicular bisector of side QR.
4. Construct ΔABC in which $AB = 6.4$ cm, $\angle A = 45°$ and $\angle B = 60°$.
5. Draw ΔABC in which $AC = 6$ cm, $\angle A = 90°$ and $\angle B = 60°$.

17.6 RHS TRIANGLE CONSTRUCTION

A triangle is said to be a right triangle or a right angled triangle, if one of its three angles is a right angle.

In Fig. 10, ΔABC is a right triangle with $\angle C$ as right angle.

HYPOTENUSE *In a right triangle, the side opposite the right angle is called the hypotenuse of the triangle.*

Each of the other two sides is called a leg or simply, a side of the triangle.

In the above right triangle ABC, $\angle C$ is a right angle. Therefore, AB is the hypotenuse and AC, BC are the sides (or legs) of the right triangle.

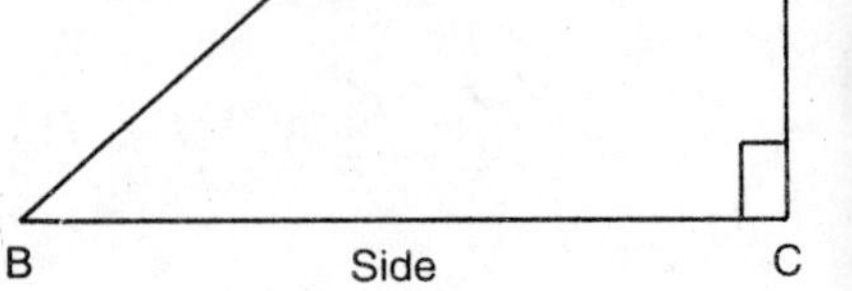

Fig. 10

From the angle sum property of a triangle, we have

$$\angle A + \angle B + \angle C = 180°$$

$\Rightarrow \quad \angle A + \angle B + 90° = 180°$

$\Rightarrow \quad \angle A + \angle B = 180° - 90°$

$\Rightarrow \quad \angle A + \angle B = 90°$

$\Rightarrow \quad \angle A$ and $\angle B$ are acute angles.

Thus, each of the other two angles of a right triangle is acute.

To construct a right triangle *ABC* right angled at *C* when its hypotenuse *AB* and one side *BC* are given, we follow the following steps:

Steps of Construction

STEP I *Draw a line segment BC of given length.*

STEP II *Draw* $\angle BCX$ *of measure 90°.*

STEP III *With centre B and radius equal to the hypotenuse AB, draw an arc of the circle to intersect ray CX at A.*

STEP IV *Join BA to obtain the required triangle ABC.*

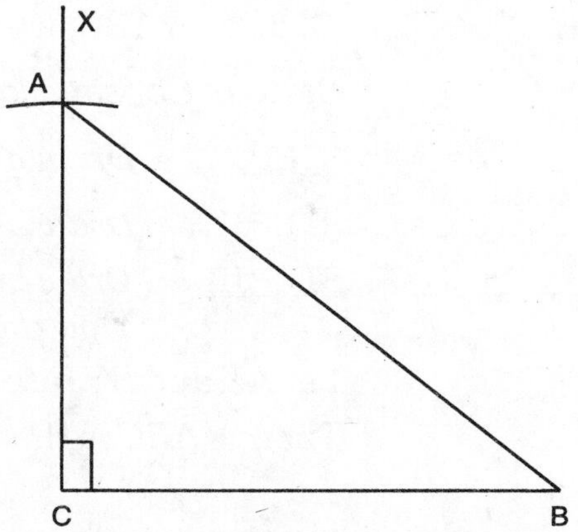

Fig. 11

Following examples will illustrate the above procedure.

ILLUSTRATIVE EXAMPLES

Example 1 Draw triangle *ABC* with $\angle C$ a right angle, $AB = 6.2$ cm and $BC = 4.5$ cm.

Solution To construct the ΔABC, we follow the following steps:

Steps of Construction:

STEP I *Draw a line segment BC of length 4.5 cm.*

STEP II *Draw* $\angle BCX$ *of measure 90°.*

STEP III *With centre B and radius AB = 6.2 cm, draw an arc of the circle to intersect ray CX at A.*

STEP IV *Join BA to obtain the desired triangle ABC.*

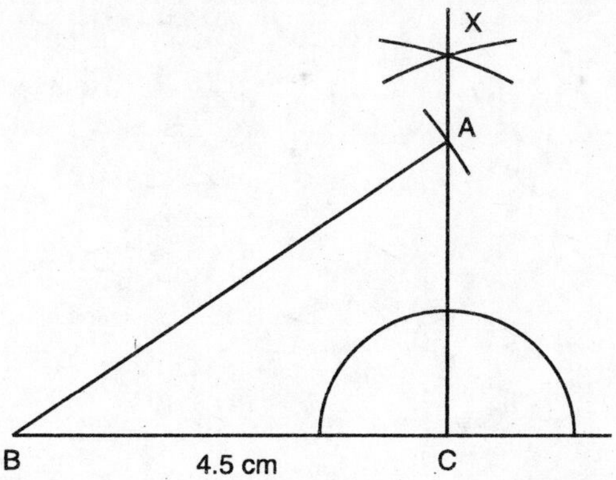

Fig. 12

Example 2 Draw a right triangle having hypotenuse of length 5.4 cm, and one of the acute angles of measure $60°$.

Solution Let ΔABC be a right triangle, right angled at C, such that hypotenuse $AB = 5.4$ cm. Further, let $\angle A = 60°$. Then by the angle sum property of ΔABC, we have

$$\angle A + \angle B + \angle C = 180°$$

$$\Rightarrow \quad 60° + \angle B + 90° = 180°$$

$$\Rightarrow \quad 150° + \angle B = 180°$$

$$\Rightarrow \quad \angle B = 180° - 150° = 30°$$

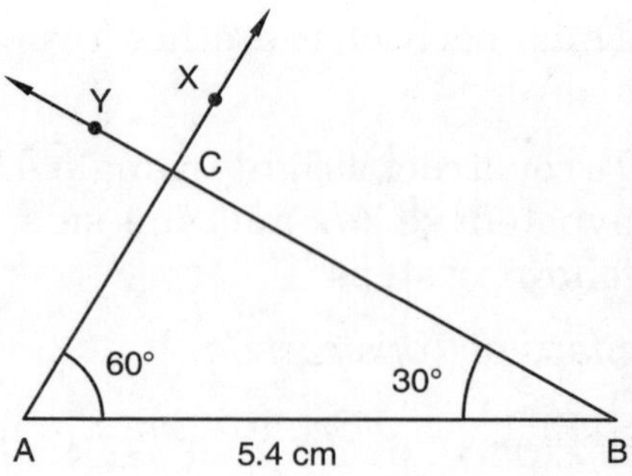

Fig. 13

To draw ΔABC, we follow the following steps:

Steps of Construction:

STEP I *Draw a line segment $AB = 5.4$ cm.*

STEP II *Draw $\angle BAX$ of measure $60°$*

STEP III *Draw $\angle ABY$ of measure $30°$ with Y on the same side of AB as X.*

Let AX and BY intersect at C.

Then, ΔABC is the required triangle.

EXERCISE 17.5

1. Draw a right triangle with hypotenuse of length 5 cm and one side of length 4 cm.
2. Draw a right triangle whose hypotenuse is of length 4 cm and one side is of length 2.5 cm.
3. Draw a right triangle having hypotenuse of length 5.4 cm, and one of the acute angles of measure $30°$.
4. Construct a right triangle ABC in which $AB = 5.8$ cm, $BC = 4.5$ cm and $\angle C = 90°$.
5. Construct a right triangle, right angled at C in which $AB = 5.2$ cm and $BC = 4.6$ cm.

18

SYMMETRY

18.1 INTRODUCTION

In class VI, we have studied about symmetry and lines of symmetry of various mathematical and non-mathematical figures and objects. Symmetry is such a nice thing that it is used almost in every field of activity. Architects, designers of jewellery or clothing, artists and many others use the idea of symmetry in their profession. Even nature has also gifted many living and non-living symmetrical objects to us. Some of them are shown below.

Fig. 1

Fig. 2

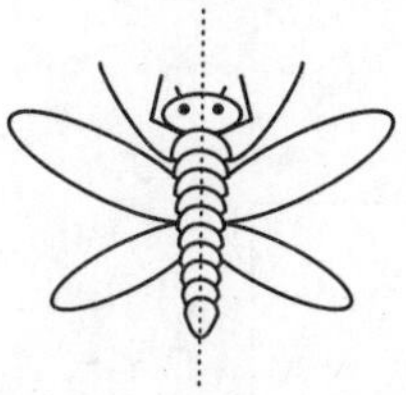

Fig. 3

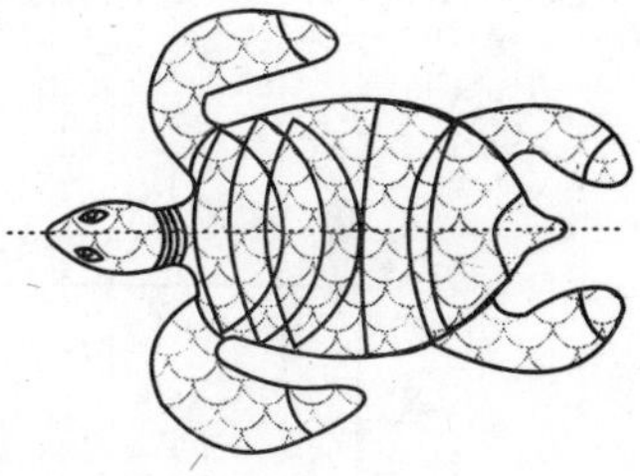

Fig. 4

Following are the pictures of some man made architectural marvels which are beautiful because of their symmetry.

Fig. 5 Tajmahal

Fig. 6

In each of the following figures dotted lines are lines of symmetry.

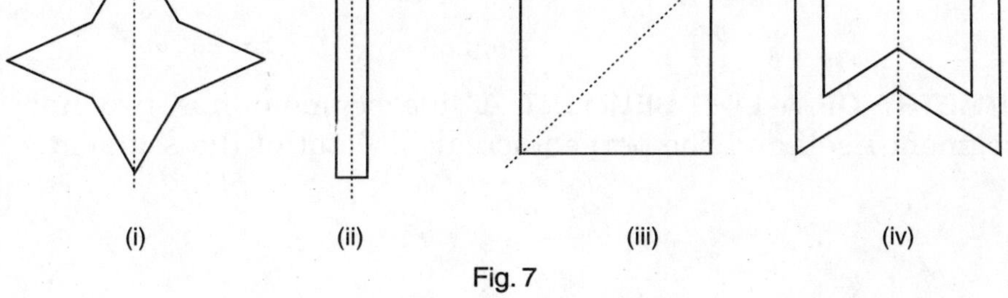

(i) (ii) (iii) (iv)

Fig. 7

18.2 LINES OF SYMMETRY

We observe that each one of the figures 1 to 7 is divided into two identical parts by the dotted lines. When we fold these figures along the dotted line, one half of the figures would fit exactly cover the other half. The dotted lines are known as the lines of symmetry of the respective figures. Thus, we may define a line of symmetry of a figure as follows.

LINE OF SYMMETRY *If a line divides a figure into two parts such that when the figure is folded about the line the two parts of the figure coincide, then the line is known as the line of symmetry.*

The line of symmetry is also known as the axis of symmetry.

In each one of the figure 1 to 7 dotted lines are lines of symmetry of the respective figures.

A figure may or may not have a line of symmetry. There may be figures having more than one line of symmetry.

The following figures have more than one line of symmetry. Such figures are said to have multiple lines of symmetry.

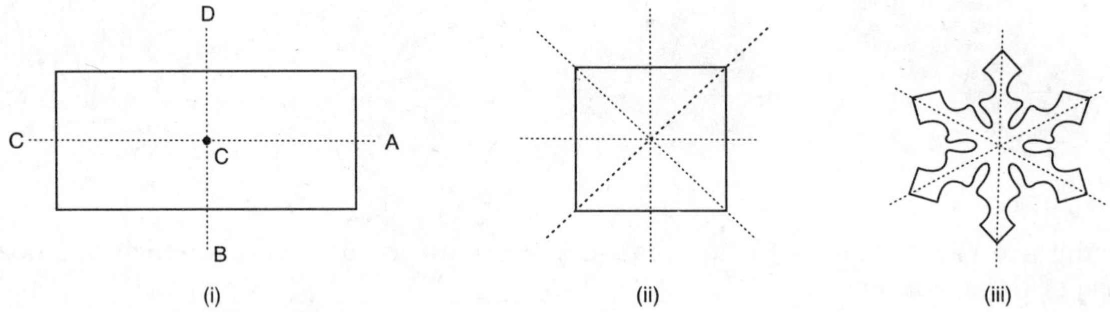

Fig. 8

Let us now discuss about the lines of symmetry of some geometrical figures.

LINES OF SYMMETRY OF A LINE A line has infinite length and hence it can be considered that each line perpendicular to the given line divide the line into two equal halves (parts). So, a line has infinite number of symmetrical lines which are perpendicular to it. Also, a line is symmetrical to itself.

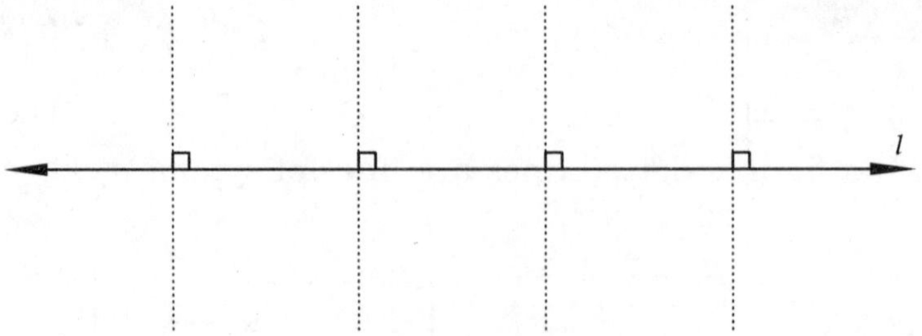

Fig. 9

LINES OF SYMMETRY OF A LINE SEGMENT A line segment has two lines of symmetry, namely, the segment itself and the perpendicular bisector of the segment.

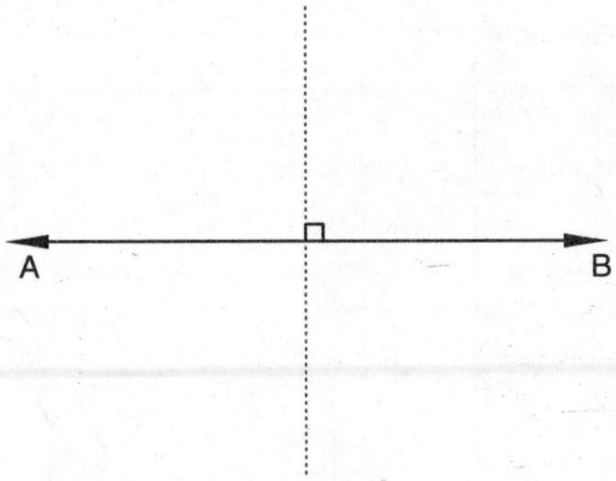

Fig. 10

LINES OF SYMMETRY OF AN ANGLE An angle with equal arms has one line of symmetry which is along the internal bisector of the angle.

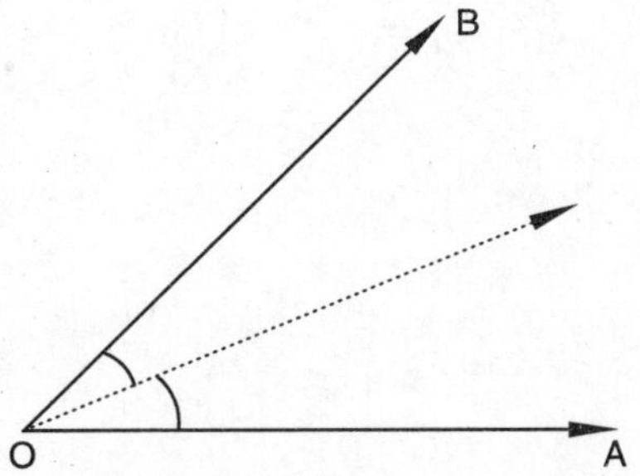

Fig. 11

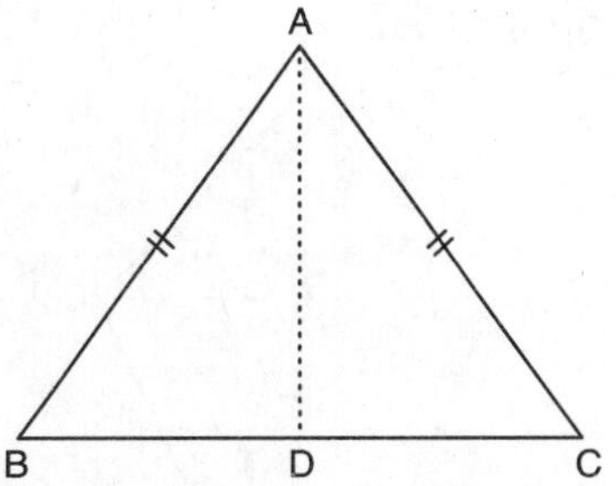

Fig. 12

LINES OF SYMMETRY OF AN ISOSCELES TRIANGLE An isosceles triangle has one line of symmetry which is along the median through the vertex. Median AD is a line of symmetry of isosceles triangle ABC as the $AB = AC$ in Fig.12.

LINES OF SYMMETRY OF A PARALLELOGRAM A parallelogram has no line of symmetry. In Fig. 13, parallelogram $ABCD$ has no line of symmetry.

Fig. 13

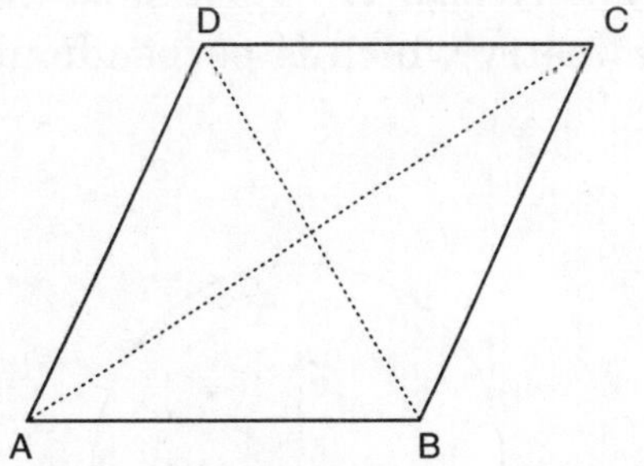

Fig. 14

LINES OF SYMMETRY OF A RHOMBUS A rhombus has two lines of symmetry along the diagonals of the rhombus.

In rhombus $ABCD$, diagonals AC and BD are two lines of symmetry. As shown in Fig 14.

LINES OF SYMMETRY OF A RECTANGLE *A rectangle has two lines of symmetry along the line segments joining the mid-points of the opposite sides.*

In the fig. 15, PQ and RS are two lines of symmetry of rectangle $ABCD$.

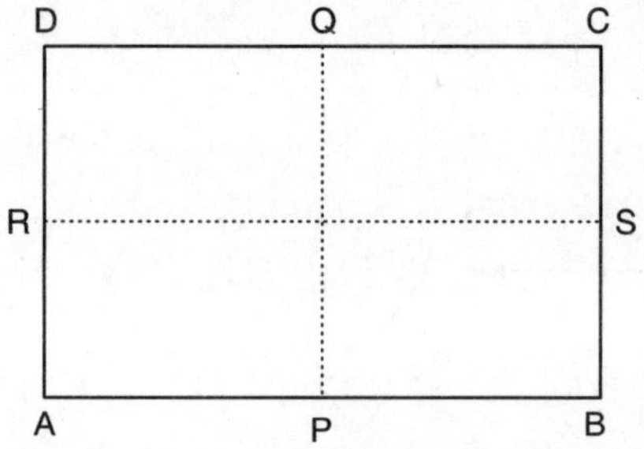

Fig. 15

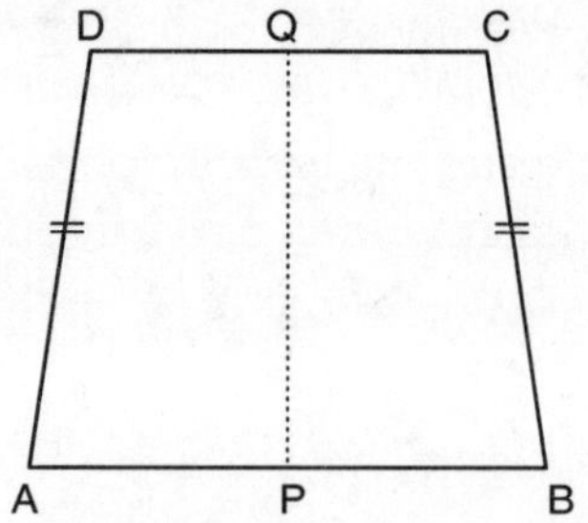

Fig. 16

LINES OF SYMMETRY OF AN ISOSCELES TRAPEZIUM An isosceles trapezium has two parallel sides and two non-parallel sides of equal length. In Fig. 16, $ABCD$ is an isosceles trapezium such that $BC = AD$ and AB is parallel to CD. It has only one line of symmetry along the line segment joining the mid-points of two parallel sides AB and CD.

LINES OF SYMMETRY OF A KITE A kite, as shown in Fig. 17 has one line of symmetry along the diagonal BD.

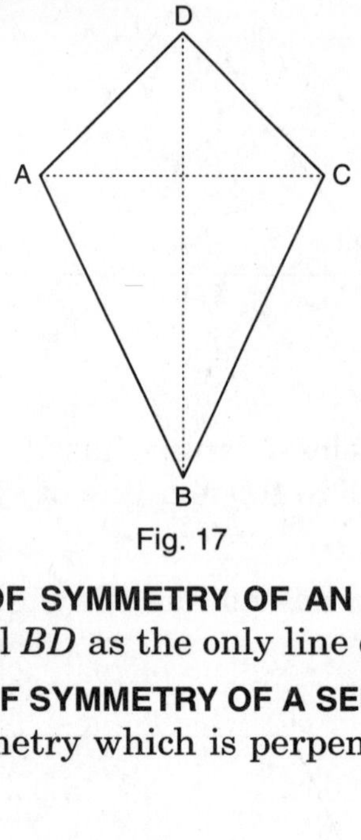

Fig. 17

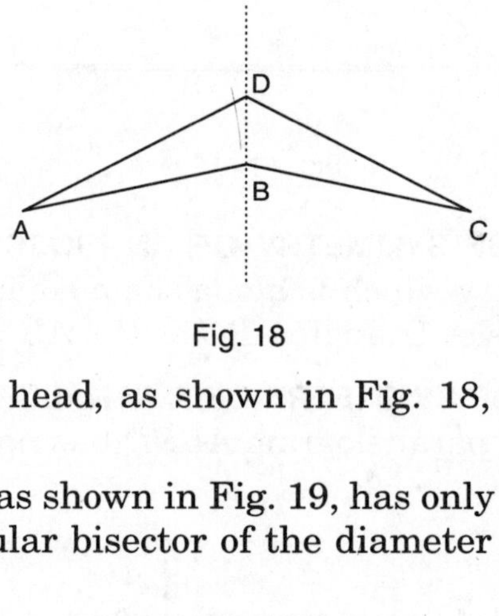

Fig. 18

LINES OF SYMMETRY OF AN ARROW HEAD An arrow head, as shown in Fig. 18, has the diagonal BD as the only line of symmetry.

LINES OF SYMMETRY OF A SEMI-CIRCLE A semi-circle, as shown in Fig. 19, has only one line of symmetry which is perpendicular to the perpendicular bisector of the diameter AB.

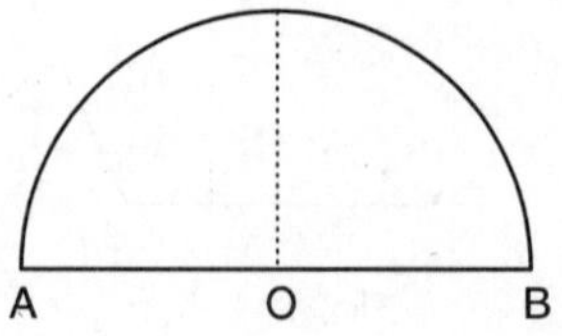

Fig. 19

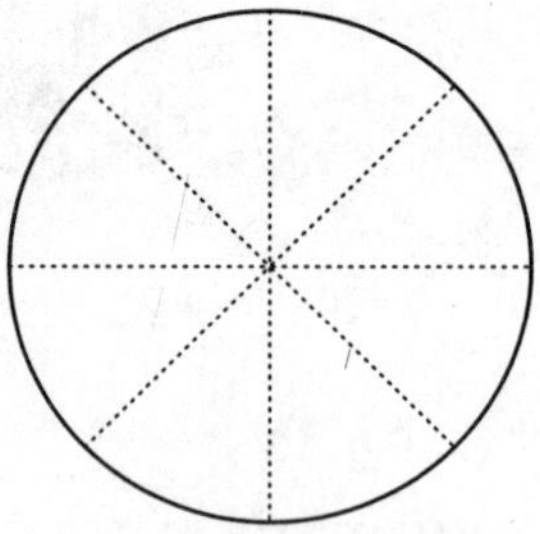

Fig. 20

LINES OF SYMMETRY OF A CIRCLE A circle has an infinite number of lines of symmetry all along the diameters.

18.3 LINES OF SYMMETRY OF SOME REGULAR POLYGONS

Regular polygons are symmetrical beauties and hence their lines of symmetry are quite interesting. In this section, we will discuss about the lines of symmetry of some regular polygons. We know that a closed figure made up of several line segments is called a polygon. Polygons made up of three, four, five and six line segments are known as triangles, quadrilaterals, pentagons and hexagons respectively. A polygon is said to be regular if all its sides are of equal length and all its angles are of equal measure.

LINES OF SYMMETRY OF AN EQUILATERAL TRIANGLE All sides of an equilateral triangle are equal in length and each angle is of measure 60°. An equilateral triangle has three lines of symmetry along the three medians of the triangle as shown in Fig. 21.

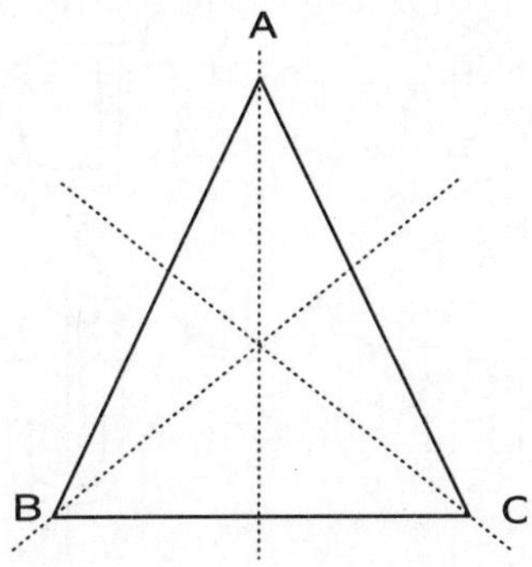

Fig. 21

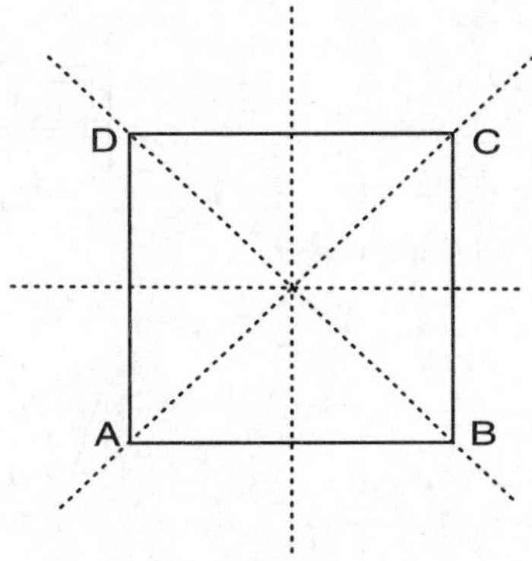

Fig. 22

LINES OF SYMMETRY OF A SQUARE A square is a quadrilateral whose all sides are of equal length and each of its angles is a right-angle i.e. 90°. Diagonals of a square are perpendicular bisector of each other.

A square has four lines of symmetry two along the diagonals and two along the line segments joining the mid-points of opposite sides as shown Fig. 22.

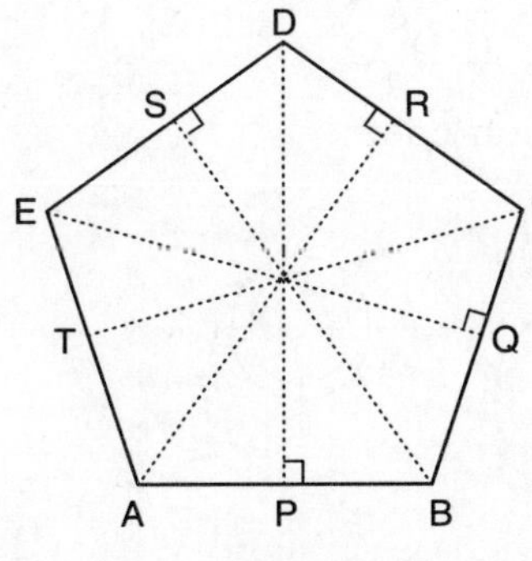

Fig. 23

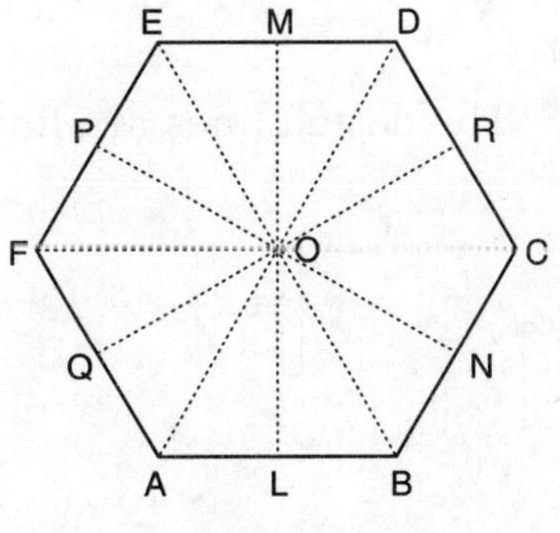

Fig. 24

LINES OF SYMMETRY OF A REGULAR PENTAGON A regular pentagon has all its sides equal in length and the measure of each of its angles is 108°.

A regular pentagon has five lines of symmetry as shown in fig. 23.

LINES OF SYMMETRY OF A REGULAR HEXAGON A regular hexagon has all its sides equal and each of its anlgles measures 120°. A regular hexagon has six lines of symmetry. Three along the lines joining the mid-points of opposite sides and three along the diagonals as shown in fig. 24.

We observe from the above discussion that each regular polygon has as many lines of symmetry as the number of its sides.

ILLUSTRATIVE EXAMPLES

Example 1 Following letters of English alphabet are symmetrical about a line. Identify, a line of symmetry in each case:

(i) A (ii) B (iii) C (iv) D (v) E (vi) M
(vii) T (viii) U (ix) V (x) W (xi) X (xii) Y.

Solution The dotted line is the line of symmetry.

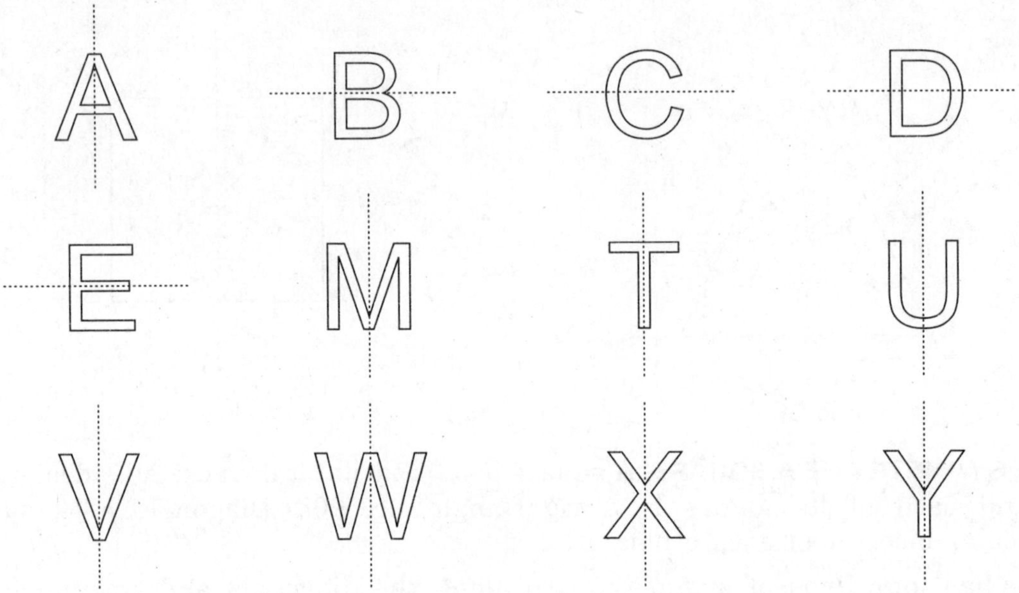

Fig. 25

Example 2 Each of the following letters from English alphabet has two lines of symmetry. Identify lines of symmetry in each case:

(i) H (ii) I (iii) O

Solution The dotted lines are lines of symmetry in each case:

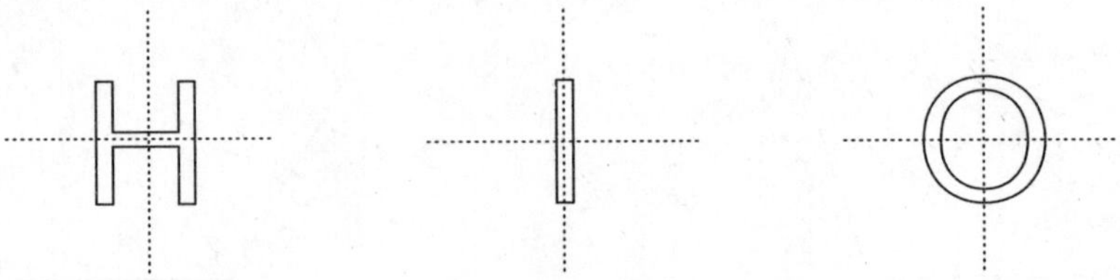

Fig. 26

EXERCISE 18.1

1. State the number of lines of symmetry for the following figures:

(i) An equilateral triangle (ii) An isosceles triangle
(iii) A scalene tringle (iv) A rectangle
(v) A rhombus (vi) A square
(vii) A parallelogram (viii) A quadrilateral
(ix) A regular pentagon (x) A regular hexagon
(xi) A circle (xii) A semi-circle

2. What other name can you give to the line of symmetry of
   (i) An isosceles triangle? (ii) A circle?
3. Identify three examples of shapes with no line of symmetry.
4. Identify multiple lines of symmetry, if any, in each of the following figures:

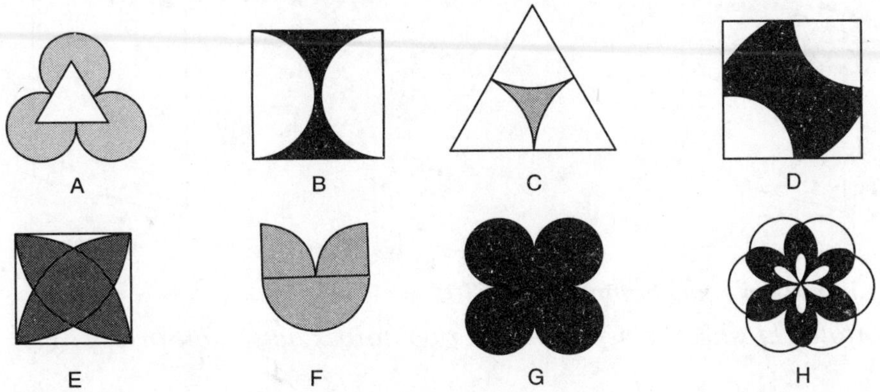

Fig. 27

ANSWERS

1. (i) 3 (ii) 1 (iii) 0 (iv) 2 (v) 2 (vi) 4
   (vii) 0 (viii) 0 (ix) 5 (x) 6 (xi) Infinitely many
   (xii) 1
2. (i) Altitude (ii) Diameter
3. Parallelogram, A scalene triangle, A quadrilateral.

18.4 LINE OF SYMMETRY AND REFLECTION

The concept of line of symmetry is closely related to the mirror reflection. If a figure has a line of symmetry and we place a mirror along the line of symmetry, then the image or reflection of one side of the figure is exactly same as the figure on the other side of the line of symmetry. That is why line symmetry of a figure is also known as the reflection symmetry. Using this, we can also draw the complete figure, if we are given a line of symmetry and one half on one side of it. For example, if the dotted line in the following figure is a line of symmetry and we wish to draw the complete figure. Then, we take the image of the figure in the mirror placed along the line of symmetry. The complete figure will look like the figure shown below.

Fig. 28

ACTIVITY

STEP I *Take sheet of paper and fold it into 2 halves (Fig. 29).*

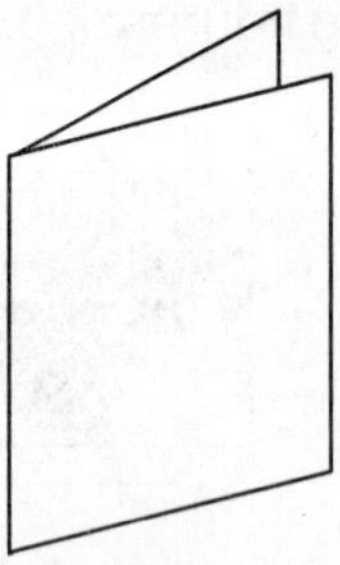

Fig. 29

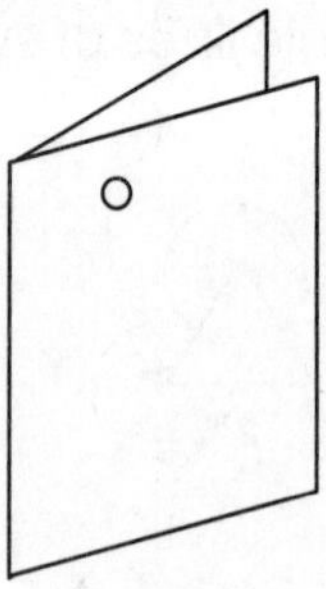

Fig. 30

STEP II *Punch a hole as shown in Fig. 30.*

STEP III *Unfold the sheet to separate the two halves as shown in Fig. 31.*

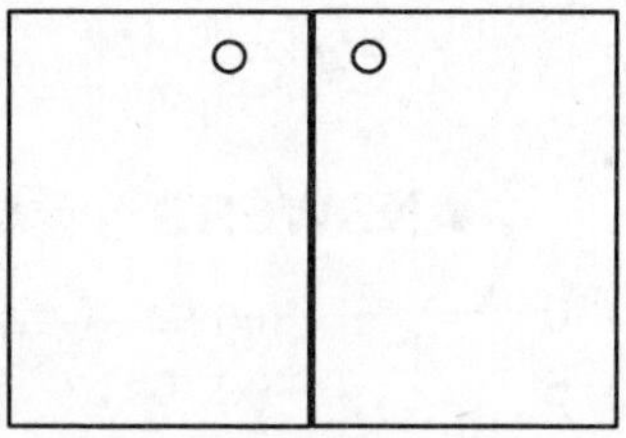

Fig. 31

You will find the fold is a line (or axis) of symmetry.

EXERCISE 18.2

1. In the following figures, the mirror line (i.e. the line of symmetry) is given as dotted line. Complete each figure performing reflection in the dotted (mirror) line. Also, try to recall the name of the complete figure.

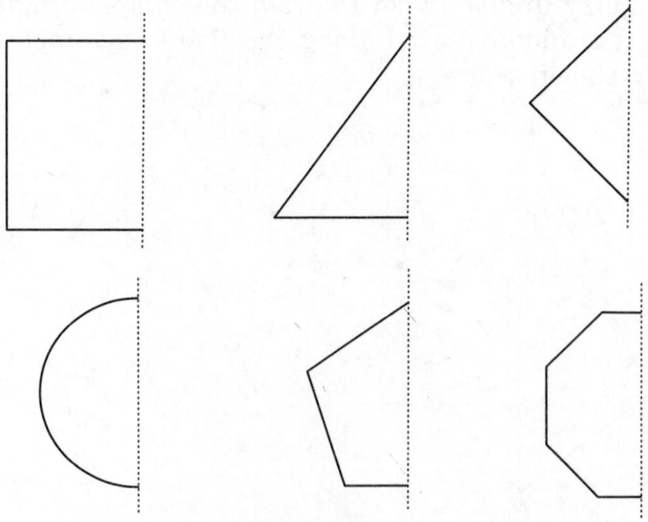

Fig. 32

2. Each of the following figures shows paper cuttings with punched holes. Copy these figures on a plane sheet and mark the axis of symmetry so that if the paper is folded along it, then the wholes on one side of it coincide with the holes on the other side.

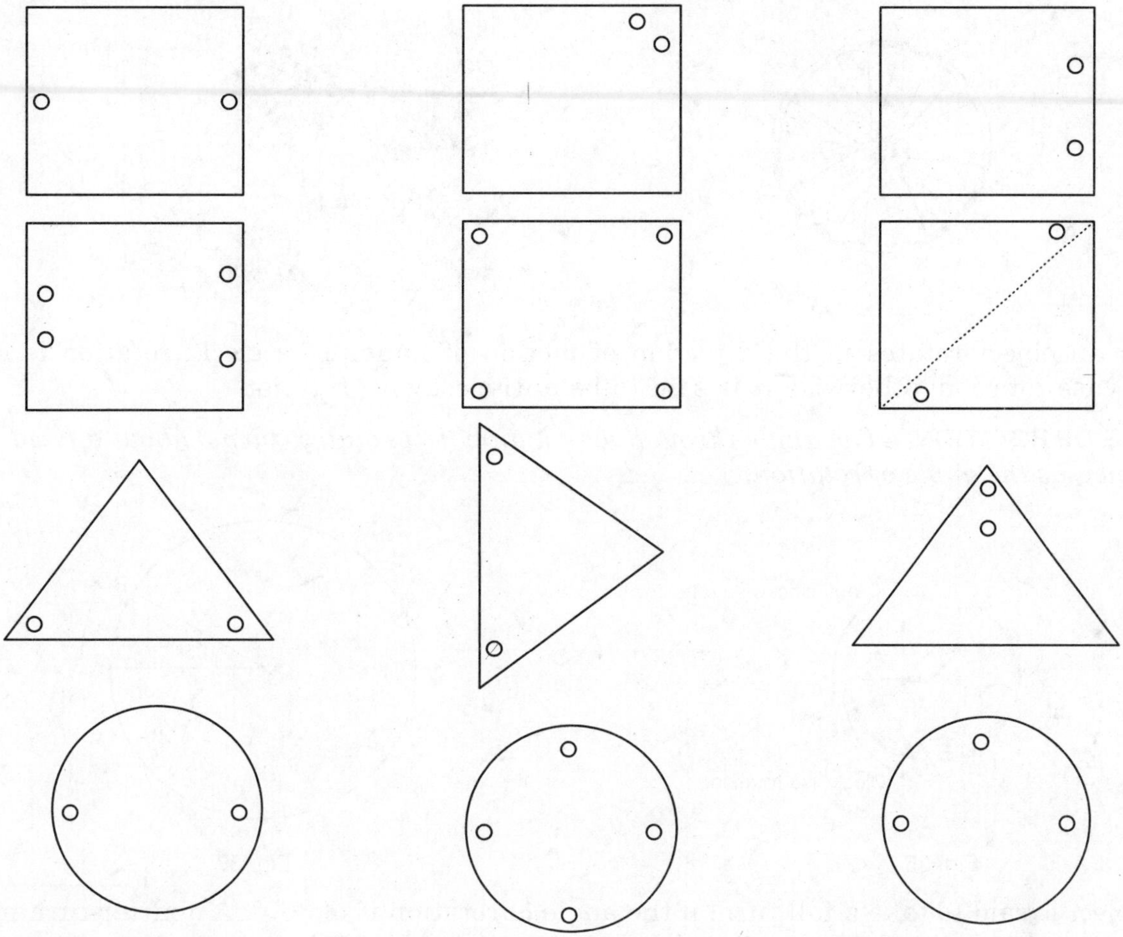

Fig. 33

3. In the following figures if the dotted lines represent the lines of symmetry, find the other hole (s).

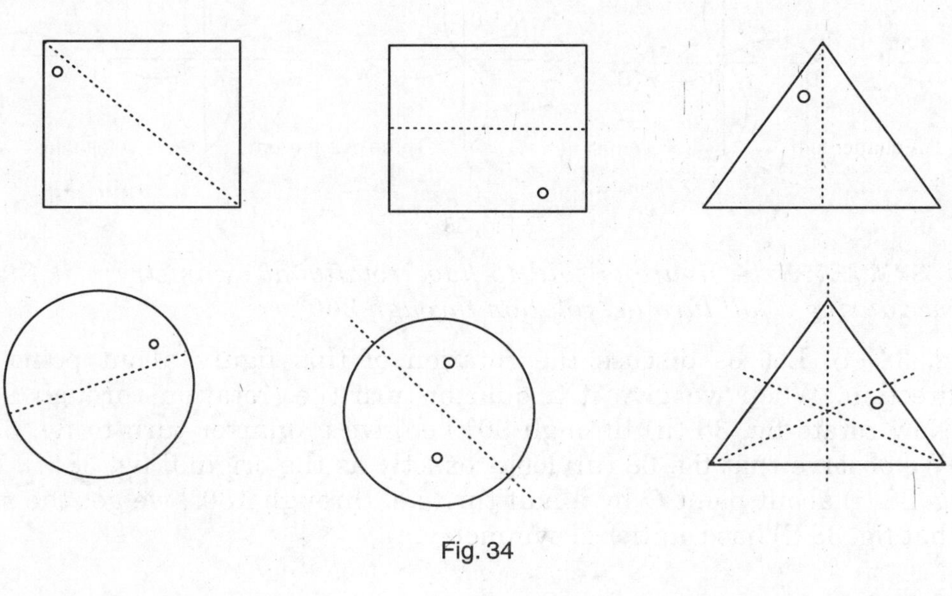

Fig. 34

18.5 ROTATIONAL SYMMETRY

Consider a rotating object, say a wheel of a bicycle or a wind-mill etc. The fixed point about which the object rotates is called the centre of rotation.

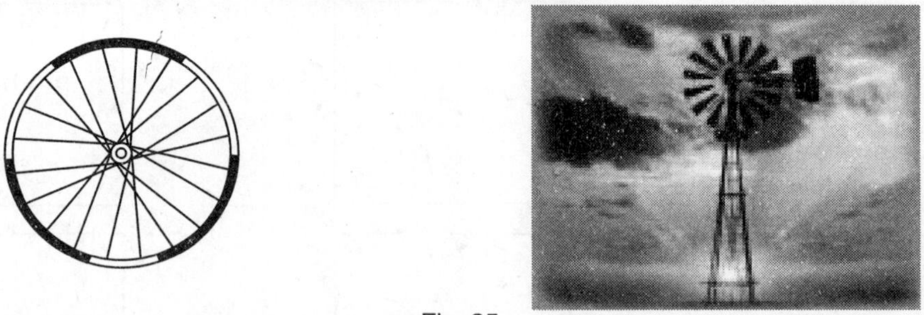

Fig. 35

When an object rotates in the direction of motion of hands of a clock, rotation is called clock wise rotation; otherwise it is said to be anti-clockwise rotation.

ANGLE OF ROTATION *The angle through which an object rotates (turns) about a fixed point is known as the angle of rotation.*

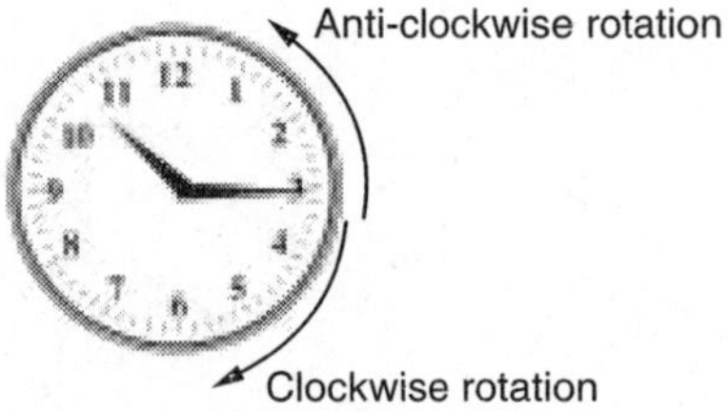

Fig. 36

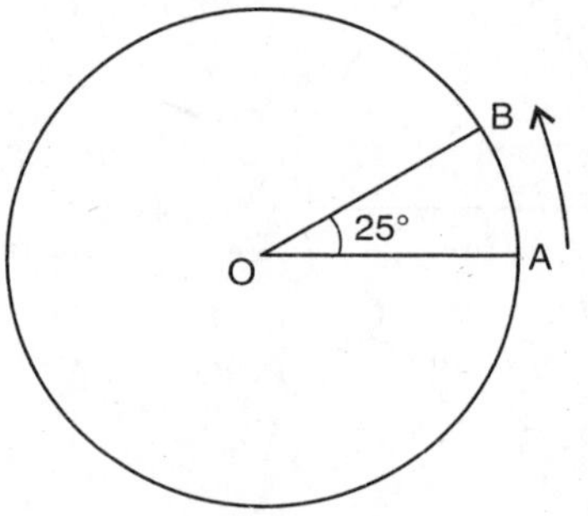

Fig. 37

An object is said to take a full turn, if the angle of rotation is of 360°. A quarter-turn means rotation by 90° and a three quarter-turn means rotation by 270° as shown below.

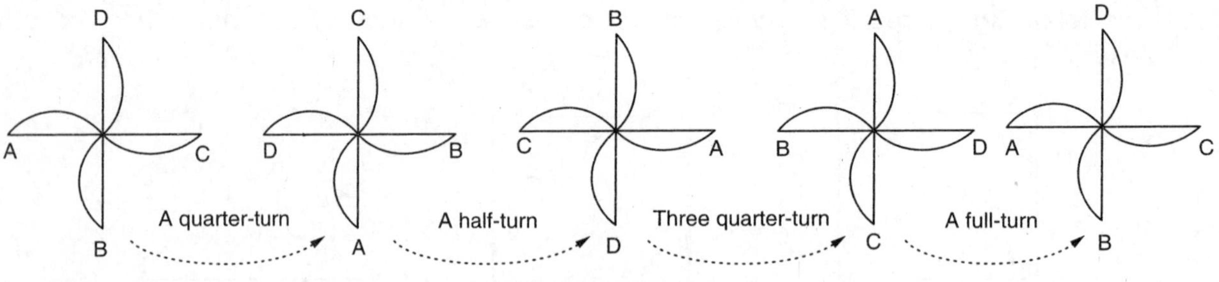

Fig. 38

ROTATIONAL SYMMETRY *A figure is said to have rotational symmetry if it fits onto itself more than once during a full turn i.e. rotation through 360°.*

Consider fig. 38 (i). Let us discuss the rotation of this figure about point O in anti-clockwise direction. When we give it a quarter-turn (i.e. rotation through 90°), we get fig. 38 (ii). Now rotate fig. 38 (ii) through 90° i.e. give a quarter turn to fig. 38 (ii) to get fig. 38 (iii). We observe that fig. 38 (iii) looks exactly as the original fig. 38 (i). Thus, when we rotate fig. 38 (i) about point O by a half-turn i.e. through 180°, we get the same figure. So, we say that fig. 38 (i) has rotational symmetry.

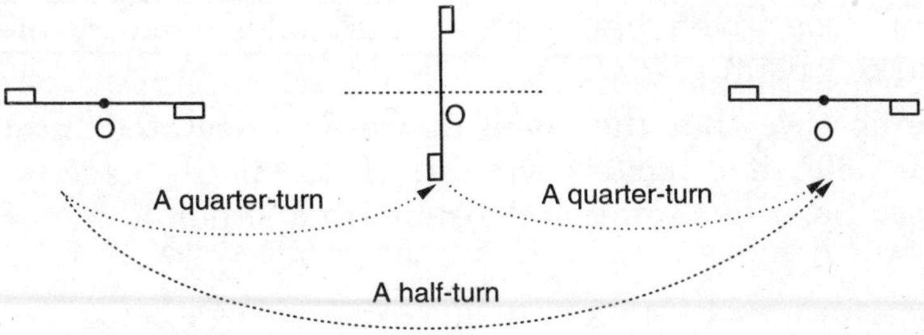

Fig. 39

We also observe that fig. 38 (i) fits onto itself twice in a full-turn i.e. rotation through 360°. So, we say that this figure has rotational symmetry of order 2.

Thus, we define the order of rotational symmetry of a figure as follows:

ORDER OF ROTATIONAL SYMMETRY The number of times a figure fits onto itself in one full-turn is called the order of rotational symmetry.

NOTE 1 *Rotating a figure through 90° clockwise direction is the same as rotating it through 270° in anti-clockwise direction. In other-words, 90° clockwise rotation is equivalent to 270° anti-clockwise rotation.*

NOTE 2 *Rotating a figure through 180° in clockwise direction is the same as rotating it through 180° in anti-clockwise direction i.e., 180° rotations in either direction are equivalent.*

ILLUSTRATIVE EXAMPLES

Example 1 Which of the following figures have rotational symmetry about the marked point (*)? Also, find the order of rotational symmetry.

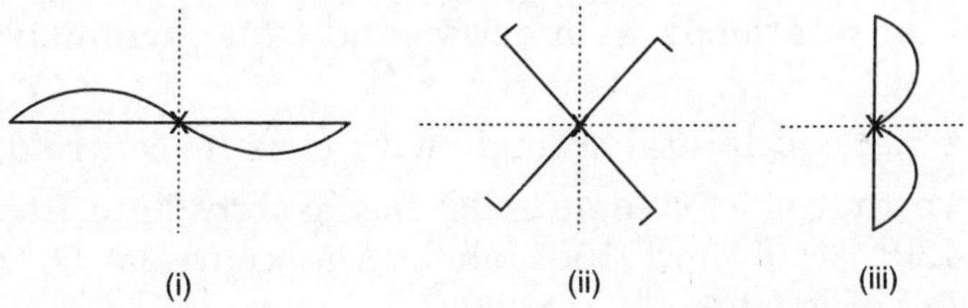

Fig. 40

Solution (i) We observe that fig.40 (i) fits onto itself when we give it a half-turn i.e. when it is rotated through 180° as shown below.

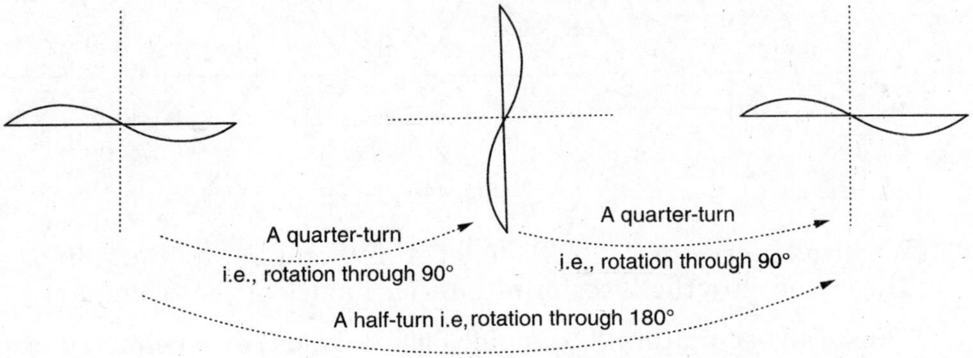

Fig. 41

Thus, the given figure has rotational symmetry of order 2 about the marked point.

(ii) We observe that the given figure when rotated through 90°, 180°, 270° and 360°, it coincides with itself i.e., it fits exactly onto itself in each case. So, it has rotational symmetry of order 4.

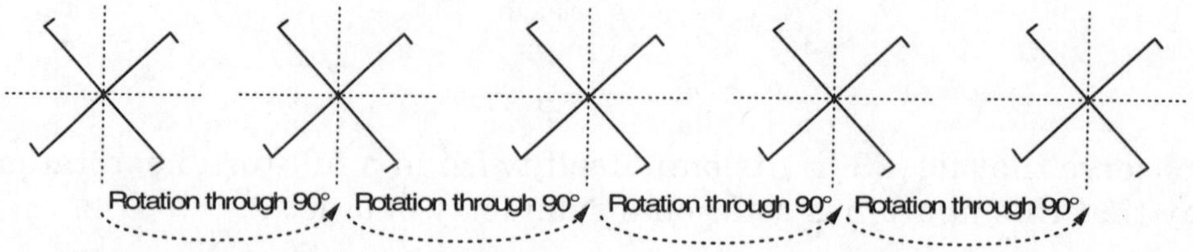

Fig. 42

(iii) Clearly, given figure coincides with itself when it is rotated through 360° i.e., when it takes a full-turn.

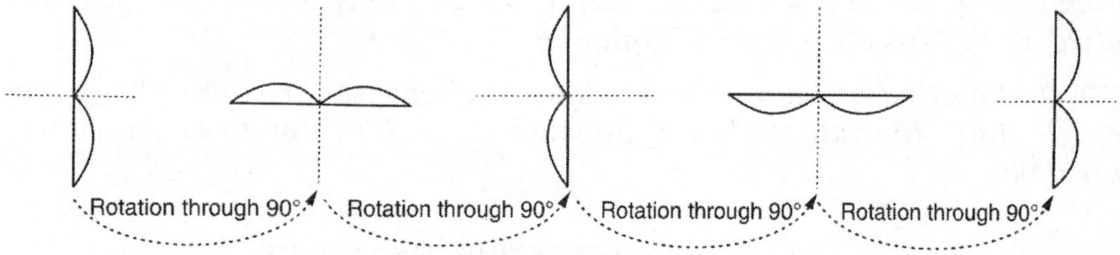

Fig. 43

So, it has rotational symmetry of order 1.

Example 2 Discuss the rotational symmetry and line symmetry of an equilateral triangle.

Solution Let *ABC* be an equilateral triangle with *O* as its centroid. We have,

We observe that the triangle *ABC* fits exactly onto itself when it is rotated through 120°, 240° and 360° about the centroid *O*. So, it has rotational symmetry of order 3.

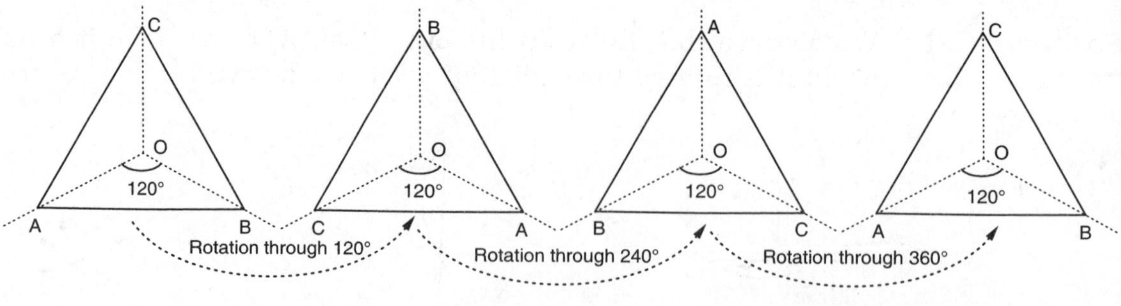

Fig. 44

We also observe that Δ *ABC* has *OA, OB* and *OC* as three lines of symmetry. These lines are the bisector of interior angles of the triangle.

Thus, an equilateral triangle has 3 lines of symmetry and rotational symmetry of order 3.

Example 3 Discuss the rotational symmetry of a square. Also, determine its lines of symmetry.

Solution Let $ABCD$ be a square with centre O as shown in fig. 45. Let us rotate it through 90°, 180°, 270° and 360° about point O to attain various positions shown below.

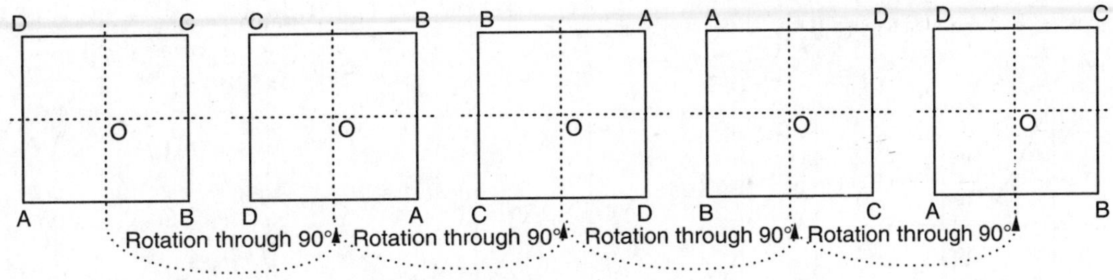

Fig. 45

We observe that the square $ABCD$ fits exactly onto itself.

Clearly, after each rotation about point O the square attains the position which exactly fits onto itself.

Hence, a square has rotational symmetry of order 4.

In section 18.3, we have seen that a square has 4 lines of symmetry, namely the diagonals and the lines joining the mid-points of opposite sides.

Example 4 Discuss the rotational and line symmetry of a rectangle.

Solution Let $ABCD$ be a rectangle such that the line joining the mid-points of opposite sides intersect at O.

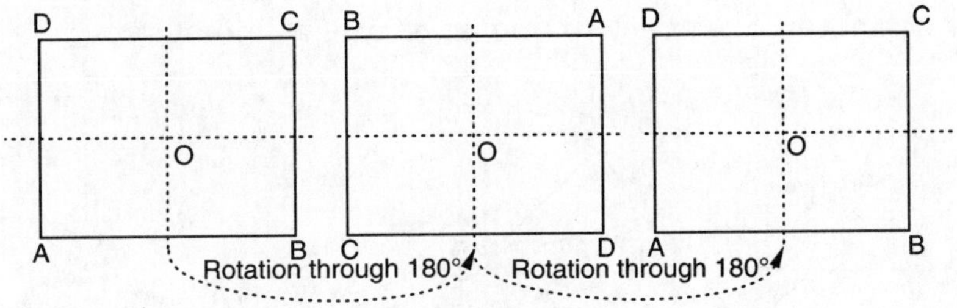

Fig. 46

Clearly, these two lines are lines of symmetry of the rectangle.

If we rotate the rectangle about point O through 180° and 360°, we find that it fits onto itself.

So, it has rotational symmetry of order 2.

Example 5 Show that each of the letters *H, I, N, S, X* and *Z* has a rotational symmetry of order 2. Also, mark the point of rotational symmetry in each case.

Solution We observe that each of the letters *H, I, N, S, X* and *Z* fits onto itself when it is rotated through 180° and 360° about point O as shown below. Thus each of the letters *H, I, N, S, X* and Z has a rotational symmetry of order 2.

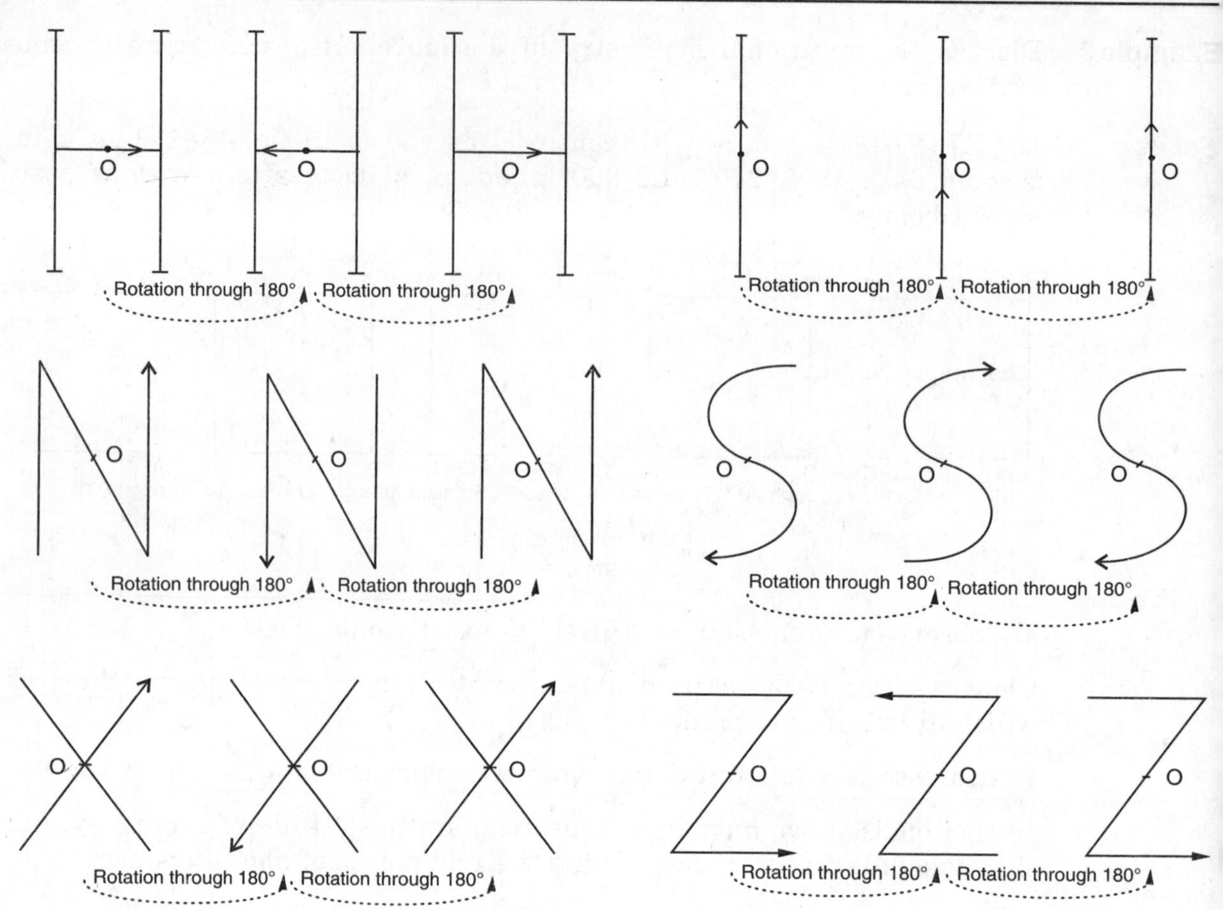

Fig. 47

Example 6 Discuss the rotational and line symmetry of a circle.

Solution Let O be the centre of circle shown in Fig. 48. Clearly, it is symmetrical about every diameter. So, every diameter of it is a line of symmetry.

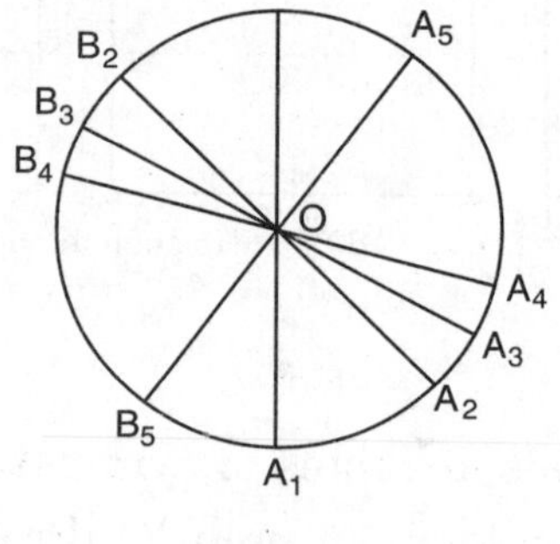

Fig. 48

Thus, a cirlce has unlimited number of lines of symmetry.

If we rotate the circle about its centre O through any angle, then it fits onto itself. Therefore, a circle has rotational symmetry around the centre for every angle. Thus, a circle has unlimited number of angles of symmetry and the order of its rotation is infinite.

Example 7 Discuss the rotational symmetry of a parallelogram. Also, find the centre of rotation, if any.

Solution In order to check the rotational symmetry of a parallelogram, let us perform the following activity.

(i) *Draw two identical parallelograms ABCD on a piece of paper and A′ B′ C′ D′ on a transparent sheet.*

(ii) *Mark the points of intersection of their diagonals as O and O′ respectively.*

(iii) *Place the parallelograms such that A′ lies on A, B′ lies on B, C′ lies on C and D′ lies on D. In such a situation O′ will fall on O.*

(iv) *Stick a pin into the shapes at the point O.*

(v) *Turn the transparent sheet in the clockwise direction so that the two shapes coincide i.e. overlap each other. You will find that the two shapes will coincide in two positions — once when A′ falls on A and secondly when A′ falls on C.*

Thus, a parallelogram has rotational symmetry of order 2. The point where we have stick the pin is the centre of rotation. It is the point of intersection of diagonals of the parallelogram.

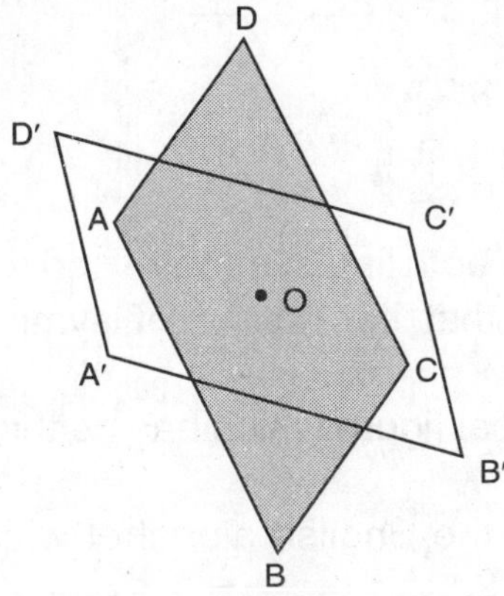

Fig. 49

Example 8 Discuss the rotational and line symmetry of the following figure.

Solution We observe that the figure fits onto itself when it is rotated through 120°, 240° and 360°.

So, it has rotational symmetry of order 3.

We also observe that the given figure has lines l, m and n as three lines of symmetry.

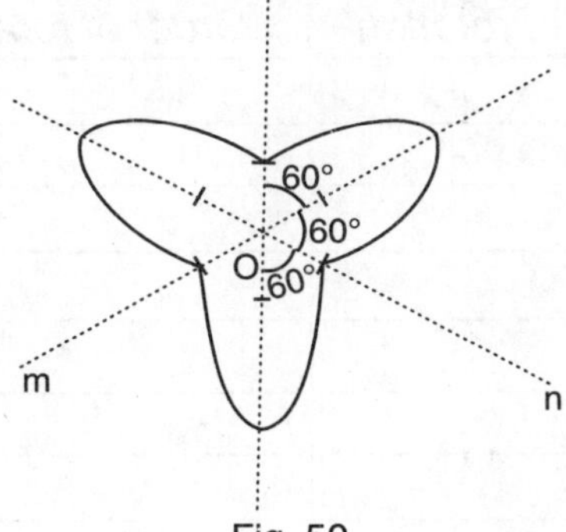

Fig. 50

EXERCISE 18.3

1. Give the order of rotational symmetry for each of the following figures when rotated about the marked point (x):

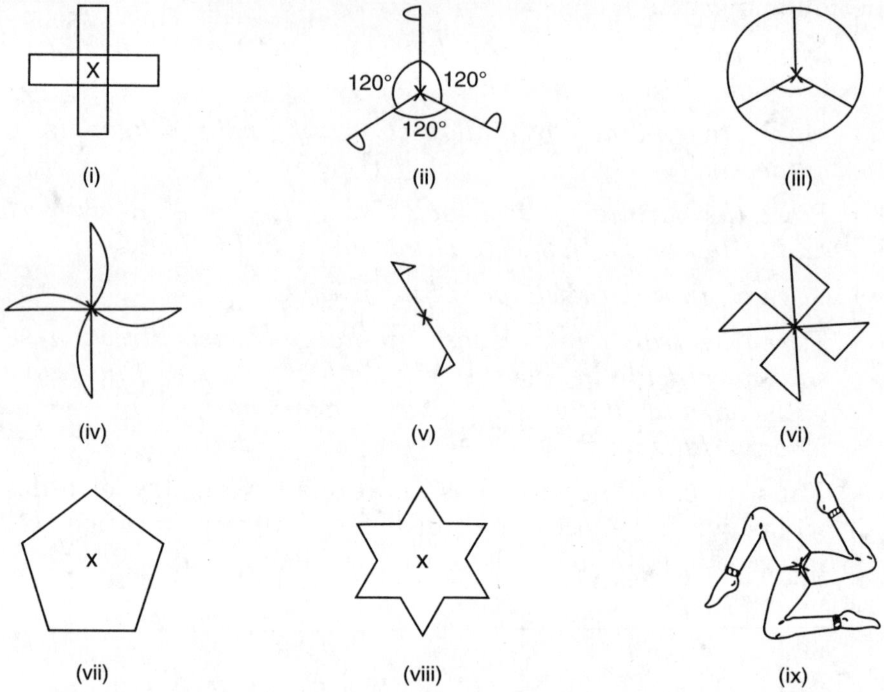

Fig. 51

2. Name any two figures that have both line symmetry and rotational symmetry.
3. Give an example of a figure that has a line of symmetry but does not have rotational symmetry.
4. Give an example of a geometrical figure which has neither a line of symmetry nor a rotational symmetry.
5. Give an example of a letter of the English alphabet which has (i) no line of symmetry and (ii) rotational symmetry of order 2.
6. What is the line of symmetry of a semi-circle? Does it have rotational symmetry?
7. Draw, whenever possible, a rough sketch of
   (i) a triangle with both line and rotational symmetries.
   (ii) a triangle with only line symmetry and no rotational symmetry.
   (iii) a quadrilateral with a rotational symmetry but not a line of symmetry.
   (iv) a quadrilateral with line symmetry but not a rotational symmetry.
8. Fill in the blanks:

Figures	*Centre of rotation*	*Order of rotation*	*Angle of rotation*
Square			
Rectangle			
Rhombus			
Equilateral triangle			
Regular hexagon			
Circle			
Semi-circle			

9. Fill in the blanks:

English alphabet Letter	*Line Symmetry*	*Number of Lines of symmetry*	*Rotational Symmetry*	*Order of rotational Symmetry*
Z	Nil	0	Yes	2
S	–	–	–	–
H	Yes	–	Yes	–
O	Yes	–	Yes	–
E	Yes	–	–	–
N	–	–	Yes	–
C	–	–	–	–

ANSWERS

1. (i) 4 (ii) 3 (iii) 3 (iv) 4 (v) 2 (vi) 4 (vii) 5 (viii) 6 (ix) 3
2. An equilateral triangle, A square
3. A semi-circle, An isosceles triangle
4. A scalene triangle
5. (i) Z (ii) N
6. Perpendicular bisector of the diameter, No
7. (i) Draw an equilateral triangle (ii) Draw an isosceles triangle

8.

Figure	*Centre of rotation*	*Order of rotation*	*Angle of rotation*
Square	Point of intersection of the line segments joining the mid-points of opposite sides.	4	90°
Rectangle	Point of intersection of the line segments joining the mid-points of opposite sides.	2	180°
Rhombus	Point of intersection of diagonals	2	180°
Equilateral triangle	Point of intersection of angle bisectors i.e. centroid	3	120°
Regular hexagon	Centre of the hexagon	6	60°
Circle	Centre of the circle	Unlimited	Any angle
Semi-circle	Nil	Nil	Nil

9.

English alphabet Letter	*Line Symmetry*	*Number of Lines of symmetry*	*Rotational Symmetry*	*Order of rotational Symmetry*
Z	No	0	Yes	2
S	No	0	Yes	2
H	Yes	2	Yes	2
O	Yes	4	Yes	2
E	Yes	1	No	0
N	No	0	Yes	2
C	Yes	1	No	0

OBJECTIVE TYPE QUESTIONS

Mark the correct alternative in each of the following:

1. Which of the following has only 2 lines of symmetry?
   (a) Equilateral triangle (b) Rhombus (c) Circle (d) None of these
2. Which of the following is/are point symmetric?
   (a) Rectangle (b) Square (c) Parallelogram (d) All of these

3. Which of the following has an infinite number of lines of symmetry?
   (a) Equilatoral trianglo (b) Ioooooloo trianglo (o) Rcgular hcxagon (d) Circlc
4. Which of the following is point symmetric?
   (a) Equilateral triangle (b) Trapezium (c) Rectangle (d) None of these
5. The number of lines of symmetry of a square is
   (a) 2 (b) 3 (c) 4 (d) Infinite
6. The number of lines of symmetry of a rectangle is
   (a) 2 (b) 3 (c) 4 (d) 1
7. The number of lines of symmetry of an equilateral triangle is
   (a) 1 (b) 2 (c) 3 (d) 0
8. The order of rotational symmetry of an equilateral triangle is
   (a) 0 (b) 1 (c) 2 (d) 3
9. A rectangle has rotational symmetry of order
   (a) 1 (b) 2 (c) 3 (d) 4
10. The number of lines of symmetry of an isosceles triangle is
   (a) 0 (b) 1 (c) 2 (d) 3

ANSWERS

1. (b) 2. (d) 3. (d) 4. (c) 5. (c) 6. (a) 7. (c)
8. (d) 9. (b) 10. (b)

THINGS TO REMEMBER

1. *If a line divides a figure into two parts such that when the figure is folded about the line the two parts of the figure coincide, then the line is known as the line of symmetry. The line of symmetry is also known as the axis of symmetry.*
2. *A figure is said to have rotational symmetry if it fits on to itself more than once during a full turn i.e. rotation through 360°.*
3. *The number of times a figure fits onto ifself in one full turn is called the order of rotational symmetry.*
4. *Following table provides the details of linear and rotational symmetries of various figures:*

Figure	*Line Symmetry*	*No. of Line Symmetry*	*Rotational Symmetry*	*Centre of Rotation*	*Order of Rotational Symmetry*
Square	*Yes*	*4*	*Yes*	*Intersection of diagonals*	*4*
Rectangle	*Yes*	*2*	*Yes*	*Intersection of diagonals*	*2*
Equilateral Triangle	*Yes*	*3*	*Yes*	*Centroid*	*3*
Regular Hexagon	*Yes*	*6*	*Yes*	*Centre of the hexagon*	*6*
Circle	*Yes*	*Unlimited*	*Yes*	*Centre*	*Unlimited*
Parallelogram	*Yes*	*2*	*Yes*	*Intersection of diagonals*	*2*
Rhombus	*Yes*	*2*	*Yes*	*Intersection of diagonals*	*2*

19

VISUALISING SOLID SHAPES

19.1 INTRODUCTION

In our day-to-day life, we come across several objects, which have different shapes and sizes. One thing common about most of these objects is that they all have some length, breadth and height. Objects or Figures having length only are known as one-dimensional objects. For example, a line is a one dimensional figure. Figures having some length and breadth are known as two dimensional figures. For example, rectangle, triangle, circle etc. are two dimensional figures. These figures can be easily represented on a plane. That is why they are called plane figures. Objects and shapes having length, breadth and height are known as three dimensional objects/shapes. Following are some three dimensional shapes about which we have learnt in earlier classes.

One-dimensional figure:

Fig. 1

Two-dimensional figures:

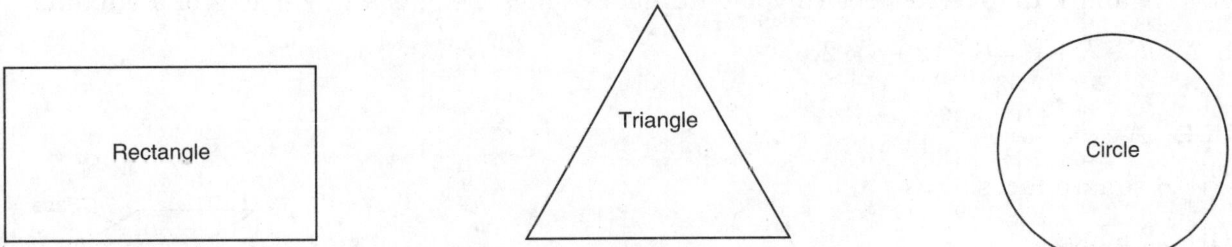

Fig. 2

Three-dimensional figures shapes:

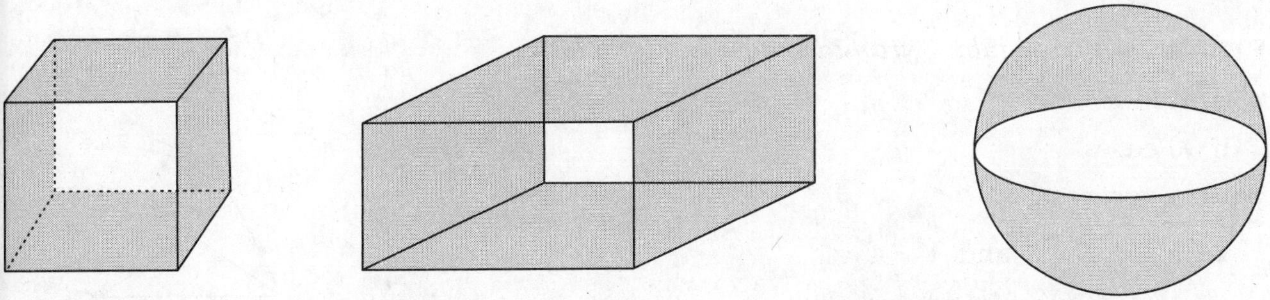

Cube Cuboid Sphere

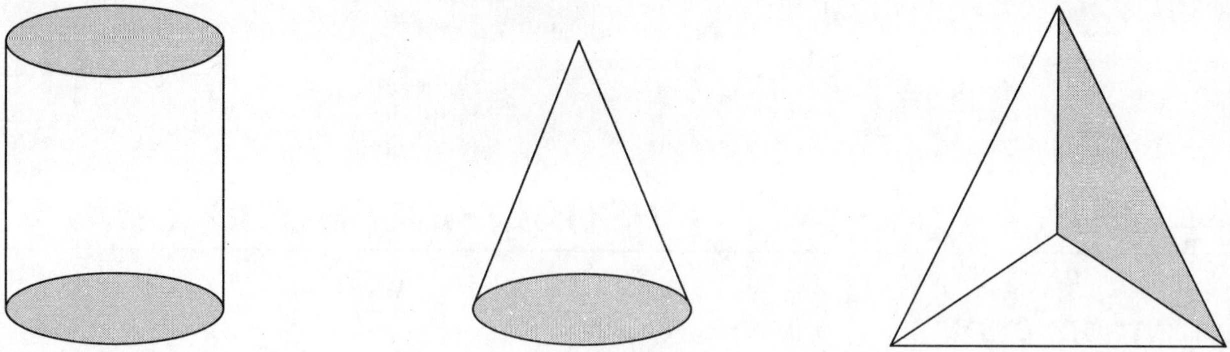

Cylinder Cone Pyramid

Fig. 3

We will write 2-D in short for 2-dimensional shapes and 3-D in short for 3-dimensional shapes.

19.2 FACES, EDGES AND VERTICES

In the previous class, we have learnt about various solids, namely, cuboid, cube, cone, cylinder, sphere etc. Let us now recall their faces, edges and vertices to strengthen our knowledge about them.

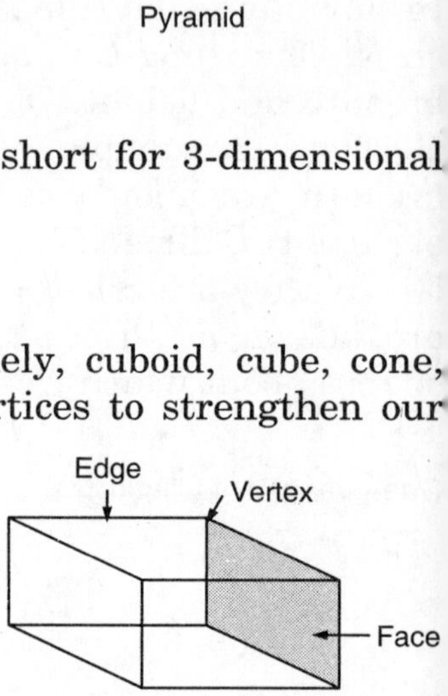

Fig. 4

CUBOID *A cuboid has*

(i) 6 rectangular faces
(ii) 12 edges
(iii) 8 vertices.

Let F, E and V denote respectively the number of faces, edges and vertices of a cuboid.

Then, $F - E + V = 6 - 12 + 8 = 2$.

CUBE *A cube has*

(i) 6 square faces
(ii) 12 edges
(iii) 8 vertices

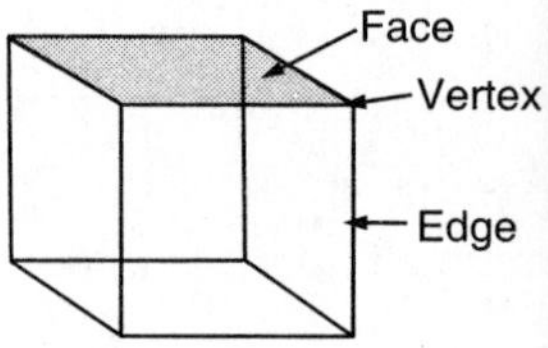

Fig. 5

Here, $F = 6, E = 12$ and $V = 8$

$\therefore \quad F - E + V = 6 - 12 + 8 = 2$

PYRAMID *A triangular pyramid shown in Fig. 6 has*

(i) 4 faces
(ii) 6 edges
(iii) 4 vertices

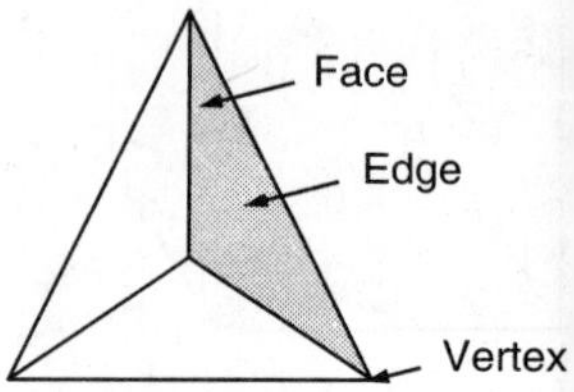

Fig. 6

Here $F = 4, E = 6$ and $V = 4$

$\therefore \quad F - E + V = 4 - 6 + 4 = 2$

<u>Remark</u> *A figure/shape whose faces are polygons (triangles, quadrilaterals etc) is called a polyhedron. If F, E and V denote respectively the number of faces, edges and vertices of a polyhedron, then* $F - E + V = 2$. *This is called Euler's formula.*

CYLINDER *A cylinder has*

(i) no vertex
(ii) two circular faces
(iii) one curved face
(iv) two curved edges

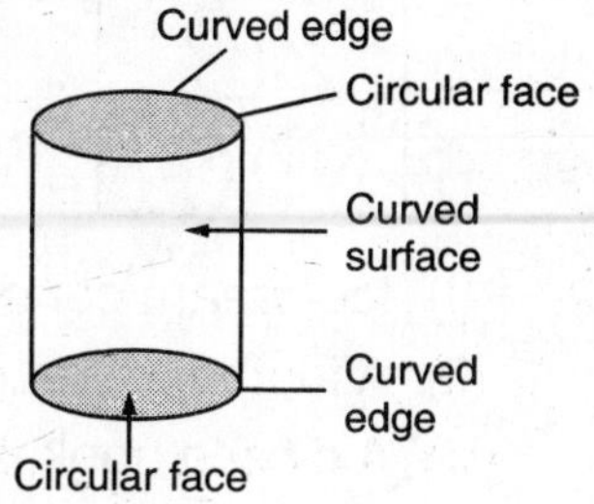

Fig. 7

CONE *A cone has*

(i) one vertex
(ii) one curved edge
(iii) one curved face and one flat face

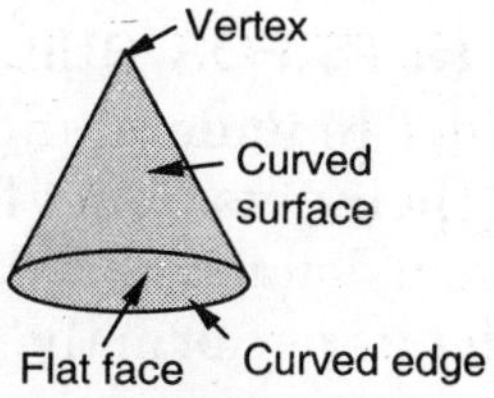

Fig. 8

SPHERE *A sphere has*

(i) no vertex
(ii) no edge
(iii) a curved surface

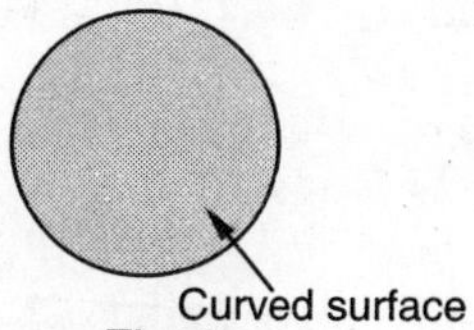

Fig. 9

We observe that the faces of three dimensional shapes are two dimensional figures. For example, a cuboid has six faces which are rectangles, a pyramid has four triangular faces.

EXERCISE 19.1

1. Complete the following table and verify Euler's formula in each case.

	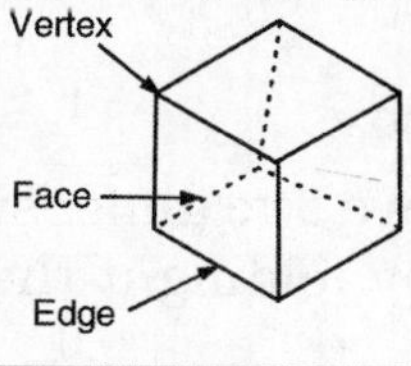	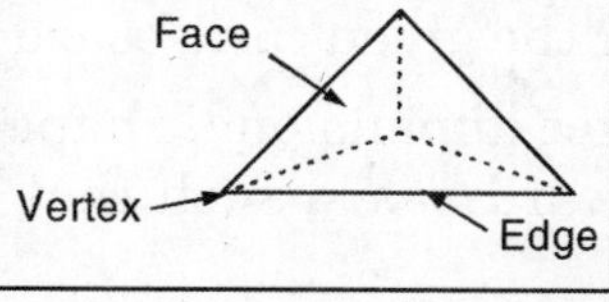	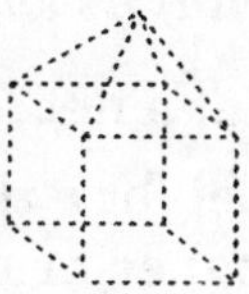	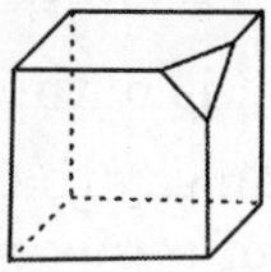
Faces (F)	6	4		
Edges (E)	12			
Vertex (V)	8	4		

2. Give three examples from our daily life which are in the form of (i) a cone (ii) a sphere (iii) a cuboid (iv) a cylinder (v) a pyramid.

ANSWER

1.

Faces (F)	6	4	9	7
Edges (E)	12	6	16	15
Vertex (V)	8	4	9	10

2. (i) Ice-cream cone, cap,
   (ii) A football, a round apple, a round orange
   (iii) A dice, a book, a brick, a duster
   (iv) A circular pipe, a glass.

19.3 NETS FOR BUILDING 3 D-SHAPES

In order to understand three dimensional objects more closely, we try to form these objects from their nets. A net for a three dimensional shape is nothing but a sort of skelton-outline in 2-dimension which, when folded, results in three dimensional shape. In order to understand this let us perform the following activity:

ACTIVITY

STEP I *Take a card-board box as shown in Fig 10.*

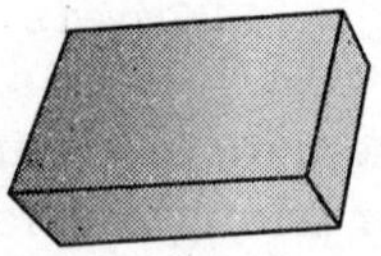

Fig. 10

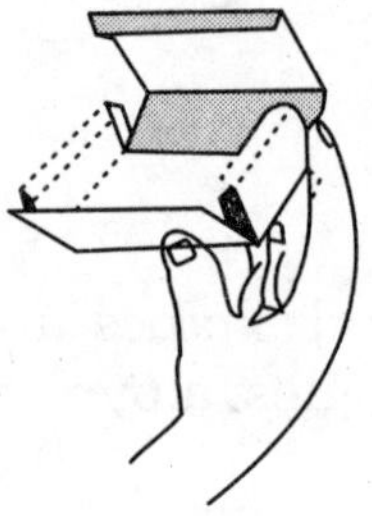

Fig. 11

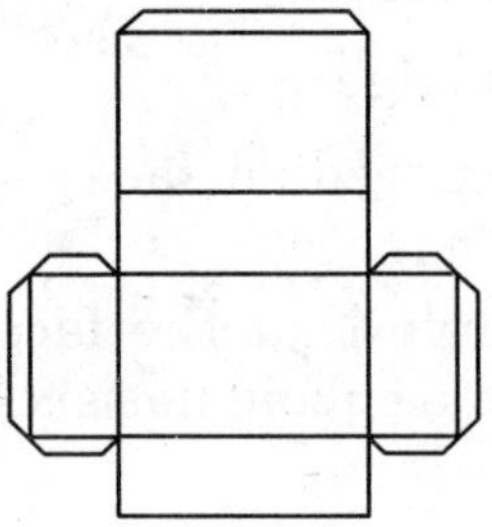

Fig. 12

STEP II *Cut the edges of the box as shown in Fig 11.*

STEP III *Lay the box flat as shown in Fig. 12.*

What we get is nothing but a net for the given card-board box.

Thus, we can say that a net for a three dimensional shape is a two dimensional shape that can be cut out of a piece of paper or a card-board such that by folding it the three dimensional shape can be formed.

Following are net patterns for different three dimensional shapes:

(i) Net pattern for a cuboid (Fig. 13). (ii) Net pattern for cube (Fig. 14).

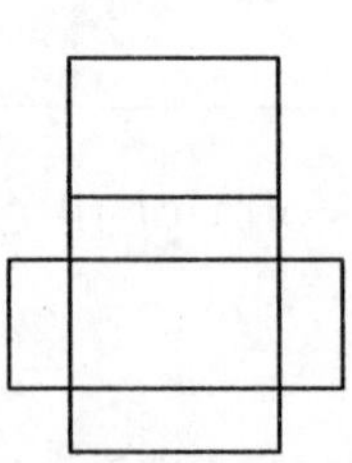

Fig. 13

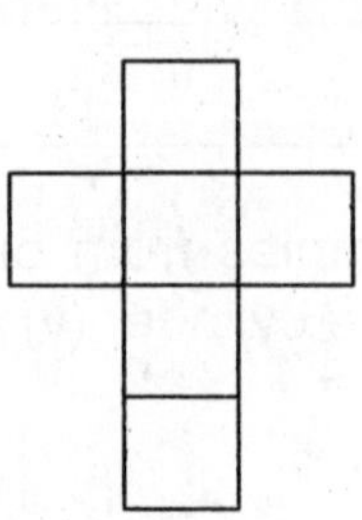

Fig. 14

(iii) Net pattern for a cylinder (Fig 15). (iv) Net pattern for a cone (Fig 16).

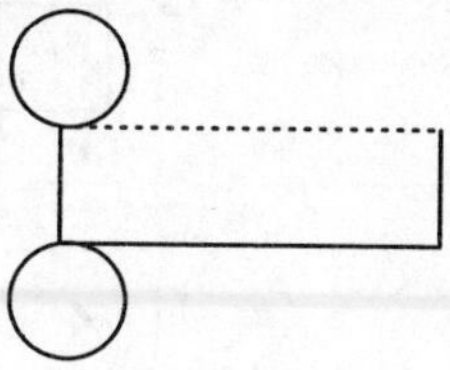

Fig. 15

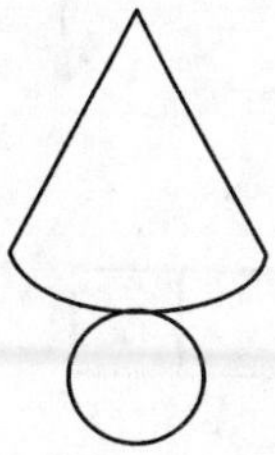

Fig. 16

(v) Net pattern for a triangular prism (Fig. 17).

(vi) Net pattern for a square pyramid (Fig. 18)

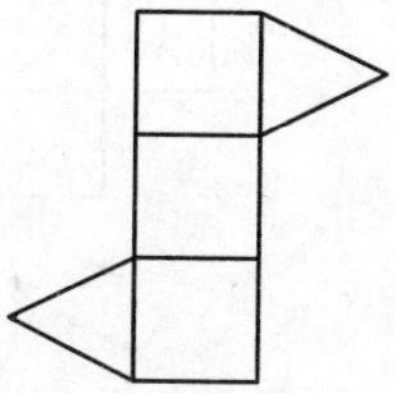

Fig. 17

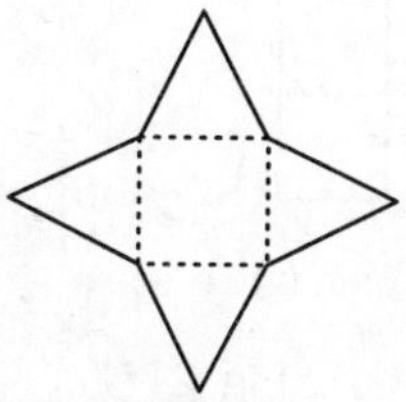

Fig. 18

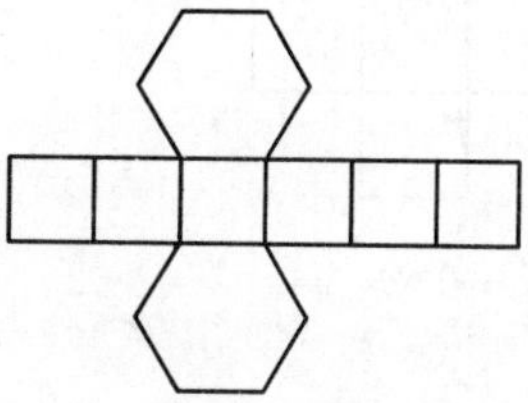

Fig. 19

(vii) Net pattern for a hexagonal prism (Fig. 19).

EXERCISE 19.2

1. Match the following nets with appropriate solids:

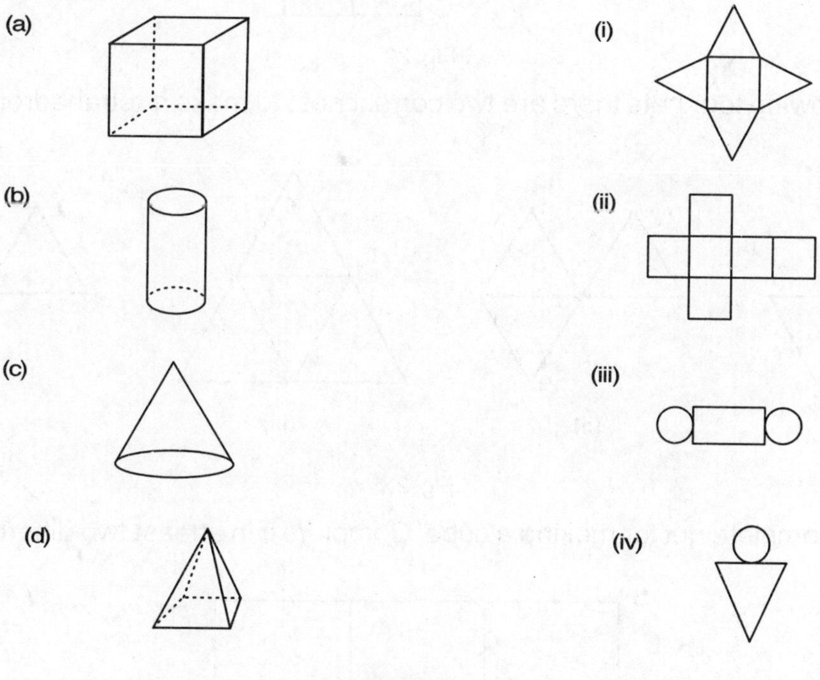

Fig. 20

2. Identify the nets which can be used to make cubes (cut-out the nets and try it):

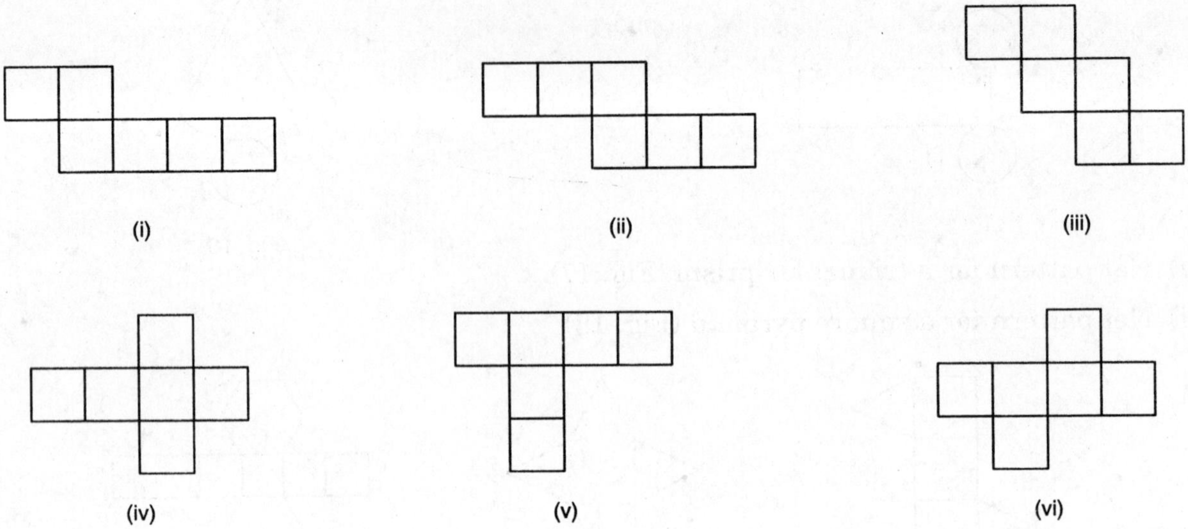

Fig. 21

3. Can the following be a net for a die? Explain your answer.

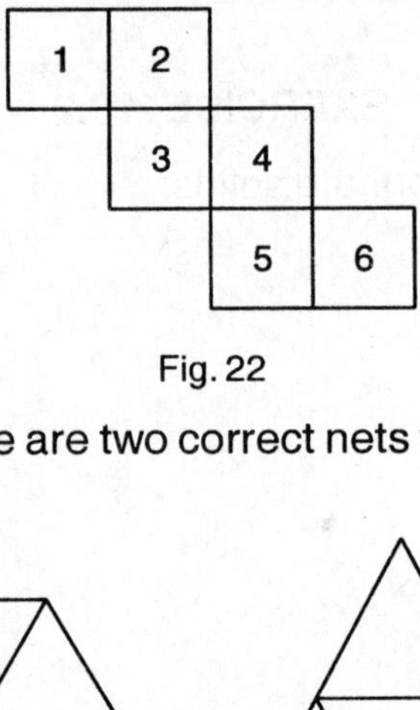

Fig. 22

4. Out of the following four nets there are two correct nets to make a tetrahedron. Identify them.

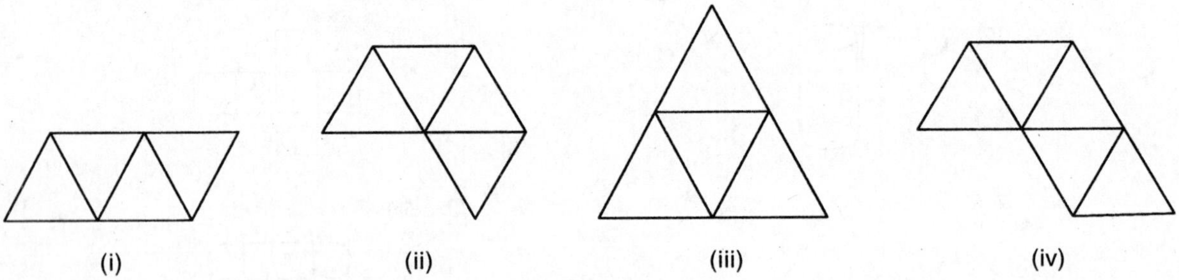

Fig. 23

5. Here is an incomplete net for making a cube. Complete it in atleast two different ways.

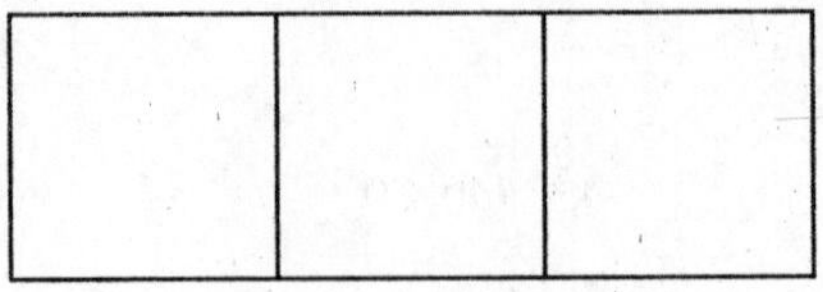

ANSWERS

1. a. $\rightarrow$ (ii), b. $\rightarrow$ (iii), c. $\rightarrow$ (iv), d. $\rightarrow$ (i)
2. (ii), (iv), (vi)
3. No, as the sum of the numbers on all opposite faces as 7 is not possible.
4. (i), (iii).
5.

(i) (ii)

Fig. 24

20

MENSURATION – I
(Perimeter and area of rectilinear figures)

20.1 INTRODUCTION

In Class VI, we have learnt about perimeters of plane figures and areas of square and rectangle. We have learnt that the perimeter is the length of the boundary of a closed figure and the magnitude of the measurement of the region enclosed by it is its area. In this chapter, we will learn about perimeter and area of few more plane figures.

20.2 UNITS OF MEASUREMENT OF AREA

Following are various units of measurement of area:

SQUARE MILLIMETRE *The area of a region formed by a square of side 1 millimetre is called a square millimetre and is written as 1 mm*^{2}.

SQUARE CENTIMETRE *The area of a region formed by a square of side 1 cm is called a square centimetre and is written as 1 cm*^{2}.

$\because$ 1 cm = 10 mm

$\therefore$ $1\text{ cm}^2 = 1\text{ cm} \times 1\text{ cm} = 10 \times 10\text{ mm}^2 = 100\text{ mm}^2$

Thus, $1\text{ cm}^2 = 100\text{ mm}^2$

SQUARE DECIMETRE *The area of a region formed by a square of side 1 decimetre is called a square decimetre, written as 1 dm*^{2}.

$\because$ 1 dm = 10 cm

$\therefore$ $1\text{ dm}^2 = 10 \times 10\text{ cm}^2 = 100\text{ cm}^2$

Also, $1\text{ dm}^2 = 100 \times 100\text{ mm}^2$

$= 10000\text{ mm}^2$ $\quad [\because 1\text{ cm}^2 = 100\text{ mm}^2]$

SQUARE METRE *The area of a region formed by a square of side 1 metre is called a square metre, written as 1 m*^{2}.

$\because$ 1 m = 100 cm

$\therefore$ $1\text{ m}^2 = 100 \times 100\text{ cm}^2 = 10000\text{ cm}^2$

Also, 1 m = 10 dm

$\therefore$ $1\text{ m}^2 = 10 \times 10\text{ dm}^2 = 100\text{ dm}^2$

and, $1\text{ m}^2 = 100 \times 10000\text{ mm}^2$ $\quad [\because 1\text{ dm}^2 = 10000\text{ mm}^2]$

$= 1000000\text{ mm}^2$

ARE *The area of a region formed by a square of side one decametre (1 dam) is called an are, written as 1 dam*^{2} *or 1 are.*

$\because$ 1 dam = 10 m

$\therefore$ $1\text{ dam}^2 = 10 \times 10\text{ m}^2 = 100\text{ m}^2$

or, 1 are $= 100\ m^2$

Also, $1\ m^2 = 100\ dm^2$

$\therefore$ 1 are $= 100 \times 100\ dm^2$

$= 10^4\ dm^2$

$= 10^6\ cm^2$ $[\because 1\ dm^2 = 100\ cm^2]$

HECTARE *The area of a region formed by a square of side 1 hectometre (1 hm) is called a hectare, written as 1 hm^2.*

$\because$ $1\ hm = 100\ m$

$\therefore$ $1\ hm^2 = 100 \times 100\ m^2$

$= 10^4\ m^2$

or, 1 hectare $= 10^4\ m^2$

Also, $100\ m^2 = 1$ are

$\therefore$ 1 hectare = 100 are or, 1 ha = 100 a.

SQUARE KILOMETRE *The area of a region formed by a square of side 1 km is called a square kilometer, written as 1 km^2.*

$\because$ $1\ km = 1000\ m$

$\therefore$ $1\ km^2 = 1000 \times 1000\ m^2 = 10^6\ m^2$.

$\because$ $100\ m^2 = 1$ are

$\therefore$ $1\ km^2 = \frac{1000000}{100}$ are $= 10000$ are

Also, $1\ ha = 10000\ m^2$

$\therefore$ $1\ km^2 = \frac{1000000}{10000}\ ha = 100\ ha$

In the above discussion, we have introduced various standard units each of which can be converted into others. The following table provides ready reference for the conversion of these units.

Conversion of units

Units of Length	*Units of Area*
1 cm = 10 mm	$1\ cm^2 = (10 \times 10)\ mm^2 = 100\ mm^2$
1 m = 10 dm	$1\ m^2 = (10 \times 10)\ dm^2 = 100\ dm^2$
1 dm = 10 cm	$1\ dm^2 = (10 \times 10)\ cm^2 = 100\ cm^2$
1 m = 100 cm	$1\ m^2 = (100 \times 100)\ cm^2 = 10000\ cm^2$
1 dam = 10 m	$1\ dam^2 = (10 \times 10)\ m^2 = 100\ m^2 = 1$ are
1 hm = 100 m	$1\ hm^2 = (100 \times 100)\ m^2 = 10000\ m^2 = 1$ hectare
1 km = 10 hm	$1\ km^2 = (10 \times 10)\ hm^2 = 100\ hm^2$
1 km = 1000 m	$1\ km^2 = (1000 \times 1000)\ m^2 = 1000000\ m^2 = 100$ hectare

20.3 PERIMETER AND AREA OF SQUARES AND RECTANGLES

In class VI, we have learnt about the perimeters and areas of rectangles and squares. In this chapter, we will review the problems related to them.

(i) Perimeter and area of a rectangle

Let l and b denote the length and breadth respectively of a rectangle. Then,

(i) Perimeter $= 2(l + b)$

(ii) Area $= l \times b$

(iii) Length $= \dfrac{\text{Area}}{\text{Breadth}}$

(iv) Breadth $= \dfrac{\text{Area}}{\text{Length}}$

(v) Diagonal $= \sqrt{l^2 + b^2}$

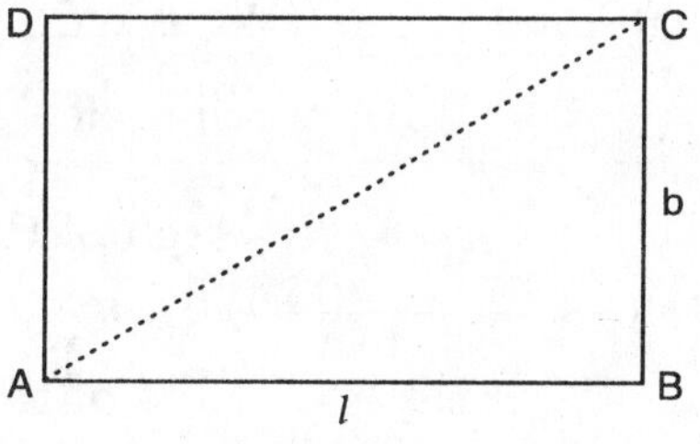

Fig. 1

(ii) Perimeter and area of a square

Let a be the length of each side of a square. Then,

(i) Perimeter $= 4a$

(ii) Area $= a^2$, Area $= \left(\dfrac{\text{Perimeter}}{4}\right)^2$

(iii) Side of the square $= \sqrt{\text{Area}}$

(iv) Diagonal $= \sqrt{2}\,a$

(v) Area $= \dfrac{1}{2}(\text{Diagonal})^2$

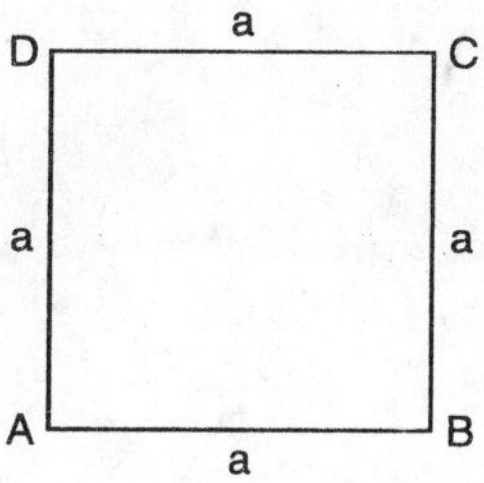

Fig. 2

(iii) Area of four walls of a room

Let l, b and h denote respectively the length, breadth and height of a room. Then,

(i) Area of the 4 walls $= 2(l + b) \times h$

(ii) Diagonal of the room $= \sqrt{l^2 + b^2 + h^2}$

ILLUSTRATIVE EXAMPLES

Example 1 Find the area, in square metres, of a rectangle whose

(i) length = 4.5 m, breadth = 1.6 m (ii) length = 720 cm, breadth = 25 cm

(iii) length = 3 dm 6 cm, breadth = 2 dm 9 cm.

Solution (i) We have,

Length = 4.5 m and, Breadth = 1.6 m

$\therefore$ Area of the rectangle $=$ Length $\times$ Breadth $= 4.5 \times 1.6\ \text{m}^2 = 7.20\ \text{m}^2$

(ii) We have,

Length $= 720\,\text{cm} = \dfrac{720}{100}\,\text{m} = 7.2\,\text{m}$, Breadth $= 25\,\text{cm} = \dfrac{25}{100}\,\text{m} = 0.25\,\text{m}$

$\therefore$ Area of the rectangle $=$ Length $\times$ Breadth $= 7.2 \times 0.25\ \text{m}^2 = 1.8\,\text{m}^2$

(iii) We have,

Length $= 3$ dm 6 cm $= (3 \times 10 + 6)$ cm $= 36$ cm $= 0.36$ m [$\because$ 1 dm = 10 cm]

Breadth $= 2$ dm 9 cm $= (2 \times 10 + 9)$ cm $= 29$ cm $= 0.29$ m

$\therefore$ Area of the rectangle $= 0.36 \times 0.29\ \text{m}^2 = 0.1044\ \text{m}^2$

Example 2 Find the area, in square centimetres, of a square whose side is

(i) 2.4 dm (ii) 20 mm

Solution (i) We have,

Side of the square $= 2.4$ dm $= (2.4 \times 10)$ cm $= 24$ cm

$\therefore$ Area of the square $= (\text{Side})^2 = (24)^2\ \text{cm}^2 = 576\ \text{cm}^2$

(ii) We have,

Side of the square $= 20$ mm $= 2$ cm [$\because$ 10 mm = 1 cm]

$\therefore$ Area of the square $= (\text{Side})^2 = (2)^2\ \text{cm}^2 = 4\ \text{cm}^2$

Example 3 Find the area, in hectare, of a field whose length is 240 m and breadth 110 m.

Solution We have,

Length of the field = 240 m, Breadth of the field = 110 m

$\therefore$ Area of the field $= (240 \times 110)\ \text{m}^2$

$= 26400\ \text{m}^2$

$= \dfrac{26400}{10000}$ hectare $= 2.64$ hectare [$\because 10000\ \text{m}^2 = 1$ hectare]

Example 4 Find the area of a rectangular plot one side of which is 48 m and its diagonal 50 m.

Solution Let the other side be x metres. Since ΔABC is a right triangle. Therefore,

$$AC^2 = AB^2 + BC^2$$

$$\Rightarrow \quad 50^2 = 48^2 + x^2$$

$$\Rightarrow \quad x^2 = (50)^2 - (48)^2$$

$$\Rightarrow \quad x^2 = (50 + 48)(50 - 48)$$

$$\Rightarrow \quad x^2 = 98 \times 2$$

$$\Rightarrow \quad x^2 = 14^2$$

$$\Rightarrow \quad x = 14.$$

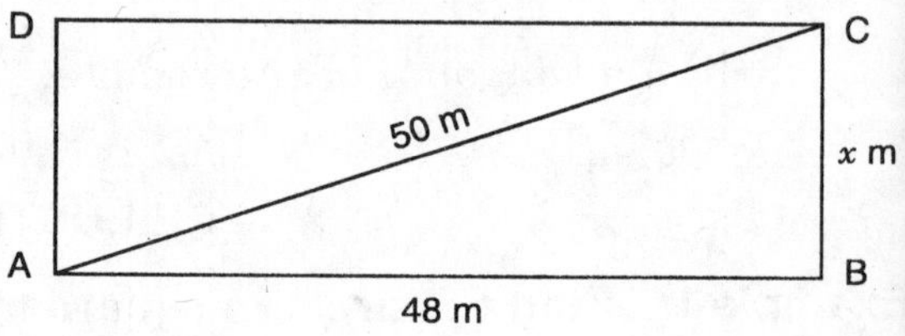

Fig. 3

Thus, the other side of the rectangle is 14 m.

$\therefore$ Area of the rectangle $= (48 \times 14)\ \text{m}^2 = 672\ \text{m}^2$

Example 5 The length and breadth of a rectangular piece of land are 500 m and 300 m respectively. Find :

(i) its area (ii) its cost, if 1 m^2 of the land costs Rs 10000.

Solution (i) We have, l = Length = 500 m, b = Breadth = 300 m

$\therefore$ Area $= l \times b = 500 \times 300\,m^2 = 150000\,m^2$

(ii) Since 1 m^2 of the land costs Rs 10000.

$\therefore$ Cost of 150000 m^2 of land $=$ Rs (150000×10000)

$=$ Rs 1500000000 $=$ Rs 1500 millions

Example 6 Find the area of a square park whose perimeter is 320 m.

Solution Let the length of each side of the square park be a metre. Then,

Perimeter = 320 m

$4a = 320$

$\Rightarrow a = \dfrac{320}{4} = 80$ m [$\because$ Perimeter of a square $= 4 \times$ Side]

$\therefore$ Area $= a^2 = (80 \times 80)\,m^2 = 6400\,m^2$

Example 7 Find the breadth of a rectangular plot of land, if its area is 440 sq. m and length is 22 m. Also, find its perimeter.

Solution We have,

l = Length of the plot = 22 m, Area of the plot = 440 sq. metre

Let the breadth of the plot be b metres. Then,

$$\text{Breadth} = \frac{\text{Area}}{\text{Length}} \qquad b = \frac{440}{22} = 20\text{ m}$$

Perimeter $= 2(l + b) = 2 \times (22 + 20)$ m $= 2 \times 42$ m 84 m.

Hence, the breadth of the plot is 20 m and the perimeter is 84 m.

Example 8 The perimeter of a rectangular sheet is 100 cm. If the length is 35 cm, find its breadth. Also, find the area.

Solution We have,

l = Length of the sheet = 35 cm, P = Perimeter of the sheet = 100 cm

Let the breadth of the sheet be b cm. Then,

Perimeter $= 2 \times (l + b)$

$100 = 2 \times (35 + b)$

$100 = 70 + 2b$

$2b = 100 - 70 \Rightarrow 2b = 30 \Rightarrow b = 15$ cm

Area of sheet $= l \times b = 35 \times 15\,cm^2 = 525\,cm^2$

Example 9 The areas of a square and rectangle are equal. If the side of the square is 40 cm and the breadth of the rectangle is 25 cm, find the length of the rectangle. Also, find the permeter of the rectangle.

Solution We have,

Side of the square = 40 cm.

$\therefore$ Area of the square $= (\text{Side})^2 = 40 \text{ cm} \times 40 \text{ cm} = 1600 \text{ cm}^2$

$\Rightarrow$ Area of the rectangle $= 1600 \text{ cm}^2$ $\left[\because \text{Area of the rectangle} = \text{Area of the square}\right]$

It is given that the breadth of the rectangle is 25 cm.

$\therefore$ Length $= \dfrac{\text{Area}}{\text{Breadth}} = \dfrac{1600}{25}$ cm $= 64$ cm

Perimeter of the rectangle $= 2\,(\text{Length} + \text{Breadth})$

$= 2 \times (64 + 25)$ cm $= 2 \times 89$ cm $= 178$ cm

Example 10 Anu wants to fence the garden infront of her house as shown in Fig. 4 on three sides. Find the cost of fencing at the rate of Rs 150 per metre.

Solution Anu wants to fence the garden on three sides, as one of the side of the house will serve the purpose of fence. Therefore, length of the fence required is the perimeter of the garden excluding the one side facing the house.

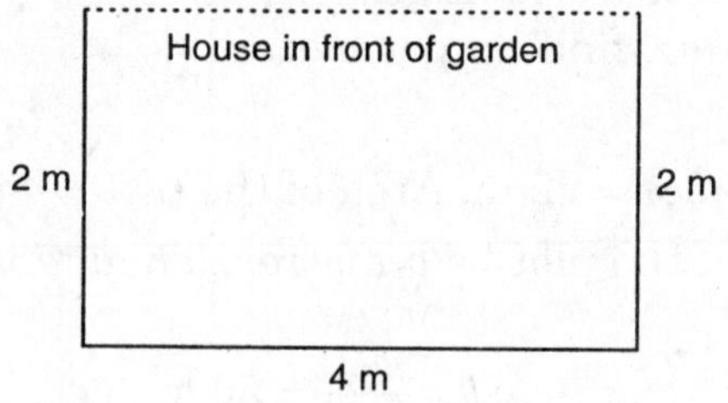

Fig. 4

$\therefore$ Length of fence $= 4 \text{ m} + 2 \text{ m} + 2 \text{ m} = 8 \text{ m}$

Hence, cost of fencing $= \text{Rs}\,(8 \times 150) = \text{Rs}\ 1200$

Example 11 A wire is in the shape of a square of side 10 cm. If the wire is rebent into a rectangle of length 12 cm, find its breadth. Which encloses more area, the square or the rectangle?

Solution We have,

Side of the square = 10 cm.

Length of the wire $=$ Perimeter of the square $= 4 \times \text{Side} = 4 \times 10 \text{ cm} = 40 \text{ cm}$

l = Length of the rectangle = 12 cm.

Let b be the breadth of the rectangle.

Now,

Perimeter of the rectangle = Perimeter of the square

$\Rightarrow$ $2\,(l + b) = 40$

$\Rightarrow$ $2\,(12 + b) = 40$

$\Rightarrow$ $24 + 2b = 40 \Rightarrow 2b = 40 - 24 \Rightarrow 2b = 16 \Rightarrow b = \dfrac{16}{2} \text{ cm} = 8 \text{ cm}$

So, Breadth of the rectangle = 8 cm.

Now, Area of the square $=(\text{Side})^2 = 10\text{ cm} \times 10\text{ cm} = 100\text{ cm}^2$

Area of the rectangle $= l \times b = 12\text{ cm} \times 8\text{ cm} = 96\text{ cm}^2$

Thus, the square encloses more area even though its perimeter is the same as that of the rectangle.

Example 12 A door of length 1 m and breadth 0.5 m is on a wall. The length of the wall is 4.5 m and the breadth is 3.6 m as shown in Fig. 5. Find the cost of white washing the wall, if the rate of white washing the wall is Rs 20 per m^2.

Solution We have,

l = Length of the wall = 4.5 m, b = Breadth of the wall = 3.6 m

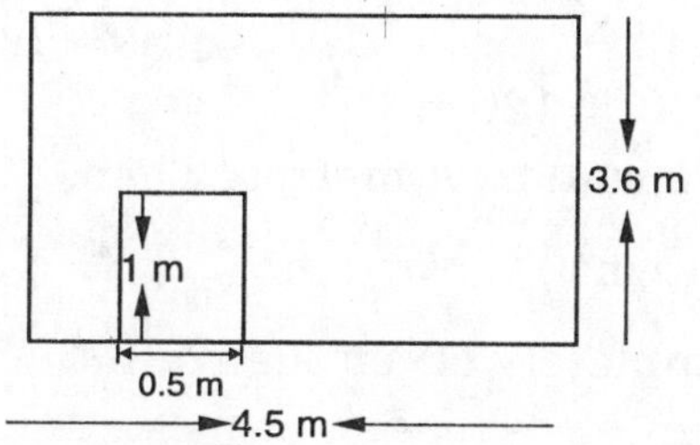

Fig. 5

$\therefore$ Area of the wall $= l \times b = 4.5\text{ m} \times 3.6\text{ m} = 16.2\text{ m}^2$

Area of the door $= 1\text{ m} \times 0.5\text{ m} = 0.5\text{ m}^2$

$\therefore$ Area to be white washed $= 16.2\text{ m}^2 - 0.5\text{ m}^2 = 15.7\text{ m}^2$

Cost of white washing the wall $= \text{Rs}\,(15.7 \times 20) = \text{Rs}\,314$.

Example 13 A wall 4.84 m long and 3.1 m high is covered with rectangular tiles of size 22 cm by 10 cm. Find the total cost of the tiles at the rate of Rs 1.50 per tile.

Solution We have,

Area of the wall $= 4.84 \times 3.1\text{ m}^2$

$= 15.004\text{ m}^2$

$= 15.004 \times 10000\text{ cm}^2$ $[\because 1\text{ m}^2 = 10000\text{ cm}^2]$

$= 150040\text{ cm}^2$

Area of one tile $= 22 \times 10\text{ cm}^2 = 220\text{ cm}^2$

$$\therefore \text{Number of tiles} = \frac{\text{Area of the wall}}{\text{Area of one tile}} = \frac{150040}{220} = 682$$

Cost of one tile = Rs 1.50

$\therefore$ Total cost = Number of tiles $\times$ Cost of one tile $= \text{Rs}\,(682 \times 1.50) = \text{Rs}\,1023$

Example 14 A black board of sides 5 m 20 cm and 3 m 40 cm is to be painted, find the cost at the rate of Rs 12 per square metre.

Solution We have,

Length of the black board = 5 m 20 cm = 5.20 m

Breadth of the black board = 3m 40 cm = 3.40 m

$\therefore$ Area of the black board $= (5.20 \times 3.40)\ m^2 = 17.68\ m^2$

Rate of painting the black board $=$ ₹ 12 per m^2

$\therefore$ Cost of painting the black board $=$ ₹ $(17.68 \times 12) =$ ₹ 212.16

Example 15 Find the height of the wall whose length is 4 m and which can be covered by 2400 tiles of size 25 cm by 20 cm.

Solution Area of a tile $= 25 \times 20\ cm^2 = 500\ cm^2$

$\therefore$ Area of 2400 tiles $= 2400 \times 500\ cm^2$

$$= 1200000\ cm^2 = \frac{1200000}{10000}\ m^2 \qquad [\because 10000\ cm^2 = 1\ m^2]$$

$$= 120\ m^2$$

Let the height of the wall be h metres. Then,

Area of the wall $= 4h\ m^2$

Since 2400 tiles completely cover the wall.

$\therefore$ Area of the wall = Area of 2400 tiles

$\Rightarrow \quad 4h = 120$

$\Rightarrow \quad \frac{4h}{4} = \frac{120}{4} = 30$ [Dividing both sides by 4]

Hence, the height of the wall is 30 metres.

EXERCISE 20.1

1. Find the area, in square metres, of a rectangle whose
   (i) Length = 5.5 m, breadth = 2.4 m (ii) Length = 180 cm, breadth = 150 cm
2. Find the area, in square centimetres, of a square whose side is
   (i) 2.6 cm (ii) 1.2 dm
3. Find in square metres, the area of a square of side 16.5 dam.
4. Find the area of a rectangular field in ares whose sides are:
   (i) 200 m and 125 m (ii) 75 m 5 dm and 120 m
5. Find the area of a rectangular field in hectares whose sides are:
   (i) 125 m and 400 m (ii) 75 m 5 dm and 120 m
6. A door of dimensions 3 m × 2m is on the wall of dimension 10 m × 10 m. Find the cost of painting the wall if rate of painting is ₹ 2.50 per sq. m.
7. A wire is in the shape of a rectangle. Its length is 40 cm and breadth is 22 cm. If the same wire is bent in the shape of a square, what will be the measure of each side. Also, find which shape encloses more area?
8. How many square metres of glass will be required for a window, which has 12 panes, each pane measuring 25 cm by 16 cm?
9. A marble tile measures 10 cm × 12 cm. How many tiles will be required to cover a wall of size 3 m × 4 m? Also, find the total cost of the tiles at the rate of ₹ 2 per tile.
10. A table top is 9 dm 5 cm long 6 dm 5 cm broad. What will be the cost to polish it at the rate of 20 paise per square centimetre?

11. A room is 9.68 m long and 6.2 m wide. Its floor is to be covered with rectangular tiles of size 22 cm by 10 cm. Find the total cost of the tiles at the rate of Rs 2.50 per tile.
12. One side of a square field is 179 m. Find the cost of raising a lawn on the field at the rate of Rs 1.50 per square metre.
13. A rectangular field is measured 290 m by 210 m. How long will it take for a girl to go two times round the field, if she walks at the rate of 1.5 m/sec?
14. A corridor of a school is 8 m long and 6 m wide. It is to be covered with convas sheets. If the available canvas sheets have the size 2 m × 1 m, find the cost of canvas sheets required to cover the corridor at the rate of Rs 8 per sheet.
15. The length and breadth of a playground are 62 m 60 cm and 25 m 40 cm respectively. Find the cost of turfing it at Rs 2.50 per square metre. How long will a man take to go three times round the field, if he walks at the rate of 2 metres per second.
16. A lane 180 m long and 5 m wide is to be paved with bricks of length 20 cm and breadth 15 cm. Find the cost of bricks that are required, at the rate of Rs 750 per thousand.
17. How many envelopes can be made out of a sheet of paper 125 cm by 85 cm; supposing one envelope requires a piece of paper of size 17 cm by 5 cm?
18. The width of a cloth is 170 cm. Calculate the length of the cloth required to make 25 diapers, if each diaper requires a piece of cloth of size 50 cm by 17 cm.
19. The carpet for a room 6.6 m by 5.6 m costs Rs 3960 and it was made from a roll 70 cm wide. Find the cost of the carpet per metre.
20. A room is 9 m long, 8 m broad and 6.5 m high. It has one door of dimensions 2 m × 1.5 m and three windows each of dimensions 1.5 m × 1 m. Find the cost of white washing the walls at Rs 3.80 per square metre.
21. A hall 36 m long and 24 m broad allowing 80 m^2 for doors and windows, the cost of papering the walls at Rs 8.40 per m^2 is Rs 9408. Find the height of the hall.

ANSWER

1. (i) 13.2 m^2 (ii) 2.7 m^2 2. (i) 6.76 cm^2 (ii) 144 cm^2 3. 27225 m^2
4. (i) 250 ares (ii) 90.6 ares 5. (i) 5 hectares (ii) 0.906 hectares 6. Rs. 235
7. 31 cm, Square 8. 0.48 m^2 9. 1000, Rs 2000 10. Rs 1235
11. Rs 6820 12. Rs 48061.50 13. $22\frac{2}{9}$ minutes 14. Rs 192
15. Rs 3975.10, 4 minutes 24 seconds 16. Rs 22500 17. 125
18. 125 cm 19. Rs 75 per metre 20. Rs 811.30 21. 10 m

20.4 AREA BETWEEN RECTANGLES

In this section, we shall apply the formulae for the areas of a rectangle and a square to determine the areas of the paths around (in or outside) a rectangle and also of the central paths.

Following examples will illustrate the same.

ILLUSTRATIVE EXAMPLES

Example 1 A rectangular grassy lawn measuring 30 m by 28 m is to be surrounded externally by a path which is 2 m wide. Find the cost of levelling the path at the rate of Rs 5 per square metre.

Solution Let $ABCD$ be the grassy lawn, and let $PQRS$ be the external boundaries of the path.

We have,

Length AB = 30 m, Breadth BC = 28 m

$\therefore$ Area of lawn $ABCD = 30 \times 28\,\text{m}^2 = 840\,\text{m}^2$

Length $PQ = (30\,\text{m} + 2\,\text{m} + 2\,\text{m}) = 34\,\text{m}$

Breadth $QR = 28\,\text{m} + 2\,\text{m} + 2\,\text{m} = 32\,\text{m}$

$\therefore$ Area $PQRS = 34 \times 32\,\text{m}^2 = 1088\,\text{m}^2$

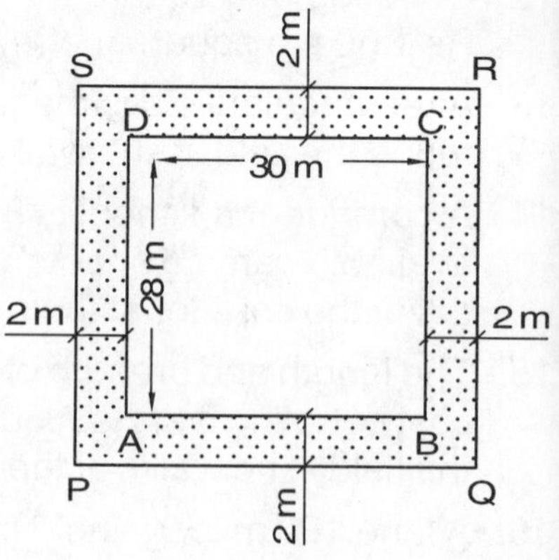

Fig. 6

Now,

Area of the path

= Area $PQRS$ – Area of the lawn

$= (1088 - 840)\,\text{m}^2 = 248\,\text{m}^2$

$\therefore$ Cost of levelling the path = Rs (248×5) = Rs 1240.

Example 2 A rectangular park is 45 m long and 30 m wide. A path 2.5 m wide is constructed outside the park. Find the area of the path.

Solution Let $ABCD$ be the rectangular park and the shaded region represents the 2.5 wide path to be constructed outside the park.

We have,

$PQ = (45 + 2.5 + 2.5)\,\text{m} = 50\,\text{m}$,

$PS = (30 + 2.5 + 2.5)\,\text{m} = 35\,\text{m}$

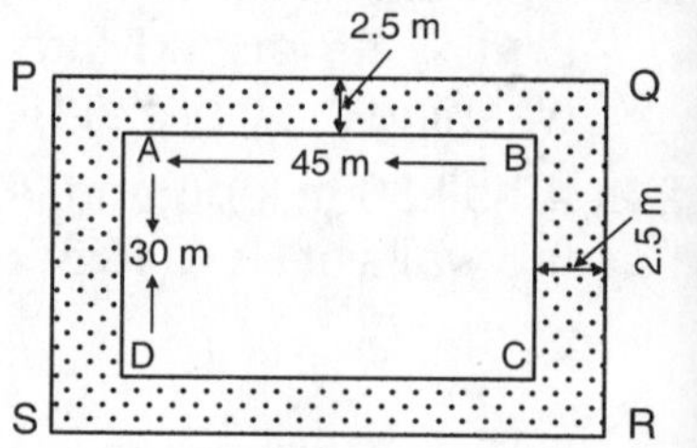

Fig. 7

Clearly,

Area of the path = Area of rectangle $PQRS$ – Area of rectangle $ABCD$

$= (50 \times 35)\,\text{m}^2 - (45 \times 30)\,\text{m}^2$,

$= 1750\,\text{m}^2 - 1350\,\text{m}^2 = 400\,\text{m}^2$

Example 3 A verandah 1.25 m wide is constructed all along the outside of a room 5.5 m long and 4 m wide. Find (i) the area of the verandah (ii) the cost of cementing the floor of the verandah at the rate of Rs 200 per m^2.

Solution Let $ABCD$ denote the floor of the room and the shaded region represents the floor of the 1.25 m wide verandah.

We have,

$PQ = 5.5 + 1.25 + 1.25)\,\text{m} = 8\,\text{m}$ and $PS = (4 + 1.25 + 1.25)\,\text{m} = 6.5\,\text{m}$

We have,

Area of verandah = Area of rectangle $PQRS$ – Area of rectangle $ABCD$

$= PQ \times PS - AB \times AD$

$= 8 \times 6.5\,\text{m}^2 - 5.5 \times 4\,\text{m}^2 = (52 - 22)\,\text{m}^2 = 30\,\text{m}^2$

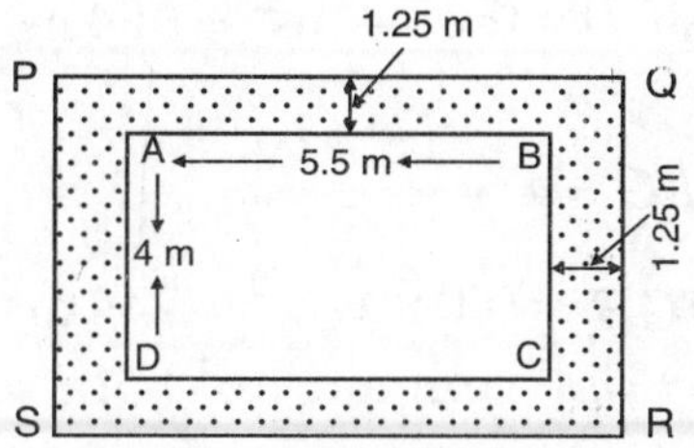

Fig. 8

(ii) We have,

Rate of cementing the floor of verandah = Rs 200 per m^2

$\therefore$ Cost of cementing the floor of verandah $=$ Rs $(30\times 200)=$ Rs 6000

Example 4 A path 1 m wide is built along the border inside a square garden of side 30 m. Find (i) the area of the path (ii) the cost of planting the grass in the remaining portion of the garden at the rate of Rs 40 per m^2.

Solution Let *ABCD* be the square of side 30 m and the shaded region represents 1 m wide path which is built along the border inside the garden.

We have,

$PQ=(30-1-1)\,m=28\,m$, $PS=(30-1-1)\,m=28\,m$

(i) Area of the path

$=$ Area of square *ABCD* – Area of square *PQRS*

$=(30\times 30)\,m^2-(28\times 28)\,m^2=(900-784)\,m^2=116\,m^2$

(ii) Area of the remaining portion in which the grass is planted

$=$ Area of square *PQRS* $=28\times 28\,m^2=784\,m^2$

Since the grass is planted in the garden at the rate of Rs 40 per m^2.

$\therefore$ Cost of planting the grass in the region *PQRS* $=$ Rs $(40\times 784)=$ Rs 31360

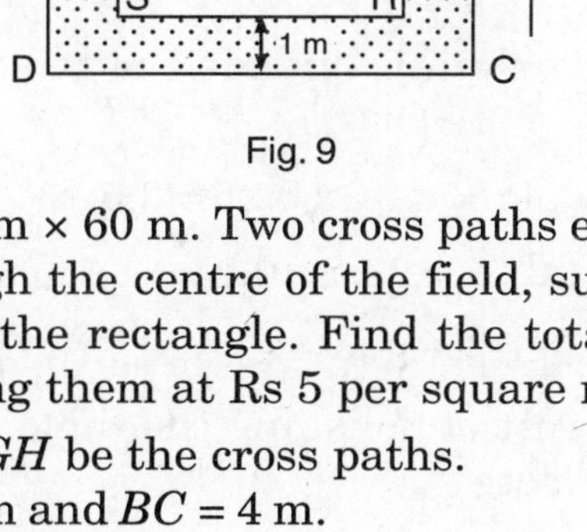

Fig. 9

Example 5 A grassy plot is 80 m × 60 m. Two cross paths each 4 m wide are constructed at right angles through the centre of the field, such that each path is parallel to one of the sides of the rectangle. Find the total area used as path. Also, find the cost of gravelling them at Rs 5 per square metre (Fig.11)

Solution Let *ABCD* and *EFGH* be the cross paths.

We have, $AB=80$ m and $BC=4$ m.

$\therefore$ Area of path $ABCD = (80 \times 4)\,\text{m}^2 = 320\,\text{m}^2$

Again,

$EF = 60\,\text{m}$ and $FG = 4\,\text{m}$

$\therefore$ Area of path $EFGH = (60 \times 4)\,\text{m}^2 = 240\,\text{m}^2$.

Clearly, area $PQRS$ is common to both the paths.

We have,

Area $PQRS = (4 \times 4)\,\text{m}^2 = 16\,\text{m}^2$

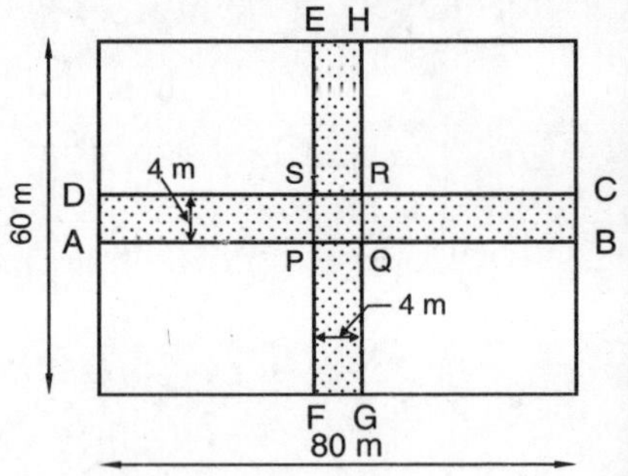

Fig. 10

$\therefore$ Total area used as path = Area of path $ABCD$ + Area of path $EFGH$ – Area $PQRS$

$= (320 + 240 - 16)\,\text{m}^2 = 544\,\text{m}^2$

Rate of gravelling the path = Rs 5 per square metre

$\therefore$ Total cost of gravelling the path = Rs (5×544) = Rs 2720

Example 6 A rectangular lawn is 30 m by 20 m. It has two roads each 2 m wide running in the middle of it, one parallel to the length and the other parallel to the breadth. Find the area of the roads.

Solution Area of road $ABCD = 30 \times 2 = 60\,\text{m}^2$

Area of road $PQRS = 20 \times 2 = 40\,\text{m}^2$

Clearly, the shaded portion is common to the two roads.

Area of the shaded portion $= 2 \times 2 = 4\,\text{m}^2$

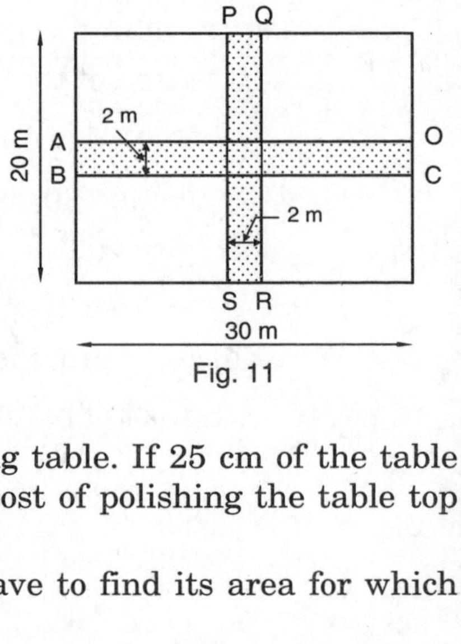

Fig. 11

Hence, Area of the roads $= 60 + 40 - 4 = 96\,\text{m}^2$.

Example 7 A table cover, 4 m × 2 m, is spread on a meeting table. If 25 cm of the table cover is hanging all around the table, find the cost of polishing the table top at Rs 2.25 per square metre.

Solution To find the cost of polishing the table top we have to find its area for which we require its length and breadth.

We have,

Length of the cloth = 4 m

Breadth of the cloth = 2 m

Since 25 cm width of cloth is outside the table on each side.

$\therefore$ Length of the table $= 4 - 2 \times 0.25 = 3.5\,\text{m}$

Breadth of the table $= 2 - 2 \times 0.25 = 1.5\,\text{m}$

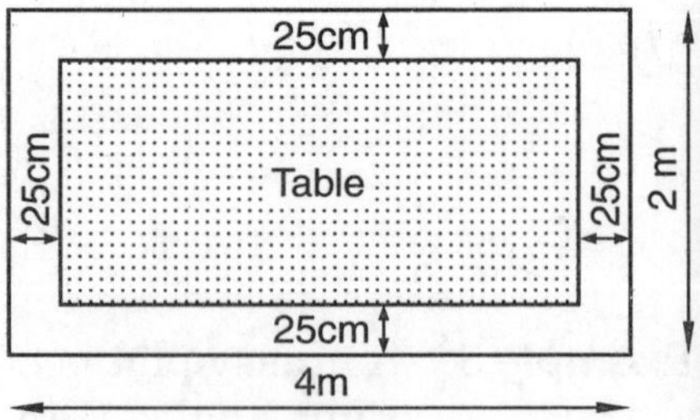

Fig. 12

$\therefore$ Area of the top of the table $= (3.5 \times 1.5)\,\text{m}^2$

It is given that the cost of polishing the table top is at the rate of Rs 2.25 per square metre. Therefore,

Cost of polishing the top = Area × Rate per sq. metre

$$= \text{Rs}\,(3.5 \times 1.5 \times 2.25)$$

$$= \text{Rs}\left(\frac{7}{2} \times \frac{3}{2} \times \frac{9}{4}\right) = \text{Rs}\,11.81$$

Example 8 The length and breadth of a park are in the ratio 2 : 1 and its perimeter is 240 m. A path of 2 m wide runs inside it, along boundary. Find the cost of paving the path at Rs 3 per m^2.

Solution Let *ABCD* be the park whose length *AB* and breadth *AD* are in the ratio 2 : 1. Let the shaded region represent the 2 m inside path that runs inside the park *ABCD*. Since length and breadth of the park are in the ratio 2:1. So, let the length and breadth of the park be $2x$ and x metre respectively. Then,

$$\text{Perimeter} = 2(2x + x)$$

But, Perimeter = 240 m

$$\therefore \quad 2(2x + x) = 240$$

$$\Rightarrow \quad 6x = 240$$

$$\Rightarrow \quad x = \frac{240}{6} = 40$$

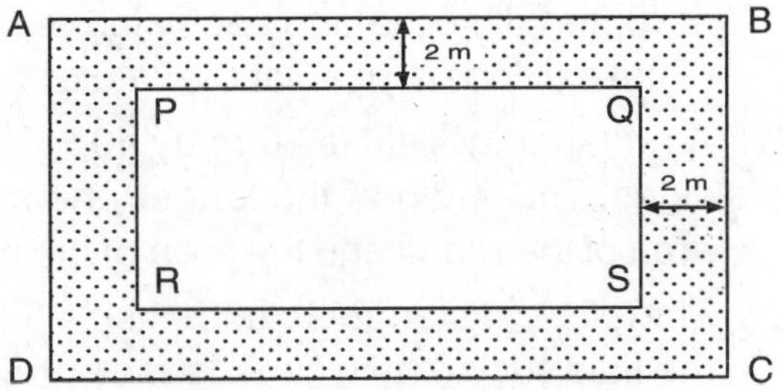

Fig. 13

$\therefore$ Length $AB = (2 \times 40)\,\text{m} = 80\,\text{m}$

and Breadth = AD = 40 m

We have,

$$PQ = (80 - 2 - 2)\,\text{m} = 76\,\text{m} \text{ and, } PR = (40 - 2 - 2)\,\text{m} = 36\,\text{m}$$

$\therefore$ Area of the path = Area of rectangle *ABCD* – Area of rectangle *PQRS*

$$= (80 \times 40 - 76 \times 36)\,\text{m}^2 = (3200 - 2736)\,\text{m}^2 = 464\,\text{m}^2$$

Hence, cost of paving the path = Rs (464×3) = Rs 1392

EXERCISE 20.2

1. A rectangular grassy lawn measuring 40 m by 25 m is to be surrounded externally by a path which is 2 m wide. Calcualte the cost of levelling the path at the rate of Rs 8.25 per square metre.
2. One metre wide path is built inside a square park of side 30 m along its sides. The remaining part of the park is covered by grass. If the total cost of covering by grass is Rs 1176, find the rate per square metre at which the park is covered by the grass.
3. Through a rectangular field of sides 90 m × 60 m, two roads are constructed which are parallel to the sides and cut each other at right angles through the centre of the field. If the width of the roads is 3 m, find the total area covered by the two roads.
4. From a rectangular sheet of tin, of size 100 cm by 80 cm, are cut four squares of side 10 cm from each corner. Find the area of the remaining sheet.

5. A painting 8 cm long and 5 cm wide is painted on a cardboard such that there is a margin of 1.5 cm along each of its sides. Find the total area of the margin.
6. Rakesh has a rectangular field of length 80 m and breadth 60 m. In it, he wants to make a garden 10 m long and 4 m broad at one of the corners and at another corner, he wants to grow flowers in two floor-beds each of size 4 m by 1.5 m. In the remaining part of the field, he wants to apply manures. Find the cost of applying the manures at the rate of Rs 300 per are.
7. Each side of a square flower bed is 2 m 80 cm long. It is extended by digging a strip 30 cm wide all around it. Find the area of the enlarged flower bed and also the increase in the area of the flower bed.
8. A room 5 m long and 4 m wide is surrounded by a verandah. If the verandah occupies an area of 22 m^2, find the width of the varandah.
9. A square lawn has a 2 m wide path surrounding it. If the area of the path is 136 m^2, find the area of the lawn.
10. A poster of size 10 cm by 8 cm is pasted on a sheet of cardboard such that there is a margin of width 1.75 cm along each side of the poster. Find (i) the total area of the margin (ii) the cost of the cardboard used at the rate of ₹ 0.60 per cm^2.
11. A rectangular field is 50 m by 40 m. It has two roads through its centre, running parallel to its sides. The width of the longer and shorter roads are 1.8 m and 2.5 m respectively. Find the area of the roads and the area of the remaining portion of the field.
12. There is a rectangular field of size 94 m × 32 m. Three roads each of 2 m width pass through the field such that two roads are parallel to the breadth of the field and the third is parallel to the length. Calculate : (i) area of the field covered by the three roads (ii) area of the field not covered by the roads.
13. A school has a hall which is 22 m long and 15.5 m broad. A carpet is laid inside the hall leaving all around a margin of 75 cm from the walls. Find the area of the carpet and the area of the strip left uncoverd. If the width of the carpet is 82 cm, find the cost at the rate of ₹ 18 per metre.
14. Two cross roads, each of width 5 m, run at right angles through the centre of a rectangular park of length 70 m and breadth 45 m parallel to its sides. Find the area of the roads. Also, find the cost of constructing the roads at the rate of ₹ 105 per m^2.
15. The length and breadth of a rectangular park are in the ratio 5 : 2. A 2.5 m wide path running all around the outside the park has an area 305 m^2. Find the dimensions of the park.
16. A square lawn is surrounded by a path 2.5 m wide. If the area of the path is 165 m^2, find the area of the lawn.

ANSWERS

1. ₹ 2277	2. ₹ 1.50 per square metre	3. 441 m^2
4. 7600 cm^2	5. 30 cm^2	6. ₹ 14244
7. 11.56 m^2, 3.72 m^2	8. 1 m	9. 225 m^2
10. (i) 75.25 cm^2	(ii) ₹ 93.15	11. 185.5 m^2, 1814.5 m^2
12. (i) 308 m^2	(ii) 2700 m^2	13. 287 m^2, 54 m^2, ₹ 6300
14. Area = 550 m^2 Cost = ₹ 57750		15. Length = 40 cm, Breadth = 16 m
16. 196 m^2		

20.5 AREAS OF A PARALLELOGRAM AND A RHOMBUS

A parallelogram is a quadrilateral, whose each pair of opposite sides are parallel. In Fig. 20, *ABCD* is a parallelogram such that *AB* and *DC* are a pair of its opposite sides so that $AB \parallel DC$. Similarly, *BC* and *AD* are a pair of opposite sides such that $BC \parallel AD$.

If $DL \perp AB$, then we find that any line segment with its end-points on the two sides *AB* and *DC* perpendicular to them, has the same length *DL*. So, we call *AB* as the base and *DL* the corresponding altitude.

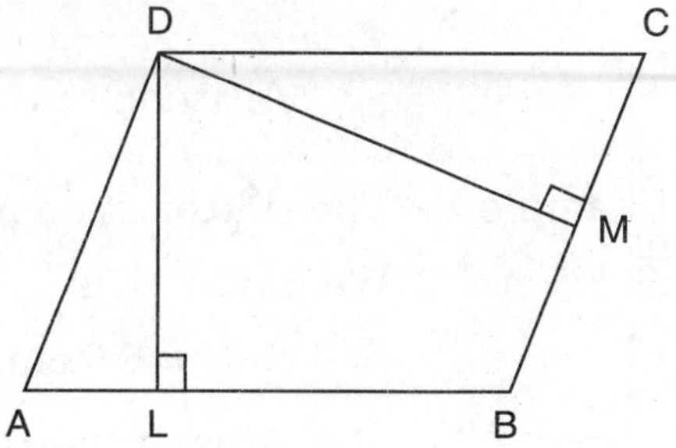

Fig. 14

Similarly, if $DM \perp BC$, then any line segment with its end-points on the two sides *AD* and *BC* and perpendicular to them, has the same length *DM*. So, we can call *BC* as the base and *DM* the corresponding altitude.

We have,

$$\text{Area of a parallelogram} = \text{Base} \times \text{Altitude}$$

$$\therefore \quad \text{Base} = \frac{\text{Area of the parallelogram}}{\text{Altitude of the parallelogram}}$$

$$\text{Altitude} = \frac{\text{Area of the parallelogram}}{\text{Corresponding base}}$$

Since a rhombus is a parallelogram with all its sides equal, therefore, the above formulae are applicable in case of a rhombus also.

$$\text{Also, Area of rhombus} = \frac{1}{2}(\text{Product of the diagonals})$$

Following examples will illustrate the use of the above formulae.

ILLUSTRATIVE EXAMPLES

Example 1 Find the area of a parallelogram with base 5 cm and altitude 4.2 cm.

Solution We have, Base = 5 cm and altitude = 4.2 cm

$\therefore$ Area of the parallelogram $= \text{Base} \times \text{height} = (5 \times 4.2)\ \text{cm}^2 = 21\ \text{cm}^2$

Example 2 Find the area in square metres of the parallelogram whose base and altitudes are as under:

(i) Base = 10 dm, altitude = 4.6 dm (ii) Base = 2 m 20 cm, altitude = 60 cm

Solution (i) We have,

Base = 10 dm = 1 m,

$\therefore$ Area of the parallelogram $= \text{Base} \times \text{Altitude} = (1 \times 0.46)\ \text{m}^2 = 0.46\ \text{m}^2$

(ii) We have,

Base = 2 m 20 cm = 2.2 m

$$\text{Altitude} = 60\ \text{cm} = \frac{60}{100}\ \text{m} = 0.6\ \text{m}$$

$\therefore$ Area of the parallelgram $= (2.2 \times 0.6)\ \text{m}^2 = 1.32\ \text{m}^2$

Example 3 Find the altitude of parallelogram whose area is 2.25 m^2 and base is 25 dm.

Solution We have,

Area of the given parallelogram = 2.25 m^2

Base of the given parallelogram $= 25\,\text{dm} = \frac{25}{10}\,\text{m} = 2.5\,\text{m}$

$\therefore$ Altitude of the given parallelogram $= \frac{\text{Area}}{\text{Base}} = \frac{2.25}{2.5}\,\text{m} = 0.9\,\text{m}$

Example 4 The side of a rhombus is 6.5 cm and its altitude is 4 cm. Find its area.

Solution We have,

Side = 6.5 cm, Altitude = 4 cm.

$\therefore$ Area of the rhombus = Base × Altitude $= (6.5 \times 4)\,\text{cm}^2 = 26\,\text{cm}^2$

Example 5 The area of a rhombus is 72 cm^2. If its perimeter is 32 cm, find its altitude.

Solution We have,

Perimeter of the rhombus = 32 cm

$\therefore$ 4 (Side) = 32 cm [$\because$ Perimeter = 4 (Side)]

$\Rightarrow$ Side $= \frac{32}{4}\,\text{cm} = 8\,\text{cm}$

Now,

Area of the rhombus = 72 cm^2

$\Rightarrow$ (Side × Altitude) = 72

$\Rightarrow$ 8 × Altitude = 72

$\Rightarrow$ Altitude $= \frac{72}{8}\,\text{cm} = 9\,\text{cm}$

Example 6 In Fig. 15 *ABCD* is a parallelogram $CM \perp AB$ and $BL \perp AD$.

(i) If *AB* = 16 cm, *AD* = 12 cm and *CM* = 10 cm, find *BL*.

(ii) If *AD* = 10 cm, *CM* = 8 cm and *BL* = 12 cm, find *AB*.

Solution (i) We have,

Base *AB* = 16 cm and Altitude *CM* = 10 cm

$\therefore$ Area of parallelogram *ABCD*

= Base × Altitude

$= (16 \times 10)\,\text{cm}^2$

$= 160\,\text{cm}^2$ ...(i)

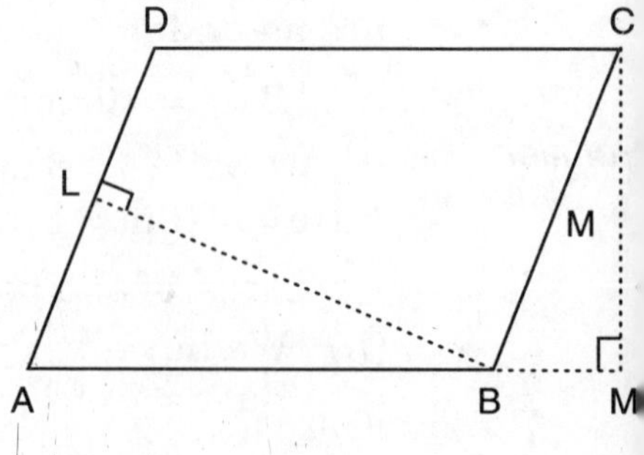

Fig. 15

Now, taking *AD* as the base, we have

Area of parallelogram *ABCD* = Base × Altitude $= (12 \times BL)\,\text{cm}^2$ ...(ii)

From (i) and (ii), we have

$$12 \times BL = 160 \Rightarrow BL = \frac{160}{12} = 13.33\,\text{cm}$$

(ii) We have,

$AD = 10$ cm, $BL = 12$ cm

$\therefore$ Area of parallelogram $ABCD = \text{Base} \times \text{height} = 10 \times 12\,\text{cm}^2 = 120\,\text{cm}^2$ ... (iii)

Now, taking AB as the base, we have

Area of parallelogram $ABCD = AB \times CM = (AB \times 8)\,\text{cm}^2$ ...(iv)

From (iii) and (iv), we get

$$AB \times 8 = 120 \Rightarrow AB = \frac{120}{8}\,\text{cm} \Rightarrow AB = 15\,\text{cm}$$

Example 7 A field in the form of a parallelogram has base 15 dam and altitude 8 dam. Find the cost of watering the field at the rate of 50 paise per square metre.

Solution We have,

Base = 15 dam $= (15 \times 10)$ m = 150 m [$\because$ 1 dam = 10 m]

Altitude = 8 dam = (8×10) m = 80 m

$\therefore$ Area of the field $= (150 \times 80)\,\text{m}^2 = 12000\,\text{m}^2$

Rate of watering the field = 50 paise per m^2 = Re $\frac{1}{2}$ per m^2

$\therefore$ Cost of watering the field = Rs $\left(12000 \times \frac{1}{2}\right)$ = Rs 6000

Example 8 The area of a parallelogram is 338 m^2. If its altitude is twice the corresponding base, determine the base and the altitude.

Solution Let the base be x metre long. Then, Altitude = $2x$ metres

$\therefore$ Area = Base $\times$ Altitude $= (x \times 2x)\,\text{m}^2 = 2x^2\,\text{m}^2$

But, the area is given to be 338 m^2.

$\therefore$ $2x^2 = 338$

$$\Rightarrow x^2 = \frac{338}{2} \Rightarrow x^2 = 169 \Rightarrow x^2 = 13^2 \Rightarrow x = 13$$

Hence, base = 13 m and altitude $= (2 \times 13)\,\text{m} = 26\,\text{m}$.

Example 9 The base of a parallelogram is thrice its height. If the area is 867 cm^2, find the base and height of the parallelogram.

Solution Let the height of the parallelogram be x cm. Then, base = $3x$ cm.

$\therefore$ Area of the parallelogram $= (x \times 3x)\,\text{cm}^2 = 3x^2\,\text{cm}^2$

But, area of the parallelogram is given as 867 cm^2

$\therefore \quad 3x^2 = 867 \Rightarrow x^2 = 289 \Rightarrow x^2 = 17^2 \Rightarrow x = 17$

Thus, height = 17 cm and base $= (3 \times 17)\,\text{cm} = 51\,\text{cm}$.

Example 10 Find the area of a rhombus having each side equal to 13 cm and one of whose diagonals is 24 cm.

Solution Let *ABCD* be the given rhombus whose diagonals intersect at *O*. Then,

$AB = 13\,\text{cm}$ and $AC = 24\,\text{cm}$

Since the diagonals of a rhombus bisect each other at right angles. Therefore, ΔAOB is a right triangle, right angled at *O* such that $OA = \frac{1}{2}AC = 12$ cm and $AB = 13$ cm.

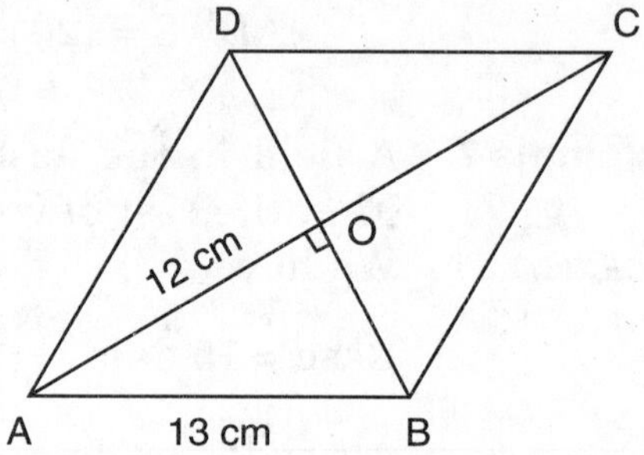

Fig. 16

$\therefore$ By Pythagoras theorem, we have

$AB^2 = OA^2 + OB^2$

$\Rightarrow \quad 13^2 = 12^2 + OB^2$

$\Rightarrow \quad OB^2 = 13^2 - 12^2$

$\Rightarrow \quad OB^2 = 169 - 144 = 25$

$\Rightarrow \quad OB^2 = 5^2$

$\Rightarrow \quad OB = 5\,\text{cm}$

$\therefore \quad BD = 2 \times OB = 2 \times 5\,\text{cm} = 10\,\text{cm}$

Hence, area of rhombus *ABCD* $= \left(\frac{1}{2} \times AC \times BD\right) = \left(\frac{1}{2} \times 24 \times 10\right)\text{cm}^2 = 120\,\text{cm}^2$

Example 11 If the area of a rhombus be 24 cm^2 and one of the its diagonals be 4 cm, find the perimeter of the rhombus.

Solution Let *ABCD* be a rhombus such that its one diagonal *AC* = 4 cm. Suppose the diagonals *AC* and *BD* intersect at *O*.

Now, Area of rhombus *ABCD* = 24 cm^2

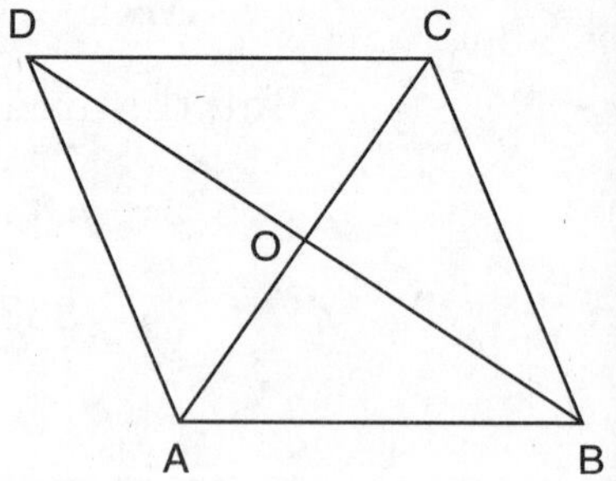

Fig. 17

$\Rightarrow \quad \frac{1}{2} \times AC \times BD = 24$

$\Rightarrow \quad \frac{1}{2} \times 4 \times BD = 24$

$\Rightarrow \quad 2 \times BD = 24$

$\Rightarrow \quad BD = 12$ cm

Thus, we have *AC* = 4 cm and *BD* = 12 cm

$\therefore \quad OA = \frac{1}{2}AC = 2\,\text{cm}$ and $OB = \frac{1}{2}BD = 6\,\text{cm}$

Since the diagonals of a rhombus bisect each other at right angles. Therefore, ΔAOB is a right triangle, right angled at *O*.

By Pythagoras theorem, we have

$$AB^2 = OA^2 + OB^2$$

$$\Rightarrow \quad AB^2 = 2^2 + 6^2 = 40 = 4 \times 10 = 2^2 \times 10$$

$$\Rightarrow \quad AB = 2\sqrt{10} \text{ cm}$$

Hence, perimeter of rhombus $ABCD = (4 \times 2\sqrt{10})\text{cm} = 8\sqrt{10}\text{ cm}$

Example 12 If the area of a rhombus be 48 cm^2 and one of its diagonals is 6 cm, find its altitude.

Solution Let $ABCD$ be the given rhombus such that diagonal AC = 6 cm.

Now, Area of rhombus $ABCD$ = 48 cm^2

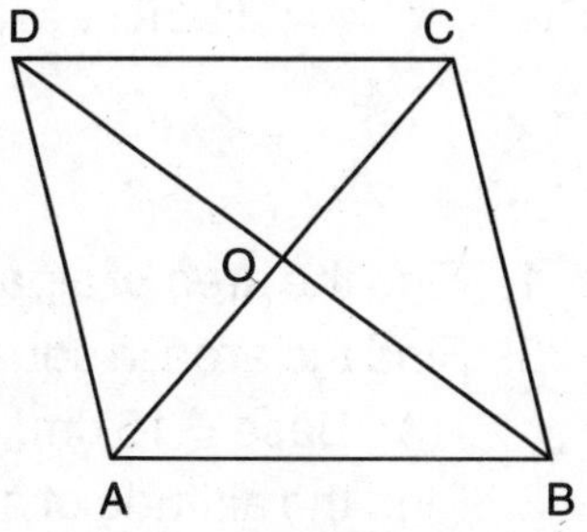

Fig. 18

$$\Rightarrow \quad \frac{1}{2} \times AC \times BD = 48$$

$$\Rightarrow \quad \frac{1}{2} \times 6 \times BD = 48$$

$$\Rightarrow \quad 3BD = 48$$

$$\Rightarrow \quad BD = \frac{48}{3} = 16 \text{ cm}$$

Since diagonals of a rhombus bisect each other at right angles.

$$\therefore \quad OA = \frac{1}{2}AC = 3 \text{ cm and } OB = \frac{1}{2}BD = 8 \text{ cm.}$$

Also, $\Delta\, OAB$ is a right triangle, right angled at O.

$$\therefore \quad AB^2 = OA^2 + OB^2 \qquad \text{[Using Pythagoras Theorem]}$$

$$\Rightarrow \quad AB^2 = 3^2 + 8^2$$

$$\Rightarrow \quad AB^2 = 9 + 64$$

$$\Rightarrow \quad AB^2 = 73$$

$$\Rightarrow \quad AB = \sqrt{73} \text{ cm}$$

Now, Area of rhombus $ABCD$ = 48 cm^2

$$\Rightarrow \quad \text{Base} \times \text{Altitude} = 48$$

$$\Rightarrow \quad AB \times \text{Altitude} = 48 \Rightarrow \sqrt{73} \times \text{Altitude} = 48 \Rightarrow \text{Altitude} = \frac{48}{\sqrt{73}} \text{ cm}$$

Example 13 If the side of a square is 4 m and it is converted into a rhombus whose major diagonal is 6 m, find the other diagonal and the area of the rhombus.

Solution Let AB = 4 m be the side of a square $ABPQ$ which is converted into a rhombus $ABCD$ such that diagonal AC = 6 m.

Since the diagonal of a rhombus bisect each other at right angles, therefore

$$OA = \frac{1}{2}AC = 3\,\text{m and } \angle AOB = 90°$$

In right $\Delta\, AOB$, we have

$$AB^2 = OA^2 + OB^2 \quad \left[\begin{array}{l}\text{Using Pythagoras} \\ \text{Theorem}\end{array}\right]$$

$$\Rightarrow \quad 4^2 = 3^2 + OB^2$$

$$\Rightarrow \quad OB^2 = 16 - 9$$

$$\Rightarrow \quad OB = \sqrt{7} \text{ m}$$

$$\therefore \quad BD = 2\,OB = 2\sqrt{7} \text{ m}$$

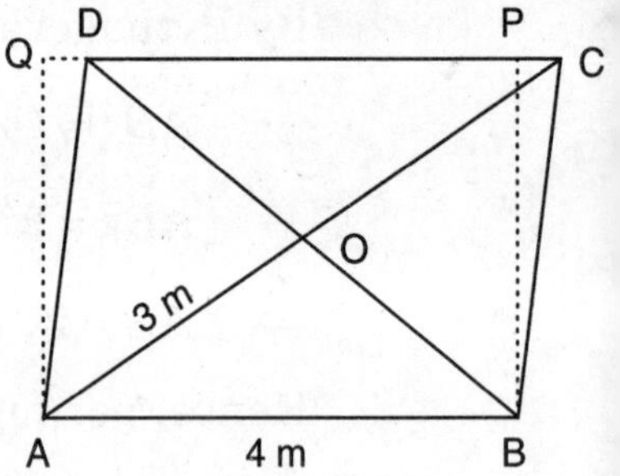

Fig. 19

Thus, the other diagonal, $BD = 2 \times \sqrt{7}$ m

Hence, area of rhombus $ABCD = \frac{1}{2} \times AC \times BD = \left(\frac{1}{2} \times 6 \times 2\sqrt{7}\right) \text{m}^2 = 6\sqrt{7} \text{ m}^2$

EXERCISE 20.3

1. Find the area of a parallelogram with base 8 cm and altitude 4.5 cm.
2. Find the area in square metres of the parallelogram whose base and altitudes are as under :
   (i) Base = 15 dm, altitude = 6.4 dm (ii) Base = 1 m 40 cm, altitude = 60 cm
3. Find the altitude of a parallelogram whose area is 54 dm^2 and base is 12 dm.
4. The area of a rhombus is 28 m^2. If its perimeter be 28 m, find its altitude.
5. In Fig. 20, *ABCD* is a parallelogram, $DL \perp AB$ and $DM \perp BC$. If AB = 18 cm, *BC* = 12 cm and *DM* = 9.3 cm, find *DL*.
6. The longer side of a parallelogram is 54 cm and the corresponding altitude is 16 cm. If the altitude corresponding to the shorter side is 24 cm, find the length of the shorter side.

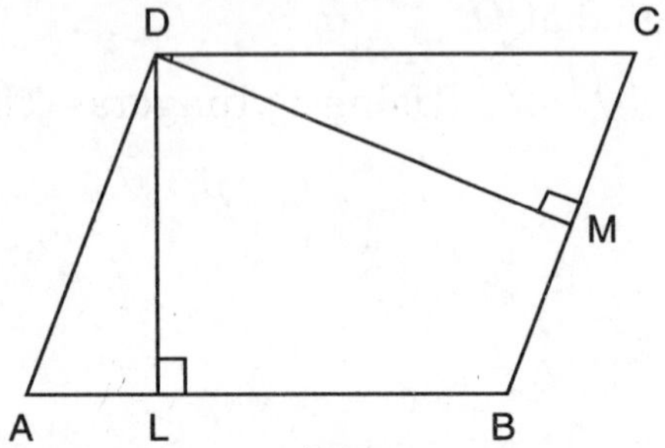

Fig. 20

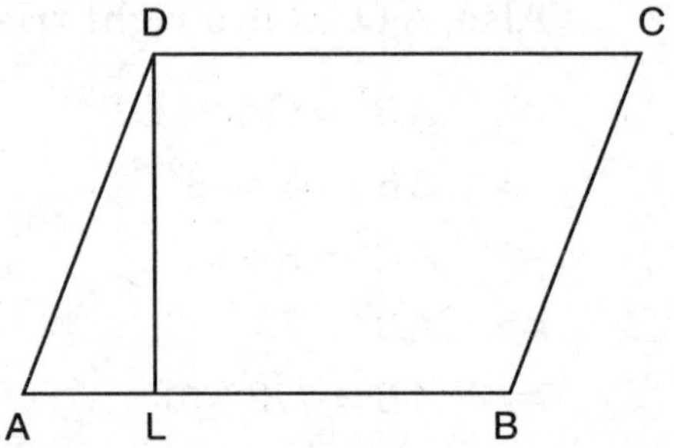

Fig. 21

7. In Fig. 21, *ABCD* is a parallelogram, $DL \perp AB$. If *AB* = 20 cm, *AD* = 13 cm and area of the parallelogram is 100 cm^2, find *AL*.
8. In Fig. 21, if *AB* = 35 cm, *AD* = 20 cm and area of the parallelogram is 560 cm^2, find *LB*.
9. The adjacent sides of a parallelogram are 10 m and 8 m. If the distance between the longer sides is 4 m, find the distance between the shorter sides.
10. The base of a parallelogram is twice its height. If the area of the parallelogram is 512 cm^2, find the base and height.
11. Find the area of a rhombus having each side equal to 15 cm and one of whose diagonals is 24 cm.
12. Find the area of a rhombus, each side of which measures 20 cm and one of whose diagonals is 24 cm.
13. The length of a side of a square field is 4 m. What will be the altitude of the rhombus, if the area of the rhombus is equal to the square field and one of its diagonals is 2 m?

14. Two sides of a parallelogram are 20 cm and 25 cm. If the altitude corresponding to the sides of length 25 cm is 10 cm, find the altitude corresponding to the other pair of sides.
15. The base and corresponding altitude of a parallelogram are 10 cm and 12 cm respectively. If the other altitude is 8 cm, find the length of the other pair of parallel sides.
16. A floral design on the floor of a building consists of 280 tiles. Each tile is in the shape of a parallelogram of altitude 3 cm and base 5 cm. Find the cost of polishing the design at the rate of 50 paise per cm^2.

ANSWERS

1. $36\ m^2$	2. (i) $0.96\ m^2$	(ii) $0.84\ m^2$	3. 4.5 dm
4. 4 m	5. 6.2 cm	6. 36 cm	7. 12 cm
8. 23 cm	9. 5 m	10. Base = 32 cm, Height = 16 cm	
11. $216\ cm^2$	12. $384\ cm^2$	13. $\frac{16}{\sqrt{65}}$ cm	14. 12.5 cm
15. 15 cm	16. ₹2100		

20.6 AREA OF A TRIANGLE

(i) Area of a triangle

We have,

$$\text{Area of } \Delta ABC = \frac{1}{2}(BC \times AL)$$

or $$\text{Area of } \Delta ABC = \frac{1}{2}(\text{Base} \times \text{Height})$$

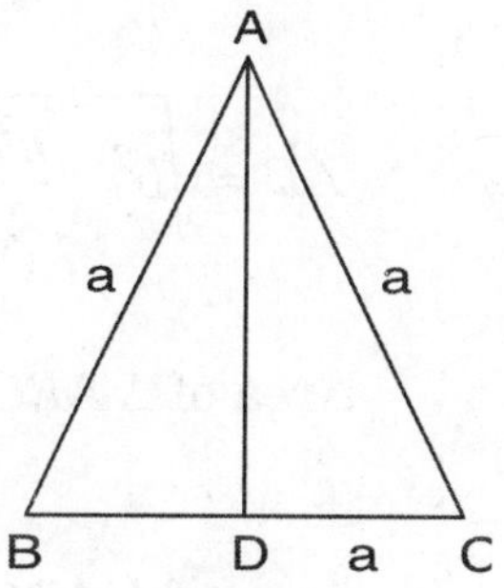

Fig. 22

From the above formula, we also obtain the following results.

$$Base = \frac{2 \times Area}{Height}, \quad Height = \frac{2 \times Area}{Base}$$

(ii) Area of an equilateral triangle

Let ABC be an equilateral triangle each of whose side is a units in length. Let $AD \perp BC$.

Then, $BD = DC = \frac{a}{2}$.

Applying Pythagoras theorem in ΔABD, we have

$$AB^2 = AD^2 + BD^2$$

$$\Rightarrow \quad AD = \sqrt{AB^2 - BD^2}$$

$$\Rightarrow \quad AD = \sqrt{a^2 - \frac{a^2}{4}} = \sqrt{\frac{3a^2}{4}} = \frac{\sqrt{3}a}{2} \text{ units}$$

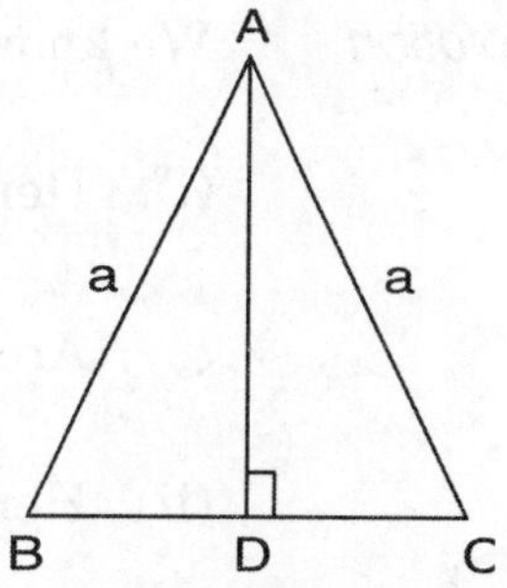

Fig. 23

$$\therefore \quad \text{Area of } \Delta ABC = \frac{1}{2} \times (\text{Base} \times \text{Height})$$

$$\text{Area of } \Delta ABC = \frac{1}{2} \times BC \times AD$$

$$\text{Area of } \Delta ABC = \left(\frac{1}{2} \times a \times \frac{\sqrt{3}a}{2}\right) \text{sq. units} = \left(\frac{\sqrt{3}}{4} \times (\text{Side})^2\right) \text{sq. units}.$$

Thus, area of an equilateral triangle $= \left(\frac{\sqrt{3}}{4} \times (\text{Side})^2\right)$ sq. units

(iii) Area of an isosceles triangle

Let ABC be an isosceles triangle such that $AB = AC = b$ units and $BC = a$ units.

Draw $AD \perp BC$. Then, $BD = DC = \frac{a}{2}$.

Applying Pythagoras theorem in ΔABD, we have

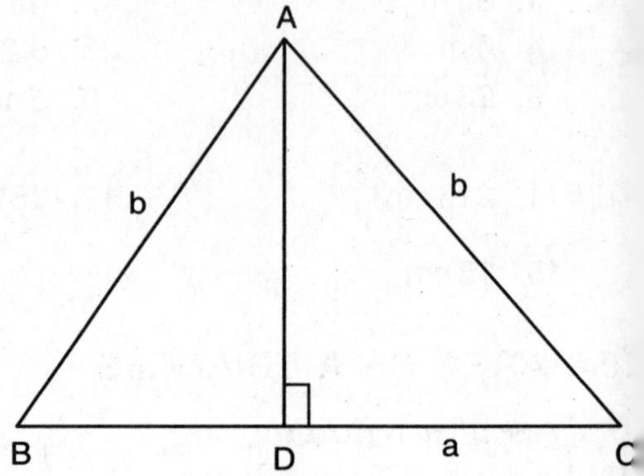

Fig. 24

$$AB^2 = AD^2 + BD^2$$

$$\Rightarrow \quad b^2 = AD^2 + \left(\frac{a}{2}\right)^2$$

$$\Rightarrow \quad AD^2 = b^2 - \frac{a^2}{4}$$

$$\Rightarrow \quad AD = \sqrt{b^2 - \frac{a^2}{4}}$$

$$\therefore \quad \text{Area of } \Delta ABC = \frac{1}{2} \times BC \times AD$$

$$\Rightarrow \quad \text{Area of } \Delta ABC = \frac{1}{2} \times a \times \sqrt{b^2 - \frac{a^2}{4}} = \frac{1}{2} \times \text{Base} \times \sqrt{(\text{Equal Side})^2 - \frac{1}{4}(\text{Base})^2}$$

ILLUSTTRATIVE EXAMPLES

Example 1 Find the area in square centimetres of the triangle whose base and altitude are as under:

(i) Base = 15 cm, Altitude = 8 cm

(ii) Base = 1.5 m, Altitude = 0.8 m

Solution We know that the area of a triangle $= \frac{1}{2} \times \text{Base} \times \text{Altitude}$

(i) Here, Base = 15 cm and Altitude = 8 cm

$$\therefore \quad \text{Area of the triangle} = \left(\frac{1}{2} \times 15 \times 8\right) \text{cm}^2 = 60\,\text{cm}^2$$

(ii) Here, Base = 1.5 m = 150 cm and Altitude = 0.8 m = 80 cm

$$\therefore \quad \text{Area of the triangle} = \left(\frac{1}{2} \times 150 \times 80\right) \text{cm}^2 = 6000\,\text{cm}^2$$

Example 2 Find the altitude of a triangle whose base is 20 cm and area is 150 cm^2.

Solution We have, Altitude of a triangle $= \frac{2 \times \text{Area}}{\text{Base}}$

Here, Base = 20 cm and Area = 150 cm^2

$\therefore$ Altitude $= \frac{2 \times 150}{20}$ cm $= 15$ cm

Example 3 The area of a right triangle is 50 m^2. If one of the legs is 20 m, find the length of the other leg.

Solution In a right angled triangle, if one side is the base, then the other side is its altitude or height.

Let the given leg be the base. Then, the other leg is the altitude.

Here, area of the triangle = 50 m^2

One leg of the triangle = 20 m

$\therefore$ The other leg of the triangle = Height of the triangle

$$= \frac{2 \times \text{Area}}{\text{Base}} = \left(\frac{2 \times 50}{20}\right) \text{m} = 5 \text{m}$$

Example 4 Find the area of an isosceles right triangle, if one of the equal sides is 20 cm long.

Solution We know that in a right angled triangle, any one of the two sides which are at right angle can be taken as the base and the other perpendicular side is the altitude.

$\therefore$ Base = 20 cm and Altitude = 20 cm.

So, area of the given triangle $= \left(\frac{1}{2} \times 20 \times 20\right) \text{cm}^2 = 200 \text{cm}^2$

Example 5 The area of a triangle is equal to that of a square whose each side measures 60 metres. Find the side of the triangle whose corresponding altitude is 90 metres.

Solution We have,

Area of the square $= (60 \times 60)\,\text{m}^2 = 3600\,\text{m}^2$

$\therefore$ Area of the triangle $= 3600\,\text{m}^2$ [$\because$ Area of triangle = Area of square]

Altitude of the triangle = 90 m

$\therefore$ Side of the triangle $= \frac{2 \times \text{Area}}{\text{Corresponding altitude}} = \left(\frac{2 \times 3600}{90}\right) \text{m} = 80 \text{m}$

Example 6 A field in the form of a parallelogram has one of its diagonals 42 m long and the perpendicular distance of this diagonal from either of the outlying vertices is 10.8 m (see Fig. 25). Find the area of the field.

Solution We have, $AC = 42$ m and $DL = BM = 10.8$ m

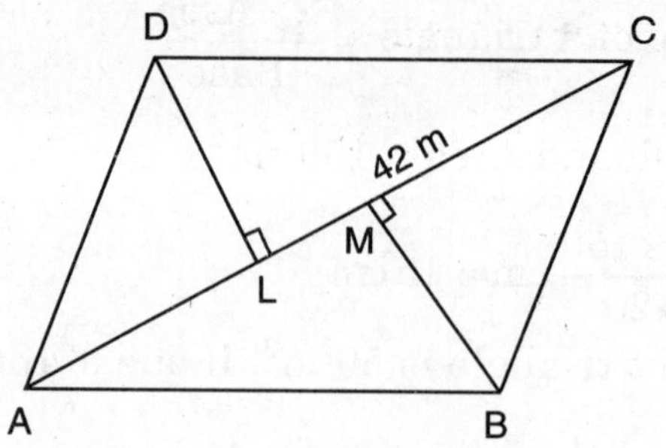

Fig. 25

$\therefore$ Area of the field $= 2 \times$ Area of ΔACD

$$= \left(2 \times \frac{1}{2} \times 42 \times 10.8\right) m^2$$

$$= 453.6\, m^2$$

Example 7 Find the area of an equilateral triangle having each side 4 cm.

Solution We know that the area of an equilateral triangle is equal to

$$\left(\frac{\sqrt{3}}{4} \times (\text{Side})^2\right) \text{sq. units}$$

Here, Side = 4 cm

$\therefore$ Area of the given triangle $= \frac{\sqrt{3}}{4} \times 4^2\ cm^2 = 4\sqrt{3}\ cm^2$

Example 8 Find the area of an isosceles triangle having the base 6 cm and the length of each equal side 5 cm.

Solution We know that :

Area of an isosceles triangle $= \frac{1}{2} \times \text{Base} \times \sqrt{(\text{Equal side})^2 - \frac{1}{4}(\text{Base})^2}$

Here, base = 6 cm, equal side = 5 cm.

$\therefore$ Area of the given triangle $= \frac{1}{2} \times 6 \times \sqrt{(5)^2 - \frac{1}{4} \times (6)^2}\ cm^2$

$$= 3 \times \sqrt{25 - 9}\ cm^2 = 3 \times \sqrt{16}\ cm^2 = 12\, cm^2$$

Example 9 Find the area of a right angled triangle with base $BC = 7$ cm and hypotenuse $AC = 25$ cm.

Solution Let ABC be the right angled triangle with base $BC = 7$ cm and hypotenuse $AC = 25$ cm.

Using Pythagoras theorem, we have

$$AC^2 = AB^2 + BC^2$$

$$\Rightarrow \quad (25)^2 = AB^2 + 7^2$$

$$\Rightarrow \quad AB^2 = 25^2 - 7^2 = 625 - 49 = 576 = 24^2$$

$$\Rightarrow \quad AB = 24 \text{ cm}$$

Hence,

$$\text{Area of } \Delta ABC = \frac{1}{2}(\text{Base} \times \text{Height}) = \frac{1}{2}(7 \times 24) = 84 \text{ cm}^2$$

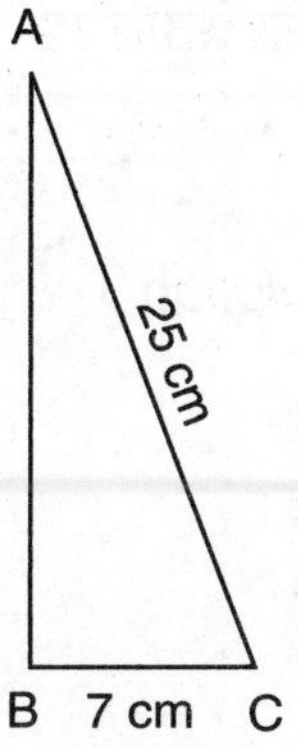

Fig. 26

Example 10 The base of an isosceles triangle is 12 cm and its perimeter is 32 cm. Find its area.

Solution We have, Base = 12 cm and Perimeter = 32 cm

Let the length of each of the two equal sides be b cm. Then,

Perimeter = 32 cm

$$\Rightarrow \quad 2b + 12 = 32 \quad \Rightarrow \quad 2b = 32 - 12 \quad \Rightarrow \quad 2b = 20 \quad \Rightarrow \quad b = 10$$

Thus, we have

Base = 12 cm and Equal side = 10 cm

$\therefore$ Area of the given triangle

$$= \frac{1}{2} \times \text{Base} \times \sqrt{(\text{Equal side})^2 - \frac{1}{4} \times (\text{Base})^2}$$

$$= \frac{1}{2} \times 12 \times \sqrt{(10)^2 - \frac{1}{4} \times (12)^2} \text{ cm}^2$$

$$= 6 \times \sqrt{100 - 36} \text{ cm}^2 = 6 \times \sqrt{64} \text{ cm}^2 = 6 \times 8 \text{ cm}^2 = 48 \text{ cm}^2$$

Example 11 Triangle ABC is right angled at A. AD is perpendicular to BC. If AB = 5 cm, BC = 13 cm and AC = 12 cm. Find the area of ΔABC. Also, find the length of AD.

Solution We have, $AB = 5 \text{ cm}$, $AC = 12 \text{ cm}$ and $\angle BAC = 90°$

$$\therefore \quad \text{Area of } \Delta ABC = \frac{1}{2}(AB \times AC)$$

$$\Rightarrow \quad \text{Area of } \Delta ABC = \frac{1}{2} \times 5 \times 12 \text{ cm}^2$$

$$\Rightarrow \quad \text{Area of } \Delta ABC = 30 \text{ cm}^2$$

Also,

$$\text{Area of } \Delta ABC = \frac{1}{2}(BC \times AD)$$

$$\Rightarrow \quad 30 = \frac{1}{2} \times 13 \times AD \quad \Rightarrow \quad AD = \frac{30 \times 2}{13} \text{ cm} = \frac{60}{13} \text{ cm}$$

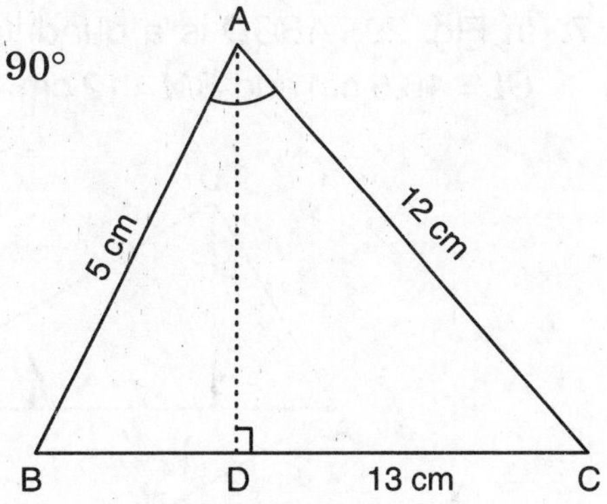

Fig. 27

Example 12 Triangle ABC is isosceles with $AB = AC = 7.5$ cm and $BC = 9$ cm. The height from A to BC i.e., AD is 6 cm. Find the area of ΔABC. What will be the height from C to AB?

Solution We have,

$$\text{Area of } \Delta ABC = \frac{1}{2} \times BC \times AD$$

$$= \frac{1}{2} \times 9 \times 6 \text{ cm}^2 = 27 \text{ cm}^2$$

Let CF be the height from C to AB. Then,

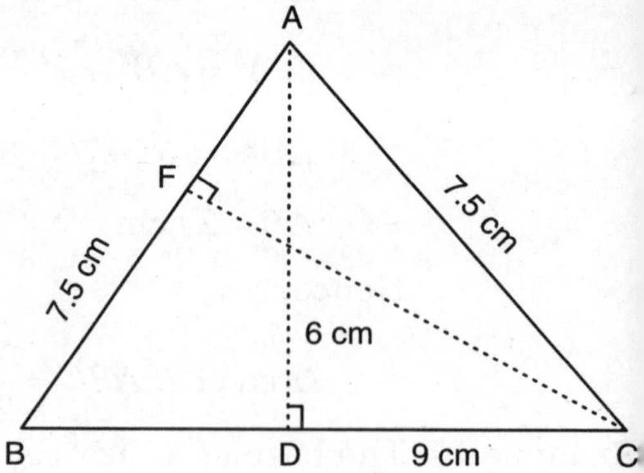

Fig. 28

$$\text{Area of } \Delta ABC = \frac{1}{2} \times AB \times CF$$

$$\Rightarrow \quad 27 = \frac{1}{2} \times 7.5 \times CF \quad [\because \text{Area of } \Delta ABC = 27 \text{ cm}^2]$$

$$\Rightarrow \quad CF = \frac{27 \times 2}{7.5} \Rightarrow CF = 7.2 \text{ cm}$$

EXERCISE 20.4

1. Find the area in square centimetres of a triangle whose base and altitude are as under :
   (i) base = 18 cm, altitude = 3.5 cm (ii) base = 8 dm, altitude = 15 cm
2. Find the altitude of a triangle whose area is 42 cm^2 and base is 12 cm.
3. The area of a triangle is 50 cm^2. If the altitude is 8 cm, what is its base?
4. Find the area of a right angled triangle whose sides containing the right angle are of lengths 20.8 m and 14.7 m.
5. The area of a triangle, whose base and the corresponding altitude are 15 cm and 7 cm, is equal to area of a right triangle whose one of the sides containing the right angle is 10.5 cm. Find the other side of this triangle.
6. A rectangular field is 48 m long and 20 m wide. How many right triangular flower beds, whose sides containing the right angle measure 12 m and 5 m can be laid in this field?
7. In Fig. 29, $ABCD$ is a quadrilateral in which diagonal $AC = 84$ cm; $DL \perp AC$, $BM \perp AC$, $DL = 16.5$ cm and $BM = 12$ cm. Find the area of quadrilateral $ABCD$.

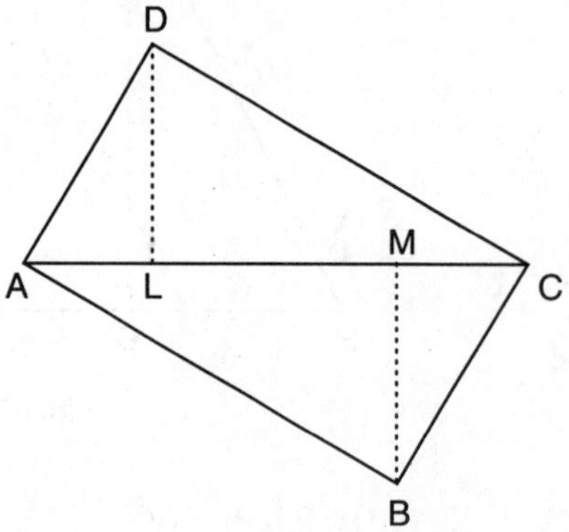

Fig. 29

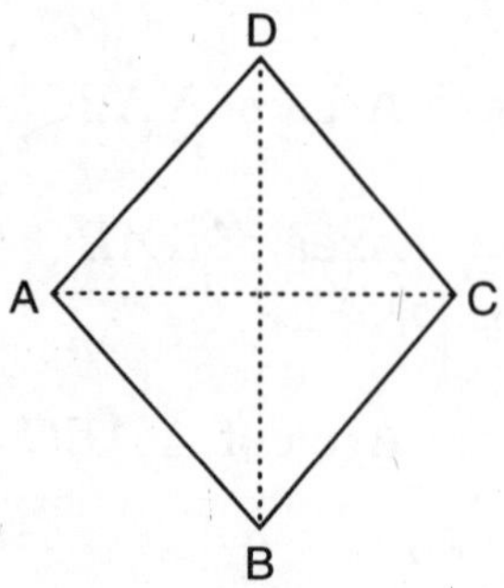

Fig. 30

8. Find the area of the quadrilateral *ABCD* given in Fig. 30. The diagonals *AC* and *BD* measure 48 m and 32 m respectively and are perpendicular to each other.
9. In Fig 31, *ABCD* is a rectangle with dimensions 32 m by 18 m. *ADE* is a triangle such that $EF \perp AD$ and $EF =$ 14 cm. Calculate the area of the shaded region.

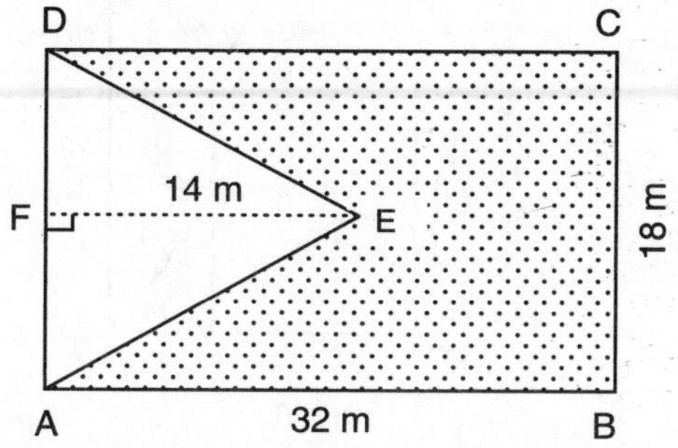

Fig. 31

10. In Fig. 32, *ABCD* is a rectangle of length $AB = 40$ cm and breadth $BC = 25$ cm. If *P, Q, R, S* be the mid-points of the sides *AB, BC, CD* and *DA* respectively, find the area of the shaded region.

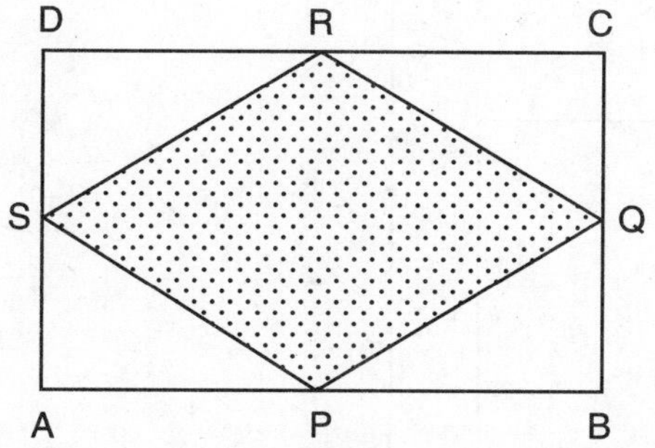

Fig. 32

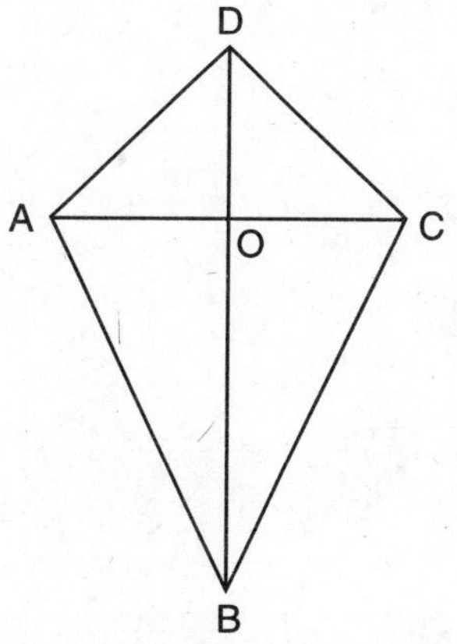

Fig. 33

11. Calculate the area of the quadrilateral *ABCD* as shown in Fig. 33, given that $BD = 42$ cm, $AC = 28$ cm, $OD = 12$ cm and $AC \perp BD$.
12. Find the area of a figure formed by a square of side 8 cm and an isosceles triangle with base as one side of the square and perimeter as 18 cm.
13. Find the area of Fig. 34 in the following ways:
    (i) Sum of the areas of three triangles
    (ii) Area of a rectangle – sum of the areas of five triangles

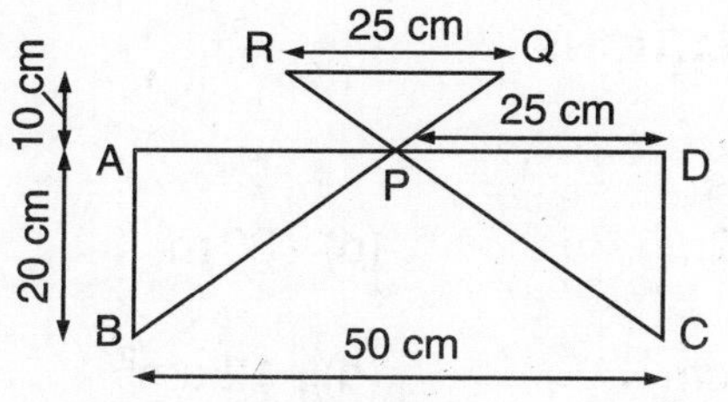

Fig. 34

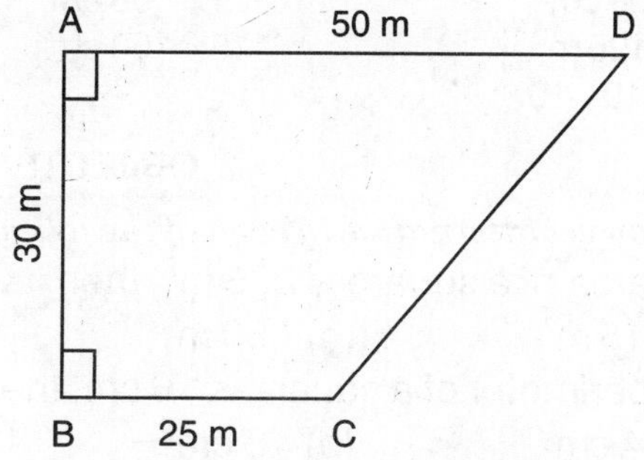

Fig. 35

14. Calculate the area of quadrilateral field *ABCD* as shown in Fig. 35, by dividing it into a rectangle and a triangle.

15. Calculate the area of the pentagon $ABCDE$, where $AB = AE$ and with dimensions as shown in Fig. 36.

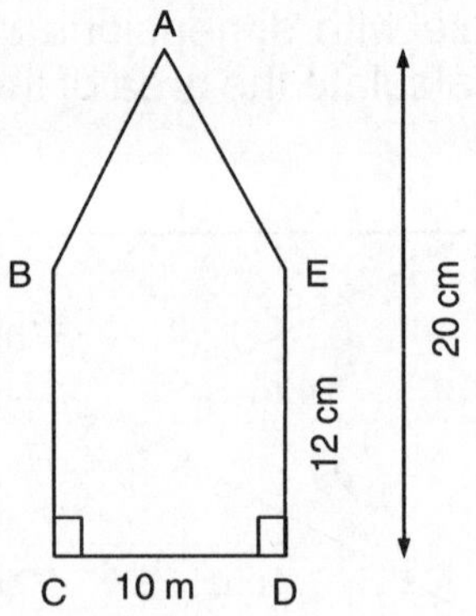

Fig. 36

16. The base of a triangular field is three times its altitude. If the cost of cultivating the field at ₹ 24.60 per hectare is ₹ 332.10, find its base and height.
17. A wall is 4.5 m long and 3 m high. It has two equal windows, each having form and dimensions as shown in Fig. 37. Find the cost of painting the wall (leaving windows) at the rate of ₹ 15 per m^2.

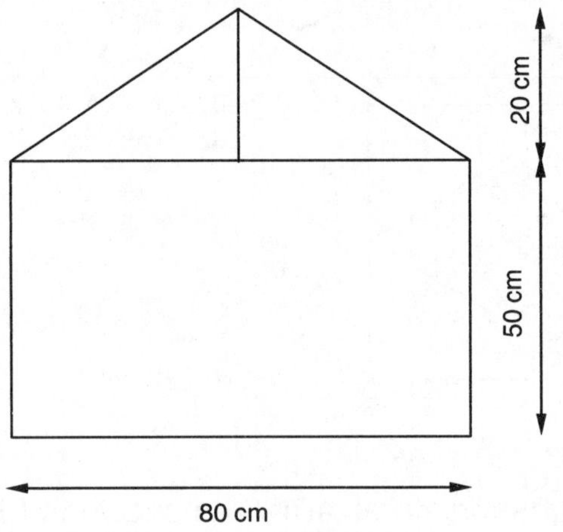

Fig. 37

ANSWERS

1. (i) 31.5 cm^2	(ii) 600 cm^2	2. 7 cm	3. 12.5 cm
4. 152.88 m^2	5. 10 cm		
6. 32	7. 1197 cm^2	8. 768 m^2	9. 450 m^2
10. 500 cm^2	11. 588 cm^2	12. 76 cm^2	13. 625 cm^2
14. 1125 m^2	15. 160 cm^2	16. Base = 900 m, height = 300 m	
17. ₹ 194.10			

OBJECTIVE TYPE QUESTIONS

Mark the correct alternative in each of the following:

1. If the area of a square is 225 m^2, then its perimeter is
   (a) 15 m (b) 60 m (c) 225 m (d) 30 m
2. If the perimeter of a square is 16 cm, then its area is
   (a) 4 cm^2 (b) 8 cm^2 (c) 16 cm^2 (d) 12 cm^2
3. The length of a rectangle is 8 cm and its area is 48 cm^2. The perimeter of the rectangle is
   (a) 14 cm (b) 24 cm (c) 12 cm (d) 28 cm

4. The area of a square and that of a square drawn on its diagonal are in the ratio
(a) $1:\sqrt{2}$ (b) $1:2$ (c) $1:3$ (d) $1:4$
5. The length of the diagonal of a square is d units. The area of the square is
(a) d^2 (b) $\frac{1}{2}d^2$ (c) $\frac{1}{4}d^2$ (d) $2d^2$
6. The ratio of the areas of two squares, one having its diagonal double that of the other, is
(a) 2 : 1 (b) 3 : 1 (c) 3 : 2 (d) 4 : 1
7. If the ratio of the areas of two squares is 9 : 1, then the ratio of their perimeters is
(a) 2 : 1 (b) 3 : 1 (c) 3 : 2 (d) 4 : 1
8. The ratio of the area of a square of side a and that of an equilateral triangle of side a, is
(a) 2 : 1 (b) $2:\sqrt{3}$ (c) 4 : 3 (d) $4:\sqrt{3}$
9. On increasing each side of a square by 25%, the increase in area will be
(a) 25 % (b) 55 % (c) 55.5 % (d) 56.25 %
10. The area of a square is 50 cm^2. The length of its diagonal is
(a) $5\sqrt{2}$ cm (b) 10 cm (c) $10\sqrt{2}$ cm (d) 8 cm
11. Each diagonal of a square is 14 cm. Its area is
(a) 196 cm^2 (b) 88 cm^2 (c) 98 cm^2 (d) 148 cm^2
12. The area of a square field is 64 m^2. A path of uniform width is laid around and outside of it. If the area of the path is 17 m^2, then the width of the path is
(a) 1 m (b) 1.5 m (c) 0.5 m (d) 2 m
13. A path of 1 m wide runs around and inside a square garden of side of 20 m. The cost of levelling the path at the rate of ₹ 2.25 per square metre is
(a) ₹ 154 (b) ₹ 164 (c) ₹ 182 (d) ₹ 171
14. The length and breadth of a rectangle are $(3x + 4)$ cm and $(4x - 13)$ cm. If the perimeter of the rectangle is 94 cm, then $x =$
(a) 4 (b) 8 (c) 12 (d) 6
15. In Fig. 38, *ABCD* and *PQRC* are squares such that *AD* = 22 cm and *PC* = y cm. If the area of the shaded region is 403 cm^2, then the value of y is
(a) 3 (b) 6 (c) 9 (d) 10

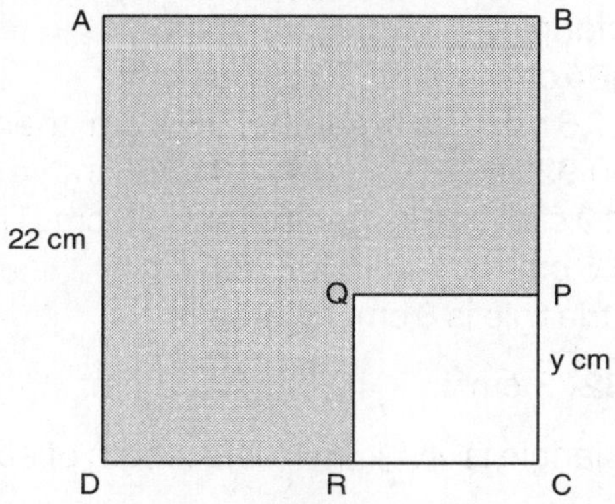

Fig. 38

16. The length and breadth of a rectangle are $(3x + 4)$ cm and $(4x - 13)$ cm respectively. If the perimeter of the rectangle is 94 cm, then its area is
(a) 432 cm^2 (b) 512 cm^2 (c) 542 cm^2 (d) 532 cm^2
17. The length and breadth of a rectangle are in the ratio 3 : 2. If its area is 216 cm^2, then its perimeter is
(a) 60 cm (b) 30 cm (c) 40 cm (d) 120 cm

18. If the length of a diagonal of a rectangle of length 16 cm is 20 cm, then its area is
(a) 192 cm^2 (b) 320 cm^2 (c) 160 cm^2 (d) 156 cm^2
19. The area of a rectangle 144 cm long is same as that of a square of side 84 cm. The width of the rectangle is
(a) 7 cm (b) 14 cm (c) 49 cm (d) 28 cm
20. The length and breadth of a rectangular field are in the ratio 5 : 3 and its perimeter is 480 m. The area of the field is
(a) 7200 m^2 (b) 13500 m^2 (c) 15000 m^2 (d) 54000 m^2
21. The length of a rectangular field is thrice its breadth and its perimeter is 240 m. The length of the field is
(a) 30 m (b) 120 m (c) 90 m (d) 80 m
22. If the diagonal of a rectangle is 17 cm and its perimeter is 46 cm, the area of the rectangle is
(a) 100 cm^2 (b) 110 cm^2 (c) 120 cm^2 (d) 240 cm^2
23. The length and breadth of a rectangular field are 4 m and 3 m respectively. The field is divided into two parts by fencing diagonally. The cost of fencing at the rate of ₹ 10 per metre is
(a) ₹ 50 (b) ₹ 30 (c) ₹ 190 (d) ₹ 240
24. The area of a parallelogram is 100 cm^2. If the base is 25 cm, then the corresponding height is
(a) 4 cm (b) 6 cm (c) 10 cm (d) 5 cm
25. The base of a parallelogram is twice its height. If its area is 512 cm^2, then the length of base is
(a) 16 cm (b) 32 cm (c) 48 cm (d) 64 cm
26. The lengths of the diagonals of a rhombus are 36 cm and 22.5 cm. Its area is
(a) 810 cm^2 (b) 405 cm^2 (c) 202.5 cm^2 (d) 1620 cm^2
27. The length of a diagonal of a rhombus is 16 cm. If its area is 96 cm^2, then the length of other diagonal is
(a) 6 cm (b) 8 cm (c) 12 cm (d) 18 cm
28. The lengths of the diagonals of a rhombus are 8 cm and 14 cm. The area of one of the 4 triangles formed by the diagonal is
(a) 12 cm^2 (b) 8 cm^2 (c) 16 cm^2 (d) 14 cm^2
29. The length of a rectangle is 8 cm more than the breadth. If the perimeter of the rectangle is 80 cm, then the length of the rectangle is
(a) 16 cm (b) 24 cm (c) 28 cm (d) 18 cm
30. The length of a rectangle is 8 cm more than the breadth. If the perimeter of the rectangle is 80 cm, then the area of the rectangle is
(a) 192 cm^2 (b) 364 cm^2 (c) 384 cm^2 (d) 382 cm^2
31. The area of a rectangle is 11.6 m^2. If its breadth is 46.4 cm, then the perimeter is
(a) 25.464 m (b) 50.928 m (c) 101.856 m (d) None of these
32. The area of a rhombus is 119 cm^2 and its perimeter is 56 cm. The height of the rhombus is
(a) 7.5 cm (b) 6.5 cm (c) 8.5 cm (d) 9.5 cm
33. Each side of an equilateral triangle is 8 cm. Its area is
(a) $16\sqrt{3}$ cm^2 (b) $32\sqrt{3}$ cm^2 (c) $24\sqrt{3}$ cm^2 (d) $8\sqrt{3}$ cm^2
34. The area of an equilateral triangle is $4\sqrt{3}$ cm^2. The length of each of its side is
(a) 3 cm (b) 4 cm (c) $2\sqrt{3}$ cm (d) $\frac{\sqrt{3}}{2}$ cm
35. The height of an equilateral triangle is $\sqrt{6}$ cm. Its area is
(a) $3\sqrt{3}$ cm^2 (b) $2\sqrt{3}$ cm^2 (c) $2\sqrt{2}$ cm^2 (d) $6\sqrt{2}$ cm^2
36. If A is the area an equilateral triangle of height h, then
(a) $A = \sqrt{3}\,h^2$ (b) $\sqrt{3}A = h$ (c) $\sqrt{3}A = h^2$ (d) $3A = h^2$

37. If area of an equilateral triangle is $3\sqrt{3}$ cm^2, then its height is

(a) 3 cm (b) $\sqrt{3}$ cm (c) 6 cm (d) $2\sqrt{3}$ cm

38. The area of a rhombus is 144 cm^2 and one of its diagonals is double the other. The length of the longer diagonal is

(a) 12 cm (b) 16 cm (c) 18 cm (d) 24 cm

39. In Fig. 39, the value of *k* is

(a) $\frac{77}{8}$ (b) $\frac{73}{8}$ (c) $\frac{71}{8}$ (d) $\frac{75}{8}$

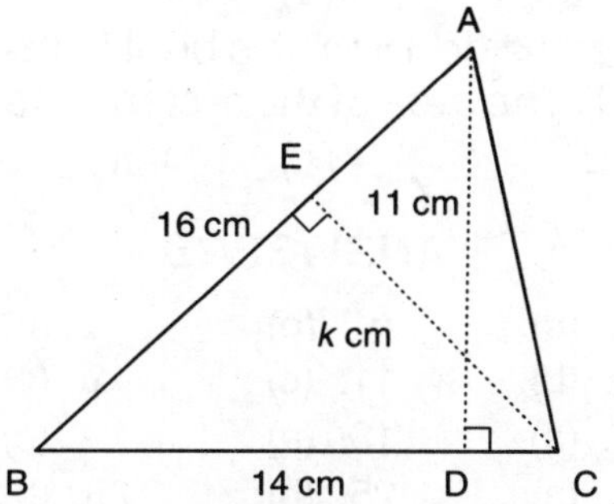

Fig. 39

40. In Fig. 40, ABCD is a parallelogram of area 144 cm^2, the value of x is

(a) 8 (b) 6 (c) 9 (d) 10

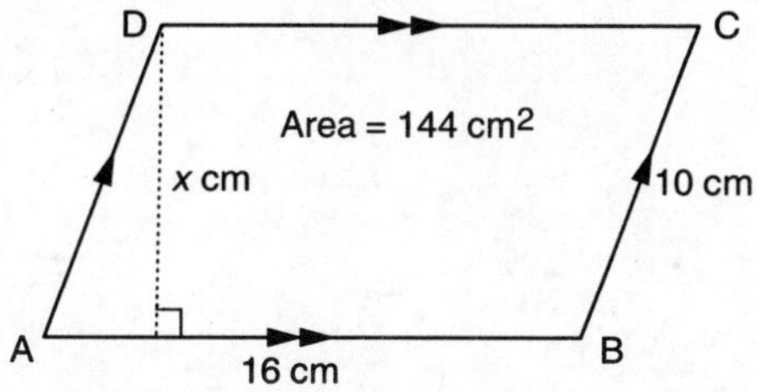

Fig. 40

41. In Fig. 41, if *ABCD* is a parallelogram of area 273 cm^2, then the value of *h* is

(a) 13 (b) 12 (c) 8 (d) 14

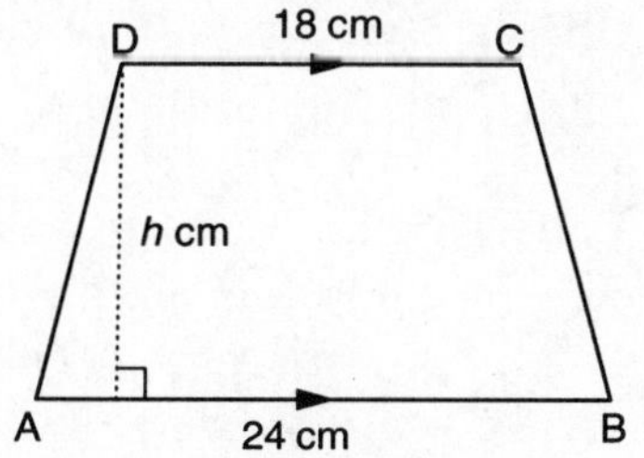

Fig. 41

42. In Fig. 42, *ABCD* is a parallelogram in which *AD* = 21 cm, *DH* = 18 cm and *DK* = 27 cm. The length of side *AB* is

(a) 63 cm (b) 63.5 cm (c) 31.5 cm (d) 31 cm

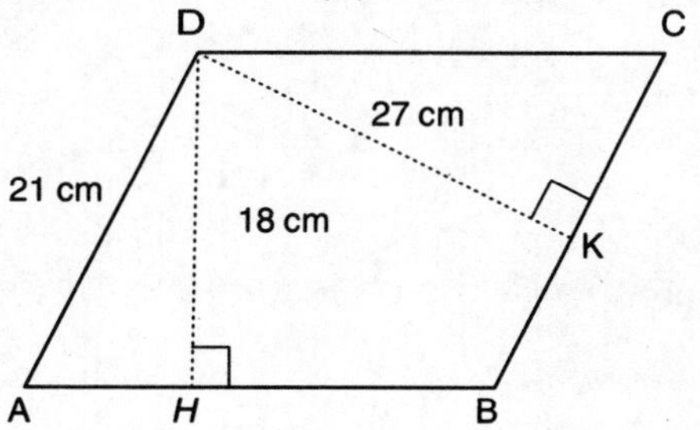

Fig. 42

43. In Fig. 42 *ABCD* is a parallelogram in which AD = 21 cm, DH = 18 cm and DK = 27 cm. The perimeter of the parallelogram is
    (a) 105 cm (b) 84.5 cm (c) 169 cm (d) 52.5 cm
44. In Fig. 42, the area of the parallelogram is
    (a) 516 cm^2 (b) 567 cm^2 (c) 416 cm^2 (d) 606 cm^2
45. A piece of wire of length 12 cm is bent to form a square. The area of the square is
    (a) 36 cm^2 (b) 144 cm^2 (c) 9 cm^2 (d) 12 cm^2
46. The area of a right isosceles triangle whose hypotenuse is $16\sqrt{2}$ cm is
    (a) 125 cm^2 (b) 158 cm^2 (c) 128 cm^2 (d) 144 cm^2
47. A wire is in the form of a square of side 18 m. It is bent in the form of a rectangle, whose length and breadth are in the ratio 3 : 1. The area of the rectangle is
    (a) 81 m^2 (b) 243 m^2 (c) 144 m^2 (d) 324 m^2

ANSWSERS

1. (b)	2. (c)	3. (d)	4. (b)	5. (b)	6. (d)	7. (b)
8. (d)	9. (d)	10. (b)	11. (c)	12. (c)	13. (d)	14. (b)
15. (c)	16. (d)	17. (a)	18. (a)	19. (c)	20. (b)	21. (c)
22. (c)	23. (a)	24. (a)	25. (b)	26. (b)	27. (c)	28. (d)
29. (b)	30. (c)	31. (b)	32. (c)	33. (a)	34. (b)	35. (b)
36. (c)	37. (a)	38. (d)	39. (a)	40. (c)	41. (a)	42. (c)
43. (a)	44. (b)	45. (c)	46. (c)	47. (b)		

THINGS TO REMEMBER

1. A square centimetre is the area of the region formed by a square of side 1 cm.
2. Standard units of area and their relations are:

   $100\ mm^2 = 1\ cm^2$, $100\ cm^2 = 1\ dm^2$

   $100\ dm^2 = 1\ m^2$, $10000\ cm^2 = 1\ m^2$

   $100\ m^2 = 1$ are, 100 ares = 1 hectare

   100 hectares = 1 sq. km.
3. Perimeter of a rectangle = 2 (Length + Breadth) or, $P = 2(l + b)$

   Perimeter of a square = 4 × (Side) or, $P = 4l$

   Area of a rectangle = Length × Breadth or, $A = l \times b$

   Also, length of a rectangle $= \dfrac{\text{Area}}{\text{Breadth}}$ or, $l = \dfrac{A}{b}$

   Breadth of a rectangle $= \dfrac{\text{Area}}{\text{Length}}$ or, $b = \dfrac{A}{l}$

   Area of a square = $(\text{Side})^2$ or, $A = l \times l$.
4. Area of a parallelogram = Base × Height or, $A = b \times h$

   Also, Base of parallelogram $= \dfrac{\text{Area}}{\text{height}}$ or, $b = \dfrac{A}{h}$

   Height of a parallelogram $= \dfrac{\text{Area}}{\text{base}}$ or, $h = \dfrac{A}{b}$
5. Area of a triangle $= \dfrac{1}{2} \times$ Base × Height or, $A = \dfrac{1}{2} \times b \times h$

   Height of a triangle $= \dfrac{2 \times \text{Area}}{\text{Base}}$ or, $h = \dfrac{2A}{b}$

   Base of a triangle $= \dfrac{2 \times \text{Area}}{\text{height}}$ or, $b = \dfrac{2A}{h}$
6. Area of a rhombus $= \dfrac{1}{2} \times$ Product of diagonals
7. Area of a trapezium $= \dfrac{1}{2} \times$ (Sum of the parallel sides) × (Distance between the parallel sides)

21

MENSURATION – II
(Area of Circle)

21.1 INTRODUCTION

In this chapter, we shall discuss problems on circumference and area of a circle. We shall also discuss problems on areas of segment and a sector of a circle.

21.2 CIRCLE

A circle is a geometrical figure consisting of all those points in a plane which are at a given distance from a fixed point in the same plane.

The fixed point is called the centre of the circle and the constant distance is known as its radius.

In Fig. 1, O is the centre and r is the radius of the circle.

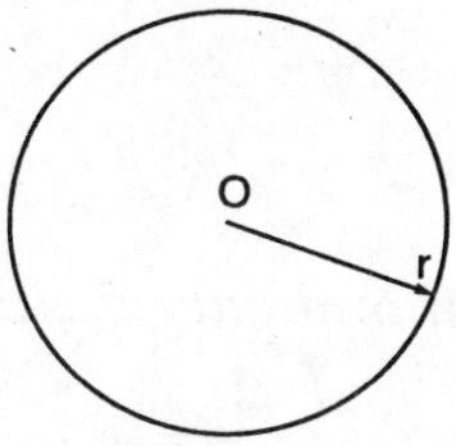

Fig. 1

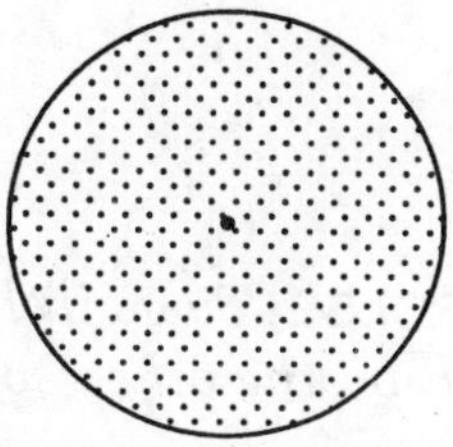

Fig. 2

A circle with centre O and radius r is generally denoted by $C(O, r)$.

CIRCULAR REGION *The part of the circle that consists of the circle and its interior is called the circular region.*

A circular region is also called a circular discuss shown in Fig. 2.

CHORD OF A CIRCLE *A line segment joining any two points on a circle is called a chord of the circle.*

It should be noted that a chord is not a part of the circle.

In Fig. 3, PQ is a chord of the circle.

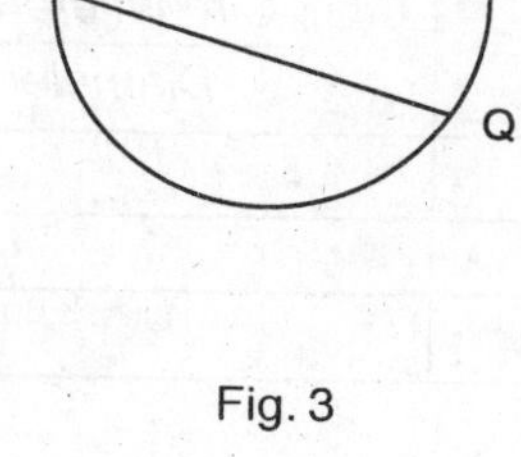

Fig. 3

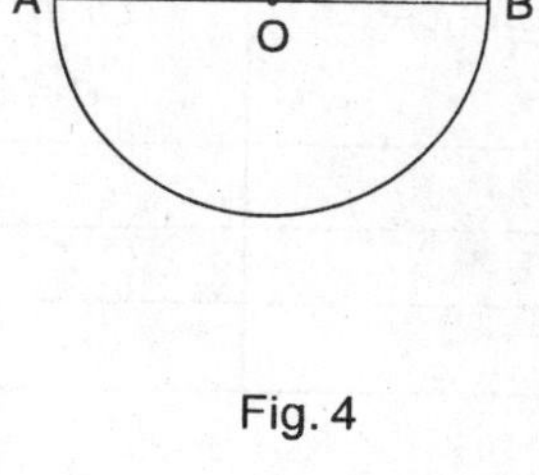

Fig. 4

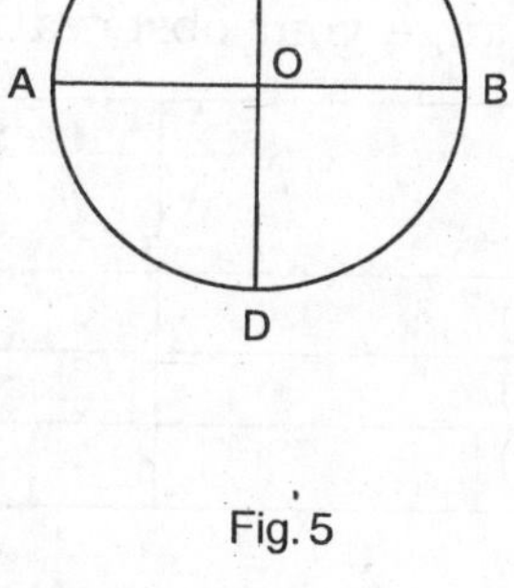

Fig. 5

DIAMETER *A chord passing through the centre of a circle is known as its diameter.*

Note that a circle has many diameters and a diameter of a given circle is one of the largest chords of the circle. Also, all diameters are of the same length.

In this book, the word 'diameter' will be used for a chord passing through the centre, and also for its length.

Clearly, if d is diameter of a circle of radius $= r$, then $d = 2r$.

A diameter of a circle divides the circumference of a circle into two equal parts each of which is called a *semi-circle*.

Two perpendicular diameters of a circle divide its circumference into four equal parts each of which is known as a *quadrant*.

CONCENTRIC CIRCLES *Circles having the same centre but with different radii are said to be concentric circles.*

Fig. 6, shows two concentric circles.

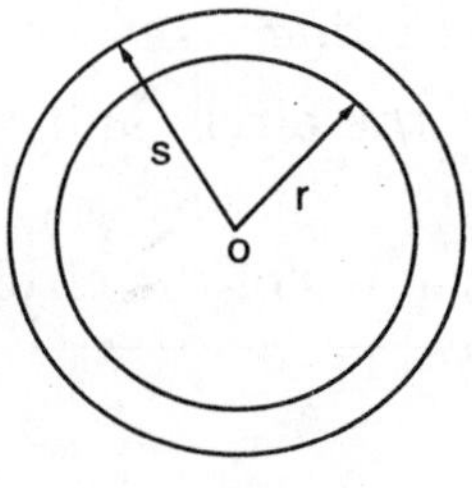

Fig. 6

CONGRUENT CIRCLES *Two circles are said to be congruent if and only if either of them can be super imposed on the other so as to cover it exactly.*

It follows from the above definition that two circles are congruent if and only if their radii are equal.

21.3 CIRCUMFERENCE OF A CIRCLE

The perimeter of a circle is called its circumference.

The length of the thread that winds around the circle exactly once, gives the circumference of the circle.

RELATION BETWEEN DIAMETER AND CIRCUMFERENCE The ratio of the circumference of a circle and its diameter is always constant.

The above result can be verified with the help of the following experiment :

Experiment Draw three circles of different radii. Use a tape or a piece of thread to measure the circumference of each circle. Also, measure the diameter of each one of them.

Arrange your observations as under :

Circle	Circumference C	Diameter $d = 2r$	$\frac{\text{Circumference}}{\text{Diameter}}\left(\frac{C}{2r}\right)$
(i)			
(ii)			
(iii)			

For each circle, compute the ratio of the circumference and diameter and enter the same against each circle in the last column of the table. You will find that in each case

$$\frac{\text{Circumference}}{\text{Diameter}} = 3.14 \text{ (approximately)}$$

This ratio is denoted by π(Pi).

Thus, we have

$$\pi = 3.14 \text{ (approximately)} = \frac{22}{7} \text{ (approximately)}$$

Now, $$\frac{\text{Circumference}}{\text{Diameter}} = \pi$$

$\Rightarrow$ $$\frac{C}{2r} = \pi$$

$\Rightarrow$ $$C = 2\pi r$$

Thus, circumference C of a circle of radius r is given by

$$C = 2\pi r$$

If d denotes the diameter of the circle. Then, $d = 2r$

$\therefore$ $$C = \pi d$$

Remark *The number π is not a rational number, but its value upto two decimal places coincides with $\frac{22}{7}$. So, we take the value of π as $\frac{22}{7}$. In the remaining part of this chapter, unless stated otherwise, the value of π will be taken as $\frac{22}{7}$.*

21.4 THE NUMBER π

In the previous section, we have observed that the circumference of a circle is in constant ratio to its diameter. This constant is denoted by the Greek letter π which is read as "pie" in the word apple-pie. It has been proved that π is not a rational number. Therefore, it cannot be written as a terminating (finite) or a non-terminating repeating decimal. The values of π correct to 2, 3, 4, 5 and 6, places of decimal are respectively 3.14, 3.142, 3.1416, 3.14159 and 3.141593. Throughout this chapter the value of π will be taken as $\frac{22}{7}$ unless specified otherwise.

ILLUSTRATIVE EXAMPLES

Example 1 Find the circumference of a circle of radius 14 cm.

Solution The circumference C of a circle of radius r is given by

$$C = 2\pi r.$$

Here, $r = 14$ cm

$\therefore$ $C = 2 \times \frac{22}{7} \times 14 \text{ cm} = 88 \text{ cm}$

Example 2 Find the circumference of a circle whose diameter is 42 cm.

Solution We have,

Diameter = 42 cm

$\therefore$ Radius $= \frac{42}{2} \text{ cm} = 21 \text{ cm}$

Let C be the circumfernce of the circle. Then,

$C = 2\pi r$

$\Rightarrow$ $C = 2 \times \frac{22}{7} \times 21 \text{ cm} = 132 \text{ cm}$

Example 3 Find the diameter of a circle whose circumference is 15.7 cm.

Solution We know that the circumference C of a circle of a diameter d is given by

$C = \pi d$

$\Rightarrow$ $d = \frac{C}{\pi}$

Here, $C = 15.7$ cm

$\therefore$ $d = \frac{15.7}{\pi} \text{ cm} = \frac{15.7}{22} \times 7 \text{ cm} = \frac{109.9}{22} \text{ cm} = 5 \text{ cm (approx.)}$

Example 4 The ratio of the radii of two circles is 2 : 5. What is the ratio of their circumferences ?

Solution We have, ratio of radii = 2 : 5.

So, let the radii of two circles be $2r$ and $5r$ respectively.

Let C_1 and C_2 be the circumferences of two circles of radii $2r$ and $5r$ respectively. Then,

$C_1 = 2\pi \times 2r = 4\pi r$ and, $C_2 = 2\pi \times 5r = 10\pi r$

$\therefore$ $\frac{C_1}{C_2} = \frac{4\pi r}{10\pi r} = \frac{2}{5} \Rightarrow C_1 : C_2 = 2 : 5$

Example 5 A piece of wire in the form of a rectangle 8.9 cm long and 5.4 cm broad is reshaped and bent into the form of a circle. Find the radius of the circle.

Solution We have,

Length of the wire = Perimeter of the rectangle

$= 2(l + b) = 2 \times (8.9 + 5.4) \text{ cm} = 28.6 \text{ cm}$

Let the wire be bent into the form of a circle of radius r cm. Then,

Circumference = 28.6 cm

$\Rightarrow$ $2\pi r = 28.6$

$$\Rightarrow \quad 2\times\frac{22}{7}\times r = 28.6$$

$$\Rightarrow \quad r = \frac{28.6\times 7}{2\times 22}\text{ cm } = \frac{286\times 7}{2\times 22\times 10}\text{ cm} = 4.55\text{ cm}.$$

Example 6 The diameter of a wheel of a cycle is 70 cm. It moves slowly along a road. How far will it go in 24 complete revolutions?

Solution It may be noted that in one revolution, the cycle covers a distance equal to the circumference of the wheel?

Now, diameter of the wheel = 70 cm

$\therefore$ Circumference of the wheel $= \pi d = \left(\frac{22}{7}\times 70\right)$ cm $= 220$ cm

Thus, the cycle travels 220 cm in one revolution.

$\therefore$ Distance covered by the cycle in 24 revolutions $= (220\times 24)$ cm

$= 5280$ cm $= 52.80$ m

Example 7 The diameter of the wheel of a car is 77 cm. How many revolutions will it make to travel 121 km?

Solution We have,

Diameter of the wheel of the car = 77 cm

$\therefore$ Circumference of the wheel of the car $= \pi d = \left(\frac{22}{7}\times 77\right)$ cm $= 242$ cm

Note that in one revolution of the wheel, the car travels a distance equal to the circumference of the wheel.

$\therefore$ Distance travelled by the car in one revolution of the wheel = 242 cm

Total distance travelled by the car = 121 km = 121000 m = 12100000 cm

$\therefore$ Number of revolutions $= \frac{12100000}{242} = 50000$

Example 8 There is a circular pond and foot-path runs along its boundary. A man walks around it, exactly once, keeping close to the edge. If his step is 66 cm long and he takes exactly 400 steps to go around the pond, what is the diameter of the pond?

Solution We have, length of one step = 66 cm

$\therefore$ Distance covered in 400 steps $= (400\times 66)$ cm $= \frac{400\times 66}{100}$ m $= 264$ m

Let d metre be the diameter of the pond. Then,

Circumference = Distance covered in 400 steps

$$\Rightarrow \quad \pi d = 264$$

$$\Rightarrow \quad \frac{22}{7}\times d = 264$$

$\Rightarrow \quad d = \dfrac{264 \times 7}{22}$ m $= 84$ m

Hence, the diameter of the pond is 84 metres.

Example 9 The circumference of a circle exceeds the diameter by 30 cm. Find the radius of the circle.

Solution Let the radius of the circle be r cm. Then,

Circumference of the circle $= 2\pi r$ cm

Diameter of the circle $= 2r$ cm

It is given that the circumference of the circle exceeds its diameter by 30 cm.

$\therefore \quad 2\pi r = 2r + 30$

$\Rightarrow \quad 2 \times \dfrac{22}{7} \times r = 2r + 30$

$\Rightarrow \quad \dfrac{44r}{7} = 2r + 30$

$\Rightarrow \quad \dfrac{44r}{7} - 2r = 30$

$\Rightarrow \quad \dfrac{44r - 14r}{7} = 30 \Rightarrow \dfrac{30r}{7} = 30 \Rightarrow r = \dfrac{30 \times 7}{30} = 7$ cm

Example 10 A race track is in the form of a ring whose inner circumference is 352 m, and the outer circumference is 396 m. Find the width of the track.

Solution Let the outer and inner radii of the ring be R metres and r metres respec-tively. Then,

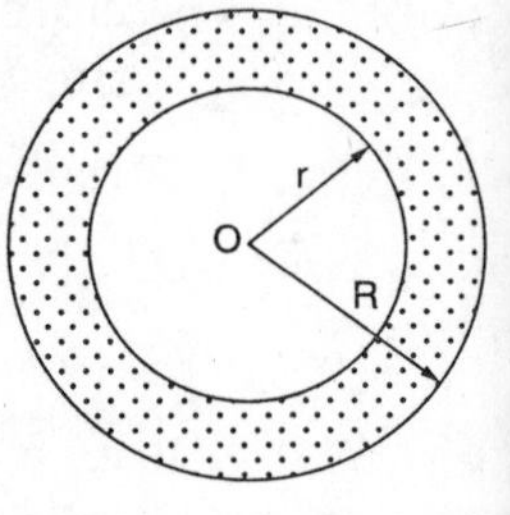

Fig. 7

$2\pi R = 396$ and $2\pi r = 352$

$\Rightarrow \quad 2 \times \dfrac{22}{7} \times R = 396$ and $2 \times \dfrac{22}{7} \times r = 352$

$\Rightarrow \quad R = 396 \times \dfrac{7}{22} \times \dfrac{1}{2}$ and $r = 352 \times \dfrac{7}{22} \times \dfrac{1}{2}$

$\Rightarrow \quad R = 63$ m and $r = 56$ m.

Hence, width of the track $= (R - r)$ metres $= (63 - 56)$ metres $= 7$ metres.

Example 11 The inner circumference of a circular track is 220 m. The track is 7 m wide everywhere. Calculate the cost of putting up a fence along the outer circle at the rate of Rs 2 per metre. (Use $\pi = 22/7$)

Solution Let the inner and outer radii of the circular track be r metres and R metres respectively. Then,

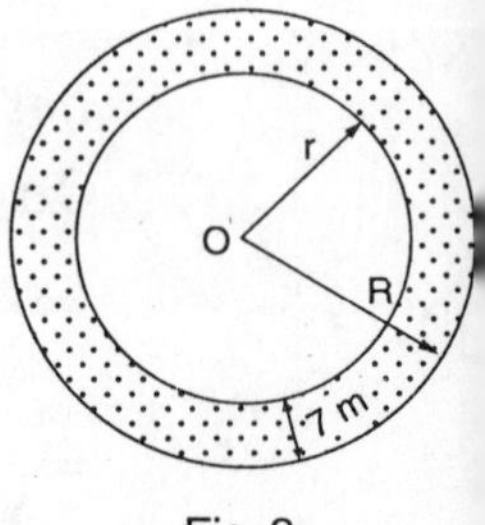

Fig. 8

Inner circumference = 220 metres

$\Rightarrow \quad 2\pi r = 220 \Rightarrow 2 \times \dfrac{22}{7} \times r = 220 \Rightarrow r = 35$ m

Since the track is 7 metre wide everywhere.

$\therefore \quad R =$ Outer radius $= r + 7 = (35 + 7)$ m $= 42$ m

$\therefore$ Outer circumference $= 2\pi R = 2\times\frac{22}{7}\times 42\text{m} = 264\text{m}$

Rate of fencing = Rs 2 per metre

$\therefore$ Total cost of fencing = (Circumference $\times$ Rate) = Rs (264×2) Rs528

EXERCISE 21.1

1. Find the circumference of a circle whose radius is
   (i) 14 cm (ii) 10 m (iii) 4 km
2. Find the circumference of a circle whose diameter is
   (i) 7 cm (ii) 4.2 cm (iii) 11.2 km
3. Find the radius of a circle whose circumference is
   (i) 52.8 cm (ii) 42 cm (iii) 6.6 km
4. Find the diameter of a circle whose circumference is
   (i) 12.56 cm (ii) 88 m (iii) 11.0 km
5. The ratio of the radii of two circles is 3 : 2. What is the ratio of their circumferences?
6. A wire in the form of a rectangle 18.7 cm long and 14.3 cm wide is reshaped and bent into the form of a circle. Find the radius of the circle so formed.
7. A piece of wire is bent in the shape of an equilateral triangle of each side 6.6 cm. It is re-bent to form a circular ring. What is the diameter of the ring?
8. The diameter of a wheel of a car is 63 cm. Find the distance travelled by the car during the period, the wheel makes 1000 revolutions.
9. The diameter of a wheel of a car is 98 cm. How many revolutions will it make to travel 6160 metres.
10. The moon is about 384400 km from the earth and its path around the earth is nearly circular. Find the circumference of the path described by the moon in lunar month.
11. How long will John take to make a round of a circular field of radius 21 m cycling at the speed of 8 km/hr ?
12. The hour and minute hands of a clock are 4 cm and 6 cm long respectively. Find the sum of the distances travelled by their tips in 2 days.
13. A rhombus has the same perimeter as the circumference of a circle. If the side of the rhombus is 2.2 m, find the radius of the circle.
14. A wire is looped in the form of a circle of radius 28 cm. It is re-bent into a square form. Determine the length of the side of the square.
15. A bicycle wheel makes 5000 revolutions in moving 11 km. Find the diameter of the wheel.
16. A boy is cycling such that the wheels of the cycle are making 140 revolutions per minute. If the diameter of the wheel is 60 cm, calculate the speed per hour with which the boy is cycling.
17. The diameter of the driving wheel of a bus is 140 cm. How many revolutions per minute must the wheel make in order to keep a speed of 66 km per hour ?

18. A water sprinkler in a lawn sprays water as far as 7 m in all directions. Find the length of the outer edge of wet grass.
19. A well of diameter 150 cm has a stone parapet around it. If the length of the outer edge of the parapet is 660 cm, then find the width of the parapet.
20. An ox in a kolhu (an oil processing apparatus) is tethered to a rope 3 m long. How much distance does it cover in 14 rounds?

ANSWER

1.	(i) 88 cm		(ii) 62.86 m		(iii) 25.142 km		
2.	(i) 22 cm		(ii) 13.2 cm		(iii) 35.2 km		
3.	(i) 8.4 cm		(ii) 6.68 cm		(iii) 1.05 km		
4.	(i) 3.99 cm		(ii) 28 m		(iii) 3.5 km		
5.	3 : 2	6.	10.5 cm	7.	6.3 cm	8.	1980 m
9.	2000	10.	2416228.57 km	11.	59.4 seconds	12.	1910.8 cm
13.	1.4 m	14.	44 cm	15.	70 cm	16.	15.84 km/hr
17.	250	18.	44 m	19.	30 cm	20.	264 m

HINTS TO SELECTED PROBLEMS

10. Take radius = 384000 km.

11. Required time $= \dfrac{\text{Distance}}{\text{Speed}} = \dfrac{2 \times \frac{22}{7} \times 21}{8}$ hr

12. The hour hand travels $\left(2 \times \dfrac{22}{7} \times 4\right)$ cm distance in 12 hours and the minute hand travels $\left(2 \times \dfrac{22}{7} \times 6\right)$ cm in one hour.

18. Wet grass forms a circular region of radius 7 m.

$\therefore$ Length of the outer edge of wet grass $= 2 \times \dfrac{22}{7} \times 7 \text{ m} = 44 \text{ m}$

19. Let the width of the parapet be x cm. Clearly, outer edge of the parapet forms of a circle of radius $(x + 75)$ cm.

$\therefore$ Length of the outer edge of parapet = 660 cm.

$$\Rightarrow \quad 2 \times \frac{22}{7} \times (x + 75) = 660$$

$$\Rightarrow \quad x + 75 = \frac{660 \times 7}{2 \times 22} \Rightarrow x + 75 = 105 \Rightarrow x = 30 \text{ cm}$$

21.5 AREA OF A CIRCLE

In this section, we shall first obtain the formula for the area of a circle and then the same will be used to solve some simple problems.

To obtain the formula for the area of a circle, let us consider the following experiment.

Experiment On a thick sheet of a paper, draw a circle with any radius, say r cm. With a pair of scissors, cut the sheet of paper along the circle. Thus, we get a circular disc of radius r cm.

Fold the circular disc so that the two parts cover each other exactly, and to get a crease. Fold again this folded disc, so that the two parts cover each other exactly and press to get another crease. Repeat the process of folding and pressing to obtain creases dividing the circular disc into 16 equal parts. Number the parts from 1 to 16, in serial order as shown in Fig. 9. Carefully cut out the sixteen parts and arrange them on a sheet of paper as shown in Fig. 10.

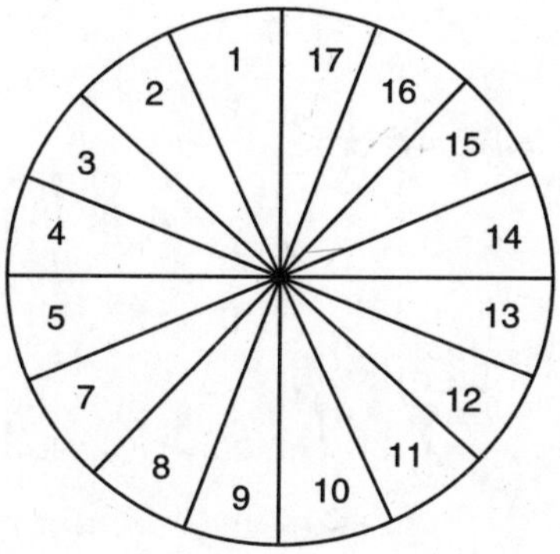

Fig. 9

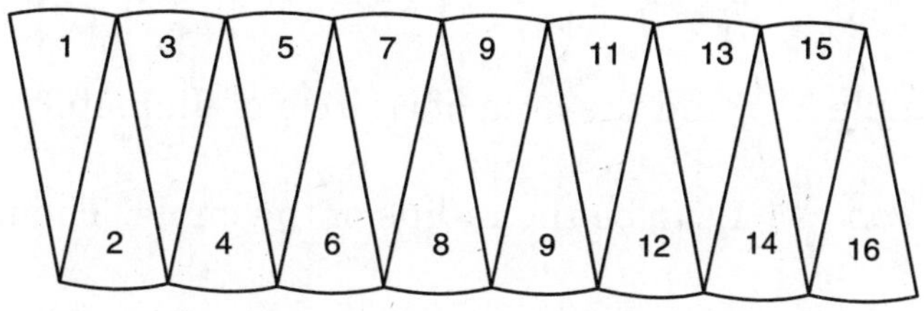

Fig. 10

This looks like a rectangular region. But it is not exactly so. However, if the disc is divided into a very large number of equal sectors and then these sectors are arranged as shown above, then the above figure will become very near to a rectangle.

Thus, the given circular region is equal in area to a near to a rectangle whose length and breadth are respectively half the circumference and the radius of the circle.

∴ Area of the circle = Area of the rectangle with length equal to half the circumference and breadth equal to its radius

$$= \frac{1}{2}(\text{Circumference}) \times \text{Radius}$$

$$= \left(\frac{1}{2} \times 2\pi r \times r\right) \text{ sq. cm}$$

$$= \pi r^2 \text{ sq. cm}$$

Hence, area A of a circle of radius r cm is given by

$$A = \pi r^2 \quad \text{Also,} \quad r = \sqrt{\frac{A}{\pi}}$$

Remark *Area of a semi-circle* $= \frac{1}{2}(\textit{Area of the circle}) = \frac{1}{2}\pi r^2$

Area of a quadrant of a circle $= \frac{1}{4}(\textit{Area of the circle}) = \frac{1}{4}\pi r^2$.

ILLUSTRATIVE EXAMPLES

Example 1 Find the area of a circle of radius 4.2 cm.

Solution We know that the area A of a circle of radius r is given by $A = \pi r^2$

Here, $r = 4.2$ cm

$\therefore \quad A = \frac{22}{7} \times (4.2)^2 \text{ cm}^2$ $\left[\because \pi = \frac{22}{7}\right]$

$\Rightarrow \quad A = \left(\frac{22}{7} \times 4.2 \times 4.2\right) \text{cm}^2 = (22 \times 0.6 \times 4.2) \text{ cm}^2 = 55.44 \text{ cm}^2$

Example 2 Find the area of a circle of diameter 7 cm.

Solution Let r be the radius of the circle. Then, $r = \frac{7}{2}$ cm $= 3.5$ cm

$\therefore$ Area of the circle $= \pi r^2$

$\Rightarrow$ Area of the circle $= \frac{22}{7} \times (3.5)^2 \text{ cm}^2$

$\Rightarrow$ Area of the circle $= \left(\frac{22}{7} \times 3.5 \times 3.5\right) \text{cm}^2 = (22 \times 0.5 \times 3.5) \text{ cm}^2 = 38.5 \text{ cm}^2$

Example 3 The circumference of a circle is 44 cm. Find its area.

Solution Let the radius of the circle be r cm. Then,
Circumference = 44 cm

$\Rightarrow \quad 2\pi r = 44$ [$\because$ Circumference $= 2\pi r$]

$\Rightarrow \quad 2 \times \frac{22}{7} \times r = 44$

$\Rightarrow \quad r = \frac{44 \times 7}{2 \times 22}$ cm $= 7$ cm

$\therefore$ Area of the circle $= \pi r^2 = \left(\frac{22}{7} \times 7^2\right) \text{cm}^2 = \left(\frac{22}{7} \times 7 \times 7\right) \text{cm}^2 = 154 \text{ cm}^2$

Example 4 The area of a circle is 616 cm^2. Find the radius of the circle.

Solution Let the radius of the circle be r cm.
We have,
Area of the circle = 616 cm^2

$\Rightarrow \quad \pi r^2 = 616$ $\left[\because \textit{Area} = \pi r^2\right]$

$\Rightarrow \quad \frac{22}{7} \times r^2 = 616$

$\Rightarrow \quad r^2 = \dfrac{616 \times 7}{22} = 28 \times 7 = 196 = 14^2$

$\Rightarrow \quad r = 14 \text{ cm}$

Hence, radius of the circle = 14 cm.

Example 5 A copper wire, when bent in the form of a square, encloses an area of 484 cm^2. If the same wire is bent in the form of a circle, find the area enclosed by it. (Use $\pi = 22/7$).

Solution We have,

Area of the square = 484 cm^2

$\Rightarrow \quad (\text{Side})^2 = (22)^2 \text{ cm}^2$

$\Rightarrow \quad \text{Side} = 22 \text{ cm}$

So, Perimeter of the square $= 4(\text{Side}) = (4 \times 22) \text{ cm} = 88 \text{ cm}$.

Let r be the radius of the circle. Then,

Circumference of the circle = Perimeter of the square

$\Rightarrow \quad 2\pi r = 88$

$\Rightarrow \quad 2 \times \dfrac{22}{7} \times r = 88 \Rightarrow r = 14 \text{ cm}$

$\therefore \quad$ Area of the circle $\pi r^2 = \dfrac{22}{7} \times (14)^2 \text{ cm}^2 = 616 \text{ cm}^2$.

Example 6 A circular grassy plot of land, 42 m in diameter, has a path 3.5 m wide running round it on the outside. Find the cost of gravelling the path at Rs 4 per square metre.

Solution Radius of the plot $= \dfrac{42}{2} \text{ m} = 21 \text{ m}$

Radius of the plot including the path $= (21 + 3.5) \text{ m} = 24.5 \text{ m}$

$$\therefore \quad \text{Area of the path} = \left[\pi(24.5)^2 - \pi(21)^2\right] \text{m}^2$$

$$= \pi\left[(24.5)^2 - \pi(21)^2\right] \text{m}^2$$

$$= \pi\left[(24.5 + 21)(24.5 - 21)\right] \text{m}^2$$

$$= \left[\pi(45.5)(3.5)\right] \text{m}^2$$

$$= \left(\frac{22}{7} \times 45.5 \times 3.5\right) \text{m}^2 = 500.5 \text{ m}^2$$

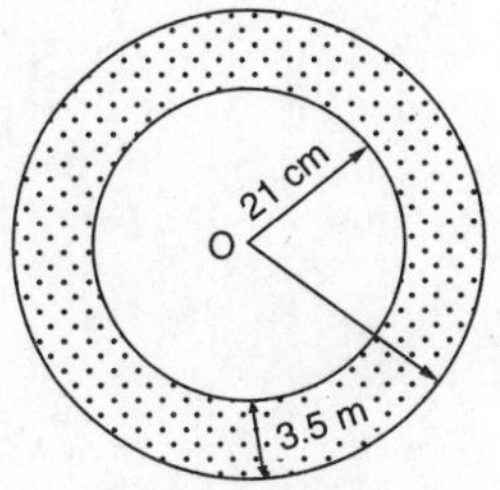

Fig. 11

Hence, cost of gravelling the path $= \text{Rs } (500.5 \times 4) = \text{Rs } 2002$

Example 7 A paper is in the form of a rectangle $ABCD$ in which AB = 20 cm and BC = 14 cm. A semicircular portion with BC as diameter is cut off. Find the area of the remaining part.

Solution Length of the rectangle $ABCD = AB = 20$ cm

Breadth of the rectangle $ABCD = BC = 14$ cm

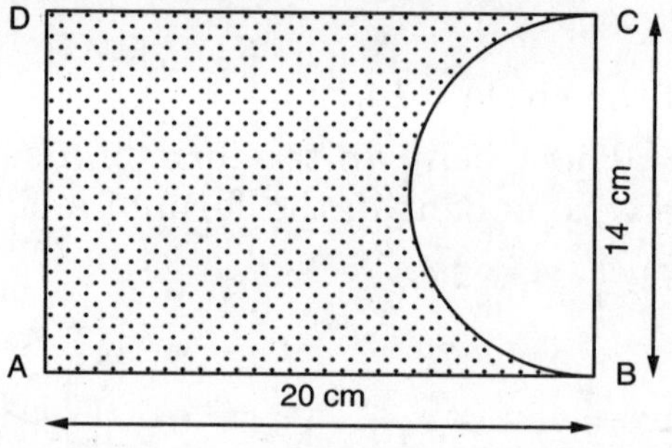

Fig. 12

$\therefore$ Area of rectangle $ABCD = (20 \times 14)\ \text{cm}^2 = 280\ \text{cm}^2$.

Diameter of the semi-circle $= BC = 14$ cm

$\therefore$ Radius of the semi-circle = 7 cm

Area of the semi-circular portion cut off from the rectangle $ABCD$

$$= \frac{1}{2}\pi r^2 = \frac{1}{2} \times \frac{22}{7} \times 7^2\ \text{cm}^2 = 77\ \text{cm}^2$$

$\therefore$ Area of the remaining part

= Area of rectangle $ABCD$ – Area of semi-circle $= (280 - 77)\ \text{cm}^2 = 203\ \text{cm}^2$

Example 8 In Fig. 13, find the area of the shaded region [Use $\pi = 3.14$]

Solution Clearly, diameter of the circle = Diagonal BD of rectangle $ABCD$

$\therefore$ Diameter $= BD = \sqrt{BC^2 + CD^2} = \sqrt{6^2 + 8^2}$ cm $= 10$ cm

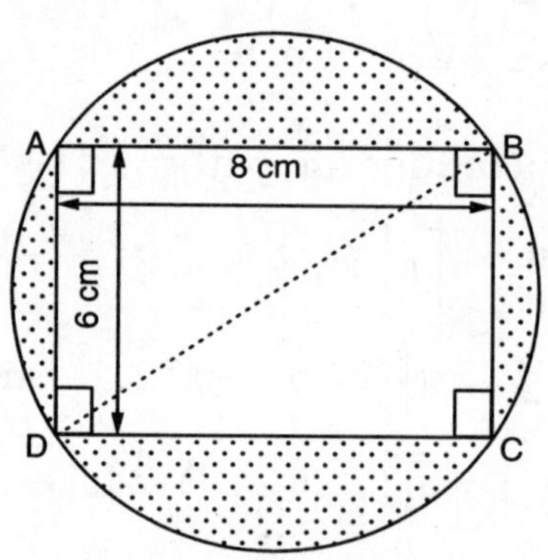

Fig. 13

Let r be the radius of the circle. Then,

r = Radius of the circle = (10 / 2) cm = 5 cm

Area of rectangle $ABCD = AB \times BC = (8 \times 6)\ \text{cm}^2 = 48\ \text{cm}^2$

Area of the circle $= \pi r^2 = 3.14 \times (5)^2\ \text{cm}^2 = 78.50\ \text{cm}^2$

Hence, area of the shaded region

$= \text{Area of the circle} - \text{Area of rectangle } ABCD$

$= (78.50 - 48)\text{ cm}^2 = 30.50\text{ cm}^2$

Example 9 The circumferences of two circles are in the ratio 2 : 3. Find the ratio of their areas.

Solution Let r_1 and r_2 be the radii of two given circles and C_1 and C_2 be their circumferences. Then,

$$C_1 = 2\pi r_1 \text{ and } C_2 = 2\pi r_2$$

Now, $C_1 : C_2 = 2 : 3$

$$\Rightarrow \quad \frac{C_1}{C_2} = \frac{2}{3} \Rightarrow \frac{2\pi r_1}{2\pi r_2} = \frac{2}{3} \Rightarrow \frac{r_1}{r_2} = \frac{2}{3}$$

Let A_1 and A_2 be the areas of two circles. Then,

$$A_1 = \pi r_1^2 \text{ and } A_2 = \pi r_2^2$$

$$\therefore \quad \frac{A_1}{A_2} = \frac{\pi r_1^2}{\pi r_2^2} = \frac{r_1^2}{r_2^2} = \frac{4}{9} \qquad \left[\because \frac{r_1}{r_2} = \frac{2}{3} \therefore \frac{r_1^2}{r_2^2} = \frac{4}{9}\right]$$

$\Rightarrow \quad A_1 : A_2 = 4 : 9$

Hence, the areas of two given circles are in the ratio 4 : 9.

Example 10 The areas of two circles are in the ratio 16 : 25. Find the ratio of their circumferences.

Solution Let r_1 and r_2 be the radii of two circles and let their areas be A_1 and A_2 respectively. Then,

$$A_1 = \pi r_1^2, A_2 = \pi r_2^2$$

Now, $A_1 : A_2 = 16 : 25$ [Given]

$\Rightarrow \quad \pi r_1^2 : \pi r_2^2 = 16 : 25$

$$\Rightarrow \quad \frac{\pi r_1^2}{\pi r_2^2} = \frac{16}{25}$$

$$\Rightarrow \quad \frac{r_1^2}{r_2^2} = \frac{4^2}{5^2} \Rightarrow \frac{r_1}{r_2} = \frac{4}{5} \qquad \text{... (i)} \quad \text{[Taking square root of both sides]}$$

Let C_1 and C_2 be the circumferences of two circles. Then,

$$C_1 = 2\pi r_1 \text{ and } C_2 = 2\pi r_2.$$

$$\therefore \quad \frac{C_1}{C_2} = \frac{2\pi r_1}{2\pi r_2} = \frac{r_1}{r_2} = \frac{4}{5} \qquad \text{[Using (i)]}$$

$\Rightarrow \quad C_1 : C_2 = 4 : 5$

Hence, the circumferences of the two circles are in the ratio 4 : 5.

Example 11 A square park has each side of 100 m. At each corner of the park, there is a flower bed in the form of a quadrant of radius 14 m as shown in Fig. 14. Find the area of the remaining part of the park. (Take $\pi = 22/7$)

Solution We have,

Area of each quadrant of radius 14 m $= \frac{1}{4}(\pi r^2)$

$= \frac{1}{4} \times \frac{22}{7} \times 14 \times 14$ $[\because r = 14]$

$= 154 \text{ m}^2$

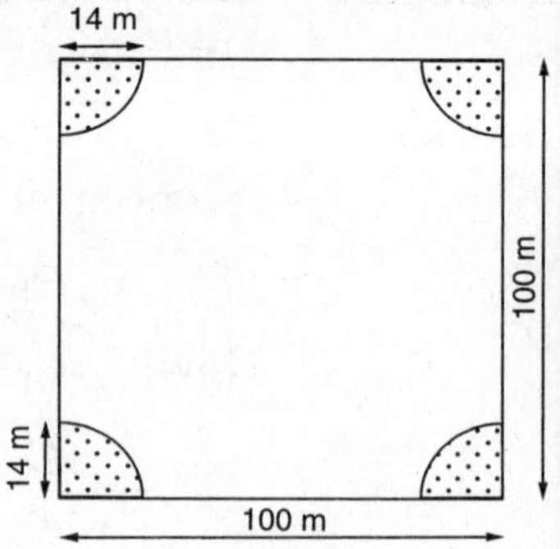

Fig. 14

$\therefore$ Area of 4 quadrants $= (4 \times 154) \text{ m}^2 = 616 \text{ m}^2$

Area of square park having side 100 m long

$= (100 \times 100) \text{ m}^2 = 10000 \text{ m}^2$

Hence, Area of the remaining part of the park $= 10000 - 616 = 9384 \text{ m}^2$.

Example 12 Four equal circles are described about the four corners of a square so that each touches two of the others as shown in Fig. 15. Find the area of the shaded region, each side of the square measuring 14 cm.

Solution Let $ABCD$ be the given square each side of which is 14 cm long. Clearly, the radius of each circle is 7 cm.

We have,

Area of the square of side 14 cm long

$= (14 \times 14) \text{ cm}^2 = 196 \text{ cm}^2$

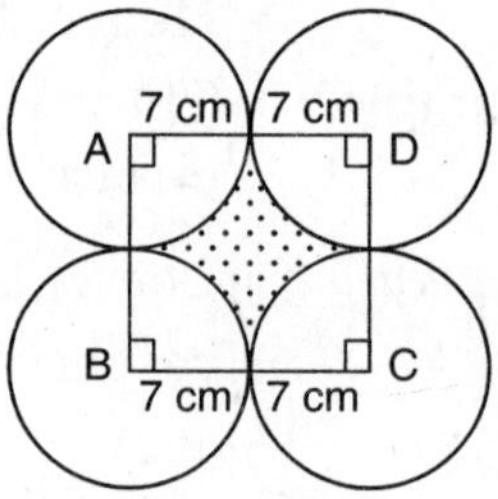

Fig. 15

Area of each quadrant of a circle of radius 7 cm

$= \frac{1}{4}(\pi r^2) = \left(\frac{1}{4} \times \frac{22}{7} \times (7)^2\right) \text{cm}^2 = 38.5 \text{ cm}^2$

$\therefore$ Area of 4 quadrants $= 4 \times 38.5 \text{ cm}^2 = 154 \text{ cm}^2$

Hence,

Area of the shaded region

= Area of the square $ABCD$ – Area of 4 quadrants $= (196 - 154) \text{ cm}^2 = 42 \text{ cm}^2$

Example 13 A horse is placed for grazing inside a rectangular field 70 m by 52 m and is tethered to one corner by a rope 21 m long. On how much area can it graze ?

Solution Shaded portion indicates the area which the horse can graze. Clearly, shaded area is the area of a quadrant of a circle of radius $r = 21$ m

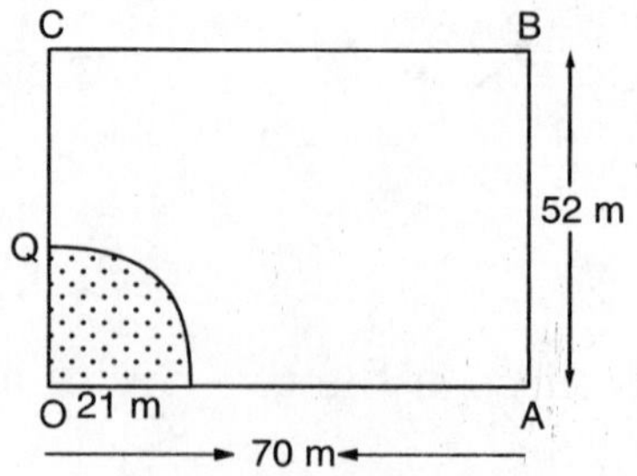

Fig. 16

Hence,

$$\text{Required area} = \frac{1}{4}\pi r^2 = \left\{\frac{1}{4}\times\frac{22}{7}\times(21)^2\right\}\text{cm}^2 = \frac{693}{2}\text{cm}^2 = 346.5\text{ cm}^2$$

Example 14 *PQRS* is a diameter of a circle of radius 6 cm. The lengths *PQ*, *QR* and *RS* are equal. Semi-circles are drawn on *PQ* and *QS* as diameters as shown in Fig. 17. Find the area of the shaded region.

Solution We have, $PS = 12$ cm.

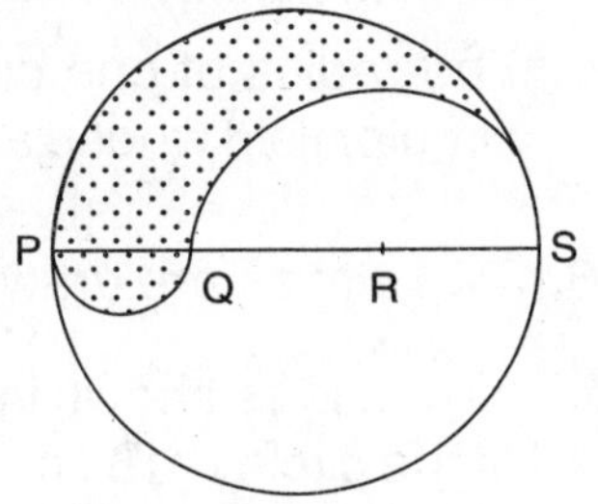

Fig. 17

$\because \quad PQ = QR = RS = \frac{1}{3}PS$

$\therefore \quad PQ = 4$ cm, $QS = 2\,PQ = 8$ cm

$\therefore$ Required Area

= Area of semi-circle with *PS* as diameter

+ Area of seme-circle with *PQ* as diameter

– Area of semi-circle with *QS* as diameter.

$$= \frac{1}{2}\times\frac{22}{7}\times(6)^2 + \frac{1}{2}\times\frac{22}{7}\times 2^2 - \frac{1}{2}\times\frac{22}{7}\times(4)^2$$

$$= \frac{1}{2}\times\frac{22}{7}\left(6^2 + 2^2 - 4^2\right)$$

$$= \frac{1}{2}\times\frac{22}{7}\times 24 = \frac{264}{7}\text{ cm}^2 = 37.71\text{ cm}^2$$

EXERCISE 21.2

1. Find the area of a circle whose radius is
   (i) 7 cm (ii) 2.1 m (iii) 7 km
2. Find the area of a circle whose diameter is
   (i) 8.4 cm (ii) 5.6 m (iii) 7 km
3. The area of a circle is 154 cm^2. Find the radius of the circle.
4. Find the radius of a circle, if its area is
   (i) 4π cm^2 (ii) 55.44 m^2 (iii) 1.54 km^2
5. The circumference of a circle is 3.14 m, find its area.
6. If the area of a circle is 50.24 m^2, find its circumference.
7. A horse is tied to a pole with 28 m long string. Find the area where the horse can graze. (Take $\pi = 22/7$).
8. A steel wire when bent in the form of a square encloses an area of 121 cm^2. If the same wire is bent in the form of a circle, find the area of the circle.
9. A road which is 7 m wide surrounds a circular park whose circumference is 352 m. Find the area of of road.
10. Prove that the area of a circular path of uniform width *h* surrounding a circular region of radius *r* is $\pi\ h\ (2r + h)$.

11. The perimeter of a circle is $4\pi r$ cm. What is the area of the circle?
12. A wire of 5024 m length is in the form of a square. It is cut and made a circle. Find the ratio of the area of the square to that of the circle.
13. The radius of a circle is 14 cm. Find the radius of the circle whose area is double of the area of the circle.
14. The radius of one circluar field is 20 m and that of another is 48 m. Find the radius of the third circular field whose area is equal to the sum of the areas of two fields.
15. The radius of one circular field is 5 m and that of the other is 13 m. Find the radius of the circuiar field whose area is the difference of the areas of first and second field.
16. Two circles are drawn inside a big circle with diameters $\frac{2}{3}$rd and $\frac{1}{3}$rd of the diameter of the big circle as shown in Fig. 18. Find the area of the shaded portion, if the length of the diameter of the circle is 18 cm.

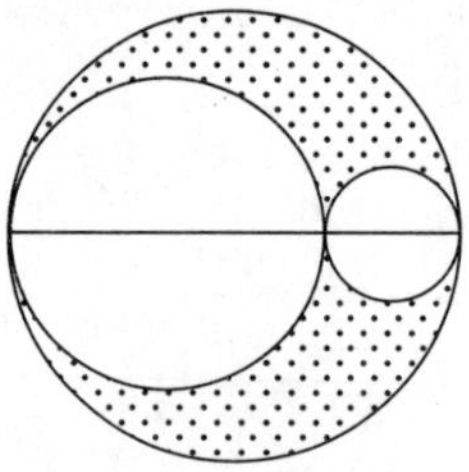

Fig. 18

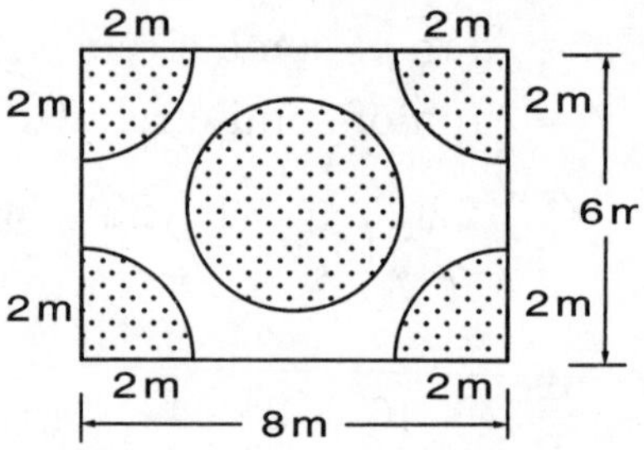

Fig. 19

17. In Fig. 19, the radius of quarter circular plot taken is 2 m and radius of the flower bed is 2 m. Find the area of the remaining field.
18. Four equal circles, each of radius 5 cm, touch each other as shown in Fig. 20. Find the area included between them. (Take $\pi = 3.14$).

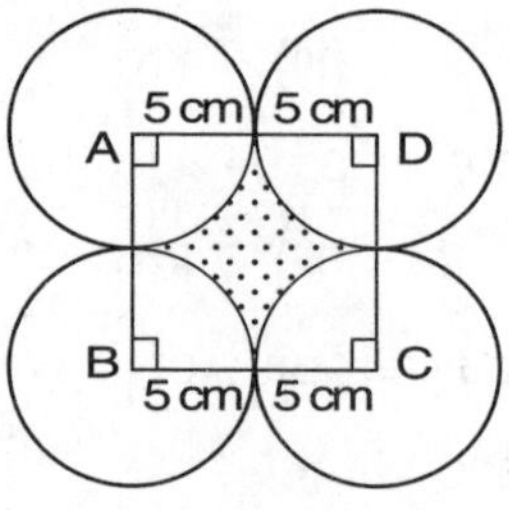

Fig. 20

19. The area of circle is 100 times the area of another circle. What is the ratio of their circumferences?

ANSWER

1. (i) 154 cm^2	(ii) 13.86 m^2	(iii) 154 km^2	
2. (i) 55.44 cm^2	(ii) 24.64 m^2	(iii) 38.5 km^2	3. 7 cm
4. (i) 2 cm	(ii) 4.2 m	(iii) 0.7 km	5. 0.785 m^2
6. 25.12 m	7. 2464 m^2	8. 154 cm^2	9. 2618 m^2
11. $4\pi r^2$ cm^2	12. 11 : 14	13. $14\sqrt{2}$ cm	14. 52 m
15.12 m	16. 36π cm^2	17. 22.86 m^2	18. 21.43 cm^2
19.10 : 1			

HINTS TO SELECTED PROBLEMS

7. Length of the string = 28 m. Area over which the horse can graze is the area of a circle of radius 28 m. Hence, required area $= \pi (28)^2 = 2464\,m^2$

18. Required area = Area of square ABCD – Area of 4 quadrants $= 10 \times 10 - 4\left(\frac{1}{4} \times \frac{22}{7} \times 5^2\right) cm^2$

OBJECTIVE TYPE QUESTIONS

Mark the correct alternative in each of the following:

1. The ratio of the perimeter (circumference) and diameter of a circle is
   (a) π (b) 2π (c) $\frac{\pi}{2}$ (d) $\frac{\pi}{4}$
2. The ratio of the area and circumference of a circle of diameter d is
   (a) d (b) $\frac{d}{2}$ (c) $\frac{d}{4}$ (d) $2d$
3. The cost of fencing a circular garden of radius 21 m at ₹ 10 per metre is
   (a) ₹ 1320 (b) ₹ 132 (c) ₹ 1200 (d) ₹ 660
4. If the diameter of a circle is equal to the diagonal of a square, then the ratio of their areas is
   (a) 7:1 (b) 1:1 (c) 11:7 (d) 22:7
5. A circle is inscribed in a square of side 14 m. The ratio of the area of the circle and that of the square is
   (a) $\pi : 3$ (b) $\pi : 4$ (c) $\pi : 2$ (d) $\pi : 1$
6. How many times should a wheel of radius 7 m rotate to go around the perimeter of a rectangular field of length 60 m and breadth 50 m?
   (a) 3 (b) 4 (c) 5 (d) 6
7. The minute hand of a clock is 14 cm long. How far does the tip of the minute hand move in 60 minutes?
   (a) 22 cm (b) 44 cm (c) 33 cm (d) 88 cm
8. The cost of fencing a semi-circular garden of radius 14 m at ₹ 10 per metre is
   (a) ₹ 1080 (b) ₹ 1020 (c) ₹ 700 (d) ₹ 720
9. The area of a square is equal to the area of a circle. The ratio between the side of the square and the radius of the circle is
   (a) $\sqrt{\pi} : 1$ (b) $1 : \sqrt{\pi}$ (c) $1 : \pi$ (d) $\pi : 1$
10. If A is the area and C is the circumference of a circle, then its radius is
    (a) $\frac{A}{C}$ (b) $\frac{2A}{C}$ (c) $\frac{3A}{C}$ (d) $\frac{4A}{C}$
11. The area of a circle of circumference C is
    (a) $\frac{C^2}{4\pi}$ (b) $\frac{C^2}{2\pi}$ (c) $\frac{C^2}{\pi}$ (d) $\frac{4C^2}{\pi}$
12. The circumference of a circle is 44 cm. Its area is
    (a) 77 cm^2 (b) 154 cm^2 (c) 208 cm^2 (d) 144 cm^2
13. Each side of an equilateral triangle is equal to the radius of a circle whose area is 154 cm^2. The area of the triangle is
    (a) $\frac{7\sqrt{3}}{4}\,cm^2$ (b) $\frac{49\sqrt{3}}{2}\,cm^2$ (c) $\frac{49\sqrt{3}}{4}\,cm^2$ (d) $\frac{7\sqrt{3}}{2}\,cm^2$

14. The area of a circle is 9π cm^2. Its circumference is
(a) 6π cm (b) 36π cm (c) 9π cm (d) $36\pi^2$ cm

15. The area of a circle is increased by 22 cm^2 when its radius is increased by 1 cm. The original radius of the circle is
(a) 6 cm (b) 3 cm (c) 4 cm (d) 3.5 cm

16. The radii of two circles are in the ratio 2 : 3. The ratio of their areas is
(a) 2:3 (b) 4:9 (c) 3:2 (d) 9:4

17. The areas of two circles are in the ratio 49 : 36. The ratio of their circumferences is
(a) 7:6 (b) 6:7 (c) 3:2 (d) 2:3

18. The circumferences of two circles are in the ratio 3 : 4. The ratio of their areas is
(a) 3:4 (b) 4:3 (c) 9:16 (d) 16:9

19. The difference between the circumference and radius of a circle is 37 cm. The area of the circle is
(a) 111 cm^2 (b) 148 cm^2 (c) 154 cm^2 (d) 258 cm^2

ANSWSERS

1. (a)	2. (c)	3. (a)	4. (c)	5. (b)	6. (c)	7. (d)
8. (d)	9. (a)	10. (b)	11. (a)	12. (b)	13. (c)	14. (a)
15. (b)	16. (b)	17. (a)	18. (c)	19. (c)		

THINGS TO REMEMBER

1. *The perimeter of a circle is called its circumference.*
2. *The ratio of the circumference of a circle to its diameter is the same for all circles, regardless of their sizes. The constant ratio is denoted by pi whose approximate value is* $\frac{22}{7}$ *or 3.14.*

i.e. $$\frac{\text{Circunference}}{\text{Diameter}} = \pi$$

$\Rightarrow$ $\frac{C}{2r} = \pi$, *where C denotes circumference and r radius of the circle.*

$\Rightarrow$ $C = 2\pi r$.

3. *The number* π *is not a rational number.*
4. *Circumference C of a circle of radius r is given by* $C = 2\pi r$.

or, $C = \pi d$, *where* $d = 2r$ = *diameter*

5. *Area A of a circle of radius r is given by* $A = \pi r^2$
6. *Radius of a circle* $= \sqrt{\frac{A}{\pi}}$.

22

DATA HANDLING – I
(Collection and Organisation of Data)

22.1 DATA

Consider the following list of marks (out of 100) scored by 30 students of class VI in a test:

55, 65, 15, 40, 35, 70, 90, 92, 84, 85

70, 75, 65, 72, 80, 78, 64, 88, 78, 76

55, 54, 52, 72, 70, 90, 85, 75, 65, 80

We find that each entry in the above list is a numerical fact which is called an observation. Such a collection of observations gathered initially is called raw data.

Data are of two types:

(i) Primary data (ii) Secondary data

PRIMARY DATA *When an investigator collects data himself with a definite plan or design in his (her) mind, it is called primary data.*

SECONDARY DATA *Data which are not originally collected by the investigator but they are obtained from published or unpublished sources are known as secondary data.*

Secondary data are collected by an individual or an institution for some purpose and are used by someone else in another context.

22.2 ORGANISATION OF DATA

After collection of data, the investigator has to find ways to condense them in tabular form in order to study their salient features. Such an arrangement is called presentation of data.

The raw data can be arranged in any one of the following ways:

(i) Serial order of alphabetical order
(ii) Ascending order
(iii) Descending order

The raw data when put in ascending or descending order of magnitude is called an array.

Let the marks obtained by 30 students of class VIII in a class test, out of 50 marks, according to their roll numbers be:

39, 25, 5, 33, 19, 21, 12, 41, 12, 21, 19, 1, 10, 8, 12,

17, 19, 17, 17, 41, 40, 12, 41, 33, 19, 21, 33, 5, 1, 21.

The data in this form are called raw data or ungrouped data. The above raw data can be arranged in serial order as follows:

Roll No.	Marks	Roll No.	Marks	Roll No.	Marks
1	39	11	19	21	40
2	25	12	1	22	12
3	5	13	10	23	41
4	33	14	8	24	33
5	19	15	12	25	19
6	21	16	17	26	21
7	12	17	19	27	33
8	41	18	17	28	5
9	12	19	17	29	1
10	21	20	41	30	21

Now suppose we wish to judge the standard of achievement of the students. The data in this form do not give us a clear picture of the group. If we arrange them in ascending or descending order, it gives us a slightly better picture. In ascending order, the data look as follow:

1, 1, 5, 5, 8, 10, 12, 12, 12, 12, 17, 17, 17, 19, 19,

19, 19, 21, 21, 21, 25, 33, 33, 33, 39, 40, 41, 41, 41

In descending order, the data look as follows:

41, 41, 41, 40, 39, 33, 33, 33, 25, 21, 21, 21, 21, 19, 19,

19, 19, 17, 17, 17, 12, 12, 12, 12, 10, 8, 5, 5, 1, 1.

The raw data when put in ascending or descending order of magnitude is called an *array or arrayed data*.

If the number of observations is large, then arranging data in ascending or descending or serial order is a tedious job and it does not tell us much except perhaps the minimum(s) and maximum(s) of data. So, to make it easily understandable and clear, we can tabulate data in the form of a table given below.

In the first column of the table, we write all marks from lowest to highest. We now look at the first value in the given raw data and put a bar (vertical line) in the second column opposite to it. Now, we see the second value in the given raw data and put a bar opposite to it in the second column. This process is repeated till all observations in the given raw data are exhausted. The bars drawn in the second column are known as *tally marks* and to facilitate we record tally marks in bunches of five, the fifth tally mark is drawn diagonally across the first four. For example, ~~||||~~ || = 7. We finally count the number of tally marks corresponding to each observation and write in the third column.

Marks	Tally Marks	No. of students
1	||	2
5	||	2
8	|	1
10	|	1
12	||||	4
17	|||	3
19	||||	4

21	||||	4
25	|	1
33	|||	3
39	|	1
40	|	1
41	|||	3

This way of presentation of data is known as *frequency distribution.* Marks are called *variates* and the number of students who have secured a particular number of marks is called frequency of the variate. *The number of times an observation occurs in the given data, is called the frequency of the observation.*

22.3 FREQUENCY DISTRIBUTION

Frequency table or frequency distribution is a method to present raw data in the form from which one can easily understand the information contained in the raw data.

The construction of a frequency distribution from the given raw data is done by the use of the method of tally marks. In the first column of the frequency table we write all possible values of the variable from the lowest to the highest.

We now look at the first value in the given raw data and put a bar (vertical line) in the second column opposite to it. Now, we see the second value in the given raw data and put a bar opposite to it in the second column. This process is repeated till all observations in the given raw data are exhausted. To facilitate counting blocks of five (~~||||~~) are prepared and some space is left in between each block. We finally count the number of bars corresponding to each value of the variable and place it in the third column of frequency. The process will be clear from the following example of the number of children in 20 families:

1, 1, 2, 3, 4, 3, 2, 1, 1, 4, 5, 2, 4, 2, 2, 1, 3, 3, 2, 5

The data may be put in the form of a frequency distribution as follows:

No. of children	*Tally Bars*	*Frequency*
1	~~||||~~	5
2	~~||||~~ |	6
3	||||	4
4	|||	3
5	||	2

22.3.1 CONSTRUCTION OF A FREQUENCY DISTRIBUTION

To prepare a frequency distribution from the given raw data we may use the following steps:

STEP I *Obtain the given raw data.*

STEP II *Prepare a table with three columns — first for variable under study such as marks, weight, height etc., second for 'Tally marks' and third for the total, representing corresponding frequency to each value of size of the variable.*

<u>STEP III</u> *Place all the values of the variable in the first column in ascending order.*

<u>STEP IV</u> *Take the first observation in the raw data and put a bar in the second column opposite to it. Then take the second observation in the given raw data and put a bar opposite to it. Continue this process till all the observations in the given raw data are exhausted. For the sake of convenience, record tally marks in bunches of five, the fifth is obtained by crossing diagonally the other four. Leave some space between each block of bars.*

<u>STEP V</u> *Count the number of bars (tally marks) in respect of each value of the variable and place it in the third column.*

<u>STEP VI</u> *Give a suitable title to the frequency distribution table so that it conveys exactly what the table is about.*

ILLUSTRATIVE EXAMPLES

Example 1 Given below are the ages of 25 students of class VIII in a school. Prepare a discrete frequency distribution.

15, 16, 16, 14, 17, 17, 16, 15, 15, 16, 16, 17, 15

16, 16, 14, 16, 15, 14, 15, 16, 16, 15, 14, 15

Solution Frequency distribution of ages of 25 students:

Age	*Tally Bars*	*Frequency*
14	||||	4
15	卌 |||	8
16	卌 卌	10
17	|||	3
Total		25

Example 2 Form a discrete frequency distribution from the following scores:

15, 18, 16, 20, 25, 24, 25, 20, 16, 15, 18, 18, 16

24, 15, 20, 28, 30, 27, 16, 24, 25, 20, 18, 28, 27

25, 24, 24, 18, 18, 25, 20, 16, 15, 20, 27, 28, 29, 16

Solution: Frequency distribution of scores:

Variate	*Tally marks*	*Frequency*
15	||||	4
16	卌 |	6
18	卌 |	6
20	卌 |	6
24	卌	5
25	卌	5
27	|||	3
28	|||	3
29	|	1
30	|	1
Total		40

EXERCISE 22.1

1. Define the following terms:
   (i) Observations (ii) data
   (iii) Frequency of an observation (iv) Frequency distribution
2. The final marks in mathematics of 30 students are as follows:

   53, 61, 48, 60, 78, 68, 55, 100, 67, 90
   75, 88, 77, 37, 84, 58, 60, 48, 62, 56
   44, 58, 52, 64, 98, 59, 70, 39, 50, 60

   (i) Arrange these marks in the ascending order. 30 to 39 one group, 40 to 49 second group, etc.
   (ii) What is the highest score?
   (iii) What is the lowest score?
   (iv) What is the range?
   (v) If 40 is the pass mark how many have failed?
   (vi) How many have scored 75 or more?
   (vii) Which observations between 50 and 60 have not actually appeared?
   (viii) How many have scored less than 50?
3. The weights of new born babies (in kg) in a hospital on a particular day are as follows:

   2.3, 2.2, 2.1, 2.7, 2.6, 3.0, 2.5, 2.9, 2.8, 3.1, 2.5, 2.8, 2.7, 2.9, 2.4

   (i) Rearrange the weights in descending order.
   (ii) Determine the highest weight.
   (iii) Determine the lowest weight.
   (iv) Determine the range.
   (v) How many babies were born on that day?
   (vi) How many babies weigh below 2.5 kg?
   (vii) How many babies weigh more than 2.8?
   (viii) How many babies weigh 2.8 kg?
4. Following data gives the number of children in 40 families:

   1, 2, 6, 5, 1, 5, 1, 3, 2, 6, 2, 3, 4, 2, 0, 0, 4, 4, 3, 2
   2, 0, 0, 1, 2, 2, 4, 3, 2, 1, 0, 5, 1, 2, 4, 3, 4, 1, 6, 2

   Represent it in the form of a frequency distribution.
5. Prepare a frequency table of the following scores obtained by 50 students in a test:

42	51	21	42	37	37	42	49	38	52
7	33	17	44	39	7	14	27	39	42
42	62	37	39	67	51	53	53	59	41
29	38	27	31	54	19	53	51	22	61
42	39	59	47	33	34	16	37	57	43

6. A die was thrown 25 times and following scores were obtained:

1	5	2	4	3
6	1	4	2	5
1	6	2	6	3
5	4	1	3	2
3	6	1	5	2

   Prepare a frequency table of the scores.

7. In a study of number of accidents per day, the observations for 30 days were obtained as follows:

6	3	5	6	4	3	2	5	4	2
4	2	1	2	2	0	5	4	6	1
6	0	5	3	6	1	5	5	2	6

Prepare a frequency distribution table.

8. Prepare a frequency table of the following ages (in years) of 30 students of class VIII in your school:

13, 14, 13, 12, 14, 13, 14, 15, 13, 14, 13, 14, 16, 12, 14
13, 14, 15, 16, 13, 14, 13, 12, 17, 13, 12, 13, 13, 13, 14,

9. Following figures relate the weekly wages (in Rs.) of 15 workers in a factory:
300, 250, 200, 250, 200, 150, 350, 200, 250, 200, 150, 300, 150, 200, 250
Prepare a frequency table.
   (i) What is the range in wages (in Rs)?
   (ii) How many Workers are getting Rs 350?
   (iii) How many workers are getting the minimum wages?

10. Construct a frequency distribution table for the following marks obtained by 25 students in a history test in class VI of a school:
9, 17, 12, 20, 9, 18, 25, 17, 19, 9, 12, 9, 12, 18, 17, 19, 20, 25, 9, 12, 17, 19, 19, 20, 9
   (i) What is the range of marks?
   (ii) What is the highest mark?
   (iii) Which mark is occurring more frequently?

11. In a mathematics test following marks were obtained by 40 students of class VI. Arrange these marks in a table using, tally marks.

8	1	3	7	6	5	5	4	4	2
4	9	5	3	7	1	6	5	2	7
7	3	8	4	2	8	9	5	8	6
7	4	5	6	9	6	4	4	6	6

   (i) Find how many students obtained marks equal to or more than 7?
   (ii) How many students obtained marks below 4?

12. Following is the choice of sweets of 30 students of class VI: Ladoo, Barfi, Ladoo, Jalebi, Ladoo, Rasgulla, Jalebi, Ladoo, Barfi, Rasgulla, Ladoo, Jalebi, Jalebi Rasgulla, Ladoo, Rasgulla, Jalebi, Ladoo, Rasgulla, Ladoo, Rasgulla, Jalebi, Ladoo, Rasgulla, Ladoo, Ladoo, Barfi, Rasgulla, Rasgulla, Ladoo.
   (i) Arrange the names of sweets in a table using tally marks.
   (ii) Which sweet is preferred by most of the students.

ANSWERS

2. (ii) 100 (iii) 37 (iv) 63 (v) 2 (vi) 8 (vii) 51, 54, 57 (viii) 5

3. (i) 3.1, 3.0, 2.9, 2.9, 2.8, 2.8, 2.7, 2.7, 2.6, 2.5, 2.4, 2.4, 2.3, 2.2, 2.1 (ii) 3.1 kg (iii) 2.1 kg (iv) 1.0 kg (v) 15 (vi) 4 (vii) 4 (viii) 2

4.

No. of Children	*Frequency*
0	5
1	7
2	11
3	5
4	6
5	3
6	3

5.

Marks	*No. of Students*	*Marks*	*No. of Students*	*Marks*	*No. of Students*
7	2	33	2	49	1
14	1	34	1	51	3
16	1	37	4	52	1
17	1	38	2	53	3
19	1	39	4	54	1
21	1	41	1	57	1
22	1	42	6	59	2
27	2	43	1	61	1
29	1	44	1	62	1
31	1	47	1	67	1

6.	Score:	1	2	3	4	5	6	
	Number of times:	5	5	4	3	4	4	
7.	Number of accidents:	0	1	2	3	4	5	6
	Number of days:	2	3	6	3	4	6	6
8.	Ages (in years):		12	13	14	15	16	17
	Number of Students:		4	12	9	2	2	1

9. (i) 200 (ii) 1 (iii) 3

10. (i) 16 (ii) 25 (iii) 9

11.

Marks	*Tally marks*	*Frequency*
1	||	2
2	|||	3
3	|||	3
4	卌 ||	7
5	卌 |	6
6	卌 ||	7
7	卌	5
8	||||	4
9	|||	1

(i) 12 (II) 8

12. (i)

Sweet	*Tally Marks*	*Frequency*
Ladoo	卌 卌 ||	12
Burfi	|||	3
Jalebi	卌 |	6
Rasgulla	卌 ||||	9

(ii) Ladoo

23

DATA HANDLING – II
(Central Values)

23.1 CENTRAL VALUE

In our day-to-day life we frequently use words average height, average price, average weight, etc. What do we mean by the word average? An average is a number indicating the central value of a group of observation i.e. data. In other words, an average is the number representing the entire data. Let us consider the following statements to understand what the term average means.

(i) The average score of class VII students in a class test is 65 marks.

(ii) The average temperature of January month in Delhi is 18°C.

(iii) The average age of pupils in class VII is 13 years.

The first statement means that the maximum number of students have scored around 65 marks. Only a few of them might have scored very high marks and some of them might have obtained very low marks.

In the second statement, the average temperature of 18 degree celsius means that, in general, the temperature in the month of January remains around 18 degree celsius. Sometimes, in the month it may be less than 18 degree celsius and at other times in the month it may be more than 18°C.

When we say that the average age of pupils in class VII is 13 years, it does not mean that every student of class VII is 13 years old. There may be some students of 14 years age and some may be of 12 years age. But, the maximum number of students are around 13 years old.

It follows from the above discussion that an average is a number indicating the representative or central value of a group of observations or data. Maximum number of observations of a data are very close to the central value and only few observations are either less than or greater than the central value. Since an average represents the entire data, therefore, its value lies somewhere in between the largest and smallest values of the variable. For this reason an average is called a measure of central value.

23.2 MEASURES OF CENTRAL VALUE

As discussed above that the central value or representative value of a group of observations or data is the value representing the entire data. It gives us a number around maximum number of observations are clustered. The question now is, how to find the central value of a group of observations or data. Different forms of data need different methods to determine the central value representing it. Various methods of determining the central values are known as the measures of central value. The most commonly used measures of central value are:

(i) Arithmetic mean (ii) Median (iii) Mode

Let us now learn about these measures.

23.3 ARITHMETIC MEAN

The most common representative value or central value of a group of observations is the arithmetic mean or the mean. The mean of a group of observations is the value which is equally shared out among all the observations. Thus, the arithmetic mean of a group of observations is defined as

$$\text{Arithmetic mean} = \frac{\text{Sum of all observations}}{\text{Number of observations}}$$

Thus, if $x_1, x_2, x_3, \ldots, x_n$ are the values of n observations, then the arithmetic mean of these observations is given by

$$\text{Arithmetic mean} = \frac{x_1 + x_2 + \ldots + x_n}{n}$$

In order to have an idea of the spread of the observations in a group of observations, we compute its range which is defined as follows:

RANGE *The difference between the highest and the lowest observations of a group of observations is defined as its range.*

i.e., Range = Value of the largest observation – Value of the smallest observation.

Following examples will illustrate the computation of arithmetic mean of given observations.

ILLUSTRATIVE EXAMPLES

Example 1 A batsman scored the following number of runs in six innings:

36, 35, 50, 46, 60, 55

Calculate the mean runs scored in an inning.

Solution We have,

$$\text{Mean runs scored} = \frac{36+35+50+46+60+55}{6} = \frac{282}{6} = 47$$

Thus, the mean runs scored in an inning is 47.

Example 2 If the heights of 5 persons are 144 cm, 152 cm, 151 cm, 158 cm and 155 cm respectively. Find the mean height.

Solution $$\text{Mean height} = \frac{144+152+151+158+155}{5} = \frac{760}{5}\text{ cm} = 152\text{ cm}$$

Example 3 Find the arithmetic mean of first 6 natural numbers.

Solution First six natural numbers are 1, 2, 3, 4, 5, 6. Let $\overline{X}$ denote their arithmetic mean. Then,

$$\overline{X} = \frac{1+2+3+4+5+6}{6} = \frac{21}{6} = \frac{7}{2} = 3.5$$

Example 4 Find the mean of first five whole numbers.

Solution First five whole numbers are 0, 1, 2, 3, 4. Let $\overline{X}$ denote their arithmetic mean. Then,

$$\overline{X} = \frac{0+1+2+3+4}{5} = \frac{10}{5} = 2$$

Example 5 The ages in years of 10 teachers in a school are: 32, 41, 28, 54, 35, 26, 23, 33, 38, 40.

(i) What is the age of the oldest teacher and that of the youngest teacher?

(ii) What is the range of the ages of the teachers?

(iii) What is the mean age of these teachers?

Solution (i) In order to find the ages of oldest and youngest teachers, Let us arrange their ages in ascending order as follows:

23, 26, 28, 32, 33, 35, 38, 40, 41, 54

We observe that the age of the oldest teacher is 54 years and the age of the youngest teacher is 23 years.

(ii) We have,

Age of the oldest teacher = 54 years

Age of the youngest teacher = 23 years

∴ Range of the ages of teachers = (54 – 23) = 31 years

(iii) We have,

$$\text{Mean age of teachers} = \frac{\text{Sum of the ages of teachers}}{\text{Total number of teachers}}$$

$$\Rightarrow \text{Mean age of teachers} = \frac{23+26+28+32+33+35+38+40+41+54}{10}$$

$$\Rightarrow \text{Mean age of teachers} = \frac{350}{10} \text{ years} = 35 \text{ years}$$

Example 6 The heights of 10 girls were measured in cm and the results are as follows:

135, 150, 139, 128, 151, 132, 146, 149, 143, 141

(i) What is the height of the tallest girl?

(ii) What is the height of the shortest girl?

(iii) What is the range of the data?

(iv) What is the mean height of the girls?

(v) How many girls have heights more than the mean height?

Solution In order to find the heights of the tallest and the shortest girls, let us arrange the heights in ascending order as follows:

128, 132, 135, 139, 141, 143, 146, 149, 150, 151

(i) Clearly, the height of the tallest girl is 151 cm

(ii) The height of the shortest girl is 128 cm.

(iii) The range of the heights = (151 – 128) cm = 23 cm.

(iv) We have,

$$\text{Mean height} = \frac{\text{Sum of the heights}}{\text{Total number of girls}}$$

$$\Rightarrow \text{Mean height} = \frac{128+132+135+139+141+143+146+149+150+151}{10} \text{ cm}$$

$$\Rightarrow \text{Mean height} = \frac{1414}{10} \text{ cm} = 141.4 \text{ cm}$$

Hence, mean height of the girls is 141.4 cm.

(v) Clearly, 5 girls have heights more than the mean height.

Example 7 If the mean of 6, 8, 5, x and 4 is 7, find the value of x.

Solution The number of observations = 5

The mean of the given observations is $\frac{6+8+5+x+4}{5}$

But, the mean is given as 7.

$$\therefore \quad \frac{6+8+5+x+4}{5}=7$$

$$\Rightarrow \quad \frac{23+x}{5}=7$$

$$\Rightarrow \quad 23+x=7\times 5 \Rightarrow x=35-23=12.$$

Example 8 If the mean of 6, 4, 7, p and 10 is 8, find the value of p.

Solution Since 8 is the mean of 6, 4, 7, p, 10.

$$\therefore \quad 8=\frac{6+4+7+p+10}{5} \Rightarrow 40=27+p \Rightarrow p=13$$

Example 9 The mean of 10 numbers is 20. If 5 is subtracted from every number, what will be the new mean?

Solution Let $x_1, x_2, x_3, \ldots x_{10}$ be 10 numbers with their mean equal to 20. Then,

$$20=\frac{x_1+x_2+x_3+\ldots+x_{10}}{10}$$

$$\Rightarrow \quad x_1+x_2+x_3+\ldots+x_{10}=20\times 10$$

$$\Rightarrow \quad x_1+x_2+x_3+\ldots+x_{10}=200 \quad \ldots \text{(i)}$$

New numbers are $x_1-5, x_2-5, x_3-5, \ldots, x_{10}-5$. Let M be their arithmetic mean. Then,

$$M=\frac{(x_1-5)+(x_2-5)+(x_3-5)+\ldots+(x_{10}-5)}{10}$$

$$\Rightarrow \quad M=\frac{(x_1+x_2+x_3+\ldots+x_{10})-5\times 10}{10} \quad \text{[Using (i)]}$$

$$\Rightarrow \quad M=\frac{200-50}{10}=15$$

Example 10 The mean of 16 numbers is 8. If 2 is added to every number, what will be the new mean?

Solution Let $x_1, x_2, x_3, \ldots, x_{16}$ be 16 numbers with their mean equal to 8. Then,

$$8=\frac{x_1+x_2+x_3+\ldots+x_{16}}{16}$$

$$\Rightarrow \quad x_1+x_2+x_3+\ldots+x_{16}=8\times 16$$

$$\Rightarrow \quad x_1+x_2+x_3+\ldots+x_{16}=128 \quad \ldots \text{(i)}$$

New numbers are $x_1+2, x_2+2, x_3+2, \ldots, x_{16}+2$. Let M be arithmetic mean of new numbers. Then,

$$M = \frac{(x_1 + 2) + (x_2 + 2) + (x_3 + 2) + \ldots + (x_{16} + 2)}{16}$$

$$\Rightarrow \quad M = \frac{(x_1 + x_2 + \ldots x_{16}) + (2 \times 16)}{16}$$

$$\Rightarrow \quad M = \frac{128 + 32}{16} \qquad \text{[Using (i)]}$$

$$\Rightarrow \quad M = \frac{160}{16} = 10$$

Example 11 If the mean of five observations $x, x + 2, x + 4, x + 6, x + 8$, is 11. find the mean of first three observations.

Solution We have,

$$11 = \frac{x + (x + 2) + (x + 4) + (x + 6) + (x + 8)}{5}$$

$$\Rightarrow \quad 11 = \frac{5x + 20}{5}$$

$$\Rightarrow \quad 55 = 5x + 20$$

$$\Rightarrow \quad 5x = 35$$

$$\Rightarrow \quad x = 7$$

$\therefore$ Mean of first three observations

$$= \frac{x + (x + 2) + (x + 4)}{3} = \frac{3x + 6}{3} = x + 2 = 7 + 2 = 9 \qquad [\because x = 7]$$

Example 12 The mean of 40 observations was 160. It was detected on re-checking that the value of 165 was wrongly copied as 125 for computation of mean. Find the correct mean.

Solution We have,

n = Number of observations = 40, Mean = 160

$$\therefore \quad \text{Mean} = \frac{\text{Sum of the observations}}{\text{Number of observations}}$$

$$\Rightarrow \quad 160 \times 40 = \frac{\text{Sum of the observations}}{40}$$

$\Rightarrow$ 160×40 = Sum of the observations.

Thus, incorrect sum of observations = 160×40

Now,

Correct sum of the observations = Incorrect sum of the observations − Incorrect observation + correct observation

$\Rightarrow$ Correct sum of the observations = $160 \times 40 - 125 + 165$

$\Rightarrow$ Correct sum of the observations = $6400 + 40 = 6440$.

$$\therefore \quad \text{Correct mean} = \frac{\text{Correct sum of the observations}}{\text{Number of observations}} = \frac{6440}{40} = 161$$

Example 13 Following table shows the points of scores each player plays:

Player	Game 1	Game 2	Game 3	Game 4
A	14	16	10	10
B	0	8	6	4
C	8	11	Did not play	13

(i) Find the average scores of three players.

(ii) Who is the best performer?

Solution (i) We have,

$$\text{Average score of player } A = \frac{14+16+10+10}{4} = \frac{50}{4} = 12.5$$

$$\text{Average score of player } B = \frac{0+8+6+4}{4} = \frac{18}{4} = 4.5$$

$$\text{Average score of player } C = \frac{8+11+13}{3} = 10.66$$

(ii) Clearly, average score of player A is more. So, player A is the best performer.

EXERCISE 23.1

1. Ashish studies for 4 hours, 5 hours and 3 hours on three consecutive days. How many hours does he study daily on an average?
2. A cricketer scores the following runs in 8 innings: 58, 76, 40, 35, 48, 45, 0, 100.
   Find the mean score.
3. The marks (out of 100) obtained by a group of students in science test are 85, 76, 90, 84, 39, 48, 56, 95, 81 and 75. Find the
   (i) highest and the lowest marks obtained by the students.
   (ii) range of marks obtained.
   (iii) mean marks obtained by the group.
4. The enrolment of a school during six consecutive years was as follows:
   1555, 1670, 1750, 2019, 2540, 2820
   Find the mean enrollment of the school for this period.
5. The rainfall (in mm) in a city on 7 days of a certain week was recorded as follows:

Day	Mon	Tue	Wed	Thu	Fri	Sat	Sun
Rainfall (in mm)	0.0	12.2	2.1	0.0	20.5	5.3	1.0

   (i) Find the range of the rainfall from the above data.
   (ii) Find the mean rainfall for the week.
   (iii) On how many days was the rainfall less than the mean rainfall.
6. If the heights of 5 persons are 140 cm, 150 cm, 152 cm, 158 cm and 161 cm respectively, find the mean height.

7. Find the mean of 994, 996, 998, 1002 and 1000.
8. Find the mean of first five natural numbers.
9. Find the mean of all factors of 10.
10. Find the mean of first 10 even natural numbers.
11. Find the mean of $x, x+2, x+4, x+6, x+8$.
12. Find the mean of first five multiples of 3.
13. Following are the weights (in kg) of 10 new born babies in a hospital on a particular day:

    3.4, 3.6, 4.2, 4.5, 3.9, 4.1, 3.8, 4.5, 4.4, 3.6. Find the mean $\overline{X}$.
14. The percentage of marks obtained by students of a class in mathematics are:
    64, 36, 47, 23, 0, 19, 81, 93, 72, 35, 3, 1. Find their mean.
15. The numbers of children in 10 families of a locality are:
    2, 4, 3, 4, 2, 3, 5, 1, 1, 5. Find the mean number of children per family.
16. The mean of marks scored by 100 students was found to be 40. Later on it was discovered that a score of 53 was misread as 83. Find the correct mean.
17. The mean of five numbers is 27. If one number is excluded, their mean is 25. Find the excluded number.
18. The mean weight per student in a group of 7 students is 55 kg. The individual weights of 6 of them (in kg) are 52, 54, 55, 53, 56 and 54. Find the weight of the seventh student.
19. The mean weight of 8 numbers is 15 kg. If each number is multiplied by 2, what will be the new mean?
20. The mean of 5 numbers is 18. If one number is excluded, their mean is 16. Find the excluded number.
21. The mean of 200 items was 50. Later on, it was discovered that the two items were misread as 92 and 8 instead of 192 and 88. Find the correct mean.
22. The mean of 5 numbers is 27. If one more number is included, then the mean is 25. Find the included number.
23. The mean of 75 numbers is 35. If each number is multiplied by 4, find the new mean.

ANSWERS

1. 4 hrs 2. 50.25 runs 3. (i) 95, 39 marks (ii) 56 marks (iii) 72.9 marks
4. 2059 5. (i) 20.5 mm (ii) 5.87 mm (iii) 5 days
6. 152.2 cm 7. 998 8. 3 9. 4.5 10. 11 11. $x+4$
12. 9 13. 4 kg 14. 39.5 15. 3 16. 39.7 17. 35
18. 61 kg 19. 30 kg 20. 26 21. 50.9 22. 15 23. 140

23.4 ARITHMETIC MEAN OF GROUPED DATA

In the previous subsection, we have learnt about the method of finding the arithmetic mean of individual observations or ungrouped data. We have learnt in the previous chapter that in case of large number of observations, data can be presented in the form of a frequency table which exhibits the values taken by the variable and the corresponding frequencies. In such a form data is known as grouped data. Sometimes, we also call it discrete frequency distribution. If $x_1, x_2, x_3, \ldots, x_n$ are n values of a variate with corresponding frequencies $f_1, f_2, \ldots, f_n$ respectively. Then, the arithmetic mean of these values is defined as

$$\text{Mean} = \frac{f_1 \times x_1 + f_2 \times x_2 + \ldots + f_n \times x_n}{f_1 + f_2 + \ldots + f_n}$$

or, $$\text{Mean} = \frac{\Sigma f_i\, x_i}{\Sigma f_i},$$ where Σ (called sigma) is the Greek letter showing summation.

In order to compute the arithmetic mean of grouped data, we may use the following steps:

STEP I *Prepare frequency table in such a way that its first column consists of the values of the variate and the second column the corresponding frequencies.*

STEP II *Multiply the frequency of each row with the corresponding values of variate to obtain third column containing $f_i\, x_i$.*

STEP III *Find the sum of all entries in III column to obtain $\Sigma f_i\, x_i$.*

STEP IV *Find the sum of all the frequencies in II column to obtain Σf_i or, N*

STEP V *Use the formula:* $\overline{X} = \dfrac{\Sigma f_i\, x_i}{N}$.

Following examples will illustrate the above algorithm.

ILLUSTRATIVE EXAMPLES

Example 1 Organise the following grades in a class assessment in a tabular form:
4, 6, 7, 5, 3, 5, 4, 5, 8, 6, 2, 5, 1, 9, 6, 7, 8, 4, 6, 7
Find the arithmetic mean of grades. Also, find the highest grade, the lowest grade and the range of the data.

Solution In the tabular form, the above data can be represented as follows:

Grade	*Tally Bars*	*Frequency* (f_i)
1	|	1
2	|	1
3	|	1
4	|||	3
5	||||	4
6	||||	4
7	|||	3
8	||	2
9	|	1

In order to compute the arithmetic mean of grades i.e. average grade, we prepare the following table.

Computation of Arithmetic mean

Grade (x_i)	*Frequency* (f_i)	$f_i \times x_i$
1	1	$1 \times 1 = 1$
2	1	$1 \times 2 = 2$
3	1	$1 \times 3 = 3$
4	3	$3 \times 4 = 12$
5	4	$4 \times 5 = 20$
6	4	$4 \times 6 = 24$
7	3	$3 \times 7 = 21$
8	2	$2 \times 8 = 16$
9	1	$1 \times 9 = 9$
	$\Sigma f_i = 20$	$\Sigma f_i\, x_i = 108$

$$\therefore \quad \text{Mean grade} = \frac{\Sigma f_i\, x_i}{\Sigma f_i} = \frac{108}{20} = 5.4$$

Hence, the mean grade is 5.4.

It is evident from the frequency table that the highest and lowest grades are 9 and 1 respectively.

$\therefore$ Range of the data = $9 - 1 = 8$

Example 2 Given below are the ages of 25 students of a class in a school. Prepare a frequency table and hence find the mean age.

15, 16, 16, 14, 17, 17, 16, 15, 15, 15, 16, 16, 17, 17, 16, 16, 17, 17, 16, 16, 16, 15, 16, 16, 17

Solution In the tabular form, the given data can be presented as follows:

Age (x_i)	*Tally Bars*	*Frequency* (f_i)
14	|	1
15	~~||||~~	5
16	~~||||~~ ~~||||~~ ||	12
17	~~||||~~ ||	7

In order to compute the average age of students in the class, we prepare following table:

Computation of Arithmetic mean

Age (x_i)	*Frequency* (f_i)	$f_i \times x_i$
14	1	$1 \times 14 = 14$
15	5	$5 \times 15 = 75$
16	12	$12 \times 16 = 192$
17	7	$7 \times 17 = 119$
Total	$\Sigma f_i = 25$	$\Sigma f_i\, x_i = 400$

We have, $\Sigma f_i = 25$ and $\Sigma f_i\ x_i = 400$

$$\therefore \quad \text{Mean age} = \frac{\Sigma f_i\ x_i}{\Sigma f_i} = \frac{400}{25} = 16 \text{ years.}$$

Example 3 Find the mean of the following distribution:

x:	4	6	9	10	15
f:	5	10	10	7	8

Solution

Calculation of Arithmetic Mean

x_i	f_i	$f_i\ x_i$
4	5	20
6	10	60
9	10	90
10	7	70
15	8	120
	$N = \Sigma f_i = 40$	$\Sigma f_i\ x_i = 360$

$$\therefore \quad \text{Mean} = \overline{X} = \frac{\Sigma f_i\ x_i}{\Sigma f_i} = \frac{360}{40} = 9.$$

Example 4 Following table shows the weights of 12 students:

Weight (in kgs)	67	70	72	73	75
Number of Students:	4	3	2	2	1

Find the mean weight.

Solution

Calculation of Arithmetic Mean

Weight (in kgs) x_i	*Frequency* f_i	$f_i\ x_i$
67	4	268
70	3	210
72	2	144
73	2	146
75	1	75
	$N = \Sigma f_i = 12$	$\Sigma f_i\ x_i = 843$

$$\therefore \quad \text{Mean} = \overline{X} = \frac{\Sigma f_i\ x_i}{N} = \frac{843}{12} = 70.25 \text{ kg}.$$

Example 5 Find the mean of the following distribution:

x:	10	30	50	70	89
f:	7	8	10	15	10

Solution

Calculation of Mean

x_i	f_i	$f_i\ x_i$
10	7	70
30	8	240
50	10	500
70	15	1050
89	10	890
	$\Sigma f_i = N = 50$	$\Sigma f_i x_i = 2750$

$$\therefore \quad \text{Mean} = \frac{\Sigma f_i x_i}{N} = \frac{2750}{50} = 55.$$

Example 6 If the mean of the following distribution is 6, find the value of p.

x:	2	4	6	10	$p + 5$
f:	3	2	3	1	2

Solution

Calculation of Mean

x_i	f_i	$f_i\ x_i$
2	3	6
4	2	8
6	3	18
10	1	10
$p + 5$	2	$2p + 10$
	$N = \Sigma f_i = 11$	$\Sigma f_i\ x_i = 2p + 52$

We have,

$N = \Sigma f_i = 11, \Sigma f_i\ x_i = 2p + 52$

$$\therefore \quad \text{Mean} = \frac{\Sigma f_i\ x_i}{N}$$

$$\Rightarrow \quad 6 = \frac{2p + 52}{11} \Rightarrow 66 = 2p + 52 \Rightarrow 2p = 14 \Rightarrow p = 7$$

Example 7 Find the value of p, if the mean of the following distribution is 7.5.

x:	3	5	7	9	11	13
f:	6	8	15	p	8	4

Solution

Calculation of Mean

x_i	f_i	$f_i\, x_i$
3	6	18
5	8	40
7	15	105
9	p	$9p$
11	8	88
13	4	52
	$N = \Sigma f_i = 41 + p$	$\Sigma f_i\, x_i = 303 + 9p$

We have,

$$\Sigma f_i = 41 + p, \Sigma f_i\, x_i = 303 + 9p.$$

$$\therefore \quad \text{Mean} = \frac{\Sigma f_i\, x_i}{\Sigma f_i}$$

$$\Rightarrow \quad 7.5 = \frac{303 + 9p}{41 + p}$$

$$\Rightarrow \quad 7.5 \times (41 + p) = 303 + 9p$$

$$\Rightarrow \quad 307.5 + 7.5p = 303 + 9p$$

$$\Rightarrow \quad 9p - 7.5p = 307.5 - 303$$

$$\Rightarrow \quad 1.5p = 4.5 \Rightarrow p = \frac{4.5}{1.5} = 3$$

EXERCISE 23.2

1. A die was thrown 20 times and the following scores were recorded:
   5, 2, 1, 3, 4, 4, 5, 6, 2, 2, 4, 5, 5, 6, 2, 2, 4, 5, 5, 1
   Prepare the frequency table of the scores on the upper face of the die and find the mean score.
2. The daily wages (in Rs) of 15 workers in a factory are given below:
   200, 180, 150, 150, 130, 180, 180, 200, 150, 130, 180, 180, 200, 150, 180
   Prepare the frequency table and find the mean wage.
3. The following table shows the weights (in kg) of 15 workers in a factory:

Weight (in kg) :	60	63	66	72	75
Numbers of workers :	4	5	3	1	2

   Calculate the mean weight.

4. The ages (in years) of 50 students of a class in a school are given below:

Age (in years) :	14	15	16	17	18
Numbers of students:	15	14	10	8	3

   Find the mean age.

5. Calculate the mean for the following distribution:

x :	5	6	7	8	9
f :	4	8	14	11	3

6. Find the mean of the following data:

x :	19	21	23	25	27	29	31
f :	13	15	16	18	16	15	13

7. The mean of the following data is 20.6. Find the value of p.

x :	10	15	p	25	35
f :	3	10	25	7	5

8. If the mean of the following data is 15, find p.

x :	5	10	15	20	25
f :	6	p	6	10	5

9. Find the value of p for the following distribution whose mean is 16.6

x :	8	12	15	p	20	25	30
f :	12	16	20	24	16	8	4

10. Find the missing value of p for the following distribution whose mean is 12.58

x :	5	8	10	12	p	20	25
f :	2	5	8	22	7	4	2

11. Find the missing frequency (p) for the following distribution whose mean is 7.68

x :	3	5	7	9	11	13
f :	6	8	15	p	8	4

12. Find the value of p, if the mean of the following distribution is 20

x :	15	17	19	$20 + p$	23
f :	2	3	4	$5p$	6

ANSWERS

1.

Score (x_i) :	1	2	3	4	5	6
Frequency (f_i) :	2	5	1	4	6	2

Mean score = 3.65

2.

Wages (x_i) :	130	150	180	200
No. of workers (f_i) :	2	4	6	3

Mean wage = Rs 169.33

3. 65 kg 4. 15.4 years 5. 7.025 6. 25 7. $p = 20$ 8. 8

9. 18 10. 15 11. 9 12. 1

23.5 MEDIAN

Mean is not the only tool or method to determine the representative value or central value of a group of observations. In different situations, we use different methods or tools to find the central value of a group of observations. Also, for different requirements from a group of observations (data) we use different measures of central value. Let us consider a group of 17 students of a school with the following heights (in cms):

101, 106, 116, 110, 109, 123, 118, 127, 120, 117, 102, 122, 115, 112, 121, 125, 111

The mean height of this group of students is

$$\frac{101+106+116+110+109+123+118+127+120+117+102+122+115+112+121+125+111}{17}$$

$$= \frac{1955}{17} = 115.$$

Clearly, there are 7 students of heights less than the mean height and 9 students are of heights greater than the mean height.

If the games teacher of the school wants to divide this group of 17 students into two groups on the basis of mean height so that one group has students of height less than the mean height and the other group has students of height more than the mean height, then the groups would be of unequal size. This means that the mean is unable to divide the group of students into two equal sub-groups. So, there must be some other representative value (or central value) to divide a group of observations into two equal groups. Such a representative value or central value is known as the median of the data. Median is the value which lies in the middle of the data with half of the observations above it and the other half below it.

Let us again look at the given heights of students and arrange them in ascending order as follows:

101, 102, 106, 109, 110, 111, 112, 115, 116, 117, 118, 120, 121, 122, 123, 125, 127

We find that the middle value in this data is 116. This value is the median. Thus, we define the median as follows:

MEDIAN *Median of a group of observations is the value of the variable which divides the group into two equal parts.*

In other words, median is the value which exceeds and is exceeded by the same number of observations i.e., it is the value such that the number of observations above it is equal to the number of observations below it.

In case of individual observations i.e., ungrouped data, we may use the following steps to find the median.

STEP I *Arrange the observations in ascending or descending order of magnitude.*

STEP II *Determine the total number of observations, say, n.*

STEP III *If n is odd, then use the following formula:*

$$\text{Median} = \text{Value of } \left(\frac{n+1}{2}\right)^{\text{th}} \text{ observation.}$$

If n is even, then use the following formula:

$$\text{Median} = \frac{\text{Value of } \left(\frac{n}{2}\right)^{\text{th}} \text{ observation} + \text{Value of } \left(\frac{n}{2}+1\right)^{\text{th}} \text{ observation}}{2}$$

Following examples will illustrate the above procedure.

ILLUSTRATIVE EXAMPLES

Example 1 Find the median of the data: 24, 36, 46, 17, 18, 25, 35

Solution Arranging the data in ascending order, we get

17, 18, 24, 25, 35, 36, 46

Here, $n = 7$, which is odd.

$$\therefore \quad \text{Median} = \text{Value of } \left(\frac{7+1}{2}\right)^{\text{th}} \text{ observation} = \text{Value of } 4^{\text{th}} \text{ observation} = 25$$

Example 2 The runs scored in a cricket match by 11 players are as follows:

6, 15, 120, 50, 100, 80, 10, 15, 8, 10, 10

Find the median score.

Solution Arranging runs scored in ascending order, we get

6, 8, 10, 10, 10, 15, 15, 50, 80, 100, 120

Here, $n = 11$, which is odd.

$$\therefore \quad \text{Median} = \text{Value of } \left(\frac{11+1}{2}\right)^{\text{th}} \text{ i.e., } 6^{\text{th}} \text{ observation} = 15$$

Example 3 Find the median of the data: 25, 34, 31, 23, 22, 26, 35, 28, 20, 32

Solution Arranging the data in ascending order, we get

20, 22, 23, 25, 26, 28, 31, 32, 34, 35

Here, the number of observation $n = 10$ (even).

$$\Rightarrow \quad \text{Median} = \frac{\text{Value of } \left(\frac{10}{2}\right)^{\text{th}} \text{ observation} + \text{Value of } \left(\frac{10}{2}+1\right)^{\text{th}} \text{ observation}}{2}$$

$$\Rightarrow \quad \text{Median} = \frac{\text{Value of } 5^{\text{th}} \text{ observation} + \text{Value of } 6^{\text{th}} \text{ observation}}{2}$$

$$\Rightarrow \quad \text{Median} = \frac{26+28}{2} = 27$$

Hence, median of the given data is 27.

Example 4 Find the median of the values: 37, 31, 42, 43, 46, 25, 39, 45, 32

Solution Arranging the data in ascending order, we have

25, 31, 32, 37, 39, 42, 43, 45, 46

Here, the number of observations $n = 9$ (odd)

$$\therefore \quad \text{Median} = \text{Value of } \left(\frac{9+1}{2}\right)^{\text{th}} \text{ observation}$$

$$\Rightarrow \quad \text{Median} = \text{Value of } 5^{\text{th}} \text{ observation} = 39$$

Example 5 The median of the observations 11, 12, 14, 18, $x + 2$, $x + 4$, 30, 32, 35, 41 arranged in ascending order is 24. Find the value of x.

Solution Here, the number of observations n is 10. Since n is even.

$$\therefore \quad \text{Median} = \frac{\left(\frac{n}{2}\right)^{\text{th}} \text{ observation} + \left(\frac{n}{2}+1\right)^{\text{th}} \text{ observation}}{2}$$

$$\Rightarrow \quad 24 = \frac{5^{\text{th}} \text{ observation} + 6^{\text{th}} \text{ observation}}{2}$$

$$\Rightarrow \quad 24 = \frac{(x+2)+(x+4)}{2}$$

$$\Rightarrow \quad 24 = \frac{2x+6}{2} \Rightarrow 24 = x + 3 \Rightarrow x = 21$$

Hence, $x = 21$.

Example 6 Find the median of the data: 19, 25, 59, 48, 35, 31, 30, 32, 51. If 25 is replaced by 52, what will be the new median.

Solution Arranging the given data in ascending order, we have

19, 25, 30, 31, 32, 35, 48, 51, 59

Here, the number of observations $n = 9$ (odd)

Since the number of observations is odd. Therefore,

$$\text{Median} = \text{Value of } \left(\frac{9+1}{2}\right)^{\text{th}} \text{ observation} = \text{Value of } 5^{\text{th}} \text{ observation} = 32.$$

Hence, median = 32

If 25 is replaced by 52, then the new observations arranged in ascending order are:

19, 30, 31, 32, 35, 48, 51, 52, 59

$\therefore$ New median = Value of 5th observation = 35.

EXERCISE 23.3

Find the median of the following data (1-8)

1. 83, 37, 70, 29, 45, 63, 41, 70, 34, 54
2. 133, 73, 89, 108, 94, 104, 94, 85, 100, 120
3. 31, 38, 27, 28, 36, 25, 35, 40
4. 15, 6, 16, 8, 22, 21, 9, 18, 25
5. 41, 43, 127, 99, 71, 92, 71, 58, 57
6. 25, 34, 31, 23, 22, 26, 35, 29, 20, 32
7. 12, 17, 3, 14, 5, 8, 7, 15
8. 92, 35, 67, 85, 72, 81, 56, 51, 42, 69
9. Numbers 50, 42, 35, $2x + 10$, $2x - 8$, 12, 11, 8, 6 are written in descending order and their median is 25, find x.
10. Find the median of the following observations : 46, 64, 87, 41, 58, 77, 35, 90, 55, 92, 33. If 92 is replaced by 99 and 41 by 43 in the above data, find the new median?
11. Find the median of the following data : 41, 43, 127, 99, 61, 92, 71, 58, 57, If 58 is replaced by 85, what will be the new median?
12. The weights (in kg) of 15 students are : 31, 35, 27, 29, 32, 43, 37, 41, 34, 28, 36, 44, 45, 42, 30. Find the median. If the weight 44 kg is replaced by 46 kg and 27 kg by 25 kg, find the new median.
13. The following observations have been arranged in ascending order. If the median of the data is 63, find the value of x:

    29, 32, 48, 50, x, $x + 2$, 72, 78, 84, 95

ANSWERS

1. 49.5 2. 97 3. 33 4. 16 5. 71 6. 27.5
7. 10 8. 68 9. 16.5 10. 58, 58 11. 61,71 12. 35 kg, 35 kg
13. 62

23.6 MODE

In the previous two sections, we have seen that in some situations arithmetic mean is an appropriate measure of central value where as in some other situations, median is the appropriate measure of central value. Let us now consider the following table showing the sizes of shoes and the number of pairs of shoes sold in a week by a shopkeeper.

Size of shoes:	5	6	7	8	9	10	11
No. of pairs of shoes sold:	10	20	38	42	10	4	2

Suppose the shop-keeper finds the arithmetic mean of the number of pairs of shoes sold in a week. He finds that the mean number of shoes sold in a week is

$$\frac{10+20+38+42+10+4+2}{7} = \frac{126}{7} = 18$$

On the basis of the mean if the shopkeeper places the order for 18 pairs of shoes of each size, then he will not be able to cater the needs of the customers demanding 6, 7, 8 sizes of shoes.

If the shopkeeper decides to find the median size of the number of pairs of shoes sold, then median size is 7. On the basis of this if he procures 38 pairs of shoes of each size, then he will not be able to cater the needs of the customers of size 8.

If follows from the above discussion that the mean and median are not appropriate measures of central value (central tendency) in such situations. We, therefore, think of an alternative measure of central tendency.

If the shopkeeper looks at the shoe size 8 that is sold most and decides to procure 42 pairs of shoes of each size, then he is able to cater the needs of customers of all sizes. We find that the highest occuring event in the sale data is the sale of size 8. This representative value of the data is called the mode of the data. Thus, we define the mode of a data as follows:

MODE *Mode of a set of observations is the value of the observation that occurs most frequently.*

The mean, median and mode of a group of observations (data) are connected by the following empirical relation:

Mode = 3 Median – 2 Mean.

In order to find the mode of a group of observations (or ungrouped data), we may follow the following steps:

STEP I *Obtain the set of obserations i.e., ungrouped data.*

STEP II *Count the number of times the various values repeat themselves. In other words, prepare the frequency table.*

STEP III *Find the value which occurs the maximum number of times i.e., obtain the value which has the maximum frequency.*

STEP IV *The value obtained in step III is the mode.*

Following examples will illustrate the above procedure.

ILLUSTRATIVE EXAMPLES

Example 1 Find the mode of the following data:

1, 1, 2, 4, 3, 2, 1, 2, 2, 4

Solution Arranging the number with the same values together, we get

1, 1, 1, 2, 2, 2, 2, 3, 4, 4.

Clearly, 2 occurs maximum number of times.

Hence, mode of the given data is 2.

Aliter Arranging the data in the form of a frequency table, we have

Value	*Tally bars*	*Frequency*
1					3
2						4
3			1
4				2

Clearly the value 2 occurs maximum number of times i.e. 4.

Hence, the mode is 2.

Example 2 Following are the margins of victory in the football matches of a league.

1, 3, 2, 5, 1, 4, 6, 2, 5, 2, 2, 2, 4, 1, 2, 3, 1, 1, 2, 3, 2, 6, 4, 3, 2, 1, 1, 4, 2, 1, 5, 3, 3, 2, 3, 2, 4, 2, 1, 2. Find the mode.

Solution Arranging the margins of victory in the tabular form, we have

Margins of victory	*Tally bars*	*Number of matches (Frequency)*
1	~~||||~~ ||||	9
2	~~||||~~ ~~||||~~ ||||	14
3	~~||||~~ ||	7
4	~~||||~~	5
5					3
6				2
	Total	40

We find that the value 2 has the maximum frequency. So, 2 is the mode which means that most of the matches have been won with a victory margin of 2 goals.

Example 3 Find the mode of the data: 2, 2, 3, 3, 2, 5, 4, 5, 5, 8, 6, 6

Solution Arranging the numbers with the same values together we get

2, 2, 2, 3, 3, 4, 5, 5, 5, 6, 6, 8

Here, 2 and 5 both occur three times. Therefore, they are both modes of the data. In such a case, we say that the data is bi-modal.

Example 4 The weights (in kg) of 15 students of a class are:

38, 42, 35, 37, 45, 50, 32, 43, 43, 40, 36, 38, 43, 38, 47

(i) Find the mode and median of this data.

(ii) Is there more than one mode?

Solution (i) Arranging the weights in the ascending order such that the same weights are put together, we get

32, 35, 36, 37, 38, 38, 38, 40, 42, 43, 43, 43, 45, 47, 50

Here, $n = 15$.

$\therefore$ Median = Value of $\left(\frac{15+1}{2}\right)^{\text{th}}$ observation = Value of 8th observation = 40

Here, 38 and 43 both occur three times. Therefore, 38 kg and 43 kg are two modes.

Example 5 Find the mode and median of the following data:

12, 14, 12, 16, 15, 13, 14, 18, 19, 12, 14, 15, 16, 15, 16, 16, 15, 17, 13, 16, 16, 15, 15, 13, 15, 17, 15, 14, 15, 13, 15, 14

Also, find the mean by using the empirical relation.

Solution Arranging the data in tabular form, we have

Value	*Tally bars*	*Frequency*
12	|||	3
13	||||	4
14	~~||||~~	5
15	~~||||~~ ~~||||~~	10
16	~~||||~~ |	6
17	||	2
18	|	1
19	|	1
	Total	32

Looking at the table, we find that the value 15 occurs most frequently. So, 15 is the mode.

We find that there are 32 observations i.e. $n = 32$.

$$\therefore \quad \text{Median} = \frac{\text{Value of } \left(\frac{n}{2}\right)^{\text{th}} \text{ observation} + \text{Value of } \left(\frac{n}{2}+1\right)^{\text{th}} \text{ observation}}{2}$$

$$\Rightarrow \quad \text{Median} = \frac{\text{Value of } 16^{\text{th}} \text{ observation} + \text{Value of } 17^{\text{th}} \text{ observation}}{2}$$

$\Rightarrow \quad \text{Median} = \frac{15+15}{2} = 15$ $\left[\because \text{Value of } 12^{th} \text{ observation is 14 and each of the observations from } 13^{th} \text{ to } 22^{nd} \text{ is of value 15}\right]$

Hence, Median = 15

Now, Mode = 3 Median – 2 Mean

$\Rightarrow \quad 15 = 3 \times 15 - 2 \text{ Mean}$

$\Rightarrow \quad 2 \text{ Mean} = 45 - 15$

$\Rightarrow \quad \text{Mean} = \frac{30}{2} = 15$

Hence, Mean = Median = Mode = 15.

EXERCISE 23.4

1. Find the mode and median of the data: 13, 16, 12, 14, 19, 12, 14, 13, 14
   By using the empirical relation also find the mean.
2. Find the median and mode of the data: 35, 32, 35, 42, 38, 32, 34
3. Find the mode of the data: 6, 5, 3, 0, 3, 4, 3, 2, 4, 6, 2, 4
4. The runs scored in a cricket match by 11 players are as follows:
   6, 15, 120, 50, 100, 80, 10, 15, 8, 10, 10
   Find the mean, mode and median of this data.
5. Find the mode of the following data:
   12, 14, 16, 12, 14, 14, 16, 14, 10, 14, 18, 14
6. Heights of 25 children (in cm) in a school are as given below:
   168, 165, 163, 160, 163, 161, 162, 164, 163, 162, 164, 163, 160, 163, 163, 165, 163, 162, 163, 164, 163, 160, 165, 163, 162
   What is the mode of heights?
   Also, find the mean and median.
7. The scores in mathematics test (out of 25) of 15 students are as follows:
   19, 25, 23, 20, 9, 20, 15, 10, 5, 16, 25, 20, 24, 12, 20
   Find the mode and median of this data. Are they same?
8. Calculate the mean and median for the following data:

Marks :	10	11	12	13	14	16	19	20
Number of students :	3	5	4	5	2	3	2	1

   Using empirical formula, find its mode.
9. The following table shows the weights of 12 persons.

Weight (in kg) :	48	50	52	54	58
Number of persons :	4	3	2	2	1

   Find the median and mean weights. Using empirical relation, calculate its mode.

ANSWERS

1. Mode = 14, Median = 14, Mean = 14
2. Median = 35, 32 and 35 are two modes.
3. 2, 3 and 4 are three modes.
4. Mode = 10, Median = 15, Mean = 17.5
5. Mode = 14
6. Mode = 163 cm = Mean = Median
7. Mode = 20, Median = 20, Yes
8. Mean = 13.28, Mode = 12.44, Median = 13.
9. Mean = 51 kg Mode = 48 kg Median = 50 kg.

OBJECTIVE TYPE QUESTIONS

Mark the correct alternative in each of the following:

1. If the mean of observations 7, 8, 9, 11 and x is 10, then $x=$
   (a) 10 (b) 15 (c) 12 (d) 13
2. If the mean of observations 20, 42, 35, 45, x is 37, then $x=$
   (a) 43 (b) 42 (c) 44 (d) 45
3. The mean of first five natural numbers is
   (a) 5 (b) 4 (c) 3 (d) 6
4. The mean of first five prime numbers is
   (a) 5.6 (b) 5.5 (c) 5.4 (d) 5.2
5. The mean of first seven even natural numbers is
   (a) 7 (b) 8 (c) 9 (d) 6
6. The mean of first six multiples of 5 is
   (a) 3.5 (b) 18.5 (c) 17.5 (d) 30
7. The mean of 5 numbers is 4. If 1 is added to each number, then the new mean is
   (a) 4 (b) 5 (c) 3 (d) 5.5
8. If the sum of 10 observations is 95, then their mean is
   (a) 9.5 (b) 10 (c) 950 (d) 95
9. If the mean of n observations is 12 and the sum of the observations is 132, then the value of n is
   (a) 9 (b) 10 (c) 11 (d) 12
10. The median of the data 9, 12, 11, 10, 8, 9, 11 is
    (a) 10 (b) 11 (c) 9 (d) None of these
11. The median of the data 5, 7, 9, 10, 11 is
    (a) 7 (b) 9 (c) 11 (d) 10
12. The mean of a data is 15 and the sum of the observations is 195. The number of observations is
    (a) 13 (b) 19 (c) 16 (d) 17
13. The median of 11 observations is 10. The number of possible observations in the data which are less than 10 is
    (a) 5 (b) 6 (c) 3 (d) 10
14. If the mode of 22, 21, 23, 24, 21, 20, 23, 26, x and 26 is 23, then $x=$
    (a) 20 (b) 21 (c) 23 (d) 24
15. If the mean of 5, 7, x, 10, 5 and 7 is 7, then $x=$
    (a) 6 (b) 7 (c) 8 (d) 9
16. The mean of p, q and r is same as the mean of q, $2r$ and s. Then which of the following is correct?
    (a) $p=q=r$ (b) $q=r=s$ (c) $q=r$ (d) $p=r+s$
17. The mean of 10, 15, 19, 30, 43, 69 and x is x. Then the median is
    (a) 19 (b) 43 (c) 30 (d) None of these
18. If the mean of 9, 10, 15, x, 6, 8 and 12 is 11. The median of the observations is
    (a) 4 (b) 10 (c) 13 (d) 5
19. The mode of the unimodular data 7, 8, 9, 8, 9, 10, 9, 10, 11, 10, 11, 12 and x is 10. The value of x is
    (a) 10 (b) 9 (c) 8 (d) 11
20. The mean weight of 21 students is 21 kg. If a student weighing 21 kg is removed from the group, then the mean of the remaining students is
    (a) 20 kg (b) 21 kg (c) 19 kg (d) 18 kg

21. There are 7 observations in the data and their mean is 11. If each observation is multiplied by 2, then the mean of new observations is
(a) 11 (b) 13 (c) 22 (d) 5.5

22. The mean of 10 observations is 15. If one observation 15 is added, then the new mean is
(a) 16 (b) 11 (c) 10 (d) 15

23. If the median of 10, 12, x, 6, 18 is 10, then which of the following is correct.
(a) $6 \leq x \leq 10$ (b) $x < 6$ (c) $x > 18$ (d) Either (a) or (b)

24. The mode of the data 9, x, 6, 3, 4, 9, 8, 6, 4, 6 is 6. Which of the following cannot be the value of x?
(a) 8 (b) 7 (c) 6 (d) 9

25. Which of the following is correct?
(a) Mode = 2 Median – 3 Mean (b) Mode = 3 Median – Mean
(c) Mode – Mean = 3 (Median – Mean) (d) Mode – Median = Median – Mean

ANSWSERS

1. (b)	2. (a)	3. (c)	4. (a)	5. (b)	6. (c)	7. (b)
8. (a)	9. (c)	10. (a)	11. (b)	12. (a)	13. (a)	14. (c)
15. (c)	16. (d)	17. (c)	18. (b)	19. (a)	20. (b)	21. (c)
22. (d)	23. (d)	24. (d)	25. (c)			

24

DATA HANDLING – III
(Construction of bar graphs)

24.1 INTRODUCTION

In class VI, we have learnt how to read bar graphs. We have learnt about reading and interpretation of bar graphs. In this chapter, we shall learn about the construction of bar graphs.

24.2 CONSTRUCTION OF BAR GRAPHS

BAR GRAPH *A bar graph is a pictorial representation of the numerical data by a number of bars (rectangles) of uniform width erected horizontally or vertically with equal spacing between them.*

In a bar graph each rectangle or bar represents only one value of the numerical data and so there are as many bars as the number of values of numerical data. The height or length of a bar indicates, on a suitable scale, the corresponding value of the numerical data. If the bars are drawn vertically on the horizontal line (i.e. x-axis), then the scale of heights of the bars or rectangles is shown along the vertical line (i.e. y-axis). If the bars are drawn horizontally on the vertical line, then the scale of heights of bars is shown along the horizontal line.

In order to construct a bar graph for the given data, we follow the following steps:

STEP I *Take a graph paper and draw two lines perpendicular to each other and call them horizontal and vertical axes.*

STEP II *Along the horizontal axis mark the information given in the data like days, weeks, months, years, places etc. at uniform gaps.*

STEP III *Choose a suitable scale to determine the heights of the rectangles or bars and then mark the heights on the vertical axes.*

STEP IV *Draw bars or rectangles of equal width and of heights marked in Step III on the horizontal axis with equal spacing between them.*

The figure so obtained will be the bar graph representing the given numerical data.

The following examples will illustrate the construction of bar graphs of given data.

ILLUSTRATIVE EXAMPLES

Example 1 The following data gives the number of students of Delhi state who went abroad for study during some years:

Year	1995	1996	1997	1998	1999	2000
Number of students	1400	1600	1250	1000	2000	2200

Represent the above data with the help of a bar graph.

Solution In order to construct a bar graph representing the above data, we follow the following steps:

STEP I Take a graph paper and draw two mutually perpendicular lines OX and OY as shown in Fig. 1. Call OX as the horizontal axis and OY as the vertical axis.

STEP II Along OX, mark years and along OY, mark number of students.

STEP III Along OX, choose the uniform (equal) width of the bars and the uniform gap between them, according to the space available for the graph.

STEP IV Choose a suitable scale to determine the heights of the bars, according to the availability of space. Here, we choose 1 big division to represent 200 students.

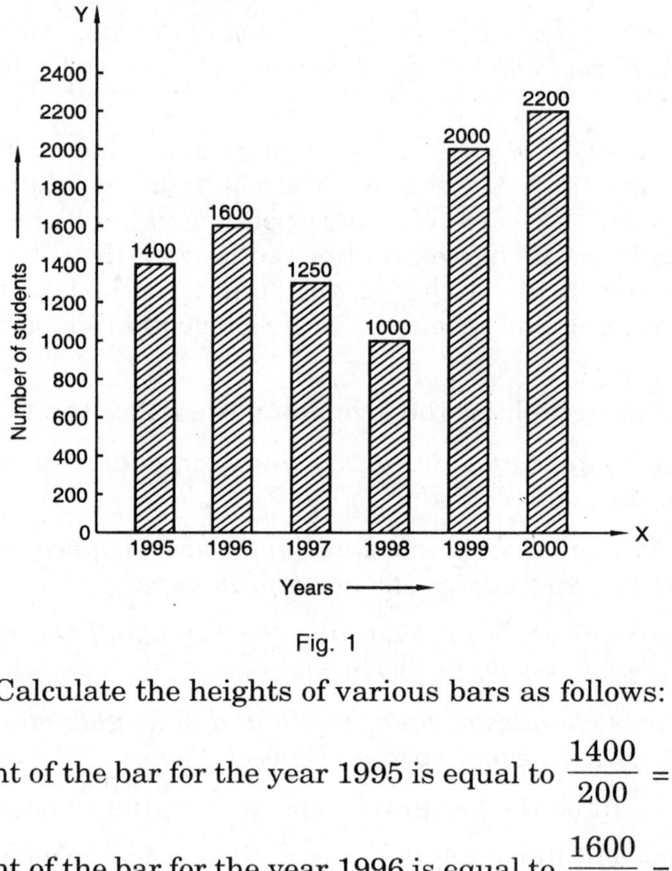

Fig. 1

STEP V Calculate the heights of various bars as follows:

The height of the bar for the year 1995 is equal to $\frac{1400}{200} = 7$ big divisions;

The height of the bar for the year 1996 is equal to $\frac{1600}{200} = 8$ big divisions

The height of the bar for the year 1997 is equal to $\frac{1250}{200} = 6\frac{1}{4}$ big divisions = 6 big divisions and 2.5 small divisions

The height of the bar for the year 1998 is equal to = $\frac{1000}{200} = 5$ big divisions

The height of the bar for the year 1999 is equal to = $\frac{2000}{200} = 10$ big divisions

The height of the bar for the year 2000 is equal to = $\frac{2200}{200}$ = 11 big divisions.

STEP VI We draw the bars as shown in Fig. 1 and on the top of each bar we write the number of students represented by it.

Example 2 In a school, there are five sections of class VII. The number of students in each section is given below. Construct a bar graph representing this data:

Section	A	B	C	D	E
Number of students	40	48	52	45	30

Solution We go through the following steps to construct the bar graph:

STEP I Take a graph paper and draw two lines *OX* and *OY* perpendicular to each other. Call the horizontal line as *OX* and the vertical line as *OY*.

STEP II Along the horizontal axis *OX*, mark "sections of Class VII" and along the vertical axis *OY* mark "No. of students".

STEP III Along the horizontal axis *OX*, choose the uniform (equal) width of the bars and the uniform gap between them.

STEP IV Choose a suitable scale to determine the heights of the bars, according to the space available for the graph. Here, we choose 1 small division to represent 1 student.

STEP V Calculate the heights of the various bars as follows:

Height of the bar for Section A = 40×1

= 40 small divisions = 4 big division

Height of the bar for Section B = 48×1

= 48 small divisions

= 4 big divisions and 8 small divisions

Height of the bar for Section C = 52×1

= 52 small divisions

= 5 big divisions and 2 small divisions.

Height of the bar for SectionD= 45 small divisions

= 4 big divisions and 5 small divisions.

Height of the bar for Section E= 30 small divisions

= 3 big divisions.

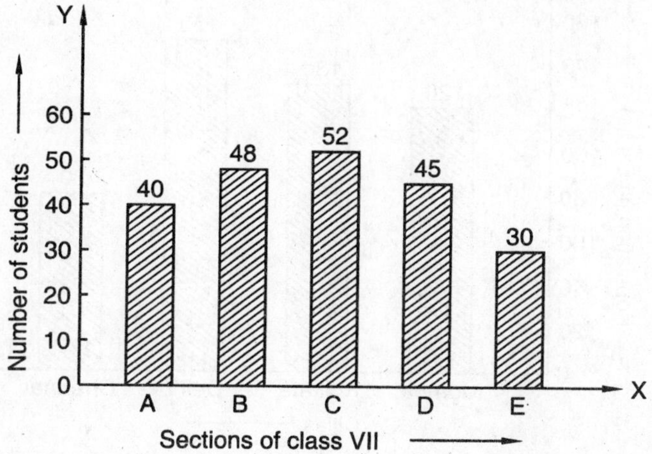

Fig. 2

STEP VI We draw the bars as shown in Fig 2 and on the top of each bar, we write the number of students represented by it.

Example 3 The population of four major cities in India in a particular year is given below:

City	Mumbai	Kolkata	Delhi	Chennai
Number of students	120	130	150	80

Construct a bar graph to represent the above data.

Solution To construct the bar graph representing the given data, we follow the following steps:

STEP I We take a graph paper and draw two mutually perpendicular lines *OX* and *OY*.

STEP II Along the horizontal line *OX*, we mark 'cities' and along the vertical line, we mark the 'population'.

STEP III Along the axis *OX*, we choose equal suitable width of each bar. The gap between the bars is chosen same.

STEP IV Choose a suitable scale to determine the heights of the bars, according to the availability of space. Here, we choose 1 big division to represent 20 lakhs population.

STEP V Calculate the height of various bars as follows:

The height of the bar for Mumbai = $\frac{120}{20}$ = 6 big divisions.

The height of the bar for Calcutta = $\frac{130}{20}$ = 6.5 big divisions.

The height of the bar for Delhi = $\frac{150}{20}$ = 7.5 big divisions.

The height of the bar for Chennai = $\frac{80}{20}$ = 4 big divisions.

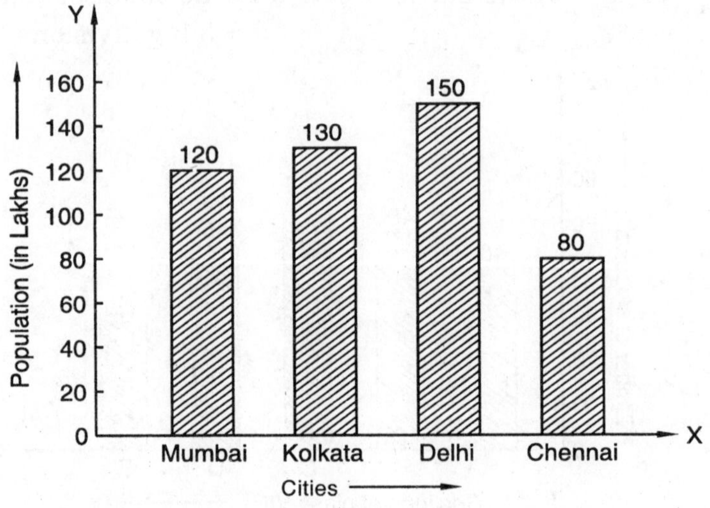

Fig. 3

<u>STEP VI</u> Now, we draw the bars as shown in Fig. 3 and at the top of each bar we write the population of the corresponding city.

Example 4 The results of pass percentage of Class X and XII in C.B.S.E. examination for 5 years are given in the following table:

Year	1994-95	1995-96	1996-97	1997-98	1998-1999
X	90	95	90	80	98
XII	95	80	85	90	95

Draw bar graphs to represent the data.

Solution We go through the following steps to construct the bar graphs:

<u>STEP I</u> *We draw two lines perpendicular to each other on a graph paper and call them horizontal and vertical axes as shown in Fig. 4.*

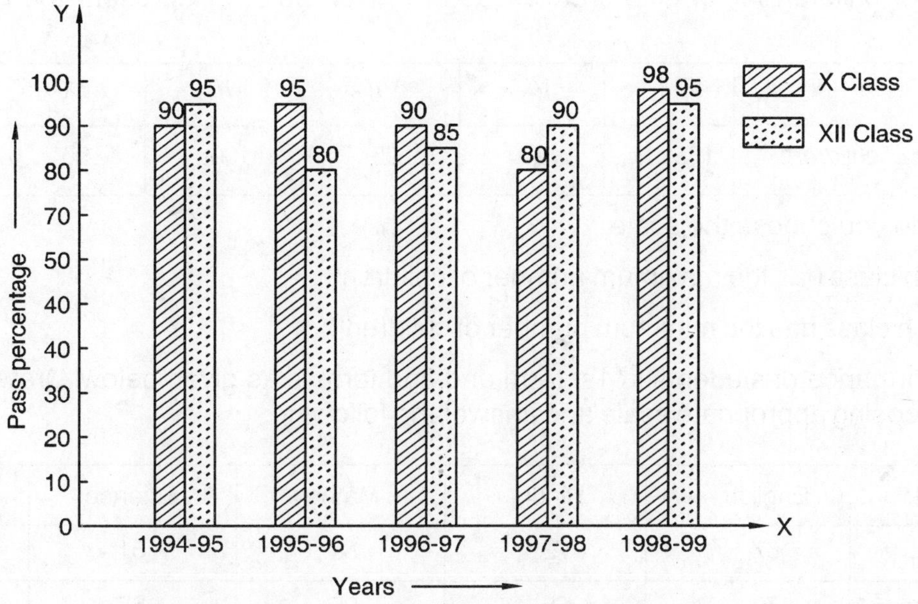

Fig. 4

<u>STEP II</u> *Along the horizontal axis, we mark the 'years' and along the vertical axis, we mark the 'pass percentage'.*

<u>STEP III</u> *We choose a suitable scale to determine the heights of bars. Here, we choose the scale as 1 big division to represent 10.*

<u>STEP IV</u> *First we draw the bars for Class X results and then bars for Class XII results for different years.*

Bars for X and XII class results are shaded separately and the shading is shown in the top right corner of the graph paper.

EXERCISE 24.1

1. Two hundred students of class VI and VII were asked to name their favourite colours so as to decide upon what should be the colour of their school house. The results are shown in the following table.

Colour:	Red	Green	Blue	Yellow	Orange
Number of students:	43	19	55	49	34

Represent the given data on a bar graph.

(i) Which is the most preferred colour and which is the least?

(ii) How many colours are there in all?

2. Following data gives total marks (out of 600) obtained by six children of a particular class.

Student:	Ajay	Bali	Dipti	Faiyaz	Gotika	Hari
Marks obtained:	450	500	300	360	400	540

Represent the data by a bar graph

3. Number of children in six different classes are given below. Represent the data on a bar graph.

Class:	V	VI	VII	VIII	IX	X
Number of children:	135	120	95	100	90	80

(i) How do you choose the scale.

(ii) Which class has the maximum number of children?

(iii) Which class has the minimum number of children?

4. The performance of students in 1st term and 2nd term is as given below. Draw a double bar graph choosing appropriate scale and answer the following:

Subject:	English	Hindi	Maths	Science	S. Science
1st term:	67	72	88	81	73
2nd term:	70	65	95	85	75

(i) In which subject, has the children improved their performance the most?

(ii) Has the performance gone down in any subject?

5. Consider the following data gathered from a survey of a colony:

Favourate Sport:	Cricket	Basket-Ball	Swimming	Hockey	Athletics
Watching	1240	470	510	423	250
Participating	620	320	320	250	105

Draw a double bar graph choosing an appropriate scale. What do you infer from the bar graph?

(i) Which sport is most popular?

(ii) What is more preferred watching or participating in sports?

5. The production of saleable steel in some of the steel plants of our country during 1999 is given below:

Plant	Bhilai	Durgapur	Rourkela	Bokaro
Production (In thousand tonnes)	160	80	200	150

Construct a bar graph to represent the above data on a graph paper by using the scale 1 big division = 20 thousand tonnes.

6. The following data gives the number (in thousands) of applicants registered with an Employment Exchange during, 1995-2000:

Year	1995	1996	1997	1998	1999	2000
Number of applicants registered (in thousands)	18	20	24	28	30	34

Construct a bar graph to represent the above data.

7. The following table gives the route length (in thousand kilometres) of the Indian Railways in some of the years:

Year	1960-61	1970-71	1980-81	1990-91	2000-2001
Route length (in thousand kilometres)	56	60	61	74	98

Represent the above data with the help of a bar graph.

8. The following data gives the amount of loans (in crores of rupees) disbursed by a bank during some years:

Year	1992	1993	1994	1995	1996
Loan (in crores of rupees)	28	33	55	55	80

(i) Represent the above data with the help of a bar graph.

(ii) With the help of the bar graph, indicate the year in which amount of loan is not increased over that of the preceding year.

9. The following table shows the interest paid by a company (in lakhs):

Year	1995-96	1996-97	1997-98	1998-99	1999-2000
Interest (in lakhs of rupees)	20	25	15	18	30

Draw the bar graph to represent the above information.

10. The following data shows the average age of men in various countries in a certain year:

Country	India	Nepal	China	Pakistan	U.K.	U.S.A.
Average age (in years)	55	52	60	50	70	75

Represent the above information by a bar graph.

11. The following data gives the production of foodgrains (in thousand tonnes) for some years:

Year	1995	1996	1997	1998	1999	2000
Production (in thousand tonnes)	120	150	140	180	170	190

Represent the above data with the help of a bar graph.

12. The following data gives the amount of manure (in thousand tonnes) manufactured by a company during some years:

Year	1992	1993	1994	1995	1996	1997
Manure (in thousand tonnes)	15	35	45	30	40	20

(i) Represent the above data with the help of a bar graph.

(ii) Indicate with the help of the bar graph the year in which the amount of manure manufactured by the company was maximum.

(iii) Choose the correct alternative:

The consecutive years during which there was maximum decrease in manure production are:

(a) 1994 and 1995 (b) 1992 and 1993

(c) 1996 and 1997 (d) 1995 and 1996

ANSWERS

1. (i) Blue, Green (ii) 5 3. (ii) V (iii) X 4. (i) Maths (ii) Hindi
5. (i) Cricket (ii) Watching 8. 1995 12. (ii) 1994 (iii) 1996 and 1997.

25

DATA HANDLING – IV (Probability)

25.1 INTRODUCTION

In our everyday life, we come across statements such as:

(i) Probably it may rain today.

(ii) He is probably right.

(iii) Most probably he may join politics.

(iv) Indian cricket team has good chances of winning world-cup.

In such statements, we generally use the words: 'probably', 'most probably', chances, etc. All these words convey the same sense that there is some uncertainty in the occurrence or happening of the event in the question. For example, in first statement 'probably it may rain' will mean it may rain or it may not rain today. We are predicting rain today on the basis of our past experiences. Similar predictions are made in other statements. Thus, the word probably connotes that there is uncertainty about what has happened or what is going to happen. The uncertainty of 'probably' etc. can be measured by means of 'probability' in many cases. The concept of probability originated in the beginning of eighteenth century in problems pertaining to games of chance such as tossing a coin, throwing a die etc. Let us try to understand and introduce the concept of probability by performing the following activities.

25.2 PROBABILITY

Let us perform the following activities which will help us in understanding the concept of probability.

ACTIVITY 1 Take a coin, toss it 10 times and note down the number of times head and tail come up. Record your observations in the form of the following table.

Number of times the coin is tossed	10	20	30	50
Number of times head comes up	4	13	16	24
Number of times tail comes up	6	7	14	26
$\dfrac{\text{Number of times a head comes up}}{\text{Total number of times the coin is tossed}}$	$\frac{4}{10} = 0.4$	$\frac{13}{20} = 0.65$	$\frac{16}{30} = 0.533$	$\frac{24}{50} = 0.48$
$\dfrac{\text{Number of times a tail comes up}}{\text{Total number of times the coin is tossed}}$	$\frac{6}{10} = 0.6$	$\frac{7}{20} = 0.35$	$\frac{14}{30} = 0.466$	$\frac{26}{50} = 0.52$

Repeat the same experiment by increasing the number of tosses to 20, 30 and 50 and record your observations in the above table.

You will find that as the number of tosses gets larger, the values of fractions in fourth and fifth row of the table come closer to 0.5.

A die is a well balanced cube with its six faces marked with numbers 1 to 6, one number on one face.

Take a die and perform the following activity.

ACTIVITY 2 Throw a die 20 times and note down the number of times the numbers 1, 2, 3, 4, 5, 6 come up. Record your observations in the form of table given below.

Number of times a die is thrown	Number of times the scores turn up					
20	1	2	3	4	5	6
30						
40						

Repeat the same experiment 30 and 40 times and record your observations in the above table. Also, find the values of the following fractions in each case.

$$\frac{\text{Number of times 1 turned up}}{\text{Total number of times the die is thrown}}$$

$$\frac{\text{Number of times 2 turned up}}{\text{Total number of times the die is thrown}}$$

$$\vdots$$

$$\frac{\text{Number of times 6 turned up}}{\text{Total number of times the die is thrown}}$$

You will find that as the number of throws of the die increases, the value of each of the above fractions comes closer to $\frac{1}{6} = 0.1666$

In activity 1, each toss of a coin is called a trial. Similarly, in activity 2, each throw of a die is called a trial. Thus, we may define the term trial as follows:

TRIAL *A trial is an action which results in one or several outcomes.*

The possible outcomes in activity 1 were Head (H) and Tail (T); whereas in activity 2, the possible outcomes were 1, 2, 3, 4, 5 and 6.

In activity 1, we have considered an experiment in which the outcome of a trial is not certain. In other words, we were not certain whether outcome of a trial will be a head (H) or a tail (T). Similarly, in activity 2 we were not sure about the number on the upper face of the die. Such experiments are called random experiments. So, we define the term random experiment as follows.

RANDOM EXPERIMENT *An experiment in which the result of a trial cannot be predicted in advance is called a random experiment.*

Tossing a coin, Throwing a die, Tossing a pair of coins, Throwing a pair of dice, Drawing a ball from a bag containing 5 red and 4 white balls etc. are random experiments.

In tossing a coin, possible outcomes of a trial are: Head (H), Tail (T)

In tossing a pair of coins, possible outcomes of a trial are: HH, HT, TH, TT

In throwing a die, possible outcomes of a trial are: 1, 2, 3, 4, 5, 6.

In activity 1, getting of a head in a particular toss is an event with outcome 'head'. Similarly, getting a tail is an event with outcome 'tail'.

Similarly, in Activity 2, the getting of a particular number, say 1, is an event with outcome 1. Similarly, getting 2 is an event with outcome 2 and so on.

In the experiment of throwing a die 'getting an even number' is an event which consists of three outcomes, namely, 2, 4 and 6. Similarly, 'getting an odd number' is an event which consists of 1, 3, 5, as outcomes.

Thus, we may define the term event as follows:

EVENT *An event associated to a random experiment is the collection of some outcomes of the experiment.*

In the experiment of throwing a die 'getting a multiple of 3' is an event which consists of outcomes 3 and 6. Similarly, 'getting a prime number' is an event consisting of outcomes 2, 3 and 5.

In the experiment of tossing two coins simultaneously possible outcomes are:

HH, HT, TH, TT

Associated to this experiment 'getting exactly one head' is an event which consists of outcomes HT and TH. Similarly, 'getting at least one head' is an event consisting of outcomes HH, HT and TH.

HAPPENING OF AN EVENT *An event associated with a random experiment is said to happen if any one of the outcomes satisfying the definition of the event is an outcome of the experiment when it is performed.*

In random experiment of throwing a die, if the outcome of the throw is 4, then we say that each one of the following events happens:

(i) Getting 4.
(ii) Getting an even number.
(iii) Getting a number greater than 3.

However, on the basis of the same outcome, one can say that none of the following events have happened:

(i) Getting an odd number.

(ii) Getting a multiple of 3.

(iii) Getting a number less than 3.

(iv) Getting a prime number.

On the basis of the above discussion, we define the experimental or empirical probability of happening of an event as follows:

EMPIRICAL PROBABILITY *Let n be the total number of trials of a random experiment. Then the empirical probability P(E) of happening of an event E is defined as*

$$P(E) = \frac{\text{Number of trials in which the event happened}}{\text{Total number of trials}}$$

Let us now discuss some examples on finding the empirical probabilities.

ILLUSTRATIVE EXAMPLES

Example 1 A coin is tossed 100 times in which head is obtained 55 times. On tossing a coin at random, find the probability of getting (i) a head (ii) a tail.

Solution We have

Total number of trials = 100

Number of times a head come up = 55

Number of times a tail come up = (100 – 55) = 45

$$\therefore \quad \text{Probability of getting a head} = \frac{\text{Number of heads}}{\text{Total number of trials}} = \frac{55}{100} = 0.55$$

$$\text{Probability of getting a tail} = \frac{\text{Number of tails}}{\text{Total number of trials}} = \frac{45}{100} = 0.45$$

Example 2 A die is thrown 200 times and the outcomes are noted as shown below:

Outcome:	1	2	3	4	5	6
Frequency:	35	30	31	28	37	39

If a die is thrown at random, find the probability of getting *a*/*an*

(i) 1 (ii) 4 (iii) 6 (iv) even number (v) odd number

Solution We have,

Total number of trials = 200

(i) $$\text{Probability of getting a 1} = \frac{\text{Frequency of 1}}{\text{Total number of times the die is thrown}}$$

$$= \frac{35}{200} = \frac{7}{40}$$

(ii) $$\text{Probability of getting a 4} = \frac{\text{Frequency of 4}}{\text{Total number of times the die is thrown}}$$

$$= \frac{28}{200} = \frac{7}{50}$$

(iii) Probability of getting a 6 $= \dfrac{\text{Frequency of 6}}{\text{Total number of times the die is thrown}}$

$$= \frac{39}{200}$$

(iv) We have,

Frequency of getting an even number

= Frequency of Getting 2 + Frequency of 4 + Frequency of 6

$= 30 + 28 + 39 = 97$

∴ Probability of getting an even number

$$= \frac{\text{Frequency of getting an even number}}{\text{Total number of times the die is thrown}} = \frac{97}{200}$$

(v) We have,

Frequency of getting an odd number

= Frequency of getting 1 + Frequency of getting 3 + Frequency of getting 5

$= 35 + 31 + 37 = 103$

∴ Probability of getting an odd number

$$= \frac{\text{Frequency of getting an odd number}}{\text{Total number of times the die is thrown}} = \frac{103}{200}$$

Example 3 In a cricket match, a batsman hits a boundary 6 times out of 90 balls he plays. Find the probability that he (i) hit a boundary (ii) did not hit a boundary.

Solution We have,

Total number of trials = 90

Number of trials in which the batsman hit a boundary = 6

Number of trials in which the batsman did not hit a boundary = 90 – 6 = 84

∴ Probability that the batsman hit a boundary

$$= \frac{\text{Number of times he hit the boundary}}{\text{Total number of trials}} = \frac{6}{90} = \frac{1}{15}$$

Probability that the batsman did not hit a boundary

$$= \frac{\text{Number of times he did not hit the boundary}}{\text{Total number of trials}} = \frac{84}{90} = \frac{14}{15}$$

Example 4 There are 6 marbles in a bag with numbers from 1 to 6 marked on each of them. What is the probability of drawing a marble with number (i) 2 ? (ii) 5 ?

Solution We have,

Total number of marbles in the bag = 6

Number of marbles, in the bag, marked with number 2 = 1

Number of marbles, in the bag, marked with number 5 = 1

$\therefore$ Probability of drawing a marble with number $2 = \frac{1}{6}$

Probability of drawing a marble with number $5 = \frac{1}{6}$

Example 5 In a survey of 200 girls it was found that 85 like tea while 115 dislike it. Out of these girls, one girl is chosen at random. What is the probability that the chosen girl (i) likes tea? (ii) dislikes tea?

Solution We have,

Total number of girls = 200

Number of girls who like tea = 85

Number of girls who dislike tea = 200 – 85 = 115

$\therefore$ Probability that a chosen girl likes tea $= \frac{85}{200} = \frac{17}{40}$

Probability that a chosen girl dislikes tea $= \frac{115}{200} = \frac{23}{40}$

EXERCISE 1

1. A coin is tossed 1000 times with the following frequencies:
   Head: 445, Tail: 555
   When a coin is tossed at random, what is the probability of getting (i) a head? (ii) a tail?
2. A die is thrown 100 times and outcomes are noted as given below:

Outcome:	1	2	3	4	5	6
Frequency:	21	9	14	23	18	15

   If a die is thrown at random, find the probability of getting *a/an.*

   (i) 3 (ii) 5 (iii) 4 (iv) Even number (v) Odd number (vi) Number less than 3.
3. A box contains two pair of socks of two colours (black and white). I have picked out a white sock. I pick out one more with my eyes closed. What is the probability that I will make a pair?
4. Two coins are tossed simultaneously 500 times and the outcomes are noted as given below:

Outcome:	Two heads (HH)	One head (HT or TH)	No head (TT)
Frequency:	105	275	120

   If same pair of coins is tossed at random, find the probability of getting (i) Two heads (ii) One head (iii) No head.

ANSWERS

1. (i) 0.445 (ii) 0.555
2. (i) $\frac{7}{50}$ (ii) $\frac{9}{50}$ (iii) $\frac{23}{100}$ (iv) $\frac{47}{100}$ (v) $\frac{53}{100}$ (vi) $\frac{3}{10}$
3. $\frac{1}{3}$
4. (i) $\frac{21}{100}$ (ii) $\frac{11}{20}$ (iii) $\frac{6}{25}$

OBJECTIVE TYPE QUESTIONS

lark the correct alternative in each of the following:

1. An unbiased coin is tossed once, the probability of getting head is

   (a) $\frac{1}{2}$ (b) 1 (c) $\frac{1}{3}$ (d) $\frac{1}{4}$

2. There are 10 cards numbered from 1 to 10. A card is drawn randomly. The probability of getting an even numbered card is

   (a) $\frac{1}{10}$ (b) $\frac{1}{5}$ (c) $\frac{1}{2}$ (d) $\frac{2}{5}$

3. A dice is rolled. The probability of getting an even prime is

   (a) $\frac{1}{6}$ (b) $\frac{1}{3}$ (c) $\frac{1}{2}$ (d) $\frac{5}{6}$

4. There are 100 cards numbered from 1 to 100 in a box. If a card is drawn from the box and the probability of an event is $\frac{1}{2}$, then the number of favourable cases to the event is

   (a) 20 (b) 25 (c) 40 (d) 50

5. When a dice is thrown, the total number of possible outcomes is

   (a) 6 (b) 1 (c) 3 (d) 4

6. There are 10 marbles in a box which are marked with the distinct numbers from 1 to 10. A marble is drawn randomly. The probability of getting prime numbered marble is

   (a) $\frac{1}{2}$ (b) $\frac{2}{5}$ (c) $\frac{9}{3}$ (d) $\frac{3}{10}$

7. The probability of getting a red card from a well shuffled pack of cards is

   (a) $\frac{1}{4}$ (b) $\frac{1}{2}$ (c) $\frac{3}{4}$ (d) $\frac{1}{3}$

8. A coin is tossed 100 times and head is obtained 59 times. The probability of getting a tail is

   (a) $\frac{59}{100}$ (b) $\frac{41}{100}$ (c) $\frac{29}{100}$ (d) $\frac{43}{100}$

9. A dice is tossed 80 times and number 5 is obtained 14 times. The probability of not getting the number 5 is

   (a) $\frac{7}{40}$ (b) $\frac{7}{80}$ (c) $\frac{33}{40}$ (d) None of these

10. A bag contains 4 green balls, 4 red balls and 2 blue balls. If a ball is drawn from the bag, the probability of getting neither green nor red ball is

    (a) $\frac{2}{5}$ (b) $\frac{1}{2}$ (c) $\frac{4}{5}$ (d) $\frac{1}{5}$

ANSWERS

1. (a) 2. (c) 3. (a) 4. (d) 5. (a) 6. (b) 7. (b)
8. (b) 9. (c) 10. (d)

THINGS TO REMEMBER

1. *A trial is an action which results in one or several outcomes.*
2. *An experiment in which the result of a trial cannot be predicted in advance is called a random experiment.*
3. *An event associated to a random experiment is the collection of some outcomes of the experiment.*
4. *An event associated with a random experiment is said to happen if any one of the outcomes satisfying the definition of the event is an outcome of the experiment when it is performed.*
5. *The Empirical probability of happening of an event E is defined as*

$$P(E) = \frac{\text{Number of trials in which the event happend}}{\text{Total number of trials}}$$